COMMUNICATION, INFORMATICS AND LIBRARIANSHIP IN INDIA

CONCEPTS IN COMMUNICATION INFORMATICS & LIBRARIANSHIP (CICIL)

For a list of titles in this series, see pp. 477-479 at the end of the book.

Concepts in Communication Informatics & Librarianship-34

General Editor: **S.P. Agrawal**

COMMUNICATION INFORMATICS AND LIBRARIANSHIP IN INDIA

An Introductory Guide to Publications Based on a Survey of Libraries in Capital City of India

S.P. AGRAWAL
Former Director
National Social Science Documentation Centre, ICSSR, New Delhi

PUSHPA RANI SHARMA
National Social Science Documentation Centre, ICSSR, New Delhi

Assisted by
Meenu Chachra
Kitti Sharma
Shakuntla Sharma

CONCEPT PUBLISHING COMPANY, NEW DELHI 110059

ISBN 81-7022-417-9

First Published 1992

Published and Printed by
Ashok Kumar Mittal
Concept Publishing Company
A/15-16, Commercial Block, Mohan Garden
NEW DELHI-110059 (India)

Lasertypeset by
Microtech Advance Printing Systems (Pvt.) Ltd.
H-13, Bali Nagar
NEW DELHI-110015

GENERAL EDITOR'S INTRODUCTION

It is truism to say that we are living in an age of rapid technological advances. Every day we have been witnessing increasing progress in every field of human knowledge. It is *Information Explosion* they say. We do not however exactly know whether it is so – or else whether it is *Mis-Information Explosion* or *Dis-Information Explosion* – be that as it may; for proper growth of any profession it is utmost desirable for its members to keep themselves face to face with the new-and-latest-thereto developments in the field of their activity. Only with the acquisition of new knowledge and new techniques, one can do one's jobs effectively and competently. Moreover, the professionals have also to play an essential part in creative process by engaging themselves in research activities and by making every endeavour to widen the frontiers of knowledge in the subjects of their interest.

Of all the major cities in India, the Capital-City Delhi with a network of well-developed and well-equipped educational (Universities and Institutions) as well government departmental and public libraries on diverse subjects has by far the richest library and information resources. Quite naturally, one shares the feeling that what is available in India as a whole, is available by and large in Delhi. The present publication which has attempted to enlist in one single sequence the national information resources in Communication, Information and Librarianship, of 33 important libraries of the city, is intended to serve three purposes among others. Firstly (and to begin with it is felt), it will help the practising Librarians and working Information Scientists to update their knowledge and skill, to broaden their horizons and to meet the challenges of the changing times. Undoubtedly, continuing education is also one of the measures to reduce the professional obsolescence and to keep the professionals abreast of the new trends and the latest techniques in their profession. But it has its own limitations. Continuing education fails to satisfy adequately those Librarians and Information Scientists who would like to deepen their understanding in their area of specialisation. The present guide, which lists items on almost every aspect of library and information science, can certainly accomplish this task; it can very well cater to the needs of this type of professionals. Secondly, it is a handy tool for the Teaching Faculty who will find it (with listing of rare and out-of-print editions) of immense value in their teaching work. Thirdly, this publication is particularly valuable for Researchers and Scholars who will not only find in it listing of most of their required material in their area of study, but will also be able to locate the place where the material is available. Additionally, to Acquisition Librarian it will help indicate the gaps and to Reference Librarian a pointer for referral service.

The entries are arranged by title in an alphabetical order with the name of the author, editor or compiler etc., if any mentioned in general entry form, on the pattern of UNESCO Catalogue, which, when first brought out, was found to be very much user friendly. The year of publication precedes the title entry. Author and Subject index have also been provided to satisfy these approaches. Besides a Library Index with Library symbol used in this publication has also been provided. Efforts have been made to restrict the number of locations – but in some cases it has been passed off to indicate the acquisition-popularity of the publication.

One word of caution, nevertheless: there are variations in some entries, since these have been recorded from secondary sources, i.e., the catalogues or listing in the process files of the library concerned.

The behaviour-pattern of individuals (cataloguers and typists) must have been on play in rendering Author entries (including names and surnames of Personal Author, and preferential treatment of corporate Authors). The ideocyncracies of survey team also perhaps did not lag behind in confounding the confusion. The blunders (or Howlers, on could say) have crept in therefore automatically and these were found under mountable. Efforts to cross-check from the publication itself, these confusing and contradictory entries yielded scanty results if only because several publications were reported 'not on self' or even 'not in this library' at the time of verification.

S.P. AGRAWAL

CONTENTS

1

DESCRIPTORS

AACR
ALA
ABSTRACTS AND ABSTRACTING SERVICES
ABSTRACTS AND ABSTRACTING SERVICES : GEOGRAPHICAL AREA : GREAT BRITAIN
ABSTRACTS AND ABSTRACTING : GEOGRAPHICAL AREA : INDIA
ACADEMIC LIBRARIES
ACADEMIC LIBRARIES : GEOGRAPHICAL AREA : AFRICA : EAST
ACADEMIC LIBRARIES : GEOGRAPHICAL AREA : CANADA
ACADEMIC LIBRARIES : GEOGRAPHICAL AREA : DEVELOPING COUNTRIES
ACADEMIC LIBRARIES : GEOGRAPHICAL AREA : EUROPE : WESTERN
ACADEMIC LIBRARIES : GEOGRAPHICAL AREA : GREAT BRITAIN
ACADEMIC LIBRARIES : GEOGRAPHICAL AREA : INDIA
ACADEMIC LIBRARIES : GEOGRAPHICAL AREA : INDIA : DELHI
ACADEMIC LIBRARIES : GEOGRAPHICAL AREA : INDIA : GUJARAT
ACADEMIC LIBRARIES : GEOGRAPHICAL AREA : INDIA : KERALA
ACADEMIC LIBRARIES : GEOGRAPHICAL AREA : INDIA : MADHYA PRADESH
ACADEMIC LIBRARIES : GEOGRAPHICAL AREA : INDIA : RAJASTHAN
ACADEMIC LIBRARIES : GEOGRAPHICAL AREA : INDIA : UTTAR PRADESH
ACADEMIC LIBRARIES : GEOGRAPHICAL AREA : PACIFIC : NORTH WEST
ACADEMIC LIBRARIES : GEOGRAPHICAL AREA : PACIFIC : SOUTH
ACADEMIC LIBRARIES : GEOGRAPHICAL AREA : PUERTO RICO
ACADEMIC LIBRARIES : GEOGRAPHICAL AREA : UNITED STATES
ACQUISITION IN LIBRARIES
ACQUISITION IN LIBRARIES : GEOGRAPHICAL AREA : GREAT BRITAIN
ACQUISITION IN LIBRARIES : GEOGRAPHICAL AREA : INDIA : DELHI
ACQUISITION IN LIBRARIES : GEOGRAPHICAL AREA : LATIN AMERICA
ACRONYMS
ADMINISTRATION AND ORGANISATION
ADULT EDUCATION AND LIBRARIES
ADVERTISING : LIBRARIES
AFRICA
AFRICA : BIBLIOGRAPHY
AFRICA : WEST
AGLIS
AGRICULTURE LIBRARIES
AGRICULTURE
AGRICULTURE : DOCUMENTATION
ALLAHABAD UNIVERSITY LIBRARY, ALLAHABAD

BIBLIOMATRICS
BLISS BIBLIOGRAPHIC CLASSIFICATION
BOMBAY
BOOK BINDING
BOOK CATALOGUES
BOOK CENSORSHIP
BOOK COLLECTION
BOOK DESIGN
BOOK INDUSTRY AND TRADE
BOOK JACKET
BOOK LENDING
BOOK MOBILES
BOOK NUMBERS
BOOK REPAIRING
BOOK REVIEWS AND BOOK REVIEWING
BOOK SELECTION
BOOK THEFT
BOOK SELLERS AND BOOK SELLING
BOOKS
BOOKS : CONSERVATION AND PRESERVATION
BOOKS : REFERENCE
BOOKS AND READING
BOOKS AND READING : GEOGRAPHICAL AREA : ASIA
BOOKS AND READING : GEOGRAPHICAL AREA : PAKISTAN
BOOKS AND READING : GEOGRAPHICAL AREA : U.S.
BRANCH LIBRARIES
BRITISH PERIODICALS
BUILDINGS : LIBRARY
BUREAU OF INDIAN STANDARDS
BUSINESS : BIBLIOGRAPHY
BUSINESS INFORMATION SERVICES
BUSINESS LIBRARIES

CALDECOTT MEDAL BOOKS
CANADA
CATALOGUE CARDS
CATALOGUE CARDS : REPRODUCTION
CATALOGUES
CATALOGUES : BOOKS
CATALOGUES : CLASSIFIED
CATALOGUES : COLLEGE
CATALOGUES : DICTIONARY
CATALOGUES : SUBJECT
CATALOGUES : UNION
CATALOGUES : UNIVERSITIES AND COLLEGES
CATALOGUES AND CATALOGUING
CATALOGUING : DICTIONARIES
CATALOGUING : COOPERATIVE
CATALOGUING OF FILMSTRIPS
CATALOGUING OF MUSIC AND MUSICAL INSTRUMENTS
CATALOGUING OF NON BOOK MATERIALS
CATALOGUING OF PERSIAN LITERATURE
CATALOGUING OF PHONORECORDS
CATALOGUING OF RARE BOOKS
CENSORSHIP
CENTRALIZED PROCESSING : LIBRARIES
CEYLON
CHAIN INDEXING
CHARGING SYSTEMS : LIBRARIES
CHEMICAL LITERATURE SEARCH
CHEMISTRY : INFORMATION SERVICES
CHICAGO PUBLIC LIBRARY
CHILDREN'S LIBRARIES
CHILDREN'S LITERATURE
CHILDREN'S LITERATURE : HINDI
CHILDREN'S LITERATURE : INFORMATION SOURCES
CIRCULATION
CITATION INDEXES AND INDEXING
CLASSIFICATION
CLASSIFICATION : BIBLIOGRAPHY
CLASSIFICATION : DICTIONARIES
CLASSIFICATION : TERMINOLOGY
CLASSIFICATION SCHEMES : BIBLIOGRAPHIC
CLASSIFICATION SCHEMES : COLON
CLASSIFICATION SCHEMES : DECIMAL
CLASSIFICATION SCHEMES : DEWEY DECIMAL
CLASSIFICATION SCHEMES : FACETED
CLASSIFICATION SCHEMES : U.S. LIBRARY OF CONGRESS
CLASSIFICATION SCHEMES :

MECHANICAL ENGINEERING : INFORMATION SERVICES
MEDIA LIBRARIES
MEDICAL LIBRARIES
MEDICAL LITERATURE ANALYSIS AND RETRIEVAL SYSTEM
MEDICINE : INFORMATION SERVICES
MEDLARS
MEETINGS
MICROFICHES
MICROFILM SERVICES
MICROFILMS/MICROFICHES
MICROFORMS
MICROFORMS : BIBLIOGRAPHY
MICROPHOTOCOPY
MOBILE LIBRARIES
MOTILAL (MASTER)
MOVING PICTURES : DOCUMENTARY : CATALOGUES
MUNICIPAL COLLEGE LIBRARIES
MUSEUMS
MUSEUMS : GEOGRAPHICAL AREA : INDIA
MUSIC : CATALOGUING
MYANMAR

NATIONAL ARCHIVES OF INDIA, NEW DELHI
NATIONAL ARCHIVES OF UNITED STATES
NATIONAL BIBLIOGRAPHY
NATIONAL BIBLIOGRAPHY : GEOGRAPHICAL AREA : AUSTRALIA
NATIONAL BIBLIOGRAPHY : GEOGRAPHICAL AREA : BANGLADESH
NATIONAL BIBLIOGRAPHY : GEOGRAPHICAL AREA : GREAT BRITAIN
NATIONAL BIBLIOGRAPHY : GEOGRAPHICAL AREA : INDIA
NATIONAL BIBLIOGRAPHY : GEOGRAPHICAL AREA : LATIN AMERICA
NATIONAL BIBLIOGRAPHY : GEOGRAPHICAL AREA : NEW ZEALAND
NATIONAL BOOK LEAGUE
NATIONAL DOCUMENTATION CENTRE OF MASS COMMUNICATION, NEW DELHI
NATIONAL LENDING LIBRARY FOR SCIENCE AND TECHNOLOGY
NATIONAL LIBRARIES
NATIONAL LIBRARIES : GEOGRAPHICAL AREA : DEVELOPING COUNTRIES
NATIONAL LIBRARIES : GEOGRAPHICAL AREA : EUROPE
NATIONAL LIBRARIES : GEOGRAPHICAL AREA : INDIA
NATIONAL LIBRARIES : GEOGRAPHICAL AREA : JAPAN
NATIONAL LIBRARIES : GEOGRAPHICAL AREA : SAUDI ARABIA
NATIONAL LIBRARY BILL, 1972
NEPAL
NEPAL : BIBLIOGRAPHY
NETWORKS : INFORMATION
NEWBERY, JOHN
NEWBERY MEDAL BOOKS
NEWSPAPERS/PERIODICALS/PRESS CLIPPINGS LIBRARIES
NEW YORK PUBLIC LIBRARY
NEW YORK REVIEW OF BOOKS (PERIODICAL)
NON-BOOK MATERIALS
NON-BOOK MATERIALS : CATALOGUING

OFFICIAL PUBLICATIONS
ON-LINE DATA PROCESSING
OPERATIONS RESEARCH
OPTICAL CHARACTER RECOGNITION DEVICES
ORIENTAL LIBRARY
OXFORD

PRECIS
PAKISTAN
PERIODICAL
PERSONALIA
PHONORECORDS : CATALOGUING
PHTOCOPYING SERVICES IN LIBRARIES
PHYSICAL VERIFICATION
PICTURES

2

BASIC GUIDE

Arranged Alphabetically by TITLE given in bold letters in the text

Varma, A.K., 1986, **AACR2** : Entries and procedure. {NASSDOC}

Uppal, O.P., 1987, **AACR2** : Practice and theory. {JNU NASSDOC}

Cook, C. Donald, comp., 1982, **AACR2 decisions and rule interpretations :** A consolidation of the decision and rule interpretations for the Anglo-American Cataloguing Rules, 2nd. edn. assisted by Glenna E. Stevens. [Canadian Library Association]. {USIS}

Anon, 1980, **AACR2 institute handbook** : The Library of Congress interpretation and application of the Anglo-American Cataloguing Rules, 2nd. edn. [U.S. Library of Congress; American Library Association]. {USIS}

Anon, n.d., **ABC : Abridged building classification for architects, builders, civil engineers**. [International Council for Building Research Studies and Documentation, Rotterdam]. {BIS}

Carter, J., 1961, **ABC for book collectors**. {IIT}

Muthuswamy, A.T., 1969, **ABC of library science**. {NASSDOC}

Sherman, Steve, 1971, **ABC's of library promotion.** {DEPT JNU}

Beetle, Clara, 1970, **ALA cataloguing rules for author and title entries**. {BIS CRRI DSSW ICA IIFT IIT MFL NIEPA SPA TDA USIS ZHL}

Anon, 1980, **ALA filing rules**. [American Library Association]. {USIS}

Yong, Heartsill, et al, eds., 1983, **The ALA glossary of library and information science**. [American Library Association]. {USIS}

Thompson, Elizabeth H., 1943, **ALA glossary of library terms**. [American Library Association]. {BIS CRRI ZHL}

Thompson, Elizabeth, H. 1971, **ALA glossary of library terms with a selection of terms in related fields**. [American Library Association]. {IIT NASSDOC}

Anon, 1979, **ALA handbook of organisation, 1979-80.** [American Library Association]. {NASSDOC USIS}

Anon, 1979, **ALA membership directory, 1979-80**. [American Library Association]. {NASSDOC USIS}

Anon, 1942, **ALA rules for filing catalogue cards**. [American Library Association]. {CRRI IIT}

Seely, Pauline A., ed., 1968, **ALA rules for filing catalogue cards**, 2nd. edn. [American Library Association]. {BIS IIT JNU NIEPA NMML USIS}

Wedgeworth, R., et al, eds., 1980, **ALA world encyclopaedia of library and information services**. [American Library Association]. {IIT NASSDOC NCERT NERC USIS}

Anon, 1980, **ALA year book**: A review of library events, 1979. [American Library Association] {IIT JNU USIS}

Anon, 1986, **APINESS** : Report : UNESCO/AASSREC regional meeting of experts to develop Asia Pacific Information Network in Social Sciences, May 12-16, 1986, Bangkok. {NASSDOC}

Wilson, Brian J., ed., 1968-70, **ASLIB directory** : Information sources in medicine, the social sciences and the humanities. 2 vols. {IIT NASSDOC}

Codlin, Ellen M., ed., 1982, **ASLIB directory of information sources in the United Kingdom**, vol. 1: Science, Technology & Commerce, 5th edn. {JNU}

Anon, 1947, **ASLIB meeting on planning and equipment of special libraries, April 6, 1946, London**. {CRRI}

Anthony, Lawrence James, ed., 1976, **ASLIB seminar for information planners and industry, May 13-14, 1976, Boaconfield**. {BCL NASSDOC}

Kimey, 1967, **Abbreviated citation**. {DEPT}

Mary, R. Kenney, 1967, **Abbreviated citation** : A bibliographical problem. {DU.}

Anon, n.d., **Abbreviations for titles of periodicals**. [Indian Standards Institution]. {AIU}

Anon, 1968, **Abbreviations of generic names in titles of periodicals**. [International Organisation for Standardisation, Geneva]. (ISO/R 833-1968) (E/F). {NASSDOC}

Anon, 1968, **Abbreviations of typical words in bibliographical references**. [International Organisation for Standardisation, Geneva]. (ISO/R 832-1968) (E/F). {NASSDOC}.

Leduss, S.T.G.S.V. and Stokolova, N.A., 1974, **About a method of constructing information languages having grammar.** {DEPT JNU}

Anon, 1969, **Abridged Bliss Classification** : The bibliographic classification of Henry Evelyn Bliss revised for school libraries. [Bliss Classification Working Party]. {DUL}

Dewey, Melvil, 1936, **Abridged Decimal Classification and Relative Index**, 5th. edn. {DEPT ZHL}

Dewey, Melvil, 1959, **Abridged Dewey Decimal Classification and Relative Index**, 8th. edn. {USIS}

Dewey, Melvil, 1965, **Abridged Dewey Decimal Classification and Relative Index**, rev. edn. {USIS}

Dewey, Melvil, 1971, **Abridged Dewey Decimal Classification and Relative Index**, rev. edn. {USIS}

Collison, Robert, 1971, **Abstract and abstracting services**. {JNU NASSDOC USIS}

Rowley, Jennifer E., 1982, **Abstracting and indexing**. {ISI JNU}

Rowley, Jennifer E., 1988, **Abstracting and indexing**, 2nd edn. {NASSDOC}

Borko, Harold and Bernier, Charles L., 1975, **Abstracting concepts and methods.** {DEPT JNU}

Kesarwani, S.K. and Bhat, S.G. eds., n.d., **Abstracting, indexing and current awareness services in environmental science**. {INSA}

Maizell, Robert E., et al, 1971, **Abstracting scientific and technical literature**. {BIS CRRI IIMC ISI JNU USIS}

Anon, n.d., **Abstracting services in science, technology, medicine agriculture, social science, humanity**. [International Federation for Documentation and Information]. {DEPT JNU}

Anon, 1961, **Abstracts and synopses**. [International Organisation for Standardisation, Geneva]. (ISO/R 214-1961) (E). {NASSDOC}

Davinson, Donald, 1965, **Academic and legal deposit libraries**, 2nd. edn. {DEPT DUL ICHR MFL ZHL}

Poole, Herbert, ed., 1977, **Academic libraries by the year 2000**. {DEPT DUL ISI JNU USIS}

Narayana Rao, B., 1982, **Academic libraries in India** : An enquiry into their organisation and professional aspect. {JNU}

Farber, Evan Ira and Walling, Ruth, 1974, **Academic library** : Essays in honour of Guy R. Lyle. {JNU}.

Osburn, Charles B., ed., 1979, **Academic research and library resources** : Changing patterns in America. {DEPT IIT JNU NIPCCD}

Datta, N., 1985, **Academic status for university and college librarians in India**. {JNU}

Grieder, T.E.D., 1978, **Acquisition** : Where, what and how. {CRRI DUL NIEPA}

Randall, William, ed., 1944, **Acquisition and cataloguing of books** : Papers presented before the library institute at the University of Chicago, July 29 to August 9, 1940. {JNU NAI ZHL}

Bloomfield, B.C., 1972, **Acquisition and provision of foreign books by national and university libraries in the United Kingdom** : Papers of the Morecamb conference, April 16, 1972. {NMML}

Kohl, David F., 1985, **Acquisition, collection development and collection use**. {JNU}

Ford, Stephen, 1973, **The acquisition of library materials**. [American Library Association]. {DUL ICA USIS}

Anon, 1964, **Acquisition, organisation and use of books and related materials**. [Trustees of New South Wales Public Library]. {JNU}

Wulfekoelter, G., ed., 1961, **Acquisition work** : Process involved in building library collections. {DUL IEG SPA}

Lee, Sul H., ed., 1988, **Acquisitions budgets and material costs** : Issues and approaches. {NASSDOC}

Clarke, D.A., ed., 1975, **Acquisitions from the Third World.** {DUL NASSDOC}

Montgomery, A.C., ed. 1982, **Acronyms and abbreviations in library and information work** : A reference handbook of British usage, 2nd. edn. {JNU}

Montgomery, A.C., 1986, **Acronyms and abbreviations in library and information work**, 3rd edn. [Library Association, London]. {NASSDOC}

Chakrabarti, Bhubaneswar and Chakraborty, A.R. 1983, **Acronyms, initialisms and abbreviations in library and information science** : An annotated guide. {NASSDOC}

Fargo, Lucile F., 1964, **Activity book for school libraries.** {JNU}

Fargo, Lucile F., 1945, **Activity book number two** : Library projects for children and young people. [American Library Association]. {NIEPA}

Mossberg, Thomas, et al, 1976, **ADDLIB** : A packaged computer programme for processing, etc. {JNU NIH}

Tripathi, S.M., 1983, **Adhunik granthalaya** : Vyavastha avam sanchalan ke mooltatva. {NASSDOC}

Tripathi, S.M., 1976, **Adhunik granthalaya vargikaran** : Sidhantik vivechan. (Modern library classification : Theoretical analysis). {BIS}

Gardiner, Jewel, 1954, **Administering library service in the elementary school**, 2nd edn. [American Library Association]. {DUL NIEPA ZHL}

Gillespie, John T. and Spirt, Diana L., 1983, **Administering the school library media centre.** {JNU}

Neal, Harcon, et al, 1969, **Administration and change** : Continuing education in library administration. {JNU}

Trehan, G.L., 1969, **Administration and organisation of college libraries in India**. {AIU DUL JNU SPA ZHL}

Trehan, G.L., 1965, **Administration and organisation of school libraries.** {NASSDOC}

McDiarmid, W.W., et al, 1942, **Administration of the American public library.** [American Library Association]. {NAI}

Hodson, J.H., 1972, **Administration of archives.** {JNU ZHL}

Lyle, Guy R., 1961, **Administration of the college library**. {DUL NERC}

Lyle, Guy R., 1974, **The administration of the college library**, 4th edn. {DUL NIEPA USIS}

Harleston, Robekah M. and Stoffle, Carla J., 1974, **Administration of government documents collections.** {USIS}

Sinclair, Dorothy, 1965, **Administration of the small public library**. [American Library Association]. {NASSDOC}

Sarkar, P.K., 1977, **Administration of technical libraries.** {BIS CRRI ICHR NCAER ZHL}

Kohl, D.F., 1985, **Administration, personnel, buildings and equipment** : A handbook for library management. {NASSDOC}

Cassata, Mary B. and Totten, Herman L., ed., 1975, **The administrative aspects of education for librarianship** : A symposium. {NIEPA USIS}

Matthis, Raimund E. and Taylor, Desmond, 1971, **Adopting the Library of Congress classification system** : A manual of methods and techniques for application or conversion. {DUL}

Thomas, Carl, et al, 1950, **Adult education activities for public libraries.** [UNESCO]. {IEG ZUL}

Tiwari, Bhaskar Nath, n.d., **Adult education and libraries.** {AIU}

Avery, Louis and Hulthciss, S.C., 1962, **Advanced data processing in university library.** {JNU}

Muhammad, Riaz, 1989, **Advanced indexing and abstracting practices.** {NASSDOC}

Vanghan, John, ed., 1973, **Advanced working seminar on national information policy and the impact of social and technological change on national information planning, Australia**. {CRRI}

Mortensen, C. David and Sereno, Kenneth K., 1973, **Advances in communication research** {NASSDOC]

Shera, Jesse H., ed., n.d., **Advances in documentation and library science**. 3 vols. {BIS}

Tou, Julius T., ed., 1969, **Advances in information systems science**, 9 vols. {CRRI MHA DUL NASSDOC USIS}

Voight, Melvin J. and Harris, Michael J., 1970-86, **Advances in librarianship**, 14 vols. {IEG NASSDOC NCAER NIH NMML USIS}

Mc Cabe, Gerard B. and Kreissman, Bernard, eds., 1983, **Advances in library administration and organisation**. {IIT}

Mittal, R.L., 1970, **Advances in library and information science**. {CRRI ICA NCAER NCDC}

Naude, Gabriel, 1976, **Advice on establishing a library.** {DUL NIPCCD}

Zell, Hans M., 1975, **African books in print** : An Index by author, title and subject, Pt. 1: English language and African language. {NASSDOC}

Anon, n.d., **Agricultural documentation** : Responsibilities of libraries and information services. {IIMC}

Subbaiah, R., 1988, **Agricultural librarianship in India**. {NASSDOC}

Grounds, Roger, 1971, **Agriculture** : Library of knowledge. {ICA}

Razvi, M.H., 1973, **Aligarh Muslim University library** : An approach paper on Fifth Five Year Plan including statistical analysis. {JNU}

Anon, 1969, **Aligned list of descriptors** : Alphabetical order. [Organisation for Economic Co-operation and Development, Paris]. {NASSDOC}

Dikshit, S.R. and Dikshit, S.D., comps., 1970-72, **All India booksellers and publishers directory, 1970, 1971, 1972.** {ICCR JNU NASSDOC}

Gupta, K.R., 1980-82, **All India directory of book trade**, vol. 1: Libraries; vol. 2; Booksellers and publishers {NASSDOC NCAER NCERT}

Anon, 1951, **Alphabetical arrangement**. (BS 1749 : 1951). [British Standards Institution]. {CRRI}

Metcalfe, John, ed., 1965, **Alphabetical subject indication of information**. {IIT USIS}

Lynn, Jeannete Murphy, 1965, **Alternative classification for catholic books**. {DUL}

Kalia, D.R., **American libraries** : Lessons for developing countries. (Mimeographed). {NASSDOC*}

Anon, 1960, **American libraries** : Report : U.S. field seminar on library reference services for Japanese librarians, June 1960. [International House of Japan]. {DUL NASSDOC}

La Montagne, Leo E., 1961, **American library classification with special reference to the Library of Congress**. {DUL}

Anon, 1973, **American library directory**: A classified list of libraries in the U.S. and Canada with personnel and statistical data. {ICWA}

Anon, 1964-72, **American library directory, 1964; 1971; 1972.** {IIT INSA JNU}

Downs, Robert B., n.d., **American library resources** : A bibliographical guide: Supplement: 1961-1970. {NASSDOC}

Anon, 1969, **American national standards for the abbreviation of titles of periodicals.** (ANSI Z39.5-1969). [American National Standards Institute]. {NASSDOC}

Anon, 1971, **American national standards for directories of libraries and information centres**. (ANSI Z39.5.-1971). [American National Standards Institute]. {NASSDOC}

Anon, 1971, **American national standards for identification number for serial publications**. (ANSI Z39.5-1971). [American National Standards Institute].{NASSDOC}

Anon, 1968, **American national standards for library statistics**. (ANSI Z39.5-1968). [American National Standards Institute]. {NASSDOC}

Anon, 1967, **American national standards for periodicals** : Format and arrangement. (ANSI Z39.5-1967). [American National Standards Institute]. {NASSDOC}

Anon, 1971, **American national standards for title leaves of a book.** (ANSI Z39.5-1971). [American National Standards Institute]. {NASSDOC}

Anon, 1971, **American national standards for writing abstracts**. (ANSI Z39.5-1971). [American National Standards Institute]. {NASSDOC}

Anon, 1970, **American national standards practice for storage of processed silver-gelatin micro-film**. (ANSI PH5.4-1970). [American National Standards Institute]. {NASSDOC}

Anon, 1972, **American national standards system for the romanisation of Arabic**, 12th rev edn. (ANSI Z39.12-1972). [American National Standards Institute]. {NASSDOC}

Anon, 1972, **American national standards system for the romanisation of Japanese**, rev edn. (ANSI Z39.11-1972). [American National Standards Institute]. {NASSDOC}

Wheeler, Joseph L. and Githens, Alfred Morton, 1941, **The American public library building** : Its planning and design with special reference to its administration and service. [American Library Association]. {USIS}

Smith, Roger H., 1963, **The American reading public** : What it reads, why it reads. {USIS}

Wynar, Bohdan S., et al, eds., 1971, **American reference books annual.** {NASSDOC}

Lucas, Henry C., 1976, **The analysis, design and implementation of information systems**. {TDA}

Bhatnagar, Manjula, 1977, **Analysis of the current serial publications being subscribed to in the Delhi University Library System (DULS), Jawahar Lal Nehru University Library and Indian Institute of Technology Library**. (University of Delhi, Department of Library Science, Sessional Project, 1977). {DUL}

Madhu Bala, 1973, **Analysis of Indian library conferences and seminars since 1947.** {JNU}

Meadow, Charles T., 1973, **Analysis of information systems.** {BIS CRRI DUL NIH NIPCCD USIS}

Thomas, P.A. and Ward, V.A., 1974, **Analysis of managerial activities in libraries**. [Association of Special Libraries and Information Bureaux]. {DUL IIT}

Leimkuhler, F.F. and Cooper, M.D., n.d., **Analytical planning for university libraries.** [University of California]. {IIT}

Lee, John A.N., 1967, **Anatomy of a compiler**. {NASSDOC}

Narasimhan, P.V.A. and Majeed Khan, M.A., 1980, **Andhra Pradesh Public Libraries Act, 1960 with latest amendments and commentaries.** [Andhra Pradesh Public Library Association]. {NASSDOC*}

Anon, 1967, **Anglo-American Cataloguing Rules**. [American Library Association]. {NASSDOC}

Anon, 1978, **Anglo-American Cataloguing Rules**, 2nd edn. [American Library Association]. {CRRI IIC ISI JNU MHA NCAER NERC NIH NIPCCD USIS ZHL}

Anon, 1975, **Anglo-American Cataloguing Rules** : Amendment bulletin. [Library Association, London] {ZHL}

Anon, 1974, **Anglo-American Cataloguing Rules** : British text. [Library Association, London]. {AIU IIT ISI JNU ZHL}

Anon, 1976, **Anglo-American Cataloguing Rules** : North American text. [Library Association, London]. {NASSDOC NMML USIS}

Anon, 1976, **Anglo-American Cataloguing Rules** : North American text : Chapter 6 : Separately published monographs. [American Library Association]. {JNU}

Anon, 1975, **Anglo-American Cataloguing Rules** : North American text : Chapter 12 : Audiovisual media and special instructional materials, rev. [American Library Association]. {USIS}

Anon, 1971, **Anglo-American Cataloguing Rules** : North American Text, with supplement of additions and changes. [American Library Association]. {JNU}

Hunter, Eric J., 1972, **Anglo-American Cataloguing Rules, 1967** : An introduction. {JNU NERC}

Ahmad, Syed Reyaz, 1979, **Annotated and classified bibliography of project reports submitted to the Department of Library Science, University of Delhi since 1968.** {DUL}

Anon, 1978, **Annotated bibliography of country serials**. [UNCTAD/GATT. International Trade Centre]. {MFL}

Minaikit, Nonglak, 1968, **Annotated bibliography on librarianship in Thailand.** {JNU}

Mechanic, Sylvia, 1971, **Annotated list of selected United States government publications available to depository libraries**. {NASSDOC}

Anon, 1972, **Annual report of the Library of Congress, 1972**. [U.S. Library of Congress]. {JNU}

Anon, 1985, **Annual report of the Library of Congress for 1985**. [U.S. Library of Congress] {NASSDOC}

Anon, 1966-84, **Annual review of information science and technology**, 19 vols {CRRI NASSDOC USIS}

Anon, 1963-74, **Annual seminar.** No. 1: 1963; No. 2: 1964; No. 3: 1965; No. 4: 1966; No. 5: 1967; No. 6 : 1968, 2 pts; No. 7: 1969; No. 8: 1970; No. 9: 1971; No. 10: 1972, 2 pts; No. 11: 1974. [Documentation Research and Training Centre, Bangalore]. {IEG IIMC ISI JNU NASSDOC}.

Weiner, Margery, 1974, **Answering any questions** : How to set up an information office. {BCL DUL}

Anon, 1967, **Application of international classification of diseases and neurology**. [World Health Organisation]. {JNU}

McDaniel, Herman, ed., 1970, **Applications of decision tables** : A reader. {NASSDOC}

Keren, Carl and Perlmutter Linda, 1985, **Applications of mini and micro computers in information, documentation and libraries**. {JNU NASSDOC}

Kapoor, S.K., ed., 1979, **Applications of management techniques to library and information system**. {JNU NIPCCD}

Chen, Ching-Chih, 1976, **Applications of operations research models to libraries.** {CRRI}

Van Gigch, John P., 1978, **Applied general systems theory**. {JNU}

Langridge, Derek, 1973, **Approach to classification for students of librarianship.** {IIC JNU NASSDOC}

McCullough, Kathleen, et al, 1977, **Approval plans and academic libraries** : An interpretive survey. {IIT}

Duchein, Michel, 1977, **Archive buildings and equipment**. {DUL}

Clark, Robert L., ed., 1976, **Archive-library relations.** {ISI}

Stueart, Robert D., 1972, **Area specialist bibliographer** : An inquiry into his role. {NASSDOC}

Anon, 1951, **Army medical library classification** : Medicine. {DUL}

Broyard, Anatole, 1974, **Aroused by books.** {USIS}

Taylor, Hugh, 1980, **Arrangement and description of archival materials**. {IIT}

Mehta, S.P., 1975, **Art and science of book preservation.** {BIS IIT MFL ZHL}

Geerge, Mackaness, 1956, **Art of the book collecting in Australia** {JNU}

McCanse, Ralph Alan, 1963, **Art of the book review** : A comprehensive working outline. {DUL}

Byrne, Brendan, 1985, **Art of systems analysis.** {JNU}

Anon, 1963, **Article and reports reprinted from the Library Association Record for December, 1963.** [Library Association, London]. {NASSDOC}

Elithorn, Alick and Jones, David, eds., 1973, **Artificial and human thinking**. {NASSDOC}

Stagle, James R., 1971, **Artificial intelligence** : The heuristic programming approach. {NASSDOC}

Mohanrajan, P.A., 1983, **Ascent of a university library**. {NMML}

Benewick, Anne J., 1974, **Asian and African collections in British libraries** : Problems and prospects. {DUL NMML}

Anon, 1983, **Asian regional seminar on information sources, systems and services in the social sciences, July 11-22, 1983, Philippines**. [Unesco Regional Office, Bangkok]. {NASSDOC}

Anon, 1973, **Aspects of public library management** : The application of new management processes to the library services. [Library Advisory Council for England]. {NIPCCD ZHL}

Richmond, Phyllis A., 1965, **Aspects of recent research in the art and science of classification**. {DUL}

Gangadhara Rao, P. and Raghavan, Q.S., eds., 1986, **Assessment of public library development in India** : Seminar papers. [University of Madras, Department of Library and Information Science]. {NASSDOC}

Hunt, K.G., 1967, **Association of metropolitan chief librarians.** {JNU}

Rice, Margaretta G., 1966, **Audio-visual aids for teaching the use of school library**. {JNU}

Anon, n.d., **Audio-visual materials** : Development of a national cataloguing and information service : Report of joint feasibility study for the British Library and the Council for Educational Technology. {IIMC}

Rufsvold, Margaret I., 1949, **Audio-visual school library service** : A handbook for librarians. [American Library Association]. {ZHL}

Auduson, Herschel V., 1969, **Audio-visual services in the small public library**. {JNU}

Anon, n.d., **Australian government publications, 1974-82**. [National Library of Australia]. {NASSDOC}

Balnaves, John, 1956, **Australian libraries**. {NASSDOC}

Anon, n.d., **Australian national bibliography**, 1974-80. [National Library of Australia]. {NASSDOC}.

Anon, n.d., **Australian public affairs information service** : A subject index to current literature, 1977-82. {NASSDOC}

Anon, n.d., **Author catalogue of printed books in European languages,** 8 vols. [National Library, Calcutta]. {NASSDOC}

Anon, 1941, **Author entry for government publications**. [U.S. Library of Congress]. {NAI}

Greenberg, Alan M., 1981, **Author index to Library of Congress classification** : Class P, Subclass PN, PR, PS, PZ. {BIS}

Anon, 1961, **Author table for Indian names**. [National Library, Calcutta]. {NMML}

Collins, F. Howard, 1956, **Author's and printer's dictionary**. {IIC}

Collins, F. Howard, 1973, **Author's and printer's dictionary**. {DUL}

Anon, 1971 **Authors and writer's who's who**, 6th. edn. {NMML RTL}

Tait, James A., 1969, **Authors' and titles** : An analytical study of the author concept in codes of cataloguing rules in the English language from that of the British Museum. {NMML}

Ward, Eads Martha and Marquardt, Dorothy A., 1964, **Authors of books for young people**. {DUL}

Nicolaus, John J., 1964, **Automated approach to technical information retrieval** : Library application. {JNU}

Anon, 1978, **Automated centre for scientific and technical information.** [UNESCO]. {ISI}

Belongov, G. and Kotov, R., 1971, **Automated information** : Retrieval system. {JNU}

Anon, 1973, **Automated information management in public administration** : Present development and impacts. [Organisation of Economic Co-operation and Development, Paris]. {TDA}

Borko, Harold, 1967, **Automated language processing**. {NASSDOC}

Dranov, Paula, 1977, **Automated library circulation systems.** {IIT}

Evans, Lynn, 1976, **Automatic aids to profile construction** : Expansion of search terms by thesaurus. [Institute of Electrical Engineers]. {BCL}

Awad, Elias M., 1966, **Automatic data processing** : Principle procedures. {JNU}

Steven, Mary Elizabeth, 1965, **Automatic indexing** : A state of the art report. [U.S. National Bureau of Standards]. {USIS}

Jones, Karen Spark, 1971, **Automatic keyword classification for information retrieval**. {BCL BIS NASSDOC}

Melton, Jessica S., 1963, **Automatic processing of metallurgical abstracts for purpose of information retrieval.** {JNU}

Boss, Richard W., 1982, **Automating library acquisitions** : Issues and outlook. {JNU}

Ian, Lovecy, 1984, **Automating library procedures** : A survivor's handbook. {NMML}

Hattery, Lowell H. and Bush, George P. eds., n.d., **Automation and electronics in publishing**. {DUL}

Anon, 1963, **Automation and the Library of Congress**. [U.S. Library of Congress]. {BIS}

Luhn, H.P., 1963, **Automation and scientific communication** : Short papers contributed to the theme sessions of the 26th annual meeting of the American Documentation Institute at Chicago. {JNU}

Rigby, Malcolm, 1981, **Automation and the UDC**, 1948-1980, 2nd edn. [International Federation for Documentation and Information]. {CRRI}

Kimber, Richard T., 1968, **Automation in libraries**. {AIU BIS IIT ISI JNU NASSDOC NCAER NIH SPA}

Kimber, Richard T., 1974, **Automation in libraries**, 2nd edn. {USIS}

Singh, S.P., 1975, **Automation in libraries.** {ICHR NASSDOC NIPCCD SPA}

Anon, n.d., **Automation in union catalogue of periodicals** : India and abroad, typed short bibliography. {NASSDOC}

Cohen, Aaron and Cohen, Elaine, 1982, **Automation, space management and productivity** : A guide for libraries. {IIT USIS}

Gautreaux, Agnes A. and Lally, Mary, comps., 1949, **Aviation subject headings** : A concise list for civil aviation libraries or collections. {DUL}

Anon, 1978, **BEPI** : Bibliography of English publications in India : An integrated author-title-subject index of scholarly and significant publications of the year, 1977-1978. {NASSDOC}

Anon, 1976, **BIBDATA network** : A draft proposal for an Australian national shared cataloguing system. [National Library of Australia]. {JNU}

Anon, 1978, **BSO manual** : The development, rationale and use of broad system of ordering. [International Federation for Documentation and Information] {CRRI}

Anon, 1985, **Bachelor degree in library and information science** : A handbook. [Andhra Pradesh Open University, Hyderabad]. {NASSDOC}

Anon, 1981, **Background papers** : Sub-regional workshop for cooperative librarians and documentation officers for South East Asia, April 14-29, 1981, Los Banos. [ICA Regional Office and Education Centre for South East Asia, New Delhi]. {ICA}

Van Orden, Phyllis and Phillips, Edith B., eds., 1979, **Background readings in building library collections**, 2nd edn. {USIS}

Martin, Lowell A., 1967, **Baltimore reaches out** : Library service to the disadvantaged. {JNU}

Anon, 1975, **Bangladesh national bibliography**. {NASSDOC}

Anon, 1987, **Bangladesh public library directory (1972-1986)**. [Ministry of Education, Cultural Affairs Division, Directorate of Archives and Libraries, Bangladesh National Library, Colombo]. {NASSDOC}

Wijasuriya, D.E.K. and Huck-Tee, Lim, 1975, **Barefoot librarian** : Library development in Southeast Asia with special reference to Malaysia. {NIEPA}

Dutt, Newton Mohun, 1928, **Baroda and its libraries**. [Central Library, Baroda]. {NAI NASSDOC}

Kudelkar, Janardan S., n.d., **The Baroda library movement** : A short account of the origin and growth of the Central Library Department of the Baroda State. [Central Library, Baroda]. {NASSDOC}

White, Carl M., ed., 1964, **Bases of modern librarianship** : A study of library theory and practice in Britain, Canada, Denmark, the Federal Republic of Germany and the United States. {IIT JNU NIPCCD NMML SPA}

Wheeler, Helen R., 1968, **Basic book collection for the community college library.** {JNU}

Anon, 1960, **Basic book collection for elementary grades**. [American Library Association]. {NIEPA USIS}

Yrumpeter, Marg C. and Rounds, Richards, 1985, **Basic budgeting practices for librarians**. {JNU}

Schlessinger, Bernard S., ed., 1983, **The basic business library** : Core resources. {USIS}

Shukla, Lalita S., 1974, **Basic foundations of library science**. {CRRI JNU ZHL}

Saxon, James A. and Stayer, Wesley W., 1967, **Basic principles of data processing**. {JNU}

Shores, Louis, 1939, **Basic reference books** : An introduction to the evaluation study and use of reference materials with special emphasis on some 300 titles. {JNU}

Shores, Louis, 1954, **Basic reference sources**. [American Library Association]. {CRRI NAI USIS}

Shores, Louis, 1972, **Basic reference sources** : An introduction to materials and methods. {DUL USIS}

Taylor, Margaret T., 1973, **Basic reference sources** : A self study manual. {DUL USIS}

Taylor, Margaret T. and Powell, Ronald R., 1981, **Basic reference sources** : A self study manual, 2nd edn. {USIS}

Powell, Ronald R., 1985, **Basic research methods for librarians**. {JNU}

Simpson, I.S., 1975, **Basic statistics for librarians**. {ISI JNU}

Simpson, I.S., 1983, **Basic statistics for librarians**, 2nd edn. {IIT}

Hott, Richard W., 1971, **Basic system analysis**. {JNU}

Bunch, Allan, 1984, **Basics of information work**. {JNU}

Harrison, Colin and Oates, Rosemary, 1981, **The basics of librarianship**. {ISIL}

Craster, H.H.E., 1941, **Bedlican library extension scheme**. {NAL}

Teh-Wci, Hu, et al, 1975, **Benefit-cost analysis of alternative library delivery systems**. {JNU}

Wynar, Bohdan S., 1976, **Best reference books**. {JNU}

Trinkner, Charles L., 1962, **Better libraries make better schools**. {JNU}

Waldo, Willis H., 1965, **Better report writing,** 2nd rev edn. {DUL}

Danton, J. Periam, 1970, **Between MLS and PHD** : A study of sixth year specialist programmes in accredited library schools. {DUL}

Bliss, Henry Evelyn, 1977, **Bibliographic Classification**, 2nd edn., ed. by J. Mills {IIT JNU}

Bliss, Henry Evelyn, 1953, **Bibliographic Classification** : Classes L-Z, 3 vols, {CRRI}

Davinson, Donald Edward, 1975, **Bibliographic control**. {AIU DUL NASSDOC}

Reichmann, Felix and Tharpe, Josephine M., 1972, **Bibliographic control of microforms**. {ISI JNU}

Grove, Pearce S. and Clement, Evelyn G., eds., 1972, **Bibliographic control of nonprint media.** [American Library Association]. {NASSDOC}

Pemberton, John E., 1982, **Bibliographic control of official publications**. {IIT}

Cowley, J.D., 1939, **Bibliographic description and cataloguing**. {DUL}

Thomas, P.A., 1973, **Bibliographic information in library systems**. [Association of Special Libraries and Information Bureaux]. {CRRI JNU}.

Renford, Beverly and Hendrickson, Linnea, 1980, **Bibliographic instruction** : A handbook. {IIT}

Sahai, S.N. 1976, **Bibliographic methods and reading behaviour**. {ICHR NASSDOC NERC NIPCCD}

Hagler, Ronald, and Simmons, Peter, 1982, **Bibliographic record and information technology**. {DUL JNU}

Stockes, Roy, 1965, **Bibliographical control and service**. {DUL IIT MFL NASSDOC}

Cameron, William J., 1978, **Bibliographical control of early books**. {JNU}

Awad, Atef Kamel, 1975, **Bibliographical control of patent literature**. [University of Delhi, Department of Library Science, Sessional Project]. {DUL}

Cowley, J.D., 1970, **Bibliographical description and cataloguing**. {NASSDOC}.

Anon, 1970, **Biographical directory of librarians in the United States and Canada**, 5th edn. {NASSDOC}

Anon, 1950, **Bibliographical references.** (BS 1629 : 1950). [British Standards Institution]. {CRRI NASSDOC}

Anon, 1968, **Bibliographical references** : Essential elements. (ISO/R 690-1968) (E). [International Organisation for Standardisation, Geneva]. {NASSDOC}

Anon, 1950, **Bibliographical services** : Their present state and possibilities of improvement. [U.S. Library of Congress]. {JNU}

Patil, P.K., 1972, **Bibliographical services for Indian studies** : A guide to printed sources of information. [Mysore Institute of Development Studies]. {NASSDOC}

Usmani, M. Adil, 1978, **Bibliographical services throughout Pakistan.** {ZHL}

Anon, 1950-1974, **Bibliographical services throughout the world,** 1950-54; 1955-59; 1960-64; 1965-69; 1970-74. [UNESCO]. {DSSW DUL IIMC JNU NASSDOC NIEPA ZHL}

Collison, R.L., 1951, **Bibliographies** : Subject and national : A guide to their contents, arrangement and use. {MFL}

Collison, R.L., 1962, **Bibliographics** : Subject and national : A guide to their contents and use, 2nd ed. {MFL}

Anon, 1968, **Bibliographies and reference works including abstract journals, library journals, books about books and standard works**, 2 parts, pt 1: A-J. {NASSDOC}

Girja Kumar, and Krishan Kumar, 1976, **Bibliography**. {CRRI ICA ISI JNU NASSDOC NIPCCD NMML}

Anon, 1977, **Bibliography** : Reports from the International Conference on Education, 1975. [UNESCO]. {ICA}

Sharma, Ram Saroop, ed., 1974, **Bibliography and documentation**. {ICHR IIT JNU NIPCCD}

Hurt, Peyton, 1968, **Bibliography and footnotes** : A style manual for students and writers. 3rd edn. [University of California]. {NASSDOC}

Gore, Daniel, 1973, **Bibliography for beginners**, 2nd edn. {NASSDOC}.

Chakraborti, M.L. 1971, **Bibliography in theory and practice**. {MFL NASSDOC}

Chakraborti, M.L. 1975, **Bibliography in theory and practice,** 2nd rev edn. {ICA ICHR IIMC INSA JNU NIPCCD}

Kalia, D.R. and Jain, M.K., 1975, **A bibliography of bibliographies on India**. {ICA}

Anon, 1964, **Bibliography of dictionaries and encyclopaedias in Indian languages**. [National Library, Calcutta]. {ZHL}

Aitchison, Jean and Allen, C.G., eds., 1982, **Bibliography of mono and multilingual vocabularies, thesauri, subject headings and classification schemes in the social sciences** : Prepared by the ASLIB Library. [UNESCO]. {NASSDOC}

Anon, 1973, **Bibliography of publications issued by UNESCO or under its auspices, 1946-1971**. [UNESCO]. {NASSDOC}

Pathak, Vijay, and Ramaiah, L.S. 1986, **Bibliography of research in library and information in India**. {NMML}

Anon, 1976, **Bibliography of selected Indian books, 1970-71**. {NASSDOC}

Schuchmann, M., 1958, **Bibliography of standards on documentation**. {BIS ISI}

Anon, n.d., **Bibliography of United Nations thesauri, classification nomenclatures.** [Inter-Organisation Board for Information Systems, Geneva]. {BIS}

Davis, Richard A. and Bailey, Catherine A., 1964, **Bibliography of use studies**. {JNU}

Anon, 1970, **Bibliography on documentation**. {JNU}

Neeland, Frances, 1967, **Bibliography on information science and technology for 1966**. {JNU}

Havelock, Ronald G., 1968, **Bibliography on knowledge utilisation and dissemination**. [University of Michigan]. {NASSDOC}

Anon, 1966, **Bibliography on work-flow in libraries**. [Council of Scientific and Industrial Research, New Delhi]. {INSDOC NASSDOC}.

Patil, G.M., 1967, **Bibliography technical** : An illuminating exposition. {NASSDOC}

Chen, Ching-Chih, 1976, **Biomedical, scientific and technical book reviewing**. {DUL}

Smith, Jessie Carney, 1977, **Black academic libraries and research collections** : An historical survey. {DUL IIT NIPCCD}

Clack, Doris H., ed., 1975, **Black literature resources** : Analysis and organisation. {IIT ISI}

Anon, 1981, **Bombay Booksellers and Publishers Association Members' Directory**. [Bombay Booksellers and Publishers Association]. {NASSDOC}

Mc Mustrie, Douglas C., 1943, **Book** : The story of printing and bookmaking, 3rd rev ed. {DUL}

Morpurgo, J.E., 1969, **Book and journal services for doctors and nurses** : An interim report on a National Book League investigation. {DUL}

Buckland, Michael K., 1975, **Book availability and the library user.** {JNU NASSDOC USIS}

Walker, Elinor, comp., 1969, **Book bait** : Detailed notes on adult books popular with young people. 2nd edn. [American Library Association]. {USIS}

Clements, Jaff, n.d., **Bookbinding**. {ISI}

Hewitt-Bates, F. S.A.M., 1954, **Bookbinding**. {NASSDOC}

Diehl, Edith, 1965, **Bookbinding** : Its background and technique, 2 vols. {DUL}

Cockerell, Douglas, 1925, **Bookbinding and the care of the books**, 5th edn. {CRRI ZHL}

Town, Laurence, 1973, **Bookbinding by hand for students and craftsmen**, 2nd edn. {BIS}

Clugh, Eric A., 1967, **Bookbinding for librarians**. [Association of Assistant Librarians, London]. {NASSDOC}

Lehmann-Haupt, Hellmut, et al, 1967, **Bookbinding in America** : Three essays. {DUL}

Kingery, Robert E. and Tauber, Maurice F., eds., 1963, **Book catalogs.** {USIS}

Tauber, Maurice F. and Feinberg, Hilda, 1971, **Book catalogs**. {NASSDOC}

Chapman, R.W., 1950, **Book collecting** : Four broadcast talks. {DUL}

Collison, Robert Lewis, 1957, **Book collection** : An introduction to modern methods of literary and bibliographical detection. {DUL}

Shaffer, Kenneth R., 1961, **Book collection** : Policy case studies in public and academic libraries. {DUL}

Punnoose, Kunnuparampil P., 1977, **Book dealers in India, Pakistan, Sri Lanka** : A directory of dealers in second hand and antiquarian books in the sub-continent of South Western Asia. {NMML}

Anon, 1967, **Book development in Asia** : A report on the production and distribution of books. [UNESCO]. {DUL}

Phillips, David, 1972, **Book display.** {USIS}

Sankaranarayanan, N., 1964, **Book distribution and promotion problems in South Asia**. {DUL}

Barker, Ronald and Escarpit, Robert, eds., 1973, **Book hunger**. {DUL}

Anderson, M.D., 1971, **Book indexing**. {NASSDOC NIEPA}

Miller, William, 1950, **The book industry** : A report of the public library enquiry. {CRRI}

Turner, Mary C., 1961, **Bookman's glossary,** 4th edn. {DUL}

Peters, Jean, ed., 1961, **The bookmen's glossary**. 5th edn. {NCERT}

Peters, Jean, ed., 1983, **The bookmen's glossary**. 61th edn. {NASSDOC}

Brown, Eleanor Frances, 1967, **Bookmobiles and bookmobile service**. {USIS}

Barden, Bertha R., 1937, **Book numbers** : A manual for students with a basic code of rules. {DUL}

Satija, M.P. and Agrawal, S.P., 1990, **Book numbers** : Some Indian methods. {NASSDOC}

Viswanathan, C.G., 1988, **A book on books**. {NASSDOC}

Liebaers, Herman, 1975, **Book promotion through libraries**. {DUL}

Madison, Charles A., 1966, **Book publishing in America**. {DUL}

Anon, 1948-1981, **Book review digest 1948-73; 1976-77; 1979-80; 1980-81.** {NASSDOC}

Drewry, John E., n.d., **Book reviewing.** {DUL}

Escarpit, Robert, 1966, **Book revolution**. {DUL}

Ranganathan, S.R. and Neelameghan, A., n.d., **Book science** : Depth classification. {DUL}

Drury, Francis K.W., 1930, **Book selection**. [American Library Association]. {ZHL}

Sengupta, Benoyendra, 1974, **Book selection**. {ICA IIT ISIL JNU NERC ZHL}

Spiller, David, 1971, **Book selection** : An introduction to principles and practice, 2nd ed. {BIS}

Spiller, David, 1986, **Book selection** : An introduction to principles and practice. {NASSDOC}

Wellard, J.H., 1937, **Book selection** : Its principles and practice. {NAI}

Lunati, Rinaldo, 1975, **Book selection** : Principles and procedures. {DUL}

Mukherjee, A.K., 1974, **Book selection** : Principles, practices and tools. {ICHR IEG}

Kee, S. Janice and Smith, Dorothy K., eds., 1955, **Book selection** : Proceedings of a work conference. {DUL}

Sharma, C.K., n.d., **Book selection and bibliography**. {ICHR}

Marjorie, Fiske, 1959, **Book selection and censorship** : A study of school and public libraries in California. {JNU}

Moon, Eric, ed., 1969, **Book selection and censorship in the sixties**. {DUL IIT USIS}.

Danton, J. Periam, 1963, **Book selection and collections** : A comparison of German and American university libraries. {JNU}

Merritt, Le Roy Charles, 1970, **Book selection and intellectual freedom**. {USIS}

Sharma, C.D., 1976, **Book selection and physical bibliography**. {CRRI}

Mukherjee, A.K., 1960, **Book selection and systematic bibliography** {IIT MFL NMML SPA}

Wofford, Azile, 1967, **Book selection for school libraries** {JNU}

Thomas, Joy, 1952, **Book selling**. {DUL}

Bahr, Alic Harrison, n.d., **Book theft and library security systems**. {BIS JNU USIS}

Kenneth, Day, ed., 1966, **Book typography, 1815-1965, in Europe and the United States of America**. {DUL}

Hickiny, Norman, 1985, **Book worms** : The insect pests of books. {JNU}

King, Marion, 1954, **Books and people** : Five decades of New York's oldest library. {NAI}

Hill, Henry H., et al, eds., 1956, **Books and publishing**, vol. 3. {DUL}

Kenyon, Frederic G., 1951, **Books and readers in ancient Greece and Rome**, 2nd edn. {DUL}

Jones, Mander, 1962, **Books and related materials**. {JNU}

Marshall, Lee, ed., 1951, **Books are for our time**. {DUL}

Dearden, James, 1969, **Books are for people** : Librarian's life educational explorers. {IIT}

Mews, Hazel, 1951, **Books are tools** : The organisation of small technical libraries for South African industry. {JNU}

David, Kaser, ed., 1966, **Books in America's past** : Essays honouring Rudolph H. Gjelsness. {DUL}

Powell, Lawrence Clark, 1960, **Books in my baggage** : Adventures in reading and collecting. {JNU}

Anon, 1969-1983, **Books in print 1969-71; 1973-74 to 1982-83**. {NASSDOC NIH}

Yefimova, A.N. et al, eds., 1974, **Books in the service of society** : Collection of articles of Soviet authors. [Ministry of Culture of the USSR, Main Library Inspectorate]. {NASSDOC}

Conlon, Eileen, 1964, **Books lead the way** : Library and reading skill-text. {JNU}

Sigel, Efrem, et al, 1982, **Books, libraries and electronics** : Essays on the future of written communication. {USIS}

Boyd, Jessie, et al, 1941, **Books, libraries and you**, {ZHL}

Boyd, Jessie, et al, 1965, **Books, libraries and you** : A handbook on the use of reference books and the reference resources of the library, 3rd edn. {USIS}

Vaswani, H.P., comp., 1964, **Books of India, 1963** : A reference catalogue of Indian book published in English in 1963. {NASSDOC}

Downs, Robert B., 1977, **Books that changed America**. {USIS}

Downs, Robert B., 1956, **Books that changed the world**, 2nd ed. [American Library Association]. {USIS}

Downs, Robert B., 1978, **Books that changed the world**, 2nd edn., [American Library Association]. {USIS}

Sabine, Gordon and Sabine, Patricia, 1983, **Books that made the difference** : What people told us. {USIS}

Anon, 1970-1984, **Bowker annual of library and book trade information**. {IIT JNU NASSDOC NCAER NIH USIS}

Mortimore, Arthur D., 1966, **Branch libraries**. {ICA}

Sharp, Henry A., 1938, **Branch libraries** : Modern problems and administration. {JNU}

Enser, A.G.S., 1950, **Branch library practice**. {CRRI}

Neal, K.W., 1973, **British academic libraries**. {JNU}

Anon, 1970-1984, **British books in print** {NASSDOC}

Margen, A. Marry, ed., 1973, **British government publications** : An index to chairmen and authors, 1941-1960. [Library Association, London]. {NASSDOC}

Whatley, H.A., ed., 1972, **British librarianship and information science**, 1966-70. {JNU NMML}

Mc Colvin, Lionel R. and Revie, James, 1949, **British libraries**. {MHA}

Taylor, P.J., 1978, **British library research and development reports** : Information guides. {JNU}

Esdaile, Arundell, 1946, **British Museum Library**. {NAL NMML}

Anon, 1950-83, **British national bibliography**, 1950-54 to 1973; 1975 to 83, 2 vols. [British Library Bibliographic Services Division]. {NASSDOC}

Pemberton, John E., 1971, **British official publications**. {NASSDOC}

Berriman, S.G. and Harrison, K.C., 1966, **British public library buildings**. {IIT}

Pocock, Guy, 1942, **Brush up your reading**. {ZHL}

Werner, Mevissen, 1958, **Buchereibau** : Public library building. {DUL}

Martin, Murray, S., 1978, **Budgetary control in academic libraries**. {AIU DUL}

Sardar, Z., 1988, **Building information systems in the Islamic world**. {NASSDOC}

Carter, Mary Duncan and Bonk, Wallace John, 1969, **Building library collections**, 3rd edn. {USIS}

Carter, Marry Duncan, et al, 1974, **Building library collections**, 4th edn. {USIS}

Bonk, Wallace John and Marymagril, Rose, 1979, **Building library collections**, 5th edn. {USIS}

Mangla, P.B., ed., 1985, **Building library collections and national policy for library** : Seminar papers : All India library conference, 30th, January 28-31, 1985, Jaipur. [Indian Library Association]. {NASSDOC}

Anon, 1980, **Buildings for small public libraries** : Remodelled and adapted including new designs for branches. [American Library Association]. {DUL}

Spencer, J., 1976, **Business information in London** : A study of the demand and supply of business information in 13 London business libraries. [Association of Special Libraries and Information Bureaux]. {NASSDOC}

Campbell, Malcolm James, 1974, **Business information services** : Some aspects of structure organisation and problems. {BCL}

Varma, A.K., 1988, **CCC** : Entries and procedure. {JNU}

Bochm, Eric H., 1967, **CUE system for bibliography and indexing**. {NASSDOC}.

Miller, Bertha Mahony and Field, Elinor Whitney, eds., 1957, **Caldecott medal books**, with the artists' acceptance: Papers and related material chiefly from the Horn Book Magazine 1938-1957. {USIS}

Munby, A., 1960, **Cambridge college libraries** : Aid for research studies. {JNU}

Anon, n.d., **Canadian library directory**, 2 vols. [Canada National Library]. {ICWA}

Anon, 1977-82, **Canadian periodical index**, 1975; 1977 to 1982, formerly *Canadian index to periodicals and documentary films*. [Canadian Library Association]. {NASSDOC}

Beard, John Robert, 1967, **Canadian provincial libraries**. {JNU}

Anon, 1976, **Canons for making abstracts**. [Indian Standards Institution]. {NASSDOC}

Bavakutty, M., 1981, **Canons of library classification**. {JNU NIH ZHL}

Anon, 1976, **Capital provision for university libraries** : Report of a working party. [University Grants Commission, London]. {IIT JNU NIFPA ZHL}

Agrawal, O.P., 1977, **Care and preservation of museum objects**. {NASSDOC}

Lydenberg, Harry Miller and Archer, John, 1980, **Care and repair of books**, 4th rev edn. {DUL IGI}

Anon, 1972, **Care of books and documents**. [Library Association, London]. {ZHL}

Morrison, Perry, D., 1969, **Career of the academic librarian** : A study of the social origins. {JNU}

Spivack, Jane, F., 1982, **Careers in information.** {USIS}

Bobinski, George S., 1969, **Carnegie libraries** : Their history and impact on American public library development. [American Library Association]. {USIS}

Comb, Lewis C. Brans, n.d., **Case for faculty status for academic librarians**. {JNU}

Tedd, L.A., 1979, **Case studies in computer based bibliographic information services**. {BCL}

Palmer, Richard Phillips, 1973, **Case studies in library computer systems**. {ISI USIS}

Grogan, Denis, 1967, **Case studies in reference work**. {DUL IIT NIH}

Burkhalter, Barten R., 1968, **Case studies in systems analysis in a university library**. {JNU}

Anon, 1960, **Cassell's dictionary of publishing in Great Britain, the commonwealth and Ireland**. {ICCR}

Rowland, Arthur Ray, 1969, **Catalogue and cataloguing**. {IIFT IIT NMML SPA}

Anon, 1965, **Catalogue card reproduction.** [American Library Association]. {IIT}

Agrawal, S.S., 1972, **Catalogue entries and procedure** : A guide to cataloguing work according to ALA and AACR and CCC. {IEG IIT ISI}

Anon, 1985, **Catalogue of back volumes of periodicals in Punjabrao Krishi Vidyapeeth Library, Akola, 1985**. [Punjabrao Krishi Vidyapeeth, Akola]. {NASSDOC}

Anon, 1959, **Catalogue of Government of India civil publications** : Subject-wise arranged corrected up to 31st December, 1959. [Controller of Publications Delhi]. {NASSDOC NIPCCD}

Anon, n.d., **Catalogue of Government of India civil publications** : Subject-wise arranged corrected up to 31st December, 1959 : Supplement for the years 1968-70. [Controller of Publications, Delhi]. {IIFT ISI NASSDOC TDA}

Anon, 1977, **Catalogue of Government of India civil publications** : Subject-wise arranged, corrected up to 31st December, 1977, 8th supplement for the year 1977. {MMTC}

Anon, 1970-71, **Catalogue of government publications**. [HMSO, Great Britain]. {NASSDOC}

Momoh, O.A., 1975, **Catalogue of new accessions in the headquarter's library, National Archives of India, April 1966 to March 1974**. {NAI}

Anon, 1967, **Catalogue of publications issued by Government of Uttar Pradesh and obtainable from the book depot, Government Press, Allahabad, for the year ending, 1965-66** : Corrected up to September, 1966. {NASSDOC}

Gaur, Ganesh, comp., 1975, **Catalogue of Punjabi printed books added to the India Office Library, 1902-1964**. [India Office Library, London]. {NASSDOC}

Shah, Ambalal P., ed., n.d. **Catalogue of Sanskrit and Prakrit manuscripts**, 4 parts. [Lalbhai Dalpatbhai Institute of Indology]. {INSA}

Anon, n.d., **Catalogue of serials** : Indian Institute of Science Library, Bangalore. [INSDOC Union Catalogue Series, 2]. {DUL}

Anon, 1980, **Catalogue of special collections in National Library, Baghdad**. [National Library, Baghdad]. {NASSDOC}.

Anon, n.d., **Catalogue of type specimens**. {DUL}

Vishva Bandhu, n.d., **Catalogue of Vishvesharananda Vedic Research Institute manuscript collection**, 2 vols. {INSA}

Dunkin, Paul S., 1969, **Cataloguing**. [American Library Association]. {USIS}

Hunter, Eric J., 1974, **Cataloguing**. {NASSDOC}

Hunter, Eric J., 1979, **Cataloguing**, 2nd rev. edn. {IIT}

Sharma, C.K., 1984, **Cataloguing**. {NASSDOC}

Sengupta, B., 1964, **Cataloguing** : Its theory and practice. {CRRI ICHR MHA NMML SPA ZHL}

Sengupta, B., 1970, **Cataloguing** : Its theory and practice, 2nd edn. {JNU NERC}

Sengupta, B., 1974, **Cataloguing** : Its theory and practice, 3rd rev. edn. {IIT ISIL}

Sharp, H.A., 1950, **Cataloguing** : A textbook for the use in libraries, 4th edn. {IIT ZHL}

Sharp, H.A., 1964, **Cataloguing** : A textbook for use in libraries. {ICA MFL NAI NIPCCD ZHL}

Vishwanathan, C.G., 1959, **Cataloguing** : Theory and practice, 2nd edn. {CRRI NAI}

Vishwanathan, C.G., 1965, **Cataloguing** : Theory and practice, 3rd edn. {ISI MMTC NASSDOC SPA ZHL}

Vishwanathan, C.G., 1970. **Cataloguing** : Theory and practice, 4th edn. {AIU ICA IIFT ISI MMTC NASSDOC NERC NIEPA SPA ZHL}

Vishwanathan, C.G., 1983, **Cataloguing** : Theory and practice, 5th edn. {ICHR IEG IIT MHA MMTC NCAER NCDC ZHL}

Kohl, D.F., 1986, **Cataloguing and catalogue** : A handbook for library management. {NASSDOC}

Chan, Lois Mai, 1985, **Cataloguing and classification** : An introduction. {JNU}

Eaton, Thelma, 1963, **Cataloguing and classification** : An introductory manual, 3rd edn. {DUL}

Manhieimer, Martha L., 1980, **Cataloguing and classification :** A workshop, 2nd edn. {NASSDOC NIPCCD}

Friedman, Joan and Jeffreys, Alan, 1967, **Cataloguing and classification in British university libraries** : A survey of practices and procedures. [Sheffield University Post Graduate School of Librarianship]. {DUL IIT}

Aman, Mohammad M., ed., 1980, **Cataloguing and classification of non-Western materials** : Concerns, issues and practices. {IIT}

Collison, Robert L., 1950, **Cataloguing arrangement and filing of special material in special libraries**. {NAL}

Fleischer, Eugene and Goodman, Helen, 1980, **Cataloguing audio-visual materials** : A manual based on the Anglo-American Cataloguing Rules-2. {IIT}

Titchler, Therea, 1926, **Cataloguing for small libraries**, 3rd edn. {ZHL}

Bennett, Frederick, 1972, **Cataloguing in practice** : Organisation of book acquisition in libraries. {CRRI ICHR NASSDOC NIPCCD}

Thornton, J.L., 1930, **Cataloguing in special libraries** : A survey of methods. {CRRI MFL NAL}

Roscoe, A., 1962, **Cataloguing made easy**. {DUL}

Singh, S.N. and Prasad, H.N., 1985, **Cataloguing manual** : AACR-2, {JNU}

Haroon, Mohammed, 1984, **Cataloguing of Indian Muslim names**. {NASSDOC NMML}

Anon, 1953, **Cataloguing of musical instruments.** [Government Museum, Madras]. {NAL}

Sharify, Nasser, 1959, **Cataloguing of Persian works including rules for transliteration, entry and description**. [American Library Association]. {JNU NASSDOC}

Daily, Jay, E., 1975, **Cataloguing phonorecordings** : Problems and possibilities. {BIS}

Ranganathan, S.R., 1974, **Cataloguing practice**, 2nd edn. {ICA ICHR IEG JNU NERC NMML ZHL}

Khan, Noorul Hassan, Kamleshwar Nath and Sardana, J.L., 1984, **Cataloguing practice** : Classified catalogue code and Anglo- American cataloguing rules. {IIMC JNU NASSDOC NIH}

Anon, 1961, **Cataloguing rules** : Author and title entries. [American Library Association; Library Association, London]. {IIT MFL}

Beetle, Clara, 1970, **Cataloguing rules for author and title entries,** 2nd edn. [American Library Association]. {NAI}

Anon, n.d., **Cataloguing rules of the American Library Association and the Library of Congress, 1949-1958**. [American Library Association; U.S. Library of Congress]. {BIS IEG ZHL}

Fellows, Doracas, 1926, **Cataloguing rules with explanations and illustrations**, 2nd edn. {NAI}

Colvin, Laura C., 1973, **Cataloguing sampler** : Comparative and interpretive guide. {IIT}

Pandey, S.K., 1986, **Cataloguing theory**. {JNU}

Viswanathan, C.G., 1965, **Cataloguing theory and practice**. {NMML}

Misra, Jogesh, 1965, **Censorship** : A literature survey. (University of Delhi, Department of Library Science. Sessional Project). {DUL}

Plump, Philip W., 1965, **Central library storage of books** : An essay awarded the Sevensma prize, 1962. {IIT}

Clark, Fife, 1970, **Central Office of Information**. {NASSDOC}

Leonard, Lawrence E., et al, 1969, **Centralised book processing** : A feasibility study based on Colorado academic libraries. {USIS}

Anon, 1967, **Centres of advanced study in Indian universities**. [University Grants Commission, New Delhi]. {NASSDOC}

Desai, Z.A., 1978, **Centres of Islamic learning in India**. [Ministry of Information and Broadcasting, New Delhi]. {NASSDOC}

Weber, David C., 1976, **Century of cooperative programme among academic libraries**. {BIS}

Jackson, Sidney L,. et al, eds., 1976, **A century of service** : Librarianship in United States and Canada. [American Library Association]. {USIS}

Maheu, Mary Helen, 1958, **Certification of school librarians** : A compilation of State requirements, 1958. {NASSDOC}

Narang, Rita, 1974, **Chain procedure** : An annotated bibliography. {JNU}

Anon, 1986, **Challenges of new technologies** : All India library convention, 6th September 1-4, Shimla, [Government of India Librarians Association]. {NMML}

Macleish, Archibald, 1971, **Champion of a cause** : Essays and addresses on librarianship. [American Library Association]. {USIS}

Suseela Kumar, 1974, **Changing concepts of reference service**. {AIU DUL ICHR IIT MHA NERC NIPCCD NMML}

McGarry, K.J., 1981, **Changing context of information** : An introductory analysis. {NIEPA}

Eastlick, John T., ed., 1971, **The changing environment of libraries** : Papers delivered at the 1970-71 colloquim series. [American Library Association]. {USIS}

Anon, 1982, **Changing information** : Concepts and technologies. {JNU USIS}

Anon, 1961, **The changing pattern of librarianship**. [Library Association, London]. {ICA}

Shiart-Shibbs, B., 1985, **Changing technology and education for librarianship and information science**. {NASSDOC}

Bonn, George S. and Faibisoff, Sulvia, eds., 1978, **Changing times, changing libraries.** {USIS}

Nicholas, David, 1975, **Characteristics of social science serials** : The construction and analysis of a file : Social science serial titles. [Bath University]. {BCL}

Geer, H.T., 1955, **Charging system**. [American Library Association]. {DUL IIFT IIT ZHL}

Kirkwood, Letla H., 1961, **Charging systems.** {USIS}

Wolman, Yecheskel, 1983, **Chemical information** : A practical guide to utilisation. {CRRI}

Fegan, E.S. and Cant M., 1958, **Chetenham classification.** {JNU}

Agrawal, S.P. and Naresh Kanta, 1990, **Child education in India**: Index to scholarly writings in Indian educational journals and newspapers. {NIPCCD}

Anon, 1969, **Children's catalogue**, 12th edn. {USIS}

Fleet, Anne, 1973, **Children's libraries**. {DUL}

Anon, 1966, **Children's literature** : A guide to reference sources. [U.S. Library of Congress]. {USIS}

Gross, Elizabeth Henry, 1983, **Children's service in public libraries** : Organisation and administration, with collaboration of Gene Inyart Namovicz. {NASSDOC}

Matthews, Joseph, R., 1980, **Choosing an automated library system** : A planning guide. [American Library Association]. {USIS}

Smith, Josephine Metcalfe, 1968, **A chronology of librarianship**. {USIS}

Thorton, John L., 1941, **Chronology of librarianship**. {CRRI}

Kohl, D.F., 1986, **Circulation, interlibrary loan, patron use and collection maintenance** : A handbook for library management. {NASSDOC}

Fry, George, et al, 1961, **Circulation systems selection manual for college and university libraries.** {JNU}

Brown, Charles Harvey and Bousfield, H.G., n.d., **Circulation work in college and university libraries.** {JNU}

Libetz, Ben Anni, 1964, **Citations for physics literature** : Experimental issue : Citations of Journal of Applied Physics : The physical review. {DUL}

Garfield, E., 1979, **Citation indexing** : Its theory and application in science, technology and humanities. {NASSDOC NIH}

Bidlack, Russel E., 1955, **City Library of Detroit, 1817-1837**. {JNU}

Anon, n.d., **Classification** : Class A : General works, polygraphy, 3rd edn. [U.S. Library of Congress] {CRRI}.

Anon, n.d., **Classification** : class B, 2nd edn. [U.S. Library of Congress]. {ISI}

Anon, n.d., **Classification** : Class H : Social sciences, 3rd edn. [U.S. Library of Congress]. {CRRI}

Anon, 1924, **Classification** : Class J : Political science with supplementary pages, 2nd edn. [U.S. Library of Congress]. {DUL}

Anon, 1922, **Classification** : Class N : Fine Arts, 3rd edn., [U.S. Libray of Congress]. {ISI}

Anon, 1948, **Classification** : Class P : Subclass PG : Russian literature. [U.S. Library of Congress]. {DUL}

Anon, 1915, **Classification** : Class P : Subclasses PNPR, PS and PZ, Literature, [U.S. Library of Congress]. {DUL}

Anon, 1937, **Classification** : Class P : Subclass PQ : Italian, Spanish and Portuguese literature with supplementary pages, part 2. [U.S. Library of Congress]. {DUL}

Anon, 1950, **Classification** : Class Q : Science, 5th edn. [U.S. Library of Congress]. {CRRI}

Anon, n.d., **Classification** : Class R : Medicine : 3rd edn. [U.S. Library of Congress]. {ISI}

Anon, 1948, **Classification** : Class S : Agriculture, plant and animal industry, fish culture and fisheries, hunting, sports, 3rd edn. [U.S. Library of Congress]. {DUL}

Anon, 1952, **Classification** : Class U : Military science, 3rd edn. [U.S. Library of Congress]. {JNU}

Anon, 1927, **Classification** : Class Z : Bibliography and library science, 3rd edn. [U.S. Library of Congress]. {CRRI}

Herdman, Margaret M., 1947, **Classification** : An introductory manual, 2nd edn. {DUL NASSDOC}

Richardson, Ernest Cushing, 1964, **Classification** : Theoretical and practical, 3rd edn. {DUL}

Ranganathan, S.R., 1951, **Classification and communication**. {ISI NERC}

Voegelin, C.F. and Voegelin, F.M., 1977, **Classification and index of the world's languages**. {JNU}

Langridge, D.W., 1976, **Classification and indexing in the humanities**. {DUL JNU NASSDOC ZHL}

Vickery, B.C., 1959, **Classification and indexing in science**. {CRRI DUL IIT NAI}

Foskett, D.J., 1963, **Classification and indexing in the social sciences**. {DSSW IEG IIMC IIT NAI NASSDOC NIEPA SPA USIS}

Foskett, D.J., 1971, **Classification and indexing in the social sciences**, 2nd edn. {BIS ICA JNU NASSDOC}

Ranganathan, S.R., 1950, **Classification, coding and machinery for search**. {DUL}

Bakewell, K.G.B., ed., 1968, **Classification for information retrieval** : Papers presented at an intensive course held in September 1967 at the School of Librarianship. [Liverpool College of Commerce]. {NIH}

Schwerin, Kurt, n.d., **Classification for international law and relations,** 2nd edn. {IEG}

Biligiri, B.S. and Sulochna, C.R., 1973, **Classification for linguistics and languages** : A modified approach based on Decimal Classification. [Central Institute of Indian Languages, Mysore]. {ICHR ZHL}

Cunninghan, Eileen R., 1967, **Classification for medical literature**. 5th edn. {DUL}

Maltby, Arthur, ed., 1972, **Classification in the 1970's** : A discussion of the development and prospects for the major schemes. {AIU IIC JNU NASSDOC NIPCCD ZHL}.

Kelley, Grace O., 1938, **Classification of books** : An inquiry into its usefulness to the reader. {DUL}

Anon, 1960, **Classification of business literature**. [Graduate School of Business Administration Library, Harvard University]. {ISI}

Daniel, Ruth and Mills, J., 1975, **Classification of library and information science**. {DUL}

Anon, 1958, **Classification of type design**. {DUL}

Davison, Keith, 1966, **Classification practice in Britain** : Report on a survey of classification opinion, etc. {DUL}

Anon, 1973, **Classification research** : India, 1968-1973. [Documentation Research and Training Centre, Bangalore]. {BIS}

Kalia, D.R., 1988, **Classification schedule for area studies**. {NASSDOC*}

Anon, 1955, **Classification schedules for printed, microcopy and phonorecord materials in the Reference Department**, 2nd edn. [New York Public Library]. {DUL}

Sigmund, Frauendorter Wein, 1960, **Classification scheme of agricultural science**, 3rd rev edn. {DUL}

Dhyani, Pushpa, 1983, **Classification schemes and Indian libraries**. {DUL IIFT IIT ISI NERC NMML}.

Shera, Jesse H. and Egan, M.E., 1956, **Classified catalogue** : Basic principles and practices. [American Library Association]. {CRRI NASSDOC}

Ranganathan, S.R., 1945, **Classified catalogue code**, 2nd edn. [Madras Library Association]. {CRRI DSSW NAI}

Ranganathan, S.R., 1951, **Classified catalogue code**, 3rd edn. {DSSW}

Ranganathan, S.R., 1958, **Classified catalogue code**, with additional rules for dictionary catalogue code, 4th edn. [Madras Library Association]. {DSSW IEG NERC}

Ranganathan, S.R., 1965, **Classified catalogue code**, with additional rules for dictionary catalogue code, 5th edn. {AIU BIS CRRI DSSW ICHR IIT ISI MHA NAI NASSDOC NMML SPA ZHL}

Varma, A.K., 1988, **Classified catalogue code** : Entries and procedure. {JNU}

Sharma, C.D., 1973, **Classified catalogue code in theory and practice.** {CRRI}

Sharma, C.D. and Dave, Meenakshi, 1990, **Classified catalogue code in theory and practice** {DUL}

Williams, James G., et al, eds., 1972, **Classified Library of Congress subject headings**, 2 vols., V. 1: Classified list; V. 2: Alphabetical list. {IIT JNU NASSDOC NIH}

Williams, James G., et al, eds., 1982, **Classified Library of Congress subject headings**, 2nd edn., Part A : Classified list; Part B : Alphabetical list. {IIT JNU NASSDOC}

Horton, Carolyn, 1967, **Cleaning and preserving bindings and related materials**. [American Library Association]. {DUL IIT}

Horton, Carolyn, 1969, **Cleaning and preserving bindings and related materials,** 2nd edn. [American Library Association]. {USIS}

Martell, Charles R., 1983, **Client-centred academic library** ; An organisational model. {JNU}

Danton, J. Periam, 1959, **Climate of book selection** : Social influences on school and public libraries. {DUL}

Anon, 1974, **Clinic on library applications of data processing**, 24th, 1974, Illinois. [University of Illinois at Urbana-Champaign]. {USIS}

Packer, Katherine H. and Phillips, Delores, eds., 1969, **Code and the cataloguer** : Proceedings of the colloquium on the Anglo-American Cataloguing Rules held at the School of Library Science, University of Toronto on March 31 and April 1, 1967. {NASSDOC}

Merril, W.S., 1939, **Code for classifiers**. 2nd edn. [American Library Association]. {BIS CRRI IIT NAI USIS ZHL}

Anon, 1972, **Code of practice for handling and storage of microtransparencies**, rev. edn., (IS : 3130-1972). [Indian Standards Institution]. {NASSDOC}

Anon, 1966, **Code of practice for library lighting**. (IS : 2672-1966). [Indian Standards Institution]. {NASSDOC}

Anon, 1966, **Code of practice for the processing of microfilms**, Silver halide. (IS : 3083-1966). [Indian Standards Institution]. {NASSDOC}

Anon, 1965, **Code of practice for reinforced binding of library books and periodicals**. (IS : 3050-1965). [Indian Standards Institution]. {CRRI NASSDOC}

Anon, 1965, **Code of practice for storage and use of microfilms of permanent value.** (IS : 3130-1965). [Indian Standards Institution]. {NASSDOC}

Anon, 1964, **Code of practice relating to primary elements in the design of buildings for archives**. (IS : 2663-1964). [Indian Standards Institution]. {NASSDOC}

Anon, 1960, **Code of practice relating to primary elements in the design of library buildings**. (IS : 1553-1960). [Indian Standards Institution]. {NASSDOC}

Anon, 1963, **Code of recommended practice for the form and presentation of periodicals of permanent value**. (CP 48 : 1963). [New Zealand Standards Institute, Wellington]. {NASSDOC}

Fasana, Paul J. and Venaner, Allen, 1971, **Collaborative library systems development**. {JNU}

Anon, 1976, **Collection building in special purpose libraries**. {USIS}

Petrova, L.G., et al, eds., 1965, **Collection of materials on the preservation of library resources**. {INSA NASSDOC}

Anon, 1931, **Colleges and reference library year book**, No. 3. [American Library Association]. {JNU}

Hanley, E.R., 1939, **College and university library building**. [American Library Association]. {IIT}

Erickson, E. Walfred, 1961, **College and university library surveys**, 1938-52. {JNU}

Burlingame, Dwight F., 1978, **College learning resource centre**. {NIEPA}

Anon, 1971, **College libraries** : Recommended standards of library provision in colleges of technology and other establishment of further education. [Library Association, London]. {DUL ICA}

Bavakutty, M., 1986, **College libraries in India** : A case study: Photocopy from: *Library management* 7(1) 1986. {NASSDOC}

Goil, N.K., n.d., **College libraries in India** : Needed a policy for development. {AIU IEG}

Jefferson, George and Burnett, C.C.K. Smith, 1978, **College library** : A collection of essays. {DUL NIEPA}

Gunjal, S.R. and Sangam, S.L., 1987, **College library** : Problems and prospects. [Gulbarga University, Gulbarga]. {NASSDOC}

Smith, D.L. and Baxter, E.G., 1965, **College library administration**. {DUL IIT SPA}

Gerould, James Thayer, n.d., **College library building** : Its planning and equipment. {DUL}

Trehan, G.L., 1985, **College library management** : Academic library system, services and use. {JNU}

Lyle, Guy R., 1935, **College library publicity**. {USIS}

Lyle, Guy R., 1986, **College library publicity**. {DUL}

Line, Maurice, B., 1986, **College students and the library** : Report of a survey in May 1964 of the use of libraries and books, by students in five teacher training colleges. {JNU}

Knapp, Particia B., n.d., **College teaching and the college library**. {AIU JNU}

Kroll, Morton, 1961, **College, university and special libraries of the Pacific North West**. {JNU}

Khanna, J.K. and Kapil, D.D., 1982, **Colon Classification**. {CRRI ICHR IIFT IIT}

Ranganathan, S.R., 1939, **Colon Classification**, 2nd edn. {DSSW}

Ranganathan, S.R., 1950, **Colon Classification**. 3rd edn. [Madras Library Association]. {CRRI}

Ranganathan, S.R., 1952, **Colon Classification**. 4th edn. [Madras Library Association]. {ISI}

Ranganathan, S.R., 1957, **Colon Classification**, 5th edn. (DSSW IEG NCAER}

Ranganathan, S.R., 1969, **Colon Classification**, 6th edn., reprinted 1960; 1963; 1964; 1969. {AIU BIS CRRI DSSW GPF ICHR IDSA IIFT IIMC IIT INSA ISI JNU MHA NAL NASSDOC NERC NIPCCD NMML SPA UGC ZHL}

Ranganathan, S.R., 1987, **Colon Classification**, 7th edn. {JNU}

Khanna, J.K. and Bhagal, S.R., 1986, **Colon Classification** : Enumerated and expanded schedules alongwith theoretical formulations. {NASSDOC}

Mohinder Pratap Chand, 1978, **Colon Classification** : Its structure and working. {ISI NERC NMML}

Ranganathan, S.R., 1969, **Colon Classification** : A perview, 7th edn. {JNU}

Neelameghan, A., et al, n.d., **Colon Classification** : Schedule of basic subjects, 7th edn. {DUL}'

Bhargava, G.D. and Sood, S.P., 1975, **Colon Classification** : Theory and practice. {CRRI ICA ICHR NIPCCD}

Sachdeva, Mohinder Singh, 1975, **Colon Classification** : Theory and practice. {ICA MHA MMTC NIPCCD}

Ranganathan, S.R., 1970, **Colon Classification for library science**. {DUL}

Gopinath, M.A., **Colon Classification for macro documents in history**. {DUL}

Neelameghan, A., and Seetharam, S., n.d., **Colon Classification for macro documents in mathematics**. {DUL}

Slamecka, Vladimir, 1965, **Coming age of information technology** : Studies in coordinate indexing. {DUL}

Collison, Robert, 1969, **Commercial and industrial records storage**. {NMML}

Lamp, J.P., 1955, **Commercial and technical libraries**. {BIS}

Piercy, Esther J., 1974, **Commonsense cataloguing** : A manual for the organization of books and other materials in school and small public libraries, 2nd rev ed., by Marian Sannar. {USIS}

Mathews, Anne J., 1983, **Communicate** : A librarian's guide to interpersonal relations. [American Library Association]. {USIS}

Rathbone, Robert R., 1972, **Communicating technical information.** {CRRI}

Bolt, A.B. and Wardle, M.E., 1970, **Communicating with a computer**. {NASSDOC}

Johnson, E.D., 1966, **Communication** : An introduction to the history of writing, printing, books and libraries, 3rd edn. {IIC MHA}

Johnson, E.D., 1973, **Communication** : An introduction to the history of writing, printing, books and libraries, 4th edn. {USIS}

De Reuck, Anthony and Knight, Julie, eds., 1967, **Communication in science** : Documentation and automation. [CIBA Foundation]. {MHA}

Penland, Patrick R., 1974, **Communication in science and technology**. {INSA}

Mc Garry, Keyin J., 1975, **Communication knowledge and the librarian**. {CRRI DUL NASSDOC}

Penland, Patrick R., 1972, **Communication manual for libraries**. {JNU}

Egan, Margret Elizabeth, 1954, **Communication of specialised information**. {JNU}

McGarry, K.J., and Burrel, T.W., 1973, **Communiçation studies**. {CRRI}

Jackson, Wills, 1953, **Communication theory**. {JNU}

Thayer, Lee, ed. and comp., 1967, **Communication theory and research** : Proceedings of the first international symposium. {NASSDOC}

Anon, 1977-83, **Communication yearbook**, 1977-78; 1982-83. {RTL}

Anon, 1976, **Community college libraries in the United States**. {USIS}

Vett, Fritz, 1975, **The community college library**. {DUL USIS}.

Wheeler, Helen Rippier, 1965, **The community college library** : A plan for action. {DUL USIS}

Wilson, Pauline, 1977, **Community elite and the public library** : The use of information in leadership. {IIT NIPCCD}

Becker, Carol A., 1974, **Community information service** : A directory of public library involvement. {JNU}

Bunch, Allan, 1982, **Community information services** : Their origin, scope and development. {IIT}

Gawrecki, Drahoslav, 1968, **Compact library shelving**. [American Library Association]. {DUL NASSDOC USIS}

Edwards, Tom, ed., 1978, **A comparative analysis of the major abstracting and indexing services for library and information science**. [UNESCO]. {NASSDOC}

Edwards, Tom, ed., 1982, **A comparative analysis of the major abstracting and indexing services for library and information science** : With notes on their coverage of archive material. [UNESCO]. {NASSDOC}

Jackson, Miles M., ed., 1970, **Comparative and international librarianship** : Essays on themes and problems. {AIU IIT}

Hendricks, Donald D., 1966, **Comparative costs of book processing in a processing centre and in five individual libraries**. {DUL}

Gidwani, N.N., ed., 1973, **Comparative librarianship** : Essays in honour of Prof. D.N. Marshall. {ICHR IIC JNU NASSDOC NIPCCD NMML ZHL}

Hanson, J.C.M., 1939, **A Comparative study of cataloguing rules** : Based on Anglo-American code of 1908. {NASSDOC*}

Chene, Steven Seapho, 1976, **Comparative study of librarian's job satisfaction** : Cataloguer and reference librarians in university libraries. {JNU}

Stevens, Norman D., n.d., **Comparative study of three systems of information retrieval**. [Graduate School of Library Science, New Brunswick]. {BIS MHA}

Almasy, Elina, et al, 1976, **Comparative survey analysis** : An annotated bibliography, 1967-1978. {NASSDOC}

Lancaster, F.W. and Smith, L.C., n.d., **Compatibility issues affecting information systems and services**. {JNU}

Chennaveerian, M.S., et al, eds., 1976, **Compendium of research, 1951-1976**. [Karnatak University]. {NASSDOC}

Pollack, Bary W., 1972, **Compilers techniques**. {NASSDOC}

Anon, 1963, **A comprehensive bibliography on operations research, 1957-58**. [Operations Research Society of America]. {INSA}

Anon, 1973, **A compressed term index language for library and information science.** [Association of Special Libraries and Information Bureaux]. {NASSDOC}

Wessel, Andrew E., 1975, **Computer-aided information retrieval**. {BIS CRRI NIH USIS}

Horn, Jack, n.d., **Computer and data processing** : Dictionary and guide. {RTL}

Tou, Julius T. and Wilcox, Richard H., eds., n.d., **Computer and information science** : Collected papers on learning, adaptation and control in information systems. {DUL}

Cox, N.S.M., 1966, **Computer and the library**. {IIT}

Madan, Som Nath, 1987, **Computer and library services**. {NASSDOC*}

Houghton, Bernard, ed., 1968, **Computer based information retrieval systems**. {DUL INSA NASSDOC}

Anon, 1979, **Computer-based information services in medicines** : A feasibility study : On behalf of the University of Otago medical libraries. [Centerbury Medical Library]. {BCL}

Lynch, Michael Felix, 1974, **Computer-based information services in science and technology** : Principles and techniques. {BCL}

Henley, J.P., 1970, **Computer based library and information systems**. {BIS IIT JNU NASSDOC NIH}

Henley, J.P., 1972, **Computer based library and information systems**, 2nd edn. {DUL NIH}

Anon, 1981, **Computer based national information systems** : Technology and public policy issues. [U.S. Office of Technology Assessment]. {USIS}

Methics, Lorraine M. and Watson, Peter G., 1976, **Computer based reference service**. {JNU}

Fosdick, Howard, 1981, **Computer basics for librarians and information scientists**. {USIS}

Sippl, Charles J., 1966, **Computer dictionary and handbook**. {NASSDOC}

Sippl, Charles J. and Sippl, Roger J., 1983, **Computer dictionary and handbook**, 3rd edn. {NASSDOC RTL}

Haleda, Prithvi, ed., 1983, **Computer directory of India, 1983.** {NASSDOC}

Haleda, Prithvi, ed., 1984, **Computer directory of India, 1984.** {NCERT}

Blessum, William T. and Sippl, Charles J., 1972, **Computer glossary for medical and health sciences**. {NASSDOC}

Schmalz, Larry C. and Sippl, Charles J., 1972, **Computer glossary for students and teachers.** {NASSDOC}

Bagley, D.E., 1966, **Computer in libraries** : A selected bibliography. {JNU}

Mahapatra, Piyushkanti, 1985, **Computer in library services**. {JNU NASSDOC NMML}

Abkin, Michael H. and Carrol, Tam W., 1976, **Computer library for agricultural systems simulation** : A progress roport. {BIS}

Barron, D.W., 1971, **Computer operating systems**. {NASSDOC}

Katzan, Harry, 1971, **Computer organisation and the system/370**. {NASSDOC}

Avedon, Don M., 1971, **Computer output microfilm**, 2nd edn. [National Microfilm Association]. {USIS}

Saffady, William, 1979, **Computer output microfilm** : Its library applications. {JNU}

Spencer, Donlad D., ed., 1968, **Computer programmer's dictionary handbook**. {RTL}

Dodd, K.N., 1969, **Computer programming and languages**. {DUL}

Dial, O. Eugene, 1968, **Computer programming and statistics for basic research**. {NASSDOC}

Emerick, Paul L. and Wilkinson, Joseph W., 1970, **Computer programming for business and social science**. {NASSDOC}

Leeds, Herbert D. and Winberg, Gerald M., 1966, **Computer programming fundamentals,** 2nd edn. {NASSDOC}

Rajaraman, V., 1971, **Computer programming in Fortran IV**. {NASSDOC}

Anon, 1973, **Computer programming problems** : Batch-I. [National Computer Centre, Manchester]. {NASSDOC}

Wainwright, Jane, 1975, **Computer provision in British libraries**. {JNU}

Williams, Martha E., et al, comps. and eds., 1982, **Computer readable data bases** : A directory and data sourcebook. 2 vols. [American Society for Information Science]. {USIS}

Hawkes, Nigel, 1971, **Computer revolution**. {NASSDOC}

Cardenas, Alfonso F., et al, eds., 1972, **Computer science**. {NASSDOC}

Forsyth, Alexandra I., et al, 1970, **Computer science** : Fortran language programming. {DUL}

Naylor, Thomas H., et al, 1968, **Computer simulation techniques**. {NASSDOC}

Swihart, Stanley J. and Heeley, Beryl F., 1973, **Computer systems in the library** : A handbook for managers and designers. {CRRI NASSDOC NIPCCD}

Kumar, P.S.G., 1987, **Computerisation in Indian libraries**. {NASSDOC}

Dolby, J.L., et al, 1969, **Computerised library catalogues** : Their growth, costs and utility. {IIT JNU NMML USIS}

Anon, 1983, **Computerised systems in library and information services**. {NASSDOC}

Philips, G.M. and Taylor, P.J., 1969, **Computers**. {DUL}

Sprowls, R. Clay, 1968, **Computers** : A programming problem approach, rev. edn. {DUL}

Taube, Mortimer, 1961, **Computers and common sense** : The myth of thinking machines. {JNU}

Anon, 1971, **Computers and computation**. {NASSDOC}

Eyre, John and Tonks, Peter, 1971, **Computers and systems** : Introduction for librarians. {IIT NASSDOC}

Rigby, M., 1974, **Computers and the UDC** : A decade of progress, 1963-1973. [International Federation for Documentation and Information]. {NIH}

Avebury, Lord, et al, eds., n.d., **Computers and the year 2000**. [National Computer Centre, Manchester]. {NASSDOC}

Chanana, Charanjit, 1973, **Computers in Asia**. {NASSDOC}

Bowles, Edmund A., ed., 1967, **Computers in humanistic research**. {NASSDOC}

Gopalakrishnan, P. and Narayanan, K.S., 1975, **Computers in India**. {NASSDOC}

Kochenburger, Ralph J. and Turcio, Corolyn J., 1974, **Computers in modern society**. {NASSDOC}

Anger, Arthur L., et al, 1972, **Computers science** : The PL/I language. {DUL}

Sterling, T.D. and Rollack, S.V., 1970, **Computing and computer science** : A first course with PL/I. {DUL}

Plaister, Jean M., 1982, **Computing in LASER regional library cooperation** : London and South Eastern library region. [Library Association, London]. {DUL}

Agrawal, S.P., gen ed., 1989-, **Concepts in communication, informatics and librarianship**. (CICIL series). {JNU NASSDOC}

Pao, M.L., 1989, **Concepts of information retrieval.** {NASSDOC}

Borka, H., 1965, **Conceptual foundations of information systems**. {JNU}

Anon, 1981, **The concise AACR2** : Being a rewritten and simplified version of Anglo-American Cataloguing Rules, 2nd edn. [American Library Association]. {NASSDOC USIS}

Anderson, R.G., 1984, **Concise dictionary of data processing and computer terms,**, 2nd edn. {NCERT}

Stokes, Adrian V., 1982, **Concise encyclopaedia of information technology**. {CRRI JNU NASSDOC RTC}

Morse, Grant W., 1966, **Concise guide to library research**. {JNU}

Naur, Peter, 1974, **Concise survey of computer methods.** {NASSDOC}

Jordain, Philip B., 1969, **Condensed computer encyclopedia.** {IDSA}

Anon, 1975, **Conference number and souvenir** : All India library conference, 22nd, January 17-20, 1976, Delhi. [Indian Library Association]. {NASSDOC}

Anon, 1967, **Conference on mechanised information storage, retrieval and dissemination.** {NMML}

Linderman, Wilfred B., 1967, **Conference on the present status and future prospects of reference information work.** {JNU}

Jones, Ken, 1984, **Conflict and change in library organisation** : People, power and service. {DUL JNU}

Ranganathan, S.R. and Bhattacharya, G., 1970, **Conflict of authorship.** [Sarada Ranganathan Endowment for Library Science]. {ZHL}

Zwirn, Jerrold, 1983, **Congressional publications** : A research guide to legislation, budgets and treaties. {USIS}

Cronin, Richard, 1981, **Congressional research service.** {USIS}

Singh A.P., 1987, **Conservation and museum techniques.** {NMML}

Kathpalia, Yash Pal, 1973, **Conservation and restoration of archive materials.** {NASSDOC}

Kuhn, Hermann, 1986, **Conservation and restoration of works of art and antiquities,** tr. by Alexandra Trone. {NMML}

Anon, 1985, **Conservation in India** : Problems and prospects : Seminar on conservation in India, 1985, Lucknow. {NMML}

Swartzburg, Susan Garretson, ed., 1983, **Conservation in the library** : A handbook of use and care of traditional and non-traditional materials. {JNU NMML}

Langwell, W.H., 1974, **Conservation of books and documents.** {NERC}

Chuna, George M. and Chuna, Dorothy G., 1972, **Conservation of library materials** : Manual of bibliography on the care, repair and restoration of library materials, 2 vols. {DUL IIT NMML USIS}

Agrawal, O.P., 1984, **Conservation of manuscripts and painting of South-East Asia.** {NMML}

Morrow, Carolyn Clark and Dual, Carole, 1986, **Conservation treatment procedure** : A manual of step by step proocdures for the maintenance and repair of library materials. {NASSDOC}

Saracevic, Tefko, and Wood, Judith B, 1981, **Consolidation of information** : A handbook on evaluation, restructuring and repackaging of scientific and technical information. [UNESCO]. {CRRI}

Mc Lilvaine, Betsy, 1983, **A consumers', researchers' and students' guide to government publications.** {USIS}

Sharma, Satinder, 1982, **Contemporary approach to school library.** {DUL NASSDOC}

Nasso, Christine, ed., 1976, **Contemporary authors** : A bibliographical guide to current authors and their work, 2 vols. {RTL}

Jackson, Miles M., ed., 1981, **Contemporary developments in librarianship** : An international handbook. [Library Association, London]. {IIT NASSDOC}

Yehawine, Wayne S., ed., 1958, **Contemporary library design.** {DUL}

Rees, Alan, ed., 1974, **Contemporary problems in technical library and information centre management** : A state-of-the-art. [American Society for Information Science]. {USIS}

Anon, 1972, **Content Analysis** : A technique for systematic inference from communications. {NASSDOC}

Berelson, Bernard, 1971, **Content analysis in communication research.** {NASSDOC}

Budd, Richard W., et al, 1967, **Content analysis of communication.** {NASSDOC}

Ellis, Lee Robert, 1966, **Continuing education for adults through the American Public Library, 1833-1964**. [American Library Association]. {USIS}

Sardana, J.L., ed., 1984, **Continuing education for librarians** : Paper : All India seminar for librarians, February 13, 1984, New Delhi. [Indian Library Association]. {NASSDOC}

Stone, Elizabeth W., et al, 1974, **Continuing library and information science education** : Final report to the National Commission on Libraries and Information Science (with bibliography). {USIS}

Stone, Elizabeth W., 1974, **Continuing library education as viewed in relation to other continuing professional movements.** [American Society for Information Science]. {NIEPA}

Anon, 1988, **Convention and exposition** : Micrographic Congress (India), 2nd, January 20-22, 1988, New Delhi. {NASSDOC}

Anon, n.d., **Convention papers** : All India library convention, 5th, May 23-26, 1985, Hardwar. [Government of India Librarians Association]. {NASSDOC}

Converse, Jean M. and Schuman, Howard, 1974, **Conversations at random** : Survey research as interviewers see it. {NASSDOC}

Metcalf, Keyes D., 1964, **Co-operation among Maine libraries** : A report prepared for the larger libraries of Maine. {DUL}

Stenstrom, Ralph H., 1970, **Cooperation between types of libraries, 1940-1968** : An annotated bibliography. [American Library Association]. {NASSDOC}

Henderson, M.M., et al, **Cooperation, convertibility and compatibility among information systems** : A literature review. {BIS}

Anon, n.d., **Cooperative cataloguing manual for the use of contributing libraries.** [U.S. Library of Congress]. {DUL}

Kenney, Brigitte L., 1959, **Cooperative centralised processing** : A report of the establishment and first year of operation of the South West Mission Library Service. {DUL}

Luquire, W., 1986, **Coordinating cooperative collection development** : A national prospective. {JNU NASSDOC}

Myrick, William J., 1975, **Coordination** : Concept or reality. {DUL}

Anon, 1976, **Copyright Act**. {NASSDOC}

Verona, Eva, 1975, **Corporate headings** : Their use in library catalogues and national bibliographies : A comparative and critical study. [International Federation of Library Associations and Institutions]. {JNU NASSDOC ZHL}

Scheuk, Gretchen Knief, 1954, **County and regional library development.** {NASSDOC}

Carnell, E.J., 1938, **County libraries** : Retrospect and forecast. {CRRI ZHL}

Anon, 1932, **County libraries in Great Britain and Ireland**. [Library Association, London]. {NASSDOC}

Cooke, A.S., ed., 1931, **County libraries manual**. [Library Association, London]. {NASSDOC}

Osborn, Egar and Sharr, F.A., 1950, **County library practice**. [Library Association, London]. {CRRI ZHL}

Sandre, Mildred W., 1942, **County library primer**. {JNU}

Long, Harriet Catherine, 1925, **County library service**. {JNU}

Macledo, Robert D., n.d., **County rural libraries** : Their policy and organisation. {JNU}

Anon, 1976, **A course in administration for managers of information services** : Design, implementation and topical outline. [UNESCO; UNISIST]. {NASSDOC}

Anon, 1986, **Course material** : Workshop on computer application to library and information activities, 2nd, September 8-13, 1986, Ahmedabad. [ILA; Physical Research Laboratory, Ahmedabad]. {NASSDOC}

Kirby, John, 1985, **Creating the library identity** : A manual of design. {NASSDOC}

Lincoln, Alan Jary, 1984, **Crime in the library** : A study of patterns, impact and security. {JNU}

Girja Kumar, 1990, **Crisis management of libraries in India**. {NASSDOC}

Sandhu, S.N., 1969, **Critical evaluation of the bibliographical sources for manuscript in modern Indian languages**. (University of Delhi, Department of Library Science. Sessional Project). {DUL}

Bavakutty, M., 1984, **A critical study of the organisation and utilisation of libraries in higher educational institutions in Kerala**. [University of Calicut]. {NASSDOC}

Atkins, Thomas V., et al, eds., 1974, **Cross reference index** : A subject heading guide. {NASSDOC USIS}

Atkins, Thomas V., ed., 1984, **Cross reference index**, 2nd edn. {USIS}

Benge, Ronald Charles, 1979, **Culture crisis and libraries in the Third World**. {IIT}

Anon, 1928-81, **Cumulated book index** : World list of books in English language, 1928-32 to 1973; 1976 to 1981. {NASSDOC}

Anon, 1928, **Cumulative instructions to depository libraries**. {NASSDOC}

Kemp, Alasdair, 1979, **Current awareness service**. {JNU}

Anon, 1981-83, **Current book review citations**, 1981 to 1983. {USIS}

Woodworth, David P., ed., 1982, **Current British journals, 1982.** [British Library Lending Division]. {NASSDOC}

Boaz, Martha, ed., 1979, **Current concepts in library management.** {USIS}

Carleton, Joecket, 1939, **Current issues in library administration.** {JNU}

Zimmerman, Irena, 1971, **Current national bibliographies of Latin America** : A state-of-the-art study. [Centre for Latin America, University of Florida]. {NASSDOC}

Khan, H.A. and Ijari, S.R., 1990, **Current problems and trends in library and information services** : Professor K.S. Deshpande felicitation volume. {DUL}

Galvin, Thomas J., 1971, **Current problems in reference service**. {DUL JNU NERC USIS}

Biggs, P.T., ed., 1985, **Current research for the information profession, 1985-86**. [Library Association, London]. {NASSDOC}

Hakam Singh and Narang, S.P., 1973, **Current trends in library organisation**. {JNU}

Anon, n.d., **Curriculum guide for the school libraries in the elementary school**. [Detroit Public School]. {JNU}

Cutter, C.A., n.d., **Cutter's three figure author table**. {IIT ISI}

Rose, J., 1974, **The cybernetic revolution**. {INSA NASSDOC}

Pask, Gordon, 1975, **Cybernetics of human learning and performance** : A guide to theory and research. {NASSDOC}

Vasarhelyi, Paul, n.d., **DARE Equal : UNESCO computerised data retrieval system for documentation in the social and human sciences**. {NASSDOC}

Anon, 1966, **DDC descriptor frequencies**. [Defence Documentation Centre]. {IIT}

Anon, 1976, **DEVSIS** : The preliminary design of an international information system for the development sciences. [International Development Research Centre, DEVSIS Study Team, Ottawa]. {NASSDOC}

Agrawal, S.P., ch. ed., 1985, **Dr. S.R. Ranganathan** : A bibliography, comp. by O.K. Choudhry. [National Social Science Documentation Centre]. {NASSDOC NMML}

Rokhan, Stein, n.d., **Data archives for the social science**. {DSSW}

Nasatir, David, 1973, **Data archives for the social sciences** : Purposes, operations and problems. {ZHL}

Westin, Alen F. and Baker, Michal A., 1972, **Databanks in a free society** : Computers, record keeping and privacy : Report. [National Academy of Sciences, Washington]. {USIS}

Abramson, Norman, 1985, **Data communication and information exchange network**. (ASTINFONET). [UNESCO]. {NASSDOC}

Schnake, M.A., 1973, **Data-processing concepts**. {NASSDOC}

Harper, William L., 1973, **Data processing documentation** : Standards, procedures and applications. {USIS}

Harvey, John, M., 1966, **Data processing in public and university libraries**. {DUL IIT}

Clifton, H.D., 1971, **Data processing systems design** : Case studies from the application of computers to business. {NASSDOC}

Jolley, J.L., 1968, **Data university**. {JNU}

Clarke, Marion G.M., 1966, **David Watkinson's library** : Hundred years in Harftord, Connecticat. {DUL}

Parkhi, R.S., 1945, **The Decimal and Colon Classifications** : A summary and a comparison. {NASSDOC}

Pollard, A.F.C., 1926, **Decimal Bibliographical Classification of the Institut International de Bibliographies**. {BIS}

Parkhi, R.S., 1964, **Decimal Classification and Colon Classification in perspective**. {CRRI IEG IIT ISI NAL NERC NMML}

Raju, A.A.N., 1984, **Decimal, Universal Decimal and Colon Classification** : A study in comparison. {ICA NASSDOC NERC NIEPA SPA}

Shaffer, Kenneth, R., 1971, **Decision making** : A seminar in public library management. {USIS}

Bommer, Michael R.W. and Chorba, Ronald W., 1982, **Decision-making for library management**. {JNU NIEPA}

Hastings, N.A. and Mello, J.M., 1978, **Decision networks**. {JNU}

Keen, Peter F. and Scott-Morten, Michael S., 1978, **Decision support systems** : An organisational perspective. {JNU}

Anon, 1979, **Decision tables in data processing** : A report. [National Computer Centre, Manchester]. {NASSDOC}

Jones, Frances M., 1983, **Defusing censorship** : The librarian's guide to handling censorship conflicts. {JNU}

Anon, 1963, **Delhi Public Library** : Constitution, regulations of Delhi Library Board and rules of the library. [Delhi Library Board]. {NASSDOC}

Gardner, Frank M., 1957, **Delhi Public Library** : An evaluation report. {DSSW DUL}

Anon, 1976, **Delhi Public Library** : Silver jubilee souvenir, 27th October, 1976. {NASSDOC}

Anon, n.d., **Delhi University Library** : The opening of the new library by S. Radhakrishnan. {JNU}

Ranganathan, S.R., 1953, **Depth classification and reference service and reference material**. [Indian Library Association]. {INSA ISI}

Pandey, S.K., 1986, **Depth schedules for Indian philosophy and religions for DDC**. {JNU]

Gorman, Michael, and Linford, John E., 1971, **Description of the BNB/MARC record** : A manual of practice. {JNU}

Ranganathan, S.R., 1967, **A descriptive account of Colon Classification.** {BIS DSSW DUL ISI JNU NAL NASSDOC NERC NMML SPA ZHL}

Anon, 1955, **Descriptive catalogue of documentary films.** [Films Division, Government of India]. {NAL}

Tait, James A. and Anderson, F. Douglas, 1968, **Descriptive cataloguing** : A students introduction to the Anglo-American Cataloguing Rules, 1967. {NASSDOC}

Tait, James A. and Anderson, F. Douglas, 1971. **Descriptive cataloguing** : A students introduction to the Anglo-American Cataloguing Rules, 1967, 2nd edn. {IIC IIT}

Delbigio, G. and Ruckenbaver, E. Inis, 1978, **Descriptive cataloguing rules**. [International Atomic Energy Agency, Vienna]. {BIS}

Anon, 1948, **Descriptive list of professional and non-professional duties in libraries** : Preliminary draft. [American Library Association]. {USIS}

Bowen, Judith, 1978, **The design and implementation of community information service in the library**. {BCL}

Pasty, Cullen and Kirby, John, 1986, **Design and production of media presentation for libraries.** {JNU}

Anon, 1957, **Design for elementary libraries**. [Department of School, City of South Bend]. {JNU}

Newbury, K.M., ed., n.d., **Design in the library**. [Library Association London]. {ISI}

Anon, 1974, **Design of information in the social sciences** : Size and growth of monograph literature with particular reference to the social sciences. [Bath University Library]. {BCL NASSDOC*}

Churchman, C. West, 1971, **Design of inquiry systems** : Basic concepts of systems and organisation. {JNU}

Myller, Rolf, 1966, **The design of the small public library**. {USIS}

Cohen, Aaron and Cohen, Elaine, 1979, **Designing and space planning for libraries** : A behavioural guide. {BIS NASSDOC USIS}

Orr, N.M., 1972, **Designing library buildings for activity**. {CRRI ICA ICHR ISI MMTC NASSDOC}

Ackoff, Rusell L., et al, 1976, **Designing national scientific and technological communication system**. {USIS}

Singer, Howard W. and Smith, Richard Daniel, eds., 1970, **Deterioration and preservation of library materials** : Conference of the Graduate Library School, 34th, August 4-6, 1969, Chicago. {AIU CRRI IIT INSA JNU NASSDOC NMML}

Rosove, Perry E., 1967, **Developing computer based information systems**. {JNU}

Corbin, John, 1981, **Developing computer based library systems.** {JNU}

Sharma, C.D. and Vyas, Kailash, 1983, **Developing horizons in library and information science**, 2 vols. {AIU IIT ISI JNU NASSDOC NMML SPA}

Harmon, Robert B., 1976, **Developing the library collection in political science**. {JNU}

Evans, G. Edward, 1979, **Developing library collections**. {USIS}

Hicks, Warren B. and Tillin, Alma, 1970, **Developing multi-media libraries**. {JNU}

Cambell, H.C., 1983, **Developing public library systems and services**. [UNESCO]. {NIEPA}

Insha, Ibne, 1967, **Developing reading habits in Asian conditions.** {ZHL}

Anon, 1977, **Development index Canada** : Index to 1976 Canadian literature on economic and social development. [International Development Research Centre]. {IIFT}

Agrawal, S.P., 1989, **Development of documentation in India** : Social science information. {BIS DSSW DUL ISI JNU NAL NASSDOC NERC NMML SPA ZHC}

Hussain, Khateeb M., 1973, **Development of information systems for education**. {AIU INSA}

Mookerjee, S.K., 1969, **Development of libraries and library science in India.** {ICA IIC IIT NASSDOC NERC NIH NIPCCD NMML}

Sen, N.B., ed., 1965, **Development of libraries in new India**. {ICA IIC IIT NASSDOC SPA}

Anon, 1968, **Development of library facilities in universities and colleges.** [University Grants Commission, New Delhi]. {AIU IIT MHA}

Morton, E.H., 1974, **Development of library services** : Trinidad and Tobago. [UNESCO]. {ISI}

Agrawal, S.P., 1989, **Development of library services in India** : Social science information. {BIS DUL ISI JNU NASSDOC NERC NMML ZHL}

Dudley, Edward, ed., 1983, **Development of national library and information service.** [Library Association, London]. {NIEPA}

Anon, 1966, **Development of performance standards for library binding**, Phase 1: Report of the survey, April, 1961; Phase 2: Report on a study conducted by library technology project. [American Library Association]. {BIS IIT}

Anon, 1954, **Development of public libraries in Africa** : Ibadan seminar. [UNESCO]. {IEG NASSDOC ZHL}

Anon, 1952, **Development of public libraries in Latin America** : The Sao Paulo conference. [UNESCO]. {IEG NASSDOC ZHL}

Samhel, Rothstein, 1955, **Development of reference services through academic traditions, public library practices and special librarianship**. {JNU}

Anon, 1985, **Development of research and information system in the Third World** : Report of the proceedings: Research and information system for the non-aligned and other developing countries, 2nd, November 20-22, 1985, New Delhi. [RISNODC]. {NASSDOC}

Anon, 1975, **Development of resource sharing networks in the framework of UNISIST World Science Information System**. [National Library of Australia]. {JNU}

Prasad, K.N., 1983, **Development of terminology in the field of library classification with special reference to Indian school of thought**: A case study in terminology development : Thesis. (Karnatak University). {NASSDOC}

Asundi, A.Y., 1983, **Development of an unified scheme of common subdivisions in general classification systems**. Thesis. [Gulbarga University]. {NASSDOC}

Schumacher, August, 1973, **Development plans and planning** : Bibliographic and computer aids to research. {JNU}

Ijari, S.R., 1983, **A development plan for public library system in the Karnataka State**. Thesis. (Karnataka University). {NASSDOC}

Anon, 1967, **Developments in classification** : DRTC annual seminar, 2 vols. [Documentation Research and Training Centre]. {NASSDOC}

Koops, William R.H. and Stellingwerff, Johannes, eds., 1977, **Developments in collection building in university libraries in Western Europe**: Symposium on . . ., March 31-April 2, 1976, Amsterdam. {IIT}

Dewey, Melvil, 1989, **Dewey Decimal Classification**, 20th edn. 4 vols, V. 1. : Introduction tables; V. 2. : Schedules 000-599; V. 3. : Schedules 600-990; V. 4. : Index manual, 20th edn. {NASSDOC}

Dewey, Melvil, 1982, **Dewey Decimal Classification** : 301-307, sociology : Expanded version based on edition 19. {NASSDOC}

Osborn, Jeanne, 1982, **Dewey Decimal Classification** : A study manual. {USIS}

Dewey, Melvil, 1935, **Dewey Decimal Classification and Relative Index,** 6th edn. {NAI}

Dewey, Melvil, 1942, **Dewey Decimal Classification and Relative Index.** 14th edn., 2 vols. {USIS ZHL}

Dewey, Melvil, 1951, **Dewey Decimal Classification and Relative Index**. 15th edn. {IEG IIT NAI USIS}

Dewey, Melvil, 1964, **Dewey Decimal Classification and Relative Index**. 16th edn. 2 vols. {CRRI NASSDOC NMML SPA USIS}

Dewey, Melvil, 1967, **Dewey Decimal Classification and Relative Index**, 17th edn., 2 vols. {CRRI NASSDOC NMML SPA USIS}

Dewey, Melvil, 1971, **Dewey Decimal Classification and Relative Index,** 18th edn., 3 vols. {IIMC ISI JNU NASSDOC NIEPA USIS}

Dewey, Melvil, 1979, **Dewey Decimal Classification and Relative Index,** 19th edn., 3 vols. {CRRI ICHR ISI JNU MHA NAI NASSDOC NMML USIS ZHL}

Sharma, Pandey S.K., 1979, **Dewey Decimal Classification for Indology** : Expansion and modification of Dewey Decimal Classification (18) for classifying Indological books with special reference to Indian philosophy and Indian religions. {DSSW ICHR IIC IIT INSA JNU MHA NIPCCD ZHL}

Baba, Abdul Majid, 1988, **Dewey Decimal Classification, Universal Decimal Classification and Colon Classification** : Development structure, comparison. {NASSDOC}

Mittal, R.L. and Gupta, Shamsher, 1966, **Dictionary catalogue** : A practical manual. {ICHR IIT IIMC NERC NIPCCD}

Ranganathan, S.R., 1952, **Dictionary Catalogue Code**, 2nd edn. [Madras Library Association]. {CRRI}

Breuer, Hans, n.d., **Dictionary for computer languages**. {RTL}

Tayyab, R. and Chanadana, K., comps., 1985, **A dictionary of acronyms and abbreviations in library and information science**, 2nd edn. [Canadian Library Association, Ottawa]. {NASSDOC}

Watson, James and Hill, Anne, 1986, **Dictionary of communication and media studies**. {JNU NASSDOC}

Camille, Claude, and Dehaine, Michel, 1970, **Dictionary of data processing**. {NASSDOC}

Wittmann, Alfred and Klos, Joel, 1977, **Dictionary of data processing**, 3rd. rev edn. {NASSDOC}

Rogers, Harold A., 1970, **Dictionary of data processing terms** : {UGC}

Trollhani, Lilian and Wittmann, Alfred, 1964, **Dictionary of information processing**, including fields of application. {RTL}

Rosenberg, Kenyon C. and Feinstein, Paul T., 1983, **Dictionary of library and educational technology,** 2nd rev edn. {NASSDOC}

Sharma, Pandey S.K. and Gupta, O.P., 1986, **Dictionary of library and information science** : English-Hindi; Hindi-English. {NASSDOC}

Gunjal, S.R. and Sangam, S.L., 1986, **Dictionary of library and information science** : English-Kannada. [University of Gulbarga, Gulbarga]. {NASSDOC}

Chopra, R.N., 1990, **Dictionary of library scinece**. {JNU}

El-Benhawy, Mohamad Amil, 1970, **Dictionary of library terms** : English-Arabic. {JNU}

Meadows, A.J., 1982, **Dictionary of new information technology**. {IIPA}

Gordon, M., et al, 1984, **Dictionary of new information technology acronym**. {JNU}

Kennlison, W.C. and Spilman, A.J.B., 1963, **Dictionary of printing paper making and book binding.** {DUL}

Goil, N.K., ed., 1973, **Dictionary of pseudonyms in Indian literature**. [Delhi Library Association]. {NASSDOC}

Anon, n.d., **Dilemma of the urban public library in developing countries**. [International Federation of Library Associations and Institutions; International Council for Adult Education]. {IIMC}

Danton, J. Periam, 1973, **Dimensions of comparative librarianship.** [American Library Association]. {NASSDOC}

Bhargava, G.D. and Tejomurty, A. eds., 1986, **Dimensions in library and information science**. {JNU}

Venkatappaiah, V., et al, eds., 1990, **Dimensions of library and information science** : Kaula festschrift. {NASSDOC}

Kirkendall, Carolyn A., ed., 1981, **Directions for the decade** : Library instruction in the 1980's : Conference on library orientation for academic libraries, 10th, May 8-9. 1980. [Eastern Michigan University]. {USIS}

Anon, 1977-79, **Directory**, 1977; 1979. [International Federation of Library Association and Institutions]. {NASSDOC}

Dadzie, E.W. and Strickland, J.T., n.d., **Directory of archives, libraries and schools of librarianship in Africa**. {IIMC}

Anon, 1968, **Directory of booksellers, publishers, libraries and librarians in India, 1968-69**. {SPA}

Khosla, Raj K., ed., 1973, **Directory of booksellers, publishers, libraries and librarians in India**, including who's who, 2nd edn, {ICA IDSA JNU NASSDOC NMML}

Sharma, Jai Kishore, 1973, **Directory of book trade in India**. JNU RTL}

Anon, n.d., **Directory of British publishers**, 1961; 1967. {DUL}

Kapoor, Pran, comp. and ed., 1979, **Directory of business Information research centres in India.** [National Industrial Documentation and Manpower Centre, New Delhi]. {NASSDOC}

Anon, 1971, **Directory of college and university libraries in New York State**. [University of the State of New York; State Education Department]. {JNU}

Anon, 1974, **Directory of co-operative libraries and documentation services**. [ICA, London]. {ICA}

Anon, 1976, **Directory of development documentation and information facilities in Asia and Pacific**. [UN Asian Development Institute, Bangkok]. {IEG IIFT NASSDOC}

Zidoemba, Dominique, 1977, **Directory of documentation, libraries and archives services in Africa**, 2nd edn. [UNESCO]. {JNU NASSDOC}

Anon, 1979, **Directory of educational documentation and information services**, 3rd edn., [UNESCO]. {NASSDOC NIPCCD}

Bhatia, Brajesh, and Goyal, M.M.L., 1971, **Directory of family planning and population libraries in India**. [National Institute of Family Planning]. {NIH}

Krishnamurty, P.G., 1980, **Directory of health science libraries and documentation centres in India**. [National Institute of Health and Family Welfare, New Delhi]. {NIH}

Dhir, S.C. and Anand, S.K., 1979, **Directory of health science libraries in South-Asia**. {NIH}

Barua, B.P. ed., 1986, **Directory of Indian public libraries** : A selected list of libraries. {NASSDOC}

Trivedi, Dinkar, ed., 1973, **Directory of Indian publishers**. [Federation of Publishers and Booksellers Association in India]. {IIPA NASSDOC RTL UGC}.

Anon, 1974, **A directory of information resources in the United States Federal Government, with a supplement of government sponsored information analysis centres**. [U.S. Library of Congress, National Referral Centre]. {USIS}

Anon, 1979, **Directory of information sources in Japan**. {JNU}

Anon, 1985, **Directory of institutions and organisations specialising in children's literature**. [International Board on Books for Young People; UNESCO]. {NASSDOC*}

Khan, Mohammad A.S., comp., 1983, **Directory of Islamic libraries and librarians**. [Islamic Library Association, California]. {ZHL}

Anon, 1979, **Directory of libraries and documentation centres in the United Nations system**. {JNU}

Anon, 1985, **Directory of libraries and information centres in Gujarat**. {Gujarat Granthalaya Seva Sangh, Ahmedabad]. {NASSDOC}

Anon, 1972, **A directory of libraries and library training programme in Thailand**. [UNESCO Regional Office for Education in Asia, Bangkok]. {NASSDOC NIEPA}

Collison, Robert, comp., 1970, **Directory of libraries and special collections on Asia and North Africa**. {NASSDOC NCERT NMML}

Goel, N.K., et al, 1964, **Directory of libraries and who's who in library profession in Delhi**. [Delhi Library Association]. {BIS CRRI DSSW ICCR ICWA IEG IIC NMML ZHL}

Bhatia, S.K. and Surender Kumar, comps., 1988, **Directory of libraries in Delhi.** {ICA ICCR IIC IIPA JNU NIEPA NASSDOC}

Keeth, Kent H., comp., 1965, **A directory of libraries in Malaysia.** [University of Malaya Library, Kaula Lumpur]. {NASSDOC}

Mwinyimvua, E.A., comp. and ed., 1984, **Directory of libraries in Tanzania**. [National Central Library, Tanzania]. {NASSDOC}

Panwar, Bhanwar Singh and Vyas, Shree Dhar, 1970, **Directory of libraries, publishers and booksellers of Udaipur city and who's who.** {NMML RTL}

Khandwala, Vidyut K. and Naidu, M.K.R., eds., 1965, **Directory of libraries, publishers, booksellers in the city of Bombay**. [SNDT Women University Library]. {NASSDOC}

Gates, Hilary and Brookes, Alison, comps., 1986, **A directory of library and information retrieval software for micro-computers**, 2nd edn. {NASSDOC}

Chopra, H.R., Kumar, P.S.G. and Tejomurty, A., 1988, **Directory of library and information science schools in India**. {NASSDOC}

Berry, John N., ed., 1969, **Directory of library consultants**. {USIS}

Casby, Brinkley, comp., n.d., **Directory of library photo duplication services in the United States, Canada and Mexico**. {DUL}

Sharma, J.K., 1973, **Directory of library schools and lecturers in librarianship in Australia**. {NASSDOC*}

Anon, 1976, **Directory of medical libraries in the British Isles**. [Library Association, London, Medical Section]. {NIH}

Anon, 1988, **Directory of members**. [Micrographic Congress of India]. {NASSDOC}

Huen, P. Lim Pui, comp., 1973, **Directory of microfilm facilities in Southeast Asia**, 2nd edn. {JNU}

Hudson, Kenneth and Micholls, Ann, 1975, **Directory of museum**. {ICCR}

Sivaramamurti, C., 1959, **Directory of museums in India**. [Ministry of Scientific Research and Cultural Affairs, New Delhi]. {ICCR NASSDOC}

Buckner, B.C., comp., 1973, **Directory of population libraries and information centres in the United States**. [Carolina Population Centre, University of North Carolina]. {NIH RTL}

Anand Sagar, comp. and ed., 1986, **Directory of publishers and booksellers in India**, based on actual mailing. [Federation of Indian Publishers]. {NASSDOC}

Woodworth, David, comp., 1971, **Directory of publishers of British journals**. {NASSDOC}

Brownstone, David M. and Franck Irene M., 1982, **The directory of publishing**. {NASSDOC}

Chatterjee, Nihar Kanti, 1980, **Directory of research and special libraries in India and Sri Lanka**, 2 vols. {MMTC ZHL}

Kalia, D.R. and Surender Kumar, 1988, **Directory of scientific and technical libraries in India.** {DUL}

Tapingkae, A., 1974, **Directory of selected scholars and researchers in Southeast Asia**. [Regional Institute of Higher Education and Development, Singapore]. {NASSDOC}

Anon, 1986, **Directory of social science libraries, information centres and data bases in Sri Lanka**. [Sri Lanka Social Science Documentation Centre]. {NASSDOC}

Anon, 1962, **Directory of special and research libraries in India**. [Indian Association of Special Libraries and Information Centres]. {IIT ISI MFL NMML ZHL}

Anon, 1985, **Directory of special and research libraries in India**. 2nd edn. [Indian Association of Special Libraries and Information Centres]. {ICCR ICWA IDSA IIPA NASSDOC NMML UGC}

Kruzas, Authony T., ed., 1963, **Directory of special libraries and information centres**. {ICCR ICWA IIPA}

Young, M.L. and Young, H.C., eds., 1974-79, **Directory of special libraries and information centres 1974; 1979**. {IIFT}

Young, M.L. and Young, H.C., eds., 1981-83, **Directory of special libraries and information centres 1981 to 1983**. {USIS}

Anon, 1976, **Directory of suppliers of library requisites**. [IDL Chemicals Limited, Hyderabad]. {NASSDOC*}

Anon, 1985, **Directory of United Nations databases and information systems** [United Nations Advisory Committee for Coordination of Information Systems]. {NASSDOC}

Anon, 1980, **Directory of United Nations information systems**, 2 vols. [United Nations Inter-Organisation Board of Information Systems, Geneva]. {MMTC RTL}

Anon, 1983 **Directory of World Bank depository libraries**. [International Bank for Reconstruction and Development] {NASSDOC}

Lipsman, Claire K., 1972, **The disadvantaged and library effectiveness**. [American Library Association]. {USIS}

Cleary, Florence D., 1966, **Discovering books and libraries** : A handbook for the upper elementary and junior high school grades. {DUL}

Muscutt, H.C., 1963, **Display techniques**. {DUL}

Rowley, J.E. and Turner, C.M.D., 1978, **The dissemination of information**. {BCL DUL ISI NASSDOC ZHL}

Wilson, T.D. and Stephenson, J., 1969, **Dissemination of information** : An examination guidebook. {BIS DUL MFL NIPCCD}

Broadbent, K.P., 1980, **Dissemination of scientific information in the People's Republic of China**. [International Development Research Centre, Ottawa]. {NASSDOC}

Konkar, S., 1985, **Dissemination services provided by special libraries in Pune**. [University of Poona, Pune]. {NASSDOC*}

Nagarajan, S., et al, eds., 1989, **Distributed data bases** : Plan for interaction and online search. {NASSDOC*}

Blagden, John, 1980, **Do we really need libraries?** {NIPCCD}

Murty, A.T., 1979, **Document bibliography**. {NIPCCD NASSDOC}

Wardle, D.B., 1971, **Document repair**. [Society of Archivists]. {NMML}

Mason, Donald, 1968, **Document reproduction in libraries**. {DUL}

Duyvis, F. Donker and Schippers, M.E., **Document reproduction services** : Their efficient organisation and management. [UNESCO]. {IIMC NASSDOC}

Montgomery, K. Leon, 1975, **Document retrieval systems** : Factors effecting search time. {DUL IIT NASSDOC USIS}

Black, Donard V., 1983, **Document storage and retrieval techniques appendix** : Indexing techniques, descriptions and background. {JNU}

Bradford, S.C., 1953, **Documentation**. {BCL BIS DUL MFL NAI SPA}

Ranganathan, S.R., ed., 1973, **Documentation** : Genesis and development. {AIU CRRI DUL ICA ICHR IIMC ISI JNU MFL MHA MMTC NASSDOC NIEPA NIPCCD NMML}

Whitehouse, Franck, 1971, **Documentation** : How to organise and control information processes in business and industry. {JNU}

Guha, Bimalendu, 1978, **Documentation and information** : Services, techniques and systems. {AIU BCL BIS IIMC ISI JNU MFL NASSDOC NCDC NERC NIEPA NIH NMML}

Guha, Bimalendu, 1988, **Documentation and information** : Services, techniques and systems, 2nd edn. {DUL ICA IIT JNU MHA NIH NIPCCD ZHL}

Sengupta, Benoyendra and Chatterjee, Mridula, 1977, **Documentation and information retrieval**. {DUL MHA ZHL}

Perry, J.W. and Kent, Allen, n.d., **Documentation and information retrieval** : An information to basic principle and cost analysis. {JNU}

Ranganathan, S.R., 1963, **Documentation and its facets** : Being a symposium of seventy papers by thirty-two authors. {BIS DUL DSSW IIFT JNU NMML SPA}

Shera, Jesse H., 1966, **Documentation and the organisation of knowledge**, ed. by D.J. Foskett. {DUL NASSDOC NMML USIS}

Aggarwal, J.C. and Agrawal, S.P., 1990, **Documentation encyclopaedia of UNESCO and education**. {NIEPA}

Shera, Jesse, H., et al, 1956, **Documentation in action**. {BIS DUL NASSDOC}

Kesavan, B.S. 1968, **Documentation in India**. {JNU}

Anon, 1961, **Documentation, indexing and retrieval of scientific information.** [US Committee on Government Operations]. {JNU}

Haworth, Carol S., 1964, **Documentation of semi-automatic bibliographic information retrieval**. {JNU}

Anon, 1980, **Documentation services in departmental libraries** : Papers : All India library convention, 2nd, March 3-6, 1980, New Delhi. [Government of India Librarians Association]. {CRRI NASSDOC NMML}

Asija, S., 1988, **Documentation services in India** : An overview of some selected documentation centres. {NASSDOC}

Schutze, Gertrude, 1965, **Documentation source book**. {BIS DUL MHA NASSDOC NIH}

Gray, Max, 1969, **Documentation standards**. {BIS DUL NIEPA}

Rubin, Martin L., ed., 1979, **Documentation standards and procedures for on-line systems**. {CRRI}

Anon, 1951, **Documentation techniques in the USA**. [Organisation for Economic Co-operation and Development, Paris]. {ISI}

Kempe, Mary E., 1977, **Documentation training needs in Eastern Africa**. {ICA}

Vashishth, C.P., 1967, **Documents of the UN and the specialised agencies** : A study of problems regarding their acquisition and organisation with special reference to India. (University of Delhi Department of Library and Information Science sessional project). {DUL}

Anon, 1985, **Documents on national policy on library and information system**. [Raja Rammohan Roy Library Foundation; Indian Library Association]. {NASSDOC*}

Anon, 1963, **Does your firm need its own information service** : An enquiry into the economic advantages of an information service in small and medium-sized firms. [Organisation of Economic Cooperation and Development, Paris]. {TDA}

Baker, Robert, K., 1981, **Doing library research** : An introduction for community college students. {USIS}

Foulkes, John, ed., 1986, **Down loading bibliographic records.** {NASSDOC*}

Sharma, B.N., 1977, **Dvibindu vargikaran ka sankshipt parichay**. {NMML}

Parkhi, R.S., 1965, **Dvibindu vargikaran paddhatiche yatharth darshan** {NMML}

Salton, Gerard, 1975, **Dynamic information and library processing.** {CRRI DUL ICHR INSA ISI NASSDOC USIS}

Pacay, Philip, 1977, **ED art library manual** : A guide to resources and practice. {IIT}

Anon, 1982, **EUDISED multilingual thesaurus** : Alphabetical list of deseriptors. {NASSDOC}

Viet, Jean, 1973, **EUDISEO multilingual thesaurus for information processing in the field of education**. {NASSDOC}

Saith, S.S., 1968, **East African School of Librarianship.** [UNESCO]. {NASSDOC*}

Swaran Kumar, 1963, **East and West**. : Delhi Public Library, India, as seen against the background of the Rochester Public Library. {NASSDOC*}

O'Connor, V.C. Scott, 1920, **Eastern library**. {ZHL}

O'Connor, V.C. Scott, 1977, **Eastern library** : An introduction to the Khuda Bakhsh Oriental Public Library, 2nd edn. {JNU NMML}

O'Connor, V.C. Scott, 1985, **An eastern library** : An introduction to the Khuda Bakhsh Oriental Public Library, 3rd edn. {NASSDOC*}

Ruok, Alice, 1959, **Easy ways to displays** : A library publicity handbook. {JNU}

Newhouse, Joseph P. and Alexender, Arthur J., 1972, **Economic analysis of public library services**. {ISI}

Anon, n.d., **Economic analysis of special libraries with special reference to CSIR libraries**, memeo short bibliography. {NASSDOC}

Getz, Malcolm, 1979, **An economic view of public libraries** [U.S. National Bureau of Economic Research]. {USIS}

Maltby, Arthur, ed., 1968, **Economics and commerce** : The sources of information and their organisation. {NASSDOC}

Baumel, W.J. and Marcus, M., n.d., **Economics of academic libraries**. [American Council of Education]. {AIU NIEPA USIS}

Hayes, R.M. and Shoffner, R.M., 1964, **Economics of book catalogue production**. {DUL}

Smith, Datus C., 1977, **Economics of book publishing in developing countries.** {DUL}

Eric, Bailey, 1965, **Economics of book selling**. {DUL}

Elisworth, Ralph E., 1969, **Economics of book storage in college and university libraries**. {NASSDOC}

Lamberton, D.M., ed., 1971, **Economics of information and knowledge** : Selected readings. {NASSDOC}

Anon, n.d., **Editor and publisher international year book** : Encyclopaedia of the newspaper industry. {DUL}

Lubrans, John, ed., 1974, **Educating the library user**. {USIS}

Tauber, Maurice F. and Orne, Jerrold, eds., 1976, **Education and libraries** : Selected papers. {AIU USIS}

Schur, H. and Saunders, W.L., 1968, **Education and training for scientific and technological library and information work.** {IIT SPA}

Schur, H., 1973, **Education and training of information specialists.** {BCL CRRI ICA}

Evans, A.J., et al, 1977, **Education and training of users of scientific and technical information** : UNISIST guide for teachers. [UNESCO]. {BCI ISI NASSDOC}

Anon, 1957, **Education clearing houses and documentation centres.** [UNESCO]. {JNU}

Borolson, Bernard, ed., n.d., **Education for librarianship.** {AIU IEG}

Danton, J. Periam, 1949, **Education for librarianship.** [UNESCO]. {IEG NASSDOC}

New, Peter G., 1978, **Education for librarianship** : Decisions in organising a system of professional education. {NIEPA}

Chakraverty, N.C., 1966, **Education for librarianship** : A survey. [Indian Association of Special Libraries and Information Centres]. {SPA}

Anon, 1965, **Education for librarianship in India**. [Indian Association of Special Libraries and Information Centres]. {IIT MFL NASSDOC}

Srivastava, A.P., 1969, **Education for library science and documentation** : Iran. [UNESCO]. {NASSDOC*}

Anon, 1972, **Education, library science, journalism** : A bibliography of doctoral dissertations, 1857-1970. [Inter-University Board of India and Ceylon, New Delhi]. {JNU NMML}

Anon, 1983, **Educational information** : Problems, issues and strategies for resolving them : Report of a regional workshop. [National Institute for Educational Research]. {NIEPA}

Haughney, John D., 1968, **Effective catalogues**. {NIPCCD}

Coplan, Kate, 1974, **Effective library exhibits** : How to prepare and promote good displays, 2nd edn. {CRRI USIS}

Anon, 1989, **Effective methods of promoting reading habits in Asia and the Pacific**. [Asian Cultural Centre for UNESCO, Tokyo]. {NASSDOC*}

Thomas, Diana M., 1981, **Effective reference librarian**. {IIT ISI NASSDOC}

Gaver, Mary Virginia, 1963, **Effectiveness of centralized library services in elementary schools**. {JNU}

Grundt, Leonard, 1968, **Efficient patterns for adequate library service in a large city** : A survey of Boston. {JNU}

O'Connor, V.C. Scott, 1950, **Ek mashriqui kutubkhana** : Kutub- khana Khuda Bakhsh, tr. by Mubarizuddin Rifat. {NMML}

Bird, E.A., 1972, **Electronic data processing computers for commercial students**. {NERC}

Kent, Allen, et al, eds., 1967, **Electronic handling of information** : Testing and evaluation. {DUL INSA}

Christien, Roger, 1978, **The electronic library** : Bibliographic data bases, 1978-79, 2nd rev. edn. {USIS}

Kroll, Morton, 1960, **Elementary and secondary school libraries of the Pacific North West**. {JNU}

Lawrie, Jean Elizabeth, 1970, **Elementary school libraries**. {JNU}

Palouec, Lora and Goodman, Elezabeth B., 1969, **Elementary school library in action**. {JNU}

Vishwanathan, C.G., 1976, **Elements of information science**. {DUL NAI NIEPA}

Ranganathan, S.R., 1945, **Elements of library classification**. {ZHL}

Ranganathan, S.R., 1960, **Elements of library classification**, 2nd edn. {INSA NERC SPA}

Ranganathan, S.R., 1962, **Elements of library classification**, 3rd edn. {BIS CRRI IIT ISI NASSDOC}

Clason, W.E., comp., 1973, **Elsevier's dictionary of library science, information and documentation**. {JNU ZHL}

Clason, W.E., comp., 1976, **Elsevier's dictionary of library science, information and documentation**, 2nd edn. {IIT}

Bry, Ilse. 1977, **Emerging field of socio-bibliography** : The collected essays of Ilse Bry, comp. and ed. by Lois Afflerback and Marga Franck {BCL IIT}

Woy, James, ed., 1980, **Encyclopaedia of business information sources**. {USIS}

Kruzas, Anthony Thomas, ed., 1974, **Encyclopaedia of information systems and services**. {MHA}

Kruzas, Anthony Thomas, ed., 1978, **Encyclopaedia of information system and services** : A guide to information storage and retrieval services, data base produces and publishers, online vendors, 3rd edn. {USIS}

Kruzas, Anthony Thomas, ed., 1981, **Encyclopaedia of information system and services** : An international guide to computer readable data bases, data base producers and publishers, online vendors and time sharing companies, 4th edn. {USIS}

Schmittroth, John, ed., 1982, **Encyclopaedia of information systems and services**, 5th edn. {USIS}

Eastlick, John T., ed., 1958, **Encyclopaedia of librarianship.** {SPA ZHL}

Landau, T., ed., 1958, **Encyclopaedia of librarianship,** 3rd edn. {SPA ZHL}

Landau, T., ed., 1967, **Encyclopaedia of librarianship**, rev. edn. {BIS CRRI DSSW IAMR IDSA IEG IIT MFL NASSDOC NCERT NIEPA}

Kent, Allen and Lancom, Harold, eds., n.d., **Encyclopaedia of library and information science**, 41 vols. {ACA IOSA IEG IIT INSA JNU NASSDOC NCERT NIH ZHL}

Meetham, A.R., ed., 1968, **Encyclopaedia of linguistics, information and control**. {NASSDOC NCERT}

Anon, 1983, **Encyclopaedias and dictionaries of the world.** {NASSDOC}

Thompson, James, 1982, **End of libraries.** {IIT}

Irwin, Raymond, 1966, **English library** : Sources and history. {JNU}

Yadubaities, E.A., ed., 1981, **English-Russian glossary of computer systems and networks terminology**. {NASSDOC}

Kubat, Libor and Zeman, Jiri, eds., 1975, **Entropy and information in science and philosophy.** {INSA}

Withington, Frederic G., 1978, **Environment for systems programmes.** {JNU}

Satija, M.P., 1979, **An epostle to dean Shera on the gravity of notation in colon classification**. {NASSDOC}

Esdaile, A., 1967, **Esdaile's manual of bibliography**, rev edn., by Roy Stockes. {MFL}

Anon, 1975, **Essays and studies in librarianship**. {NASSDOC}

Foskett, D.J. and Palmer, B.I., 1961, **Essays in librarianship** : In memory of William Charles Berwick Sayers. {MFL}

Rajagopalan, T.S., comp., 1973, **Essays in library science**, 3rd edn. {JNU}

Dasgupta, A.K., 1967, **Essays in personnel bibliography** : A bibliography of the writings on and by S.R. Ranganathan. {DUL NASSDOC NMML}

Garfield, Eugene, 1981, **Essays of an information scientist.** {CRRI JNU}

Brenni, Vito J., comp. and ed., 1975, **Essays on bibliography.** {NASSDOC}

Barr, Keith and Line, Maurice, eds., 1975, **Essays on information and libraries.** {CRRI DUL ICA IIMC INSA JNU NASSDOC NIPCCD ZHL}

Anon, 1980, **Essential problems in terminology for informatics and documentation**. [International Federation for Documentation and Information]. {BIS CRRI}

Mc Collough, Ethel Farguhar and Van Buren, Maud, 1931, **Essentials in library education**. [American Library Association]. {NASSDOC*}

Lodewycks, K.A., 1961, **Essentials of library planning.** {DUL}

Sewell, P.H., et al, 1977, **Establishing a legislative framework for the implementation of NATIS**. [UNESCO]. {NASSDOC}

Katzer, Zeffery, et al, 1978, **Evaluating information** : A guide for users of social science research. {NCAER}

Lancaster, F.W. and Cleverdon, C.W., eds., 1977, **Evaluation and scientific management of libraries and information centres**. {NIEPA}

Sircar, Pankti, 1970, **Evaluation of the acquisition policy and procedure of periodicals in the Indian Institute of Foreign Trade Library and Rattan Tata Library**. {DUL}

Gupta, S.R., 1978, **Evaluation of collection of Jawahar Lal Nehru University Library from the point of view of Indian reference sources**. [University of Delhi, Department of Library and Information Science Sessional Project]. {DUL}

Gupta, Shamsher, 1973, **Evaluation of Indian reference sources published during last ten years available in Delhi University Library**. (University of Delhi, Department of Library and Information Science, Sessional Project). {DUL}

Anon, 1968, **Evaluation of the MEDLARE demand research services**. [U.S. National Library of Medicine]. {USIS}

Veaner, Allen B., 1970, **Evaluation of micropublications** : A handbook for librarians. [American Library Association]. {NASSDOC}

Houghton, Bernard, 1977, **The evaluation of a programme designed for teaching on-line information retrieval techniques** : Final report for the period June-September 1976. [Liverpool Polytechnic, Department of Library and Information Studies]. {BCL}

Mushtaq Ahmed, 1958, **Evaluation of reading materials for neo-literates and a study of their reading needs and interests.** {NMML}

Majumdar, S., 1980, **Evaluation of reference service in JNU library.** {JNU}

Sachdev, Surinder Mohan, 1976, **Evaluation of the reference sources in the field of Hindi language and literature serving the needs of post-graduates and faculty of Delhi University campus college libraries**. (University of Delhi, Department of Library and Information Science, Sessional Project). {DUL}

Abidi, Syed Ameer Haider, 1967, **Evaluation of selected reference tools published in India**. (University of Delhi, Department of Library Science, Sessional Project). {DUL}

Gaver, Mary Virginia, 1962, **Every child needs a school library.** {JNU}

Kaul, B.K., 1962, **Examination of current practices in Delhi college libraries and suggestion for improvement.** {JNU}

Adamson, Edith, 1963, **Examination of public library finance in Canada in relation to minimum standards of the Canadian Library Association**. {JNU}

Hunter, Eric J. and Fox, Nicholas J., 1980, **Examples illustrating AACR2** : Anglo-American Cataloguing Rules, 2nd ed. [Library Association, London]. {NASSDOC}

Anon, 1972, **Examples illustrating Anglo-American Cataloguing Rules** : British text. [Library Association, London]. {ZHL}

Georgi, C. and Bellanti, Robert, eds., 1985, **Excellence in library management**. {NASSDOC*}

Anon, 1957, **Exchange of ideas** : East and West meet the challenge : Final report : Seminar on the international exchange of publications in the Indo-Pacific area, 1957, Tokyo. {IEG}

Asha Rani, 1964, **Exchange of publications and organisation of national exchange centres**. (University of Delhi, Department of Library and Information Science, Sessional Project). {DUL}

Anon, 1968, **Exhibition of scientific and technical books** : Catalogue. {DUL}

Boyle, Deirdre, ed., 1977, **Expanding media.** {IIT}

Sharma, Pandey Suraj Kant, 1976, **Expansion and modification of Dewey Decimal Classification (18) for classifying Indological books with special reference to Indian philosophy and Indian religions**. {NASSDOC}

Luquire, W., ed., 1984, **Experiences of library network administrators** : Papers based on the symposium 'From our past : Towards 2000'. {NASSDOC}

Line, Maurice B., et al, 1971, **Experimental information service in the social sciences** : Report on work carried out in 1970, [University Library, Bath University of Technology]. {NASSDOC}

De Rossi, Claude J., 1975, **Exploring the world of data processing.** {NASSDOC}

Anon, 1956, **Extensions and corrections to the UDC**. [International Federation for Documentation and Information]. {IIT INSA}

Anon, 1978, **FID congress on new trends in documentation and information, 1978, Edinburg**. [International Federation of Documentation and Information] {CRRI}

Anon, 1985, **FID directory 1985-86**. [International Federation of Documentation and Information]. {NASSDOC}

Vickery, B.C., 1960, **Faceted classification**. [Association of Special Libraries and Information Bureaux]. {CRRI}

Croghan, Antony, 1968, **Faceted classification for an essay on the literature of the performing arts.** {DUL}

Stone, Elizabeth W., 1969, **Factors related to the professional development of librarians**. {USIS}

Bagley, W.A., 1948, **Facts and how to find them**. {CRRI MFL}

Bagley, W.A., 1950, **Facts and how to find them**, 4th edn. {BIS DUL}

Bagley, W.A., n.d. **Facts and how to find them**, 7th edn. {DSSW}

Bagley, William, 1958, **Facts and how to find them** : A guide to source of information and to the method of systematic research. {JNU}

Harrison, K.C., 1964, **Facts at your fingertips** : Everyman's guide to reference books. {MFL}

Rader, Hannelore B., 1976, **Faculty involvement in library instruction**. {JNU}

Anon, 1975, **Faculty status for university and college librarian in India** : Basic documents. {JNU NASSDOC ZHL}

Edwards, Margaret A., 1974, **The fair garden and the swarm of beasts** : The library and the young adult. {USIS}

Lewis, P.R., 1982, **The fall and rise of national bibliography**. [Sarada Ranganathan Endowment for Library Science, Bangalore]. {NASSDOC*}

Horowitiz, Blanche, 1975, **A family planning library manual**. [Planned Parenthood Federation of America]. {NIH}

Korloztury D., n.d., **Famous Hungarian libraries**. [National Szecheni Library]. {NASSDOC}

Williams, Edwin Everitt, 1953. **Farminton plan handbook**. [Association of Research Libraries]. {USIS}

Rees, Alan M., et al, n.d., **Feasibility study for continuing education of medical librarians** : Interim report. {DUL}

Benton, Milored, comp., 1973, **Federal library resources** : A user's guide to research collections. {USIS}

Mason, Merilyn Gell, 1983, **The federal role in library and information services.** {USIS}

Moranjian, Lorig and Boss, Richard W., 1980, **Fee based information services**: A study of a growing industry. {IIT USIS}

Dupuy, Trevor N., 1968, **Ferment in college libraries** : The impact of information technology. {JNU}

Anon, 1967, **Fifteen years of activity of the association, 1953-67**. [Delhi Library Association]. {NASSDOC*}

Anon, 1983, **Fifty years of Government of India Librarians Association.** [Government of India Librarians Association]. {NASSDOC NMML}

Anon, 1983, **Fifty years of Indian Library Association, 1933-83** : Golden jubilee. [Indian Library Association]. {JNU MMTC ZHL}

Mangla, P.B., et al, eds., 1983, **Fifty years of librarianship in India** : Past, present and future : Papers : All India library conference, 29th, December 5-9, 1983. [Indian Library Association]. {MMTC NASSDOC ZHL}

Alexs, Phillip, 1935, **Filing and preserving stock and records,** in libraries and other institutions including museums and art galleries. {JNU}

Anon, 1956, **Filing rules for dictionary catalogues of the Library of Congress.** [U.S. Library of Congress]. {IEC NASSDOC}

Anon, 1963, **Film cataloguing rules**. [Association of Special Libraries and Information Bureaux]. {SPA}

Harrison, Helen P., 1973, **Film library techniques** : Principles of administration. {NMML USIS}

Rehrauer, George, 1975, **The film user's handbook** : A basic manual for managing library film services. {USIS}

Anon, 1972, **Final report** : International congress on the universal availability of publications. [UNESCO]. {NASSDOC}

Anon, 1982, **Final report** : International congress on the universal availability of publications. [UNESCO]. {NASSDOC}

Anon, 1969, **Final report** : Project for evaluating the benefits from university libraries. [University of Durham]. {NIEPA}

Anon, 1968, **Final report** : UNESCO meeting of experts on the national planning of library services in Asia, December 11-19, 1967, Colombo. {NASSDOC}

Anon, 1985-1986, **Final report, 1985 and 1986**. [Inter-Governmental Committee for the UNESCO; Inter-Governmental Informatics Programme]. {JNU}

Anon, n.d., **Final report on the ICAR institutions and Agricultural University libraries**. [ICAR]. {IEG}

Anon, n.d., **Final report on mechanised information services in the university library** : Phase-I : Planning. 13 pts. Pt 1 : Mechanised information services in the university library : Introduction and summary; Pt 2 : Summary of symposium on mechanised information services in the university library; Pt 3 : Inventory of available data bases; Pt 4 : Standards for cataloguing of magnetic tape material; Pt 5 : Nature of typical data bases; Pt 6 : Evaluation of generalised file management systems; Pt 7 : Experience with Library of Congress rare tapes; Pt 8 : Experimental on-line mathematics citation data base; Pt 9 : Development programme for a centre for information services; Pt 10 : Preliminary specifications (hardware and software) for a centre for information and documentation services (Interim report); Pt 11 : On the development of social science information; Pt 12 : Joint design and development of library systems; and Pt 13 : Library and human memory. [Institute of Library Research, University of California]. {BIS}

Carey, R.J.P., 1966, **Finding and using technical information.** {MHA}

Kolatkar, Ram S., 1970, **Finding the facts** : Newspaper information retrieval system. {IIMC JNU NIPCCD}

Shearer, Benjamin F. and Shearer, Barbara Smith, comps., 1981, **Finding the source** : A thesaurus index to the reference collection. {NASSDOC USIS}

Anon, 1973, **First All India workshop on the methods of teaching and evaluation in library science, May 15-30, 1973, Delhi.** {DUL}

Anon, n.d., **First seminar of university librarians in India, Jaipur.** {NMML}

Sayers, W.C., Berwick, 1955, **First steps in annotation in catalogues,** 2nd rev ed. {DUL}

Harrison, K.C., 1964, **First steps in librarianship.** {CRRI ICHR IIT MFL SPA}

Ranganathan, S.R., 1963, **Five laws of library science**. {BIS CRRI IIT MHA NAI NCAER NMML SPA ZHL}

Sivaswami Iyyar, P.S., 1931, **The five laws of library science**. [Madras Library Association, Madras]. {NASSDOC*}

Sewell, P.H., ed., 1963, **Five year work in librarianship.** [Library Association, London]. {IIT}

Plaster, C.D., 1939, **Floor and floor coverings**. [American Library Association]. {NAI}

Bohe, Marilyn, 1971, **Flow charting techniques**. {JNU}

Fhessle, Barbara Ruth, 1965, **Focus on information and communication.** {JNU}

Mahapatra, Piyushkanti, 1966, **Folklore library**. {IIMC NASSDOC NMML}

Delavenay, Emile, 1974, **For books**. [UNESCO]. {ICA}

Cole, John Y., 1979, **For Congress and the nation** : A chronological history of the Library of Congress. [U.S. Library of Congress]. {USIS}

Seymour, Whitney North and Layne, Elizabeth N., 1979, **For the people** : Fightings for public libraries. {USIS}

Anon, 1964, **Forecast of the cost of academic library services in Canada, 1965-1975**. [Association of College and University Libraries, Canada]. {JNU}

Morehouse, Ward, ed., 1965, **Foreign area studies and the college library** : Bibliographies, reference service, acquisitions programmes and other activities and services for undergraduate librarians in African, Asian, Latin American and Russian studies. [Foreign Area Materials Center, University of the State of New York]. {NASSDOC}

Johnson, R.S., 1971, **Foreign theses in British libraries**. [University of Birmingham]. {NASSDOC}

Anon, 1979, **Formation of necessary standards for different types of libraries in India** : Working paper : ILA seminar, 1979, Trivandrum. [Indian Library Association]. {NASSDOC}

Montgomery, Edward B., ed., 1968, **Foundations of access to knowledge** : A symposium. {NASSDOC}

Carpenter, Michael and Svenonius, E., eds., 1985, **Foundations of cataloguing** : A source book. {NASSDOC}

Shera, Jesse H., 1972, **Foundations of education for librarianship.** {AIU IIFT ISI NIPCCD USIS ZHL}

Shera, Jesse H., 1949, **Foundations of the public library** : The origins of the public library movement in New England, 1629-1855. {USIS}

Moodey, Edgar C., 1977, **Fraser-Hickson library** : An informal history. {IIT}

Ranganathan, S.R., et al, 1968, **Free book service for all** : An international survey. {ICA ISI JNU MFL NMML SPA}

Mosher, Frederic J., ed., 1954, **Freedom of book selection** : Proceedings : Conference on intellectual freedom, 2nd, June 20-21, 1953. [American Library Association]. {AIU USIS}

Gournay, Bernard, 1963, **French bibliographical digest** : Public administration. {MFL}

Wallace, Sarah Leslie, ed., 1962, **Friends of the library** : Organisation and activities. [American Library Association]. {NASSDOC USIS}

Mann, Peter, 1982, **From author to reader** : A social study of books. {AIU}

Palmer, B.I., 1966, **From little acorns** : The library profession in Britain. {IEG NERC}

Wasserman, Paul, ed., 1972, **Frontiers in librarianship** : Proceedings of Change Institute, 1969. [Change Institute, University of Maryland]. {JNU NIPCCD}

Seal, Alan and Bryant, Philip, 1982, **Full and short entry catalogues** : Library needs and uses. [Centre for Catalogue Research]. {NASSDOC}

Schutz, H., 1975, **Function and organisation of a national documentation centre in developing country**. [FID/DC Working Group]. {ICA JNU NASSDOC}

Hants, Roy Stokes, 1982, **The function of bibliography**. {AIU NASSDOC}

Booth, Grayce M., 1973, **Functional analysis of information processing** : A structured approach for simplifying systems design. {NASSDOC}

Domanovszky, A., 1975, **Functions and objects of author and title cataloguing** : A contribution to cataloguing theory. {NMML}

Fussler, Herman, ed., 1954, **Functions of the library in the modern college** : Conference of the Graduate Library School, 19th, 1954, Chicago. {IIT SPA}

Cheney, Frances Neel and Williams, Wiley J., 1971, **Fundamental reference sources**. [American Library Association]. {DUL INSA JNU MMTC NASSDOC NERC}

Cheney, Frances Neel, 1980, **Fundamental reference sources**. [American Library Association]. {DUL}

Shypla, Bana Bihari, 1984. **Fundamental theories in abstracting and fundamental laws in library science**. {JNU}

Sharma, Jagdish Saran, 1977. **Fundamentals of bibliography with special reference to India**. {JNU NASSDOC}

Kawatra, P.S., 1984, **Fundamentals of documentation** : With special reference to India. {DSSW DUL ICA ISI NCDC NMML}

Ram Shobhit Prasad Singh, 1990, **Fundamentals of library administration and management**. {NMML}

Sharma, Madhusudan, 1990, **Fundamentals of library and information science**. {NMML}

Palmer, B.I., 1951, **Fundamentals of library classification**. {BIS CRRI NAI SPA}

Khanna, J.K., 1984, **Fundamentals of library organisation**. {DSSW IIMC}

Corbett, Edmund V., 1978, **Fundamentals of library organisation and administration** : A practical guide. {NCDC NERC NIEPA ZHL}

Sharma, J.S., 1977, **Fundamentals of library science** : A modern approach. {ICA ISI JNU ZHL}

Taylor, Margaret S., 1948, **Fundamentals of practical cataloguing**. {BIS CRRI ICA IIFT MHA NAI NASSDOC ZHL}

Mukherjee, A.K., 1969, **Fundamentals of special librarianship and documentation**. [Indian Association of Special Libraries and Information Centres]. {AIU DUL IIT}

Fitzgerald, John M. and Fitzgerald, Andra F., 1973, **Fundamentals of systems analysis**. {JNU}

Pierce, William S., 1980, **Furnishing the library interior**. {BIS USIS}

Anon, 1982, **Future development of libraries and information services**. [Department of Education and Science, Great Britain]. {ISI}

Malinconico, Michael and Fasana, Paul J., 1979, **The future of the catalog** : The library's choices. {USIS}

Anon, 1975, **The future of cataloguing**. {USIS}

Anon, 1982, **Future of libraries** : Panel discussion by librarians, administrators, faculty and students : Papers from the millionth volume celebration. [New York State University]. {NASSDOC}

Clapp, Vener W., 1964, **Future of the research library**. {IEG JNU}

Westlake, Duncan R., 1987, **GEAC** : A guide for librarians and system managers. {NASSDOC}

Anon, 1946-67, **General catalogue of UNESCO publications and UNESCO sponsored publications**. supplements : 1946/59-1964/67. [UNESCO]. {NASSDOC}

Anon, 1971, **A general description of an approach to computerised bibliographical control.** [International Labour Office, Intergrated Scientific Information System]. {TDA}

Stone, Phillip, J., et al, 1966, **General inquirer** : A computer approach to content analysis. {NASSDOC}

Guinchat, Claire and Menou, Michel, 1983, **General introduction to the techniques of information and documentation work.** [UNESCO]. {JNU NMML}

Barton, Mary N. and Watson, Ellen F., 1950, **General reference department staff manual.** [Enoch Pratt Free Library, Baltimore]. {USIS}

Von Bertalanffy, Ludwig, 1968, **General system theory** : Foundations, development, applications. {NASSDOC*}

Sutherland, John W., 1973, **General systems philosophy for the social and behavioural sciences,** ed. by Erwinlaszlo. {NASSDOC}

Bhattacharya, G., n.d., **A general theory of SIL, POPSI and CLASSAURUS** : Results of current classification research in India. {NASSDOC*}

Campey, Lucille H., 1972, **Generating and printing indexes by computer.** [Association of Special Libraries and Information Bureaux]. {CRRI}

Hutchins, W.J., 1971, **Generation of syntactic structures from a semantic base.** {JNU}

Dixit, R.S., 1990, **Geography of marketing and commercial activities in India** : Documentation on research information. {IIT}

Hoffmann, Christa F., 1980, **Getting ready for AACR2** : The cataloguer's guide. {JNU USIS}

Singh, R.S.P., 1981, **Glimpses of librarianship**. {JNU}

Hayes, Robert M. and Becker, Joseph, 1971, **Glossary from handbook of data processing for libraries**. {USIS}

Askall, Glaister A., Geoffrey, 1960, **Glossary of the book** : Terms used in paper making, printing, binding book printing and publishing with notes on illuminated manuscripts bibliographies, private presses and printing societies. {DUL}

Anon, 1967, **Glossary of cataloguing terms**. (IS : 796-1966). [Indian Standards Institution]. {NAI NASSDOC}

Anon, 1964, **Glossary of cataloguing terms in Indian regional languages**. [Indian Association of Special Libraries and Information Centres]. {NASSDOC SPA}

Anon, 1963, **Glossary of classification terms**. (IS : 2550-1963). [Indian Standards Institutions]. {ISI NASSDOC}

Anon, 1976, **Glossary of documentation terms**. (BS : 5408-1976). [British Standards Institution]. {CRRI}

Buchanan, Brian W., 1976, **Glossary of indexing terms**. {BCL NASSDOC NERC}

Venkatappaiah, V., 1986, **Glossary of library and information science** : English-Telugu and Telugu-English. [Zilla Granthalaya Samstha, Machilipatnam]. {NASSDOC*}

Gour, P.N., 1980, **Glossary of library science technical terms**. {JNU NASSDOC RTL}

Barrett, W.J., 1961, **Glossary of photocopying terms**. {DUL}

Barrocal, Ramon, 1969, **A glossary of technical service terms for library science students**. [School of Library Science, Syracuse University]. {NASSDOC*}.

Anon, 1967, **Glossary of terms for wooden furniture.** (IS : 4415-1967). [Indian Standards Institution]. {NASSDOC}

Anon, 1974, **Glossary of terms relating to wooden furniture and fixtures**, rev. edn. (IS : 4415-1974). {NASSDOC}

Anon, 1986, **Glossary of terms used in the Public Libraries Department** : English-Telugu. [Government of Andhra Pradesh, Official Language Commission, Hyderabad]. {NASSDOC*}

Thornley, Arthur, 1968, **Going into print** : Notes for the guidance of authors in preparing copy for the printer, correcting proofs, etc. {DUL}

Stockham, K.A., n.d., **The government and control of libraries**, 2nd edn. {DUL ICHR}

Mohinder Singh, 1982, **Government of India publications**. {MHA}

Fry, Bernard, 1979, **Government publications** : Their role in the national programme for library and information services. [U.S. National Commission on Libraries and Information Science]. {USIS}

Schmeckebier, K.F. and Eastin, R.B., 1961, **Government publications and their use**, rev edn. {MFL}

Mohinder Singh, 1967, **Government publications of India** : A survey of their nature, bibliographical control and distribution systems. {MFL NASSDOC NIPCCD}

Overton, C. David, 1951, **Gramophone recording library**. {CRRI}

Sharma, Chandra Kant, 1978, **Granthalaya mein sandhrab seva**. {JNU NMML}

Anon, 1982, **Granthalaya pragati** : Souvenir : Andhra Pradesh libraries conference, December 10-12, 1982, Tirupati. [Andhra Pradesh Public Library Association]. {NASSDOC*}

Ranganathan, S.R. and Nagar, M.L., 1951, **Granthalaya pratikriya**. {JNU}

Agarwal, Shyam Sunder, 1978, **Granthalaya sangathan**. {BIS}

Anon, 1974, **Granthalaya shastra paribhasha kosh**. {NASSDOC NMML}

Bhargava, G.D., 1971, **Granthalaya vargikaran**. [Madhya Pradesh Hindi Granth Academi]. {NMML}

Girja Kumar and Krishan Kumar, 1978, **Granthvigyan**. {CRRI NMML}

Hutchins, Robert M., 1954, **Great books** : The foundation of liberal education. {USIS}

Thomas, Alan G., 1975, **Great books and book collectors**. {NASSDOC*}

Jagjit Singh, 1967, **Great ideas in information theory, language and cybernetics**. {INSA}

Hobson, Anthony, 1970, **Great libraries**. {NMML USIS}

Charles, Rosner, n.d., **Growth of the book-jacket**. {DUL}

Kochen, Manfred, ed., 1967, **The growth of knowledge** : Readings on organisation and retrieval of knowledge. {NIEPA USIS}

Ohdedar, A.K., 1966, **Growth of the library in modern India, 1498-1836**. {ICHR IIT NMML ZHL}

Anon, 1970, **Guide for abbreviations of words in titles of periodicals using Roman alphabet**, rev edn. (IS : 18-1970). [Indian Standards Institution]. {NASSDOC}

Anon, n.d., **A guide for authors in the preparation of manuscripts and illustrations**. {IIPA}

Anon, 1977, **Guide for the conversion of school libraries into media centres.** [UNESCO]. {DUL ICA JNU NIEPA}

Anon, 1984, **Guide for drafting Indian standards**, 2nd edn. (IS : 12-1984). [Indian Standards Institution]. {NASSDOC}

Meyriat, Jean and Beauchet, Micheline, 1968, **Guide for the establishment of national social science documentation centres in developing countries**. [UNESCO] {IEG JNU NMML}

Anon, 1971, **Guide for handling, testing and storage of monochrome photographic prints**, (IS : 6299-1971). [Indian Standards Institution]. {NASSDOC}

Anon, 1976, **Guide for layout of learned periodicals**, rev edn. (IS : 795-1976). [Indian Standards Institution]. {NASSDOC}

Anon, 1976, **Guide for preparation of abstracts**, rev. edn. (IS : 795-1976). [Indian Standards Institution]. {NASSDOC}

Anon, 1968, **Guide for preparation of manuscript of an article in a learned periodical**. (IS : 4731-1968). [Indian Standards Institution]. {NASSDOC}

Anon, 1977, **Guide for standard book numbering**. {IS : 8310-1977). [Indian Standards Institution]. {NAI NASSDOC}

Hamer, Philip M., ed., 1961, **A guide to archives and manuscripts in the United States**. [U.S. National Historical Publications Commission]. {USIS}

Walls, Chamberlin Mary, 1959, **Guide to art reference books**. {DUL}

Smith, Datus C., 1966, **Guide to book publishing**. {DUL}

Kane, Lucile M., 1966, **Guide to the care and administration of manuscripts**, 2nd edn. [American Association for State and Local History]. {NMML}

Mukhopadhyay, Ajoy, 1976, **Guide to Colon Classification practical.** {CRRI ICHR}

Negus, Ron, 1972, **Guide to Computer Bureau Services**. {NASSDOC}

Pritchard, Alan, 1969, **Guide to computer literature** : An introductory survey of the sources of information. {NASSDOC}

Conning, Arthur M., 1983, **Guide to the computerisation of population documentation storage and retrieval systems**. [United Nations]. {NASSDOC}

Woodworth, David, ed., 1973, **Guide to current British journals**, Vol. 1, 2nd edn. [Library Association, London]. {NASSDOC}

Dhyani, Pushpa, n.d., **Guide to Dewey Decimal Classification**. {DUL}

Elliott, C.K., 1971, **Guide to the documentation of psychology**. {NIH}

Sutton, S.C., 1967, **Guide to the India Office Library** : With a note on the India Office Records. [India Office Library]. {NMML}

Sutton, S.C., 1968, **Guide to the India Office Library** : With a note on the India Office Records, 2nd edn. [India Office Library]. {IEG IIT JNU MFL NASSDOC NMML RTL}

Davis, Charles H. and Ruse, James E., 1979, **Guide to information science**. {BCL JNU}

Pry, Barnard M. and Mohrarot, Foster E., 1963, **Guide to information sources in space science and technology**. {DUL}

Strauss, William, et al, 1968, **Guide to laws and regulation on federal libraries** : A compilation and analysis. {USIS}

Immroth, John Philip, 1968, **Guide to Library of Congress classification**. {USIS}

Immroth, John Philip, 1971, **A guide to Library of Congress classification**, 2nd edn. {USIS}

Immroth, John Philip, 1980, **Guide to Library of Congress classification**, 3rd edn., by Lois Mai Chan. {USIS}

Mann, Thomas, 1987, **Guide to library research methods**. {JNU}

Calder, Rose E., et al, comps., **A guide to library resources in Rangoon**. {IEG}

Black, Dorothy M., 1975, **Guide to lists of Master's theses**. [American Library Association]. {NASSDOC}

Hammond, George P., 1972, **Guide to the manuscript collections of the Bancroft Library**, 2 Vols. {JNU}

Ballou, Hubbard, W., ed., 1968, **Guide to micro reproduction equipment,** 4th edn. [National Microfilm Association]. {NASSDOC}

Anon, n.d., **A guide to micrographics**. [Bhabha Atomic Research Centre; Micrographic Congress of India]. {NASSDOC*}

Anon, 1974, **Guide to the National Archives of the United States**. [U.S. National Archives and Records Service]. {USIS}

Anon, 1970, **Guide to national bibliographical centres.** [UNESCO]. {DUL IIMC NASSDOC USIS}

Duckworth, Walter E., 1962, **Guide to operational research**. {NASSDOC}

Foskett, A.C., 1970, **Guide to personal indexes** : Using edgenotched and peek-a-boo cards, 2nd edn. {BIS IEG IIT JNU NASSDOC}

Thompson, Anthony H., 1983, **Guide to production and use of audio-visual aids in library and information science teaching.** [UNESCO]. {NASSDOC*}

Winchell, C.M., 1967, **Guide to reference books**, 8th edn. [American Library Association]. {JNU NASSDOC}

Dority, G. Kim, 1984, **Guide to reference books for small and medium sized libraries, 1970-82**. {NASSDOC}

Walford, A.J., ed., n.d., **Guide to reference material,** 3 vols. [Library Association, London]. {INSA NASSDOC NIPCCD ZHL}

Gidwani, N.N. and Navalani, K., 1974, **A guide to reference materials on India**, 2 vols. {INSA NAI NASSDOC NCAER NERC ZHL}

Kennedy, James R., ed., 1972, **Guide to reference sources on Africa, Asia, Latin America and the Caribbean, Middle East and North Africa and Russia and East Europe** : Selected and annotated. {NASSDOC}

Hewitt, A.R., 1957, **Guide to resources for Commonwealth studies in London, Oxford and Cambridge with bibliographical and other information**. {IEG JNU NIEPA}

Bardeh, Bertha R. and Denison, Barbara, n.d., **Guide to the SLA loan collection, classification schemes and subject heading lists**. [Special Libraries Association] {DUL}

Panchanathan, A., 1984, **Guide to Saraswati Mahal**. [Saraswati Mahal Library, Tanjore]. {NASSDOC*}

Maureen, J., 1966, **Guide to scientific periodicals** : Annotated bibliography. {DUL}

Anon, 1972, **Guide to selected computer-based information services.** [Association of Special Libraries and Information Bureaux]. {CRRI}

Mukherjee, A.K., 1979, **Guide to selected reference tools and Indological source materials** : Classified and annotated. {DUL NASSDOC}

Olle, James G., 1984, **A guide to sources of information in libraries**. {NASSDOC}

Anon, 1963, **Guide to the Universal Decimal Classification**. (BS 1000 C : 1963). [British Standards Institution]. {AIU IIT JNU NASSDOC}

Staveley, Ronald, ed., n.d., **Guide to unpublished research materials**. {IEG}

Gates, J.K., 1962, **Guide to the use of books and libraries.** {DUL IIT MFL}

Gates, J.K., 1969, **Guide to the use of books and libraries**, 2nd edn. {NIH USIS}

Gates, J.K., 1979, **Guide to the use of books and libraries**, 4th edn. {USIS}

Anon, 1962, **Guide to use of Dewey Decimal Classification**. [Lake Placid Club Education Foundation]. {IIT USIS}

Brimmer, Brenda, et al, 1962, **A guide to the use of United Nations documents, including reference to the specialised agencies and special U.N. bodies.** {MFL USIS}

Perkins, David, ed., 1979, **Guidelines for collection development.** [American Library Association]. {USIS}

Anon, 1982, **Guidelines for curriculum development in records management and administration of modern archives**. [UNESCO]. {NASSDOC}

Anon, 1978, **Guidelines for curriculum development on information studies**. [UNESCO]. {NASSDOC*}

Anon, 1988, **Guidelines for drafting and presentation of India standards**. [Bureau of Indian Standards]. {BIS NASSDOC}

Anon, 1979, **Guidelines for the establishment and development of monolingual thesauri.** (BS 5723-1979). [British Standards Institution]. {CRRI}

Lancaster, F.W., 1978, **Guidelines for the evaluation of information systems and services**. [UNESCO]. {JNU}

Anon, 1975, **Guidelines for the evaluation of training courses, workshops and seminars in scientific and technical information and documentation**. [UNESCO]. {NASSDOC}

Neelameghan, A., ed., 1977, **Guidelines for formulation of a policy on education, training and development of library and information personnel** . All India seminar on library and information science education, October 3-8, 1977, Delhi. [Indian Statistical Institution]. {NASSDOC}.

Anon, 1960, **Guidelines for library planners.** [American Library Association]. {IIT}

Anon, 1979, **Guidelines for national bibliographic agency and national bibliography**. [UNESCO]. {NASSDOC}

Anon, 1976, **Guidelines for newspaper libraries**. [American Newspaper Publishers Association]. {USIS}

Anon, 1982, **Guidelines for the preparation of bibliography**. [U.S. National Agricultural Library]. {NASSDOC}

Hildesheimer, Francoise, 1983, **Guidelines for the preparation of general guides to national archives**. [UNESCO]. {NASSDOC}

Venderborght, G., 1979, **Guidelines for preparation of texts of dissertations for their presentation and publication**. {DUL}

Anon, 1983, **Guidelines for presentation of abstract sheets in serial publications**. (IS : 10455-1983). [Indian Standards Institution]. {CRRI}

Anon, 1983, **Guidelines for presentation of translations.** (IS : 10454-1983). [Indian Standards Institution]. {NASSDOC}

Anon, 1974, **Guidelines for thesaurus structure, construction and use.** [American National Standard Institute]. {CRRI}

Wolman, Perctz, 1975, **Guidelines on the conduct of a national inventory of current research and development projects**. {DUL}

Anon, 1981, **Guidelines on studies of information users**. [UNESCO]. {NASSDOC}

Maxwell, Margaret F., 1980, **Handbook for AACR2** : Explaining and illustrating Anglo-American Cataloguing Rules, 2nd ed. [American Library Association]. {USIS}

Atherton, Pauline, 1978, **Handbook for information systems and services.** [UNESCO]. {ICA IIMC NASSDOC NIEPA TDA USIS}

Anon, 1980, **Handbook for information systems and services**. [UNESCO] {IDSA}

Atkinson, Jean, 1968, **Handbook for interviewers** : A manual for Government social survey interviewing staff, describing practice and procedures on structured interviewing. {NASSDOC}

Winser, Marian Marley, 1959, **Handbook for library trustees**. {DUL}

Isaac, Stephen and Michael, William B, 1972, **Handbook in research and evaluation** : A collection of principles, methods and strategies useful in the planning, design and evaluation of studies in education and the behavioural sciences. {NASSDOC}

Narasimharao, K.V.V.L., 1988, **Handbook of AP Government Oriental Manuscripts Library and Research Institute**. [Andhra Pradesh Government Oriental Manuscripts Library and Institute, Hyderabad], {NASSDOC*}

Grabbe, Eugene M., et al, eds., 1961, **Handbook of automation, and computation and control**. {IDSA}

Pool, Ithiel de Sola, et al, eds., 1973, **Handbook of communication**. {NASSDOC}

Simsova, S. and Mackee, Monique, 1970, **Handbook of comparative librarianship**. {NASSDOC}

Simsova, S. and Mackee, Monique, 1975, **Handbook of comparative librarianship,** 2nd edn. {BIS IICL ISI NIPCCD}

Mackee, Monique, 1983, **Handbook of comparative librarianship**, 3rd edn. {NASSDOC}

Rubin, Martin L., 1970-71, **Handbook of data management**, 6 vols, vol 1 : Introduction to the system life cycle; vol 2 : System life cycle standards; vol. 3 : System life cycle standards forms methods, by Peter Zuckerman; vol 4 : Advanced technology input and output; vol. 5 : Advanced technology systems concepts; vol. 6 : Data processing administration. {NASSDOC}

Hayes, Robert M. and Becker, Joseph, 1970, **Handbook of data processing for libraries** : A comprehensive guide to the use of modern data processing equipment in libraries. {CRRI IIT INSA NASSDOC NCAER NIH NMML USIS}

Hayes, Robert M. and Becker, Joseph, 1974, **Handbook of data processing for libraries**, 2nd edn. {BIS CRRI DUL ISI JNU USIS}

Rubin, Martin L., 1970-71, **Handbook of data processing management,** 6 vols. {NASSDOC}

Struening, Elmer L. and Guttentag, Marcia, eds., 1975, **Handbook of evaluation research**, 2 vols. {NASSDOC}

Fowles, Jib, ed., 1978, **Handbook of futures research.** {NASSDOC}

Jain, M.K., 1990, **Handbook of government libraries.** {CRRI}

Kaul, H.K., ed., 1975, **Handbook of Indian writers**. {ICCR MMTC NASSDOC UGC}

Kaul, Neelima, comp., 1980, **Handbook of information scientists and librarians in India**. {BIS CRRI IIPA IIT ISI MMTC NASSDOC NCAER NIEPA NMML RTL}

Atherten, Pauline, 1977, **Handbook of information systems services**. {JNU}

Gupta, B.M., et al, eds., 1984-89, **Handbook of libraries, archives and information centres in India**, 8 vols. : Vol. 1 : Libraries and archives; Vol. 2 : Libraries and archives; Vol. 3 : Information policy system and network; Vol. 4 : Asia-Pacific co-operative information systems and networks and programmes; Vol. 5 : Information technology industry and networks; Vol. 6 : International co-operative information systems, network and programmes; Vol. 7 : Science and technology information systems and centres; Vol. 8 : Social sciences information systems and centres. {DSIW IDSA JNU NASSDOC NCAER NMML}

Murphy, Marcy and Johns, Claude J., 1977, **Handbook of library regulations**. {INSA JNU USIS}

Majeed Khan, M.A., 1982, **Handbook of library science education in India**. [Andhra Pradesh Library Association, Hyderabad]. {NASSDOC}

Prytherch, Ray, 1986, **Handbook of library training practice**. {NASSDOC}

Fang, Josephine Riss and Songe, Alice H., 1973, **Handbook of national and international library associations**. [American Library Association]. {NASSDOC USIS}

Raju, A.A.N., 1974, **Handbook of pseudonymous authors in Telugu**. {NASSDOC*}

Ashworth, W., ed., 1955, **Handbook of special librarianship and information work**. [Association of Special Libraries and Information Bureaux]. {BIS IEG}

Ashworth, W., ed., 1962, **Handbook of special librarianship and information work**. 2nd edn. [Association of Special Libraries and Information Bureaux]. {IIT SPA}

Ashworth, W., ed., 1967, **Handbook of special librarianship and information work**, 3rd edn. [Association of Special Libraries and Information Bureaux]. {MHA MMTC NASSDOC NIH}

Batten, W.E., ed., 1975, **Handbook of special librarianship and information work**, 4th edn. [Association of Special Libraries and Information Bureaux]. {CRRI IIT}

Anon, 1956, **Handbook on the international exchange of publications**. [UNESCO]. {CRRI IEG}

Von Busse, Gisela, ed., 1964, **Handbook on the international exchange of publications**, 3rd edn. [UNESCO]. {NASSDOC NMML}

Vanwijngaerden, Frans, ed., 1978, **Handbook on the international exchange of publications**, 4th edn, [UNESCO]. {JNU NASSDOC USIS}

Sears, Donald A., (1984), **Harbrace guide to the library and the research paper**, 4th ed. {IIMC}

Harrod, Leonard Mortague and Prytherch, R.J., ed., 1984, **Harrod's librarians' glossary and reference book**. {NCERT}

Ranganathan, S.R., 1955, **Heading and canons.** {BIS IEG ISI}

Riggs, Fred W., 1986, **Help for social scientists** : A new kind of information process. {NASSDOC}

Chancellor, John Miller, 1938, **Helping the reader toward self education**. {JNU}

Lal, S.S., comp., 1985, **Herald of Library Science** : Trend report, citation and index, 1962-83. {NASSDOC}

Gringhuis, Drik, n.d., **Here comes the book mobile.** {JNU}

Lee, Charles, 1958, **The hidden public** : The story of the book-of-the- Month Club. {USIS}

Vishwanathan, C.G., 1957, **High school library** : Organisation and administration. {DUL NERC}

Magnanand and Vaish, J.D., n.d., **Higher secondary school libraries**. {DUL IEG}

Agrawal, Suren, et al, 1972, **Hindi mein bal sahitya** : Children literature in Hindi since independence, Pratham khand 1947-1960. {NASSDOC}

Nadvi, Salman Shamsi, 1973, **Hindustan ke mashraqi kutubkhane**. {NMML}

Rolland, E. Stevens, ed., n.d., **Historical and bibliographical methods in library research**. {ICHR}

Evans, Frank B., comp., 1979, **The history of archives administration** : A select bibliography. [UNESCO] {NASSDOC}

Parish, Charles, 1966, **History of the Birmingham Library**. {JNU}

Curwin, Henry, 1968, **History of booksellers** : The old and new. {DUL}

Norris, Dorothy May, 1939, **History of cataloguing and cataloguing methods, 1100-1880, with an introductory survey of ancient times**. {CRRI}

Marshall, D.N., 1983, **History of libraries** : Ancient and mediaeval. {JNU}

Misra, Jogesh, 1979, **History of libraries and librarianship in modern India since 1850**. {JNU NERC NMML}

Johnson, Elmer D., 1965, **History of libraries in the Western world**. {NASSDOC}

Raju, A.A.N., 1988, **History of library movement in Andhra Pradesh, 1900-1956**. {NASSDOC*}

Lydenberg, H.M., 1932, **History of the New York Public Library.** {NAI}

Thompson, James, 1968, **History of the principles of librarianship.** {IIT}

Rhodes, Dennis E., 1969, **History of printing in the India, Pakistan, Ceylon, Burma and Thailand.** {DUL}

Mahajan, S.G., 1984, **History of public library movement in Maharashtra**. {JNU NASSDOC*}

Mahajan, S.G., 1979, **History of the public library movement in western Maharashtra, 1805-1921** : Thesis. (Poona University). {NASSDOC}

Kronick, David A., 1962, **History of scientific and technical periodicals** : The origins and development of the scientific and technical press. {DUL}

Going, Mona E., comp. and ed., 1963, **Hospital libraries and work with the disabled in the community**. {DUL}

Anon, 1962, **Hospital library in Sweden**, tr. by Frykman. {DUL}

Phebe, Snow, 1960, **How a book is made**. {DUL}

Murphey, R.W., 1958, **How and where to look it up**. {IIT}

Dunkin, Paul Shaner, 1973, **How to catalogue a rare book**, 2nd edn. {JNU}

Lehnus, Donal J., 1971, **How to determine author and title entries according to AACR** : An interpretive guide with card examples. {AIU USIS}

Downs, Robert B., 1966, **How to do library research.** {ICA IIT JNU NIH USIS}

Chandler, G., 1967, **How to find out** : A guide to sources of information for all, arranged by the Dewey Decimal Classification, 2nd edn. {MHA}

Chandler, G., 1974, **How to find out** : A guide to sources of information for all, arranged by the Dewey Decimal Classification, 4th rev. edn. {NASSDOC}

Chandler, G., 1982, **How to find out** : Printed and on-line sources, 5th rev edn. {DUL NASSDOC}

Parsons, S.A.J., 1972, **How to find out about engineering.** {CRRI}

Chandler, G., 1968, **How to find out about literature**. {DUL}

Smith, D.L., 1967, **How to find out in architecture and building**. {SPA}

Alexander, C. and Burke, A.J., 1958, **How to locate educational information and data,** 4th edn. {NIEPA}

Currie, Dorothy H., 1965, **How to organise a children's library**. {DUL}

Bakewell, K.G.B., n.d., **How to organise information** : A manager's guide to techniques and sources with a check list for secretaries and assistants. {JNU}

Lynes, Alice, 1974, **How to organise a local collection.** {NASSDOC}

Soule, Charles C., n.d., **How to plan a library building for library work.** {IEG}

Adler, Mortimer J. and Van Doren, Charles, 1972, **How to read a book**, rev. edn. {USIS}

Shankman, Florence V. and Kranyik, Robert, 1964, **How to teach reference and research skills.** {JNU}

Marjarum, E. Warne, 1947, **How to use a book.** {JNU}

Johnson, Herbert Weber, et al, 1972, **How to use the business library** : With sources of business information, 4th edn. {USIS}

Santa, Beauel M. and Hardy, Lois Lynn, 1955, **How to use the library**. {JNU}

Morton, Leslie T., 1979, **How to use a medical library**. {NIH}

Berry, Ralph, 1966, **How to write a research paper**. {DUL}

Johnson, Edwin G. and Corliss, William R., 1971, **Human factors applications in tele-operator design and operation**. {INSA}

Asheim, Lester, 1957, **The humanities and the library** : Problems in the interpretation, evaluation and use of library materials. [American Library Association]. {AIU USIS}

Stone, Sue, ed., 1980, **Humanities information research** : Proceedings of a seminar. {JNU}

Anon, 1987, **Hundred years of library education.** [Nagpur University, Department of Library and Information Science, Nagpur]. {NASSDOC}

Kumar, P.S.G., ed., 1987, **Hundred years of library education and its future** : Pre-seminar volume : ILA-IASLIC-GILA-IATLIS library education centenary seminar, October 10-12, 1987, Nagpur. [Nagpur University, Department of Library and Information Science, Nagpur]. {NASSDOC}

Kapur, Gopal K., 1970, **IBM 360 assembler language programming**. {NASSDOC]

Foubert, Charles Henri, 1982, **The IDOC documentation handbook**. [IDOC]. {NASSDOC}

Anon, 1983, **IENS press handbook**. [Indian and Eastern Newspaper Society, New Delhi]. {JNU}

Anon, 1987, **IFLA and the Third World** : The IFLA core on the advancement of librarianship in the Third World. (ALP). {NASSDOC}

Anon, 1988, **IFLA annual** : Proceedings of the general conferences; Annual reports. [International Federation of Library Associations and Institutions]. {NASSDOC}

Anon, n.d., **IFLA directory** : 1977; 1979; 1982-84; 1984-85; 1986-87; 1988-89. [International Federation of Library Associations and Institutions]. {NASSDOC}

Anon, 1987, **IFLA round-table on research on reading, August 13-15, 1987, Manchester** : Preparatory meeting before Brighton Congress. {NASSDOC*}

Anon, 1986, **IFLA statutes, rules of procedure terms of reference**. [International Federation of Library Associations and Institutions] {NASSDOC}

Vashishth, C.P., ed., 1987, **ILA members directory**. [Indian Library Association]. {NASSDOC}

Anon, 1985, **ILO thesaurus**. [International Labour Office, Geneva]. {NASSDOC}

Anon, 1966, **INSDOC seminar on work-flow in libraries**, November 21-24, 1966, New Delhi, 3 pts. Pt-1 : Special libraries; Pt-2 : University libraries; Pt-3 : Government libraries. {BIS}

Anon, n.d., **ISBD (B)** : International standard bibliographic description for books. [International Federation of Library Associations and Institutions]. {JNU}

Anon, 1977, **ISBD (CH)** : International standard bibliographic description for cartographic material. [International Federation of Library Association and Institutions]. {NASSDOC}

Anon, 1977, **ISBD (G)** : General international standard bibliographic description : Annotated text. [International Federation of Library Associations and Institution, Working Group on the General International Standard Bibliographic Description]. {NASSDOC}

Anon, 1978, **ISBD (M)** : International standard bibliographic description for monographic publications, rev edn. [International Federation of Library Associations and Institutions]. {NASSDOC}

Anon, 1977, **ISBD (NBM)** : International standard bibliographic description for non-book materials. [International Federation of Library Associations and Institutions, Working Group on the International Standard Bibliographic Description for Non-Book Materials]. {NASSDOC}

Anon, 1974, **ISBD (S)** : International standard bibliographic description for serials. [International Federation of Library Associations and Institutions, Joint Working Group on the International Standard Bibliographic Description for Serials]. {NASSDOC}

Anon, 1972, **ISBN** : International standard book numbering (incorporating the recommendations for implementing the Standard Book Numbering Scheme). [Standard Book Numbering Agency, London]. {NASSDOC}

Mullis, A.A., ed., 1983, **ISDS manual**. (International Serial Data System). {NASSDOC}

Anon, 1973, **ISIS** : A general description of an approach to computerised bibliographical control. [International Labour Office]. {NASSDOC}

Anon, 1982, **ISO standards handbook, 1982** : Information transfer. [UNESCO]. {NASSDOC}

Peereault, Jean M., 1978, **Idea of order in bibliography**. {JNU}

Oboler, Eli M., 1977, **Ideas and the university library** : Essays of an unorthodox academic librarian. {DUL}

Curran, Ann T. and Auram, Henriette D., n.d., **Identification of data elements in bibliographic records**. {BIS}

Lancaster, F.W., 1988, **If you want to evaluate your library**. [Library Association, London]. {NASSDOC}

Diringer, David, 1967, **Illuminated book** : Its history and production. 2nd edn. {DUL}

Davis, Charles H. and Lundeen, Gerald W., 1974, **Illustrative computer programming for libraries**. {JNU}

Davis, Charles H. and Lundeen, Gerald W., 1981, **Illustrative computer programming for libraries** : Selected examples for information specialists, 2nd edn. {NASSDOC USiS}

Chan, Lois Mai, 1980, **Immroth's guide to the Library of Congress Classification**, 3rd edn. {USIS}

Anon, 1977, **Impact of information services on national development**. [COSTED, Bangalore]. {NASSDOC}

Cancaster, F.W., et al, 1980, **Impact of a paperless society on the research library of the future** : A report to the NSF. [Library Research Centre, Illinois]. {ISI}

Anon, n.d., **Impact of technology on the library building**. [Educational Facilities Laboratories, New Delhi]. {AIU}

Aziz, Abdul, 1974, **The imperial library of the moghuls**. [Idarah-I Adabiyat-I Delhi]. {INSA NMML}

Wessel, Andrew E., 1979, **Implementation of complex information system**. {CRRI IIT USIS}

Anon, 1979, **Implication of modern information technology for national information policy and planning**. [UNESCO]. {NASSDOC}

Gates, Arthur I., 1947, **Improvement of reading**. 3rd edn. {ZHL}

Guha, B., ed., 1986, **In the library and information science horizon** : A collection of essays in honour of Dr. V.A. Kamath, presented by the Bombay Science Librarians Association (BOSLA). {JNU NASSDOC}

Daedalus, 1976, **In praise of books**. [Academy of Arts and Sciences, Cambridge]. {USIS}

Anon, 1969, **Index of a publication**. (ISO/R 999-1969. (E). [International Organisation for Standardisation, Geneva]. {NASSDOC}

Harrod, Leonard Montague, ed., 1978, **Indexers on indexing** : Selection of articles published in the Indexer. {BIS}

Collison, Robert L., 1959, **Indexes and indexing**. {BIS CRRI IEG IIT MFL MHA SPA}

Collison, Robert L., 1969, **Indexes and indexing** : Guide to the indexing of books and collections of books, periodicals, music recordings, films and other materials, with a reference section and suggestions for further reading, 3rd rev. edn. {USIS}

Collison, Robert L., 1972, **Indexes and indexing** : Guide to the indexing of books and collections of books, periodicals, music recordings, films and other materials, with a reference section and suggestions for further reading, 4th edn. {JNU NASSDOC NIPCCD NMML}

Prasher, R.G., 1990, **Index and indexing systems**. {JNU}

Knight, G. Norman, 1979, **Indexing, the art of** : A guide to the indexing of books and periodicals. {BCL NASSDOC}

Collison, Robert L., 1969, **Indexing books** : A manual of basic principles. {IEG IIT INSA NIPCCD}

Borko, Harold and Bernier, Charles L., 1978, **Indexing concepts and methods**. {BCL BIS}

Hunnisett, R.F., 1972, **Indexing for editors.** { NASSDOC NMML}

Soergel, Dagobert, 1074, **Indexing languages and thesauri** : Construction and maintenance. {CRRI IIT NASSDOC}

Devsare, H.K., n.d., **Indexing of children's magazines in Hindi with particular reference to its impact on society and social sciences**. (typed copy). {NASSDOC}

Rajan, T.N., 1981, **Indexing systems** : Concepts, models and techniques. [Indian Association of Special Libraries and Information Centres]. {BIS CRRI JNU MFL MMTC NASSDOC}

Anon, 1976, **Indexing systems** : IASLIC special course, November 1—December 14, 1976 : Course material. [Indian Association of Special Libraries and Information Centres]. {JNU}

Ramakrishnan, M.N., 1986, **Indexing systems and techniques**. {NASSDOC}

Janker, Frederic, 1964, **Indexing theory, indexing methods and search devices.** {IIT JNU USIS}

Spiker, Sina K., n.d., **Indexing your book** : A practical guide for authors. {DUL}

Arberry, A.J., 1967, **India Office Library** : A historical sketch, [Commonwealth Office, London]. {NASSDOC}

Sharma, Ravindra Nath, 1986, **Indian academic libraries and Dr. S.R. Ranganathan** : A critical study. {JNU NMML}

Banerjee, S.B., ed., 1980, **Indian Association of Special Libraries and Information Centres** : Perspective, performance, promise : Silver jubilee commemorative volume. [Indian Association of Special Libraries and Information Centres]. {JNU}

Sethi, A.R., and Moodgal, H.M.K., 1978, **Indian book review index,** 1975-76. {JNU NASSDOC}

Prasher, Ram Gopal, et al, 1971-72, **Indian books** : An annual bibliography. {NASSDOC}

Sharma, H.D., ed., 1984, **Indian books** : A bibliography of Indian books published or reprinted in 1983 in the English language, comp. by Ram Lal. [Indian Bibliographic Centre, Varanasi]. {NASSDOC}

Anon, 1955-1983, **Indian books in print** : A bibliography of Indian books in English language, 3 vols, Vol 1 : Author; Vol 2 : Title; Vol 3 : Subject guide. {ICA INSA NASSDOC}

Duggal, K.S., 1982, **Indian broadcast media yearbook**. {NASSDOC}

Goyal, Satpaul, ed, n.d., **Indian librarianship**. {JNU}

Sharma, Ravindra N., ed., 1981, **Indian librarianship** : Perspectives and prospects. {IEG NASSDOC}

George, K.M., 1985, **Indian libraries** : Trends and prospectives. {JNU NMML}

Kipp, Laurence, 1961, **Indian libraries and India Wheat Loan Education Exchange Programme** : A report. {JNU}

Kumar, P.S.G., 1977, **Indian library chronology**. {BIS JNU NERC NIPCCD}

Ranganathan, S.R. and Das Gupta, S., 1951, **Indian library directory**, 3rd edn. [Indian Library Association]. {BIS INSA NASSDOC}

Joginder Singh and Sethi, A.R., eds., 1987, **Indian library directory**; 4th edn. [Indian Library Association]. {JNU NMML}

Venkatappaiah, V. and Vashishth, C.P., 1990, **Indian library legislation**, 2 vols., Vol. 1 : Union Library Bills and Acts; Vol. 2 : State Library Bills and Acts. {NASSDOC}

Prasher, R.G., 1971, **Indian library literature** : An annotated bibliography. {ICHR NASSDOC NIPCCD NMML}

Ranganathan, S.R., n.d., **Indian library manifesto**. {IDSA}

Anon, 1967, **Indian library science abstracts**. [Indian Association of Special Libraries and Information Centres]. {NASSDOC}

Anon, 1958-77, **Indian National Bibliography**. [Central Reference Library, Calcutta]. {DSSW INSA NASSDOC}

Anon, 1958-62, **Indian National Bibliography** : Cumulated Index 1958-62. [Central Reference Library, Calcutta]. {NASSDOC}

Gupta, R.C., 1975, **Indian Press Index** : Procedure manual. (University of Delhi, Department of Library Science, Sessional project, 1975). {DUL}

Anon, n.d., **Indian publishers directory**, {NASSDOC}

Sengupta, B., 1981, **Indian reference and information services**. {ICA NIH}

Sharma, H.D., et al, n.d., **Indian reference sources** : An annotated guide to Indian reference books. {ICHR IIC NASSDOC ZHL}

Anon, 1960, **Indian scientific and technical publications** : Exhibition. (National Library, Calcutta). {DUL}

Anon, 1967, **Indian standard glossary of cataloguing terms**, rev edn. [Indian Standards Institution]. {ICA IIMC JNU NASSDOC}

Anon, 1963, **Indian standard glossary of classification terms**. [Indian Standards Institution]. {NASSDOC}

Surinder Kumari, 1975-76, **Indian Standards Institution and its role in the development of library and documentation standards**. (University of Delhi, Department of Library and Information Science, Sessional project 1975-76). {BIS}

Anon, 1977, **Indian trade classification**, 2nd rev edn. [Directorate General of Commercial Intelligence and Statistics, New Delhi]. {TDA}

Jain, M.K., 1989, **Indiana** : A bibliography of bibliographical sources. {NASSDOC}

Kesavan, B.S., 1961, **India's national library**. [National Library, Calcutta]. {IIT JNU MFL ZHL}

Majumdar, 1987, **India's national library** : Systematisation. [National Library, Calcutta]. {NASSDOC}

Kaul, R.K., 1980, **Indic names** : Documentation list. {BIS NASSDOC ZHL}

West, Roland, 1965, **Individualised reading instructions** : Its implication for teacher and librarian. {JNU}

Jackson, Eugene B. and Jackson, Ruth L., 1978, **Industrial information systems** : A manual for higher management and their information officer, librarian/associates. {USIS}

Bakewell, K.G.B., 1969, **Industrial libraries throughout the world**. {IIFT IIT ISI NASSDOC}

Anon, n.d., **Industrial technical libraries of paperback books** : Little Libraries. [U.S. State Department]. {BIS}

Tiihonen, Pertti, n.d., **Influence of television on the use of libraries**. {IIMC}

Hammer, Donald P., ed., 1976, **The information age, its development, its impact**. {DUL USIS}

Kent, Allen, 1971, **Information analysis and retrieval**. {CRRI JNU MHA NASSDOC NIPCCD}

Singer, T.E.R., ed., n.d., **Information and communication practice in industry**. {IEG}

Wiio, Osmo, 1984, **Information and communication system** : Introduction to the concepts of information, communication and research. {JNU}.

Anon, n.d., **Information and its dissemination**. [Institute of Petroleum, London]. {BIS}

Brittain, J.M., 1970, **Information and its users** : A review with special reference to the social sciences. {JNU NASSDOC}

Schutze, Gertrude, 1972, **Information and library science source book** : Supplement to documentation source book. {NERC}

Long, Nicholas, 1975, **Information and referral services** : Research findings. [U.S. Department of Health, Education and Welfare]. {NASSDOC}

Meltzer, Morton F., 1967, **The information center** : Management's hidden asset. [American Management Association]. {USIS}

Tolly, Roy D., 1979, **Information choice and policies** : Proceedings : American society for information science annual meeting, 42nd, October 14-18, 1979, Minneapoles. {USIS}

Lunin, Lois F., et al, 1981, **Information Community** : An alliance for progress : Proceedings : ASIS annual meeting, 44th, 1981. {NASSDOC}

Kibirige, Harry M., 1983, **Information dilemma**. {NIEPA}

Pratt, Gordon, 1976, **Information economics** : Costs and prices of machine-readable information in Europe. [Association of Special Libraries and Information Bureaux]. {BCL}

Porat, Marc Uri, 1977, **The information economy** : Definition and measurement. {USIS}

Mclean, M., ed., 1985, **The information explosion** : The new electronic media in Japan and Europe. {NASSDOC}

McClure, Charles R., 1980, **Information for academic library decision making** : The case for organisational information management. {JNU}

Kohen, Manfred, ed., 1975, **Information for action** : From knowledge to wisdom. {JNU}

Howerton, Paul W., 1963, **Information handling** : First principles. {JNU}

Anon, 1966, **Information handling in the National Standard Reference Data System**. (NBS, Technical Note 290). [U.S. National Bureau of Standards]. {BIS}

Anthony, Lawrence James, ed., 1976, **Information in the 1980's** : Proceedings : ASLIB seminar for information planners and industry, May 13-14, 1976, Beaconfield. [Association of Special Libraries and Information Bureaux]. {BCL NASSDOC}

Anderla, Georges, 1986, **Information in 1985** : A forecasting study of information needs and resources. [Organisation for Economic Cooperation and Development]. {BCL BIS CRRI JNU MMTC}

Stamper, Ronald, 1973, **Information in business and administrative systems**. {DUL NASSDOC}

Freeman, Robert R., et al, eds., 1968, **Information in the language sciences** : Proceedings of the conference held at Airlic House, Warrenton, Virginia, March 4-6, 1966. {NASSDOC}

Metcalfe, J., 1957, **Information indexing and subject cataloguing** : Alphabetical classified, coordinate, mechanical. {DUL IEG IIT}

Agrawal, S.P. and Aggarwal, J.C., 1989, **Information India, 1988** : Global view {IDSA IIPA NIEPA NMML}

Agrawal, S.P. and Aggarwal, J.C., 1990, **Information India, 1990-91** : Global view. {AIU BIS CPR DUL ICA IEG IIT ISI JNU NASSDOC NIEPA NMML ZHL}

Anon, 1978-83, **Information Industry Market Place** : An international directory of information products and services, **1978; 1982; 1983**. {USIS}

Breivick, Patrica Senn and Gel, E. Gordon, 1989, **Information literacy** : Revolution in the library. {NASSDOC}

Smith, J.C. and Hisson, N.J., 1965, **Information maintenance system documentation**. {JNU}

Mason, Donald, 1978, **Information management**. {IIT}

Taylor, Peter J. and Crown, Blaise, 1983, **Information management research in Europe** : Proceedings of the EURIMS conference, Paris. {JNU}

Anon, 1986, **Information market with special regard to social science information**. (FID studies in social science information and documentation). [Hungarian Academy of Science; International Federation for Documentation and Information]. {NASSDOC}

Steurat, Robert D., 1982 : **Information needs of the 80's**. {JNU}

Stater, Margaret, 1989, **Information needs of social scientists.** [British Library Research and Development Department]. {NASSDOC}

Anon, 1977, **Information networks for on-line bibliography retrieval.** [UNESCO]. {BIS}

Anon, 1976, **Information policy for development** : National and international responsibilities. [UNESCO]. {NASSDOC}

Clark, F.J., 1970, **Information processing.** {NASSDOC NIH}

Anon, n.d., **Information processing** : Proceedings : International conference on information processing. {JNU}

Anon, 1960, **Information processing** : Proceedings : International conference on information processing. {JNU}

Hill, H.C., 1973, **Information processing and computer programming** : An introduction. {NIH}

Doss, Milburn Price, 1955, **Information processing equipment.** {JNU}

Mc Maron, et al, 1969, **Information processing laboratory for education and research in library science** : Phase-I. {IIT}

Szweda, Ralph A., 1981, **Information processing systems.** {JNU}

Davis, William S., 1981, **Information processing systems**, 2nd edn. {JNU}

Debons, Anthony, 1981, **Information professional** : Survey of an emerging field. {IIT JNU USIS}

Wood, D.N. and Hamilton, D.R.L., 1967, **Information requirements of mechanical engineers** : Report of a recent survey. {DUL}

Shera, Jesse H., 1958, **Information resources** : A challenge to American science and industry. {JNU}

Gyawali, Bharat M. and Standrodd, Garland L., n.d., **Information resources on Nepal.** {IEG}

Doednikoff, Basic, 1973, **Information retrieval.** {JNU}

Van Rijsbergen, C.J., 1979, **Information retrieval,** 2nd edn. {BCL CRRI DUL IEG MMTC NIH}

Metcalfe, John, 1976, **Information retrieval** : British and American. {JNU}

Scheeter, George, 1967, **Information retrieval** : A critical view. {JNU}

Heaps, H.S., 1978, **Information retrieval** ; Computational and theoretical aspects. {BCL CRRI NIH}

Sharp, John Raymond, 1970, **Information retrieval** : Notes for students. {BCL}

Paice, D.B., 1977, **Information retrieval and the computer**. {BCL}

Kent, Allen, ed., 1960, **Information retrieval and machine translation.** {CRRI DUL}

Doyle, Lauren B., 1975, **Information retrieval and processing.** {BIS CRRI DUL IIMC ISI NASSDOC NIH USIS}

Jones, Karen Spark, ed., 1981, **Information retrieval experiment.** {BIS IIMC IIT}

Haltery, Loweld H. and McCormik, Edmaral M., 1962, **Information retrieval management.** {JNU}

Lancaster, F.W. and Fayen, E.G., 1973, **Information retrieval on-line.** {DUL INSA ISI NASSDOC USIS}

Oddy, R.N., et al, eds., 1981, **Information retrieval research.** {IIMC JNU NASSDOC}

Lancaster, F.W., 1968, **Information retrieval systems** : Characteristics, testing and evaluation. {TDA}

Lancaster, F.W., 1979, **Information retrieval systems** : Characteristics, testing and evaluation, 2nd edn. {CRRI DUL IIT USIS}

Anon, 1970, **Information retrieval systems** : Subject authority list, 7th edn. [American Petroleum Institute]. {IIT}

Barhydt, Gordon, C. and Schmidt, Charles T., n.d., **Information retrieval thesaurus of education terms**. {AIU}

Lamberton, Donald M., ed., 1974, **The information revolution : Annals.** [American Academy of Political and Social Science]. {USIS}

Bose, H., 1986, **Information science** : Principles and practice. {NASSDOC}

Debons, Anthony, ed., 1974, **Information science** : Search for identity. {INSA}

Anon, 1978, **Information science** : A unified view through a systems approach. [Indian Association of Special Libraries and Information Bureaux]. {DUL MMTC}

Mitchell, Ruth K., 1971, **Information science and computer basics**. {BIS}

Dhyani, Pushpa, 1990, **Information science and libraries**. {CRRI ICHR JNU ZHL}

Debons, Anthony and Larson, Arvid G., eds., n.d., **Information science in action** : System design, 2 vols. {DUL}

Anon, 1965, **Information sciences**. [U.S. Air Force Office of Scientific Research]. {JNU}

Chen, Ching-Chih and Hernon, Peter, 1982, **Information seeking** : Assessing and anticipating user needs. {JNU}

Bagg, Thomas C. and Stevens, Mary Elizabeth, 1961, **Information selection systems retrieving replica copies** : A state-of-art report. {JNU}

Taneja, Ram D., n.d., **Information service for the small enterprise** : Need, source and organisation. {BIS}

Norris, Willa, et al, 1972, **Information service in guidance for career development and planning**. {NIPCCD}

Foskett, D.J., 1967, **Information service in libraries**. {CRRI IEG JNU NAI}

Kashyap, Subhash C., 1988, **Information service in the Parliament of India**. {NASSDOC}

Collison, R.L., n.d., **Information services** : Their organisation and administration. {JNU}

Sharma, C.D. and Boonlia, Naresh, n.d., **Information services for college librarians.** {JNU}

Anon, 1977, **Information services for world trade centres.** [World Trade Centre Association]. {TDA}

Roy, A.K. and Kapoor, S.K., eds., 1982, **Information services in India** : Papers: IASLIC national seminar, 10th, December 21-24, 1982, Kanpur. [Indian Association of Special Libraries and Information Centres]. {ICA JNU MMTC NASSDOC NIPCCD}

Josey, E.J., ed., 1979, **The information society** : Issues and answers. [American Library Association]. {JNU}

Umapathy, K.S., 1978, **Information sources** : An international selective guide. {DUL ICA IIFT INSA}

Meachan, Mary, 1978, **Information sources in children's literature** : A practical reference guide. {NIPCCD}

Parper, C.C. and Turley, R.V., 1986, **Information sources in science and technology** : A practical guide to traditional and on-line use. {JNU}

Taube, Mortimer and Wooster, Harold, eds., 1958, **Information storage and retrieval** : Theory, system and devices. {CRRI DUL}

Becker, Joseph and Hayes, Robert M., 1963, **Information storage and retrieval** : Tools, elements, theories. {DUL ICA IEG MFL NASSDOC USIS}

Politt, A.S., 1989, **Information storage and retrieval systems** : Origin, development and applications. {NASSDOC}

Jahoda, Gerald, 1970, **Information storage and retrieval systems for individual researchers.** {ISI MHA USIS}

Murdick, Robert G. and Ross, Jod E., 1977, **Information system for modern management.** {ICA}

Vickery, B.C., 1973, **Information systems.** {DUL ICA ISI MMTC NASSDOC}

Burch, John G., et al, 1979, **Information systems** : Theory and practice. {JNU NIPCCD TDA}

Sherrod, John, 1975, **Information systems and networks** : Eleventh annual symposium {JNU}

Newman, Simon M., 1965, **Information systems compatibility**. {JNU}

Anon, 1976, **Information systems design for socio-economic development** : Retrospect and prospect. [International Federation for Documentation and Information]. {JNU}

Radford, K.J., 1978, **Information systems for strategic decisions.** {DUL}

Shera, J.H., et al, 1975, **Information systems in documentation.** {CRRI DUL JNU}

Anon, 1979, **Information systems in UK agriculture.** [UK Agriculture Information Review Committee; British Library Research and Development Department]. {BCL}

Weisman, Herman M., 1972, **Information systems, services and centres**. {CRRI DUL NASSDOC USIS}

Kent, Allen and Galvin, Thomas J., eds., 1982, **Information technology** : Critical choices for library decision makers : Pittsburg conference on electronic information technology and its impact on library and information services, 1981, 4th, Pittsburg. {BIS CRRI IIT JNU USIS}

Anon, 1982, **Information technology and its impact on American education**. {USIS}

Anon, 1974, **Information technology in local government** : A survey of the development of urban and regional information systems in five European countries. [Organisation for Economic Cooperation and Development]. {BCL}

Smith, Robert Irvine and Combell, Bob, 1981, **Information technology revolution**. {NASSDOC}

Chartrand, Robert Lee and Morentz, James W., eds., 1979, **Information technology serving society.** {USIS}

Abramson, Norman, 1963, **Information theory and coding**. {INSA}

Anon, 1982, **Information trade directory** : An International directory of information products and services. {USIS}

Anon, 1982, **Information transfer,** 2nd edn. [International Organisation for Standardisation]. {CRRI MMTC}

Rowland, J.F.B., 1978, **Information transfer and use in chemistry** : Final report of the Chemical Information Review Committee. {BCL}

Lesko, Matthew, 1983, **Information U.S.A.** {USIS}

Houghton, Bernard, 1967, **Information work today** : Symposium on information work today, September, 1966, Liverpool. {ICA IIMC MHA}

Holloway, A.M., et al, 1976, **Information work with unpublished reports**. {NASSDOC}

El-Hadidy, Barbara and Horne, Estic E., 1984, **The infrastructure of an information society**. {JNU}

Weiss, Harry B. and Carruthers Ralph, H., 1945, **Insect** : Enemies of books. {JNU}

Trehan, G.L., 1981, **Inside library India** : North meets South. {JNU NASSDOC}

Davis, Harold S., ed., 1971, **Instructional Media Centre** : Bold new venture. {USIS}

Naude, Gabriel, 1961, **Instructions concerning erecting of a library**. {DUL}

Myers, Gerald E., 1977, **Insurance manual for libraries**. [American Library Association]. {BIS}

Genaway, David, C., 1984, **Integrated online library systems** : Principles, planning and implementation. {NASSDOC}

Swanson, Don R., ed., 1965, **Intellectual foundations of library education.** {IIT}

Nobile, Philip, 1974, **Intellectual skywriting** : Literary politics and the New York Review of Books. {USIS}

Fisher, Margery, 1962, **Intent upon reading** : A critical appraisal of modern fiction for children. {DUL}

Coward, R.E. and Yelland, H., eds., 1975, **Interchange of bibliographic information in machine readable form** : Papers given at the Western European seminar, May 12-16, 1974, England. [Library Association, London]. {BCL}

Balmforth, C.L. and Cox, N.S., eds., 1971, **Interface** : Library automation with special reference to computing activity. {JNU NASSDOC}

Brooks, James and Draper, James, 1979, **Interior design for libraries**. [American Library Association]. {USIS}

Becker, Joseph, ed., 1971, **Interlibrary communications and information networks.** {JNU}

Anon, 1967, **Inter-library cooperation** : A sampling of inter-library cooperation programmes. [American Library Association; Committee on Inter Library Co-operation]. {DUL}

Anon, 1962, **Inter-library cooperation in England and Wales**. [H.M.S.O., London]. {NASSDOC}

Thomson, Sarah Katharin, 1970, **Interlibrary loan involving academic libraries**. [American Library Association]. {NASSDOC}

Thomson, Sarah Katharin, 1979, **Interlibrary loan procedure manual**. [American Library Association]. {DUL NASSDOC USIS}

Agrawal, S.P., ed., 1984, **Inter-Library Resources Centre** : Holding of periodicals. {NASSDOC}

Anon, 1975, **Inter-Library Resources Centre** : Indian Council of Social Science Research—Jawaharlal Nehru University. [Indian Council of Social Science Research]. {NASSDOC}

Horsnell, Verina, 1974, **Intermediate lexicon for information science** : Feasibility study. [Polytechnic of North London]. {BCL JNU}

Clarke, Tom, 1975, **International academic and specialist publishers directory**. {NASSDOC}

Chandler, George, 1982, **International and national library and information services** : A review of some recent developments, 2 vols. {IIT NASSDOC NERC}

Garnoosky, Leon, ed., n.d., **International aspects of librarianship**. {IEG}

Anon, 1978, **International bibliography of directories**, 6th edn. {NASSDOC}

Jell, Hans and Machesney, Robert, 1965, **International bibliography of non-periodical literature on documentation and information.** {JNU}

Rugh, Archie, ed., 1983, **International books-in-print** : English- language titles published outside the United States and the United Kingdom. 2 vols. {NASSDOC}

Wegman, Edward, 1982, **International circulation of books**. [UNESCO]. {NASSDOC}

Anon, 1968-71, **International computer bibliography,** 1968; 1971. {NASSDOC}

Bishop, Enid and Waller, Jean M., eds. 1972, **International co-operation in orientalist librarianship.** {JNU NMML}

Rangra, V.K., 1982, **International dictionary of acronyms in data processing, library and information systems.** {CRRI MFL NASSDOC NMML}

Vaillancourt, Pauline M., 1980, **International directory of acronyms in library, information and computer sciences**. {NASSDOC USIS}

Goyal, S.P., 1973, **International directory of dealers of back-sets of periodicals.** {NASSDOC}

Cousineau, Marie Josee, comp., 1986, **International directory of libraries and documentation centres in terminology**. [Documentation Directorate, Ottawa]. {NASSDOC}

Anon, 1986, **International directory of library, archives and information science associations**, 2nd edn. [UNESCO General Information Programme; UNISIST]. {NASSDOC}

Gleiter, Karin, ed., 1975, **International directory of population information**, Pt. 2 : Address list. [Carolina Population Center, USA]. {NIH}

Giljarevskij, R.S., 1968-74, **International distribution of catalogue cards** : Present situation and future prospects 1968; 1969; 1974. [UNESCO]. {CRRI IIMC IIT JNU NERC NIEPA NIPCCD}

Dimitrov, Th. and Maruli, L., 1982, **International documents for 80's** : Their role and use : Proceedings : World symposium on international documentation, 2nd, 1980, Brussels. {JNU NMML}

Fang, Josephine Riss and Nauta, Paul, eds., 1985, **International guide to library and information science education** : A reference source for educational programmes in the information fields world-wide. [International Federation of Library Associations and Institutions]. {NASSDOC}

Fang, Josephine Riss and Songe, Alice H., 1976, **International guide to library, archival and information science associations**. {USIS}

Fang, Josephine Riss and Songe, Alice H., 1980, **International guide to library, archival and information science associations**, 2nd edn. {USIS}

Jackson, Miles M., ed., 1981, **International handbook of contemporary developments in librarianship.** {USIS}

Anon, 1962, **International inter-library lending** : A review of the literature, [International Federation of Library Associations and Institutions]. {NASSDOC}

Chandler, George, ed., 1972, **International librarianship** : Surveys of recent developments in developing countries and in advanced librarianship submitted to the 1971 IFLA pre-session seminar for developing countries, August 24—September 1, 1971. [Library Association, London]. {NASSDOC}

Anon, 1963, **International library directory** : A world directory of libraries. {ICWA}

Anon, 1986 **International literary market place, 1986-87**. {NASSDOC}

Chakmakhchev, A.G., 1970, **International organisation and their activities in the field of scientific and technical information.** [UNESCO]. {NASSDOC}

Anon, 1981, **The international provision and supply of publications**. [UNESCO]. {NASSDOC}

Anon, 1962, **International scientific organisations** : A guide to their library, documentation and information services. [U.S. National Science Foundation, International Science Information Studies]. {DUL}

Anon, 1970, **International seminar on electronic data processing in libraries, Regersburg**. {JNU}

Aiyepeku, Wilson O., 1983, **International socio-economic information systems** : An evaluating directory of DEVSIS-type programs. {NASSDOC}

Sharma, M.S., 1987, **International standard book numbering system in India.** {NASSDOC}

Anon, 1972, **International standard classification of education** (ISCED) : Three stage classification system, 2pts. [UNESCO]. {AIU}

Anon, 1972, **International standardisation of library and documentation techniques**. [UNESCO]. {ICA}

Anon, n.d., **International standards for computers and information processing**. [International Organisation for Standardisation]. {BIS}

Anon, n.d., **International standards for documentation and terminology**, 3rd edn. [International Organisation for Standardisation]. {BIS}

Anon, 1969, **International subscription agents** : An annotated directory, 2nd edn. [American Library Association]. {DUL}

Anon, 1961, **International system for the transliteration of Arabic characters.** (ISO/R 233-1961) (E). [International Organisation for Standardisation]. {NASSDOC}

Anon, 1968, **International system for the transliteration of Greek characters into Latin characters.** (ISO/R 843-1968) (E). [International Organisation for Standardisation, Geneva]. {NASSDOC}

Anon, 1968, **International system for the transliteration of Slavic Cyrillic characters**, 2nd edn. (ISO/R 9-1968) (E). [International Organisation for Standardisation, Geneva]. {NASSDOC}

Gorden, Raymond L., 1969, **Interviewing** : Strategy, techniques and tactics. {NASSDOC}

Escreet, P.K., 1971, **Introduction to the Anglo-American cataloguing rules.** {MFL NASSDOC ZHL}

Winkler, Paul Walter, 1980, **Introduction to the Anglo-American cataloguing rules** : History and development. [American Library Association]. {USIS}

Saffady, William,1983, **Introduction to automation for librarians.** [American Library Association]. {USIS}

Wynar,, Bohdan S., 1967, **Introduction to bibliography and reference work** : A guide to materials and sources. {JNU}

Mc Kerrow, Ronald B., 1965, **Introduction to bibliography for literary students.** {DUL}

Darley, Lionel S., 1965, **Introduction to bookbinding**. {CRRI}

Boll, John J., 1970, **Introduction to cataloguing**, 2 vols, Vol. 1: Descriptive cataloguing and an overview of catalogues and cataloguing; Vol 2: Entry headings. {IIT JNU NERC NASSDOC NMML ZHL}

Krishan Kumar, 1983, **Introduction to cataloguing,** 2nd edn. {ZHL}

Wynar, Bohdan S. 1967, **Introduction to cataloguing and classification**, 3rd edn. {IIT}

Wynar, Bohdan S., et al, 1980, **Introduction to cataloguing and classification,** 6th edn. {USIS}

Wynar, Bohdan S., et al, 1985, **Introduction to cataloguing and classification.** (Library Science Text Series). {NASSDOC}

Mann, Margaret, 1943, **Introduction to cataloguing and classification of books.** [American Library Association]. {BIS CRRI ICA NAI NMML SPA USIS ZHL}

Anon, 1965, **Introduction to cataloguing and classification of books**, 2nd edn. [American Library Association]. {IIFT}

Krishan Kumar, 1981, **Introduction to cataloguing practice.** {ISI JNU NASSDOC NERC NMML}

Wilson, T.D., 1971, **Introduction to chain indexing.** {BCL ICHR IIT JNU NASSDOC}

Bloomberg, Marty and Weber, Hans, 1976, **Introduction to classification and number building in Dewey.** {IIFT}

Batty, C.D., 1966, **Introduction to Colon Classification.** {ICHR IIFT IIT JNU NASSDOC NMML SPA ZHL}

Tedd, L.A., 1977, **Introduction to computer-based library systems.** {JNU NIH}

Bergman, Samuel and Bruckner, Steven, 1972, **Introduction to computers and computer programming.** {DUL}

Artandi, Susan B., 1972, **Introduction to computers in information science.** {JNU}

Caldwell, William, 1956, **Introduction to county library practice.** {JNU}

Ashby, W. Ross, 1964, **Introduction to cybernetics.** {NASSDOC}

Price, Wilson T., 1972, **Introduction to data processing.** {JNU}

Wendel, Thomas M. and Williams, William H., 1969, **Introduction to data processing and COBOL.** {NASSDOC}

Battey, C.D., 1966, **Introduction to the Dewey Decimal Classification.** {IIFT IIT MFL SPA ZHL}

Chambers, Marjori, comp., 1968, **Introduction to Dewey Decimal Classification for British schools.** {DUL}

Chakrabarti, A.K., 1980, **An introduction to documentation science.** {NASSDOC}

Batty, C.D. 1971, **Introduction to the eighteenth edition of the Dewey Decimal Classification.** {CRRI IIC JNU NIE USIS}

Binns, Norman, E., 1962, **Introduction to historical bibliography,** rev edn. {DUL}

Ramsden, Michael John, 1974, **An introduction to index language construction** : A programmed text. {BCL}

Anon, 1973, **Introduction to indexing and abstracting for technical information systems.** {TDA}

Saracevic, Tefko, ed., 1970, **Introduction to information science.** {DUL NASSDOC}

Gates, J.K., 1968, **Introduction to librarianship.** {IIT MFL NCAER ZHL}

Gates, J.K., 1976, **Introduction to librarianship,** 2nd edn. {USIS}

Neal, K.W., 1975, **Introduction to library administration.** {JNU}

Rice, James, 1984, **Introduction to library automation.** {NASSDOC NMML}

Dutta, D., 1958-1969, **Introduction to library cataloguing,** 1958; 1959; 1969. {CRRI IIT NERC NIPCCD NMML}

Dewey, Harry, 1957, **Introduction to library cataloguing and classification,** 4th rev. edn. {DUL}

Sayers, W.C. Berwick, 1938, **Introduction to library classification.** {NAI}

Sayers, W.C. Berwick, 1950, **An introduction to library classification.** {CRRI}

Sayers, W.C. Berwick, 1958, **Introduction to library classification,** 9th edn. {BIS}

Martinson, Tom L., 1972, **Introduction to library research in geography.** {DUL}

Butler, Pierce, 1961, **Introduction to library science.** {AIU IIT MFL}

Shera, Jesse H., 1976, **Introduction to library science** : Basic elements of library science. {DUL}

Wisdom, Aline C., 1974, **Introduction to library services for library media technical assistants.** {ICA}

Young, Micki Jo, et al, 1978, **Introduction to minicomputers in federal libraries.** [U.S. Library of Congress]. {USIS}

Salton, Gerard and Mc Gill, Michael J., 1983, **Introduction to modern information retrieval.** {BIS}

Colin, A.J.T., 1971, **Introduction to operating systems.** {NASSDOC}

Churchman, C. West, et al, 1969, **Introduction to operations research.** {NASSDOC}

Mott, Thomas H. Jr., et al, 1972, **Introduction to PL-1 programming for library and information science.** {BCL IIT JNU}

Hospers, John, ed., 1971, **Introduction to philosophical analysis**, rev edn. {NASSDOC}

Richmond, Phyllis A., 1981, **Introduction to PRECIS for North American usage.** {USIS}

Satija, M.P. and Comarona, John P., 1987, **Introduction to the practice of Dewey Decimal Classification**. {NASSDOC}

Corbett, Edmund V., 1950, **Introduction to public librarianship for entrance examination students.** {ZHL}

Vishwanathan, C.G., 1955, **Introduction to public library organisation.** {NAI}

Vishwanathan, C.G., 1961, **An introduction to public library organisation**, 2nd edn. {SPA}

Vishwanathan, C.G., 1978, **Introduction to public library organisation with special reference to India**. {NERC}

Taverekere, Srikantaid and Hoffman, Herbert H., 1978, **Introduction to quantitative research methods for librarians**, 2nd rev edn. {DUL}

Roberts A.D., 1948-1956, **Introduction to reference books, 1948; 1952; 1956.** {CRRI JNU SPA}

Hutchins, Margaret, 1944, **Introduction to reference work**. [American Library Association]. {BIS CRRI DUL ICHR IIFT NMML USIS}

Katz, William A., 1969, **Introduction to reference work**, 2 vols, V. 1 : Basic information services; V. 2 : Reference services. {AIU BIS DUL ICHR IIT ISI NASSDOC}

Katz, William A., 1974, **Introduction to reference work**, 2nd edn, 2 vols. {CRRI DUL JNU MMTC}

Katz, William A., 1978, **Introduction to reference work**, 3rd edn., 2 vols. {CRRI MMTC NIPCCD}

Katz, William A., 1982, **Introduction to reference work**, 4th edn., 2 vols. {CRRI IIC USIS}

Corrigan, Phillip, 1967, **Introduction to Sears list of subject headings**. {IIMC IIT}

Horne, Thomas Hartwell, 1981, **Introduction to the study of bibliography, to which is prefixed a memour on the public libraries of America**, 2 vols. {DUL}

Brown, A.G., 1976, **An introduction to subject indexing.** {ICA NIEPA NIH ZHL}

Brown, A.G., 1982, **Introduction to subject indexing** : A programmed text. 2nd edn. {IIT}

Stavley, Ronald, et al, 1967, **Introduction to subject study**. {AIU IIT NASSDOC}

Bloomberg, Marty and Evans, G. Edward, 1976, **Introduction to technical services for library technicians**, 3rd edn. {MHA}

Bloomberg, Marty and Evans, G. Edward, 1985, **Introduction to technical services for library technicians**, 5th edn. {NASSDOC}

Perreault, Jean M., 1969, **Introduction to UDC**. {BIS IIT ISI JNU SPA}

Thompson, James, 1980, **Introduction to university library administration**, 3rd edn. {DUL IIT NIH ZHL}

Anon, 1963, **Introduction to the University of Chicago library** : A brief guide to the location and use of the library's service and resources. {NMML}

Mikhailov, A.I. and Giljarevaskij, R.S., n.d., **Introductory course in informatics/documentations**. [UNESCO]. {DUL NASSDOC}

Anon, 1976, **Inventory of bibliographic data bases produced in the UK** : Report. [British Library, Department of Research and Development]. {JNU}

Anon, n.d., **Investigation concerning the SFS information service and its users**. [Finnish Standards Association]. {BIS}

Baker, C.A., 1977, **An investigation of man-computer interaction in an online bibliographic information retrieval system**. {BCL}

Sardar, Ziauddin, 1979, **Islam** : Outline of a classification scheme. {ZHL}

Anon, n.d., **Islamic libraries**, mimeo short bibliography. {NASSDOC}

Qaisar, Mahmood Hasan, 1965, **Islamic sciences** : Expansion of Dewey Decimal Classification (16th edn.) for oriental libraries, {ZHL}

Anon, 1972, **Issues in library administration** : Papers presented at the U.S.-Japan conference on libraries and information science in higher education, 2nd, 1972. {JNU}

Anwar, H., 1985, **Issues in South East Asian librarianship** : A selection of papers and articles. {NASSDOC}

Moore, Everett L., 1964, **Issues of freedom in American libraries**. [American Library Association]. {USIS}

Palmer, B.I., 1962, **Itself an education**. [Library Association, London]. {IIT}

Palmer, B.I., 1971, **Itself an education** : Six lectures on classification, 2nd edn. [Library Association, London]. {NASSDOC NMML}

Kasliwal, Kastoor Chand, comp., 1967, **Jaina grantha bhandars in Rajasthan**. {INSA}

Azad, Asadollah, 1978, **Job satisfaction of para-professional librarians** : Comparative study of public and technical services departments in selected university libraries. {JNU}

Schatz, Birdie B., 1968, **Joint university libraries** ; Staff handbook. {JNU}

Moore, Everett Leroy, 1968, **Junior college libraries development needs and proopectlve.** {JNU}

Anon, 1970, **Junior high school library catalog**, 2nd edn. {USIS}

Homanyunfarokh, Ruknuddin, n.d., **Ketab va ketab khana**. {JNU}

Wolters, Marthin F., ed., 1972, **Key to the computer**, 2 vols. V. 1 : Text book; V. 2 : Training manual. {NASSDOC}

Gover, Harvey R., 1981, **Keys to library research on the graduate level** : A guide to guides. {JNU}

Williams, Raymond, 1976, **keywords** : A vocabulary of culture and society {NMML}

Athar, Shere, 1965, **Khuda Bakhsh Oriental Public Library, Patna**. {Khuda Bakhsh Oriental Public Library]. {ZHL}

Wasserman, Paul, et al, eds, 1974, **LIST** : Library and information services today : An international registry of research and innovation, vol-4. {USIS}

Deshpande, K.S., 1958, **Land of libraries** : Story of a study tour of the USA. [Gurudev Literary Association, Hubli]. {AIU ZHL}

Anon, 1970, **Landscape filling index**. [Institute of Landscape Architects]. {SPA}

Hutchins, W.J., 1975, **Languages of indexing and classification** : A linguistic study of structures and function. {DUL}

Savary, M.J., 1968, **Latin American cooperative acquisitions programme.** {IIFT}

Jain, H.C., 1972, **Law library administration and reference.** {CRRI MMTC}

Anon, 1954, **Layout of periodicals.** (ISO/R 8-1954) (E). [International Organisation for Standardisation, Geneva]. {NASSDOC}

Burrel, T.W., 1969, **Learn to use books and libraries** : A programmed text. {JNU}

Mohinder Singh, comp., 1975, **Learned societies and institutions in India** : Activities and publications, including over 4000 research oriented titles. {JNU UGC}

Trehan, G.L., 1975, **Learning and libraries in ancient India** : A study. {JNU}

Beaubien, Anne K. and George, Mary W., 1982, **Learning the library** : Concepts and methods for effective bibliographic instruction. {AIU}

Meredith, Patrick, 1961, **Learning, remembering and knowing**. {NASSDOC}

Shantilata, 1985, **Learning to read** : Use of orthographic and semantic cues. {NASSDOC}

Thiagrajan, R., 1978, **Lecture notes** : NISSAT training course on systems analysis for information sciences, December 12-23, 1978, New Delhi. [Department of Science and Technology, New Delhi]. {BIS}

Aggarwal, D.S., 1985, **Lectures on universe of knowledge**. {NMML}

Kartashou, N.S., ed., 1983, **Lenin and library cooperation**. {NASSDOC*}

Anon, 1964, **Let's read together** : Books for family enjoyment, 2nd edn. [American Library Association; Association for Library Service to Children]. {USIS}

Gardner, Frank M., 1951, **Letters to a younger librarian**. {DUL NASSDOC}

Savage, Ernest A., 1942, **The librarian and his committee**. {CRRI}

Sogani, Kamal Chand and Vijay Narain, eds., 1973, **Librarian and libraries** : In the memory of the Master Moti Lal ji and his Shri Sanmati Pustakalaya. {JNU NASSDOC}

Ganguly, N., 1933, **Librarian and library administration**. {NAI}

Wasserman, Paul, 1965, **Librarian and the machine** : Observations on the applications of machines in administration of college and university libraries. {JNU}

Jahoda, Gerald and Braunagel, J.S., 1980, **Librarian and reference queries** : A systematic approach. {CRRI ISI USIS}

Lyle, Guy R., 1970, **Librarian speaking** : Interview with university librarians. {JNU USIS}

Atherton, Pauline and Chiristian, Roger W., 1977, **Librarians and online services.** {BCL IIT}

Harrod, L.M., 1971, **Librarians' glossary of terms used in librarianship and the book crafts and reference book**, 3rd edn. {CRRI IIT JNU NASSDOC}

Harrod, L.M., 1977, **Librarians' glossary of terms used in librarianship, documentation and the book crafts and reference book**, 4th edn. {ICA IIC MMTC NCDC NCERT NERC NIH NMML ZHL}

Gakhar, Attam Prakash, 1982, **Librarians' guide to Broad System of ordering.** [British Standards Institution]. {JNU}

Balwinder, Kaur comp., n.d., **Librarians' guide to Indian periodicals published for free distribution**. {NASSDOC}

Woods, Lawrence A. and Pope, Nolan F., 1983, **Librarians' guide to microcomputer technology and applications.** {JNU NIEPA USIS}

Taylor, L.J., ed., 1976, **Librarians' handbook** [Library Association London]. 2 vols. {JNU NASSDOC NIPCCD}

Ghazi, Muhammad Ismail, 1963, **A librarian's musing**. {JNU}

Press, Jaques Cattel, ed., 1979, **The Librarians' phone book.** {USIS}

Pipics, Zoltan, ed., 1969, **Librarians' practical dictionary in twenty two languages.** {JNU}

De Hart, Florence E, 1979, **Librarian's psychological commitments** : Human relations in librarianship. {INSA NIPCCD USIS}

Gujarati, B.S., 1964, **Librarianship.** {NERC NIPCCD ZHL}

Tomlinson, N., 1963, **Librarianship.** {NIH}

Umapathy Setty, K. 1977, **Librarianship** : Change or status quo. {CRRI JNU}

Irwin, Raymond, 1949, **Librarianship** : Essays on applied bibliography. {CRRI}

Atkinson, Frank, 1974, **Librarianship** : Introduction to the profession. {ICA USIS}

Mukherjee, A.K., 1966, **Librarianship** : Its philosophy and history. {BIS IIT NASSDOC NIH SPA}

Sharma, Ravindra N., ed., 1981, **Librarianship** : Perspectives and prospects. {AIU NIEPA}

Hutchings, F.G.B., 1969, **Librarianship** : A short manual with special reference to developing countries. {IIMC SPA}

Jayaswal, P.K., 1990, **Librarianship and bureaucratic organisation** : A study in the sociology of library profession in India. {JNU NASSDOC}

Coblans, Herbert, 1974, **Librarianship and documentation** : An international perspective. {BIS ICHR ISI NASSDOC NERC}

Abdul Haq, A.M. and Aman, Mohammad M., 1977, **Librarianship and the Third World** : An annotated bibliography of selected literature on developing nations, 1960-1975. {NASSDOC}

Myson, William, 1963, **Librarianship as a career.** {ICA}

Anon, n.d., **Librarianship as a profession**, mimeo short bibliography. {NASSDOC}

Chopra, H.R., 1984, **Librarianship as a profession** : A study of socio-economic background and professional orientation of the libraries in Delhi : Thesis. [Punjab University]. {NASSDOC}

Chopra, H.R., 1989, **Librarianship as a profession in India.** {NASSDOC}

Borcharat, D.H. and Horacek, J.I., 1975, **Librarianship in Australia, New Zealand and Oceania.** {NASSDOC}

Saunders, W.L., ed., 1967, **Librarianship in Britain today**. [Library Association, London]. {IIT}

Asheim, Lester, 1966, **Librarianship in developing countries.** {NIPCCD}

Bhargava, G.D.,1977, **Librarianship in India and abroad** : Retrospect and prospect. {CRRI ICA IIT JNU NASSDOC NCAER NIEPA NIPCCD ZHL}

Gerard, David E., ed., 1970, **Libraries and the arts** : A symposium of papers and discussions at the seminar held in the College of Librarianship, September 1-6, 1969, Wales. {NASSDOC}

Markuson, B.E., 1964, **Libraries and automation.** {IIT}

Horecky, Paul L., **Libraries and bibliographic centres in the Soviet Union.** {IEG}

Bergen, Dan and Duryea, E.D., 1964, **Libraries and college climate of learning.** {JNU}

Benge, Ronald C., 1970-75, **Libraries and cultural change, 1970; 1975.** {AIU IIT MMTC NASSDOC USIS}

Melin, Johns, **Libraries and data processing** : Where do we stand. {JNU}

Martyn, John, 1987, **Libraries and information centres in Britain.** [British Council, London]. {NASSDOC*}

Andersen, A., et al, 1985, **Libraries and information centres in the Soviet Union.** {NASSDOC*}

Edelman, H., ed., 1986, **Libraries and information science in the electronic age.** {NASSDOC}

Anon, 1972, **Libraries and information technology** : A national system challenge : A report to the Council of Library Resources. [National Academy of Sciences, Washington]. {USIS}

Lancaster, F.W., 1982, **Libraries and librarians in an age of electronics**. {USIS}

Ambhnwong, Suthilak, 1967, **Libraries and librarianship in Thailand**. {JNU}

Datta, Bimal Kumar, 1970, **Libraries and librarianship of ancient and medieval India**. {IIC IIT JNU NAI NERC NMML}

Anders, Mary Edna, 1976, **Libraries and library services in the Southeast** : A report of the Southeastern states cooperative library survey, 1972-74. {BIS ISI}

Anon, 1977, **Libraries and the life of the mind in America** : Addresses delivered at the centennial celebration of the American Library Association, [American Library Association]. {IIT NIPCCD USIS}

Marshall, Margaret R., n.d., **Libraries and literature for teenagers**. {ICHR}

Karunakarnan Nayar, 1947, **Libraries and mass education**. [Sri Setha Parvathi Bayi Library, Kottayam]. {NASSDOC*}

Hobbs, John L., 1984, **Libraries and the materials of local history**. {CRRI NAI}

Shera, Jesse H., 1965, **Libraries and the organisation of knowledge**. {IIT USIS}

McColvin, L.R., 1937, **Libraries and the public**. {NAI}

Waples, Douglas and Carnovsky, Leon, 1939, **Libraries and readers in the State of New York**. {NASSDOC*}

Kaufman, Paul, 1969, **Libraries and their users** : Collected papers in library history. [Library Association, London]. {NIPCCD}

Dutta, D.N. 1975, **Libraries and their uses.** {ICA IIT}

Buck, Paul, 1964, **Libraries and universities** : Addresses and reports, ed. by E.E. Williams {JNU}

Goodell, John S. and Kemper, Robert E., eds., 1975, **Libraries and work sampling**. {BIS}

Brawne, Michael, 1970, **Libraries architecture and equipment**. {IIT ZHL}

Orr, James Mconnell, 1977, **Libraries as communication systems**. {IIMC USIS}

Anon, 1971, **Libraries as educational tools**. [Sri Venkateswara University, Tirupati]. {JNU}

Knight, Douglas M. and Nourse, E. Shapley, eds., 1969, **Libraries at large** : Tradition, innovation and the national interest : The resource book based on the materials of the National Advisory Commission on Libraries. {JNU USIS}

Chandler, George, 1972, **Libraries, documentation and bibliography in the USSR, 1917-1971** : Survey and critical analysis of Soviet studies. {JNU NASSDOC}

Vosper, Robert and Koops, William R.H., 1977, **Libraries for all** : A world of books and their readers : World congress on libraries for all, 50th, 1977, Brussels. [International Federation of Library Association and Institutions]. {IIT}

McColvin, Lionel R., 1961, **Libraries for children**. {DUL}

Lewis, M. Joy, 1969, **Libraries for the handicapped**. {DUL}

Calderhead, Particia, ed., 1972, **Libraries for professional practice**. {CRRI IIT}

Hillian, Margret P.. 1955, **Libraries for research and industry planning and equipment**. {DUL}

Wild, Friedemann, 1972, **Libraries for schools and universities**. {CRRI}

Houle, Cyril O., ed., 1951, **Libraries in adult and fundamental education** : Report of the Malmo Seminar. [UNESCO]. {IEG NASSDOC ZHL}

Houle, Cyril O., ed., 1957, **Libraries in adult and fundamental education** : Report of the Malmo Seminar, (Hindi Translation). [Indian Adult Education Association]. {NIEPA}

Harrison, K.C., n.d., **Libraries in Britain.** {IEG}

McColvin, Lianol R., 1961, **Libraries in Britain**. {NASSDOC}

Bhatia, S.K., ed., 1979, **Libraries in Delhi** : A comprehensive list. {AIU IIT}

Chandler, George, 1971, **Libraries in the East** : An international and comparative study. {ICA IIMC JNU NASSDOC NMML}

Anon, 1971, **Libraries in Finland**. [Finnish Library Association, Helsinki]. {NASSDOC*}

Ferguson, John, 1971, **Libraries in France**. {NASSDOC}

Cowley, John, ed., 1975, **Libraries in higher education** : The user approach to service. {INSA NIEPA}

Kan, Lai-Bing, comp., 1963, **Libraries in Hongkong** : A directory {ICWA}

Kiss, Jeno, 1972, **Libraries in Hungary**. [National Szechenyi Library, Budapest]. {NASSDOC}

Anon, 1951, **Libraries in India**. [Ministry of Education, New Delhi]. {BIS NMML}

Anon, 1960, **Libraries in India**. [Ministry of Education, New Delhi]. {MHA NASSDOC}

Chandler, George, 1966, **Libraries in the modern world.** {AIU IIC SPA}

Anon, 1962, **Libraries in the Netherlands.** [Netherlands Librarians Association]. {NASSDOC}

Luczynska, Alfreda and Krystyna, Remerowa, comps., n.d., **Libraries in Poland**. {BIS}

Anon. 1974, **Libraries in the political science** : Georg Legh and German librarianship, 1933-53, tr. by Marta L. Dosa {JNU}

Estabrook, Leigh, ed., 1977, **Libraries in post-industrial society.** {IIT}

Harrison, K.C., 1969, **Libraries in Scandinavia**, 2nd edn. {IIT}

Leyland, Eric, 1961, **Libraries in schools.** {JNU}

Anon, 1985, **Libraries in social education** : Report of the national seminar on libraries in social education, 6th, September 26—October 5, 1955, 2nd ed. [Indian Adult Education Association]. {NIPCCD}

Gerard, David, 1978, **Libraries in society**. {IIT NIEPA}

Francis, Simon, ed., 1971, **Libraries in the USSR**. {NASSDOC}

Kodiyan, Cicily, 1987, **Libraries in the USSR**. [USSR Embassy in India, New Delhi]. {NASSDOC*}

Huck-Tee, Edward Lim, 1970, **Libraries in West Malaysia and Singapore** : A short history. [University of Malaysia, Kuala Lumpur] {CRRI NASSDOC}

Kabir, Abulfazal M. Fazle, 1987, **Libraries of Bengal 1700-1947**. {NMML}

Licklider, J.C., 1965, **Libraries of the future.** {JNU NMML SPA USIS}

Anon, 1966, **Libraries of the United Nations** : A descriptive guide. [United Nations]. {ICWA IIC IIT JNU NIH}

Kujoth, Jean Spealman, 1969, **Libraries, readers and book selection**. {USIS}

Rajagopalan, T.S. and Ramaswami, K., n.d., **Libraries serving the CSIR complex**. [Indian National Scientific Documentation Centre]. {IIT NASSDOC}

Petru, William C., ed., 1967, **Library** : Introduction for library assistants. [Special Library Association, New York]. {IIT}

Wynar, Bohdan S., 1968, **Library acquisition** : A classified bibliographic guide to the literature and reference tools. {JNU}

Futas, Elizabeth, 1977, **Library acquisition policies and procedures.** {IIT}

Gujarati, B.S., 1966, **Library administration**, 2nd edn. {DUL NASSDOC ZHL}

Lock, Reginald Northwood, 1961, **Library administration**. {CRRI IIT}

Lock, Reginald Northwood, 1973, **Library administration**, 3rd edn. {DUL ICA}

Ranganathan, S.R., 1959, **Library administration**, 2nd edn. {AIU BIS CRRI DSSW DUL IEG IIC IIT JNU MMTC NAI NASSDOC NIH NMML SPA ZHL}

Mittal, R.L., 1964, **Library administration** : Theory and practice. {DUL ICA NAI NCAER NIH NMML SPA ZHL}

Mittal, R.L., 1969, **Library administration** : Theory and practice, 2nd edn. {DUL JNU NASSDOC NIEPA SPA}

Mittal, R.L., 1973, **Library administration** : Theory and practice, 3rd edn. {CRRI DUL JNU NIH TDA}

Mittal, R.L., 1978, **Library administration** : Theory and practice, 4th edn. {BIS DUL JNU NIEPA ZHL}

Mittal, R.L., **Library administration** : Theory and practice, 5th edn. {ZHL}

Krishan Kumar, 1987, **Library administration and management**. {JNU NASSDOC}

Monroe, Margaret Ellen, 1963, **Library adult education** : The biography of an idea. {USIS}

Harrison, K.C., 1963, **Library and the community**. {MFL}

Harrison, K.C., 1977, **The library and the community**, 3rd rev. edn. {USIS}

Harrison, K.C., 1966, **Library and the community**. {ICA}

Sahai, Shrinath, 1973, **Library and the community**. {JNU NASSDOC NMML}

Anon, 1985, **Library and the community** : Units 1-9. [Andhra Pradesh Open University, Hyderabad]. {NASSDOC*}

Anon, 1961, **Library and documentation journals**. [International Federation for Documentation and Information]. {NASSDOC}

Hoover, Ryan E., ed., 1980, **The library and information manager's guide to online services.** {USIS}

Kumar, P.S.G., ed., 1988, **Library and information manpower development** : Papers and proceedings : Nagpur Seminar. {NASSDOC}

Burkett, Jack, 1983, **Library and information network in the United Kingdom**. [Association of Special Libraries and Information Bureaux]. {CRRI JNU}

Gupta, Pawan K. and Usha Pawan, 1986, **Library and information science** : Current trends in India. {JNU}

Stephen, Parker J., 1984, **Library and information science and archive administration** : A guide to building a basic collection for library schools. {JNU}

Mangla, P.B., ed., 1981, **Library and information science education in India** : Papers and recommendations of an All India seminar held at the Department of Library Science, University of Delhi, during October 3-8, 1977, {AIU ICA JNU NASSDOC NIEPA}

Anon, n.d., **Library and information science journals in India**, typed short bibliography. {NASSDOC}

Agrawal, S.P., ch. ed., 1985, **Library and information science literature** : SSDC resources. {NASSDOC}

Anon, 1976, **Library and information science manpower development in the Asian Region** : Report : Meeting of supervisors of library and documentation schools in the Asian region, Bangalore. {CRRI}

Anon, 1972, **Library and information sciences** : An ERIC bibliography [Educational Resources Information Centre]. {NASSDOC}

Anon, 1974, **Library and information service needs of the nation**. {JNU}

Vashishth, C.P., ed., 1989, **Library and information services in India** : Assessment and effectiveness. [Indian Library Association]. {NASSDOC}

Agrawal, S.P., 1987, **Library and information services in India** : The current scenario. {NASSDOC}

Vernon, Ken, 1986, **Library and information services of management development institutions** : A practical guide. {NASSDOC}

Taylor, Peter J., ed., 1976, **Library and information studies in the United Kingdom and Ireland, 1950-1974** : An index to theses. [Association of Special Libraries and Information Bureaux]. {NASSDOC}

Hernon, Peter, et al, 1973, **Library and library related publications** : A directory of publishing opportunities in journals, serials and annuals. {NASSDOC}

Khanna, J.K., 1987, **Library and society**. [Kurukshetra University, Kurukshetra]. {JNU NMML}

Khandwala, Vidyut K., ed., 1982, **Library architecture**. [Indian Association of Special Libraries and Information Centres]. {MMTC NIEPA}

Penland, Partick R. and Mathai, Aleyamma, 1978, **Library as a learning service centre**. {JNU}

Collison, Robert L., 1869, **Library assistance to readers**. [DUL MHA}

Chirgwin, F. John and Oldfield, Phyllis, 1983, **Library assistant's manual.** 2nd rev. edn. {IIT}

Foskett, D.J., 1962, **Library association** : Creed of librarian. {IIT}

Anon, 1968, **Library Association**. [Committee on Scientific Library Service, Library Association, London]. {IIT}

Fullard, Harold and Darby, H.C., eds., 1973, **Library atlas**. {JNU}

Heiliger, Edward M. and Henderson, Paul B., 1971, **Library automation** : Experience, methodology and technology of the library as an information system. {AIU INSA JNU NASSDOC NIPCCD NMML}

Reynolds, Dennis, 1985, **Library automation** : Issues and applications. {JNU NASSDOC NMML}

Salmon, Stephen R., ed., 1969, **Library automation** : A state of art review : Papers : Pre-conference institute on library automation, 1967, San Francisco. [American Library Association]. {USIS}

Butler, Brett and Martin, Susan K. eds., 1975, **Library automation-II** : The state of art : Papers : Pre-conference institute on library automation, June 22-23, 1973, Las Vegas. [American Library Association, Information Science and Automation Division]. {USIS}

Lucy, Te-Chu Lee, 1985, **Library automation and information science** : A collection of essays. {NASSDOC}

Anon, 1970, **Library automation at the New York Public Library and the Association of New York Libraries for Technical Services**. [LARC]. {USIS}

Salmon, Stephen R., 1975, **Library automation systems**, 2nd edn. {CRRI JNU NIH}

Anon, n.d., **Library binding handbook**. [Library Building Institute]. {ISI}

Anon, 1951, **Library binding manual**. [American Library Association]. {IIT}

Ranganathan, S.R., 1952, **Library book selection**. [Indian Library Association]. {BIS DSSW INSA}

Ranganathan, S.R., 1966, **Library book selection**, 2nd rev edn. {BIS CRRI IIT ISI NMML SPA}

Ranganathan, S.R., 1989, **Library book selections**. [Sarada Ranganathan Endowment for Library Sciences, Bangalore]. {NASSDOC}

Sharma, H.D., 1972, **Library building and furniture with special reference to college libraries**. {CRRI ICA ICHR INSA MFL NASSDOC NIEPA NIH NIPCCD ZHL}

Deprospo, Ernest R., 1969, **Library building consultant role and responsibility.** {IIT}

Reynolds, J.D., ed., 1967, **Library buildings.** {DUL}

Berriman, S.G., 1969, **Library buildings, 1967-1968**. {DUL}

Trezza, Alphonse F., ed., 1967, **Library buildings** : Innovation for changing needs : Proceedings. {AIU}

Kaula, Prithvi N., 1971, **Library buildings** : Planning and design. {ICA IIMC IIT NASSDOC NIEPA NIH NIPCCD ZHL}

Shaw, Robert J., ed., 1967, **Library buildings for the future** : Proceedings. Library buildings institute and American libraries trustee association workshop, 1965, Detroit. {DUL}

Thompson, Anthony, 1963, **Library buildings of Britain and Europe**. {CRRI IIT NASSDOC}

Strout, Ruth French, ed., 1964, **Library catalogs** : Changing damnations. {IIT}

Ranganathan, S.R., n.d., **Library catalogue** : Fundamentals and procedure. [Madras Library Association]. {BIS}

Henderson, James W. and Rosenthal, Joseph A., eds., 1968, **Library catalogues** : Their preservation and maintenance by photographic and automated techniques. {AIU IIT SPA}

Jayne, Sears, et al, 1956, **Library catalogues of the English renaissance**. {DUL}

Olney, John C., 1963, **Library cataloguing and classification.** {DUL}

Anon, 1985, **Library cataloguing practice** : Solutions to assignments 1-26. [Andhra Pradesh Open University, Hyderabad]. {NASSDOC*}

Anon, 1985, **Library cataloguing practice** : Unit 1 : Lessons 1-14. [Andhra Pradesh Open University, Hyderabad]. {NASSDOC}

Sengupta, B. and Ohdedar, A.K., 1977, **Library classification**. {CRRI IIT NMML}

Parkhi, R.S., 1972, **Library classification** : Evolution of a dynamic theory. {AIU BIS IIT ISI JNU MHA NMML}

Ranganathan, S.R., 1964, **Library classification** : Fundamentals and procedure, with graded examples and exercises. [Madras Library Association]. {BIS}

Dutta, D.N., 1962, **Library classification** : Theory and practice. {IIT}

Gliden, Sophia Hall, 1942, **Library classification for public administration materials.** [American Library Association]. {NAI}

Dutta, D.N., 1978, **Library classification manual**. {IIT ZHL}

Anon, 1985, **Library classification practice** : Unit 2 : Lessons 1-16. [Andhra Pradesh Open University, Hyderabad]. {NASSDOC*}

Anon, 1985, **Library classification practice** : Units 1-13. [Andhra Pradesh Open University, Hyderabad]. {NASSDOC*}

Anon, 1985, **Library classification theory** : Units 1-10. [Andhra Pradesh Open University, Hyderabad]. {NASSDOC*}

Wright, Alice E., 1973, **Library clerical workers and wagers**. {BIS}

Gardner, Richard K., 1981, **Library collections** : Their origin, selection and development. {DUL}

Shores, Louis, et al, ed., 1966, **The library college** : Contributions for American higher education at the Jamestown college workshop. {USIS}

Devarajan, G. and Rahelamma, A.V., 1990, **Library computerisation in India** : Isaac festschrift. {JNU}

Jefferson, G., 1966-1977, **Library co-operation, 1966; 1968; 1977.** {AIU ICA IIT NIH}

Humphry, John A., 1963, **Library co-operation** : Brown university study of university school community library coordination in the State of Rhode Island. {DUL}

Verma, Subash Chandra, 1977-78, **Library co-operation in India, 1977; 1978.** {NASSDOC}

Bryan, J.F.W., et al, 1956, **Library co-operation in the North West** : A report. {DUL}

Girja Kumar, 1986, **Library development in India**. {JNU NMML}

Anon, 1975, **Library development in Pakistan** : Resume and recommendation : National seminar, February 7-9, 1974, Lahore. [Society for the Promotion and Improvement of Libraries]. {NASSDOC*}

Tirkha, R.N. and Arneja, M.S., 1983, **Library development oriented education.** {ICA}

Ranganathan, S.R., 1950, **Library development plan** : Thirty-year programme for India. [University of Delhi]. {BIS MFL NERC SPA}

Ranganathan, S.R., 1947, **Library development plan for Allahabad University.** {AIU NASSDOC}

Morris, John, 1986, **Library disaster preparedness handbook**. {JNU}

Garvey, Mona, 1969, **Library displays** : Their purpose, construction and use. {USIS}

Malhan, Inder Vir and Kapoor, Shabad, 1982, **Library education** : A bibliography. {IIT JNU NASSDOC}

Kohl, David F., 1986, **Library education and professional issues** : A handbook for library management. {JNU NASSDOC}

Bonn, G.S., 1966, **Library education and training in developing countries**. {ICA NIEPA}

Khurshid, A., 1987, **Library education in India, Pakistan and Iran.** {NASSDOC*}

Bowden, Russel E., ed., 1980, **Library education programme in developing countries with special reference to Asia** : UNESCO pre-IFLA conference seminar on library education programme in developing countries, August 15-18, 1980, Philippines. [Library Association, London]. {IIT NASSDOC}

Morse, Philip M., 1968, **Library effectiveness** : A systems approach. {AIU DUL JNU NASSDOC NMML SPA USIS}

Poole, Frazer G., ed., 1965, **The library environment** : Aspects of interior planning : Proceedings : Library equipment institute, 2nd, 1964, St. Louis. {JNU USIS}

Sycnawine, Wayne, n.d., **Library evaluation**. [American Library Association]. {DUL}

Taylor, James L., 1966, **Library facility for elementary and secondary schools.** {JNU}

Anon, 1963, **Library furniture and equipment**. [American Library Association]. {DUL IIT NASSDOC ZHL}

Landau, T., 1963, **Library furniture and equipment**. {IIT NMML ZHL}

Kessler, Margaret and Hall-Quest, Alfred L., 1941, **Library guidance for teachers.** {DUL ZHL}

Olle, James G., 1967, **Library history** : An examination guide book, 2nd rev edn. {ICHR IIT}

Stevens, N.D., ed., 1971, **Library humor** : A bibliothecal miscellany to 1970. {NASSDOC}

Wilson, Louis Round, et al, 1951, **Library in college instruction**. {ZHL}

Wright, Gordon H., ed., 1966, **Library in colleges of commerce and technology.** {DUL IIT}

Gujarati, Balwant Singh, 1961, **Library in education** : With special reference to school libraries. {JNU}

Rossoft, Martin, 1955, **Library in the high school teaching**. {JNU}

Anon, 1983, **Library in the information revolution** : Proceedings : Congress of South-East Asian librarians, 6th, May 30 - June 3, 1983, Singapore. {JNU}

Anon, n.d., **Library in the primary schools** : A report by sub-committee of School Library Association. {JNU}

Fargo, Lucile F., 1947, **Library in the school**, 4th edn. [American Library Association]. {DUL ZHL}

Anon, 1967, **The library in the university** : The University of Tennessee library lectures, 1949-1967. {USIS}

Anon, 1968, **Library, information and archive work**. [Ministry of Labour, Great Britain]. {JNU}

Lockwood, Deborah, L., comp., 1979, **Library instruction** : A bibliography. {NIPCCD}

Anon, 1930, **Library instruction** : Junior and senior high schools. {ZHL}

Cowles, Betty M. and Orr, Robert W., 1952, **Library instruction manual**, 3rd edn. {ZHL}

Moon, Eric and Nyren, Karl, eds., 1970, **Library issues** : The sixties. {ICHR USIS}

Ranganathan, S.R., 1953, **Library legislation**. [Madras Library Association]. {BIS IEG}

Sadhu, S.H. and Saraf, B.N., 1967, **Library legislation in India** : A historical and comparative study. {BIS ICA IIMC NASSDOC NERC SPA}

Rout, R.K., 1986, **Library legislation in India** : Problems and prospects. {NASSDOC*}

Hakam Singh, 1962 **Library legislation in the Punjab**. [Punjab Library Literary Circle]. {IIT}

Plotnik, Arthur, 1975, **Library life — American style** : A journalist's field report. {USIS}

Anon, 1949-83, **Library literature** : An index to library and information science, 1949-51 to 1982-83. {NASSDOC USIS}

Vijaya Kumar, P., 1981, **Library literature in Telugu, 1915-1981**. {NASSDOC*}

Sayers, W.C. Berwick, 1939, **Library local collections**. {DUL NAI}

Panwar, B.S. and Vyas, S.D., 1986, **Library management**. {JNU}

Stueart, Robert D. and Eastlick, John Taylor, 1977, **Library management**. {DUL USIS}

Stueart, Robert D. and Eastlick, John Taylor, 1981, **Library management**, 2nd edn. {BIS DUL USIS}

Anon, 1985, **Library management** : Units 1-10. [Andhra Pradesh Open University, Hyderabad]. {NASSDOC*}

Sharma, C.K., 1983, **Library management and organisation**, Vol. I. {DUL ICHR IIFT IIT}

Hewitt, Roy, 1969, **Library management case studies**. {JNU}

Boss, Richard W., 1983, **The library manager's guide to automation**, 2nd edn. {NASSDOC USIS}

Krishan Kumar, 1982, **Library manual**. {BIS DSSW ICA IIC IIFT IIMC IIT ISI JNU NCDC NERC NIH ZHL}

Ranganathan, S.R. and Sivaraman, K.M., 1951, **Library manual**. [Indian Library Association]. {BIS DSSW INSA NERC ZHL}

Ranganathan, S.R., 1966, **Library manual**, 2nd edn. {BIS CRRI DSSW ICHR IIT INSA MMTC NASSDOC NERC NIPCCD}

Toser, Marie A., 1964, **Library manual** : A study work manual of lessons on the use of books and libraries, 6th edn. {USIS}

Ranganathan, S.R., 1960, **Library manual for library authorities, librarians and honorary library workers**. {ICA}

Ranganathan, S.R., 1966, **Library manual for library authorities, librarians and honorary library workers**, 2nd edn. {BIS ISI JNU NIEPA NMML ZHL}

Haman, Albert C. and Bakin, Marg K., comps., 1964, **Library materials for elementary science**. {DUL}

Coburn, Louis, 1973, **Library media centre problems :** Case studies. {USIS}

Goschen, Viscount, n.d., **Library movement**. {AIU}

Chakravarty, N.C., 1962, **Library movement in India**. {NASSDOC}

Kaula, P.N., ed., 1968, **Library movement in India**. [Delhi Library Association]. {CRRI}

Sharma, Jagdish Saran, 1986, **Library movement in India and abroad**. {JNU}

Ramanujam Nair, P., 1974, **Library movement in Kerala** : The need for reform and legislation. {NERC}

Martin, Susan K., 1978, **Library networks, 1978-79**. {IIT USIS}

Martin, Susan K., 1980, Library network, 1981-82, 4th edn. {USIS}

Carnovsky, Leon, ed., 1969, **Library networks** : Promises and performance. {IIT}

Goodrum, Charles A. and Dalrymple, Helen W., 1982, **The Library of Congress**, 2nd edn. {IIC JNU NASSDOC NMML USIS}

Small, Herbert, 1982, **The Library of Congress** : Its architecture and decoration ed. by Henry Hope Reed. {USIS}

Gurney, Gene and Apple, Nick, 1981, **The Library of Congress** : A picture story of the world's largest library, rev. edn. {JNU}

Anon, 1979, **The Library of Congress** : A portrait of an institution. {USIS}

Cole, John, Y., ed., 1978, **The Library of Congress in perspective** {NASSDOC}

Anon, 1975, **U.S. Library of Congress subject headings**, 8th edn., 2nd vols. [Library of Congress, Subject Cataloguing Division]. {NASSDOC USIS}

Anon, 1980, **Library of Congress subject headings**, 9th edn. [U.S. Library of Congress, Subject Cataloguing Division]. {USIS}

Chan, Lois Mai, 1986, **Library of Congress subject headings** : Principles and application, 2nd edn. (Research studies in library science, No. 19). {NASSDOC}

Anon, 1975, **Library of Congress subject headings** : Quarterly cumulative supplement to the 8th edn. [U.S. Library of Congress]. {NASSDOC}

Anon, 1982, **Library of Congress subject headings** : Quarterly cumulative supplements to the 9th edn., 1979-80. [Library of Congress]. {NASSDOC}

Arberry, A.J., 1938, **Library of the India Office** : A historical sketch. [India Office, London]. {NAI}

Nicholas, Charles L., 1964, **Library of Rameses, the Great**. {DUL}

Daiute, Robert J. and Gorman, Kenneth A., 1974, **Library operations research** : Computer programming for circulation. {USIS}

Gujarati, B.S., 1963, **Library organisation**. {SPA}

Krishan Kumar, 1987, **Library organisation**. {JNU NASSDOC}

Sharma, J.S., 1981, **Library organisation**. {CRRI ISI MMTC NIEPA}

Gujarati, B.S., 1970, **Library organisation and its development in India**, 2nd edn. {NIH}

Mookerjee, S.K. and Sengupta, B., 1972, **Library organisation and library administration**. {NIEPA NIH}

Mookerjee, S.K. and Sengupta, B., 1977, **Library organisation and library administration**, 2nd edn. {DUL ICA IIT ISI NIEPA NMML}

Saini, B.S., 1976, **Library organisation for higher education** : The status and role of university librarian. {AIU JNU NIEPA}

Shaffer, Kenneth Raymond, 1963, **Library personnel administration and supervision**, 2nd edn. {DUL}

Wilson, Louis Round, 1944, **Library planning** : A working memorandum. {DUL}

Hamburg, Morris, et al, 1974, **Library planning and decision-making systems**. {DUL NIEPA}

Furlong, Norman, 1966, **Library practice for colleges of education**. {JNU}

Anderson, Florence, 1963, **Library programme, 1911-61.** {ZHL}

Robotham, John S. and Lafleur, Lydia, 1976, **Library programmes** : How to select, plan and produce them. {USIS}

Robotham, John S. and Lafleur, Lydia, 1981, **Library programmes** : How to select, plan and produce them, 2nd edn. {USIS}

Edsall, Marian S., 1980, **Library promotion handbook.** {IIT USIS}

Eliott, Charles A., 1951, **Library publicity and service**. {DUL MHA}

Kent, A. and Galuin, T.J., 1977, **Library resource sharing.** {ISI JNU NIH}

Lee, C.P., 1971, **Library resources** : How to research and write a paper. {IIMC IIT NASSDOC NCAER}

Smith, C. and Walker, R., n.d., **Library resources in Scotland**. {JNU}

Siddiqui, Akhtar H., n.d., **Library resources of Pakistan.** {JNU}

Anon, 1967, **Library resources on East Asia** : Reports and working papers for the 10th meeting of the committee on American library resources. [Association for Asian Studies]. {JNU}

Martin, Lowell A., et al, 1969, **Library response to urban change** : A study of the Chicago Public Library. [American Library Association]. {USIS}

Kapoor, S.K. ed., 1977, **Library scene in Calcutta** : Seminar on the occasion of the 100th meeting of the IASLIC study circle, February 26-27, 1977. [Indian Association of Special Libraries and Information Centres]. {NASSDOC*}

Ranganathan, S.R., 1969, **Library science based service**. {NERC}

Cohen, Nathan M., et al, 1963, **Library science dissertations, 1925-1960** : An annotated bibliography of doctoral studies. {USIS}

Chandrasekharan, K., 1953, **Library science in India**. [Madras Library Association]. {BIS SPA}

Anon, 1963, **Library science in India today** : A symposium. [Bengal Library Association, Calcutta]. {NASSDOC*}

Anon, 1965, **Library science in Indian universities** : Report. [University Grants Commission, New Delhi]. {ICA IIC JNU NASSDOC NIEPA}

Venkatappaiah, V., comp., n.d., **Library science literature in Andhra Pradesh, 1924-1989**. {NASSDOC*}

Magnoti, Shirley, 1982, **Library science research, 1974-79.** {DUL}

Kaula, P.N., ed., 1965, **Library science today** : Ranganathan festschrift. {BIS CRRI ICHR IIT INSA MFL NIH SPA ZHL}

Anon, 1962, **Library service yearbook and directory**. [Punjab Library Association]. {IIT}

Gupta, B.L., comp., 1989, **Library services** : Important documents. {NASSDOC*}

Ranganathan, S.R. and Neelameghan, A., 1966, **Library services for all**. [Mysore Library Association, Bangalore]. {BIS SPA}

Fenwick, Sara Innis, 1975, **Library services for children in New Zealand schools and public libraries** : A report. [New Zealand Library Association]. {JNU}

Ellis, Alec, 1971, **Library services for young people in England and Wales, 1830-1970**. {DUL}

Sanders, Brenda M., n.d., **Library services in hospitals** : A survey of their present provision and possible future development in the Southeast Metropolitan region. {DUL}

Khan, Sadiq Ali, 1982, **Library services in Pakistan** : Being the proceedings of the departments of library science. . . . {JNU}

Anon, 1978, **Library services in rural areas**. [Library Advisory Council, Wales]. {NIEPA}

Sharr, F.A., 1962, **Library services in a sparsely populated area**. [UNESCO]. {NASSDOC*}

Buckland, Michael K., 1963, **Library services in theory and context**. {IIT}

Martin, William, ed., 1975, **Library service to the disadvantaged**. {NIPCCD}

Ray, Sheila G., 1982, **Library service to schools**. {JNU}

Ray, Colin, 1979, **Library service to schools and children.** {JNU NIPCCD}

McColvin, L.R., 1909, **Library staff**. {IIT}

Conroy, Barbara, 1978, **Library staff development and continuing education** : Principles and practices. {USIS}

Anon, 1966, **Library statistics** : A handbook of concepts, definitions and terminology. [American Library Association, Statistics Coordinating Project]. {USIS}

McColvin, L.R., et al, 1939, **Library stock and assistance to readers** : A textbook. {NAI}

Dewe, Michael, 1968, **Library supply agencies in Europe**. {JNU}

Tauber, Maurice Falcolm and Irlene, R. Stephens, eds., 1967, **Library surveys**. {DUL}

Line, Maurice, B., 1969, **Library surveys** : An introduction to their use, planning, procedure and presentation. {CRRI IIT NASSDOC USIS}

Line, Maurice B., 1982, **Library surveys** : An introduction to their use, planning, procedure and presentation, 2nd edn. {JNU NASSDOC}

Chapman, Edward A., et al, 1970, **Library systems analysis guidelines**. {DUL ICA IIT JNU NASSDOC NIH NMML USIS}

Foskett, D.J., 1970, **Library systems and information services**. {IIMC NASSDOC}

Godden, Irene P., 1984, **Library technical service** : Operations and management. {JNU}

Elliott, Charles A., 1954, **Library technique**. {CRRI DUL}

Cross, Otti, n.d., **Library terms**. {ISI}

Ranganathan, S.R., 1950, **Library tour, 1948** : Europe and America : Impressions and reflections. [Indian Library Association]. {INSA MFL}

Hall, Anna Gertrude, n.d., **Library trustee**. {DUL}

Anon, 1952, **Library trustees manual**. [Ohio Library Trustees Association]. {JNU}

Parsons, C.J., 1973, **Library use in further education**. {DUL}

Smith, G.L. and Meyer, R.S., eds., 1969, **Library use of computers** : Introduction. [Special Libraries Association, New York]. {IIT USIS}

Harrod, Leonard Montague, 1969, **Library work with children** : With special reference to developing countries. {DUL}

Pinehes, Stella, 1966, **Library work with young people** : An examination guide book. {DUL}

Berelson, Bernard and Asheim, Lester, 1949, **Library's public** : Report of the public library inquiry. [Social Science Research Council]. {IEG}

Lehmann-Haupt, Hellmut, 1957, **Life of the book** : How the book is written, published, sold and read. {DUL}

Anon, 1976, **Life sciences information network**. [National Library of Australia]. {JNU}

Jones, Karen Sparck and Kay, Martin, 1973, **Linguistic and information science**. {DUL}

Shaw, Charles B., comp., 1940, **List of books for college libraries, 1931-38**. [American Library Association]. {ZHL}

Anon, 1977-81, **List of documents and publications of General Information Programme and UNISIST, 1977-81**. [UNESCO]. {JNU}

Anon, 1967, **List of official publications not included in the general catalogue of Government of India publications issued during the period 1-1-1940 to 31-12-1960**. {NASSDOC}

Sears, Minnie Earl, 1959, **List of subject headings**, 8th edn., ed by Bertha Margret Frick. {DUL}

Sears, Minnie Earl, 1944, **List of subject headings for small libraries including practical suggestings for the beginner in subject heading work**, 5th edn. {MHA}

Anon, 1911, **List of subject headings for use in dictionary catalogue**, 3rd rev. edn. [American Library Association]. {NAI}

Fox, Gertrude, 1964, **List of subject headings in home building and allied fields**. [National Housing Centre Library, Washington]. {SPA}

Nicholas, David and Ritchies, Maureen, 1978, **Literature and bibliometrics**. {BCL IIT NASSDOC}

Welch, Helen, M., 1963, **Literature of technical services**. {DUL}

Anon, n.d., **Literature recommendation** : Basic reference list for establishing an industrial library. [U.S. International Cooperation Administration]. {BIS}

Isaac, K.A., 1990, **Literature search**. {UGC}

Anon, 1975, **Literature survey and trends in library cataloguing, 1970-1975**. (Mimeo; short bibliography). {NASSDOC}

Kirsch, Robert, 1978, **Lives, works and transformations** : A quarter century of book reviews and essays, ed. by Linda Rolens. {USIS}

Boaz, Martha, ed. 1951, **Living library** : Planning public library buildings for cities of 100,000 or less. {CRRI}

Haines, Helen E., 1965, **Living with books** : Art of book selection, 2nd edn. {DUL IIC IIT USIS}

Hobbs, John L., 1962, **Local history and the library**. {IIC NMML SPA}

Bowler, Reberta, ed., 1964, **Local public library administration**. [International Managers Association, Illinois]. {SPA USIS}

Nichols, H., 1979, **Local studies librarianship**. {NIH}

Foskett, D.J., 1963, **London education classification.** {University of London]. {IIT}

Wallick, Clair H., 1970, **Looking for ideas** : A display manual for libraries and bookstores. {USIS}

Anon, 1964, **Looking forward in documentation**. [Association of Special Libraries and Information Bureaux]. {BIS}

Tauber, Maurice Falcolm, 1967, **Louis Round Wilson** : Librarian and administrator. {USIS}

Avram, Henriette D., et al, 1968, **The MARC II format** : A communications format for bibliographic data, 2 vols. [U.S. Library of Congress]. {USIS}

Avram, Henriette D., et al, 1968, **The MARC pilot project** : Final report on a project. [US Library of Congress]. {USIS}

Anon, 1978, **MIMC microforms annual, 1977-78**. [Microform International Marketing Corporation]. {NASSDOC}

Christ, Alam G.L., n.d., **MINIS, MICROS and terminals for libraries and information services**. {JNU}

Helms, Harry, ed., 1983, **McGraw Hill computer handbook**. {RTL}

Perry, James W., et al, 1956, **Machine literature searching**. {CRRI}

Longley, Dennis and Shain, Michael, 1985, **Macmillan dictionary of information**. {NASSDOC}

Viet, Jean, 1978, **Macrothesaurus for information processing in the field of economic and social development**. {JNU}

Martin, Laura Katherine, 1950, **Magazine for school libraries**, rev edn. {ZHL}

Katz, William Armstrong, 1971, **Magazine selection** : How to build a community-oriented collection. {USIS}

Anon, 1978, **Maintaining library services** : A study in six countries. [Education and Science Department, Great Britain]. {IIMC NIEPA}

Steele, Colin, 1976, **Major libraries of the world** : A selective guide. {NMML}

Alex, M., 1963, **Making book work** : A course for the school library. {JNU}

Carey, G.V., 1951, **Making an Index**. {IIT}

Jennett, Sean, 1973, **The making of books**, 5th edn. {INSA}

Clack, Doris Hargrett, 1979, **The making of a code** : The issues underlying AACR2 : Papers : International conference on AACR2, March 11-14, 1979, Florida. [American Library Association]. {USIS}

Taylor, Robert S., 1972, **Making of a library** : Academic library in transition. {CRRI DUL JNU}

Sackman, Harold, 1970, **Man-computer problem solving** : Experimental evaluation of time-sharing and batch processing. {NASSDOC}

Meadow, Charles T., 1970, **Man-machine communication**. {INSA NASSDOC}

Shericlam, Thomas B. and Farrell, William R., 1974, **Man, machine systems** : Information control and decision models of human performance. {JNU}

Jacker, Corinne, 1964, **Man, memory and machines** : An introduction to cybernetics. {INSA}

Beckett, John A., 1975, **Management dynamics** : The new synthesis. {JNU}

Cloke, J., ed., 1986, **Management for librarians** : Based on a course of lectures at the Library Association in 1967. {JNU}

Rizzo, John R., 1980, **Management for librarians** : Fundamentals and issues. {NIEPA USIS}

Ponder, John, 1971, **Management in libraries**. {NASSDOC}

Peter, Braphy, 1986, **Management information and decision support systems in libraries**. {JNU NASSDOC}

Blagden, John Frederick, 1969, **Management information retrieval** : A new indexing language. {BCL NASSDOC}

Goldberg, Walter, n.d., **Management information systems** : Selected papers from MIS conferences. {JNU}

Schellenberg, T.R., 1965, **The management of archives.** {NASSDOC USIS}

Arnold, Denis Victor, 1976, **The management of the information department.** {BCL}

Cook, Michael, 1986, **Management of information from archives.** {NMML}

Howerton, Paul W., ed., 1974, **Management of information handling systems.** {NIEPA}

Anon, 1978, **Management of information resources at the national level.** [UNESCO]. {NASSDOC*}

Lowell, Milred Hawksworth, n.d., **The management of libraries and information centres,** 4 vols. {DUL NIPCCD USIS}

Rouse, William B., 1980, **Management of library networks** : Policy analysis, implementation and control. {IIT}

Cowley, J., ed., 1985, **The management of polytechnic libraries.** {NASSDOC}

Vyas, S.D., 1990, **Management of technical services in libraries.** {JNU}

Hingwe, K.S., 1982, **Management of university libraries in India** : Principles and practices. {AIU IIT}

Anon, 1976, **Management services** : Report on the library system of the Jawaharlal Nehru University. [Institute of Secretariat Training and Management, New Delhi]. {JNU ZHL}

Evans, G. Edward, 1976, **Management techniques for librarians.** {AIU IIT JNU NIEPA USIS}

Evans, G. Edward, 1983, **Management techniques for librarians**, 2nd edn. {BCL DUL IIT JNU NMML USIS}

Anderson, Ursula, 1977, **Management training for libraries**. [Library Association, London]. {NIEPA NIPCCD}

Cortz, Edwin M. and Kazlaushas, Edwin John, 1986, **Managing informations systems and technologies** : A basic guide for design, selection, evaluation and use. {NASSDOC}

Hicks, Warren B. and Tillin, Alma M., 1977, **Managing multimedia libraries**. {DUL USIS}

Taylor, David C., 1982, **Managing the serials explosion** : 1982 {JNU NMML}

White, Herbert S., 1984, **Managing the special library** : Strategies for success within the larger organisation. {NASSDOC}

Anon, 1973, **Manpower in the field of documentation and library services**. [UNESCO]. {CRRI ICA}

Sharma, H.D. and Singh, B.N., 1990, **Manual for college libraries**. {UGC}

Annette, Mary, 1955, **Manual for cataloguing school libraries.** {JNU}

Kelierhals, W. and Kamp, C.. 1964, **Manual for co-operative libraries and documentation services**. {DSSW ICA}

Anon, 1969, **Manual for new members of the staff**. [County Library]. {JNU}

Hopper, Rohn, 1974, **Manual for the operation of an information/public relations department in standards organisation**. [Industrial Standards Institute]. {BIS}

Mortin-Labatut, Girele and Sly, Mureen, 1982, **Manual for the preparation of records in development information systems**. [International Development Research Centre]. {NASSDOC}

Turabian, Kate L., 1966, **Manual for writers of term papers, theses and dissertations**. {DUL}

Strassberg, Richard, 1974, **Manual of archival and manuscript processing procedures**. {DUL}

Jenkinson, Hilary, 1973, **Manual of archive administration**. {NAI}

Anon, 1983, **Manual of bibliographic control**. [UNESCO]. {NASSDOC*}

Johnson, Arthur W., 1978, **Manual of book binding**. {ZHL}

Savage, E.A., 1949, **Manual of book classification and display for public libraries**. {BIS MMTC NAI NIH SPA ZHL}

Anderson, Charles B., et al, 1969, **Manual of book selling**. {DUL}

Quinn, J.H. and Aconib, H.M., 1937, **Manual of cataloguing and indexing**. {NAI}

Bakewell, K.G.B., 1972, **Manual of cataloguing practice**. {IIT JNU NASSDOC NIPCCD NMML ZHL}

Sayers, W.C. Berwick, 1967, **Manual of children libraries**. {DUL}

Sayers, W.C. Berwick, 1955, **Manual of classification**. {NMML}

Sayers, W.C. Berwick, 1962, **Manual of classification**, 3rd edn. {BIS CRRI IIT JNU NAI SPA ZHL}

Sayers, W.C. Berwick, 1975, **Mannual of Classification**. 5th edn., ed. by Arthur Maltby {BIS ICA ICHR MMTC NERC NIPCCO NMML ZHL}

Dugdale, Kathleen, 1962, **Manual of form for theses and term reports**, rev edn. {DUL}

Brown, Everett S., 1950, **Manual of government publications** : United States and foreign. {CRRI}

Doubleday, W.E., 1933, **Manual of library classification**. {NAI}

Duff, Brown James, 1949, **Manual of library economy**. {JNU}

Duff, Brown James, 1977, **Manual of library economy**, ed. by R.N. Lock. {BIS CRRI DUL MFL MHA NIH SPA}

Anon, 1985, **Manual of library management**. [Physical Research Laboratory, Ahmedabad]. {JNU}

Dutta, D.N., 1978, **Manual of library management**. {DUL IIT}

Headicar, B.M., 1935, **Manual of library organisation**. {NAI}

Anon, 1933, **Manual of library routine**. {JNU}

Bonny, Harold V., 1939, **A manual of practical book selection for public libraries**. {CRRI DUL}

Clarke, Archibald Loycester, 1933, **Manual of practical indexing including arrangement of subject catalogues**. {NAI}

Anon, n.d., **Manual of procedures for evaluation visits under standards for accredition**. {USIS}

Jessup, Libby, F., et al, 1962, **Manual of procedures for private law libraries**. [American Association of Law Libraries]. {USIS}

Mukherjee, Ajit Kumar, 1957, **Manual of reference work**. {DUL SPA}

Anon, 1963, **Manual of style**, 11th edn. {INSA}

Anon, 1969, **Manual of style**, 12th edn. {INSA}

Ebeling, Elinor H., comp., 1966, **Manual of technical services processes**. {DUL}

Cundiff, Ruby Ethel, 1954, **Manual of techniques in library organisation**. {DUL}

Comarona, John P. and Warren, Margaret J., 1982, **Manual on the use of the Dewey Decimal Classification**, 19th edn. {NASSDOC}

Wilcox, Jerome K., ed., 1940, **Manual on the use of the state publications**. [American Library Association]. {CRRI}

Anon, 1946, **Manuals** : Stack and reader division reference department. [U.S. Library of Congress]. {JNU}

Barrow, W.J., 1972, **Manuscripts and documents** : Their deterioration and restoration. {NASSDOC NMML}

Weiss, Edward C., ed., 1977, **The many faces of information science**. {INSA JNU USIS}

Carrington, David K., comp., 1970, **Map collection in the United States and Canada** : A directory, 2nd edn. [Special Libraries Association, New York]. {USIS}

Carrington, David K. and Stephenson, Richard W., comps., 1978, **Map collections in the United States and Canada** : A directory, 3rd edn. [Special Libraries Association, New York]. {USIS}

Nichols, Harold, 1976, **Map librarianship**. {NASSDOC NMML}

Larsgaard, Mary, 1978, **Map librarianship** : An introduction. {USIS}

Date, Shankar Ganesh, ed., 1943, **Marathi granth suchi**, 2 vols, Vol. 1 : 1800-1937; Vol. 2 : 1938-1951 {NASSDOC}

Venkatappaiah, V., ed., 1979, **March of library science** : Kaula festschrift : Papers presented in honour of Prof. P.N. Kaula. {CRRI ICA ICHR IIC IIFT INSA ISI JNU NCAER NIEPA ZHL}

Viguers, Ruth Hill, 1964, **Margin for surprise** : About books, children and librarians. {USIS}

McGaw, Howard F., 1952, **Marginal punched cards in college and research libraries**. {JNU}

Anon, 1979, **Mariamali Adigal library** : 20th Anniversary celebrations souvenir. {NMML}

Kapoor, S.K. and Chatterjee Amitabha, eds., 1988, **Marketing of library and information services in India**. [Indian Association of Special Libraries and Information Centres]. {NASSDOC}

Leerburger, Benedict A., 1982, **Marketing the library**. {JNU USIS}

Yorke, D.A., 1977, **Marketing the library service,** ed. by A. Wilson. [Library Association, London]. {JNU}

McGarry, K.J., 1972, **Mass communications** : Selected readings for librarians. {NIPCCD}

Leimkuhler, F.F., 1967, **Mathematical models for library systems analysis.** {JNU}

Qureshi, Ishrat Ali, 1990, **The Maulana Azad Library** : A major library of the world, 1977-1988. {DUL JNU UGC ZHL}

Goldhor, Herbert, ed., n.d., **Measurement and evaluation** : Papers presented at a conference conducted by the University of Illinois, Graduate School of Library Science, September 10-12, 1967. {DUL}

Joncich, M.I. and Lancaster, F.W., 1977, **Measurement and evaluation of library services.** {IIT USIS}

Beeler, M. Fancher, et al, 1974, **Measuring the quality of library service**. {NIEPA USIS}

Kutuzona, N.P., et al, 1979, **Mechanisation information retrieval and processing** : Application of punched. {NASSDOC}

Jeffreys, A.E., 1974, **Mechanisation of the national library catalogues**. [UNESCO]. {NASSDOC}

Flannery, Anne and Mack, James D., 1966, **Mechanised circulation system, Leh University Library**. {JNU}

Rowley, J.E., 1979, **Mechanised in-house information systems**. {BCL CRRI NIPCCD}

Samuelson, Kjell, 1968, **Mechanised information storage, retrieval and dissemination** : Proceedings. {JNU}

Thakur, B.S. and Agrawal, Binod C., 1990, **Media utilization for the development of women and children**. {NIPCCD}

Anon, 1955, **Medical classification**, 3rd edn. [Boston Medical Library]. {DUL}

Picken, F.M. and Mathews, D.A., 1979, **Medical librarianship** : Outlines of modern librarianship. {NIH USIS}

Thornton, John L., 1963, **Medical librarianship** : Principles and practice. {DUL}

Anon, 1982, **Medium term programme, 1981-85**. [International Federation of Library Associations and Institutions]. {NASSDOC}

Anon, 1985, **Medium term programme, 1986-91**. [International Federation of Library Associations and Institutions, Professional Board]. {NASSDOC}

Saual, Margaret and Melcher, Daniel, 1971, **Melcher on acquisition.** [American Library Association]. {AIU NASSDOC}

Stevenson, Gordon and Kramer-Greene, Judith, eds., 1983, **Melvil Dewey** : The man and the classification. {NASSDOC}

Stevenson, Gordon and Kramer-Greene, Judith, eds., n.d., **Melvil Dewey** : The man and the classification. {DUL}

Anon, 1941, **Memoirs**. [Madras Library Association]. {NASSDOC}

Schramm, Wilbur, 1973, **Men, messages and media** : A look at human communication. {NASSDOC}

Khosla, Raj K. and Gaur, M.K., eds., 1967, **Men of library science and libraries in India**. {SPA USIS}

Boorer, David, 1967, **Mental hospital library**. {DUL}

Evans, Lynn, 1976, **Merging of databases for the production of secondary information publications** : Phase-1. {BCL}

Anon, 1976, **Method for writing calendar dates in all-numeric form**. (IS : 7900-1976). [Indian Standards Institution]. {NASSDOC}

Kunz, Werener, 1977, **Methods of analysis and evaluation of information needs** : A critical review. {JNU}

Williamson, Hugh, 1966, **Methods of book design** : The practices of an industrial craft, 2nd edn. {INSA}

Bourne, Charles P., 1966, **Methods of information handling**. {DUL IIMC IIT JNU NASSDOC}

Good, Carter V. and Scates, Dughlas E., 1954, **Methods of research** : Educational, psychological and sociological. {NASSDOC}

Sabor, Josefa E., 1969, **Methods of teaching librarianship**. [UNESCO]. {IIMC JNU NASSDOC NIEPA NIPCCD}

Guthman, Judith, ed., 1969, **Metropolitan libraries** : The challenge and the promise. [American Library Association]. {USIS}

Cambell, H.C., 1967, **Metropolitan public library planning throughout the work.** {DUL JNU NASSDOC SPA USIS}

Burton, Paul F., 1986, **Micro computer in library and information services** : An annotated bibliography. {JNU}

Walton, Robert A., 1983, **Microcomputers** : A planning and implementation guide for librarians and information professionals. {JNU}

Rorvig, Mark E., 1981, **Microcomputers and libraries** : A guide to technology, products and applications. [American Society for Information Science]. {USIS}

Verry, H.R., 1967, **Microcopying methods**, ed. by Gordon H. Wright. {DUL}

Zemsky, Robert, 1979, **Microfiche reader**. {USIS}

Dranov, Paula, 1976, **Microfilm** : The librarians' view, 1976-77. {USIS}

Anon, 1975-83, **Microfilming of technical drawings and other drawing office equipments** : Pt-1 : operation procedures (ISO 3272/I-1983); Pt-II : Quality criteria and control (ISO 3272/II-1978); Pt-III : Unitized 35 mm microfilm carriers (ISO 3272/III-1975). [International Organisation for Standardisation, Geneva]. {NASSDOC}

Folcarelli, Ralph F., et al, 1982, **The microform connection** : A basic guide for libraries. {USIS}

Teague, S.J., 1977, **Microform librarianship**. {NASSDOC}

Teague, S.J., 1979, **Microform librarianship**, 2nd edn. {IDA ZHL}

Anon, 1970, **Microform retrieval equipment guide**. [Bastuibak Archives and Records Service, Washington]. {BIS}

Ladd, Dorothy P. and Gabriel, Michael R., 1980, **Microform revolution in libraries**. {BIS}

Teague, S. John, 1985, **Microform, video and electronic media librarianship**. {NMML}

Anon, n.d., **Microforms annual, 1982-83** : An international guide to microforms. {NASSDOC}

Anon, n.d., **Microforms annual, 1984-85** : An international guide to microforms. {NASSDOC}

Joshi, M., 1985, **Microforms as an alternative to physical growth in libraries**. [University of Poona, Pune]. {NASSDOC*}

Spreitzer, Francis, ed., 1985, **Microforms in libraries**. [American Library Association]. {NASSDOC}

Diaz, Albert J., ed., 1975, **Microforms in libraries** : A reader. {BIS JNU USIS}

Llewellyn, Raney M., ed., 1936, **Microphotography for libraries**. {DUL}

Gunther, A., 1962, **Microphotography in the library**. [UNESCO]. {IDA NASSDOC}

Lewis, Chester M. and Affen, Hauser William H., 1956, **Microrecording** : Industrial and library applications. {DUL}

Anon, 1958, **Microtext and microreading**. [County Technical Library Service, Hertfordshire]. {DUL}

Lehnus, Donald J., 1974, **Milestones in cataloguing** : Famous cataloguers and their writings, 1835-1969. {USIS}

Williams, Bernard J.S., 1970, **Miniaturised communications** : A review of microforms. [Library Association, London]. {NASSDOC}

Anon, 1976, **Minicomputers and bibliographic information retrieval**. [British Library Lending Division]. {BCL}

Grosch, Audrey N., 1979-82, **Minicomputers in libraries**, 1979-80; 1981-82 {USIS}

Anon, 1967, **Minimum standards for public library systems, 1966**. [Standards committee and subcommittees of the Public Library Association; American Library Association]. {USIS}

Ingraham, Mark H., 1968, **Mirror of brass** : Compensation and working condition of college and university administrators. {JNU}

Eastwood, C.R., 1967, **Mobile libraries and other public library transport**. [Association of Assistant librarians, London]. {BIS}

Dorothy, Harrop, n.d., **Modern book production**. {DUL}

Tripathi, S.M., 1969, **Modern cataloguing theory and practice**. {AIU IIC IIT JNU}

Arnold, Robert R., et al, 1972, **Modern data processing,** 2nd edn. {NASSDOC}

Edgar, Mansfield, 1966, **Modern design in book binding.** {DUL}

Frank, O., ed., 1961, **Modern documentation and information practices** : A basic manual. [International Federation for Documentation and Information]. {BIS DUL ICA NASSDOC NIEPA}

Continolo, G., n.d., **Modern filing methods and equipment.** {IIMC}

Gessford, J.E., 1980, **Modern information systems**. {NIH}

Dupuy, Trevor N., 1968 **Modern libraries for modern colleges**. {JNU}

Millard, Patrica, ed., 1968, **Modern library equipment**. {CRRI IIT NIH NMML}

Sharma, C.K., 1990, **Modern library systems**. {NMML}

Bordin, Ruth B. and Warner, Robert M., 1966, **Modern manuscript library**. {NMML}

Whatmore, Geoffrey, n.d., **Modern news library** : Documentation of current affairs in newspaper and broadcasting libraries. {IIMC}

Mills, J., 1960, **Modern outline of library classification,** 2nd edn. {BIS CRRI IIT MFL NAI NMML}

Mullish, Henry, 1971, **Modern programming** : PL/I. {DUL}

Ashburner, E.H., **Modern public libraries** : Their planning and design. {CRRI}

Trehan, G.L., 1982, **Modern public library movement and services in India.** {JNU}

Barzun, Jacques and Graff, Henry F., 1977, **Modern researcher,** 3rd edn. {NASSDOC}

Saunders, Helen E., 1968, **Modern school library** : Its administration as a material centre. {JNU}

Muhammad, Riaz, 1989, **Modern techniques of documentation and information work**. {NASSDOC}

Boaz, Martha, ed., 1959, **Modern trends in documentation**. {ISI}

Bhattacharya, K.K., 1979, **Modern trends in librarianship in India**. {IIMC IIT NMML}

Vashishth, C.P., ed., 1987, **Modernisation in libraries** : Seminar Papers : All India Library Conference, 33rd, December 28-31, 1987, Tiruchirapalli. [Indian Library Association]. {NASSDOC}

Bean, Donald E. and Ellsworth, Ralph E., 1948, **Modular planning for college and small university libraries**. {DUL}

Anon, 1977, **Monograph on use of library as enrichment to teaching**. [State Council for Education Research and Teaching, Hyderabad]. {NASSDOC*}

Grogan, Denis, 1972, **More case studies in reference work**. {DUL IIT}

Kurth, William H. and Grim, Ray W., 1966, **Moving a library**. {USIS}

Durey, Peter Spayers, 1965, **Moving library materials**. {JNU}

Cabeceiras, James, 1978, **Multimedia library** : Materials selection and use. {IIFT JNU NIPCCD}

Cabeceiras, James, 1982, **Multimedia library** : Materials selection and use, 2nd edn. {NIEPA}

Hamilton, Beth A. and Ernst, William B. Jr., eds., 1977, **Multitype library cooperation**. {NASSDOC USIS}

Agrawal, S.P., ch. ed., 1987, **NASSDOC** : How it works. {NASSDOC}

Agrawal, S.P., ch. ed., 1987-88, **NASSDOC dockets**. {NASSDOC}

Agrawal, S.P., ch. ed., 1982-88, **NASSDOC research information series,** 62 vols. {NASSDOC}

Anon, 1976, **NATIS** : Design and planning of national information systems. [UNESCO]. {NASSDOC*}

Anon, 1976, **NATIS** : National information policy. {NASSDOC*}

Foskett, D.J., 1976, **NATIS** : Preliminary survey of education and training programmes at university level in information and library science. [UNESCO]. {NIEPA}

Anon, 1972, **NCC thesaurus of computing terms**, 4th edn, 2 vols, Vol. 1 : Alphabetic; Vol. 2 : Hierarchy listing. {NASSDOC}

Anon, 1974, **NCC thesaurus of computing terms**, 7th edn. {NASSDOC}

Chaplin, A.H., comp., 1967, **Names of person** : National usages for entry in catalogues. [International Federation of Library Association and Institutions]. {NASSDOC}

Jain, Nem Chand, 1975, **National abstracting services** : Need, purpose and scope. {JNU}

Anon, n.d., **National agency for International Standard Book Numbering System** : A manual. [Raja Rammohan Roy National Educational Resources Centres, New Delhi]. {NASSDOC}

Vosper, Robert and Newskirk, Leone I., 1976. **National and international library planning**. {DUL}

Mc Coy, Donald R., comp., 1978, **The National Archives** : America's Ministry of Documents, 1934-1968. {USIS}

Larsen, Knud, n.d., **National bibliographical services**. {IEG}

Kesavan, B.S., ed., 1978, **National bibliography of Indian literature 1901-1953,** 4 vols. [Sahitya Akademi, New Delhi]. {DSSW INSA MFL NASSDOC}

Anon, 1971, **National catalogue of university level books**. {DSSW NASSDOC}

Anon, n.d., **National Diet Library** : Organisation, functions and activities. [National Diet Library, Japan]. {AIU}

Carter, Launor F., et al, 1967, **National document handling systems for science and technology.** {BIS IIMC NIH USIS}

Anon, n.d., **National Documentation Centre on Mass Communication** : Report. [Ministry of Information and Broadcasting, New Delhi]. {IIMC}

Anon, n.d., **National information** : Guide to Indian periodicals, 1953-1956. {DSSW}

Krishnamurty, P.G., 1979, **National information base for health population and family welfare in India** : Manual for preparation of input for computerised bibliographic information base. [National Institute of Health and Family Welfare, New Delhi]. {NIH}

Agrawal, S.P., ch. ed., 1985, **National information literature in SSDC**. {NASSDOC*}

Anon, 1977, **National information system** : Library and information science manpower development in Asian region : Meeting of supervisors of library and documentation schools in the Asian region, Bangalore. [UNESCO; DRTC]. {JNU}

Anon, 1985, **National Information System for Science and Technology (NISSAT)** : Detailed project report, (1985-1990). [Ministry of Science and Technology, New Delhi]. {NASSDOC}

Anon, n.d., **National information system for social sciences**, typed Short bibliography. {NASSDOC}

Anon, 1963, **National libraries** : Their problems and prospects : Symposium on national libraries in Europe, September 8-27, Vienna. [UNESCO]. {AIU BIS CRRI IEG IIMC MFL NASSDOC NIEPA NIPCCD}

Penna, C.V., et al, eds., 1977, **National library and information services** : Handbook for planners. {CRRI DUL IIT INSA JNU NASSDOC NCAER NIEPA}

Verma, Subash Chandra, 1985, **National library and information system**. {NASSDOC NMML}

Anon, 1972, **National Library Bill, 1972** : Report and evidence : India, Lok Sabha, Joint Committee on the National Library Bill. {AIU NMML}

Allison, Anne Manne and Allan, Ann, eds., 1979, **National library network**. {IIT}

Kaula, P.N., 1970, **National library of India** : Critical study. {AIU ICHR IIC IIFT IIMC IIT ISI NERC NIEPA NIH NIPCCD NMML SPA ZHL}

Nagaraj, M.N. and Ghosh, A.K., eds., 1978, **The National Library of India, 1903-1978** : A pictorial history released on the occasion of platinum jubilee of the National Library, Calcutta. [National Library, Calcutta]. {NASSDOC}

Anon, 1969, **National Library of Medicine classification** : A scheme for the shelf arrangement of books in the field of medicine and its related sciences, 3rd edn. [U.S. National Library of Medicine]. {USIS}

Ranganathan, S.R., 1946, **National library system** : A plan for India. {ZHL}

Anon, 1978, **National library week souvenir, 1976.** [Kerala Library Association, Trivandrum]. {ICA JNU MMTC}

Inamdar, N.B. and Ramaiah, L.S., eds., 1990, **National policy for university libraries on India** : Problems and perspectives. {NASSDOC}

Anon, 1986, **National policy on library and information system** : A presentation. [Government of India, Committee on National Policy on Library and Information System]. {NASSDOC*}

Kalia, D.R., 1955, **National public library system**. {NASSDOC}

Mahajan, S.G. and Riswadker, M.R., 1984, **National seminar on social science documentation in India**. {JNU}

Choudhary, Anil Roy, 1959, **National standards for cataloguing and indexing art museum objects and documents**. {ZHL}

Houghton, A.G. and Nixon, M., 1976, **National transport system for inter-library loan**. {JNU}

Anon, 1978, **Nationwide location data base and service**. [U.S. Library of Congress]. {MMTC}

Anon, 1984, **Need for National Information Policy** : Its parameters : Papers : Convention and conference of the Society for Information Science, 4th, December 27-28, 1984, Madras. {NASSDOC*}

Anon, 1966, **Neighbourhood library centres and services**. [National Book Trust, New Delhi]. {JNU}

Miller, Bertha M. and Field, Elinor W., eds., 1955, **Newbery medal books, with their authors' acceptance** : Papers and related material, chiefly from the Horn Book magazine, 1922-55. {USIS}

Fenwick, Sara Innis, 1960, **New definitions of school library service**. {JNU}

Josey, E.J., ed., 1975, **New dimensions for academic library service**. {USIS}

Iyengar, T.K.S., 1977, **New dimensions in library science**. {CRRI DUL ICHR IIT ISI NIEPA}

Stone, Elizabeth W., ed., 1971, **New directions in staff development moving from ideas to action** : The papers : Microworkshop on staff development, June 28, 1970, Detroit. [American Library Association]. {USIS}

Ranganathan, S.R., 1973, **New education and school library** : Experience of half a century. {DUL ICA JNU NIEPA}

Anon, 1986, **New Education Policy** : Libraries and information system : Papers and proceedings. [NCERT; Raja Rammohan Roy Library Foundation, Calcutta]. {NMML}

Vashishth, C.P., ed., 1986, **New education policy vis-a-vis library development** : Papers presented in the seminar held at New Delhi on February 13, 1986. [Indian Library Association]. {NASSDOC}

Anon, 1985, **New frontiers in library and information science**. [Zilla Granthalaya Samstha, Machilipatnam]. {NASSDOC*}

Anon, n.d., **New India directory of libraries and educational institutions of India, Pakistan, Burma and Ceylon**. {AIU IIT}

Gaskell, Philip, 1972, **New introduction to bibliography**. {INSA}

Wassermann, Paul, 1972, **The new librarianship** : A challenge for change. {USIS}

Herbert, Ward, ed., 1976, **New library buildings** : Architect-librarian assessment, 1973-74. {DUL}

Langmead, Staphen and Beckman, Margaret, 1970, **New library design** : Guidelines to planning academic library buildings. {AIU BIS CRRI IIT JNU NIPCCD USIS}

Cook, Margaret G., 1975, **The new library key,** 3rd edn. {USIS}

Enright, B.J., 1972, **New media and the library in education**. {IIT NIH}

Brown, James W., 1976, **New media in public libraries** : Survey of current practices. {USIS}

Sellen, B.C., ed., 1984, **New options for librarians**. {NASSDOC*}

McInnis, Raymond G., 1978, **New perspectives for reference service in academic libraries**. {CRRI IIT NIPCCD}

Delaney, Jalk J., 1968, **New school librarian**. {JNU}

Mohanrajan, P.A., ed., 1984, **New trends in international librarianship**. {NASSDOC NMML}

Bhattacharya, I.S., 1962, **New trends in scientific communication**. [Indian Association of Special Libraries and Information Centres]. {SPA}

Anon, 1978, **New Zealand national bibliography**, 1978. [National Library of New Zealand]. {NASSDOC}

Whatmore, Geoffrey, 1964, **News information** : Organisation of press cuttings in the libraries of newspapers and broadcasting services. {IIMC IIT NMML SPA}

Anon, n.d., **Newspaper libraries**, mimeo short bibliography. {NASSDOC}

Majumdar, Gopal Kumar, 1974, **Newspaper microfilming** : A plea for newsprint documentation. {NASSDOC ZHL}

Shashi Bala, 1982, **Non-book material available in Nehru Memorial Museum and Library** : A brief survey. {NMML}

Riddle, Jean, et al, 1970, **Non-book materials** : The organisation of integrated collections. [Canadian Library Association]. {NERC USIS}

Riddle, Jean, et al., 1979, **Non-book materials** : The organisation of integrated collections, 2nd edn. [Canadian Library Association]. {NERC USIS}

Weihs, Jean, 1989, **Non book materials** : The organisation of integrated collections, 3rd edn. [Canadian Library Association]. {NASSDOC}

Anon, 1973, **Non-book materials cataloguing rules** : Integrated code of practice and draft revision of the Anglo-American Cataloguing Rules. [Library Association Media Cataloguing Rules Committee; National Council for Educational Technology, London]. {NASSDOC}

Fothergill, Richard and Butchart, I., 1972, **Non-book materials in libraries** : A practical guide. {ISIR}

Grove, Pearce S., ed., 1975, **Non-print media in academic libraries**. [American Library Association]. {USIS}

Thomas, Nancy G. and O'Neil, Rosanna, comp., 1986, **Notes for serials cataloguing**. {NASSDOC*}

Staveley, Ronald, 1962, **Notes on subject bibliography**. {DUL IEG MFL}

Maruskin, Albert F., 1980, **OCLC : Its governance, function, financing and technology**. {JNU}

Hussain, Mahmud, 1974, **Of libraries and librarians**. [University of Karachi]. {ZHL}

Tory, Bruce E., 1957, **Offset lithography**. {DUL}

Bean, Jared, 1909, **The old librarians almanac**. {NASSDOC*}

Loosjes, T.P., 1973, **On documentation of scientific literature**. {JNU}

Hall, James L. and Brown, Marjorie J., 1981, **On-line bibliographic databases** : An international directory, 2nd edn. [Association of Special Libraries and Information Bureaux]. {USIS}

Mildreth, C.R., ed., 1989, **On line catalogue**. [Library Association, London. {NASSDOC}

Fayen, Emily Gallup, 1973, **The online catalogue** : Improving public access to library materials. {USIS}

Harter, Stephen P., 1986, **On-line information retrieval** : Concepts, principles and techniques. {JNU}

Holmes, P.L., 1978, **On-line information retrieval** : An introduction and guide to British library's short term experimental information network project, Vol. 1 : Experimental use of non-medical information services; Vol. 2 : Experimental use of medical information services. [British Library]. {BCL}

Hall, J.L., comp., 1977, **On-line information retrieval, 1965-76** : A bibliography with a guide to on-line data bases and systems. [Association of Special Libraries and Information Bureaux]. {BCL CRRI NASSDOC}

Houghton, Bernard and Convey, John, 1977, **On-line information retrieval systems** : An introductory manual to principles and practices. {BCL CRRI DUL NIH}

Kent, Allen and Galvin, Thomas J., eds., 1978, **The on-line revolution in libraries** : Proceedings of the 1977 conference in Pittsburgh. {JNU}

Sieburth, J.F., 1988, **Online search services in the academic library** : Planning, management and operation. [American Library Association]. {NASSDOC}

Hoover, Ryan, E., ed., 1982, **On-line search strategies**. {USIS}

Henry, W.M., 1980, **Online searching**. {IIT}

Byerly, Greg, 1983, **Online searching** : A dictionary and bibliographic guide. {NASSDOC USIS}

Maloney, James J., ed., 1983, **Online searching technique and management**. [American Library Association]. {USIS}

Garvin, Paul L., 1972, **On machine translation** : Selected papers. {USIS}

Anon, 1969, **On research libraries** : Statement and recommendations. [American Council of Learned Societies Devoted to Humanistic Studies, Committee on Research Libraries]. {IIT INSA USIS}

Vickery, B.C., 1965, **On retrieval system theory**, 2nd edn. {CRRI DUL IIT}

Costello, John C., et al, n.d., **Operating manual for use in abstracting and coordinate indexing**. [Battelle Memorial Institute, Ohio]. {BIS}

Katzan, Harry, 1973, **Operating systems** : A pragmatic approach. {NASSDOC}

White, Douglas, et al, 1969, **Operational research techniques**, Vol. 1 : Introduction. {NASSDOC}

Swanson, Don R. and Bookstein, Abraham, eds., 1972, **Operations research** : Implications for libraries. {NASSDOC}

Taha, Handy A., 1971, **Operations research** : An introduction. {NASSDOC}

House, William C., 1972, **Operations research** : An introduction to modern applications. {NASSDOC}

Rowley, J. E. and Rowley, Petter J., 1981, **Operations research** : A tool for library management. [American Library Association]. {USIS}

Anon, 1986, **Opinion poll survey among visitors to the New Delhi World Book Fair** : A report. [National Book Trust, New Delhi]. {NASSDOC*}

Groenewegena, H.W. and Marshall, J., 1976, **Optical character recognition** : Use of OCR techniques in decentralised data collection for bibliographic information systems. [International Development Research Centre, Ottawa]. {NASSDOC}

Dohlbery, Ingetraut, 1978, **Optical structures and Universal Classification**. {DUL JNU}

Boulding, Kenneth E. and Senesh, Lawrence, 1983, **Optimum utilisation of knowledge** : Making knowledge serve human betterment. {NMML}

Casey, Robert S., 1958, **Oral communication of technical information**. {CRRI}

Meckler, Alan M. and Mc Mullin, Ruth, 1975, **Oral history collections**. {USIS}

Wildman, Panline G., 1980, **Order procedure**. {JNU}

Neelameghan, A., ed., 1979, **Ordering systems for global information networks** : Proceedings : International study conference on classification research, 3rd, January 6-11, 1975, Bombay, [FID/CR; Sarada Ranganathan Endowment for Library Science]. {BIS NASSDOC}

Sharma, Hari Krishan, 1977, **Organisation and administration of college libraries.** {DUL ICA}

Allen, Kenneth W. and Allen, Loren, 1973, **Organisation and administration of the learning resources centre in the community college.** {USIS}

Perlman, M., ed., 1977, **Organisation and retrieval of economic knowledge** : Proceedings of the conference held by the International Economic Association. {NASSDOC}

Johnson, Edward R. and Mann, Stuart H., **Organisation development for academic libraries**. {JNU}

Taraboi, Vasile, 1973, **Organisation, functioning and activities of national documentary information systems in the scientific, technical and economic fields**. [National Institute for Scientific and Technical Information and Documentation, Romania]. {BIS}

Kapoor, S.K., et al, eds., 1981, **Organisation of data services in India**. [Indian Association of Special Libraries and Information Centres]. {NASSDOC}

De Grolier, Eric, 1979, **Organisation of information systems for government and public administration**. {BIS JNU}

Mabbs, A.W., 1974, **Organisation of intermediate records storage**. [UNESCO]. {NIEPA NMML}

Bliss, Henry Evelyn, 1929, **Organisation of knowledge and system of the sciences**. {DUL}

Bliss, Henry Evelyn, 1939, **Organisation of knowledge in libraries and the subject-approach to books,** 2nd edn. {BIS IEG USIS}

Ranganathan, S.R., 1963, **Organisation of libraries**, 3rd edn. {JNU NIH}

Chaplin, H., ed., 1976, **Organisation of the library profession**. {CRRI}

Allen, Joan, 1961, **Organisation of small libraries** : A manual of educational institutions in tropical countries. {JNU NIEPA}

Heintze, Ingeborg, 1963, **The organisation of the small public library**. [UNESCO]. {ICA IEG NASSDOC NERC NIEPA}

Anon, 1983, **Organisation of social science information and documentation**: Reports on 11 Asian countries. [UNESCO Regional Adviser for Social Science in Asia and the Pacific, Bangkok]. {NASSDOC}

Soergel, Dagobert, 1985, **Organising information** : Principle of data base and retrieval. {JNU}

Needham, C.D., 1966, **Organising knowledge in libraries** : An introduction to classification and cataloguing. {IIC MFL SPA ZHL}

Needham, C.D., 1971, **Organising knowledge in libraries** : An introduction to information retrieval, 2nd rev edn. {ICA IIFT NASSDOC}

Vakata, Yuri, et al, 1979, **Organising local government documents collection**. [American Library Association]. {USIS}

Daily, Jay E., 1972, **Organising nonprint materials** : A guide for librarians. {ICHR IIT JNU NASSDOC ZHL}

Beswick, Norman, 1975, **Organising resources** : Six case studies : Final report of the Schools Council Resources Centre project. {NIPCCD}

Mittal, S.R., 1964, **Organising village library** : A guide book for social education workers and village librarians. [National Council for Educational Research and Training, New Delhi]. {ICA ISI NIPCCD}

Shiflett, Orvin Lee, 1981, **Origins of American academic librarianship**. {JNU}

Anon, 1966, **Origins of the America's college library, 1838-1900**. {JNU}

Mac Closkey, Monro, 1968, **Our national attic**. [U.S. Library of Congress; Smithsonian Institution; U.S. National Archives]. {USIS}

Houghton, Bernard, 1972, **Out of the dinosaurs** : The evolution of the National Lending Library for Science and Technology. {NASSDOC}

Frick, B.M., 1959, **Outline for the courses in problems in cataloguing and classification**. {DUL}

Robinow, Beatrix H., 1967, **Outline for the organisation of hospital libraries.** {DUL}

Mohinder Singh, 1969, **Outline of library classification**. {NERC}

Srinath, Laxmipuram Srinivasascher, 1975, **PERT and CPM** : Principles and applications. {JNU}

Sfrigai, Frances and Jacor, Marry, 1968, **PILOT** : An on-line library acquisition system. {JNU}

Austin, Derek, 1974, **PRECIS** : A manual of concept analysis and subject indexing. {CRRI JNU}

Austin, Derek and Butcher, Peter, 1969, **PRECIS** : A rotatod subject index system. [Council of British National Bibliography]. {NASSDOC}

Wellisch, H.H., ed., 1977, **The PRECIS index system** : Principles, applications and prospects : Proceedings : International PRECIS workshop, October 15-17, 1976, Maryland. {NASSDOC}

Vanghan, John, ed., 1973, **Papers** : Advanced working seminar on national information policy and the impact of social and technological change on national information planning, Australia. {CRRI}

Ranganathan, S.R., ed., 1953, **Papers** : All India library conference, 10th, June 1-4, 1953, Hyderabad. [Indian Library Association]. {NASSDOC}

Anon, 1963, **Papers** : All India library conference, 15th, 1963, Mysore. [Indian Library Association]. {NASSDOC}

Anon, 1966, **Papers** : All India library conference, 1965, Mysore. [Indian Library Association]. {CRRI}

Anon, 1975, **Papers** : All India library conference, 21st, 1975, Bhubaneswar. [Indian Library Association]. {NASSDOC}

Anon, 1980, **Papers** : All India library conference, 1980, New Delhi. [Indian Library Association]. {NASSDOC*}

Anon, 1981, **Papers** : All India library conference, 27th, 1981, Hyderabad. [Indian Library Association]. {NMML}

Anon, 1986, **Papers** : All India library conference, 1986. [Indian Library Association]. {NMML}

Anon, 1987, **Papers** : All India library conference, 32nd, 1987, Anantpur. [Indian Library Association]. {NASSDOC}

Anon, 1978, **Papers** : All India public library convention, November, 16-18, 1978, New Delhi. [Delhi Library Association, Delhi]. {MMTC NMML}

Anon, 1981, **Papers** : All India seminar on agricultural library and information services, December 29-January 16, 1980. [Andhra Pradesh Agricultural University, Hyderabad; Indian Council of Agricultural Research, New Delhi]. {IIMC}

Anon, 1982, **Papers** : All India seminar on libraries and the book trade, February 1982, New Delhi. [Indian Library Association]. {IIMC IIT JNU ZHL}

Anon, 1982, **Papers** : All India seminar on library resources in university education and research, 1982, Hyderabad. [Osmania University Library, Hyderabad]. {ZHL}

Anon, 1983, **Papers** : All India seminar on national policy for library and information science education, 1983, Nagpur. {NASSDOC}

Anon, 1981, **Papers** : Conference on electronic information technology and its impact on library and information service, 4th, 1981, Pittsburg. {IIT}

Anon, 1973, **Papers** : Conference on informatics, 1973, Durham. [Association of Special Libraries and Information Bureaux]. {CRRI}

Horsnell, Verina, ed., 1974, **Papers** : Conference on informatics, 1974, Oxford. [Association of Special Libraries and Information Bureaux]. {CRRI}

Anon, 1975, **Papers** : Conference on informatics, 1975, Cambridge. [Association of Special Libraries and Information Bureaux]. {CRRI}

Anon, 1975, **Papers** : Conference on use of computers in libraries and information centres, 1975, London. [Association of Special Libraries and Information Bureaux]. {CRRI}

Anon, 1981, **Papers** : DRTC annual seminar on information analysis and consolidation, 1981, Bangalore. [Documentation Research and Training Centre, Bangalore]. {CRRI}

Anon, 1983, **Papers** : DRTC refresher seminar, 1983, Bangalore. [Documentation Research and Training Centre, Bangalore]. {JNU}

Anon, 1980, **Papers** : DRTC refresher seminar on data accessibility and dissemination, 1980, Bangalore. [Documentation Research and Training Centre, Bangalore]. {CRRI}

Mac Cafferty, Maxine, n.d., **Papers** : EUSIDIC conference on user education, 1976, Graz. {CRRI}

Dewe, A. and Deunelle, J., n.d., **Papers** : European conference on the contribution of users to planning and policy making for information systems and networks, 1978, Germany. {CRRI}

Anon, 1978, **Papers**: FID congress on new trends in documentation and information, 1978, Edinburg. {CRRI}

Anon, 1968, **Papers** : FID pre-congress seminar on education and training : Theory and provision with a look at new developments and an example of the challenges confronting information workers, 1978, Edinburg. [International Federation for Documentation and Information]. {NASSDOC}

Anon, 1972, **Papers** : IASLIC conference, 9th, 1972, Calcutta. [Indian Association of Special Libraries and Information Centre]. {IIT INSA JNU MMTC}

Anon, 1975, **Papers** : IASLIC conference, 10th, 1975, Lucknow, Pt. A. : Library documents aspects of utilisation; Pt. B. : Procurement of periodicals : Current problems in India [Indian Association of Special Libraries and Information Centres]. {IIMC}

Chakraborty, A.R. and Kapoor, S.K., eds., 1983, **Papers** : IASLIC conference, 14th, December 26-29, 1983, New Delhi, I : Information flow in non R and D context; II : Grey literature. [Indian Association of Special Libraries and Information Centres]. {JNU MMTC NASSDOC NCAER NIEPA NIPCCD}

Anon, 1969, **Papers** : IASLIC conference on library profession in India : Its status and responsibilities and standardised library practices and job classification, 1969, Bombay. [Indian Association of Special Libraries and Information Centres]. {CRRI}

Kapoor, S.K. and Ghosh, S.B., eds., 1977, **Papers** : IASLIC conference on planning of national information network, 11th, November 2-5, 1977, Dharwar. [Indian Association of Special Libraries and Information Centres]. {CRRI ISI JNU NIEPA NIPCCD}

Anon, 1966, **Papers** : IASLIC national seminar, 4th, 1966, Hyderabad. [Indian Association of Special Libraries and Information Centres]. {NASSDOC}

Anon, 1984, **Papers** : IASLIC national seminar, 11th, November 26-29, 1984, Hyderabad, I : Toward a code of professional ethics; II : Document delivery, reproduction, translation. [Indian Association of Special Libraries and Information Centres]. {NASSDOC}

Anon, 1970, **Papers** : IASLIC seminar, 6th, November 2-5, 1970, Bangalore. [Indian Association of Special Libraries and Information Centres]. {BIS JNU NMML}

Anon, 1976, **Papers** : IASLIC seminar, 7th, December 28-31, 1976, Burdwan. [Indian Association of Special Libraries and Information Centres]. {BIS JNU NASSDOC}

Kapoor, S.K., et al, eds., 1980, **Papers** : IASLIC seminar, 9th, October 23-26, 1980, Nagpur, I : Role of information centres in technology transfer; II : Role of State-level and national library association in library development in India. [Indian Association of Special Libraries and Information Centres]. {CRRI INSA JNU NASSDOC}

Anon, 1982, **Papers** : IASLIC seminar on information services in India, 1982, Kanpur. [Indian Association of Special Libraries and Information Centres]. {CRRI}

Anon, n.d., **Papers** : IASLIC symposium on the development of libraries in India under the Third Five Year Plan with particular reference to special libraries, January 23-25, 1960, Calcutta. [Indian Association of Special Libraries and Information Centres]. {BIS}

Anon, 1987, **Papers** : IFLA General Conference, 53rd, August 16-21, 1987, Bringhton. [International Federation of Library Associations and Institutions]. {NASSDOC*}

Ingram, K.E. and Jefferson, Albert A., 1976, **Papers** : International library conference on libraries and the challenge of change, April 24-29, 1976, Kingsten. [Jamaica Library Association]. {IIT}

Anon, 1980, **Papers** : National conference, 1980, Tirupati. [Indian Association of Academic Librarians]. {ZHL}

Stueart, Robert D. and Johnson, Richard D., 1979, **Papers** : National conference on new horizons for academic libraries, November 8-11, 1978, Boston, {IIT}

Gangadhara Rao, P. and Raghavan, Q.S., eds., 1986, **Papers** : National seminar on assessment of public library development in India, March 3-6, 1986, Madras. [University of Madras, Department of Library Science; University Grants Commission, New Delhi]. {NASSDOC}

Kumar, P.S.G., ed., 1985, **Papers** : National seminar on library and information manpower development, December 6-9, 1985, Nagpur. [Nagpur University, Department of Library and Information Science; University Grants Commission, New Delhi]. {NASSDOC}

Anon, 1986, **Papers** : National seminar on library and information science education in India : New perspective, December 10-12, 1986, Trivandrum. [Kerala State Committee on Science, Technology and Environment]. {NASSDOC}

Anon, 1978, **Papers** : Seminar on information for engineering industry, February 10, 1978, New Delhi. [Association of Engineering Industry; Indian National Scientific Documentation Centre, New Delhi]. {BIS}

Anon, 1977, **Papers** : Seminar on library and information science education in India, 1977, New Delhi. {JNU}

Anon, 1980, **Papers** : Seminar on library buildings in India, February 11-13, 1980, New Delhi. [National Information System for Science and Technology, New Delhi]. {BIS CRRI IIT}

Anon, 1965, **Papers** : Seminar on library science in Southeast Asia, December 18-20, 1964, Bangkok. [Association of Southeast Asian Institutions of Higher Learning]. {NASSDOC NIEPA}

Wall, Rayond Alwyn, ed., 1974, **Papers** : Seminar on mechanical engineering information : Provision and use, March 27-29, 1974, Loughborough. {BCL}

Anon, 1979, **Papers** : Seminar on reference sources on South Asia, 1979, Jaipur. {JNU}

Anon, 1961, **Papers** : Seminar on the rendering of Indic names, 1960-61, Calcutta. [Indian Association of Special Libraries and Information Centres]. {NASSDOC}

Anon, 1979, **Papers** : Seminar on the role of the National Library of India, November 23, 1978, Calcutta. [National Library Employee's Association, Calcutta]. {NASSDOC}

Anon, 1975, **Papers** : Seminar on thesaurus in information systems, December 1-5, 1975, Bangalore. [DRTC, Bangalore; Indian National Scientific Documentation Centre, New Delhi]. {BIS CRRI DUL IIMC ZHL}

Anon, 1966, **Papers** : Seminar on work flow in libraries, November 21-24, 1966, New Delhi; 3 vols., Vol. 1 : Special libraries; Vol II : University libraries; Vol. III : Government libraries. [Indian National Scientific Documentation Centre, New Delhi]. {NASSDOC NMML SPA}

Boaz, Martha, ed., n.d., **Papers** : Symposium on modern trends in documentation, 1958, California. {CRRI}

Anon, n.d., **Papers** : Symposium on new technology in libraries : Prospects and problems for libraries in the Gulf States, 1982, Teheran. [Ministry of Petroleum and Minerals, Teheran]. {CRRI}

Motiwale, Sushila A. and Jagtar Singh, eds., 1986, **Papers** : UGC sponsored national seminar on documentation services in university and college libraries, January 12-14, 1986, Jabalpur. {NASSDOC}

Anon, 1980, **Papers** : Workshop on computer techniques in information processing. [University of Delhi, Department of Library and Information Science]. {AIU}

Venkatappaiah, V., ed., 1989, **Papers** : Workshop on norms, guidelines and standards for public libraries. [Zilla Granthalaya Samstha, Eluru]. {NASSDOC*}

Kapoor, S.K., ed., 1979, **Papers and proceedings** : IASLIC conference, 8th, December 26-29, 1978, Madras, Pt I : Standardisation of techniques and procedures for information handling; Pt II : Library and information system for rural development. [Indian Association of Special Libraries and Information Centres]. {BIS NIPCCD}

Anon, 1984, **Papers and proceedings** : Round table discussion on the concepts of Australian national bibliography, 1983, South Wales. {JNU}

Pearson, J.D., ed., 1971, **Papers on oriental library collections submitted to a library panel** : International congress of orientalists, 27th, August 17, 1967, Ann Arbor, Michigan. {NMML}

Kashyap, S.C., 1986, **Parliaments and information dissemination**. {NASSDOC}

Marchant, Maurice P., 1976, **Participative management in academic libraries**. {DUL NIEPA}

Freeman, Patricia, 1975, **Pathfinder** : An operational guide for the school librarian. {JNU}

Foskett, D.J., 1984, **Pathways for communication** : Books and libraries in the information age. {AIU NIEPA}

Wallace, Sarah Leslie, 1956, **Patrons are people** : How to be a model librarian, 2nd rev edn. [American Library Association]. {DUL USIS}

Fussler, Herman H. and Simon, Julian L., 1969, **Patterns in the use of books in large research libraries**. {NMML}

Agrawal, Binod C., 1982, **Patterns of communication in international meeting** : A pilot study of tenth international congress of anthropological and ethnological sciences. {NASSDOC}

Powell, Judith W. and Lelieuvre, Robert B., 1979, **People work, communications dynamics for libraries**. [American Library Association]. {USIS}

Mayes, Paul, ed., 1978, **Periodicals administration in libraries** : A collection of essays. {IIT NASSDOC NCAER NIPCCD}

Davinson, D.E., 1969, **Periodicals collection** : Its purpose and uses in libraries. {NMML}

Barrow, W.J., 1961, **Permanence and durability of library catalogue cards.** {DUL}

Stibic, V., 1983, **Personal documentation for professionals** : Means and methods. {JNU}

Duke, Richard D., 1961, **Personal filing system for the professional concerned with community planning**. {SPA}

Anon, 1982, **Personnel administration for libraries** : A bibliographic essay. [American Library Association]. {BIS DUL}

Martin, Lowell, 1946, **Personnel administration in libraries**. {JNU}

Stebbins, K.B., 1966, **Personnel administration in libraries**, 2nd edn. rev. by P.G. Mohrhardt. {JNU NIH USIS}

Herbert, Clara W., 1939, **Personnel administration in public libraries**. [American Library Association]. {CRRI}

Maloney, R. Kay, ed., 1977, **Personnel development in libraries**. [Bureau of Library and Information Science Research, Rutgers University Graduate School of Library Science]. {NIPCCD USIS}

Katz, Bill and Fraley, Ruth A., eds., 1986, **Personnel issues in reference services**, {JNU NASSDOC}

Savage, A.W., 1977, **Personnel management.** {JNU}

Khanna, J.K., 1981, **Personnel management in libraries**. {BIS IIFT IIMC ISI JNU NIEPA ZHL}

Juggal Kishore, 1981, **Personnel management in libraries.** {JNU}

Cowley, John, 1982, **Personnel management in library**. {DUL IIT}

Goswami, Badri Prasad, 1972, **Personnel motivation and work efficiency in libraries**. {NASSDOC}

Anon, 1966, **Personnel organisation and procedure** : A manual suggested for use in public libraries, 2nd edn. [American Library Association]. {DUL USIS}

Debons, Anthony and Cameron, William J., 1975, **Perspectives in information science**. {JNU}

Agarwal, S.N., et al, 1982, **Perspectives in library and information science** : Viswanathan festschrift. 2 vols. {AIU ICHR ISI JNU MMTC NASSDOC NCDC NIEPA NIPCCD SPA ZHL}

Broadffield, A., 1946, **Philosophy of classification**. {IEG IIT}

Broadffield, A., 1949, **Philosophy of librarianship**. {CRRI IEG IIT}

Ranganathan, S.R., 1951, **Philosophy of library classification**. {DUL}

Girja Kumar and Krishan Kumar, 1983, **Philosophy of user education**. {DUL IIT ISI JNU NASSDOC NIEPA ZHL}

Corbett, Edmund V., 1957, **Photo charging** : Its operation and installation in British Public Library. {JNU}

Whitestone, Patricia, 1977, **Photocopying in libraries** : The librarians speak. {IIT}

Anon, 1950, **Photoduplication service**. [U.S. Library of Congress]. {DUL}

Cogoli, John E., 1960, **Photo-offset** : Fundamentals. {DUL}

Ranganathan, S.R. and Neelameghan, A., 1974, **Physical bibliography for librarians**, 2nd ed. {AIU ICA INSA}

Anon, 1969, **Physics and astronomy classification scheme**. [American Institute of Physics]. {IIT}

Ireland, Norma Olin, 1952, **Picture file in school, college and public libraries**, rev edn. {ZHL}

Valls, J., 1974, **Pilot project on the mechanisation of documentation services in Asia** : Thailand. [UNESCO]. {NASSDOC*}

Luhn, Hans Peter, 1968, **Pioneer of information science** : Selected works. {JNU}

Metcalf, Keyes D., 1965, **Planning academic and research library buildings**. {BIS IIT NASSDOC NIH USIS}

Brown, Harry Faulkner, 1971, **Planning the academic library**. {JNU}

Overton, David, 1983, **Planning the administrative library**. {DUL}

Anon, 1964, **Planning agency library manual**. [Council of Planning Librarians]. {SPA}

Thompson, Godfrey, 1973, **Planning and design of library buildings**. {IIT ISI}

Thompson, Godfrey, 1977, **Planning and design of library buildings**, 2nd edn. {CRRI}

Ellsworth, Ralph Eugene, 1960, **Planning college and university library** : A book for campus planners and architects. {USIS}

Havelock, Ronald G., et al, 1971, **Planning for innovation through dissemination and utilisation of knowledge**. {NASSDOC*}

Gehrke, U., 1975, **Planning for a national information and documentation system** : Kenya. [UNESCO]. {NASSDOC}

Burke, J.E., 1961, **Planning functional college library**. {IIT}

Chandel, A.S., ed., 1987, **Planning in library resource sharing** : Proceedings : Seminar on coordination in resource sharing held at Isabella Thouburn College, Lucknow. {NASSDOC}

Anon, 1950, **Planning the library** : A guide to those considering problems of library design, book storage and shelving. {DUL}

Galvin, Hoyt R. and Devereaux, Kathryn A., eds., 1955, **Planning a library building**. {DUL}

Roth, Harold, L., ed., 1964, **Planning library buildings for service** : Proceedings : Library building and equipment institute, July 6-8, 1961, Kent. [American Library Association]. {BIS DUL}

Dean, John, 1972, **Planning library education programmes** : A study of the problems involved in the management and operation of library schools in the developing countries. {MFL NIEPA}

McKee, B., 1989, **Planning library service**. {NASSDOC}

Casteleyn, Mary, 1981, **Planning library training programmes**. {NIEPA}

Warncke, Ruth, 1976, **Planning library workshops and institutes.** [American Library Association]. {USIS}

Ellsworth, Ralph E., 1973, **Planning manual for academic library buildings.** {JNU}

D'Olier, J.H. and Delmas, B., 1975, **Planning national infrastructures for documentation, libraries and archives** : Outline of a general policy. {DUL IIMC JNU NASSDOC NIEPA}

Pushp Lata, 1979, **Planning national technical information centre for child development in India** : A blueprint, Thesis : Associateship in Documentation and Information Science. [Documentation Research and Training Centre]. {NIPCCD}

Jast, L. Stanley, 1928, **Planning of great library**. {ZHL}

Anon, 1976, **The planning of indexing and abstracting services in the social sciences** : Coverage overlap and content. [Bath University Library]. {BCL}

Penna, C.V. and Sewell, P.H., 1967, **The planning of library and documentation services.** [UNESCO]. {AIU ICA NIEPA SPA}

Penna, C.V., 1970, **Planning of library and documentation services**, 2nd edn. [UNESCO]. {IIMC INSA MFL NASSDOC NCAER NERC NIH NIPCCD NMML TDA}

Kapoor, S.K. and Ghosh, S.B., eds., 1977, **Planning of national information network** : 11th, IASLIC conference at Dharwar, 1977. {JNU}

Lee, Sul H., 1973, **Planning programming budgeting system** : Implications for library management. {JNU}

Anon, 1968, **Planning the public library**. [American Society of Planning Officials]. {SPA}

Kennon, Mary Frances and Doyle, Leila Ann, 1962, **Planning school library development** : A report of the school library development project. {DUL NASSDOC}

Burchard, John E., et al, eds., 1949, **Planning the university library building** : A summary of discussions by librarians, architects and engineers. {NASSDOC ZHL}

Anon, 1959, **Plans for six public library buildings**. [American Library Association]. {USIS}

Schunk, Russell J., 1945, **Pointers for public library building planners.** {DUL}

Kim, Ung C., 1976, **Policies of publishers** : A handbook for order librarians. {JNU}

Girja Kumar, 1965, **Politics, international relations and law** : Scope, methodology and classification. {BIS ICHR IEG IIT JNU MFL MHA NASSDOC NMML ZHL}

Anon, 1951, **Position classification and salary administration in libraries**. [American Library Association]. {IIT}

Ranganathan, S.R., 1944, **Post-war reconstruction of libraries in India**. [Punjab Library Association, Lahore]. {ZHL}

Wheeler, Joseph L. and Goldhor, Herbert, 1962, **Practical administration of public libraries.** {IIT NMML USIS}

Anon, 1966, **Practical approach to information and data retrieval**. [Boston Industrial Education Institute]. {ISI}

Cargill, Jennifer S. and Alley, Brian, 1979, **Practical approval plan management**. {IIT}

Dent, Flu W., 1966, **Practical cataloguing**. {ICHR IIC IIT ZHL}

Johnson, A.F., 1962, **Practical cataloguing**. [Association of Assistant Librarians, London]. {IIT}

Zubair, Mohamad, 1951, **Practical cataloguing**. {ZHL}

Sharma, C.D., 1972, **Practical cataloguing** : Classified catalogue. {INSA JNU NCAER}

Sharma, C.D., 1972, **Practical cataloguing** : Classified catalogue, 2nd edn. [ICA ICHR IEC JNU NIPCCD}

Rajjan Lal, 1980, **Practical cataloguing procedure**. {IIT NIPCCD}

Kumar, P.S.G., n.d., **Practical classification**, V.I : Colon Classification. {NIH NIPCCD ZHL}

Whitchall, Tom, 1986, **Practical current awareness services from libraries**. {JNU}

Navalani, K. and Gidwani, N.N., 1981, **Practical guide to Colon Classification**. {AIU IIT JNU NERC NIEPA}

Datta, Bimal Kumar, 1956, **A practical guide to library procedure**. {NASSDOC}

Datta, Bimal Kumar, 1962, **Practical guide to library procedure**. {CRRI DUL IIT NERC SPA ZHL}

Lydall, G.O.E., 1955, **Practical guide to precis writing and indexing**. {DUL}

Anon, 1955, **Practical information for seminar members** : Working paper : International seminar on the development of public libraries in Asia, October 6-26, 1966, Delhi. [UNESCO]. {NASSDOC}

Whetton, Harry, ed., 1963, **Practical printing binding.** {INSA}

Uppal, O.P., n.d., **Practical procedure of cataloguing**. {ICHR}

Uppal, O.P., n.d., **Practical procedure of classification**. {IIMC}

Anon, 1962, **Practice for alphabetical arrangement**. (IS : 382-1952). [Indian Standards Institution]. {NAI NASSDOC}

Anon, n.d., **Practice for layout of library catalogue code**. (IS : 1358-1950). [Indian Standards Institution]. {NAI}

Anon, n.d., **Practice for layout of library catalogue code**, rev edn., (IS : 1358-1967). [Indian Standards Institution]. {NASSDOC}

Sood, S.P. and Jotwani, D., 1981, **Pralekhan** {JNU NASSDOC}.

Kipp, Laurence and Kipp, Re Cedlia, 1968, **Prediction of the future** : The development programme of the University of Delhi. {JNU}

Ranganathan, S.R., 1948, **Preface to library science.** {BIS}

Heys, H., 1965, **Preparation and production of technical books.** {DUL}

Crutchky, Brooke, 1967, **Preparation of manuscripts and correction of proofs**. {DUL}

Barnes, R.C.M., 1964, **Present state of information retrieval by computer**. {JNU}

Anon, 1961, **Presentation of contributions to periodicals**. (ISO/R 215-1961) (E). [International Organisation for Standardisation, Geneva]. {NASSDOC}

Neelameghan, A., 1975, **Presentation of ideas in technical writing**. {ICHR IIC NIH}

Kapp, Reginold O., 1961, **Presentation of technical information** : Based on four public lectures given at University College, London. {DUL}

Morrow, Carolyn Clark and Walker, Gay, 1983, **Preservation challenge** : A guide to conserving library materials. {JNU NMML}

Plumbe, Wilfred J., 1964, **Preservation of books in tropical and subtropical countries**. {JNU}

Flyate, D.M., ed., 1968, **Preservation of documents and papers**. [Israel Programme for Scientific Transactions, Jerusalem]. {INSA}

Mukherjee, B.B., 1973, **Preservation of library materials, archives and documents**. {DUL ICHR NASSDOC NERC NIH NIPCCD NMML ZHL}

Gupta, R.D., 1970, **Preserving manuscripts and other research material in the Braj area of India**, (reprinted from the Bulletin of the British Association of Orientalists). [Vrindaban Research Institute]. {NMML}

Howcraft, B. and Wagner, I., 1980, **Press cuttings** : Cooperative library guide. {ICA}

Douglas, Mary Peacock, 1974, **Primary school library and its services**. [UNESCO]. {DUL IEG NERC NIPCCD}

Phillips, W. Howard, 1951, **Primer of book classification**, rev. edn. [Association of Assistant Librarians, London]. {INSA ZHL}

Winterich, John Tracy and Randall, David A., 1966, **Primer of book collecting**. {DUL}

Simsova, Sylva, 1982, **Primer of comparative librarianship**. {IIT}

Satija, M.P., 1987, **A primer on Ranganathan's book number**. {NASSDOC*}

Mathur, Lalit Mohan, 1970, **Principles and techniques of educational library displays and exhibits**. {IIT NMML}

Williams, William F., 1966, **Principles of automated information retrieval**. {JNU}

Fredson, Bowers, 1949, **Principles of bibliographical description**. {DUL}

Hulme, E. Wyndham, 1950, **Principles of book classification**. {DUL}

Jolley, L., 1961, **Principles of cataloguing**. {IEG IIT NAI SPA}

Martin, James, 1982, **Principles of data-base management**. {NASSDOC}

Kochen, Manfred, 1974, **Principles of information retrieval**. {CRRI DUL ISI MHA USIS}

Parkhi, R.S., 1950, **Principles of library classification with special reference to Colon and Decimal Classification**, Pt. 1 : General theory of classification. {CRRI}

Vanners, Robert G., 1965, **Principles of punched card data processing**. {JNU}

George, Mann, 1951, **Print** : A manual for librarians and students describing in detail the history, methods and applications of printing and paper making. {DUL}

Mac Robert, T.M., 1957, **Printed books** : A short introduction to fine typography. {DUL}

Higgins, Gavin, ed., 1980, **Printed reference material**. {NASSDOC ZHL}

Priolker, Anant Kakba, 1958, **Printing presses in India** : Its beginning and early development. {DUL}

Jelinek, Frederick, 1968, **Probabilistic information theory** : Discrete and memoryless models. {INSA}

Anon, 1979, **Problems and failures in library automation** : Clinic on library applications of data processing, 1978, Illinois. [University of Illinois at Urbana-Champaign]. {USIS}

Anon, 1972, **Problems and prospects of fundamental research in multidisciplinary fields** : Computer science. [Organisation for Economic Co-operation and Development, Paris; Committee for Science Policy]. {NASSDOC}

Williams, Edwin E., ed., n.d., **Problems and prospects of the research library.** {IEG}

Schad, J.G. and Tanis, N.E., 1974, **Problems in developing academic library collections**. {DUL IIT ISI}

Samore, Theodore, ed., 1968, **Problems in library classification** : Dewey 17 and conversion. {ISI}

Umapathy, K.S., 1984, **Problems in library management.** {DUL ICA ICHR ISI JNU NIEPA NIH NIPCCD}

Kies, Cosette, 1974, **Problems in library public relations**. {ISI}

Hickec, Doralyn J., 1972, **Problems in organising library collections.** {JNU NERC}

Katz, William A. and Swarţ, Roderick G., eds., 1964, **Problems in planning library facilities**, Consultants, architects, plans and critiques : Proceedings : Library building institute, July 12-13, 1963, Chicago. [American Library Association]. {BIS DUL NASSDOC*}

Galvin, Thomas J., 1965, **Problems in reference service** : Case studies in method and policy. {DUL USIS}

Mikhailov, A.I., n.d., **Problems of information user needs.** [International Federation for Documentation and Information]. {CRRI DUL}

Goswami, Badri Prasad, n.d., **Problems of misplacement, mutilation and theft of books in libraries**. {JNU}

Thomas, P.A., 1970, **Procedural model for the use of bibliographic records in libraries**. [Association of Special Libraries and Information Bureaux]. {DUL NASSDOC}

Anon, 1935, **Proceedings** : All India library conference, 2nd, 1935, Lucknow. [Indian Library Association]. {NASSDOC}

Anon, 1942, **Proceedings** : All India library conference, 5th, April 4-6, 1942, Bombay. [Indian Library Association]. {NASSDOC}

Anon, 1946, **Proceedings** : All India library conference, 7th, January 25-28, 1946, Baroda. [Indian Library Association]. {NASSDOC}

Krishan Kumar and Vashishth, C.P., eds., 1980, **Proceedings** : All India library conference, 26th, March 6-9, 1980, New Delhi. [Indian Library Association]. {NASSDOC}

Anon, 1987, **Proceedings** : All India library conference, 32nd, 1987. [Indian Library Association]. {NASSDOC}

Anon, 1988, **Proceedings** : All India library conference, 34rd, 1988. [Indian Library Association]. {NASSDOC}

Anon, 1989, **Proceedings** : All India library conference, 35th, 1989. [Indian Library Association] {NASSDOC}

Anon, n.d., **Proceedings** : All India library convention. [Government of India Librarians Association]. {NMML}

Anon, 1927, **Proceedings** : Anniversary conference of Library Association, 15th, 1927, Edinburg. [Library Association, London]. {NASSDOC}

Kent, Allen and Galvin, Thomas J., eds., 1978, **Proceedings** : Conference on the on-line revolution in libraries, 1978, Pittsburg. {JNU}

Kapoor, S.K., et al, eds., n.d., **Proceedings** : Conference on organisation of data services in India and user education and training programmes, 13th, 1981, Waltair. [Indian Association of Special Libraries and Information Centres]. {BIS MMTC NIPCCD}

Whatley, Allen, ed., 1974, **Proceedings** : International and comparative librarianship group conference, June 28-July 1, 1974, {NASSDOC}

Amarsinghe, N., ed., 1987, **Proceedings** : International conference of directors of national libraries of Asia and Oceania, 3rd, November 18-23, Colombo. {NASSDOC}

Keren, Carl, and Perlmutter, Linda, n.d., **Proceedings** : International conference on the application of mini and micro computers in information, documentation and libraries, March 13-18, 1983, Tel Aviv. {IIT}

Radhakrishnan, S., and Iyengar, T.K.S., eds., 1977, **Proceedings** : International conference on technical information services for developing countries, March, 1977, Madras. [International Council of Scientific Unions, Committee of Science and Technology in Developing Countries]. {BCL BIS CRRI IIT JNU}

Perti, R.K., ed., 1987, **Proceedings** : International seminar on conservation of traditional records, paper and allied materials. [National Archives of India]. {NAT}

Anon, 1957, **Proceedings** : International study conference on classification for information retrieval, 1957, {IEC IIT}

Atherton, Pauline, ed., 1965, **Proceedings** : International study conference on classification research, 2nd, September 14-18, 1969, Elsinore. {BIS IIT}

Perreault, Jean M. and Dohlberg, Ingetraut, eds., 1983, **Proceedings** : International study conference on classification research : Universal classification, 4th, June 28-July 2, 1982, Ausburg. {BIS}

Anon, 1988, **Proceedings** : National seminar on strategies for survival by Nigerian academic and research libraries during austere times, November 9-11, 1987, Ibadan. [Nigerian Association of Agricultural Librarians and Documentalists; Nigerian Librarian Association, Academic and Research Libraries Section]. {NASSDOC*}

Anon, 1966, **Proceedings** : National symposium on information display, 7th, Technical session. [Society for Information Display]. {JNU}

Anon, 1987, **Proceedings** : Regional seminar on measurement and application of micrographics, 3rd, 1987, Pune. {NASSDOC}

Anon, 1967, **Proceedings** : Seminar of university librarians in India, 1967, Jaipur. [Rajasthan University]. {DUL IIT}

Dowing, J.C. and Sharp, N.F., 1969, **Proceedings** : Seminar on the Anglo-American Cataloguing Rules, 1967. [Library Association, London]. {ZHL}

Anon, 1980, **Proceedings** : Seminar on international cooperative information systems, July 9-13, 1979. [International Development Research Centre]. {CRRI USIS}

Moreland, Carroll C. and Usmani, M. Adil, eds., n.d., **Proceedings** : Seminar on the purpose and function of library in national education, April 7-10, 1961, Nazimabad. [Society for the Promotion and Improvement of Libraries]. {NASSDOC*}

Anon, 1982, **Proceedings and list of government of Indian libraries of Delhi**: All India library convention, 3rd, February 10-12, 1982, New Delhi. [Government of India Librarians Association]. {CRRI NASSDOC}

Anon, 1977, **Proceedings and papers** : IASLIC seminar on library scene in Calcutta, 1977, Calcutta. [Indian Association of Special Libraries and Information Centres]. {JNU}

Anon, 1981, **Proceedings and papers** : International conference on delivery mechanisms for engineering and technological information, November 3-5, 1980, Budapest. {BIS}

Anon, 1969, **Proceedings of the General Council** : IFLA annual. [International Federation of Library Association and Institutions]. {NASSDOC}

Herald, Alther Canley, 1963, **Processing manual** : A pictorial work book of catalogue cards, rev. edn. {DUL}

Frarey, Carlyle J., 1959, **Processing services of the Dallas Public Library** : A report on their organisation, operation and administration. {DUL}

Poole, Frazer G. and Trezza, Alphonse F., eds., 1969, **The procurement of library furnishings** : Specifications BID documents and evaluation : Proceedings : Library equipment institute, 3rd, 1966, New York. [American Library Association]. {USIS}

Falk, Leslie K., n.d., **Procurement of library materials in the federal government** : An orientation prepared for Federal Library Committee. {JNU}

Tiwari, Bhaskar Nath, n.d., **Prodh siksha aur pustakalaya**. {NIEPA NIPCCD}

Mechluip, Fritz, 1972, **Production and distribution of knowledge in the United States.** {NASSDOC}

Anon, 1974, **Professional and non-professional duties in libraries**, 2nd edn. [Research and Development Committee, Library Association, London]. {IIT ZHL}

Jain, T.C., 1971, **Professional associations and development of librarianship** Case studies. [Library Association, London; American Library Association]. {AIU NASSDOC NCAER}

Anon, 1986, **Profession education and training for library and information work** : A review. [Library Association, London]. {NASSDOC}

Anon, 1980, **The professional librarian's reader in library automation and technology**. {JNU USIS}

Isenberg, Arthur, 1968, **A profile of Andhra book readers**. {NASSDOC*}

Polak, Fred L., 1971, **Prognostics** : A science in the making surveys and creates the future. {NASSDOC}

Johnson, A.F., 1968, **Programmed course in cataloguing and classification** {CRRI IIC IIFT IIT INSA NCAER}

Sherman, Philip M., 1970, **Programming and coding digital computers** {NASSDOC}

Lancaster, G.T., n.d., **Programming in COBOL**. {NASSDOC}

Lubrans, John, ed., 1978, **Progress in educating the library user**. {CRRI IIT}

Collison, R.L., ed., 1966, **Progress in library science**. {CRRI IEG IIFT NIH NMML}

Peaks, Gilbert L., et al, 1957, **Progress report in chemical literature retrieval** {CRRI}

Ranganathan, S.R., 1937, **Prolegomena to library classification**. [Madras Library Association]. {CRRI NMML}

Ranganathan, S.R., 1957, **Prolegomena to library classification**, 2nd edn [Madras Library Association]. {IEG IIMC ISI MFL NAI}

Ranganathan, S.R., 1967, **Prolegomena to library classification**, 3rd edn assisted by M.H. Gopinath, [Madras Library Association]. {AIU ICA IIC INSA JNU NASSDOC NCAER}

Bamberger, Richard, 1975, **Promoting the reading habit**. {JNU}

Anon, 1981, **Promotion of reading habits in Pakistan** : A study on methods and measures to promote reading habits in Pakistan. [Pakistan National Book Council]. {ZHL}

Anon, 1958, **Proof corrections for printers and authors.** (IS : 1250-1958). [Indian Standards Institution]. {NASSDOC}

Brodman, Estelle, 1968, **Proposal for documentation centre at the Central Family Planning Institute, New Delhi** : Report. {NASSDOC}

Anon, 1963, **Prospects for library co-operation in New York city** : Planning for more effective utilisation of reference and research resources submitted by Nelson Associations Incorporated, New York. {DUL}

Trehan, G.L., et al, 1982, **Prospects of library services in India** : A study. {JNU}

Anon, 1963, **Protecting the library and its resources** : A guide to physical protection and insurance : Report on a study conducted by Gage Babcock and Associates, Incorporated. [American Library Association]. {DUL IIT NASSDOC IIT}

Saunders, W.L., ed., 1966, **Provision and use of library and documentation services** : Some contributions. [University of Sheffield Postgraduate School of Librarianship]. {DUL JNU MHA NIH SPA USIS}

Weinberg, Gerald M., 1971, **Psychology of computer programming**. {NASSDOC}

Wilson, Patrick, 1977, **Public knowledge and private ignorance** : Towards a library and information policy. {CRRI USIS}

Reilly, Jane A., 1981, **The public librarian as adult learners' advisor** : An innovation in human services. {USIS}

Robbins-Carter, Jane, ed., 1982, **Public librarianship** : A reader. {USIS}

Anon, n.d., **Public libraries**, mimeo short bibliography. {NASSDOC}

Kalia, D.R., n.d., **Public libraries** : Collection of papers on public libraries written at different times. {NASSDOC*}

Anon, 1975, **Public libraries and cultural activities.** [Department of Education and Science, Great Britain]. {NIPCCD}

Maurois, Andre, 1961, **Public libraries and their mission**. [UNESCO]. {ICA}

Anon, 1973, **Public libraries and their use.** [Department of Education and Science, Great Britain]. {NIPCCD}

Anon, 1956, **Public libraries for Asia** : The Delhi seminar. [UNESCO]. {NASSDOC NIEPA ZHL}

Daniel, Hawthorne, 1961, **Public libraries for every one**. {NASSDOC}

McColvin, Lionel R., 1947, **Public libraries in Australia** : Present conditions and future possibilities. {JNU}

Singh, R.S.P., 1988, **Public libraries in Bihar**. [Bihar Library Service Association, Patna].

Thorsen, Leif, 1972, **Public libraries in Denmark**, tr. by Megens Hay Larsen from Danish. {NASSDOC}

Anon, 1982, **Public libraries in developing society and planning for national information system** : Seminar papers : All India library conference, 28th, October 20-23, 1982, Lucknow. [Indian Library Association]. {ICA NASSDOC NIPCCD ZHL}

Sharma, Pandey S.K., 1985, **Public libraries in India**. {JNU}

Patil, P.K., n.d., **Pubic libraries in Karnataka** : Their scope and development. {AIU}

Cambell, H.C., 1973, **Public libraries in the urban metropolitan setting**. {DUL IIT}

Ekbole, Gopal Rao, 1987, **Public libraries system**. {NASSDOC*}

Harrison, K.C., 1963, **Public libraries today**. {DUL IIT NASSDOC}
Rayward, W. Boyd, ed., 1978, **The public library** : Circumstances and prospects : Papers presented at the 39th Annual Conference. {IIT USIS}
Viswandhan, C.G., 1985, **Public library** : Operations and services : A short manual, rev edn. {NASSDOC}
Brown, Royston, 1979, **Public library administration.** {IIT NIEPA}
Jefferson, George, 1965, **Public library administration** : An examination guide book. {MFL NERC SPA ZHL}
Conant, Ralph W., ed., 1965, **Public library and the city.** {JNU SPA}
Wellisch, J.B., et al, 1974, **Public library and federal policy**. {NIPCCD}
Davies, D.W., 1974, **Public library as culture and social centres** : The origin of the concept. {USIS}
Mevissen, W., 1958, **Public library building**. {IIT}
Mc Comb, Dana Quick, n.d., **Public library buildings** : Their financing, design, construction, equipment and operation. {DUL}
Wellard, James Howard, 1940, **The public library comes of age.** {CRRI}
Anon, 1985, **Public library development perspectives.** [Indian Library Association]. {NASSDOC*}
McColvin, Lionel R., 1950, **Public library extension**. [UNESCO]. {NASSDOC ZHL}
Guruswamy Naidu, N., 1990, **Public library finance**. {CRRI}
Adamson, Edith, 1962, **Public library finance** : A literature review. {JNU}
Rose, Ernstine, 1954, **Public library in American life**. {NAI USIS}
Brooks, Jean S. and Reich, David L., 1974, **The public library in non-traditional education.** {NASSDOC USIS}
Sykes, Paul, 1979, **Public library in perspective** : An examination of its origins and modern role. {IIT}
Leigh, Robert D., n.d., **Public library in the United States.** {IEG}
Carnovsky, Leon, 1968, **Public library in the urban setting** : The thirty second conference of the Graduate Library School, July 31-August 2, 1967. {NMML}
Jones, Clara Station, ed., 1978, **Public library information and referral service.** {USIS}
Mittal, R.L., 1971, **Public library law** : An international survey. {ICA NASSDOC NMML}
Gradiner, Frank M., 1971, **Public library legislation** : A comparative study. [UNESCO]. {JNU NASSDOC NIEPA}
Viswanathan, C.G., 1961, **Public library operations and services** : A short manual. {CRRI IIT MHA NERC SPA ZHL}
Anon, 1956, **Public library service**. [American Library Association]. {USIS}
Anon, 1943, **Public library service** : Its post-war reorganisation and development. [Library Association, London]. {NAI}
Anon, 1973, **Public library service** : Reorganisation and after. [Department of Education and Science, Great Britain]. {NIPCCD}
Anon, 1970, **Public library services** : Bahamas. [UNESCO]. {NASSDOC*}
McColvin, Lionel R., 1957, **Public library services for children,** [UNESCO]. {IEG JNU NASSDOC NERC NIPCCD}
Ranganathan, S.R. and Neelameghan, A., eds., 1972, **Public library system** : India, Sri Lanka, UK, USA. {BIS IEG IIC JNU NAI NMML ZHL}
Venkatappaiah, V., 1982, **Public library system in Andhra Pradesh**. [Andhra University]. {NASSDOC}
Augustine, C.A. and Devarajan, G., 1990, **Public library system in India**. {ZHL}

Anon, 1969, **Public library systems in the United States** : A survey of multi-jurisdictional systems. [American Library Association]. {USIS}

Harrison, K.C., 1973, **Public relations for librarians.** {ICA MMTC ZHL}

Rice, Betty, 1972, **Public relations for public libraries** : Creative problem solving. {USIS}

Winton, Harry N.M., comp. and ed., 1972, **Publications of the United Nations systems.** {NASSDOC}

Loizeaux, Marie Duvernoy, 1959, **Publicity primer** : An ABC of telling all about the public library, 4th edn. {USIS}

Collison, Robert, 1973, **Published library catalogues** : An introduction to their contents and use. {IIT}

Gorkhoff, Boris I., n.d., **Publishing in the USSR.** {DUL}

Scheele, Martin, 1961, **Punch-card methods in research and documentation with special reference to biology.** {CRRI DUL IIMC NASSDOC}

Casey, Robert S., 1958, **Punched cards** : Their application to science and industry. {JNU}

Dickinson, Ass Don, 1916, **Punjab library primer.** [University of Punjab, Lahore]. {ZHL}

Anon, 1972, **Purchase of books by public libraries.** [Department of Education and Science, Great Britain]. {NIPCCD}

Anon, 1979, **Purchasing an encyclopaedia** : 12 point to consider. [American Library Association]. {USIS}

Sharma, Chandra Kant, 1975, **Pustak chayan evam rachna** : Book selection and physical bibliography. {BIS NMML}

Zubair, Mohamad and Agrawal, S.P., 1954, **Pustak sankhya praveshika** : Introduction to book numbers in Hindi. {NASSDOC}

Shastri, A., 1967, **Pustakalaya andolan, Bihar.** {NMML}

Sharma, Pandey S.K., **Pustakalaya aur hum** {RTL}

Shastri, Dwarka Prasad, 1958, **Pustakalaya aur sandarbh seva.** {BIS DUL}

Vajpayee, Hanuman Prasad, 1958, **Pustakalaya Karyapadhati.** {JNU}

Bagari, N.D., 1973, **Pustakalaya paddhati.** {DUL}

Shastri, Dwarka Prasad, 1959, **Pustakalaya parichay.** {BIS}

Shastri, Dwarka Prasad, 1974, **Pustakalaya parichay**, 2nd edn. {BIS NMML}

Shastri, A., 1967, **Pustakalaya-Prakriya, Patna.** {NMML}

Gupta, Chandra Prakash, n.d., **Pustakalaya prashasan** : Sidhant evam vyavahar. {BIS}

Singh, R.S.P., 1973, **Pustakalaya sanghatan evam prashasan.** {DUL}

Srivastava, Shyam Nath and Verma, Subhash Chandra, n.d., **Pustakalaya sangathan evam sanchalan.** {DUL IIMC}

Sharma, B.N., 1977, **Pustakalaya siddhant and vyavahar** : College pustakalaya ke sandarbh men. {NMML}

Agarwal, Shyam Sunder, 1971, **Pustakalaya soochikaran** : Ek adhyayan. [Madhya Pradesh Hindhi Granth Academy]. {NMML}

Shastri, Dwarka Prasad, 1974, **Pustakalaya vargikarna** : Siddhant aur prayog. {BIS MFL}

Ranganathan, S.R., 1968, **Pustakalaya vargikaran ke mool tatva**, 3rd edn. {DUL}

Ranganathan, S.R., 1980, **Pustakalaya vigyan ke panch sutra.** [Rajasthan Hindi Granth Academy, Jaipur]. {BIS}

Atherton, Pauline A., 1973, **Putting knowledge to work** : American view of Ranganathan's Five Laws of Library Science. {AIU IIMC JNU NIEPA USIS}

Vashishth, C.P., ed., 1986, **Quality in libraries**. [Indian Library Association]. {NASSDOC*}

Woolf, Harry, ed., 1961, **Quantification** : A history of the meaning of measurement in the natural and social sciences. {NASSDOC}

Chen, Ching-Chih, ed., 1978, **Quantitative measurement and dynamic library service.** {BIS IIT}

Ravichandrarao, I.K., 1983, **Quantitative methods for library and information science.** {BIS ISI JNU NASSDOC}

Hoadley, Irene Braden and Clark, Alice S., eds., 1974, **Quantitative methods in librarianship** : Standards, research and management. {IIT ISI JNU}

Bhatt, Narayan Singh, 1986, **Rajasthan ke granthagar**. {NASSDOC*}

Anon, 1975, **Rampur Raza Library Bill**. [Lok Sabha, New Delhi]. {JNU}

Satija, Mohinder Partap, 1978, **Ranganathan** : Method and style : A pastiche of opinions. {JNU}

Srivastava, A.P., 1977, **Ranganathan** : A pattern maker : A synthetic study of his contributions. {CRRI ISI JNU NIEPA.NIPCCD ZHL}

Rajagopalan, T.S., ed., 1968, **Ranganathan's philosophy** : Assessment, impact and relevance. {JNU NMML}

Archer, H. Richard, ed., 1965, **Rare book collections** : Some theoretical and practical suggestions for use by librarians and students. [American Library Association]. {NAI}

Cave, Roderick, 1976, **Rare book librarianship.** {NASSDOC}

Simpson, Murray, C.T., 1976, **Rare book librarianship** : A select annotated bibliography. {JNU}

Breillat, Pierre, 1965, **Rare books section in the library**. [UNESCO]. {IIMC IIT NASSDOC}

Kesavan, B.S, et al, eds., n.d., **Rashtriya granth-suchi**, 1961-63. {NASSDOC}

Anon, 1965, **Reaching readers** : The library's responsibility and opportunity : Papers with a summary of discussions and recommendations. Regional conference workshop for librarians, 6th, December 6-13, 1964, Albay. {NASSDOC}

Narasimharao, K.V.V.L. and Oommen, Chinna, 1972, **Read faster and understand better**, 2 pts. [Central Institute of Indian Languages, Mysore]. {MHA}

Webster, O., 1965, **Read well and remember**. {IIT}

Reynolds, Michael M., ed., 1970, **Reader in the academic library**. {USIS}

O'Hara, Frederick J., ed., 1973, **Reader in government documents.** {NASSDOC}

Wasserman, Paul and Bundy, Mary Lee, eds., 1970, **Reader in library administration**. {DUL USIS}

Simmon, Ross, 1976, **Reader in library management**. {JNU}

Lubrans, John, ed., 1977, **Reader in library systems analysis**. {USIS}

Bundy, Mary Lee and Wasserman, Paul, eds., 1970, **Reader in research methods for librarianship**. {USIS}

Mews, Hazel, 1942, **Reader instruction in colleges and universities** : An introduction handbook. {AIU JNU NIEPA}

Fox, Peter, 1974, **Reader instruction methods in academic libraries**. {JNU}

Anon, 1983, **Reader's guide to Madras University Library** : Platinum jubilee celebration, 1907-1982. [Madras University Library]. {NMML}

Sood, P.K., 1988, **Reading habits among college students** : The role of library. {NASSDOC}

Earuqui, Jalees A., ed., 1974, **Reading habits in Pakistan** : A report. {ZHL}

Anon, 1984, **Reading material** : Orientation seminar on planning and management for senior administrators of public library services, February 6-10, 1984, New Delhi. {NASSDOC NIEPA}

Karetzkey, Stephen, 1982, **Reading research and librarianship** : A history and analysis. {CRRI IIT JNU}

Anon, n.d., **Reading research in the Centre for Library Science and Methodology, 1981-85**. [Centre for Library Science and Methodology, Budapest]. {NASSDOC}

Sharp, Harold S., 1964, **Readings in information retrieval**. {JNU}

Olding, R.K., ed., 1967, **Readings in library cataloguing**. {NASSDOC NMML SPA ZHL}

Kujoth, Jean S., 1968, **Readings in nonbook librarianship**. {NMML USIS}

Sharp, Harold S., 1963, **Readings in special librarianship**. {USIS}

Carroll, Frances Laverne, 1981, **Recent advances in school librarianship.** {NIEPA}

Anon, 1967, **Recommendations for the abbreviation of titles of periodicals** (BS. 4148-1967). [British Standards Institution]. {CRRI}

Anon, 1973, **Recommendations for bibliographical catalogue reference**. [Indian Standards Institution]. {NAI}

Anon, 1963, **Recommendations for bibliographical references**, (IS : 2380-1963). [Indian Standards Institution]. {NASSDOC}

Anon, 1978, **Recommendations for bibliographical references**. Essential and supplementary elements, rev. edn., (IS : 2381-1978). [Indian Standards Institution]. {NASSDOC}

Anon, 1964, **Recommendations for the preparation of indexes for books, periodicals and other publications**, (BS 3700 : 1964). [British Standards Institution]. {CRRI NASSDOC}

Anon, 1975, **Recommendations for the processing and storage of silver gelatin-type microfilm**. (BS : 1153 : 1975). [British Standards Institution]. {CRRI}

Anon, 1955, **Recommendations for the storage of microfilm**. (BS : 1153 : 1955). [British Standards Institution]. {CRRI NASSDOC NMML}

Anon, 1977, **Recommendations relating to primary elements in the design of library buildings**. [Indian Standards Institution]. {NASSDOC}

Sudman, Seymour, 1967, **Reducing the cost of surveys**. {NASSDOC}

Sager, Donald J., 1968, **Reference** : A programmed instruction. [Ohio Library Association]. {USIS}

Shores, Hous, 1976, **Reference as the promotion of free enquiry**. {JNU}

Nelson, Edward C., 1967, **Reference books for regional reference collection**. {NAI}

Hingwe, K.S., 1967, **Reference books in academic libraries** : A brief survey. {DUL JNU}

Stevens, Rolland E., 1966, **Reference books in the social sciences and humanities.** {DUL}

Anon, n.d., **Reference catalogue of Indian books in print**, 3 vols. {NASSDOC}

Buter, Pierce, 1943, **Reference function of the library**. {DUL NAL}

Khosla, Raj K., 1973, **Reference guide of India** : Who's who incorporating men of library science in India, men of science and technology in India, and men of education in India. {JNU NASSDOC}

Bushnell, George H., 1951, **Reference librarian in university, municipal and specialised libraries**. {BIS CRRI DUL}

Warner, J., 1928, **Reference library methods**. {NAI}

McColvin, Lionel R., 1952, **Reference library stack** : An informal guide. {CRRI}

Fenton, F.H., 1960, **Reference library stacks** : An enquiry into reference book provision in the rate-supported libraries of England and Wales. {JNU}

Dierickx, Harold and Hopkinson, Alan, eds., 1981, **Reference manual for machine-readable bibliographic descriptions**, 2nd rev edn. [UNESCO]. {NASSDOC}

Ziskind, Sylvia, 1977, **Reference readiness** : A manual for librarians and students. {DUL NASSDOC}

Anon, 1966, **Reference research and the regionalism** : Selected papers from 53rd conference of Texas Library Association. {JNU}

Doyle, James M. and Grimes, George H., 1976, **Reference resources** : A systematic approach. {DUL NASSDOC}

Davinson, Donald, 1980, **Reference service**. {DUL ICA}

Krishan Kumar, 1984, **Reference service**. {JNU NMML}

Ranganathan, S.R., 1961, **Reference service**, 2nd edn. {BIS CRRI DSSW DUL JNU MHA NASSDOC NIH NMML SPA ZHL}

Murfin, Marjorie E. and Wynar, Lubomyr R., 1984, **Reference service** : An annotated bibliographic guide supplement, 1976-1982. {JNU}

Ranganathan, S.R., 1940, **Reference service and bibliography**, Vol. 1, Pts. 1-4. {DSSW DUL}

Gleaves, Edwin S. and Tucker, John Mark, 1983, **Reference service and library education** : Essays in honour of Neel Chaney. {JNU}

Sharma, Jagdish Saran and Grover, D.R., 1987, **Reference service and sources of information**. {NMML}

Sewa Singh, 1986, **Reference service in academic libraries in India**. {JNU NASSDOC NMML}

Anon, 1970, **Reference service-in-action** : Processing and servicing of special material in libraries. [Indian Association of Special Libraries and Information Centres, Calcutta]. {IEG NAI}

Rowland, Arthur Ray, 1964, **Reference services**. {DUL USIS}

Kohl, David F., 1985, **Reference services and library instruction** : A handbook for library management. {NASSDOC}

Irving, Richard D. and Katz, Bill, 1988, **Reference services and public policy**. {NASSDOC}

Wyer, James I., 1930, **Reference work**. [American Library Association]. {ZHL}

Mukherjee, A.K., 1964, **Reference work and its tools**. {CRRI ICA NMML SPA}

Mukherjee, A.K., 1971, **Reference work and its tools**, 2nd edn. {DUL JNU NASSDOC NERC NIEPA NMML}

Mukherjee, A.K., 1975, **Reference work and its tools**, 3rd ed. {CRRI ICA IIT NIH NIPCCD}

Stevens, Rolland E. and Smith, Linda C., 1986, **Reference work in the university library**. {JNU}

Finer, Ruth, 1979, **Referral centres and services** : A review. [Association of Special Libraries and Information Bureaux]. {CRRI}

Urquhart, J.A., 1976, **Relegation and stock control in libraries**. {DUL IIT ZHL}

Chambers, A., 1969, **Reluctant reader**. {DUL}

Bhargava, K.D., 1967, **Repair and preservation of records**. [National Archives of India]. {NASSDOC}

Cockerell, S.M., 1960, **Repairing of books**, 2nd edn. {NAI}

Anon, 1947, **Report** : ASLIB meeting on planning and equipment of special libraries, April 6, 1946, London. [Association of Special Libraries and Information Bureaux]. {CRRI}

Anon, 1961, **Report** : Advisory committee for libraries. [Ministry of Education, New Delhi]. {NASSDOC}

Anon, 1989, **Report** : Asia Pacific information network in social science : Regional advisory group (APINESS/RAG) meeting. [UNESCO Principal Regional Office for Asia and the Pacific, Bangkok]. {NASSDOC}

Anon, 1987, **Report** : Asia Pacific POPIN experts working group on population information networking. [U.N. Economic and Social Commission for Asia and the Pacific, Bangkok]. {NASSDOC}

Anon, 1983, **Report** : Asian regional seminar on information sources, systems and services in the social sciences, July 11-22, 1983, Philippines [UNESCO Regional Office, Bangkok]. {NASSDOC*}

Anon, 1976, **Report** : Australia committee on inquiry on public libraries. {JNU}

Anon, 1978, **Report** : Committee appointed by the Government of Andhra Pradesh to review the working of the Andhra Pradesh Public Library Act, 1960, and to suggest amendments to the act. [Government of Andhra Pradesh, Hyderabad]. {NASSDOC*}

Anon, 1982, **Report** : Committee appointed for developing the Tagore Memorial Library, Vijayawada. [Zilla Granthalaya Samstha, Machilipatnam]. {NASSDOC*}

Anon, 1978, **Report** : Committee on private libraries. [Government of Andhra Pradesh, Hyderabad]. {NASSDOC*}

Anon, 1976, **Report** : Committee on the re-organisation of libraries, research centres and museums for the government of Jammu and Kashmir. [Punjab Agricultural University, Ludhiana]. {NASSDOC*}

Anon, 1984, **Report** : Expert working group on development of population information centres and networks, June 20-23, 1984. [U.N. Economic and Social Commission for Asia and the Pacific]. {NASSDOC}

Anon, 1963, **Report** : International conference on cataloguing principles, October 9-14, 1961, Paris. [International Federation of Library Associations and Institutions]. {IIT ISI NIEPA NMML}

Anon, 1960, **Report** : National Archives committee on archival legislation. [National Archives of India, New Delhi]. {MFL}

Anon, 1970, **Report** : National Library committee to enquire into the strained relations among the members of staff, 1969. [National Library, Calcutta]. {JNU}

Anon, 1968, **Report** : National Library reviewing committee, 1968. [National Library, Calcutta]. {JNU}

Anon, 1977, **Report** : Orientation course for the libraries of cooperative training colleges and apex level organisations/institutions in India, June 1977, New Delhi. [National Council for Cooperative Training, New Delhi]. {ICA}

Overhagem, Carl F.J. and Herman, R. Joyce, eds., 1965, **Report** : Planning conference on information transfer experiments, September 3, 1965, Massachusetts. {USIS}

Anon, 1985, **Report** : Regional seminar on curriculum development in information studies, September 17-21, 1985, Bangkok. [UNESCO]. {NASSDO*}

Anon, 1985, **Report** : Seminar on documentation and information systems for vocational training, November 5-16, 1985, Pattaya, Thailand. [International Labour Office; Asian and Pacific Skill Development Programme, Islamabad]. {NASSDOC}

Anon, 1986, **Report** : Seminar on library education, December 1-4, 1965, Bombay. [Shreemati Nathibai Damodar Thachery Women's University, Bombay]. {AIU NASSDOC}

Anon, 1972, **Report** : Seminar on public library system, 1972, Bangalore. {JNU}

Anon, 1981, **Report** : Sub-regional workshop for cooperative librarians and documentation officers for S.E. Area, April, 14-29, 1981, Los Banos. [ICA Regional Office and Education Centre for South-East Asia, New Delhi]. {ICA NASSDOC}

Anon, 1974, **Report** : University Grants Commission committee on scales of pay and qualification, etc., for library staff in universities and colleges. [University Grants Commission, New Delhi]. {NIEPA}

Anon, 1958, **Report** : University Grants Commission library committee. [University Grants Commission, New Delhi]. {SPA}

Khandwala, Vidyut K. and Sales-Pontes, A. Hilda, 1982, **Report** : Western regional conference on library architecture, October 8-10, 1980, Bombay. [Indian Association of Special Libraries and Information Centres]. {JNU NASSDOC}

Anon, 1974, **Report** : Working meeting on Asian resources for a population library network, September 13-15, 1973, Bangkok. [UN Economic Commission for Asia and the Far East]. {NIH}

Anon, 1966, **Report** : Working group on libraries, 1964, New Delhi. [Planning Commission, New Delhi]. {AIU CRRI JNU MFL MHA NASSDOC NCAER NERC NIEPA NIPCCD NMML}

Anon, 1980, **Report** : Workshop on road research and information for South East Asia, 1980, Melbourne. {CRRI}

Anon, 1981, **Report**, 1981. [ICA Regional Office and Education Centre for South-East Asia, New Delhi]. {ICA NASSDOC}

Anon, n.d., **Report, 1984-85**. [British Library Department of Oriental Manuscripts and Printed Books]. {NMML}

Pandey, B.D., 1979, **Report of expert consultative services rendered to Cooperative Training Centre in Nepal for organising their library and documentation services**. [International Cooperation Alliance Regional Office and Education Centre for South-East Asia, New Delhi]. {ICA}

Picache, U.G., 1986, **Report on feasibility of establishing a regional network of social science information and documentation centres in Asia and Pacific**. [Institute of Library Science]. {NASSDOC}

Singla, M.L., 1988, **Report on feasibility study for a computer based circulation control system**. [NASSDOC]. {NASSDOC}

Hendricks, Donald D., 1973, **Report on library networks**. {DUL}

Humphrey, K.W., 1966, **Report on the library of the Indian Institute of Technology, New Delhi**. [Indian Institute of Technology]. {IIT}

Stewart, James D., **Report on the municipal library system**. {JNU}

Carnovsky, Leon, n.d., **Report on a programme of library education in Israel**. (Technical assistance : Special report, No. 1). [UNESCO]. {IEG NASSDOC}

Anon, 1968, **A report on the supply and training of librarians**. [Department of Education and Science, Great Britain]. {NIEPA}

Hrgg, H.N., 1961, **Report on a survey made of book charging systems at present in use in England.** {JNU}

Cleverdon, Cysil W., 1962, **Report on the testing and analysis of an investigation into the comparative efficiency of indexing systems.** {BIS IIT}

Simon, Herbert A. and Siklossy, Leurent, 1972, **Representation and meaning** : Experiments with information processing systems. {NASSDOC}
Anon, 1961, **Reproductions reference guide**. 2nd edn. {NASSDOC}
Crix, F.C., 1975, **Reprographic management handbook**. {ISI}
Lahood, Charles G. and Sullivan, Robert C., 1975, **Reprographic services in libraries** : Organisation and administration. [American Library Association]. {BIS NMML}
New, Peter C., 1975, **Reprography for librarians**. {AIU JNU}
Gore, Daniel, et al, eds., 1979, **Requiem for the card catalogue** : Management issues in automated cataloguing. [Associated College of the Midwest]. {IIT NIPCCD USIS}
Ross, Robert, 1974, **Research** : An introduction. {NASSDOC}
Palmer, Archie M., 1972, **Research centres directory**, 4th edn. {NASSDOC}
Holmes, W. Robert and Raj Gopal, S., 1968, **Research facilities in Bangalore, Mysore, Ahmedabad**. {NMML}
Holmes, W. Robert and Raj Gopal, S., 1968, **Research facilities in Bombay, Calcutta and Madras.** {NIPCCD NMML USIS}
Holmes, W. Robert and Raj Gopal, S., 1967, **Research facilities in Delhi**. {DSSW ICA NIEPA NIPCCD NMML USIS}
Holmes, W. Robert and Raj Gopal, S., 1967, **Research facilities in Hyderabad**. {NIPCCD NMML}
Jafar, S.M., 1971, **Research facilities in Uttar Pradesh**. {NMML}
Swisher, Robert and Mc Clure, Charles R., 1984, **Research for decision making** : Methods for librarians. {DUL}
Brooks, Philip C., 1969, **Research in archives** : The use of unpublished primary sources. {NASSDOC USIS ZHL}
Kumar, P.S.G., comp., 1987, **Research in library in information science in India** : A bibliography of Ph.D, M.Phil. and MLIS dissertation. {NASSDOC NMML}
Anon, n.d., **Research in progress**, 4 vols. [Inter University Board of India and Ceylon]. {NASSDOC}
Harlow, Jacquis, 1963, **Research information retrieval**. {JNU}
Orne, Jerrold, ed., 1971, **Research librarianship** : Essays in honour of Robert B. Downs. {JNU NASSDOC USIS}
Roberts, Stephen, et al, eds., 1978, **Research libraries and collections in the United Kingdom** : A selective inventory and guide. {DUL ZHL}
Fussler, Herman H., 1974, **Research libraries and technology** : A report. [Sloan Foundation]. {USIS}
Krishan Kumar, 1973, **Research libraries in developing countries**. {AIU DUL IEG IIT JNU NASSDOC NIEPA NIPCCD NMML}
Williams, Cecil B. and Stevenson, Allan H., 1951, **Research manual for college studies and papers**, rev. edn. {ZHL}
Mumfort, Erid, et al, eds., 1985, **Research methods in information systems** : Proceedings of the IFIP WG 8.2 colloquium, Manchester Business School, September 1-3, 1984. {NASSDOC}
Stevens, Rolland E., ed., 1971, **Research methods in librarianship** : Historical and bibliographical methods in library research. {NASSDOC}
Busha, Charles H. and Herter, Stephen P., eds., 1980, **Research methods in librarianship** : Techniques and interpretation. {ISI}
Slater, M., ed., 1990, **Research methods in library and information studies**. [Library Association, London].{DUL}

Wynar, Bohdan S., 1974, **Research methods in library science** : A bibliographic guide with tropical outlines. {NASSDOC}

Anon, 1981, **Research services directory.** {USIS}

Kent, Allen, ed., 1974, **Resource sharing in libraries** : Why, how when : Next action steps. {IIT INSA NASSDOC}

Vervliet, H.D.L., 1979, **Resource sharing of libraries in developing countries** : Proceedings : IFLA/UNESCO pre-session seminar for librarians from developing countries, August 30-September 3, 1977, [Antwerp University]. {NASSDOC}

Downs, Robert B., n.d., **Resources of Canadian academic and research libraries.** {AIU}

Williams, Edwin E., 1962, **Resources of Canadian university libraries for research in the humanities and social sciences** : Report of a survey. [National Conference of Canadian Universities and Colleges, Ottawa]. {DUL NASSDOC}

Anon, n.d., **Responsibilities of libraries and information service.** [Organisation for European Economic Co-operation]. {BIS}

Slavens, Thomas P., ed., 1981, **Retrieval of information in the humanities and the social sciences.** {NIEPA}

Anon, 1971, **Review of national scientific and technical information policy** : Germany. [Organisation for Economic Co-operation and Development, Paris]. {CRRI ICA JNU}

Merritt, LeRoy C., 1958, **Reviews in library book selection.** {DUL}

West, Celeste and Katz, Elizabeth, eds., 1972, **Revolting librarians.** {USIS}

Rider, Fremond, n.d., **Rider's international classification for the arrangement of books on the shelves of the general libraries**, Preliminary edn. {DUL}

Anon, 1974, **The right to read and the nation's libraries.** [American Association of School Libraries, Children's Services Division; Public Library Association; American Library Association]. {USIS}

Narayana Rao, Kodati and Ramachandra Rao, T., 1981, **Rise and growth of public library movement in India**. [Iyyanki Library Awards Committee, Eluru]. {NASSDOC*}

Eaton, F. Thelma and Strout, Donald Everett, eds., 1959, **Role of classification in the modern American library** : Papers presented at an institute conducted by the University of Illinois, Graduate School of Library Science, 1959. {DUL}

Girja Kumar, et al, 1978, **Role of libraries in national development.** {JNU}

Anon, 1978, **Role of libraries in socio-economic development** : Papers : All India library convention, 1st, February 13, 1978, Delhi. [Government of India Librarians Association]. {NASSDOC}

Anon, 1965, **Role of the library in the development of the community** : Society for the promotion and improvement of libraries seminar, April 12-18, 1964, Karachi. [Hamdard National Foundation, Karachi]. {NASSDOC}

Lancaster, F.W., 1980, **The role of the library in an electronic society** : Proceedings : Library applications of data processing clinic, 1979, Illinois. [University of Illinois at Urbana-Champaign]. {USIS}

Anon, 1971, **Role of the library in national reconstruction** : Society for the promotion and improvement of libraries seminar, October 30—November 3, 1967, Rawalpindi. [Hamdard National Foundation, Karachi]. {NASSDOC}

Al-Nahari, Abdulaziz Mohamed, 1984, **Role of national libraries in developing countries with special reference to Saudi Arabia.** {NMML}

Dyer, C., 1970, **Role of school libraries in education.** {JNU}

Anon, 1989, **Roles and responsibilities of librarians and library technicians** : Report. [Canada Library Association, Ottawa].

Anon, 1981, **Root thesaurus.** 2 pts., Pt.-1 : Subject display; Pt.-2 : Alphabetical list. [British Standards Institution]. {NASSDOC}

Anon, 1948, **Rules for the catalog of printed book** : Vatican Library. [American Library Association]. {NAI}

Anon, 1951, **Rules for compiling the catalogues of printed books, maps and music in the British Museum.** [British Museum, London]. {NAI}

Anon, 1913, **Rules for compiling the catalogues of printed books, maps, etc., in the Imperial Library, Calcutta**. [National Library, Calcutta]. {NAI}

Anon, n.d., **Rules for descriptive cataloguing in the Library of Congress**. [U.S. Library of Congress]. {BIS NAI SPA}

Anon, n.d., **Rules for descriptive cataloguing in the Library of Congress** : Supplement 1949-1951. [U.S. Library of Congress]. {ISI}

Anon, 1954, **Rules for descriptive cataloguing in the Library of Congress** : Phonorecords. [U.S. Library of Congress]. {IEG ZHL}

Cutter, C.A., 1891, **Rules for a dictionary catalog**. {IIT}

Cutter, C.A., 1953, **Rules for dictionary catalog**, 4th edn. [Library Association, London]. {BIS CRRI JNU MFL NAI NIEPA NMML}

Anon, 1942, **Rules for indexing records**. [Imperial Record Department]. {NML}

Anon, n.d., **Rules for making alphabetical indexes**. [Indian Standards Institution]. {AIU NASSDOC}

Anon, n.d., **Rules for making alphabetical indexes,** rev. edn., (IS : 1275-1976). [Indian Standards Institution]. {NASSDOC}

Anon, 1918, **Rules for press listing**. [Imperial Record Department]. {NAI}

Sarada, K., 1986, **Rural library services in India**. {NASSDOC*}

Salton, Gerald, ed., 1971, **The SMART retrieval system** : Experiments in automatic document processing. {MHA NASSDOC}

Dudley, Edward, ed., 1974, **S.R. Ranganathan, 1892-1972** : Papers : Memorial meeting, January 25, 1973. {JNU}

Burr, Nelson R., 1952, **Safeguarding our cultural heritage** : A bibliography on the protection of museums, works of art, monuments, archives and libraries in time of war. {JNU}

Slocum, R.B., 1962, **Sample catalog cards**. {IIT}

Anon, 1951, **Sample catalog cards**, 2nd edn. [School of Library Science, Columbia University]. {ZHL}

Leitch, L. and Billewicz, W.Z., 1963, **Scheme for classification of information on nutrition coded for machine retrieval**. {DUL}

Gorst, S.M., 1953, **Scheme for the organisation of co-operative libraries**. [Plunkett Foundation for Co-operative Studies]. {ICA}

Fenwick, Sara Innis, 1966, **School and children's libraries in Australia**. {JNU}

Ranganathan, S.R., 1942, **School and college libraries**. {JNU}

Marshall, Faya Dix, 1979, **School librarians' encyclopedic dictionary**. {NIEPA}

Smeaton, J., 1959, **School libraries** : A series of talks delivered. [Ministry of Education, New Delhi]. {NMML}

Stoff, C.A., 1955, **School libraries** : A short manual, {JNU}

Dyer, C., 1970, **School libraries** : Theory and practice. {JNU}

Gaver, Mary Virginia and Velazquer, Gonzal, 1963, **School libraries in Puerto Rico** : A survey and plan for development. {NASSDOC}

Crookall, R.E., 1961, **School libraries in West Africa**. {JNU NIEPA}

Anon, 1967, **School library.** [Department of Education and Science, Great Britain]. {JNU}

Ellsworth, Ralph E. and Wagener, Hobart E., n.d., **School library**. {AIU DUL}

Davies, Ruth Ann, 1969, **The school library** : A force for educational excellence. {JNU USIS}

Mukherjee, A.K., 1965, **School library** : Some practical hints. {ISI MFL}

Wofford, Azile, 1959, **School library at work** : Acquisition, organisation and maintenance of materials in the school library. {JNU}

Vashishth, C.P., ed., 1986, **School library development**. [Indian Library Association]. {NASSDOC*}

Trehan, G.L. and Malhan, I.V., 1980, **School library management**. {NERC}

Allan, Margaret, 1974, **School library resource centre**. {JNU}

Cecil, Henry L. and Heap, Willard A., 1940, **School library service in the United States**. {ZHL}

Winstanley, Baroda, 1959, **School loan services.** {JNU}

Prostano, Emanuel T., 1974, **School media programmes** : Case studies in management, 2nd edn. {NIEPA}

Coblans, H., et al, 1974, **Science and technology policies information exchange systems (SPINES) feasibility study**. {JNU}

Foskett, D.J., 1964, **Science, humanism and libraries**. {IIT JNU}

Anon, 1980, **Science information services in India**. [Indian National Scientific Documentation Centre, New Delhi]. {NASSDOC*}

Jenkins, Frances Briggs, 1965, **Science reference sources**, 4th edn. {DUL}

Anon, n.d., **Scientific and technical documentation centres**. [UNESCO]. {AIU}

Mikhailov, A.I., 1982, **Scientific and technical information** : Its impact on the development of science and technology. [UNESCO; UNIDO, Moscow]. {NASSDOC*}

Anon, 1969, **Scientific and technical information in Canada**. [Science Council of Canada]. {JNU}

Subramanyan, Krishna, 1981, **Scientific and technical information resources**. {DUL}

Chen, Ching-Chih, 1987, **Scientific and technical information sources**, 1977. {IIT INSA JNU NERC}

Pruett, Nancy Jones, 1986, **Scientific and technical libraries**, 2 vols. {JNU}

Strauss, Lucille J., et al, 1964, **Scientific and technical libraries** : Their organisation and administration. {BIS CRRI IIT INSA}

Strauss, Lucille J., et al., 1972, **Scientific and technical libraries** : Their organisation and administration, 2nd edn. {BIS ISI INSA JNU}

Anon, 1985, **Scientific and technological information for development**. [United Nations Information Systems]. {JNU}

Thornton, John L. and Tully, R.I.J., 1962, **Scientific books, libraries and collectors** : A study of bibliography and the book trade in relation to science, 2nd edn. {DUL}

Gray, John and Perry, Brian, 1975, **Scientific information**. {BCL INSA}

Rozsa, Gyorgy, 1973, **Scientific information and society**. {NASSDOC}

Dougherty, Richard M. and Heinritz, Fred J., 1966, **Scientific management of library operations**. {DUL USIS}

Ackoff, Russell L., et al, 1962, **Scientific method** : Optimising applied research decision. {NASSDOC}

Houghton, Bernard, 1975, **Scientific periodicals** : Their historical development, characteristics and control. {DUL}

Speterson, Martin, 1966, **Scientific thinking and scientific writing**. {DUL}

Voigt, Melvin J., n.d., **Scientist approaches to information**. [American Library Association]. {BIS}

Collison, Robert, n.d., **Scolma directory of libraries and special collections of Africa**, 2nd edn. {IIC IIT}

Anon, 1972, **Scope for automatic data processing in the British library**, 2 pts. [Department of Education and Science, Great Britain]. {NASSDOC}

Lowy, George, 1965, **Searcher's manual**. {IIT USIS}

Anon, n.d., **Secondary school libraries in Uttar Pradesh**. [Department of Education, Allahabad University]. {IEG}

Farr, M.A.L., et al, 1973, **Security for computer systems**. {NIPCCD}

Denison, Barbara, comp., 1968, **Selected material in classification** : A bibliography. {JNU}

Broadus, Robert N., 1973, **Selecting materials for libraries**. {USIS}

Dewey, Melvil, 1976, **Selective Hindi Dewey Decimal Classification and Relative Index** tr. by Prabhu Narayan Gour. {DUL}

Anon, 1988, **Selective inventory of social science information and documentation services**, 3rd edn. [UNESCO Social and Human Sciences Documentation Centre]. {NASSDOC}

Anon, 1979, **Selective list of activities in the field of information** : UNESCO Intergovernmental conference on scientific and technical information for development, 1979, Paris. {JNU}

Mc Garry, K.J. and Burrell, T.W., 1972, **Semantics in the organisation of knowledge** : A programmed text for students in information retrieval. {NASSDOC}

Anon, 1975, **Seminar and exhibition on information for industry, 1975, Bangalore**. {CRRI}

Anon, 1967, **Seminar of college librarians in Rajasthan, Jaipur, 1966**. {JNU NMML}

Anon, 1967, **Seminar on library and information services for management**. [Liverpool College of Commerce]. {NMML}

Ranganathan, S.R. and Neelameghan, A., eds., 1972, **A seminar on public library system**. [Sarada Ranganathan Endowment for Library Science, Bangalore]. {NASSDOC*}

Leong, C.L.H., 1989, **Serial cataloguing handbook** : An illustrative guide to the use of AACR2 and LC rule interpretations. [American Library Association]. {DUL}

Osborn, Andrew D., 1955, **Serial publications** : Their place and treatment in libraries. {MFL}

Osborn, Andrew D., 1973, **Serial publications** : Their place and treatment in libraries, 2nd edn. [American Library Association]. {NASSDOC}

Osborn, Andrew D., 1980, **Serial publications** : Their place and treatment in libraries, 3rd edn. [American Library Association]. {USIS}

Rodgers, Frank, comp., 1971, **Serial publications in the British Parliamentary papers, 1900-1968** : A bibliography. [American Library Association]. {NASSDOC}

Potter, William Gray and Sirkin, Arlne Farber, eds., 1981, **Serials automation for acquisition and inventory control.** [American Library Association]. {USIS}

Gellatly, P., ed., 1980, **Serials librarianship in transition** : Issues and development. {NASSDOC}

Walsh, Patricia M., 1979, **Serials management and microforms**. {IIT}

Turock, Betty J., 1982, **Serving the older adult** : A guide to library programs and information sources. {USIS}

Ennis, Philip H. and Winger, Howard W., eds., 1962, **Seven questions about the profession of librarianship** : Proceedings of the 26th Annual Conference of the Graduate Library School. {IEG}

Silva, M., ed., 1985, **Sharing of information** : South Asian initiatives. {NASSDOC*}

Hyman, Richard Joseph, 1982, **Shelf access in libraries**. [American Library Association]. {DUL NASSDOC}

Jesse, W.H., 1952, **Shelf work in library**. [American Library Association]. {DUL IIT}

Anon, 1955, **Short contents list of periodicals or other documents**, (ISO/R 18-1955) (E). [International Organisation for Standardisation, Geneva]. {NASSDOC}

Sherrie, Heather and Jones, Phyllis Mander, comps., 1950, **Short list of subject headings**. {CRRI}

Venkatarangayya, M., ed., 1942, **Shree Iyyanki Venkata Ramanayya commemoration volume** : Presented to him on Shashtipurti celebration (60th birthday). {NASSDOC}

Pollett, Dorothy and Haskell, Peter C., eds., 1979, **Sign systems for libraries** : Solving the way finding problems. {BIS IIT USIS}

Akers, Susan Grey, 1944, **Simple library cataloguing**, 3rd edn. [American Library Association]. {BIS}

Akers, Susan Grey, 1954, **Simple library cataloguing**, 4th edn. [American Library Association]. {CRRI DSSW MHA SPA ZHL}

Akers, Susan Grey, 1969, **Simple library cataloguing**, 5th edn. {JNU NASSDOC NMML USIS ZHL}

Akers, Susan Grey, 1977, **Simple library cataloguing**, 6th rev and rewritten edn., ed. by Arthur Curlly and Jana Varlejs. {MHA NIEPA}

Dennis, Donald D., 1965, **Simplifying work in small public libraries**. {Drexel Institute of Technology]. {NASSDOC}

Williams, James G. and Pope, Elspeth, 1976, **Simulation activities in library, communication and information science**, ed. by Patrick R. Penland. {NASSDOC}

Scott, Andrew M., et al, 1966, **Simulation and national development**. {NASSDOC}

Wyman, Forest Paul, 1970, **Simulation modelling** : A guide to using SIMSCRIPT. {NASSDOC}

Anon, 1965, **Sizes of correspondence envelopes**. (IS : 3338-1965). [Indian Standards Institution]. {NASSDOC}

Zemanck, H., 1972, **Skyline of information processing** : Proceedings of the 10th anniversary of IFIP, Amsterdom. {JNU}

Jenssen, Gudbrand, n.d., **A small country in the world of standards** : ANSINBS symposium on international standards information and ISONET. {BIS}

Galvin, Hoyt R. and Van Buren, Martin, 1959, **The small public library building**, 2nd edn. [UNESCO]. {CRRI IEG IIMC IIT BIS NASSDOC NERC ZHL}

Judge, Peter and Gerrie, Brenda, 1987, **Small scale bibliographic database**. {JNU}

Campbell, D.J., 1973, **Small technical libraries**. [UNESCO]. {DUL ICA NERC NIEPA}

Ranganathan, S.R., 1952, **Social bibliography or physical bibliography for libraries**. {BIS CRRI DSSW}

Kister, Kenneth F., 1968, **Social issues and library problems** : Case studies in the social science. {NMML}

Binwal, J.C., et al, ed., 1990, **Social science information** : Problems and prospects. {NASSDOC}

Agrawal, S.P., 1987, **Social science information and documentation** : Search and relevance in India. {BIS DUL JNU NASSDOC NIH NIEPA NMML ZHL}

Ranganathan, S.R. and Girja Kumar, 1960, **Social science research and libraries** : Papers and summary proceedings of the library seminar on research in the social science, January 2-4, 1959. {NMML}

Anon, 1967, **Social science research and library development** : Summary proceedings. [Indian Council of World Affairs; Indian School of International Studies]. {NASSDOC*}

Anon, 1985, **The social sciences** : Information system. [USSR Academy of Sciences, Moscow]. {NASSDOC*}

Wessel, Andrew E., 1976, **The social use of information ownership and access.** {BCL NASSDOC USIS}

Shera, J.H., 1970, **Sociological foundations of librarianship**. {IEG NASSDOC NIEPA NMML ZHL}

Schaetz, Chaire K., n.d., **Some characteristics of an efficient information retrieval system**. {JNU}

Sharp, John R., 1965, **Some fundamentals of information retrieval**. {BIS CRRI DUL JNU TDA}

Gibson, Strickland, 1914, **Some Oxford libraries**. {JNU}

Mac Pherson, H.D., 1936, **Some practical problems in cataloguing**. {DUL}

Kochen, Manfred, 1965, **Some problems in information science**. {JNU}

East, H., 1979, **Some statistical indicators of UK abstracting and indexing services**. {BCL}

Girja Kumar and Krishan Kumar, 1976, **Soochikaran ke siddhant**, tr. by Prem Kumar Jayaswal. {BIS DUL NMML}

Prytherch, Ray, comp., 1983, **Sources of information librarianship and information science** : A grafton book. {NIH}

Patterson, Maureen L.P., ed., 1975, **South Asian library resources in North America** : A survey prepared for the Boston conference, 1974. {NASSDOC}

Tast, Margret, 1984, **South Pacific region pilot project on school library development** ; Training programmes for teachers. {JNU}

Anon, 1979, **Souvenir** : AP libraries conference, 1st, 1979, Hyderabad. {NASSDOC*}

Anon, 1980, **Souvenir** : AP libraries conference, 2nd, 1980, Narasaropet. {NASSDOC*}

Anon, 1982, **Souvenir** : AP libraries conference, 3rd, 1982, Tirupati. {NASSDOC*}

Anon, n.d., **Souvenir** : All India library conference, 14th, 1964, Indore. [Indian Library Association]. {NASSDOC}

Anon, 1965, **Souvenir** : All India library conference, 15th, 1965, Mysore. [Indian Library Association]. {NASSDOC}

Anon, 1966, **Souvenir** : All India library conference, 16th, 1966, Chandigarh. [Indian Library Association]. {NASSDOC}

Anon, 1973, **Souvenir** : All India library conference, 20th, 1973, Hyderabad. [Indian Library Association]. {NASSDOC}

Anon, 1975, **Souvenir** : All India library conference, 21st, 1975, Bhubneswar. [Indian Library Association]. {NASSDOC}

Anon, 1976, **Souvenir** : All India library conference, 22nd, 1976, New Delhi. [Indian Library Association]. {NASSDOC}

Anon, 1978, **Souvenir** : All India library conference, 24th, 1978, Bangalore. [Department of Public Libraries, Bangalore; Indian Library Association]. {NASSDOC}

Augustine, C.A., ed., 1979, **Souvenir** : All India library conference, 25th, May 14-18, 1979, Trivandrum. [Indian Library Association]. {ICA}

Anon, 1980, **Souvenir** : All India library conference, 26th, March 6-9, 1980, New Delhi, [Indian Library Association]. {ICA}

Anon, 1981, **Souvenir** : All India library conference, 27th, January 9-12, 1981, Hyderabad; Indian Library Association. [Academy of Library Science and Documentation, Hyderabad]. {ICA NASSDOC}

Anon, 1985, **Souvenir** : All India library conference, 31st, 1985, Baroda. [Indian Library Association]. {NASSDOC}

Anon, n.d., **Souvenir** : All India library conference, 32nd, Anantpur. [Indian Library Association]. {NASSDOC}

Anon, 1987, **Souvenir** : All India library conference, 33rd, 1987, Tiruchirapalli. [Indian Library Association]. {NASSDOC}

Anon, 1988, **Souvenir** : All India library conference, 1988, Calcutta. [Indian Library Association]. {NASSDOC}

Anon, 1989, **Souvenir** : All India library conference, 1989, Pune. [Indian Library Association]. {NASSDOC}

Anon, 1987, **Souvenir** : Golden jubilee celebration. [Department of Library and Information Science, Andhra University]. {NASSDOC}

Anon, 1981, **Souvenir** : IASLIC all India conference, 13th, 1981, Waltaire. [Indian Association of Special Libraries and Information Centres]. {NASSDOC}

Anon, 1967, **Souvenir** : IASLIC conference, 7th, December 27-30, 1967, Delhi. [University of Delhi]. {NASSDOC}

Anon, 1980, **Souvenir** : IASLIC national seminar, 9th, 1980, Nagpur [IASLIC]. {NASSDOC}

Anon, 1984, **Souvenir** : IASLIC national seminar, 11th, 1984, Hydrabad [IASLIC]. {NASSDOC*}

Anon, 1987, **Souvenir** : Library education centenary celebration. [Nagpur University]. {NASSDOC*}

Anon, 1985, **Souvenir** : Platinum Jubilee. [Central Library, Baroda]. {NASSDOC*}

Anon, 1972, **Souvenir** : Shri Sanmati Pustakalaya Trust, Jaipur. {NASSDOC*}

Anon, n.d., **Souvenir** : Silver Jubilee. [British Council Library, Madras]. {NASSDOC*}

Anon, 1986, **Souvenir** : Silver Jubilee. [City Granthalaya Samstha, Hyderabad]. {NASSDOC*}

Anon, 1976, **Souvenir** : Silver Jubilee. [Delhi Public Library, Delhi]. {NASSDOC*}

Anon, 1952, **Souvenir** : Silver Jubilee. [State Regional Library, Guntur]. {NASSDOC*}

Ruggles, Melville J. and Swank, Paynard C., 1962, **Soviet libraries and librarianship** : Report of the visit of the delegation of U.S. librarians to the Soviet Union, May-June, 1961 under the U.S.-Soviet cultural exchange agreement. [American Library Association]. {NASSDOC NMML}

Horner, John, 1973, **Special cataloguing with particular reference to music, films, maps, serials and the multi-media computerised catalogue**. {CRRI ICHR IIC IIT JNU NASSDOC NMML ZHL}

Melville, Annette, comp., 1980, **Special collection in the Library of Congress** : A selective guide. [U.S. Library of Congress]. {USIS}

Worth, Wilfred Ash, 1979, **Special librarianship**. {JNU}

Anon, 1985, **Special librarianship**. [Andhra Pradesh Open University, Hyderabad]. {NASSDOC*}

Silva, Mail, 1970, **Special libraries**. {INSA JNU NERC NMML}

Ada, Winifred John, 1968, **Special libraries** : Development of the concept, their organization and their service. {JNU}

Strable, Edward G., ed., 1966, **Special libraries** : Guide for management. [Special Libraries Association, New York]. {IIC IIT}

Ahrensfelf, Janet L., et al, 1981, **Special libraries** : Guide for management, 2nd edn. {MMTC}

Lewis, Chester M., n.d., **Special libraries** : How to plan and equip them. [Special Libraries Association, New York]. {BIS NMML}

Burkett, Jack, 1963, **Special libraries and documentation centres in the Netherlands** {IIT JNU NASSDOC SPA}

Astall, Raland, 1966, **Special libraries and information bureau** : An examination guidebook. {BIS ICA IIC IIFT IIT MFL NMML SPA}

Saha, J., 1969, **Special libraries and information services in India and in the U.S.A.** {IEG IIT NASSDOC}

Anderson, Beryl L., 1968, **Special libraries in Canada** : A directory. {JNU}

Anon, 1963, **Special libraries of Greater New York**, 10th edn. [Special Libraries Association, New York]. {DUL}

Burkett, J., ed., 1965, **Special library and information services in the United Kingdom**, 2nd edn. [Library Association, London]. {NIEPA}

Thornton, J.L., 1940, **Special library methods** : An introduction to special librarianship. {IEG NAI}

Tower, Isable L., comp., 1947, **Special library resources**, vol. 4. [Special Libraries Association, New York]. {CRRI}

Burkett, J. and Morgan, T.S., 1963, **Special materials in the library**. [Library Association, London]. {IIT}

Markley, Arme Ethelyn, and Fruge, Grete W., 1963, **Special problems in classification and cataloguing.** {DUL}

Harvey, John M., 1976, **Specialised information centres.** {BCL CRRI ICA USIS}

Kent, Allen, 1965, **Specialised information centres.** {JNU}

Anon, n.d., **Specification for the abbreviation of titles of periodicals**, 2 pts., Pt. 1 : Principles; Pt. 2 : World abbreviation. [British Standards Institution]. {CRRI NASSDOC}

Anon, n.d., **Specification for alphabetical arrangement and the filing order of numerals and symbols**. (BS 1749 : 1969). [British Standards Institution]. {CRRI NASSDOC}

Anon, n.d., **Specification for bibliographic information interchange format for magnet tape**. (BS 4748 : 1971). [British Standards Institution]. {CRRI}

Anon, n.d., **Specification for book binding leather**. (IS : 2960-1964). [Indian Standards Institution]. {CRRI}

Anon, n.d., **Specification for book numbering**. (BS 4762 : 1971). [British Standards Institution]. {NASSDOC}

Anon, n.d., **Specification for data elements for the generation and exchange of serials records**. (BS 3532 : 1982). [British Standards Institution]. {CRRI}

Anon, n.d., **Specification for drawing filling equipment,** rev. edn. (IS : 2695-1974). [Indian Standards Institution]. {NASSDOC}

Anon, n.d., **Specification for general structure of preliminary pages of a book (tentative)**. (IS : 790-1956). [Indian Standards Institution]. {NASSDOC}

Anon, n.d., **Specification for librachine (mobile library)**. (IS : 2661-1964). [Indian Standards Institution]. {NASSDOC}

Anon, n.d., **Specification for library catalogue and abstract card**. (IS : 7150-1974) [Indian Standards Institution]. {NASSDOC}

Anon, n.d., **Specification for library furniture and fittings**. (IS : 785-1829 (Pt 1) : 1961). 2 pts. Pt. 1 : Timber; Pt. 2 : Steel. [Indian Standards Institution]. {CRRI NASSDOC}

Anon, n.d., **Specification for packages for use of libraries**. (IS : 2662-1964). [Indian Standards Institution]. {CRRI}

Anon, n.d., **Specification for page sizes for books**. (BS 1413 : 1970). [British Standards Institution]. {NASSDOC}

Anon, n.d., **Specification for the presentation of library directories**. (BS 4605 : 1970) [British Standards Institution]. {CRRI NASSDOC}

Anon, n.d., **Specification for the presentation of serial of publications, including periodicals**. (BS 2509 : 1970). [British Standards Institution]. {NASSDOC}

Anon, n.d., **Specification for sizes of folders and files**. (IS : 5457-1969). [Indian Standards Institution]. {NASSDOC}

Anon, n.d., **Specification for steel filing cabinets for general office purposes,** rev. edn. (IS : 3313-1974). [Indian Standards Institution]. {NASSDOC}

Anon, n.d., **Specification for steel shelving cabinets**, rev. edn. (IS : 3312-1974). [Indian Standards Institution]. {NASSDOC}

Anon, n.d., **Specification for the title leaves of a book**. (BS 4719 : 1971). [British Standards Institution]. {NASSDOC}

Anon, n.d., **Specification for title-page and back of title-page of a book**, rev. edn. (IS : 792-1964). [Indian Standards Institution]. {NASSDOC}

Anon, n.d., **Specification for wooden shelving cabinets (adjustable type)**. (IS : 4116-1967). [Indian Standards Institution]. {NASSDOC}

Nathan, Henry, 1973, **Stable rules** : Science and social transmission. [Organisation for Economic Co-operation and Development, Paris]. {NASSDOC}

Mery, Richard E., 1975, **Staff communication in libraries**. {JNU}

Jones, Noragh and Jordon, Peter, 1982, **Staff management in library and information work**. {IIT NASSDOC NIH}

Durey, Peter, 1976, **Staff management in university and college libraries**, ed. by G. Chandler. {ISI}

Prytherch, R., ed., 1986, **Staff training in libraries** : The British experience. {NASSDOC}

Anon, 1976, **Staffing of public libraries** : A report. [Department of Education and Science, Great Britain]. {BIS IIT ZHL}

Winger, Peter Van and Davis, Stephen Paul, 1982, **Standard citation forms for published bibliographies and catalog used in rare book cataloguing**. [U.S. Library of Congress]. {NASSDOC}

Thillainayagam, V., 1968, **Standard for a book** : The Tamils view. {NASSDOC*}

Anon, 1972, **Standard industrial classification manual**. {TDA}

Anon, 1975, **Standard international trade classification**, 2nd edn. [United Nations Department of Economic and Special Affairs]. {TDA}

Houghton, Bernard, 1969, **Standardization for documentation**. {JNU}

Anon, 1975, **Standardisation in computerised information system** : Papers for technical session. [Indian Standards Institution]. {JNU}

Anon, n.d., **Standardization in the domain of documentation**. [International Organization for Standardization, Hague]. {BIS}

Vashishth, C.P., ed., 1989, **Standardisation in library and information work and services**. [Indian Library Association]. {NASSDOC}

Deshmukh, P.P., 1990, **Standardisation of library and information services** : With special reference to scientific and agricultural libraries. {JNU}

Anon, 1968, **Standards and objectives for school libraries**. [Library Association of Australia]. {JNU}

Anon, 1970, **Standards for library functions at the state level**, rev edn., [American Association of State Libraries, Standards Revision Committee. {USIS}

Withers, E.N., 1976, **Standards for library services** : An international survey. [UNESCO]. {BIS IEG JNU NASSDOC NIEPA NMML}

Anon, 1967, **Standards for library services for the blind and visually handicapped.** [American Library Association]. {DUL}

Anon, 1977, **Standards for public libraries**. (CIFLA publications). {NASSDOC*}

Anon, 1960, **Standards for school library programmes**. [American Association of School Librarians]. {JNU}

Anon, 1967, **Standards for teachers college libraries**. [New Zealand Library Association]. {JNU}

Buhler, Curt F., et al, 1949, **Standards of bibliographical description**. {DUL}

Anon, 1962, **Standards of public library service in England and Wales** : Report of the working party appointed by the Minister of Education in March, 1961. {NASSDOC}

Comey, A.C. and McNamara, Katherine, 1937, **State and national planning.** {ISI}

Maheu, Mary Helen, 1960, **State Department of Education responsibilities for school libraries**. {JNU}

Anon, 1983, **The State Lenin Library of USSR**. {NASSDOC*}

Angelo, Douglas St., et al, 1971, **State library policy** : Its legislative and environmental contexts. {USIS}

Narula, Manju, 1973, **State of the art report on social science documentation in India**. {JNU}

Khurshid, Anis, 1982, **State of library resources in Pakistan**. {JNU}

Lane, Margaret T., 1981, **State publications and depository libraries** : A reference handbook. {USIS}

Verona, Eva, 1971, **Statement of principles adopted at the international conference on cataloguing principles,** October 1961, Paris. [IFLA Committee on Cataloguing, London]. {NASSDOC}

John, Peter W., 1971, **Statistical design and analysis of experiments**. {NASSDOC}

Carpenter, Ray L. and Vasu, Ellan Storey, 1979, **Statistical methods for librarians**. {ISI}

Sardana, J.L. and Sehgal, R.L., 1982, **Statistical methods for librarians**. {ICHR ISI JNU NASSDOC}

Fisher, Ronald A., 1970, **Statistical methods for research workers**, 14th edn. {NASSDOC}

Agrawal, S.P., ch. ed., 1985, **Statistics and data sources**, Pt. 1 : SSDC sources. {NASSDOC}

Eckard, Helen Mary, n.d., **Statistics of public libraries**, 1960-61. {JNU}

Downs, Robert B., 1958, **Status of American college and university librarian**. {JNU}

Anon, 1974, **Status of documentation in India**. [Indian National Scientific Documentation Centre, New Delhi]. {JNU}

Steele, Colin, ed., 1978, **Steady-state, zerogrowth and the academic library** : A collection of essays. {DUL NASSDOC NIEPA}

Gupta, S.R., 1990, **Stock verification in libraries** : Problems and solutions. {DUL}

Hug, William E., ed., 1974, **Strategies for change in information programs**. {DUL USIS}

Caless, T.W., et al, 1970, **Strategies for manipulating Universal Decimal Classification relationships for computer retrieval.** {JNU}

Boaz, Martha, ed., 1981, **Strategies for meeting the information needs of society in the year 2000.** {USIS}

Wilson, Vivian, 1970, **Strategies for problem solving** : Programmed instruction. {NASSDOC}

Cravan, Timothy, 1986, **String indexing**. {JNU NASSDOC}

Kent, Allen and Galvin, Thomas J., eds., 1979, **Structure and governance of library networks** : Proceedings of the 1978 conference in Pittsburg. {JNU}

Bulick, Stephen, 1982, **Structure and subject interaction** : Toward a sociology of knowledge in the social sciences. {BIS}

Kaimann, Richard A., 1973, **Structured information files.** {NASSDOC}

Dahl, O.J., et al, 1972, **Structured programming**. {NASSDOC}

Anon, 1964, **Student use of libraries** : An inquiry into the needs of students, libraries and the educational process. [American Library Association]. {USIS}

Esdaile, Arundell, 1964, **Student's manual of bibliography,** 3rd edn. {CRRI}

Taube, Mortimer, n.d., **Studies in coordinate indexing**. {JNU}

Metcalf, Keyes D., ed., 1960, **Studies in library administrative problems** : Eight reports from a seminar on library administration. {DUL USIS}

Holroyd, Gileon, ed., 1974, **Studies in library management**, vol. 2. {DUL ICA NIPCCD}

Redfern, Brian, ed., 1977, **Studies in library management**, vol. 4. {ICA JNU NAL NIEPA NIPCCD}

Vaughan, Anthony, ed., 1979, **Studies in library management**, vol. 5. {DUL IIT}

Vernon, Jackson William, 1988, **Studies in library resources.** {JNU}

Veaner, Allen B., ed., 1977, **Studies in micropublishing**, 1853-1976. {USIS}

Belson, W.A., 1962, **Studies in readership**. {IIT}

Anon, 1967, **Study of 1967 annual salaries of members of Special Library Association**. [Personnel Committee of Special Libraries Association]. {JNU}

Mukherji, Sudhir Kumar, 1939, **Study of Bengali surnames**. [Linguistic Society of India]. {ZHL}

Anon, 1971, **Study of characteristics, costs and magnitude of inter-library loans in academic libraries**. [Association of Research Libraries, Washington]. {JNU}

Anon, 1961, **Study of circulation control systems** : Public libraries, college and university libraries, special libraries. (Library Technology Project). [American Library Association]. {DUL IIT USIS}

Sudame, G.R., 1972, **Study of the effect of library use on academic achievement of post-graduate students in the M.S. University of Baroda.** {NASSDOC}

Reagon, Agnes Lytton, 1959, **Study of factors influencing college students to become librarians.** {JNU}

De Grolier, E., 1962, **Study of general categories applicable to classification and coding in documentation**, rev edn. tr. by Anthony Thompson. [UNESCO]. {BIS DSSW IEG IIT JNU}

Bikewell, Kenneth Graham Bartlett, 1978, **A study of indexers reactions to the PRECIS indexing system**. [Department of Library and Information Studies, Faculty of Humanities and Social Studies, Liverpool Polytechnic]. {BCL}

Machlup, Fritz and Mansfield, Una, n.d., **Study of information** : Inter- disciplinary messages. {JNU}

Anon, n.d., **Study of the information in the Philippine population programs**. [Population Center Foundation of the Philippines]. {NIH}

Gorman, Michael, 1968, **Study of the rules for entry and heading in the Anglo-American Cataloguing Rules, 1967** : British text. [Library Association, London]. {ZHL}

Estes, Rice, 1953, **Study of seven academic libraries in Brooklyn and their cooperative potential**. {JNU}

Needham, Christopher D. and Herman, Esther, eds., 1970, **Study of subject bibliography with special reference to the social sciences**. [School of Library and Information Services, Maryland]. {NASSDOC}

Anon, 1973, **Study on national structures for documentation and library services in countries with different levels of development, with particular reference to the needs of developing countries**. [UNESCO]. {ICA}

Anon, 1982, **Study report on the feasibility of an international data bank for the non-aligned countries**. [UNESCO]. {NASSDOC}

Oehlerts, Donald E., 1962, **Study to determine the feasibility of establishing a cooperative technical processing program and direct transmission of interlibrary loans**. {DUL}

Anon, 1960, **Studying the community** : A basis for planning library adult education services. (Library Community Project). [American Library Association]. {USIS}

Anon, 1967, **Style manual**, rev. edn. [U..S. Government Printing Office]. {NASSDOC}

Manhiemer, Martha L., 1973, **Style manual** : A guide for the preparation of reports and dissertations. {DUL}

Anon, 1966, **Style manual for authors and printers of Australian Government publications**. [Australia Style Manual Committee, 1964]. {DUL}

Fleischer, Eugene B., 1978, **Style manual for citing microform and non-print media.** [American Library Association]. {BIS}

Arvinda Chandra and Saxena, T.P., 1979, **Style manual for writing theses, dissertations and papers in social sciences.** {DUL}

Milstead, Jessica L., 1984, **Subject access systems** : Alternatives in design. {NASSDOC}

Harris, Jessica Lee, 1970, **Subject analysis** : Computer implications of rigorous definition. {BIS JNU}

Foskett, A.C., 1971, **The subject approach to information**, 2nd edn. {IIMC INSA ISIL JNU NASSDOC ZHL}

Foskett, A.C., 1977, **Subject approach to information**, 3rd edn. {JNU NMML}

Anon, 1981, **Subject authorities** : A guide to subject cataloguing. {USIS}

Hale, Barbara M., 1970, **Subject bibliography of the social sciences and humanities**. {IEG NASSDOC}

Lewin, Evan, 1967, **Subject catalogue of the library of the Royal Empire Society**. {NASSDOC}

Coates, E.J., 1960, **Subject catalogues** : Headings and structure. [Library Association, London]. {IIT NASSDOC}

Berman, Sanford, 1984, **Subject cataloguing**. : Critique and innovation. {JNU}

Brown, James Duff, 1939, **Subject classification for the arrangement of libraries and the organisation of information**, 3rd edn. {DUL}

Ellinger, Werner B., n.d., **Subject classification of law.** {DUL}

Metcalfe, J., 1959, **Subject classifying and indexing of libraries and literature.** {IEG IIT MFL}

Ash, Lee, comp., 1978, **Subject collections** : A guide to special book collections and subject emphasis as reported by university, college, public and special libraries and museums in the United States and Canada, 5th edn. {USIS}

Lewanski, Richard C., ed. and comp., 1978, **Subject collections in European libraries**, 2nd edn. {IIT}

Anon, 1976, **Subject cross reference guide.** {JNU}

Young, M.L., et al, eds., 1975, **Subject directory of special libraries and information centres.** {IIFT}

Anon, n.d., **Subject guide to books in print,** 1970-71; 1974; 1978-79; 1980-81; 1983-84. {NASSDOC}

Anon, 1973, **Subject guide to class 'Ref'** : Current reference books. [University of Cambridge Library]. {NASSDOC}

Kujoth, J.S., 1969, **Subject guide to periodical indexes and review indexes.** {NIH}

Rue, Eloise and Laplanie, Effie, 1952, **Subject heading for children's materials.** [American Library Association]. {ZHL}

Pettee, Julla, 1947, **Subject headings** : The history and theory of the alphabetical subject approach to books. {NAI}

Saifuddin, comp., 1962, **Subject headings** : A list with CC and DDC numbers. {NASSDOC}

Anon, 1951, **Subject headings** : A practical guide. [U.S. Library of Congress]. {CRRI USIS}

Anon, 1954, **Subject headings for financial libraries**. [Special Libraries Association, New York]. {ISI}

Martin, Nella Jane, 1948, **Subject headings used in the dictionary catalogues,** 5th edn. [U.S. Library of Congress]. {ZHL}

Quattlebaum, Marguerite V., ed., n.d., **Subject headings used in the dictionary catalogs of the Library of Congress from 1897 through December 1955,** 6th edn. [U.S. Library of Congress]. {BIS IEG USIS}

Quattlebaum, Marguerite V., ed., n.d., **Subject headings used in the dictionary catalogs of the Library of Congress from 1897 through December 1955** : Supplement to the 6th edn., January 1956-December 1959. [U.S. Library of Congress]. {IEG}

Quattlebaum, Marguerite V., ed., 1966, **Subject headings used in the dictionary catalogs of the Library of Congress,** 7th edn. [U.S. Library of Congress]. {USIS}

Anon, 1969, **Subject indices list.** [Central Reference Library, Calcutta]. {NASSDOC*]

Wellisch, Hans and Wilson, Thomas D., n.d., **Subject retrieval in the seventies** : New directions. {ICHR}

Hunt, K.G., 1955, **Subject specialisation and cooperative book purchase in the libraries of Great Britain**. {DUL}

Sharma, J.S., 1965, **Substance of library science.** {ICHR IIC IIT MFL NIH NERC SPA}

Girja Kumar and Krishan Kumar, 1976, **Suchikaran ke siddhant**. {DUL}

Ranganathan, S.R., 1964, **Suggestions for the organisations of libraries in India**. {NASSDOC}

Hewitt, A.R., 1947, **Summary of public library law in England and Wales, Scotland, Northern Ireland and Eira**, 2nd edn. [Association of Assistant Librarians, London]. {NASSDOC}

Sayers, Frances Clarke, 1965, **Summoned by books** : Essays and speeches, comp. by Marjeanne Jensen Blinn. {USIS}

Fay, Adra M., 1950, **Supervising library personnel**. {DUL}

Anon, 1914, **Supplementary cataloguing rules for the guidance of assistants**. [Imperial Record Department]. {NAI}

Plant, Marjorie, n.d., **Supply of foreign books and periodicals to the libraries of the United Kingdom**. {DUL}

Purton, Rowland W., 1962, **Surrounded by books** : Libraries in primary and middle schools. {JNU NASSDOC}

Anon, 1967, **A survey of the contents of existing national bibliographies**. [UNESCO]. {NASSDOC*}

Ravilious, C.P., 1975, **Survey of existing systems and current proposals for the cataloguing and description of non-book materials collected by libraries with preliminary suggestions for their international co-ordination**. [UNESCO]. {BIS}

Arora, Meena, 1980, **Survey of government documents in Central Secretariat Library 1979-80**. (University of Delhi, Department of Library Science, sessional project). {DUL}

Taylor, James C. and Bowers, David G., 1967, **Survey of organisations : A machine standardised questionnaire instruments.** [Institute of Social Research, Michigan]. {NASSDOC}

Bracken, Marlyn C. and Shilling, Charles W., 1967, **Survey of practice training in information science**. {JNU}

Kalia, D.R., 1965, **Survey of public library services in India** : Tabulated and analysed : Working group on libraries, [Planning Commission, New Delhi]. {NASSDOC*}

Anon, 1957, **Survey of secondary school libraries in U.P.** : Report. [Ministry of Education, New Delhi]. {MHA}

Anon, 1968, **Survey of special libraries serving the Federal Government.** [U.S. Department of Health Education and Welfare]. {BIS}

White, Carl M., 1965, **Survey of the University of Delhi library**. {AIU DSSW DUL IEG IIC NASSDOC NERC SPA}

Ashoor, Mohammed Salem, 1978, **Survey of user attitude towards resource and services of three university libraries in Saudi Arabia**. {JNU}

Tull, Donald S. and Albaum, Gerald S., 1973, **Survey research** : A decisional approach. {NASSDOC}

Srivastava, S.S., 1971, **Survey research technique**. {NASSDOC}

Hjelmquist, Bengt, comp., n.d., **Swedish public libraries in pictures** : Country and small town libraries. {IIT}

Brugghen, W. Van Den, 1975, **Syllabus for a documentation course.** [International Federation for Documentation and Information]. {BIS}

Wynar, Bohdan S., 1962, **Syllabus for research methods in librarianship**. {DUL}

Anon, n.d., **Symbols and notations for correction of illustration and illustration proofs**. (IS : 7140-1971). [Indian Standards Institution]. {NASSDOC}

Pomassel, Gerhand, 1975, **Synoptic tables concerning the current national bibliographies**. {NASSDOC}

Gangadhara Rao, P., 1983, **Synthesis in D.D.C., 18th edn.** [Andhra University, Waltair]. {NASSDOC*}

Gardin, J.C., 1965, **SYNTOL**, ed. by Susan Artandi, 2 vols. [New Jersy Graduate School of Library Science]. {IIT MFL}

Stabley, Don H., 1967, **System/360 Assembler language.** {NASSDOC}

Parkin, Andrew, 1980, **System analysis.** {JNU}

Youssef, Leon A., 1975, **System analysis and design**. {JNU}

Thieravht, Robert J. and Reynolds, George W., 1966, **Systems analysis and design** : A Case study approach. {JNU}

Townley, Helen M., 1978, **System analysis for information retrieval.** {BCL}

Anon, n.d., **System analysis for information sciences**. [Department of Science and Technology, New Delhi]. {BIS CRRI JNU}

Robinson, F., 1969, **System analysis in libraries.** {JNU}

Katzan, Harry, 1976, **System design and documentation**. {JNU}

Hice, G.F., 1974, **System development methodology**. {DUL}

Bliss, H.E., 1936, **System of bibliographic classification**, 2nd edn. {NAI}

Grishiani, J.M., et al, 1984, **System research** : Methodological problems. {JNU}

Anon, 1970, **System scope for library automation and generalised information storage and retrieval at Stanford University**. {IIT}

Kramer, N. and De Smit, Jacob, 1977, **System thinking** : Concepts and notions. {JNU}

Raffel, J.A. and Shiskho, Robert, 1969, **Systematic analysis of university libraries** : Application of cost benefit analysis to the M.I.T. libraries. {AIU DUL IIT JNU NIPCCD SPA}

Roy, R. Paul Mohan, 1984, **Systematic bibliography** : An introduction. {NASSDOC}

Robinson, A.M. Lewin, 1966, **Systematic bibliography** : A practical guide to the work of compilation. {ICHR NASSDOC SPA}

Robinson, A.M. Lewin, 1971, **Systematic bibliography** : A practical guide to the work of compilation, 3rd edn. {NASSDOC}

Ohdedar, A.K., 1975, **Systematic bibliography and documentation**. {ICA ICHR NASSDOC NIH}

Rayward, W. Boyd, 1967, **Systematic bibliography in England, 1850-95**. {DUL}

Optner, Stanford L., ed., 1973, **Systems analysis**. {NASSDOC}

Semprevivo, Philip C., 1976, **Systems analysis** : Definition, process and design. {NASSDOC}

Gough, Chet and Taverekere, Srikantaiah, 1978, **Systems analysis in libraries** : A question and answer approach. {BCL DUL}

Goldberg, Robert L., 1976, **A systems approach to library program development.** {JNU USIS}

Manzoor, Suhail, 1982, **Systems bibliography** : A thirty years' literature survey. {NASSDOC}

Whitehouse, Frank, 1978, **Systems documentation**. {JNU}

Parkin, Anorew, 1980, **Systems management**. {NASSDOC}

Smith, David, 1980, **Systems thinking in library and information management**. {DUL NIPCCD}

Stewart, James D., 1947, **Tabulation of librarianship** : Classified tables for the arrangement of all material relating to library economy. {CRRI}

Moir, P.H., ed., 1952, **Talks on book collecting**. {DUL}

Borko, Harold, ed., 1973, **Targets for research in library education**. [American Library Association]. {USIS}

Thomas, P.A., 1971, **Task analysis of library operations**. [Association of Special Libraries and Information Bureaux]. {DUL IIT}

Easterby, Ronald, ed., 1978, **Tasks, process and information display design** : NATO conference on visual presentation of information, September 4-8, 1978, Birmingham. {BIS}

Grimshaw, Ernest, 1960, **Teacher librarian**. {JNU}

Douglas, M.P., 1949, **Teacher librarians handbook**. [American Library Association]. {DUL NIEPA ZHL}

Ernest, Roe, 1966, **Teachers, librarians and children** : A study of libraries in education. {IIT}

Hostrop, Richard W., 1968, **Teaching and the community college library**. {JNU}

Finn, David, et al, 1978, **Teaching manual for tutor-librarians**. {JNU}

Branscomb, Harvie, 1940, **Teaching with books** : A study of college libraries. [American Library Association]. {ZHL}

Branscomb, Harvie, 1964, **Teaching with books** : A study of college libraries. {DUL}

Anon, 1979, **Technical and specialised periodicals published in Britain, 1972-73**. [Central Office of Information, London]. {NASSDOC}

Neal, K.W., 1965, **Technical college libraries** : Finchfield. {DUL IIT}

Thompson, G.A., 1969, **Technical college library** : A primer for its development. {AIU DUL IIT}

Houghton, Bernard, 1972, **Technical information sources** : A guide to patent specification, standards and technical reports literature. {BIS}

Slater, M., 1964, **Technical libraries.** {IIT}

Jackson, Lucile, ed., 1951, **Technical libraries** : Their organisation and management. [Special Libraries Association, New York]. {CRRI ISI}

Maltha, D.J., 1976, **Technical literature search and the written report**. {BCL}

Charen, Thelma, 1975, **Technical notes** : MEDLARS indexing instructions. [National Library of Medicine, Maryland]. {CRRI}

Tauber, Maurice F., et al, 1953, **Technical services in libraries** : Acquisitions, cataloguing, classification, binding, photographic. {IEG NAI ZHL}

Kochen, Manfred, 1963, **Techniques for document retrieval research** : State of art. {JNU}

Willemin, Silvere, 1966, **Technique of union catalogue** : A practical guide. [UNESCO]. {IIMC NASSDOC NERC}

Vickery, B.C., 1970, **Techniques of information retrieval**. {AIU BCL IEG IIMC INSA JNU}

Hattery, Lowell H. and Bush, George P., 1973, **Technological change in printing and publishing**. {INSA}

Anon, 1980, **Technology in support of library science and information service**. [Sarada Ranganathan Endowment for Library Science, Bangalore]. {BIS}

King, Donald W., 1981, **Telecommunications and libraries** : A primer for librarians and information managers. {USIS}

Schieber, William D. and Schofler, Ralph M., 1968, **Telefascimile in libraries** : A report of an experiment in fascimile transmission and an analysis of implication for inter library loan system. {JNU}

Morehouse, H.G., 1966, **Telefascimile services between libraries with the xerox management telescopier**. {JNU}

Anon, 1955, **Ten years of United Nations publication, 1945-55** : A complete catalogue. [United Nations]. {DSSW}

Wersig, Gernot and Neveling, Ulrich, comps., 1976, **Terminology of documentation**. [UNESCO]. {JNU NASSDOC NIPCCD ZHL}

Boswell, David, B., 1952, **Text-book on bibliography.** {DUL}

Kent, Allen, 1962, **Textbook on mechanised information retrieval**. {CRRI}

Anon, 1979, **Theoretical problems of informatics** : Forecasting of the development of scientific information activities. [International Federation for Documentation and Information]. {CRRI}

Anon, 1981, **Theoretical problems of information** : Criteria of the quality of information systems and processes : Collection of papers. [International Federation for Documentation and Information]. {BIS}

Anon, 1979, **Theoretical problems of information** : New trends in information and its terminology. [International Federation for Documentation and Information]. {CRRI}

Oberman, Cerise and Strauch, Katina, eds., 1982, **Theories of bibliographic education** : Designs for teachings. {JNU}

Harbo, Ols, ed., 1980, **Theory and applications of information research** : Proceedings : International research forum on information science, 2nd, August 3-6, 1977, Copenhagen. {BCL}

Schneider, George, 1961, **Theory and history of bibliography**, tr. by Ralph Robert Shaw. {NASSDOC}

Johnson, Richard A., et al, 1973, **Theory and management of systems**. {JNU}

Job, M.M., 1978, **Theory of book selection**. {NERC NIPCCD}

Girja Kumar and Krishan Kumar, 1977, **Theory of cataloguing**, 2nd edn. {ICHR IIT ISIL JNU MMTC NASSDOC NCAER NCDC NERC NIPCCD ZHL}

Girja Kumar and Krishan Kumar, 1982, **Theory of cataloguing**, 4th edn. {ZHL}

Olligg, P.J., 1966, **Theory of cataloguing** : An examination guide book. {NASSDOC SPA}

Davison, Fla Keith, 1966, **Theory of classification**. {ICHR IIT MFL NERC ZHL}

Krishan Kumar, 1979, **Theory of classification**. {BIS ICA ISI JNU ZHL}

Krishan Kumar, 1981, **Theory of classification**, 2nd rev. edn. {NASSDOC NMML}

Krishan Kumar, 1983, **Theory of classification**, 3rd edn. {ZHL}

Landry, Bertrand Clovis, 1971, **Theory of indexing** : Indexing theory as a model for information storage and retrieval. [Computer and Information Science Research Centre, Ohio State University]. {IIT}

Srivastava, A.P., 1973, **Theory of knowledge classification in libraries**. {CRRI ICA ICHR IIT JNU NASSDOC NERC SPA ZHL}

Rawski, Conrad H. and Towaid, A., eds., 1973, **Theory of librarianship** : Papers in honour of Jesse H. Shera. {NASSDOC*}

Buchanan, Brian, 1979, **Theory of library classification**. {DUL}

Chan, Lois Mai, et al, eds., 1985, **Theory of subject analysis** : A source book, {NASSDOC}

Mac Cafferty, Maxine, 1977, **Thesauri and thesauri construction**. [Association of Special Libraries and Information Bureaux]. {CRRI NASSDOC}

Agrawal, S.P., ch ed., 1987, **Thesauri, glossaries, terminologies and dictionaries**. {NASSDOC}

Gilchrist, Alan, 1971, **Thesauri in retrieval**. [Association of Special Libraries and Information Bureaux]. {BCL CRRF DUL IIT NASSDOC}

Anon, 1969, **Thesaurus and faceted classification for engineering and related subjects.** {IIT}

Aitchison, Jean and Gilchrist, Alan, 1972, **Thesaurus construction** : A practical manual. {CRRI}

Lancaster, F.W., 1985, **Thesaurus construction and use** : A condensed course. [UNESCO]. {NASSDOC}

Townley, Helen M. and Goe, Ralph C., 1980, **Thesaurus-making** : Grow your own word-stock. {NASSDOC}

Weiss, Irving and Weiss, Anne De Lavergne, eds., and comps., 1981, **Thesaurus of book digests, 1950-1980.** {USIS}

Anon, 1976, **Thesaurus of descriptors used for information processing in the ILO library**. [ILO]. {NASSDOC}

Goodman, Frederick, 1970, **Thesaurus of ERIC descriptors, with a special chapter on the role and function of thesaurus in education.** [U.S. Educational Resources Information Centre]. {USIS}

Anderson, Janathan, et al, 1970, **Thesis and assignment writing**. {DUL}

Anon, 1977, **Third European congress on information systems and networks overcoming the language barrier, Luxembourg**. {JNU}

Makkar, G.C., 1974, **Three number author table**. {BIS ZHL}

Mumford, W.A. comp., 1939, **Three thousand books for a public library** : Some significant and representative works for basic stock. {NAI}

Anon, 1969, **Title-leaves of a book**. (ISO/R 1086-1969) (E). [International Organisation for Standardisation, Geneva]. {NASSDOC*}

Baer, Eleanora A., 1971, **Titles in series** : A handbook for libraries and students : Supplement to 2nd edn. {NASSDOC}

Daniel, Gore, 1978, **To know a library** : Essays and annual report, 1975-76. {JNU}

Jordan, Robert Thayer, 1970, **Tomorrow's library** : Direct access and delivery. {USIS}

Ramachandra Rao, T., 1974, **Torch-bearer of public library movement** : Andhra Pradesh library field workers conference, 1974, Gudiwada. {NASSDOC*}

French, Ruth, ed., n.d., **Toward a better cataloguing code**. {IEG}

Trezza, Alphonse F., 1982, **Toward a federal library and information services network** : A proposal. {USIS}

Fairthorne, Robert Arthur, 1961, **Towards information retrieval**. {JNU}

Barquin, Raman C. and Mead, Graham P., n.d., **Towards the information society**. {DUL}

Rubinoff, Morris, ed., 1965, **Towards a national information system** : Second annual national colloquium on information retrieval. {IIT}

Anon, 1975, **Toward a national program for library and information services** : Goals for action. [U.S. National Commission on Libraries and Information Science]. {USIS}

Lancaster, F.W., 1978, **Toward paperless information system**. {BCL DUL IIFT ISI ISIL USIS}

Perreault, Jean M., 1969, **Towards a theory for U.D.C.** : Essays aimed at structural understanding and operational improvement. {ICHR NASSDOC}

Anon, 1970, **Training course in documentation techniques in Asia, July 20—August 21, 1970, Tokyo**. [Japanese National Commission for UNESCO]. {NASSDOC}

Stene, Elizabeth, 1967, **Training for the improvement of library administration.** {JNU}

Knight, G. Norman, ed., 1970, **Training in indexing** : A course. [Society of Indexers]. {IEG IIFT IIT NASSDOC}

Costello, John C., n.d., **Training manual and work book for use in abstracting and coordinate indexing**. [Battelle Memorial Institute, Ohio]. {BIS}

Anon, 1964, **Transactions** : Prague conference on information theory, statistical decision function, random processes, June 3, 1962. {INSA}

Kaiser, Frances E., 1959, **Translators and translations** : Services and sources. {JNU}

Anon, 1962, **Transliteration of Hebrew** (ISO/R 259-1962) (E). [International Organisation for Standardisation, Geneva]. {NASSDOC}

Konnur, M.B., 1990, **Transnational library relations** : The Indo-American experience. {NASSDOC}

Goodrum, Charles A., 1980, **Treasures of the Library of Congress.** {USIS}

Chakrabarti, A.K., 1983, **A treatise on book selection.** {NERC NIH ZHL}

Kaula, P.N., 1985, **A treatise on Colon Classification appended with a select bibliography on the scheme**. {NASSDOC NMML}

Collison, R.L., 1957, **Treatment of special material in libraries.** {MFL}

Anon, 1987, **Trends 1985-86** : Report to the Council by the Secretary General. [International Federation of Library Associations and Institutions]. {NASSDOC*}

Hills, Philip J., ed., 1982, **Trends in information transfer**. {ISI NASSDOC}

Burkett, Jack, ed., 1968, **Trends in special librarianship**. {IEG IIT MMTC}

Varma, A.K., 1984, **Trends in subject indexing.** {NASSDOC NMML}

Ghosh, G.B. and Banerjee, B.N., 1974, **Trends of information service in India.** {AIU CRRI ICHR NASSDOC NERC NIH NIPCCD ZHL}

Vashishth, C.P., ed., 1983, **Twenty years of Library Herald** : A cumulative index to Vols. 1-20, 1958-59 to 1981. [Delhi Library Association]. {IIT NASSDOC}

Anon, 1961, **UDC**, 3rd edn. [British Standards Institution]. {ICCR}

Bose, H., 1987, **U.D.C.** : Theory and practice. {JNU}

Anon, 1975, **UK MARC manual**. {Bibliographic Services Division, British Library, London]. {JNU}

Anon, 1980, **UK MARC manual**, 2nd edn. [Bibliographic Services Division, British Library, London]. {BIS}

Jeffreys, A.E. and Wison, T.D., 1970, **UK MARC project** : Proceedings of seminar organised by the cataloguing and indexing group of the Library Association at the University of Southampton, March 28-30, 1976. {NASSDOC}

Anon, 1974, **U.N. report** : Working meeting on Asian resources for a Population Library Information Network, September 13-15, 1973, Bangkok. [U.N. Economic Commission for Asia and the Far East]. {NIH}

Anon, 1981, **UNBIS thesaurus** : List of terms used in indexing and cataloguing of documents and other materials relevant to United Nations programmes and activities. [Dag Hammerskjold Library]. {JNU}

Parker, J. Stephen, 1985, **UNESCO and library development planning.** {DUL}

Anon, n.d., **UNESCO list of documents and publications** : 1972/76, 1980-81. [UNESCO]. {NASSDOC}

Aitchison, Jean, comp., 1977, **UNESCO thesaurus**, Vol. 1 : Introduction, classified thesaurus permitted index hierarchical display; Vol. 2 : Alphabetical thesaurus. [UNESCO]. {NASSDOC}

Anon, 1978, **UNISIST** : A study on the application of scientific and technological information in development. [UNESCO]. {JNU}

Anon, 1971, **UNISIST** : Synopsis of the feasibility study on a World Science Information System. [UNESCO; International Council of Scientific Unions]. {BIS DSSW IIMC NASSDOC ZHL}

Anon, 1980, **UNISIST guide for the establishment and evaluation of services for selective dissemination of information.** [UNESCO]. {CRRI}

Anon, 1980, **UNISIST guide to standards for information handling.** [UNESCO]. {BIS DUL MMTC}

Anon, 1979, **UNISIST guidelines for editors of scientific and technical journals.** [UNESCO]. {DUL}

Anon, 1981, **UNISIST guidelines for the establishment and development of monolingual thesauri**, 2nd edn. [UNESCO]. {BIS}

Anon, 1978, **UNISIST guidelines for the evaluation of information systems and services.** [UNESCO]. {BIS}

Anon, 1978, **UNISIST guidelines for formulating policy on education, training and development of library and information personnel.** [UNESCO]. {BIS}

Anon, 1975, **UNISIST guidelines for the organisation of training courses, workshops and seminars in scientific and technical information and documentation.** [UNESCO]. {BIS}

Anon, 1974, **UNISIST information policy objectives.** [UNESCO]. {JNU}

Anon, 1977, **UNISIST information networks for online bibliographic retrieval.** [UNESCO]. {BIS DUL}

Anon, 1973, **UNISIST International Serials Data Systems (ISDS).** [UNESCO]. {BIS}

Anon, 1978, **UNISIST international system and networks for technology transfer.** [UNESCO]. {BIS}

Anon, 1971, **UNISIST study report on the feasibility of a world science information.** [UNESCO]. {BIS DSSW IIMC NASSDOC ZHL}

Anon, n.d., **USA standard** : Basic criteria for indexes, rev edn., (USAS Z 39. 4-1968). [American National Standards Institute]. {NASSDOC}

Anon, 1968, **USA standard for compiling book publishing statistics.** (USAS Z 39.8 1968). [American National Standards Institute]. {NASSDOC}

Anon, 1969, **USA standard for permanent and durable library catalogue cards.** (USAS Z 35.1-1969). [American National Standards Institute]. {NASSDOC}

Braden, Irene A., 1970, **The undergraduate library.** [American Library Association]. {USIS}

Donohue, Joseph C., 1973, **Understanding scientific literatures** : A bibliometric approach. {INSA}

Hall, David E., 1971, **Union catalogue of Asian publications, 1965-1970.** {NASSDOC}

Das, A.R., n.d., **Union catalogue of the books in the libraries of the Botanical Survey of India**, 3 vols. [Botanical Survey of India]. {INSA}

Dutta, Rajeshwari, 1970, **Union catalogue of the Central Government of India publications held by libraries in London, Oxford and Cambridge**. [Centre of South Asian Studies, University of Cambridge, Mansell]. {NASSDOC}

Mac Donald, Teresa, 1970, **Union catalogue of the Government of Ceylon publications held by libraries in London, Oxford and Cambridge**. [Centre of South Asian Studies, University of Cambridge, Mansell]. {NASSDOC}

Agrawal, S.P., ch. ed., 1986, **Union catalogue of library and information science publications** : Delhi libraries. {NASSDOC}

Chopra, R.N., 1979, **Union catalogue of library science periodical holdings in Delhi University Library system, Jawahar Lal Nehru University Library and National Science Library**. [Indian National Scientific Documentation Centre]. {DUL}

Agrawal, S.P., ch. ed., 1983, **Union catalogue of newspapers** : Delhi libraries. {NASSDOC}

Agrawal, S.P., ch. ed., 1973-76, **Union catalogue of social science periodicals/serials**, 32 vols. {NASSDOC}

Brummel, L., 1956, **Union catalogues** : Their problems and organisation. [UNESCO]. {CRRI}

Agrawal, S.P., ch. ed., 1983, **Union list of current social science periodicals** : Delhi libraries. {NASSDOC}

Agrawal, S.P., ch. ed., 1986, **Union list of social science periodicals** : Lucknow. {NASSDOC}

Agrawal, S.P., ch. ed., 1982, **Union list of social science periodicals received in Delhi libraries**. {NASSDOC}

Anon, 1978, **United Nations document series symbols, 1946-1977** : Cumulative list with index. [United Nations]. {IIFT}

Garde, P.K., 1970, **The United Nations family of libraries**. {ICA ICHR INSA NASSDOC NMML}

Dale, Doris Cruger, 1970, **United Nations library** : Its origin and development. {JNU NASSDOC USIS}

Anderson, Dorothy, 1974, **Universal bibliographic control** : A long term policy, a plan for action. {JNU}

Foskett, A.C., 1973, **Universal Decimal Classification.** {ZHL}

Govrilova, S.A., 1979, **Universal Decimal Classification** : Its structure, application and tables : Revision procedure. [UNESCO; UNION, Moscow]. {NASSDOC}

Kyle, Barbara and Vickery, B.C., 1961, **The Universal Decimal Classification** : Present position and future developments. [UNESCO]. {ICA}

Anon, 1965, **Universal Decimal Classification** : Special subject edition for education. {DUL}

Anon, 1964, **Universal Decimal Classification** : Special subject edition for metallurgy. {DUL}

Sardana, J.L., 1983, **Universal Decimal Classification** : Structure and methodology. {BIS ICHR IIT JNU ZHL}

Anon, 1969, **Universal Decimal Classification** : Ten years supplement to abridged UDC editions, 1958-1968. [UNESCO; FID]. {ICA IIMC IIT NASSDOC}

Anon, 1958, **Universal Decimal Classification** : Trilingual abridged edition. {JNU}

Anon, 1969, **Universal reference system**, 10 vols. {NMML}

Rayward, W. Boyd, 1975, **The universe of information**. [International Federation of Documentation and Information]. {CRRI}

Anon, 1965, **University and college libraries.** [University Grants Commission, New Delhi]. {BIS DUL IEG IIMC IIT JNU NIEPA}

Anon, 1959, **University and college libraries** : Containing the report and the proceedings of the Seminar on 'from publisher to reader' held on March 4-7, 1966. [University Grants Commission, New Delhi]. {DUL NASSDOC}

Saunders, W.L., ed., 1968, **University and research library studies**. {AIU DUL IIC IIT ISI JNU SPA}

Stirling, John K., 1987, **Univesity librarianship**. {JNU}

Kesavan, B.S., 1967, **University libraries and education for librarianship in India**. {JNU}

Lincoln, Cynthia Mary, ed., 1976, **University libraries as information centres** : Proceedings of IATUL sixth meeting, 1975. {DCL}

Gelfand, M.A., 1971, **University libraries for developing countries**. [UNESCO]. {AIU DUL ICA IIMC IIT JNU NIEPA NMML USIS}

Bryan, Harrison, 1976, **University libraries in Britain** : A network. {JNU NIEPA}

Srivastava, Shyam Nath, 1980, **University libraries in India** : Their organisation and administration. {DUL IIT ISI JNU NERC NIEPA NIPCCD}

Viswanathan, C.G., 1972, **University libraries of India** : Principles and policy. {AIU DUL IIC JNU NIEPA NMML}

Sharma, Chandra Kant, 1977, **University library** : Its management and organisation. {DUL JNU}

Wilson, Louis Round and Tauber, Maurice F., 1945, **University library** : Its organisation, administration and functions, 2nd edn. {JNU}

Rogers, Rutherford D. and Weber, David C., 1971, **University library administration**. {DUL NASSDOC USIS}

Rajwant Singh, 1984, **University library buildings in India**. {AIU BIS DUL IIT JNU MMTC NASSDOC NIEPA}

Tejomurty, A., 1981, **University library finances in Madhya Pradesh** : A comparative study. {NASSDOC}

Deshpande, K.S., 1985, **University library system in India**. {JNU NASSDOC NMML}

Mount, Ellis, 1975, **University science and engineering libraries** : Their operations, collections and facilities. {CRRI IIT}

Smith, Lillian H., n.d., **Unreluctant years**. [American Library Association]. {ZHL}

Durr, W.T. and Rosenberg, Paul, comp., 1977, **Urban information thesaurus** : A vocabulary for social documentation. {JNU}

Garfield, Eugene, 1964, **Use of citation data in writing the history of science** {DUL}

Anon, 1982, **Use of computer in libraries** : Summary of the proceedings of a seminar held on March 15, 1982, New Delhi. {NASSDOC}

Sarin, Ashok Kumar, 1987, **Use of journals in libraries** : A cost effectiveness analysis. {JNU}

Sharma, C.D., 1978, **Use of libraries** : A guide to better use of libraries and their resources. {CRRI ICA IIT MMTC NASSDOC NCAER NCDC NIPCCD NMML}

Smith, Paul, 1980, **Use of libraries and the literature of human geography**. {SPA}

Dhyani, Pushpa, 1979, **Use of library classification schemes in Indian libraries with special reference to Delhi**. {NASSDOC}

Kent, Allen, et al, 1979, **Use of library materials** : The University of Pittsburg study. {CRRI USIS}

Schimmelpfeng, Richard H. and Cook, C. Donald, 1968, **The use of Library of Congress Classification** : Proceedings : Institute on the use of the Library of Congress classification, 1966, New York. [American Library Association]. {USIS}

Vernon, D.C., 1975, **Use of management and business literature.** {MMTC}

Coblans, Herbert, 1966, **Use of mechanized methods in documentation work.** {JNU}

Anon, 1985, **Use of microprocessors in information analysis and library applications.** [Society for Information Science]. {NASSDOC}

Nagarajan, S., ed., 1988, **Use of microprocessor in information analysis and library applications.** {NASSDOC}

Cowley, J.D., 1947, **Use of reference material.** {ZHL}

Auger, Charles P., ed., 1975, **Use of reports in literature.** {INSA JNU}

Anon, n.d., **Use of television by public library.** [American Library Association]. {JNU}

Anon, 1965, **User and library information service.** [Indian Association of Special Libraries and Information Centres]. {IIFT}

Mac Cafferty, Maxine, 1977, **User education** : Towards a better use of information resources. {BCL}

Fjallbrant, Nancy and Malley, Ian, 1984, **User education in libraries.** {DUL JNU NASSDOC NIEPA}

Fjallbrant, Nancy, 1977, **User education programmes in Swedish academic libraries** : A study of developments in the year 1973-77. {JNU}

Ford, Geoffrey, 1979, **User studies** : An introduction guide and select bibliography. [Centre for Research of User Studies, University of Sheffield, Sheffield]. {NASSDOC}

Anon, 1981, **User surveys and evaluation of library services** [Association of Research Libraries, Washington]. {NASSDOC}

Stone, Phillip J., 1968, **User's manual for the general inquirer.** {NASSDOC}

Anon, 1970, **Users of documentation.** {JNU}

Baker, E.A., ed., n.d., **Uses of libraries.** {AIU}

Aldrich, Ella V., 1960, **Using books and libraries**, 4th edn. {ZHL}

Aldrich, Ella V., 1967, **Using books and libraries**, 5th edn. {DUL NASSDOC USIS}

Whittaker, Kenneth, 1965, **Using libraries.** {CRRI IIT MFL}

Whittaker, Kenneth, 1972, **Using libraries** : An information guide for students and general users, 3rd edn. {ICA}

Brogan, Gerald E. and Buck, Jeanne T., 1969, **Using libraries effectively.** {ICA}

Dresser, Maxwell, 1957, **Using the library for reference and research.** {JNU}

Rossoff, Martin, 1964, **Using your high school library.** {JNU}

Grisnshaw, E., 1963, **Using your library.** {JNU}

Sehgal, R.L., 1985, **Vargikaran siddhant evam vyavhar.** {NASSDOC}

Miller, Shirley, 1971, **The vertical file and its satelites** : A handbook. {DUL USIS}

Katz, Bill and Fraley, Ruth A., 1983, **Video to online** : Reference services and the new technology. {JNU}

Howerton, P.W., 1963, **Vistas in information handling** : The augmentation of man's intellect by machine. {MHA}

Williams, Patrick and Pearce, Joan T., 1978, **The vital network** : A theory of communication and society. {USIS}

Thempson, Anthony, comp., n.d., **Vocabularium bibliothecari** {IEG}

Jennings, Jerdson T., 1930, **Voluntary education through the public library.** [American Library Association]. {NASSDOC*}

Rajjan Lal and Kidwai, Nasira, 1980, **Vyavaharik suchikaran vidhi**. {NASSDOC}

Slote, Stanley J., 1982, **Weeding library collections**, 2nd rev edn. {DUL USIS}

Khurshid, Anis, 1976, **What children read** : A survey. [National Book Council of Pakistan, Karachi]. {ZHL}

Cooper, M.J., 1969, **What computers can do** : A guide to the plain man. {DUL}

Sellen, Betty Carol, ed., 1980, **What else can you do with a library degree**. {IIT}

Burke, Remend A., 1952, **What is the index**. {NAI}

Waples, Douglas, et al, 1940, **What reading does to people**. {NAI}

Kaula, P.N., ed., 1965, **What they say**. [Ranganathan Volume Committee, Varanasi]. {NASSDOC*}

Thomas, P.A. and Ward, Valerie A., 1973, **Where the time goes.** [Association of Special Libraries and Information Bureaux]. {AIU CRRI IIT}

Hillard, James M., 1975, **Where to find what** : A handbook to reference service. {JNU}

Landau, T., 1972, **Who's who in librarianship and information science,** 2nd edn. {JNU}

Ward, Patricia Layzell, 1966, **Women and librarianship** : An investigation into certain problems of library staffing. {DUL}

Anon, 1987, **Women's information network for Asia and Pacific**. [United Nations Economic and Social Commission for Asia and Pacific, Bangkok]. {NASSDOC}

Stefferud, Alfred, ed., 1972, **Wonderful world of books**. {ZHL}

Eddison, Elizabeth B. and Lyman, Lois B., eds. and comps., 1981, **Words that mean business** : 3,000 terms for access to business information. {USIS}

Corrigan, Dorothy D., 1967, **Workbook for a successful workshop**. [American Library Association]. {USIS}

Anon, 1964, **Working conditions in Canadian public libraries**. [Canadian Library Association]. {JNU}

Anon, 1983, **Working document on scientific and technological information in Asia and the Pacific.** [UNESCO]. {NASSDOC}

Kumar, P.S.G., ed., 1989, **Working documents** : Workshop on norms, guidelines and standards for library and information science education. [Nagpur University Department of Library and Information Science, Nagpur]. {NASSDOC}

Anon, 1968, **Working of central museums** : Report : Central museums review committee, 1968, New Delhi. {AIU}

Anon, 1979, **Working papers** : All India library conference, 25th, May 14-18, 1979, Trivandrum. [Indian Library Association]. {ICA NCDC NMML}

Anon, 1980, **Working papers** : Seminar on library buildings in India, February 11-13, 1980, New Delhi. [NISSAT].

Anon, 1964, **Working papers** : Seminar on use of microforms and space management in libraries. [Sri Venkateshwar University Library, Tirupati].

Anon, 1970, **Working papers and proceedings** : DRTC seminar on cataloguing, 1970, Bangalore. [Documentation Research and Training Centre, Bangalore]. {NASSDOC}

Anon, 1971, **Working papers and proceedings** : DRTC seminar on reference service. [Documentation Research and Training Centre, Bangalore]. {NASSDOC}

Anon, 1967, **Working papers and proceedings** : IASLIC conference, 4th, 1967, Dhanbad. [Indian Association of Special Libraries and Information Centres]. {SPA}

Anon, 1965, **Working papers and proceedings** : IASLIC seminar, 2nd, 1965, Chandigarh : Part-I : Users and library information services. [Indian Association of Special Libraries and Information Centres]. {SPA}

Anon, n.d., **Working papers and proceedings of the three symposia**, I : General vs special classification schemes; II : Inter library loan and exchange of materials in India; III : Social science documentation in India : IASLIC seminar, 3rd, 1964, Lucknow; [Indian Association of Special Libraries and Information Centres]. {NASSDOC SPA}

Anon, 1966, **Working papers for the symposia** : IASLIC conference, 5th, 1963, Pune, Pt. I : Document and data processing in academic research and special libraries in India; Pt. II : Problems and prospects of library associations in India. [Indian Association of Special Libraries and Information Centres]. {NASSDOC}

Anon, 1967, **Working papers for the symposia** : IASLIC conference, 6th, 1965, Trivandrum, Pt 1-3 : Colon Classification local documentation lists, library organisation and social science research, 1967; Pt. 4 : Colon Classification, local documentation lists, library organisation and social science research, 1967. [Indian Association of Special Libraries and Information Centres]. {NASSDOC SPA}

Anon, 1966, **Working papers of the two symposia** : IASLIC seminar, 4th 1966, Hyderabad, Pt. 1 : Procurement of government publications and technical reports; Pt. 2 : Devaluation : Its impact on the development of libraries in India. [Indian Association of Special Libraries and Information Centres]. {NASSDOC SPA}

Anon, 1968, **Working papers for the symposia** : IASLIC seminar, 5th, October 7-9, 1968, Durgapur, Pt. I : Selective dissemination of information for India; Pt. II : Functions and problems of library personnel in special libraries of India. [Indian Association of Special Libraries and Information Centres]. {NASSDOC}

Anon, 1986, **Workshop on computer application to library and information activities.** [ILA NISSAT]. {JNU}

Anon, 1972, **World guide to library school and training course in documentation**. [UNESCO]. {ICA IIT JNU NASSDOC NERC NIEPA USIS}

Anon, 1969, **World guide to technical information and documentation services.** [UNESCO]. {CRRI NMML}

Anon, 1975, **World guide to technical information and documentation services**, 2nd edn. [UNESCO]. {JNU NASSDOC}

Benz, Magdalena Krommer, 1977, **World guide to terminological activities**. {JNU}

Krzys, Richard, 1983, **World librarianship**. {IIT NMML}

Wilson, John H., ed., 1973, **A world of information** : American society for information science meeting, 35th, October 23-26, 1972, Washington, D.C. {USIS}

Bramley, Gerald, 1975, **World trends in library education**. {AIU IIT NERC NIEPA USIS}

Esdaile, Arundell, n.d., **World's great libraries,** 1934-1937 2 vols. {NAI}

Charles, Compbell, 1963, **Writer's reference book** : A reference work for authors, freelance journalists and writers for film, radio and television. {DUL}

Drewry, John Eldridge, 1966, **Writing book reviews**. {DUL}

Khawar, Rafiq, comp., 1963, **Writing for new readers** : A handbook. [Pakistan National Book Council, Karachi]. {ZHL}

Colby, Jean Polndexter, 1967, **Writing, illustrating and editing children's books,** rev. edn. {DUL}

Rajagopalan, T.S., ed., 1988, **Year's work in Indian librarianship, 1987**. [Indian Library Association]. {NASSDOC}

Kohn, Rita T. and Tepper, Krysta, 1981, **You can do it** : Manual for librarians. {USIS}

Clarke, J.D., 1963, **Your future as a librarian.** {IIFT}
Anon, 1963, **Your library** : Readers guide to Karnatak University Library, Dharwar. {NASSDOC}
Katz, William A., 1979, **Your library** : A reference guide. {USIS}
Katz, William A., 1984, **Your library** : A reference guide, 2nd edn. {JNU NASSDOC}
Lolley, John L., 1974, **Your library** : What's in it for you. {CRRI}
Barnes, Melvyn, 1978, **Youth library work** : Exploratory essays, 2nd edn. {IIT}

3

SUBJECT APPROACH

AACR2 : Entries and procedure. {NASSDOC}

AACR2 : Practice and theory. {JNU NASSDOC}

AACR2 decisions and rule interpretations : A consolidation of the decision and rule interpretations for the Anglo-American Cataloguing Rules, 2nd. edn. assisted by Glenna E. Stevens. [Canadian Library Association]. {USIS}

AACR2 institute handbook : The Library of Congress interpretation and application of the Anglo-American Cataloguing Rules, 2nd. edn. [U.S. Library of Congress; American Library Association]. {USIS}

ABC : Abridged building classification for architects, builders, civil engineers. [International Council for Building Research Studies and Documentation, Rotterdam]. {BIS}

ABC for book collectors. {IIT}

ABC of library science. {NASSDOC}

ABC's of library promotion. {DEPT JNU}

ADDLIB : A packaged computer programme for processing, etc. {JNU NIH}

ALA cataloguing rules for author and title entries. {BIS CRRI DSSW ICA IIFT IIT MFL NIEPA SPA TDA USIS ZHL}

ALA filing rules. [American Library Association]. {USIS}

The ALA glossary of library and information science. [American Library Association]. {USIS}

ALA glossary of library terms. [American Library Association]. {BIS CRRI ZHL}

ALA glossary of library terms with a selection of terms in related fields. [American Library Association]. {IIT NASSDOC}

ALA handbook of organisation, 1979-80. [American Library Association]. {NASSDOC USIS}

ALA membership directory, 1979-80 [American Library Association]. {NASSDOC USIS}

ALA rules for filing catalogue cards. [American Library Association]. {CRRI IIT}

ALA rules for filing catalogue cards, 2nd. edn. [American Library Association]. {BIS IIT JNU NIEPA NMML USIS}

ALA world encyclopaedia of library and information services. [American Library Association]. {IIT NASSDOC NCERT NERC USIS}

ALA year book: A review of library events, 1979. {IIT JNU USIS}

APINESS : Report : UNESCO/AASSREC regional meeting of experts to develop Asia Pacific Information Network in Social Sciences, May 12-16, 1986, Bangkok. {NASSDOC}

ASLIB directory : Information sources in medicine, the social sciences and the humanities. 2 vols. {IIT NASSDOC}

ASLIB directory of information sources in the United Kingdom, vol. 1: Science, Technology & Commerce, 5th edn. {JNU}

ASLIB meeting on planning and equipment of special libraries, April 6, 1946, London. {CRRI}

ASLIB seminar for information planners and industry, May 13-14, 1976, Boaconfield. {BCL NASSDOC}

Abbreviated citation. {DEPT}

Abbreviated citation : A bibliographical problem. {DUL}

Abbreviations for titles of periodicals. [Indian Standards Institution]. {AIU}

Abbreviations of generic names in titles of periodicals. [International Organisation for Standardisation, Geneva]. (ISO/R 833-1968) (E/F). {NASSDOC}

Abbreviations of typical words in bibliographical references. [International Organisation for Standardisation, Geneva]. (ISO/R 832-1968) (E/F). {NASSDOC}.

About a method of constructing information languages having grammar. {DEPT JNU}

Abridged Bliss Classification : The bibliographic classification of Henry Evelyn Bliss revised for school libraries. [Bliss Classification Working Party]. {DUL}

Abridged Decimal Classification and Relative Index, 5th. edn. {DEPT ZHL}

Abridged Dewey Decimal Classification and Relative Index, 8th. edn. {USIS}

Abridged Dewey Decimal Classification and Relative Index, rev. edn. {USIS}

Abridged Dewey Decimal Classification and Relative Index, rev. edn. {USIS}

Abstract and abstracting services. {JNU NASSDOC USIS}

Abstracting and indexing. {ISI JNU}

Abstracting and indexing, 2nd edn. {NASSDOC}

Abstracting concepts and methods. {DEPT JNU}

Abstracting, indexing and current awareness services in environmental science. {INSA}

Abstracting scientific and technical literature. {BIS CRRI IIMC ISI JNU USIS}

Abstracting services in science, technology, medicine agriculture, social science, humanity. [International Federation for Documentation and Information]. {DEPT JNU}

Abstracts and synopses. [International Organisation for Standardisation, Geneva]. (ISO/R 214-1961) (E). {NASSDOC}

Academic and legal deposit libraries, 2nd. edn. {DEPT DUL ICHR MFL ZHL}

Academic libraries by the year 2000. {DEPT DUL ISI JNU USIS}

Academic libraries in India : An enquiry into their organisation and professional aspect. {JNU}

Academic library : Essays in honour of Guy R. Lyle. {JNU}.

Academic research and library resources : Changing patterns in America. {DEPT IIT JNU NIPCCD}

Academic status for university and college librarians in India. {JNU}

Acquisition : Where, what and how. {CRRI DUL NIEPA}

Acquisition and cataloguing of books : Papers presented before the library institution at the University of Chicago, July 29 to August 9, 1940. {JNU NAI ZHL}

Acquisition and provision of foreign books by national and university libraries in the United Kingdom : Papers of the Morecamb conference, April 16, 1972. {NMML}

Acquisition, collection development and collection use. {JNU}

The acquisition of library materials. [American Library Association]. {DUL ICA USIS}

Acquisition, organisation and use of books and related materials. [Trustees of New South Wales Public Library]. {JNU}

Acquisition work : Process involved in building library collections. {DUL IEG SPA}
Acquisitions budgets and material costs : Issues and approaches. {NASSDOC}
Acqulsitions from the Third World. {DUL NASSDOC}
Acronyms and abbreviations in library and information work : A reference handbook of British usage, 2nd. edn. {JNU}
Acronyms and abbreviations in library and information work, 3rd edn. [Library Association, London]. {NASSDOC}
Acronyms, initialisms and abbreviations in library and information science : An annotated guide. {NASSDOC}
Activity book for school libraries. {JNU}
Activity book number two : Library projects for children and young people. [American Library Association]. {NIEPA}
Adhunik granthalaya : Vyavastha avam sanchalan ke mooltatva. {NASSDOC}
Adhunik granthalaya vargikaran : Sidhantik vivechan. (Modern library classification : Theoretical analysis). {BIS}
Administering library service in the elementary school, 2nd edn. [American Library Association]. {DUL NIEPA ZHL}
Administering the school library media centre. {JNU}
Administration and change : Continuing education in library administration. {JNU}
Administration and organisation of college libraries in India. {AIU DUL JNU SPA ZHL}
Administration and organisation of school libraries. {NASSDOC}
Administration of the American public library. [American Library Association]. {NAI}
Administration of archives. {JNU ZHL}
Administration of the college library. {DUL NERC}
The administration of the college library, 4th edn. {DUL NIEPA USIS}
Administration of government documents collections. {USIS}
Administration of the small public library. [American Library Association]. {NASSDOC}
Administration of technical libraries. {BIS CRRI ICHR NCAER ZHL}
Administration, personnel, buildings and equipment : A handbook for library management. {NASSDOC}
The administrative aspects of education for librarianship : A symposium. {NIEPA USIS}
Adopting the Library of Congress classification system : A manual of methods and techniques for application or conversion. {DUL}
Adult education activities for public libraries. [UNESCO]. {IEG ZUL}
Adult education and libraries. {AIU}
Advanced data processing in university library. {JNU}
Advanced indexing and abstracting practices. {NASSDOC}
Advanced working seminar on national information policy and the impact of social and technological change on national information planning, Australia. {CRRI}
Advances in communication research. {NASSDOC}
Advances in documentation and library science. 3 vols. {BIS}
Advances in information systems science, 9 vols. {CRRI MHA DUL NASSDOC USIS}
Advances in librarianship, 14 vols. {IEG NASSDOC NCAER NIH NMML USIS}
Advances in library administration and organisation. {IIT}

Advances in library and information science. {CRRI ICA NCAER NCDC}

Advice on establishing a library. {DUL NIPCCD}

African books in print : An Index by author, title and subject, Pt. 1: English language and African language. {NASSDOC}

Agricultural documentation : Responsibilities of libraries and information services. {IIMC}

Agricultural librarianship in India. {NASSDOC}

Agriculture : Library of knowledge. {ICA}

Aligarh Muslim University library : An approach paper on Fifth Five Year Plan including statistical analysis. {JNU}

Aligned list of descriptors : Alphabetical order. [Organisation for Economic Co-operation and Development]. {NASSDOC}

All India booksellers and publishers directory, 1970, 1971, 1972. {ICCR JNU NASSDOC}

All India directory of book trade, vol. 1: Libraries; vol. 2; Booksellers and publishers {NASSDOC NCAER NCERT}

Alphabetical arrangement. (BS 1749 : 1951). [British Standards Institution]. {CRRI}

Alphabetical subject indication of information. {IIT USIS}

Alternative classification for catholic books. {DUL}

American libraries : Lessons for developing countries. (Mimeographed). {NASSDOC*}

American libraries : Report : U.S. field seminar on library reference services for Japanese librarians, June 1960. [International House of Japan]. {DUL NASSDOC}

American library classification with special reference to the Library of Congress. {DUL}

American library directory: A classified list of libraries in the U.S. and Canada with personnel and statistical data. {ICWA}

American library directory, 1964; 1971; 1972. {IIT INSA JNU}

American library resources : A bibliographical guide: Supplement: 1961-1970. {NASSDOC}

American national standards for the abbreviation of titles of periodicals. (ANSI Z39.5-1969). [American National Standards Institute]. {NASSDOC}

American national standards for directories of libraries and information centres. (ANSI Z39.5.-1971). [American National Standards Institute]. {NASSDOC}

American national standards for identification number for serial publications. (ANSI Z39.5-1971). [American National Standards Institute].{NASSDOC}

American national standards for library statistics. (ANSI Z39.5-1968). [American National Standards Institute]. {NASSDOC}

American national standards for periodicals : Format and arrangement. (ANSI Z39.5-1967). [American National Standards Institute]. {NASSDOC}

American national standards for title leaves of a book. (ANSI Z39.5-1971). [American National Standards Institute]. {NASSDOC}

American national standards for writing abstracts. (ANSI Z39.5-1971). [American National Standards Institute]. {NASSDOC}

American national standards practice for storage of processed silver-gelatin micro-film. (ANSI PH5.4-1970). [American National Standards Institute]. {NASSDOC}

American national standards system for the romanisation of Arabic, 12th rev edn. (ANSI Z39.12-1972). [American National Standards Institute]. {NASSDOC}

American national standards system for the romanisation of Japanese, rev edn. (ANSI Z39.11-1972). [American National Standards Institute]. {NASSDOC}

The American public library building : Its planning and design with special reference to its administration and service. [American Library Association]. {USIS}

The American reading public : What it reads, why it reads. {USIS}

American reference books annual. {NASSDOC}

The analysis, design and implementation of information systems. {TDA}

Analysis of the current serial publications being subscribed to in the Delhi University Library System (DULS), Jawahar Lal Nehru University Library and Indian Institute of Technology Library. (University of Delhi, Department of Library Science, Sessional Project, 1977). {DUL}

Analysis of Indian library conferences and seminars since 1947. {JNU}

Analysis of information systems. {BIS CRRI DUL NIH NIPCCD USIS}

Analysis of managerial activities in libraries. [Association of Special Libraries and Information Bureaux]. {DUL IIT}

Analytical planning for university libraries. [University of California]. {IIT}

Anatomy of a compiler. {NASSDOC}

Andhra Pradesh Public Libraries Act, 1960 with latest amendments and commentaries. [Andhra Pradesh Public Library Association]. {NASSDOC*}

Anglo-American Cataloguing Rules. [American Library Association]. {NASSDOC}

Anglo-American Cataloguing Rules, 2nd edn. [American Library Association]. {CRRI IIC ISI JNU MHA NCAER NERC NIH NIPCCD USIS ZHL}

Anglo-American Cataloguing Rules : Amendment bulletin. [Library Association, London] {ZHL}

Anglo-American Cataloguing Rules : British text. [Library Association, London]. {AIU IIT ISI JNU ZHL}

Anglo-American Cataloguing Rules : North American text. [Library Association, London]. {NASSDOC NMML USIS}

Anglo-American Cataloguing Rules : North American text : Chapter 6 : Separately published monographs. [American Library Association]. {JNU}

Anglo-American Cataloguing Rules : North American text : Chapter 12 : Audiovisual media and special instructional materials, rev. [American Library Association]. {USIS}

Anglo-American Cataloguing Rules : North American Text, with supplement of additions and changes. [American Library Association]. {JNU}

Anglo-American Cataloguing Rules, 1967 : An introduction. {JNU NERC}

Annotated and classified bibliography of project reports submitted to the Department of Library Science, University of Delhi since 1968. {DUL}

Annotated bibliography of country serials. [UNCTAD/GATT. International Trade Centre]. {MFL}

Annotated bibliography on librarianship in Thailand. {JNU}

Annotated list of selected United States government publications available to depository libraries. {NASSDOC}

Annual report of the Library of Congress, 1972. [Library of Congress]. {JNU}

Annual report of the Library of Congress for 1985. {NASSDOC}

Annual review of information science and technology, 19 vols {CRRI NASSDOC USIS}

Annual seminar. No. 1: 1963; No. 2: 1964; No. 3: 1965; No. 4: 1966; No. 5: 1967; No. 6 : 1968, 2 pts; No. 7: 1969; No. 8: 1970; No. 9: 1971; No. 10: 1972, 2 pts; No. 11: 1974. [Documentation Research and Training Centre, Bangalore]. {IEG IIMC ISI JNU NASSDOC}.

Answering any questions : How to set up an information office. {BCL DUL}

Applications of decision tables : A reader. {NASSDOC}

Application of international classification of diseases and neurology. [World Health Organisation]. {JNU}

Applications of mini and micro computers in information, documentation and libraries. {JNU NASSDOC}

Applications of management techniques to library and information system. {JNU NIPCCD}

Applications of operations research models,to libraries. {CRRI}

Applied general systems theory. {JNU}

Approach to classification for students of librarianship. {IIC JNU NASSDOC}

Approval plans and academic libraries : An interpretive survey. {IIT}

Archive buildings and equipment. {DUL}

Archive-library relations. {ISI}

Area specialist bibliographer : An inquiry into his role. {NASSDOC}

Army medical library classification : Medicine. {DUL}

Aroused by books. {USIS}

Arrangement and description of archival materials. {IIT}

Art and science of book preservation. [BIS IIT MFL ZHL}

Art of the book collecting in Australia {JNU}

Art of the book review : A comprehensive working outline. {DUL}

Art of systems analysis. {JNU}

Article and reports reprinted from the Library Association Record for December, 1963. [Library Association, London]. {NASSDOC}

Artificial and human thinking. {NASSDOC}

Artificial intelligence : The heuristic programming approach. {NASSDOC}

Ascent of a university library. {NMML}

Asian and African collections in British libraries : Problems and prospects. {DUL NMML}

Asian regional seminar on information sources, systems and services in the social sciences, July 11-22, 1983, Philippines. [Unesco Regional Office, Bangkok]. {NASSDOC}

Aspects of public library management : The application of new management processes to the library services. [Library Advisory Council for England]. {NIPCCD ZHL}

Aspects of recent research in the art and science of classification. {DUL}

Assessment of public library development in India : Seminar papers. [University of Madras, Department of Library and Information Science]. {NASSDOC}

Association of metropolitan chief librarians. {JNU}

Audio-visual aids for teaching the use of school library. {JNU}

Audio-visual materials : Development of a national cataloguing and information service : Report of joint feasibility study for the British Library and the Council for Educational Technology. {IIMC}

Audio-visual school library service : A handbook for librarians. [American Library Association]. {ZHL}

Audio-visual services in the small public library. {JNU}

Australian government publications, 1974-82. [National Library of Australia]. {NASSDOC}

Australian libraries. {NASSDOC}

Australian national bibliography, 1974-80. [National Library of Australia]. {NASSDOC}

Australian public affairs information service : A subject index to current literature, 1977-82. {NASSDOC}

Author catalogue of printed books in European languages, 8 vols. [National Library, Calcutta]. {NASSDOC}

Author entry for government publications. [U.S. Library of Congress]. {NAI}

Author index to Library of Congress classification : Class P, Subclass PN, PR, PS, PZ. {BIS}

Author table for Indian names. [National Library, Calcutta]. {NMML}

Author's and printer's dictionary. {IIC}

Author's and printer's dictionary. {DUL}

Authors and writer's who's who, 6th. edn. {NMML RTL}

Authors' and titles : An analytical study of the author concept in codes of cataloguing rules in the English language from that of the British Museum. {NMML}

Authors of books for young people. {DUL}

Automated approach to technical information retrieval : Library application. {JNU}

Automated centre for scientific and technical information. [UNESCO]. {ISI}

Automated information : Retrieval system. {JNU}

Automated information management in public administration : Present development and impacts. [Organisation of Economic Co-operation and Development]. {TDA}

Automated language processing. {NASSDOC}

Automated library circulation systems. {IIT}

Automatic aids to profile construction : Expansion of search terms by thesaurus. [Institute of Electrical Engineers]. {BCL}

Automatic data processing : Principle procedures. {JNU}

Automatic indexing : A state of the art report. [U.S. National Bureau of Standards]. {USIS}

Automatic keyword classification for information retrieval. {BCL BIS NASSDOC}

Automatic processing of metallurgical abstracts for purpose of information retrieval. {JNU}

Automating library acquisitions : Issues and outlook. {JNU}

Automating library procedures : A survivor's handbook. {NMML}

Automation and electronics in publishing. {DUL}

Automation and the Library of Congress. [U.S. Library of Congress]. {BIS}

Automation and scientific communication : Short papers contributed to the theme sessions of the 26th annual meeting of the American documentation institute at Chicago. {JNU}

Automation and the UDC, 1948-1980, 2nd edn. [International Federation for Documentation and Information]. {CRRI}

Automation in libraries. {AIU BIS IIT ISI JNU NASSDOC NCAER NIH SPA}

Automation in libraries, 2nd edn. {USIS}

Automation in libraries. {ICHR NASSDOC NIPCCD SPA}

Automation in union catalogue of periodicals : India and abroad. [Typed short bibliography]. {NASSDOC}

Automation, space management and productivity : A guide for libraries. {IIT USIS}

Aviation subject headings : A concise list for civil aviation libraries or collections. {DUL}

BEPI : Bibliography of English publications in India : An integrated author-title-subject index of scholarly and significant publications of the year, 1977-1978. {NASSDOC}

BIBDATA network : A draft proposal for an Australian national shared cataloguing system. [National Library of Australia]. {JNU}

BSO manual : The development, rationale and use of broad system of ordering. [International Federation for Documentation and Information] {CRRI}

Bachelor degree in library and information science : A handbook. [Andhra Pradesh Open University, Hyderabad]. {NASSDOC}

Background papers : Sub-regional workshop for cooperative librarians and documentation officers for South East Asia, April 14-29, 1981, Los Banos. [ICA Regional Office and Education Centre for South East Asia, New Delhi]. {ICA}

Background readings in building library collections, 2nd edn. {USIS}

Baltimore reaches out : Library service to the disadvantaged. {JNU}

Bangladesh national bibliography. {NASSDOC}

Bangladesh public library directory (1972-1986). [Ministry of Education, Cultural Affairs Division, Directorate of Archives and Libraries, Bangladesh National Library, Colombo]. {NASSDOC}

Barefoot librarian : Library development in Southeast Asia with special reference to Malaysia. {NIEPA}

Baroda and its libraries. [Central Library, Baroda]. {NAI NASSDOC}

The Baroda library movement : A short account of the origin and growth of the Central Library Department of the Baroda State. [Central Library, Baroda]. {NASSDOC}

Bases of modern librarianship : A study of library theory and practice in Britain, Canada, Denmark, the Federal Republic of Germany and the United States. {IIT JNU NIPCCD NMML SPA}

Basic book collection for the community college library. {JNU}

Basic book collection for elementary grades. [American Library Association]. {NIEPA USIS}

Basic budgeting practices for librarians. {JNU}

The basic business library : Core resources. {USIS}

Basic foundations of library science. {CRRI JNU ZHL}

Basic principles of data processing. {JNU}

Basic reference books : An introduction to the evaluation study and use of reference materials with special emphasis on some 300 titles. {JNU}

Basic reference sources. [American Library Association]. {CRRI NAI USIS}

Basic reference sources : An introduction to materials and methods. {DUL USIS}

Basic reference sources : A self study manual. {DUL USIS}

Basic reference sources : A self study manual, 2nd edn. {USIS}

Basic research methods for librarians. {JNU}

Basic statistics for librarians. {ISI JNU}

Basic statistics for librarians, 2nd edn. {IIT}

Basic system analysis. {JNU}
Basics of information work. {JNU}
The basics of librarianship. {ISIL}
Bedlican library extension scheme. {NAL}
Benefit-cost analysis of alternative library delivery systems. {JNU}
Best reference books. {JNU}
Better libraries make better schools. {JNU}
Better report writing, 2nd rev edn. {DUL}
Between MLS and PHD : A study of sixth year specialist programmes in accredited library schools. {DUL}
Bibliographic Classification, 2nd edn., ed. by J. Mills {IIT JNU}
Bibliographic Classification : Classes L-Z, 3 vols, {CRRI}
Bibliographic control. {AIU DUL NASSDOC}
Bibliographic control of microforms. {ISI JNU}
Bibliographic control of nonprint media. [American Library Association]. {NASSDOC}
Bibliographic control of official publications. {IIT}
Bibliographic description and cataloguing. {DUL}
Bibliographic information in library systems. [Association of Special Libraries and Information Bureaux]. {CRRI JNU}.
Bibliographic instruction : A handbook. {IIT}
Bibliographic methods and reading behaviour. {ICHR NASSDOC NERC NIPCCD}
Bibliographic record and information technology. {DUL JNU}
Bibliographical control and service. {DUL IIT MFL NASSDOC}
Bibliographical control of early books. {JNU}
Bibliographical control of patent literature. [University of Delhi, Department of Library Science, Sessional Project]. {DUL}
Bibliographical description and cataloguing. {NASSDOC}.
Biographical directory of librarians in the United States and Canada, 5th edn. {NASSDOC}
Bibliographical references. (BS 1629 : 1950). [British Standards Institution]. {CRRI NASSDOC}
Bibliographical references : Essential elements. (ISO/R 690-1968) (E). [International Organisation for Standardisation, Geneva]. {NASSDOC}
Bibliographical services : Their present state and possibilities of improvement. [U.S. Library of Congress]. {JNU}
Bibliographical services for Indian studies : A guide to printed sources of information. [Mysore Institute of Development Studies]. {NASSDOC}
Bibliographical services throughout Pakistan. {ZHL}
Bibliographical services throughout the world, 1950-54; 1955-59; 1960-64; 1965-69; 1970-74. [UNESCO]. {DSSW DUL IIMC JNU NASSDOC NIEPA ZHL}
Bibliographies : Subject and national : A guide to their contents, arrangement and use. {MFL}
Bibliographies : Subject and national : A guide to their contents and use, 2nd ed. {MFL}
Bibliographies and reference works including abstract journals, library journals, books about books and standard works, 2 parts, pt 1: A-J. {NASSDOC}
Bibliography. {CRRI ICA ISI JNU NASSDOC NIPCCD NMML}

Bibliography : Reports from the international conference on Education, 1975. [UNESCO]. {ICA}

Bibliography and documentation. {ICHR IIT JNU NIPCCD}

Bibliography and footnotes : A style manual for students and writers. 3rd edn. [University of California]. {NASSDOC}

Bibliography for beginners, 2nd edn. {NASSDOC}.

Bibliography in theory and practice. {MFL NASSDOC}

Bibliography in theory and practice, 2nd rev edn. {ICA ICHR IIMC INSA JNU NIPCCD}

A bibliography of bibliographies on India. {ICA}

Bibliography of dictionaries and encyclopaedias in Indian languages. [National Library, Calcutta]. {ZHL}

Bibliography of mono and multilingual vocabularies, thesauri, subject headings and classification schemes in the social sciences : Prepared by the Astib Library. [UNESCO]. {NASSDOC}

Bibliography of publications issued by UNESCO or under its auspices, 1946-1971. [UNESCO]. {NASSDOC}

Bibliography of research in library and information in India. {NMML}

Bibliography of selected Indian books, 1970-71. {NASSDOC}

Bibliography of standards on documentation. {BIS ISI}

Bibliography of United Nations thesauri, classification nomenclatures. [Inter-Organisation Board for Information Systems, Geneva]. {BIS}

Bibliography of use studies. {JNU}

Bibliography on documentation. {JNU}

Bibliography on information science and technology for 1966. {JNU}

Bibliography on knowledge utilisation and dissemination. [University of Michigan]. {NASSDOC}

Bibliography on work-flow in libraries. [Council of Scientific and Industrial Research, New Delhi]. {INSDOC NASSDOC}.

Bibliography technical : An illuminating exposition. {NASSDOC}

Biomedical, scientific and technical book reviewing. {DUL}

Black academic libraries and research collections : An historical survey. {DUL IIT NIPCCD}

Black literature resources : Analysis and organisation. {IIT ISI}

Bombay Booksellers and Publishers Association Members' Directory. [Bombay Booksellers and Publishers Association]. {NASSDOC}

Book : The story of printing and bookmaking, 3rd rev ed. {DUL}

Book and journal services for doctors and nurses : An interim report on a National Book League investigation. {DUL}

Book availability and the library user. {JNU NASSDOC USIS}

Book bait : Detailed notes on adult books popular with young people. 2nd edn. [American Library Association]. {USIS}

Bookbinding. {ISI}

Bookbinding. {NASSDOC}

Bookbinding : Its background and technique, 2 vols. {DUL}

Bookbinding and the care of the books, 5th edn. {CRRI ZHL}

Bookbinding by hand for students and craftsmen, 2nd edn. {BIS}

Bookbinding for librarians. [Association of Assistant Librarians, London]. {NASSDOC}

Bookbinding in America : Three essays. {DUL}

Book catalogs. {USIS}
Book catalogs. {NASSDOC}
Book collecting : Four broadcast talks. {DUL}
Book collection : An introduction to modern methods of literary and bibliographical detection. {DUL}
Book collection : Policy case studies in public and academic libraries. {DUL}
Book dealers in India, Pakistan, Sri Lanka : A directory of dealers in second hand and antiquarian books in the sub-continent of South Western Asia. {NMML}
Book development in Asia : A report on the production and distribution of books. [UNESCO]. {DUL}
Book display. {USIS}
Book distribution and promotion problems in South Asia. {DUL}
Book hunger. {DUL}
Book indexing. {NASSDOC NIEPA}
The book industry : A report of the public library enquiry. {CRRI}
Bookman's glossary, 4th edn. {DUL}
The bookmen's glossary. 5th edn. {NCERT}
The bookmen's glossary. 61th edn. {NASSDOC}
Bookmobiles and bookmobile service. {USIS}
Book numbers : A manual for students with a basic code of rules. {DUL}
Book numbers : Some Indian methods. {NASSDOC}
A book on books. {NASSDOC}
Book promotion through libraries. {DUL}
Book publishing in America. {DUL}
Book review digest 1948-73; 1976-77; 1979-80; 1980-81. {NASSDOC}
Book reviewing. {DUL}
Book revolution. {DUL}
Book science : Depth classification. {DUL}
Book selection. [American Library Association]. {ZHL}
Book selection. {ICA IIT ISIL JNU NERC ZHL}
Book selection : An introduction to principles and practice. {NASSDOC}
Book selection : An introduction to principles and practice, 2nd ed. {BIS}
Book selection : Its principles and practice. {NAI}
Book selection : Principles and procedures. {DUL}
Book selection : Principles, practices and tools. {ICHR IEG}
Book selection :.Proceedings of a work conference. {DUL}
Book selection and bibliography. {ICHR}
Book selection and censorship : A study of school and public libraries in California. {JNU}
Book selection and censorship in the sixties. {DUL IIT USIS}.
Book selection and collections : A comparison of German and American university libraries. {JNU}
Book selection and intellectual freedom. {USIS}
Book selection and physical bibliography. {CRRI}
Book selection and systematic bibliography {IIT MFL NMML SPA}
Book selection for school libraries {JNU}
Book selling. {DUL}
Book theft and library security systems. {BIS JNU USIS}
Book typography, 1815-1965, in Europe and the United States of America. {DUL}

Book worms : The insect pests of books. {JNU}

Books and people : Five decades of New York's oldest library. {NAI}

Books and publishing, vol. 3. {DUL}

Books and readers in ancient Greece and Rome, 2nd edn. {DUL}

Books and related materials. {JNU}

Books are for our time. {DUL}

Books are for people : Librarian's life educational explorers. {IIT}

Books are tools : The organisation of small technical libraries for South African industry. {JNU}

Books in America's past : Essays honouring Rudolph H. Gjelsness. {DUL}

Books in my baggage : Adventures in reading and collecting. {JNU}

Books in print 1969-71; 1973-74 to 1982-83. {NASSDOC NIH}

Books in the service of society : Collection of articles of Soviet authors. [Ministry of Culture of the USSR, Main Library Inspectorate]. {NASSDOC}

Books lead the way : Library and reading skill-text. {JNU}

Books, libraries and electronics : Essays on the future of written communication. {USIS}

Books, libraries and you, {ZHL}

Books, libraries and you : A handbook on the use of reference books and the reference resources of the library, 3rd edn. {USIS}

Books of India, 1963 : A reference catalogue of Indian book published in English in 1963. {NASSDOC}

Books that changed America. {USIS}

Books that changed the world. [American 2nd ed. Library Association]. {USIS}

Books that changed the world. [America Library Association]. {USIS}

Books that made the difference : What people told us. {USIS}

Bowker annual of library and book trade information. {IIT JNU NASSDOC NCAER NIH USIS}

Branch libraries. {ICA}

Branch libraries : Modern problems and administration. {JNU}

Branch library practice. {CRRI}

British academic libraries. {JNU}

British books in print {NASSDOC}

British government publications : An index to chairmen and authors, 1941-1960. [Library Association, London]. {NASSDOC}

British librarianship and information science, 1966-70. {JNU NMML}

British libraries. {MHA}

British library research and development reports : Information guides. {JNU}

British Museum Library. {NAL NMML}

British national bibliography, 1950-54 to 1973; 1975 to 83, 2 vols. [British Library Bibliographic Services Division]. {NASSDOC}

British official publications. {NASSDOC}

British public library buildings. {IIT}

Brush up your reading. {ZHL}

Buchereibau : Public library building. {DUL}

Budgetary control in academic libraries. {AIU DUL}

Building information systems in the Islamic world. {NASSDOC}

Building library collections, 3rd edn. {USIS}

Building library collections, 4th edn. {USIS}

Building library collections, 5th edn. {USIS}

Building library collections and national policy for library : Seminar papers : All India library conference, 30th, January, 28-31, 1985, Jaipur. [Indian Library Association]. {NASSDOC}
Buildings for small public libraries : Remodelled and adapted including new designs for branches. [American Library Association]. {DUL}
Business information in London : A study of the demand and supply of business information in 13 London business libraries. [Association of Special Libraries and Information Bureaux]. {NASSDOC}
Business information services : Some aspects of structure organisation and problems. {BCL}

CCC : Entries and procedure. {JNU}
CUE system for bibliography and indexing. {NASSDOC}.
Caldecott medal books, 1938-1957, with the artists' acceptance papers and related material chiefly from the Horn Book Magazine. {USIS}
Cambridge college libraries : Aid for research studies. {JNU}
Canadian library directory, 2 vols. [Canada National Library]. {ICWA}
Canadian periodical index, 1975; 1977 to 1982, formerly *Canadian index to periodicals and documentary films.* [Canadian Library Association]. {NASSDOC}
Canadian provincial libraries. {JNU}
Canons for making abstracts. [Indian Standards Institution]. {NASSDOC}
Canons of library classification. {JNU NIH ZHL}
Capital provision for university libraries : Report of a working party. [University Grants Commission, London]. {IIT JNU NIEPA ZHL}
Care and preservation of museum objects. {NASSDOC}
Care and repair of books, 4th rev edn. {DUL ISI}
Care of books and documents. [Library Association, London]. {ZHL}
Career of the academic librarian : A study of the social origins. {JNU}
Careers in information. {USIS}
Carnegie libraries : Their history and impact on American public library development. [American Library Association]. {USIS}
Case for faculty status for academic librarians. {JNU}
Case studies in computer based bibliographic information services. {BCL}
Case studies in library computer systems. {ISI USIS}
Case studies in reference work. {DUL IIT NIH}
Case studies in systems analysis in a university library. {JNU}
Cassell's dictionary of publishing in Great Britain, the commonwealth and Ireland. {ICCR}
Catalogue and cataloguing. {IIFT IIT NMML SPA}
Catalogue card reproduction. [American Library Association]. {IIT}
Catalogue entries and procedure : A guide to cataloguing work according to ALA and AACR and CCC. {IEG IIT ISI}
Catalogue of back volumes of periodicals in Punjabrao Krishi Vidyapeeth Library, Akola, 1985. [Punjabrao Krishi Vidyapeeth, Akola]. {NASSDOC}
Catalogue of Government of India civil publications : Subject-wise arranged corrected up to 31st December, 1959. [Department of Publication Delhi]. {NASSDOC NIPCCD}
Catalogue of Government of India civil publications : Subject-wise arranged corrected up to 31st December, 1959 : Supplement for the years 1968-70 [Department of Publications, Delhi]. {IIFT ISI NASSDOC TDA}

Catalogue of Government of India civil publications : Subject-wise arranged, corrected up to 31st December, 1977, 8th supplement for the year 1977. {MMTC}

Catalogue of government publications. [HMSO, Great Britain]. {NASSDOC}

Catalogue of new accessions in the headquarters' library, National Archives of India, April 1966 to March 1974. {NAI}

Catalogue of publications issued by Government of Uttar Pradesh and obtainable from the book depot, Government Press, Allahabad, for the year ending, 1965-66 : Corrected up to September, 1966. {NASSDOC}

Catalogue of Punjabi printed books added to the India Office Library, 1902-1964. [India Office Library, London]. {NASSDOC}

Catalogue of Sanskrit and Prakrit manuscripts, 4 parts. [Lalbhai Dalpatbhai Institute of Indology]. {INSA}

Catalogue of serials : Indian Institute of Science Library Bangalore. [INSDOC Union Catalogue Series, 2]. {DUL}

Catalogue of special collections in National Library, Baghdad. [National Library, Baghdad]. {NASSDOC}.

Catalogue of type specimens. {DUL}

Catalogue of Vishvesharananda Vedic Research Institute manuscript collection, 2 vols. {INSA}

Cataloguing. [American Library Association]. {USIS}

Cataloguing. {NASSDOC}

Cataloguing, 2nd rev. edn. {IIT}

Cataloguing. {NASSDOC}

Cataloguing : Its theory and practice. {CRRI ICHR MHA NMML SPA ZHL}

Cataloguing : Its theory and practice, 2nd edn. {JNU NERC}

Cataloguing : Its theory and practice, 3rd rev. edn. {IIT ISIL}

Cataloguing : A textbook for the use in libraries, 4th edn. {IIT ZHL}

Cataloguing : A textbook for use in libraries. {ICA MFL NAI NIPCCD ZHL}

Cataloguing : Theory and practice, 2nd edn. {CRRI NAI}

Cataloguing : Theory and practice, 3rd edn. {ISI MMTC NASSDOC SPA ZHL}

Cataloguing : Theory and practice, 4th edn. {AIU ICA IIFT ISI MMTC NASSDOC NERC NIEPA SPA ZHL}

Cataloguing : Theory and practice, 5th edn. {ICHR IEG IIT MHA MMTC NCAER NCDC ZHL}

Cataloguing and catalogue : A handbook for library management. {NASSDOC}

Cataloguing and classification : An introduction. {JNU}

Cataloguing and classification : An introductory manual, 3rd edn. {DUL}

Cataloguing and classification : A workshop, 2nd edn. {NASSDOC NIPCCD}

Cataloguing and classification in British university libraries : A survey of practices and procedures. [Sheffield University Post Graduate School of Librarianship]. {DUL IIT}

Cataloguing and classification of non-Western materials : Concerns, issues and practices. {IIT}

Cataloguing arrangement and filing of special material in special libraries. {NAL}

Cataloguing audio-visual materials : A manual based on the Anglo-American Cataloguing Rules-2. {IIT}

Cataloguing for small libraries, 3rd edn. {ZHL}

Cataloguing in practice : Organisation of book acquisition in libraries. {CRRI ICHR NASSDOC NIPCCD}

Cataloguing in special libraries : A survey of methods. {CRRI MFL NAL}
Cataloguing made easy. {DUL}
Cataloguing manual : AACR-2, {JNU}
Cataloguing of Indian Muslim names. {NASSDOC NMML}
Cataloguing of musical instruments. [Government Museum, Madras]. {NAL}
Cataloguing of Persian works including rules for transliteration, entry and description. [American Library Association]. {JNU NASSDOC}
Cataloguing phonorecordings : Problems and possibilities. {BIS}
Cataloguing practice, 2nd edn. {ICA ICHR IEG JNU NERC NMML ZHL}
Cataloguing practice : Classified catalogue code and Anglo- American cataloguing rules. {IIMC JNU NASSDOC NIH}
Cataloguing rules : Author and title entries. [American Library Association; Library Association, London]. {IIT MFL}
Cataloguing rules for author and title entries, 2nd edn. [American Library Association]. {NAI}
Cataloguing rules of the American Library Association and the Library of Congress, 1949-1958. [American Library Association; Library of Congress, U.S.]. {BIS IEG ZHL}
Cataloguing rules with explanations and illustrations, 2nd edn. {NAI}
Cataloguing sampler : Comparative and interpretive guide. {IIT}
Cataloguing theory. {JNU}
Cataloguing theory and practice. {NMML}
Censorship : A literature survey. (University of Delhi, Department of Library Science. Sessional Project). {DUL}
Central library storage of books : An essay awarded the Sevensma prize, 1962. {IIT}
Central Office of Information. {NASSDOC}
Centralised book processing : A feasibility study based on Colorado academic libraries. {USIS}
Centres of advanced study in Indian universities. [University Grants Commission, New Delhi]. {NASSDOC}
Centres of Islamic learning in India. [Ministry of Information and Broadcasting]. {NASSDOC}
Century of cooperative programme among academic libraries. {BIS}
A century of service : Librarianship in United States and Canada. [American Library Association]. {USIS}
Certification of school librarians : A compilation of State requirements, 1958. {NASSDOC}
Chain procedure : An annotated bibliography. {JNU}
Challenges of new technologies : All India library convention, Shimla, [Government of India Librarian Associations]. {NMML}
Champion of a cause : Essays and addresses on librarianship. [American Library Association]. {USIS}
Changing concepts of reference service. {AIU DUL ICHR IIT MHA NERC NIPCCD NMML}
Changing context of information : An introductory analysis. {NIEPA}
The changing environment of libraries : Papers delivered at the 1970-71 colloquim series. [American Library Association]. {USIS}
Changing information : Concepts and technologies. {JNU USIS}
The changing pattern of librarianship. [Library Association, London]. {ICA}

Changing technology and education for librarianship and information science. {NASSDOC}
Changing times, changing libraries. {USIS}
Characteristics of social science serials : The construction and analysis of a file : Social science serial titles. [Bath University]. {BCL}
Charging system. [American Library Association]. {DUL IIFT IIT ZHL}
Charging systems. {USIS}
Chemical information : A practical guide to utilisation. {CRRI}
Chetenham classification. {JNU}
Child education in India: Index to scholarly writings in Indian educational journals and newspapers. {NIPCCD}
Children's catalogue, 12th edn. {USIS}
Children's libraries. {DUL}
Children's literature : A guide to reference sources. [U.S. Library of Congress]. {USIS}
Children's service in public libraries : Organisation and administration, with collaboration of Gene Inyart Namovicz. {NASSDOC}
Choosing an automated library system : A planning guide. [American Library Association]. {USIS}
A chronology of librarianship. {USIS}
Chronology of librarianship. {CRRI}
Circulation, interlibrary loan, patron use and collection maintenance : A handbook for library management. {NASSDOC}
Circulation systems selection manual for college and university libraries. {JNU}
Circulation work in college and university libraries. {JNU}
Citations for physics literature : Experimental issue : Citations of Journal of Applied Physics : The physical review. {DUL}
Citation indexing : Its theory and application in science, technology and humanities. {NASSDOC NIH}
City Library of Detroit, 1817-1837. {JNU}
Classification : Class A : General works, polygraphy, 3rd edn. [U.S. Library of Congress] {CRRI}.
Classification : class B, 2nd edn. [U.S. Library of Congress]. {ISI}
Classification : Class H : Social sciences, 3rd edn. [U.S. Library of Congress]. {CRRI}
Classification : Class J : Political science with supplementary pages, 2nd edn. [U.S. Library of Congress]. {DUL}
Classification : Class N : Fine Arts, 3rd edn., [U.S. Libray of Congress]. {ISI}
Classification : Class P : Subclass PG : Russian literature. [U.S. Library of Congress]. {DUL}
Classification : Class P : Subclasses PNPR, PS and PZ, Literature, [U.S. Library of Congress]. {DUL}
Classification : Class P : Subclass PQ : Italian, Spanish and Portuguese literature with supplementary pages, part 2. [U.S. Library of Congress]. {DUL}
Classification : Class Q : Science, 5th edn. [U.S. Library of Congress]. {CRRI}
Classification : Class R : Medicine : 3rd edn. [U.S. Library of Congress]. {ISI}
Classification : Class S : Agriculture, plant and animal industry, fish culture and fisheries, hunting, sports, 3rd edn. [U.S. Library of Congress]. {DUL}

Classification : Class U : Military science, 3rd edn. [U.S. Library of Congress]. {JNU}
Classification : Class Z : Bibliography and library science, 3rd edn. [U.S. Library of Congress]. {CRRI}
Classification : An introductory manual, 2nd edn. {DUL NASSDOC}
Classification : Theoretical and practical, 3rd edn. {DUL}
Classification and communication. {ISI NERC}
Classification and index of the world's languages. {JNU}
Classification and indexing in the humanities. {DUL JNU NASSDOC ZHL}
Classification and indexing in science. {CRRI DUL IIT NAI}
Classification and indexing in the social sciences. {DSSW IEG IIMC IIT NAI NASSDOC NIEPA SPA USIS}
Classification and indexing in the social sciences, 2nd edn. {BIS ICA JNU NASSDOC}
Classification, coding and machinery for search. {DUL}
Classification for information retrieval : Papers presented at an intensive course held in September 1967 at the School of Librarianship. [Liverpool College of Commerce]. {NIH}
Classification for international law and relations, 2nd edn. {IEG}
Classification for linguistics and languages : A modified approach based on Decimal Classification. [Central Institute of Indian Languages, Mysore]. {ICHR ZHL}
Classification for medical literature. 5th edn. {DUL}
Classification in the 1970's : A discussion of the development and prospects for the major schemes. {AIU IIC JNU NASSDOC NIPCCD ZHL}.
Classification of books : An inquiry into its usefulness to the reader. {DUL}
Classification of business literature. [Graduate School of Business Administration Library, Harvard University]. {ISI}
Classification of library and information science. {DUL}
Classification of type design. {DUL}
Classification practice in Britain : Report on a survey of classification opinion, etc. {DUL}
Classification research : India, 1968-1973. [Documentation Research and Training Centre, Bangalore]. {BIS}
Classification schedule for area studies. {NASSDOC*}
Classification schedules for printed, microcopy and phonorecord materials in the Reference Department, 2nd edn. [New York Public Library]. {DUL}
Classification scheme of agricultural science, 3rd rev edn. {DUL}
Classification schemes and Indian libraries. {DUL IIFT IIT ISI NERC NMML}.
Classified catalogue : Basic principles and practices. [American Library Association]. {CRRI NASSDOC}
Classified catalogue code, 2nd edn. [Madras Library Association]. {CRRI DSSW NAI}
Classified catalogue code, 3rd edn. {DSSW}
Classified catalogue code, with additional rules for dictionary catalogue code, 4th edn. [Madras Library Association]. {DSSW IEG NERC}
Classified catalogue code, with additional rules for dictionary catalogue code, 5th edn. {AIU BIS CRRI DSSW ICHR IIT ISI MHA NAI NASSDOC NMML SPA ZHL}
Classified catalogue code : Entries and procedure. {JNU}
Classified catalogue code in theory and practice. {CRRI}

Classified catalogue code in theory and practice {DUL}

Classified Library of Congress subject headings, 2 vols., V. 1: Classified list; V. 2: Alphabetical list. {IIT JNU NASSDOC NIH}

Classified Library of Congress subject headings, 2nd edn., Part A : Classified list; et al, ed., Part B : Alphabetical list. {IIT JNU NASSDOC}

Cleaning and preserving bindings and related materials. [American Library Association]. {DUL IIT}

Cleaning and preserving bindings and related materials, 2nd edn. [American Library Association]. {USIS}

Client-centred academic library : An organisational model. {JNU}

Climate of book selection : Social influences on school and public libraries. {DUL}

Clinic on library applications of data processing, 24th, 1974, Illinois. [University of Illinois at Urbana-Champaign]. {USIS}

Code and the cataloguer : Proceedings of the colloquium on the Anglo-American Cataloguing Rules held at the School of Library Science, University of Toronto on March 31 and April 1, 1967. {NASSDOC}

Code for classifiers. 2nd edn. [American Library Association]. {BIS CRRI IIT NAI USIS ZHL}

Code of practice for handling and storage of microtransparencies, rev. edn., (IS : 3130-1972). [Indian Standards Institution]. {NASSDOC}

Code of practice for library lighting. (IS : 2672-1966). [Indian Standards Institution]. {NASSDOC}

Code of practice for the processing of microfilms, Silver halide. (IS : 3083-1966). [Indian Standards Institution]. {NASSDOC}

Code of practice for reinforced binding of library books and periodicals. (IS : 3050-1965). [Indian Standards Institution]. {CRRI NASSDOC}

Code of practice for storage and use of microfilms of permanent value. (IS : 3130-1965). [Indian Standards Institution]. {NASSDOC}

Code of practice relating to primary elements in the design of buildings for archives. (IS : 2663-1964). [Indian Standards Institution]. {NASSDOC}

Code of practice relating to primary elements in the design of library buildings. (IS : 1553-1960). [Indian Standards Institution]. {NASSDOC}

Code of recommended practice for the form and presentation of periodicals of permanent value. (CP 48 : 1963). [New Zealand Standards Institute, Wellington]. {NASSDOC}

Collaborative library systems development. {JNU}

Collection building in special purpose libraries. {USIS}

Collection of materials on the preservation of library resources. {INSA NASSDOC}

Colleges and reference library year book, No. 3. [American Library Association]. {JNU}

College and university library building. [American Library Association]. {IIT}

College and university library surveys, 1938-52. {JNU}

College learning resource centre. {NIEPA}

College libraries : Recommended standards of library provision in colleges of technology and other establishment of further education. [Library Association, London]. {DUL ICA}

College libraries in India : A case study. Photocopy from :*Library management* 7(1) 1986. {NASSDOC}

College libraries in India : Needed a policy for development. {AIU IEG}

College library : A collection of essays. {DUL NIEPA}

College library : Problems and prospects. [Gulbarga University, Gulbarga]. {NASSDOC}

College library administration. {DUL IIT SPA}

College library building : Its planning and equipment. {DUL}

College library management : Academic library system, services and use. {JNU}

College library publicity. {USIS}

College library publicity. {DUL}

College students and the library : Report of a survey in May 1964 of the use of libraries and books, by students in five teacher training colleges. {JNU}

College teaching and the college library. {AIU JNU}

College, university and special libraries of the Pacific North West. {JNU}

Colon Classification. {CRRI ICHR IIFT IIT}

Colon Classification, 2nd edn. {DSSW}

Colon Classification. 3rd edn. [Madras Library Association]. {CRRI}

Colon Classification. 4th edn. [Madras Library Association]. {ISI}

Colon Classification, 5th edn. (DSSW IEG NCAER}

Colon Classification, 6th edn., reprinted 1960; 1963; 1964; 1969. {AIU BIS CRRI DSSW GPF ICHR IDSA IIFT IIMC IIT INSA ISI JNU MHA NAL NASSDOC NERC NIPCCD NMML SPA UGC ZHL}

Colon Classification, 7th edn. {JNU}

Colon Classification : Enumerated and expanded schedules alongwith theoretical formulations. {NASSDOC}

Colon Classification : Its structure and working. {ISI NERC NMML}

Colon Classification : A perview, 7th edn. {JNU}

Colon Classification : Schedule of basic subjects, 7th edn. {DUL}'

Colon Classification : Theory and practice. {CRRI ICA ICHR NIPCCD}

Colon Classification : Theory and practice. {ICA MHA MMTC NIPCCD}

Colon Classification for library science. {DUL}

Colon Classification for macro documents in history. {DUL}

Colon Classification for macro documents in mathematics. {DUL}

Coming age of information technology : Studies in coordinate indexing. {DUL}

Commercial and industrial records storage. {NMML}

Commercial and technical libraries. {BIS}

Commonsense cataloguing : A manual for the organization of books and other materials in school and small public libraries, 2nd rev ed., by Marian Sannar. {USIS}

Communicate : A librarian's guide to interpersonal relations. [American Library Association]. {USIS}

Communicating technical information. {CRRI}

Communicating with a computer. {NASSDOC}

Communication : An introduction to the history of writing, printing, books and libraries, 3rd edn. {IIC MHA}

Communication : An introduction to the history of writing, printing, books and libraries, 4th edn. {USIS}

Communication in science : Documentation and automation. [CIBA Foundation]. {MHA}

Communication in science and technology. {INSA}

Communication knowledge and the librarian. {CRRI DUL NASSDOC}

Communication manual for libraries. {JNU}

Communication of specialised information. {JNU}
Communication studies. {CRRI}
Communication theory. {JNU}
Communication theory and research : Proceedings of the first international symposium. {NASSDOC}
Communication yearbook, 1977-78; 1982-83. {RTL}
Community college libraries in the United States. {USIS}
The community college library. {DUL USIS}.
The community college library : A plan for action. {DUL USIS}
Community elite and the public library : The use of information in leadership. {IIT NIPCCD}
Community information service : A directory of public library involvement. {JNU}
Community information services : Their origin, scope and development. {IIT}
Compact library shelving. [American Library Association]. {DUL NASSDOC USIS}
A comparative analysis of the major abstracting and indexing services for library and information science. [UNESCO]. {NASSDOC}
A comparative analysis of the major abstracting and indexing services for library and information science : With notes on their coverage of archive material. [UNESCO]. {NASSDOC}
Comparative and international librarianship : Essays on themes and problems. {AIU IIT}
Comparative costs of book processing in a processing centre and in five individual libraries. {DUL}
Comparative librarianship : Essays in honour of Prof. D.N. Marshall. {ICHR IIC JNU NASSDOC NIPCCD NMML ZHL}
A Comparative study of cataloguing rules : Based on Anglo-American code of 1908. {NASSDOC*}
Comparative study of librarian's job satisfaction : Cataloguer and reference librarians in university libraries. {JNU}
Comparative study of three systems of information retrieval. [Graduate School of Library Science, New Brunswick]. {BIS MHA}
Comparative survey analysis : An annotated bibliography, 1967-1978. {NASSDOC}
Compatibility issues affecting information systems and services. {JNU}
Compendium of research, 1951-1976. [Karnatak University]. {NASSDOC}
Compilers techniques. {NASSDOC}
A comprehensive bibliography on operations research, 1957-58. [Operations Research Society of America]. {INSA}
A compressed term index language for library and information science. [Association of Special Libraries and Information Bureaux]. {NASSDOC}
Computer-aided information retrieval. {BIS CRRI NIH USIS}
Computer and data processing : Dictionary and guide. {RTL}
Computer and information science : Collected papers on learning, adaptation and control in information systems. {DUL}
Computer and the library. {IIT}
Computer and library services. {NASSDOC*}
Computer based information retrieval systems. {DUL INSA NASSDOC}
Computer-based information services in medicines : A feasibility study : On behalf of the University of Otago medical libraries. [Centerbury Medical Library]. {BCL}

Computer-based information services in science and technology : Principles and techniques. {BCL}

Computer based library and information systems. {BIS IIT JNU NASSDOC NIH}

Computer based library and information systems, 2nd edn. {DUL NIH}

Computer based national information systems : Technology and public policy issues. [U.S. Office of Technology Assessment]. {USIS}

Computer based reference service. {JNU}

Computer basics for librarians and information scientists. {USIS}

Computer dictionary and handbook. {NASSDOC}

Computer dictionary and handbook, 3rd edn. {NASSDOC RTL}

Computer directory of India, 1983. {NASSDOC}

Computer directory of India, 1984. {NCERT}

Computer glossary for medical and health sciences. {NASSDOC}

Computer glossary for students and teachers. {NASSDOC}

Computer in libraries : A selected bibliography. {JNU}

Computer in library services. {JNU NASSDOC NMML}

Computer library for agricultural systems simulation : A progress report. {BIS}

Computer operating systems. {NASSDOC}

Computer organisation and the system/370. {NASSDOC}

Computer output microfilm, 2nd edn. [National Microfilm Association]. {USIS}

Computer output microfilm : Its library applications. {JNU}

Computer programmer's dictionary handbook. {RTL}

Computer programming and languages. {DUL}

Computer programming and statistics for basic research. {NASSDOC}

Computer programming for business and social science. {NASSDOC}

Computer programming fundamentals, 2nd edn. {NASSDOC}

Computer programming in Fortran IV. {NASSDOC}

Computer programming problems : Batch-I. [National Computer Centre, Manchester]. {NASSDOC}

Computer provision in British libraries. {JNU}

Computer readable data bases : A directory and data sourcebook. 2 vol. [American Society for Information Science]. {USIS}

Computer revolution. {NASSDOC}

Computer science. {NASSDOC}

Computer science : Fortran language programming. {DUL}

Computer simulation techniques. {NASSDOC}

Computer systems in the library : A handbook for managers and designers. {CRRI NASSDOC NIPCCD}

Computerisation in Indian libraries. {NASSDOC}

Computerised library catalogues : Their growth, costs and utility. {IIT JNU NMML USIS}

Computerised systems in library and information services. {NASSDOC}

Computers. {DUL}

Computers : A programming problem approach, rev. edn. {DUL}

Computers and common sense : The myth of thinking machines. {JNU}

Computers and computation. {NASSDOC}

Computers and systems : Introduction for librarians. {IIT NASSDOC}

Computers and the UDC : A decade of progress, 1963-1973. [International Federation for Documentation and Information]. {NIH}

Computers and the year 2000. [National Computing Centre, Manchester]. {NASSDOC}
Computers in Asia. {NASSDOC}
Computers in humanistic research. {NASSDOC}
Computers in India. {NASSDOC}
Computers in modern society. {NASSDOC}
Computers science : The PL/I language. {DUL}
Computing and computer science : A first course with PL/I. {DUL}
Computing in LASER regional library cooperation : London and South Eastern library region. [Library Association, London]. {DUL}
Concepts in communication, informatics and librarianship. (CICIL series). {JNU NASSDOC}
Concepts of information retrieval. {NASSDOC}
Conceptual foundations of information systems. {JNU}
The concise AACR2 : Being a rewritten and simplified version of Anglo-American Cataloguing Rules, 2nd edn. [American Library Association]. {NASSDOC USIS}
concise dictionary of data processing and computer terms,, 2nd edn. {NCERT}
Concise encyclopaedia of information technology. {CRRI JNU NASSDOC RTC}
Concise guide to library research. {JNU}
Concise survey of computer methods. {NASSDOC}
Condensed computer encyclopedia. {IDSA}
Conference number and souvenir : All India library conference, 22nd, January 17-20, 1976, Delhi. [Indian Library Association]. {NASSDOC}
Conference on mechanised information storage, retrieval and dissemination. {NMML}
Conference on the present status and future prospects of reference information work. {JNU}
Conflict and change in library organisation : People, power and service. {DUL JNU}
Conflict of authorship. [Sarada Ranganathan Endowment for Library Science]. {ZHL}
Congressional publications : A research guide to legislation, budgets and treaties. {USIS}
Congressional research service. {USIS}
Conservation and museum techniques. {NMML}
Conservation and restoration of archive materials. {NASSDOC}
Conservation and restoration of works of art and antiquities, tr. by Alexandra Trone. {NMML}
Conservation in India : Problems and prospects : Seminar on conservation in India, 1985, Lucknow. {NMML}
Conservation in the library : A handbook of use and care of traditional and non-traditional materials. {JNU NMML}
Conservation of books and documents. {NERC}
Conservation of library materials : Manual of bibliography on the care, repair and restoration of library materials, 2 vols. {DUL IIT NMML USIS}
Conservation of manuscripts and painting of South-East Asia. {NMML}
Conservation treatment procedure : A manual of step by step procedures for the maintenance and repair of library materials. {NASSDOC}
Consolidation of information : A handbook on evaluation, restructuring and repackaging of scientific and technical information. [UNESCO]. {CRRI}

A consumers', researchers' and students' guide to government publications. {USIS}

Contemporary approach to school library. {DUL NASSDOC}

Contemporary authors : A bibliographical guide to current authors and their work, 2 vols. {RTL}

Contemporary developments in librarianship : An international handbook. [Library Association, London]. {IIT NASSDOC}

Contemporary library design. {DUL}

Contemporary problems in technical library and information centre management : A state-of-the-art. [American Society for Information Science]. {USIS}

Content Analysis : A technique for systematic inference from communications. {NASSDOC}

Content analysis in communication research. {NASSDOC}

Content analysis of communication. {NASSDOC}

Continuing education for adults through the American Public Library, 1833-1964. [American Library Association]. {USIS}

Continuing education for librarians : Paper : All India seminar for librarians, February 13, 1984, New Delhi. [Indian Library Association]. {NASSDOC}

Continuing library and information science education : Final report to the National Commission on Libraries and Information Science (with bibliography). {USIS}

Continuing library education as viewed in relation to other continuing professional movements. [American Society for Information Science]. {NIEPA}

Convention and exposition : Micrographic Congress (India), 2nd, January 20-22, 1988, New Delhi. {NASSDOC}

Convention papers : All India library convention, 5th, May 23-26, 1985, Hardwar. [Government of India Librarians Association]. {NASSDOC}

Conversations at random : Survey research as interviewers see it. {NASSDOC}

Co-operation among Maine libraries : A report prepared for the larger libraries of Maine. {DUL}

Cooperation between types of libraries, 1940-1968 : An annotated bibliography. [American Library Association]. {NASSDOC}

Cooperation, convertibility and compatibility among information systems : A literature review. {BIS}

Cooperative cataloguing manual for the use of contributing libraries. [Library of Congress]. {DUL}

Cooperative centralised processing : A report of the establishment and first year of operation of the South West Mission Library Service. {DUL}

Coordinating cooperative collection development : A national prospective. {JNU NASSDOC}

Coordination : Concept or reality. {DUL}

Copyright Act. {NASSDOC}

Corporate headings : Their use in library catalogues and national bibliographies : A comparative and critical study. [International Federation of Library Associations and Institutions]. {JNU NASSDOC ZHL}

County and regional library development. {NASSDOC}

County libraries : Retrospect and forecast. {CRRI ZHL}

County libraries in Great Britain and Ireland. [Library Association, London]. {NASSDOC}

County libraries manual. [Library Association, London]. {NASSDOC}
County library practice. [Library Association, London]. {CRRI ZHL}
County library primer. {JNU}
County library service. {JNU}
County rural libraries : Their policy and organisation. {JNU}
A course in administration for managers of information services : Design, implementation and topical outline. [UNESCO; UNISIST]. {NASSDOC}
Course material : Workshop on computer application to library and information activities, 2nd, September 8-13, 1986, Ahmedabad. [ILA; Physical Research Laboratory, Ahmedabad]. {NASSDOC}
Creating the library identity : A manual of design. {NASSDOC}
Crime in the library : A study of patterns, impact and security. {JNU}
Crisis management of libraries in India. {NASSDOC}
Critical evaluation of the bibliographical sources for manuscript in modern Indian languages. (University of Delhi, Department of Library Science. Sessional Project). {DUL}
A critical study of the organisation and utilisation of libraries in higher educational institutions in Kerala : University of Calicut. {NASSDOC}
Cross reference index : A subject heading guide. {NASSDOC USIS}
Cross reference index, 2nd edn. {USIS}
Culture crisis and libraries in the Third World. {IIT}
Cumulated book index : World list of books in English language, 1928-32 to 1973; 1976 to 1981. {NASSDOC}
Cumulative instructions to depository libraries. {NASSDOC}
Current awareness service. {JNU}
Current book review citations, 1981 to 1983. {USIS}
Current British journals, 1982. [British Library Lending Division]. {NASSDOC}
Current concepts in library management. {USIS}
Current issues in library administration. {JNU}
Current national bibliographies of Latin America : A state-of-the-art study. [Centre for Latin America, University of Florida]. {NASSDOC}
Current problems and trends in library and information services : Professor K.S. Deshpande felicitation volume. {DUL}
Current problems in reference service. {DUL JNU NERC USIS}
Current research for the information profession, 1985-86. [Library Association, London]. {NASSDOC}
Current trends in library organisation. {JNU}
Curriculum guide for the school libraries in the elementary school. [Detmt Public School]. {JNU}
Cutter's three figure author table. {IIT ISI}
The cybernetic revolution. {INSA NASSDOC}
Cybernetics of human learning and performance : A guide to theory and research. {NASSDOC}

DARE Equal : UNESCO computerised data retrieval system for documentation in the social and human sciences. {NASSDOC}
DDC descriptor frequencies. [Defence Documentation Centre]. {IIT}
DEVSIS : The preliminary design of an international information system for the development sciences. [International Development Research Corporation, DEVSIS Study Team, Ottawā]. {NASSDOC}

Dr. S.R. Ranganathan : A bibliography, comp. by O.K. Choudhry. [National Social Science Documentation Centre]. {NASSDOC NMML}

Data archives for the social science. {DSSW}

Data archives for the social sciences : Purposes, operations and problems. {ZHL}

Databanks in a free society : Computers, record keeping and privacy : Report. [National Academy of Sciences, Washington]. {USIS}

Data communication and information exchange network. (ASTINFONET). [UNESCO]. {NASSDOC}

Data-processing concepts. {NASSDOC}

Data processing documentation : Standards, procedures and applications. {USIS}

Data processing in public and university libraries. {DUL IIT}

Data processing systems design : Case studies from the application of computers to business. {NASSDOC}

Data university. {JNU}

David Watkinson's library : Hundred years in Harftord, Connecticat. {DUL}

The Decimal and Colon Classifications : A summary and a comparison. {NASSDOC}

Decimal Bibliographical Classification of the Institute International de Bibliographies. {BIS}

Decimal Classification and Colon Classification in perspective. {CRRI IEG IIT ISI NAL NERC NMML}

Decimal, Universal Decimal and Colon Classification : A study in comparison. {ICA NASSDOC NERC NIEPA SPA}

Decision making : A seminar in public library management. {USIS}

Decision-making for library management. {JNU NIEPA}

Decision networks. {JNU}

Decision support systems : An organisational perspective. {JNU}

Decision tables in data processing : A report. [National Computing Centre, Manchester]. {NASSDOC}

Defusing censorship : The librarian's guide to handling censorship conflicts. {JNU}

Delhi Public Library : Constitution, regulations of Delhi Library Board and rules of the library. [Delhi Library Board]. {NASSDOC}

Delhi Public Library : An evaluation report. {DSSW DUL}

Delhi Public Library : Silver jubilee souvenir, 27th October, 1976. {NASSDOC}

Delhi University Library : The opening of the new library by S. Radhakrishnan. {JNU}

Depth classification and reference service and reference material. [Indian Library Association]. {INSA ISI}

Depth schedules for Indian philosophy and religions for DDC. {JNU]

Description of the BNB/MARC record : A manual of practice. {JNU}

A descriptive account of Colon Classification. {BIS DSSW DUL ISI JNU NAL NASSDOC NERC NMML SPA ZHL}

Descriptive catalogue of documentary films. [Films Division, Government of India]. {NAL}

Descriptive cataloguing : A students introduction to the Anglo-American Cataloguing Rules, 1967. {NASSDOC}

Descriptive cataloguing : A students introduction to the Anglo-American Cataloguing Rules, 1967, 2nd edn. {IIC IIT}

Descriptive cataloguing rules. [International Atomic Energy Agency, Vienna]. {BIS}

Descriptive list of professional and non-professional duties in libraries : Priliminary draft. [American Library Association]. {USIS}

The design and implementation of community information service in the library. {BCL}

Design and production of media presentation for libraries. {JNU}

Design for elementary libraries. [Department of School City of South Bend]. {JNU}

Design in the library. [Library Association London]. {ISI}

Design of information in the social sciences : Size and growth of monograph literature with particular reference to the social sciences. [Bath University Library]. {BCL NASSDOC*}

Design of inquiry systems : Basic concepts of systems and organisation. {JNU}

The design of the small public library. {USIS}

Designing and space planning for libraries : A behavioural guide. {BIS NASSDOC USIS}

Designing library buildings for activity. {CRRI ICA ICHR ISI MMTC NASSDOC}

Designing national scientific and technological communication system. {USIS}

Deterioration and preservation of library materials : Conference of the Graduate Library School, 34th, August 4-6, 1969, Chicago. {AIU CRRI IIT INSA JNU NASSDOC NMML}

Developing computer based information systems. {JNU}

Developing computer based library systems. {JNU}

Developing horizons in library and information science, 2 vols. {AIU IIT ISI JNU NASSDOC NMML SPA}

Developing the library collection in political science. {JNU}

Developing library collections. {USIS}

Developing multi-media libraries. {JNU}

Developing public library systems and services. [UNESCO]. {NIEPA}

Developing reading habits in Asian conditions. {ZHL}

Development index Canada : Index to 1976 Canadian literature on economic and social development. [International Development Research Centre]. {IIFT}

Development of documentation in India : Social science information. {BIS DSSW DUL ISI JNU NAL NERC NASSDOC NMML SPA ZHC}

Development of information systems for education. {AIU INSA}

Development of libraries and library science in India. {ICA IIC IIT NASSDOC NERC NIH NIPCCD NMML}

Development of libraries in new India. {ICA IIC IIT NASSDOC SPA}

Development of library facilities in universities and colleges. [University Grants Commission, New Delhi]. {AIU IIT MHA}

Development of library services : Trinidad and Tobago. [UNESCO]. {ISI}

Development of library services in India : Social science information. {BIS DUL ISI JNU NASSDOC NERC NMML ZHL}

Development of national library and information service. [Library Association, London]. {NIEPA}

Development of performance standards for library binding, Phase 1: Report of the survey, April, 1961; Phase 2: Report on a study conducted by library technology project. [American Library Association]. {BIS IIT}

Development of public libraries in Africa : Ibadan seminar. [UNESCO]. {IEG NASSDOC ZHL}

Development of public libraries in Latin America : The Sao Paulo conference. [UNESCO]. {IEG NASSDOC ZHL}

Development of reference services through academic traditions, public library practices and special librarianship. {JNU}

Development of research and information system in the Third World : Report of the proceedings: Research and information system for the non-aligned and other developing countries, 2nd, November 20-22, 1985, New Delhi. [RISNODC]. {NASSDOC}

Development of resource sharing networks in the framework of UNISIST World Science Information System. [National Library of Australia]. {JNU}

Development of terminology in the field of library classification with special reference to Indian school of thought: A case study in terminology development : Thesis. (Karnatak University). {NASSDOC}

Development of an unified scheme of common subdivisions in general classification systems. Thesis. (Gulbarga University. {NASSDOC}

Development plans and planning : Bibliographic and computer aids to research. {JNU}

A development plan for public library system in the Karnataka State. Thesis. (Karnataka University). {NASSDOC}

Developments in classification : DRTC annual seminar, 2 vols. [Documentation Research And Training Centre]. {NASSDOC}

Developments in collection building in university libraries in Western Europe: Symposium on . . ., March 31-April 2, 1976, Amsterdam. {IIT}

Dewey Decimal Classification, 20th edn. 4 vols, V. 1. : Introduction tables; V. 2. : Schedules 000-599; V. 3. : Schedules 600-990; V. 4. : Index manual, 20th edn. {NASSDOC}

Dewey decimal Classification : 301-307, sociology : Expanded version based on edition 19. {NASSDOC}

Dewey Decimal Classification : A study manual. {USIS}

Dewey Decimal Classification and Relative Index, 6th edn. {NAI}

Dewey Decimal Classification and Relative Index. 14th edn., 2 vols. {USIS ZHL}

Dewey Decimal Classification and Relative Index. 15th edn. {IEG IIT NAI USIS}

Dewey Decimal Classification and Relative Index. 16th edn. 2 vols. {CRRI NASSDOC NMML SPA USIS}

Dewey Decimal Classification and Relative Index, 17th edn., 2 vols. {CRRI NASSDOC NMML SPA USIS}

Dewey Decimal Classification and Relative Index, 18th edn., 3 vols. {JNU IIMC ISI NASSDOC NIEPA USIS}

Dewey Decimal Classification and Relative Index, 19th edn., 3 vols. {CRRI ICHR ISI JNU MHA NAI NMML NASSDOC USIS ZHL}

Dewey Decimal Classification for Indology : Expansion and modification of Dewey Decimal Classification (18) for classifying Indological books with special reference to Indian philosophy and Indian religions. {DSSW ICHR IIC IIT INSA JNU MHA NIPCCD ZHL}

Dewey Decimal Classification, Universal Decimal Classification and Colon Classification : Development structure, comparison. {NASSDOC}

Dictionary catalogue : A practical manual. {ICHR IIT IIMC NERC NIPCCD}

Dictionary Catalogue Code, 2nd edn. [Madras Library Association]. {CRRI}

Dictionary for computer languages. {RTL}

A dictionary of acronyms and abbreviations in library and information science, 2nd edn. [Canadian Library Association, Ottawa]. {NASSDOC}

Dictionary of communication and media studies. {JNU NASSDOC}

Dictionary of data processing. {NASSDOC}

Dictionary of data processing, 3rd. rev edn. {NASSDOC}

Dictionary of data processing terms : {UGC}

Dictionary of information processing, including fields of application. {RTL}

Dictionary of library and educational technology, 2nd rev edn. {NASSDOC}

Dictionary of library and information science : English-Hindi; Hindi-English. {NASSDOC}

Dictionary of library and information science : English-Kannada. [University of Gulbarga, Gulbarga]. {NASSDOC}

Dictionary of library scinece. {JNU}

Dictionary of library terms : English-Arabic. {JNU}

Dictionary of new information technology. {IIPA}

Dictionary of new information technology acronym. {JNU}

Dictionary of printing paper making and book binding. {DUL}

Dictionary of pseudonyms in Indian literature. [Delhi Library Association]. {NASSDOC}

Dilemma of the urban public library in developing countries. [International Federation of Library Associations and Institutions; International Council for Adult Education]. {IIMC}

Dimensions of comparative librarianship. [American Library Association]. {NASSDOC}

Dimensions in library and information science. {JNU}

Dimensions of library and information science : Kaula festschrift. {NASSDOC}

Directions for the decade : Library instruction in the 1980's : Conference on library orientation for academic libraries, 10th, May 8-9. 1980. [Eastern Michigan University]. {USIS}

Directory [International Federation of Library Association and Institutions]. {NASSDOC}

Directory of archives, libraries and schools of librarianship in Africa. {IIMC}

Directory of booksellers, publishers, libraries and librarians in India, 1968-69. {SPA}

Directory of booksellers, publishers, libraries and librarians in India, including who's who, 2nd edn, {ICA IDSA JNU NASSDOC NMML}

Directory of book trade in India. JNU RTL}

Directory of British publishers, 1961; 1967. {DUL}

Directory of business Information research centres in India. [National Industrial Documentation and Manpower Centre, New Delhi]. {NASSDOC}

Directory of college and university libraries in New York State. [University of the State of New York, State Education Department]. {JNU}

Directory of co-operative libraries and documentation services. [ICA, London]. {ICA}

Directory of development documentation and information facilities in Asia and Pacific. [UN Asian Development Institute, Bangkok]. {IEG IIFT NASSDOC}

Directory of documentation, libraries and archives services in Africa, 2nd edn. [UNESCO]. {JNU NASSDOC}

Directory of educational documentation and information services, 3rd edn., [UNESCO]. {NASSDOC NIPCCD}

Directory of family planning and population libraries in India. [National Institute of Family Planning]. {NIH}

Directory of health science libraries and documentation centres in India. [National Institute of Health and Family Welfare, New Delhi]. {NIH}

Directory of health science libraries in South-Asia. {NIH}

Directory of Indian public libraries : A selected list of libraries. {NASSDOC}

Directory of Indian publishers. [federation of Publishers and Booksellers Association in India]. {IIPA NASSDOC RTL UGC}.

A directory of information resources in the United States Federal Government, with a supplement of government sponsored information analysis centres. [U.S. Library of Congress, National Referral Centre]. {USIS}

Directory of information sources in Japan. {JNU}

Directory of institutions and organisations specialising in children's literature. [International Board on Books for Young People, UNESCO]. {NASSDOC*}

Directory of Islamic libraries and librarians. [Islamic Library Association, California]. {ZHL}

Directory of libraries and documentation centres in the United Nations system. {JNU}

Directory of libraries and information centres in Gujarat. {Gujarat Granthalaya Seva Sangh, Ahmedabad]. {NASSDOC}

A directory of libraries and library training programme in Thailand. [UNESCO Regional Office for Education in Asia, Bangkok]. {NASSDOC NIEPA}

Directory of libraries and special collections on Asia and North Africa. {NASSDOC NCERT NMML}

Directory of libraries and who's who in library profession in Delhi. [Delhi Library Association]. {BIS CRRI DSSW ICCR ICWA IEG IIC NMML ZHL}

Directory of libraries in Delhi. {ICA ICCR IIC IIPA JNU NIEPA NASSDOC}

A directory of libraries in Malaysia. [University of Malaya Library, Kaula Lumpur]. {NASSDOC}

Directory of libraries in Tanzania. [National Central Library, Tanzania]. {NASSDOC}

Directory of libraries, publishers and booksellers of Udaipur city and who's who. {NMML RTL}

Directory of libraries, publishers, booksellers in the city of Bombay. [SNDT Women University Library]. {NASSDOC}

A directory of library and information retrieval software for micro-computers, 2nd edn. {NASSDOC}

Directory of library and information science schools in India. {NASSDOC}

Directory of library consultants. {USIS}

Directory of library photo duplication services in the United States, Canada and Mexico. {DUL}

Directory of library schools and lecturers in librarianship in Australia. {NASSDOC*}

Directory of medical libraries in the British Isles. [Library Association, Medical Section]. {NIH}

Directory of members. [Micrographic Congress of India]. {NASSDOC}

Directory of microfilm facilities in Southeast Asia, 2nd edn. {JNU}

Directory of museum. {ICCR}

Directory of museums in India. [Ministry of Scientific Research and Cultural Affairs, New Delhi]. {ICCR NASSDOC}

Directory of population libraries and information centres in the United States. [Carolina Population Centre, University of North Carolina]. {NIH RTL}

Directory of publishers of British Journals. {NASSDOC}

Directory of publishers and booksellers in India, based on actual mailing. [Federation of Indian Publishers]. {NASSDOC}

The directory of publishing. {NASSDOC}

Directory of research and special libraries in India and Sri Lanka, 2 vols. {MMTC ZHL}

Directory of scientific and technical libraries in India. {DUL}

Directory of selected scholars and researchers in Southeast Asia. [Regional Institute of Higher Education and Development, Singapore]. {NASSDOC}

Directory of social science libraries, information centres and data bases in Sri Lanka. [Sri Lanka Social Science Documentation Centre]. {NASSDOC}

Directory of special and research libraries in India. [Indian Association of Special Libraries and Information Centres]. {IIT ISI MFL NMML ZHL}

Directory of special and research libraries in India. 2nd edn. [Indian Association of Special Libraries and Information Centres]. {ICCR ICWA IDSA IIPA NASSDOC NMML UGC}

Directory of special libraries and information centres. {ICCR ICWA IIPA}

Directory of special libraries and information centres 1974; 1979. {IIFT}

Directory of special libraries and information centres 1981 to 1983. {USIS}

Directory of suppliers of library requisites. [IDL Chemicals Limited, Hyderabad]. {NASSDOC*}

Directory of United Nations databases and information systems [United Nations Advisory Committee for Coordination of Information Systems]. {NASSDOC}

Directory of United Nations information systems, 2 vols. [United Nations Inter-Organisation Board of Information Systems, Geneva]. {MMTC RTL}

Directory of World Bank depository libraries. [International Bank for Reconstruction and Development] {NASSDOC}

The disadvantaged and library effectiveness. [American Library Association]. {USIS}

Discovering books and libraries : A handbook for the upper elementary and junior high school grades. {DUL}

Display techniques. {DUL}

The dissemination of information. {BCL DUL ISI NASSDOC ZHL}

Dissemination of information : An examination guidebook. {BIS DUL MFL NIPCCD}

Dissemination of scientific information in the People's Republic of China. [International Development Research Centre, Ottawa]. {NASSDOC}

Dissemination services provided by special libraries in Pune. [University of Poona, Pune]. {NASSDOC*}

Distributed data bases : Plan for interaction and online search. {NASSDOC*}

Do we really need libraries? {NIPCCD}

Document bibliography. {NIPCCD NASSDOC}

Document repair. [Society of Archivists]. {NMML}

Document reproduction in libraries. {DUL}

Document reproduction services : Their efficient organisation and management. [UNESCO]. {IIMC NASSDOC}

Document retrieval systems : Factors effecting search time. {DUL IIT NASSDOC USIS}

Document storage and retrieval techniques appendix : Indexing techniques, descriptions and background. {JNU}

Documentation. {BCL BIS DUL MFL NAI SPA}

Documentation : Genesis and development. {AIU CRRI DUL ICA ICHR IIMC ISI JNU MFL MHA MMTC NASSDOC NIEPA NIPCCD NMML}

Documentation : How to organise and control information processes in business and industry. {JNU}

Documentation and information : Services, techniques and systems. {AIU BCL BIS IIMC ISI JNU MFL NASSDOC NCDC NERC NIEPA NIH NMML}

Documentation and information : Services, techniques and systems, 2nd edn. {DUL ICA IIT JNU MHA NIH NIPCCD ZHL}

Documentation and information retrieval. {DUL MHA ZHL}

Documentation and information retrieval : An information to basic principle and cost analysis. {JNU}

Documentation and its facets : Being a symposium of seventy papers by thirty-two authors. {BIS DUL DSSW IIFT JNU NMML SPA}

Documentation and the organisation of knowledge, ed. by D.J. Foskett. {DUL NASSDOC NMML USIS}

Documentation encyclopaedia of UNESCO and education. {NIEPA}

Documentation in action. {BIS DUL NASSDOC}

Documentation in India. {JNU}

Documentation, indexing and retrieval of scientific information. [US Committee on Government Operations]. {JNU}

Documentation of semi-automatic bibliographic information retrieval. {JNU}

Documentation services in departmental libraries : Papers : All India library convention, 2nd, March 3-6, 1980, New Delhi. [Government of India Librarians Association]. {CRRI NASSDOC NMML}

Documentation services in India : An overview of some selected documentation centres. {NASSDOC}

Documentation source book. {BIS DUL MHA NASSDOC NIH}

Documentation standards. {BIS DUL NIEPA}

Documentation standards and procedures for on-line systems. {CRRI}

Documentation techniques in the USA. [Organisation for European Economic Co-operation, Paris]. {ISI}

Documentation training needs in Eastern Africa. {ICA}

Documents of the UN and the specialised agencies : A study of problems regarding their acquisition and organisation with special reference to India. (University of Delhi Department of Library and Information Science sessional project). {DUL}

Documents on national policy on library and information system. [Rammohan Roy Library Foundation; Indian Library Association]. {NASSDOC*}

Does your firm need its own information service : An enquiry into the economic advantages of an information service in small and medium-sized firms. [Organisation of Economic Cooperation and Development]. {TDA}

Doing library research : An introduction for community college students. {USIS}

Down loading bibliographic records. {NASSDOC*}

Dvibindu vargikaran ka sankshipt parichay. {NMML}

Dvibindu vargikaran paddhatiche yatharth darshan {NMML}

Dynamic information and library processing. {CRRI DUL ICHR INSA ISI NASSDOC USIS}

ED art library manual : A guide to resources and practice. {IIT}

EUDISED multilingual thesaurus : Alphabetical list — of deseriptors. {NASSDOC}

EUDISEO multilingual thesaurus for information processing in the field of education. {NASSDOC}

East African School of Librarianship. [UNESCO]. {NASSDOC*}

East and West. : Delhi Public Library, India, as seen against the background of the Rochester Public Library. {NASSDOC*}

Eastern library. {ZHL}

Eastern library : An introduction to the Khuda Bakhsh Oriental Public Library, 2nd edn. {JNU NMML}

An eastern library : An introduction to the Khuda Bakhsh Oriental Public Library, 3rd edn. {NASSDOC*}

Easy ways to displays : A library publicity handbook. {JNU}

Economic analysis of public library services. {ISI}

Economic analysis of special libraries with special reference to CSIR libraries. (Memeo short bibliography). {NASSDOC}

An economic view of public libraries [U.S. National Bureau of Economic Research]. {USIS}

Economics and commerce : The sources of information and their organisation. {NASSDOC}

Economics of academic libraries. [American Council of Education]. {AIU NIEPA USIS}

Economics of book catalogue production. {DUL}

Economics of book publishing in developing countries. {DUL}

Economics of book selling. {DUL}

Economics of book storage in college and university libraries. {NASSDOC}

Economics of information and knowledge : Selected readings. {NASSDOC}

Editor and publisher international year book : Encyclopaedia of the newspaper industry. {DUL}

Educating the library user. {USIS}

Education and libraries : Selected papers. {AIU USIS}

Education and training for scientific and technological library and information work. {IIT SPA}

Education and training of information specialists. {BCL CRRI ICA}

Education and training of users of scientific and technical information : UNISIST guide for teachers. [UNESCO]. {BCL ISI NASSDOC}

Education clearing houses and documentation centres. [UNESCO]. {JNU}

Education for librarianship. {AIU IEG}

Education for librarianship. [UNESCO]. {IEG NASSDOC}

Education for librarianship : Decisions in organising a system of professional education. {NIEPA}

Education for librarianship : A survey. [Indian Association of Special Libraries and Information Centres]. {SPA}

Education for librarianship in India. [Indian Association of Special Libraries and Information Centres]. {IIT MFL NASSDOC}

Education for library science and documentation : Iran. [UNESCO]. {NASSDOC*}

Education, library science, journalism : A bibliography of doctoral dissertations, 1857-1970. [Inter-University Board of India and Ceylon, New Delhi]. {JNU NMML}

Educational information : Problems, issues and strategies for resolving them : Report of a regional workshop. [National Institute for Educational Research]. {NIEPA}

Effective catalogues. {NIPCCD}

Effective library exhibits : How to prepare and promote good displays, 2nd edn. {CRRI USIS}

Effective methods of promoting reading habits in Asia and the Pacific. [Asian Cultural Centre for UNESCO, Tokyo]. {NASSDOC*}

Effective reference librarian. {IIT ISI NASSDOC}

Effectiveness of centralized library services in elementary schools. {JNU}

Efficient patterns for adequate library service in a large city : A survey of Boston. {JNU}

Ek mashriqui kutub khana : Kutub- khana Khuda Bakhsh, tr. by Mubarizuddin Rifat. {NMML}

Electronic data processing computers for commercial students. {NERC}

Electronic handling of information : Testing and evaluation. {DUL INSA}

The electronic library : Bibliographic data bases, 1978-79, 2nd rev. edn. {USIS}

Elementary and secondary school libraries of the Pacific North West. {JNU}

Elementary school libraries. {JNU}

Elementary school library in action. {JNU}

Elements of information science. {DUL NAI NIEPA}

Elements of library classification. {ZHL}

Elements of library classification, 2nd edn. {INSA NERC SPA}

Elements of library classification, 3rd edn. {BIS CRRI IIT ISI NASSDOC}

Elsevier's dictionary of library science, information and documentation. {JNU ZHL}

Elsevier's dictionary of library science, information and documentation, 2nd edn. {IIT}

Emerging field of socio-bibliography : The collected essays of Ilse Bry, comp. and ed. by Lois Afflerback and Marga Franck {BCL IIT}

Encyclopaedia of business information sources. {USIS}

Encyclopaedia of information systems and services. {MHA}

Encyclopaedia of information system and services : A guide to information storage and retrieval services, data base produces and publishers, online vendors, 3rd edn. {USIS}

Encyclopaedia of information system and services : An international guide to computer readable data bases, data base producers and publishers, online vendors and time sharing companies, 4th edn. {USIS}

Encyclopaedia of information systems and services, 5th edn. {USIS}

Encyclopaedia of librarianship. {SPA ZHL}

Encyclopaedia of librarianship, 3rd edn. {SPA ZHL}

Encyclopaedia of librarianship, rev. edn. {BIS CRRI DSSW IAMR IDSA IEG IIT MFL NASSDOC NCERT NIEPA}

Encyclopaedia of library and information science, 41 vols. {ACA IOSA IEG IIT INSA JNU NASSDOC NCERT NIH ZHL}

Encyclopaedia of linguistics, information and control. {NASSDOC NCERT}

Encyclopaedias and dictionaries of the world. {NASSDOC}

End of libraries. {IIT}

English library : Sources and history. {JNU}

English-Russian glossary of computer systems and networks terminology. {NASSDOC}

Entropy and information in science and philosophy. {INSA}

Environment for systems programmes. {JNU}

An epostle to dean Shera on the gravity of notation in colon classification. {NASSDOC}

Esdaile's manual of bibliography, rev edn., by Roy Stockes. {MFL}

Essays and studies in librarianship. {NASSDOC}

Essays in librarianship : In memory of William Charles Berwick Sayers. {MFL}

Essays in library science, 3rd edn. {JNU}

Essays in personnel bibliography : A bibliography of the writings on and by S.R. Ranganathan. {DUL NASSDOC NMML}

Essays of an information scientist. {CRRI JNU}

Essays on bibliography. {NASSDOC}

Essays on information and libraries. {CRRI DUL ICA IIMC INSA JNU NASSDOC NIPCCD ZHL}

Essential problems in terminology for informatics and documentation. [International Federation for Documentation and Information]. {BIS CRRI}

Essentials in library education. [American Library Association]. {NASSDOC*}

Essentials of library planning. {DUL}

Establishing a legislative framework for the implementation of NATIS. [UNESCO]. {NASSDOC}

Evaluating information : A guide for users of social science research. {NCAER}

Evaluation and scientific management of libraries and information centres. {NIEPA}

Evaluation of the acquisition policy and procedure of periodicals in the Indian Institute of Foreign Trade Library and Rattan Tata Library. {DUL}

Evaluation of collection of Jawaharlal Nehru University Library from the point of view of Indian reference sources. [University of Delhi, Department of Library and Information Science Sessional Project]. {DUL}

Evaluation of Indian reference sources published during last ten years available in Delhi University Library. (University of Delhi, Department of Library and Information Science, Sessional Project). {DUL}

Evaluation of the MEDLARE demand research services. [U.S. National Library of Medicine]. {USIS}

Evaluation of micropublications : A handbook for librarians. [American Library Association]. {NASSDOC}

The evaluation of a programme designed for teaching on-line information retrieval techniques : Final report for the period June-September 1976. [Liverpool Polytechnic, Department of Library and Information Studies]. {BCL}

Evaluation of reading materials for neo-literates and a study of their reading needs and interests. {NMML}

Evaluation of reference service in JNU library. {JNU}

Evaluation of the reference sources in the field of Hindi language and literature serving the needs of post-graduates and faculty of Delhi University campus college libraries. (University of Delhi, Department of Library and Information Science, Sessional Project). {DUL}

Evaluation of selected reference tools published in India. (University of Delhi, Department of Library Science, Sessional Project). {DUL}

Every child needs a school library. {JNU}

Examination of current practices in Delhi college libraries and suggestion for improvement. {JNU}

Examination of public library finance in Canada in relation to minimum standards of the Canadian Library Association. {JNU}

Examples illustrating AACR2 : Anglo-American Cataloguing Rules, 2nd ed. [Library Association, London]. {NASSDOC}

Examples illustrating Anglo-American Cataloguing Rules : British text. [Library Association, London]. {ZHL}

Excellence in library management. {NASSDOC*}

Exchange of ideas : East and West meet the challenge : Final report : Seminar on the international exchange of publication in the Indo-Pacific area, 1957, Tokyo. {IEG}

Exchange of publications and organisation of national exchange centres. (University of Delhi, Department of Library and Information Science, Sessional Project). {DUL}

Exhibition of scientific and technical books : Catalogue. {DUL}

Expanding media. {IIT}

Expansion and modification of Dewey Decimal Classification (18) for classifying Indological books with special reference to Indian philosophy and Indian religions. {NASSDOC}

Experiences of library network administrators : Papers based on the symposium 'From our past : Towards 2000'. {NASSDOC}

Experimental information service in the social sciences : Report on work carried out in 1970, [University Library, Bath University of Technology]. {NASSDOC}

Exploring the world of data processing. {NASSDOC}

Extensions and corrections to the UDC. [International Federation for Documentation and Information]. {IIT INSA}

FID congress on new trends in documentation and information, 1978, Edinburg. [International Federation of Documentation and Information] {CRRI}

FID directory 1985-86. [International Federation of Documentation and Information]. {NASSDOC}

Faceted classification. [Association of Special Libraries and Information Bureaux]. {CRRI}

Faceted classification for an essay on the literature of the performing arts. {DUL}

Factors related to the professional development of librarians. {USIS}

Facts and how to find them. {CRRI MFL}

Facts and how to find them, 4th edn. {BIS DUL}

Facts and how to find them, 7th edn. {DSSW}

Facts and how to find them : A guide to source of information and to the method of systematic research. {JNU}

Facts at your fingertips : Everyman's guide to reference books. {MFL}

Faculty involvement in library instruction. {JNU}

Faculty status for university and college librarian in India : Basic documents. {JNU NASSDOC ZHL}

The fair garden and the swarm of beasts : The library and the young adult. {USIS}

The fall and rise of national bibliography. [Sarada Ranganathan Endowment for Library Science, Bangalore]. {NASSDOC*}

A family planning library manual. [Planned Parenthood Federation of America]. {NIH}

Famous Hungarian libraries. [National Szecheni Library]. {NASSDOC}

Farminton plan handbook. [Association of Research Libraries]. {USIS}

Feasibility study for continuing education of medical librarians : Interim report. {DUL}

Federal library resources : A user's guide to research collections. {USIS}

The federal role in library and information services. {USIS}

Fee based information services : A study of a growing industry. [IIT USIS}

Ferment in college libraries : The impact of information technology. {JNU}

Fifteen years of activity of the association, 1953-67. [Delhi Library Association]. {NASSDOC*}

Fifty years of Government of India Librarians Association. [Government of India Librarians Association]. {NASSDOC NMML}

Fifty years of Indian Library Association, 1933-83 : Golden jubilee. [Indian Library Association]. {JNU MMTC ZHL}

Fifty years of librarianship in India : Past, present and future : Papers : All India library conference, 29th, December 5-9, 1983. [Indian Library Association]. {MMTC NASSDOC ZHL}

Filing and preserving stock and records, in libraries and other institutions including museums and art galleries. {JNU}

Filing rules for dictionary catalogues of the Library of Congress. [Library of Congress]. {IEC NASSDOC}

Film cataloguing rules. [Association of Special Libraries and Information Bureaux]. {SPA}

Film library techniques : Principles of administration. {NMML USIS}

The film user's handbook : A basic manual for managing library film services. {USIS}

Final report : International congress on the universal availability of publications. [UNESCO]. {NASSDOC}

Final report : International congress on the universal availability of publications. [UNESCO]. {NASSDOC}

Final report : Project for evaluating the benefits from university libraries. [University of Durham] {NIEPA}

Final report : UNESCO meeting of experts on the national planning of library services in Asia, December 11-19, 1967, Colombo. {NASSDOC}

Final report, 1985 and 1986. [Inter Governmental Committee for the UNESCO, Inter Governmental Informatics Programme]. {JNU}

Final report on the ICAR institutions and Agricultural University libraries. [ICAR]. {IEG}

Final report on mechanised information services in the university library : Phase-I : Planning. 13 pts. Pt 1 : Mechanised information services in the university library : Introduction and summary; Pt 2 : Summary of symposium on mechanised information services in the university library; Pt 3 : Inventory of available data bases; Pt 4 : Standards for cataloguing of magnetic tape material; Pt 5 : Nature of typical data bases; Pt 6 : Evaluation of generalised file management systems; Pt 7 : Experience with Library of Congress rare tapes; Pt 8 : Experimental on-line mathematics citation data base; Pt 9 : Development programme for a centre for information services; Pt 10 : Preliminary specifications (hardware and software) for a centre for information and documentation services (Interim report); Pt 11 : On the development of social science information; Pt 12 : Joint design and development of library systems; and Pt 13 : Library and human memory. [Institute of Library Research, University of California]. {BIS}

Finding and using technical information. {MHA}

Finding the facts : Newspaper information retrieval system. {IIMC JNU NIPCCD}

Finding the source : A thesaurus index to the reference collection. {NASSDOC USIS}

First All India workshop on the methods of teaching and evaluation in library science, May 15-30, 1973, Delhi. {DUL}

First seminar of university librarians in India, Jaipur. {NMML}

First steps in annotation in catalogues, 2nd rev ed. {DUL}

First steps in librarianship. {CRRI ICHR IIT MFL SPA}

Five laws of library science. {BIS CRRI IIT MHA NAI NCAER NMML SPA ZHL}

The five laws of library science. [Madras Library Association, Madras]. {NASSDOC*}

Five year work in librarianship. [Library Association, London]. {IIT}

Floor and floor coverings. [American Library Association]. {NAI}

Flow charting techniques. {JNU}

Focus on information and communication. {JNU}

Folklore library. {IIMC NASSDOC NMML}

For books. [UNESCO]. {ICA}

For Congress and the nation : A chronological history of the Library of Congress. [Library of Congress]. {USIS}

For the people : Fightings for public libraries. {USIS}

Forecast of the cost of academic library services in Canada, 1965-1975. [Association of College and University Libraries, Canada]. {JNU}

Foreign area studies and the college library : Bibliographies, reference service, acquisitions programmes and other activities and services for undergraduate librarians in African, Asian, Latin American and Russian studies. [Foreign Area Materials Center, University of the State of New York]. {NASSDOC}

Foreign theses in British libraries. [University of Birmingham]. {NASSDOC}

Formation of necessary standards for different types of libraries in India : Working paper : ILA seminar, 1979, Trivandrum. [Indian Library Association]. {NASSDOC}

Foundations of access to knowledge : A symposium. {NASSDOC}

Foundations of cataloguing : A source book. {NASSDOC}

Foundations of education for librarianship. {AIU IIFT ISI NIPCCD USIS ZHL}

Foundations of the public library : The origins of the public library movement in New England, 1629-1855. {USIS}

Fraser-Hickson library : An informal history. {IIT}

Free book service for all : An international survey. {ICA ISI JNU MFL NMML SPA}

Freedom of book selection : Proceedings : Conference on intellectual freedom, 2nd, June 20-21, 1953. [American Library Association]. {AIU USIS}

French bibliographical digest : Public administration. {MFL}

Friends of the library : Organisation and activities. [American Library Association]. {NASSDOC USIS}

From author to reader : A social study of books. {AIU}

From little acorns : The library profession in Britain. {IEG NERC}

Frontiers in librarianship : Proceedings of Change Institute, 1969. [Change Institute, University of Maryland]. {JNU NIPCCD}

Full and short entry catalogues : Library needs and uses. [Centre for Catalogue Research]. {NASSDOC}

Function and organisation of a national documentation centre in developing country. [FID/DC Working Group]. {ICA JNU NASSDOC}

The function of bibliography. {AIU NASSDOC}

Functional analysis of information processing : A structured approach for simplifying systems design. {NASSDOC}

Functions and objects of author and title cataloguing : A contribution to cataloguing theory. {NMML}

Functions of the library in the modern college : Conference of the Graduate Library School, 19th, 1954, Chicago. {IIT SPA}

Fundamental reference sources. [American Library Association]. {DUL INSA JNU MMTC NASSDOC NERC}

Fundamental reference sources. [American Library Association]. {DUL}

Fundamental theories in abstracting and fundamental laws in library science. {JNU}

Fundamentals of bibliography with special reference to India. {JNU NASSDOC}

Fundamentals of documentation : With special reference to India. {DSSW DUL ICA ISI NCDC NMML}

Fundamentals of library administration and management. {NMML}

Fundamentals of library and information science. {NMML}

Fundamentals of library classification. {BIS CRRI NAI SPA}

Fundamentals of library organisation. {DSSW IIMC}

Fundamentals of library organisation and administration : A practical guide. {NCDC NERC NIEPA ZHL}

Fundamentals of library science : A modern approach. {ICA ISI JNU ZHL}

Fundamentals of practical cataloguing. {BIS CRRI ICA IIFT MHA NAI NASSDOC ZHL}

Fundamentals of special librarianship and documentation. [Indian Association of Special Libraries and Information Centres]. {AIU DUL IIT}

Fundamentals of systems analysis. {JNU}

Furnishing the library interior. {BIS USIS}

Future development of libraries and information services. [Department of Education and Science, Great Britain]. {ISI}

The future of the catalog . The library's choices. {USIS}

The future of cataloguing. {USIS}

Future of libraries : Panel discussion by librarians, administrators, faculty and students : Papers from the millionth volume celebration. [New York State University]. {NASSDOC}

Future of the research library. {IEG JNU}

GEAC : A guide for librarians and system managers. {NASSDOC}

General catalogue of UNESCO publications and UNESCO sponsored publications. supplements : 1946/59-1964/67. [UNESCO]. {NASSDOC}

A general description of an approach to computerised bibliographical control. [International Labour Office, Intergrated Scientific Information System]. {TDA}

General inquirer : A computer approach to content analysis. {NASSDOC}

General introduction to the techniques of information and documentation work. [UNESCO]. {JNU NMML}

General reference department staff manual. [Enoch Pratt Free Library, Baltimore]. {USIS}

General system theory : Foundations, development, applications. {NASSDOC}

General systems philosophy for the social and behavioural sciences, ed. by Erwinlaszlo. {NASSDOC}

A general theory of SIL, POPSI and CLASSAURUS : Results of current classification research in India. {NASSDOC*}

Generating and printing indexes by computer. [Association of Special Libraries and Information Bureaux]. {CRRI}

Generation of syntactic structures from a semantic base. {JNU}

Geography of marketing and commercial activities in India : Documentation on research information. {IIT}

Getting ready for AACR2 : The cataloguer's guide. {JNU USIS}

Glimpses of librarianship. {JNU}

Glossary from handbook of data processing for libraries. {USIS}

Glossary of the book : Terms used in paper making, printing, binding book printing and publishing with notes on illuminated manuscripts bibliographies, private presses and printing societies. {DUL}

Glossary of cataloguing terms. (IS : 796-1966). [Indian Standards Institution]. {NAI NASSDOC}

Glossary of cataloguing terms in Indian regional languages. [Indian Association of Special Libraries and Information Centres]. {NASSDOC SPA}

Glossary of classification terms. (IS : 2550-1963). [Indian Standards Institutions]. {ISI NASSDOC}

Glossary of documentation terms. (BS : 5408-1976). [British Standards Institution]. {CRRI}

Glossary of indexing terms. {BCL NASSDOC NERC}

Glossary of library and information science : English-Telugu and Telugu-English. [Zilla Granthalaya Samstha, Machilipatnam]. {NASSDOC*}

Glossary of library science technical terms. {JNU NASSDOC RTL}

Glossary of photocopying terms. {DUL}

A glossary of technical service terms for library science students. [School of Library Science, Syracuse University]. {NASSDOC}.

Glossary of terms for wooden furniture. (IS : 4415-1967). [Indian Standards Institution]. {NASSDOC}

Glossary of terms relating to wooden furniture and fixtures rev. edn. (IS : 4415-1974). {NASSDOC}

Glossary of terms used in the Public Libraries Department : English-Telugu. [Government of Andhra Pradesh, Official Language Commission, Hyderabad]. {NASSDOC*}

Going into print : Notes for the guidance of authors in preparing copy for the printer, correcting proofs, etc. {DUL}

The government and control of libraries, 2nd edn. {DUL ICHR}

Government of India publications. {MHA}

Government publications : Their role in the national programme for library and information services. [U.S. National Commission on Libraries and Information Science]. {USIS}

Government publications and their use, rev edn. {MFL}

Government publications of India : A survey of their nature, bibliographical control and distribution systems. {MFL NASSDOC NIPCCD}
Gramophone recording library. {CRRI}
Granthalaya mein sandhrab seva. {JNU NMML}
Granthalaya pragati : Souvenir : Andhra Pradesh libraries conference, December 10-12, 1982, Tirupati. [Andhra Pradesh Public Library Association]. {NASSDOC*}
Granthalaya pratikriya. {JNU}
Granthalaya sangathan. {BIS}
Granthalaya shastra paribhasha kosh. {NASSDOC NMML}
Granthalaya vargikaran. [Madhya Pradesh Hindi Granth Academi]. {NMML}
Granthvigyan. {CRRI NMML}
Great books : The foundation of liberal education. {USIS}
Great books and book collectors. {NASSDOC*}
Great ideas in information theory, language and cybernetics. {INSA}
Great libraries. {NMML USIS}
Growth of the book-jacket. {DUL}
The growth of knowledge : Readings on organisation and retrieval of knowledge. {NIEPA USIS}
Growth of the library in modern India, 1498-1836. {ICHR IIT NMML ZHL}
Guide for abbreviations of words in titles of periodicals using Roman alphabet, rev edn. (IS : 18-1970). [Indian Standards Institution]. {NASSDOC}
A guide for authors in the preparation of manuscripts and illustrations. {IIPA}
Guide for the conversion of school libraries into media centres. [UNESCO]. {DUL ICA JNU NIEPA}
Guide for drafting Indian standards, 2nd edn. (IS : 12-1984). [Indian Standards Institution]. {NASSDOC}
Guide for the establishment of national social science documentation centres in developing countries. [UNESCO] {IEG JNU NMML}
Guide for handling, testing and storage of monochrome photographic prints, (IS : 6299-1971). [Indian Standards Institution]. {NASSDOC}
Guide for layout of learned periodicals, rev edn. (IS : 795-1976). [Indian Standards Institution]. {NASSDOC}
Guide for preparation of abstracts, rev. edn. (IS : 795-1976). [Indian Standards Institution]. {NASSDOC}
Guide for preparation of manuscript of an article in a learned periodical. (IS : 4731-1968). [Indian Standards Institution]. {NASSDOC}
Guide for standard book numbering. {IS : 8310-1977). [Indian Standards Institution]. {NAI NASSDOC}
A guide to archives and manuscripts in the United States. [U.S. National Historical Publications Commission]. {USIS}
Guide to art reference books. {DUL}
Guide to book publishing. {DUL}
Guide to the care and administration of manuscripts, 2nd edn. [American Association for State and Local History]. {NMML}
Guide to Colon Classification practical. {CRRI ICHR}
Guide to Computer Bureau Services. {NASSDOC}
Guide to computer literature : An introductory survey of the sources of information. {NASSDOC}
Guide to the computerisation of population documentation storage and retrieval systems. [United Nations]. {NASSDOC}

Guide to current British journals, Vol. 1, 2nd edn. [Library Association, London]. {NASSDOC}

Guide to Dewey Decimal Classification. {DUL}

Guide to the documentation of psychology. {NIH}

Guide to the India Office Library : With a note on the India Office Records. [India Office Library]. {NMML}

Guide to the India Office Library : With a note on the India Office Records, 2nd edn. [India Office Library]. {IEG IIT JNU MFL NASSDOC NMML RTL}

Guide to information science. {BCL JNU}

Guide to information sources in space science and technology. {DUL}

Guide to laws and regulation on federal libraries : A compilation and analysis. {USIS}

Guide to Library of Congress classification. {USIS}

A guide to Library of Congress classification, 2nd edn. {USIS}

Guide to Library of Congress classification, 3rd edn., by Lois Mai Chan. {USIS}

Guide to library research methods. {JNU}

A guide to library resources in Rangoon. {IEG}

Guide to lists of Master's theses. [American Library Association]. {NASSDOC}

Guide to the manuscript collections of the Bancroft Library, 2 Vols. {JNU}

Guide to micro reproduction equipment, 4th edn. [National Microfilm Association]. {NASSDOC}

A guide to micrographics. [Bhabha Atomic Research Centre; Micrographic Congress of India]. {NASSDOC*}

Guide to the National Archives of the United States. [U.S. National Archives and Records Service]. {USIS}

Guide to national bibliographical centres. [UNESCO]. {DUL IIMC NASSDOC USIS}

Guide to operational research. {NASSDOC}

Guide to personal indexes : Using edgenotched and peek-a-boo cards, 2nd edn. {BIS IEG IIT JNU NASSDOC}

Guide to production and use of audio-visual aids in library and information science teaching. [UNESCO]. {NASSDOC*}

Guide to reference books, 8th edn. [American Library Association]. {JNU NASSDOC}

Guide to reference books for small and medium sized libraries, 1970-82. {NASSDOC}

Guide to reference material, 3 vols. [Library Association, London]. {INSA NASSDOC NIPCCD ZHL}

A guide to reference materials on India, 2 vols. {INSA NAI NASSDOC NCAER NERC ZHL}

Guide to reference sources on Africa, Asia, Latin America and the Caribbean, Middle East and North Africa and Russia and East Europe : Selected and annotated. {NASSDOC}

Guide to resources for Commonwealth studies in London, Oxford and Cambridge with bibliographical and other information. {IEG JNU NIEPA}

Guide to the SLA loan collection, classification schemes and subject heading lists. [Special Libraries Association] {DUL}

Guide to Saraswati Mahal. [Saraswati Mahal Library, Tanjore]. {NASSDOC*}

Guide to scientific periodicals : Annotated bibliography. {DUL}

Guide to selected computer-based information services. [Association of Special Libraries and Information Bureaux]. {CRRI}

Guide to selected reference tools and Indological source materials : Classified and annotated. {DUL NASSDOC}

A guide to sources of information in libraries. {NASSDOC}

Guide to the Universal Decimal Classification. (BS 1000 C : 1963). [British Standards Institution]. {AIU IIT JNU NASSDOC}

Guide to unpublished research materials. {IEG}

Guide to the use of books and libraries. {DUL IIT MFL}

Guide to the use of books and libraries, 2nd edn. {NIH USIS}

Guide to the use of books and libraries, 4th edn. {USIS}

Guide to use of Dewey Decimal Classification. [Lake Placid Club Education Foundation]. {IIT USIS}

A guide to the use of United Nations documents, including reference to the specialised agencies and special U.N. bodies. {MFL USIS}

Guidelines for collection development. [American Library Association]. {USIS}

Guidelines for curriculum development in records management and administration of modern archives. [UNESCO]. {NASSDOC}

Guidelines for curriculum development on information studies. [UNESCO]. {NASSDOC*}

Guidelines for drafting and presentation of India standards. [Bureau of Indian Standards]. {BIS NASSDOC}

Guidelines for the establishment and development of monolingual thesauri. (BS 5723-1979), [British Standards Institution]. {CRRI}

Guidelines for the evaluation of information systems and services. [UNESCO]. {JNU}

Guidelines for the evaluation of training courses, workshops and seminars in scientific and technical information and documentation. [UNESCO]. {NASSDOC}

Guidelines for formulation of a policy on education, training and development of library and information personnel : All India seminar on library and information science education, October 3-8, 1977, Delhi. [Indian Standards Institution]. {NASSDOC}.

Guidelines for library planners. [American Library Association]. {IIT}

Guidelines for national bibliographic agency and national bibliography. [UNESCO]. {NASSDOC}

Guidelines for newspaper libraries. [American Newspaper Publishers Association]. {USIS}

Guidelines for the preparation of bibliography. [U.S. National Agricultural Library]. {NASSDOC}

Guidelines for the preparation of general guides to national archives. [UNESCO]. {NASSDOC}

Guidelines for preparation of texts of dissertations for their presentation and publication. {DUL}

Guidelines for presentation of abstract sheets in serial publications. (IS : 10455-1983). [Indian Standards Institution]. {CRRI}

Guidelines for presentation of translations. (IS : 10454-1983). [Indian Standards Institution]. {NASSDOC}

Guidelines for thesaurus structure, construction and use. [American National Standard Institute]. {CRRI}

Guidelines on the conduct of a national inventory of current research and development projects. {DUL}

Guidelines on studies of information users. [UNESCO]. {NASSDOC}

Handbook for AACR2 : Explaining and illustrating Anglo-American Cataloguing Rules, 2nd ed. [American Library Association]. {USIS}

Handbook for information systems and services. [UNESCO]. {ICA IIMC NASSDOC NIEPA TDA USIS}

Handbook for information systems and services. [UNESCO] {IDSA}

Handbook for interviewers : A manual for Government social survey interviewing staff, describing practice and procedures on structured interviewing. {NASSDOC}

Handbook for library trustees. {DUL}

Handbook in research and evaluation : A collection of principles, methods and strategies useful in the planning, design and evaluation of studies in education and the behavioural sciences. {NASSDOC}

Handbook of AP Government Oriental Manuscripts Library and Research Institute. [Andhra Pradesh Government Oriental Manuscripts Library and Institute, Hyderabad], {NASSDOC*}

Handbook of automation, and computation and control. {IDSA}

Handbook of communication. {NASSDOC}

Handbook of comparative librarianship. {NASSDOC}

Handbook of comparative librarianship, 2nd edn. {BIS IICL ISI NIPCCD}

Handbook of comparative librarianship, 3rd edn. {NASSDOC}

Handbook of data management, 6 vols, vol 1 : Introduction to the system life cycle; vol 2 : system life cycle standards; vol. 3 : system life cycle standards forms methods, by Peter Zuckerman; vol 4. Advanced technology input and output; vol. 5 : Advanced technology systems concepts; vol. 6 : Data processing administration. {NASSDOC}

Handbook of data processing for libraries : A comprehensive guide to the use of modern data processing equipment in libraries. {CRRI IIT INSA NASSDOC NCAER NIH NMML USIS}

Handbook of data processing for libraries, 2nd edn. {BIS CRRI DUL ISI JNU USIS}

Handbook of data processing management, 6 vols. {NASSDOC}

Handbook of evaluation research, 2 vols. {NASSDOC}

Handbook of futures research. {NASSDOC}

Handbook of government libraries. {CRRI}

Handbook of Indian writers. {ICCR MMTC NASSDOC UGC}

Handbook of information scientists and librarians in India. {BIS CRRI IIPA IIT ISI MMTC NASSDOC NCAER NIEPA NMML RTL}

Handbook of information systems services. {JNU}

Handbook of libraries, archives and information centres in India, 8 vols. : Vol. 1 : Libraries and archives; Vol. 2 : Libraries and archives; Vol. 3 : Information policy system and network; Vol. 4 : Asia-Pacific co-operative information systems and networks and programmes; Vol. 5 : Information technology industry and networks; Vol. 6 : International co-operative information systems, network and programmes; Vol. 7 : Science and technology information systems and centres; Vol. 8 : Social sciences information systems and centres. {DSIW IDSA JNU NASSDOC NCAER NMML}

Handbook of library regulations. {INSA JNU USIS}

Handbook of library science education in India. [Andhra Pradesh Library Association, Hyderabad]. {NASSDOC}

Handbook of library training practice. {NASSDOC}

Handbook of national and international library associations. [American Library Association]. {NASSDOC USIS}

Handbook of pseudonymous authors in Telugu. {NASSDOC*}

Handbook of special librarianship and information work. [Association of Special Libraries and Information Bureaux]. {BIS IEG}

Handbook of special librarianship and information work. 2nd edn. [Association of Special Libraries and Information Bureaux]. {IIT SPA}

Handbook of special librarianship and information work, 3rd edn. [Association of Special Libraries and Information Bureaux]. {MHA MMTC NASSDOC NIH}

Handbook of special librarianship and information work, 4th edn. [Association of Special Libraries and Information Bureaux]. {CRRI IIT}

Handbook on the international exchange of publications. [UNESCO]. {CRRI IEG}

Handbook on the international exchange of publications, 3rd edn. [UNESCO]. {NASSDOC NMML}

Handbook on the international exchange of publications, 4th edn, [UNESCO]. {JNU NASSDOC USIS}

Harbrace guide to the library and the research paper, 4th ed. {IIMC}

Harrod's librarians' glossary and reference book. {NCERT}

Heading and canons. {BIS IEG ISI}

Help for social scientists : A new kind of information process. {NASSDOC}

Helping the reader toward self education. {JNU}

Herald of Library Science : Trend report, citation and index, 1962-83. {NASSDOC}

Here comes the book mobile. {JNU}

The hidden public : The story of the book-of-the- Month Club. {USIS}

High school library : Organisation and administration. {DUL NERC}

Higher secondary school libraries. {DUL IEG}

Hindi mein bal sahitya : Children literature in Hindi sinoc independence, Pratham khand 1947-1960. {NASSDOC}

HIndustan ke mashraqi kutubkhane. {NMML}

Historical and bibliographical methods in library research. {ICHR}

The history of archives administration : A select bibliography. [UNESCO] {NASSDOC}

History of the Birmingham Library. {JNU}

History of booksellers : The old and new. {DUL}

History of cataloguing and cataloguing methods, 1100-1880, with an introductory survey of ancient times. {CRRI}

History of libraries : Ancient and mediaeval. {JNU}

History of libraries and librarianship in modern India since 1850. {JNU NERC NMML}

History of libraries in the Western world. {NASSDOC}

History of library movement in Andhra Pradesh, 1900-1956. {NASSDOC*}

History of the New York Public Library. {NAI}

History of the principles of librarianship. {IIT}

History of printing in the India, Pakistan, Ceylon, Burma and Thailand. {DUL}

History of public library movement in Maharashtra. {JNU NASSDOC*}

History of the public library movement in western Maharashtra, 1805-1921 : Thesis. (Poona University). {NASSDOC}

History of scientific and technical periodicals : The origins and development of the scientific and technical press. {DUL}

Hospital libraries and work with the disabled in the community. {DUL}

Hospital library in Sweden, tr. by Frykman. {DUL}

How a book is made. {DUL}

How and where to look it up. {IIT}

How to catalogue a rare book, 2nd edn. {JNU}

How to determine author and title entries according to AACR : An interpretive guide with card examples. {AIU USIS}

How to do library research. {ICA IIT JNU NIH USIS}

How to find out : A guide to sources of information for all, arranged by the Dewey Decimal Classification, 2nd edn. {MHA}

How to find out : A guide to sources of information for all, arranged by the Dewey Decimal Classification, 4th rev. edn. {NASSDOC}

How to find out : Printed and on-line sources, 5th rev edn. {DUL NASSDOC}

How to find out about engineering. {CRRI}

How to find out about literature. {DUL}

How to find out in architecture and building. {SPA}

How to locate educational information and data, 4th edn. {NIEPA}

How to organise a children's library. {DUL}

How to organise information : A manager's guide to techniques and sources with a check list for secretaries and assistants. {JNU}

How to organise a local collection. {NASSDOC}

How to plan a library building for library work. {IEG}

How to read a book, rev. edn. {USIS}

How to teach reference and research skills. {JNU}

How to use a book. {JNU}

How to use the business library : With sources of business information, 4th edn. {USIS}

How to use the library. {JNU}

How to use a medical library. {NIH}

How to write a research paper. {DUL}

Human factors applications in tele-operator design and operation. {INSA}

The humanities and the library : Problems in the interpretation, evaluation and use of library materials. [American Library Association]. {AIU USIS}

Humanities information research : Proceedings of a seminar. {JNU}

Hundred years of library education. [Nagpur University, Department of Library and Information Science, Nagpur]. {NASSDOC}

Hundred years of library education and its future : Pre-seminar volume : ILA-IASLIC-GILA-IATLIS library education centenary seminar, October 10-12, 1987, Nagpur. [Nagpur University, Department of Library and Information Science, Nagpur]. {NASSDOC}

IBM 360 assembler language programming. {NASSDOC}

The IDOC documentation handbook. [IDOC]. {NASSDOC}

IENS press handbook. [Indian and Eastern Newspaper Society, New Delhi]. {JNU}

IFLA and the Third World : The IFLA core on the advancement of librarianship in the Third World. (ALP). {NASSDOC}

IFLA annual : Proceedings of the general conferences; Annual reports. [International Federation of Library Associations and Institutions]. {NASSDOC}

IFLA directory : 1977; 1979; 1982-84; 1984-85; 1986-87; 1988-89. [International Federation of Library Associations and Institutions]. {NASSDOC}

IFLA round-table on research on reading, August 13-15, 1987, Manchester : Preparatory meeting before Brighton Congress. {NASSDOC}

IFLA statutes, rules of procedure terms of reference. {NASSDOC}

ILA members directory. [Indian Library Association]. {NASSDOC}

ILO thesaurus. [International Labour Office, Geneva]. {NASSDOC}

INSDOC seminar on work-flow in libraries, November 21-24, 1966, New Delhi, 3 pts. Pt-1 : Special libraries; Pt-2 : University libraries; Pt-3 : Government libraries. {BIS}

ISBD (B) : International standard bibliographic description for books. [International Federation of Library Associations and Institutions]. {JNU}

ISBD (CH) : International standard bibliographic description for cartographic material. [International Federation of Library Association and Institutions]. {NASSDOC}

ISBD (G) : General international standard bibliographic description : Annotated text. [International Federation of Library Associations and Institution, Working Group on the General International Standard Bibliographic Description]. {NASSDOC}

ISBD (M) : International standard bibliographic description for monographic publications, rev edn. [International Federation of Library Associations and Institutions]. {NASSDOC}

ISBD (NBM) : International standard bibliographic description for non-book materials. [International Federation of Library Associations and Institutions, Working Group on the International Standard Bibliographic Description for Non-Book Materials]. {NASSDOC}

ISBD (S) : International standard bibliographic description for serials. [International Federation of Library Associations and Institutions, Joint Working Group on the International Standard Bibliographic Description for Serials]. {NASSDOC}

ISBN : International standard book numbering (incorporating the recommendations for implementing the Standard Book Numbering Scheme). [Standard Book Numbering Agency, London]. {NASSDOC}

ISDS manual. [International Serial Data System]. {NASSDOC}

ISIS : A general description of an approach to computerised bibliographical control. [International Labour Office]. {NASSDOC}

ISO standards handbook, 1982 : Information transfer. [UNESCO]. {NASSDOC}

Idea of order in bibliography. {JNU}

Ideas and the university library : Essays of an unorthodox academic librarian. {DUL}

Identification of data elements in bibliographic records. {BIS}

If you want to evaluate your library. [Library Association, London]. {NASSDOC}

Illuminated book : Its history and production. 2nd edn. {DUL}

Illustrative computer programming for libraries. {JNU}

Illustrative computer programming for libraries : Selected examples for information specialists, 2nd edn. {NASSDOC USIS}

Immroth's guide to the Library of Congress Classification, 3rd edn. {USIS}

Impact of information services on national development. [COSTED, Bangalore]. {NASSDOC}

Impact of a paperless society on the research library of the future : A report to the NSF. [Library Research Centre, Illinois]. {ISI}

Impact of technology on the library building. [Educational Facilities Laboratories, New Delhi]. {AIU}

The imperial library of the moghuls. [Idarah-I Adabiyat-I Delhi]. {INSA NMML}

Implementation of complex information system. {CRRI IIT USIS}

Implication of modern information technology for national information policy and planning. [UNESCO]. {NASSDOC}

Improvement of reading. 3rd edn. {ZHL}

In the library and information science horizon : A collection of essays in honour of Dr. V.A. Kamath, presented by the Bombay Science Librarians Association (BOSLA). {JNU NASSDOC}

In praise of books. [Academy of Arts and Sciences, Cambridge]. {USIS}

Index of a publication. (ISO/R 999-1969. (E). [International Organisation for Standardisation, Geneva]. {NASSDOC}

Indexers on indexing : Selection of articles published in the Indexer. {BIS}

Indexes and indexing. {BIS CRRI IEG IIT MFL MHA SPA}

Indexes and indexing : Guide to the indexing of books and collections of books, periodicals, music recordings, films and other materials, with a reference section and suggestions for further reading, 3rd rev. edn. {USIS}

Indexes and indexing : Guide to the indexing of books and collections of books, periodicals, music recordings, films and other materials, with a reference section and suggestions for further reading, 4th edn. {JNU NASSDOC NIPCCD NMML}

Index and indexing systems. {JNU}

Indexing, the art of : A guide to the indexing of books and periodicals. {BCL NASSDOC}

Indexing books : A manual of basic principles. {IEG IIT INSA NIPCCD}

Indexing concepts and methods. {BCL BIS}

Indexing for editors. { NASSDOC NMML}

Indexing languages and thesauri : Construction and maintenance. {CRRI IIT NASSDOC}

Indexing of children's magazines in Hindi with particular reference to its impact on society and social sciences. (typed copy). {NASSDOC}

Indexing systems : Concepts, models and techniques. [Indian Association of Special Libraries and Information Centres]. {BIS CRRI JNU MFL MMTC NASSDOC}

Indexing systems : IASLIC special course, November 1—December 14, 1976 : Course material. [Indian Association of Special Libraries and Information Centres]. {JNU}

Indexing systems and techniques. {NASSDOC}

Indexing theory, indexing methods and search devices. {IIT JNU USIS}

Indexing your book : A practical guide for authors. {DUL}

India Office Library : A historical sketch, [Commonwealth Office, London]. {NASSDOC}

Indian academic libraries and Dr. S.R. Ranganathan : A critical study. {JNU NMML}

Indian Association of Special Libraries and Information Centres : Perspective, performance, promise : Silver jubilee commemorative volume. [Indian Association of Special Libraries and Information Centres]. {JNU}

Indian book review index, 1975-76. {JNU NASSDOC}

Indian books : An annual bibliography. {NASSDOC}

Indian books : A bibliography of Indian books published or reprinted in 1983 in the English language, comp. by Ram Lal. [Indian Bibliographic Centre, Varanasi]. {NASSDOC}

Indian books in print : A bibliography of Indian books in English language, 3 vols, Vol 1 : Author; Vol 2 : Title; Vol 3 : Subject guide. {ICA INSA NASSDOC}

Indian broadcast media yearbook. {NASSDOC}

Indian librarianship. {JNU}

Indian librarianship : Perspectives and prospects. {IEG NASSDOC}

Indian libraries : Trends and prospectives. {JNU NMML}

Indian libraries and India Wheat Loan Education Exchange Programme : A report. {JNU}

Indian library chronology. {BIS JNU NERC NIPCCD}

Indian library directory, 3rd edn. [Indian Library Association]. {BIS INSA NASSDOC}

Indian library directory; 4th edn. [Indian Library Association]. {JNU NMML}

Indian library legislation, 2 vols., Vol. 1 : union library bills and acts; Vol. 2 : State library bills and acts. {NASSDOC}

Indian library literature : An annotated bibliography. {ICHR NASSDOC NIPCCD NMML}

Indian library manifesto. {IDSA}

Indian library science abstracts. [Indian Association of Special Libraries and Information Centres]. {NASSDOC}

Indian National Bibliography. [Central Reference Library, Calcutta]. {DSSW INSA NASSDOC}

Indian National Bibliography : Cumulated Index 1958-62. [Central Reference Library, Calcutta]. {NASSDOC}

Indian Press Index : Procedure manual. (University of Delhi, Department of Library Science, Sessional project, 1975). {DUL}

Indian publishers directory, {NASSDOC}

Indian reference and information services. {ICA NIH}

Indian reference sources : An annotated guide to Indian reference books. {ICHR IIC NASSDOC ZHL}

Indian scientific and technical publications : Exhibition. (National Library, Calcutta). {DUL}

Indian standard glossary of cataloguing terms, rev edn. [Indian Standards Institution]. {ICA IIMC JNU NASSDOC}

Indian standard glossary of classification terms. [Indian Standards Institution]. {NASSDOC}

Indian Standards Institution and its role in the development of library and documentation standards. (University of Delhi, Department of Library and Information Science, Sessional project 1975-76). {BIS}

Indian trade classification, 2nd rev edn. [Directorate General of Commercial Intelligence and Statistics, New Delhi]. {TDA}

Indiana : A bibliography of bibliographical sources. {NASSDOC}

India's national library. [National Library, Calcutta]. {IIT JNU MFL ZHL}

India's national library : Systematisation. [National Library, Calcutta]. {NASSDOC}

Indic names : Documentation list. {BIS NASSDOC ZHL}

Individualised reading instructions : Its implication for teacher and librarian. {JNU}

Industrial information systems : A manual for higher management and their information officer, librar· n/associates. {USIS}
Industrial libraries throughout the world. {IIFT IIT ISI NASSDOC}
Industrial technical libraries of paperback books : Little Libraries. [U.S. State Department]. {BIS}
Influence of television on the use of libraries. {IIMC}
The information age, its development, its impact. {DUL USIS}
Information analysis and retrieval. {CRRI JNU MHA NASSDOC NIPCCD}
Information and communication practice in industry. {IEG}
Information and communication system : Introduction to the concepts of information, communication and research. {JNU}.
Information and its dissemination. [Institute of Petroleum, London]. {BIS}
Information and its users : A review with special reference to the social sciences. {JNU NASSDOC}
Information and library science source book : Supplement to documentation source book. {NERC}
Information and referral services : Research findings. [U.S. Department of Health, Education and Welfare]. {NASSDOC}
The information center : Management's hidden asset. [American Management Association]. {USIS}
Information choice and policies : Proceedings : American society for information science annual meeting, 42nd, October 14-18, 1979, Minneapoles. {USIS}
Information community : An alliance for progress : Proceedings : ASIS' annual meeting, 44th, 1981. {NASSDOC}
Information dilemma. {NIEPA}
Information economics : Costs and prices of machine-readable information in Europe. [Association of Special Libraries and Information Bureaux]. {BCL}
The information economy : Definition and measurement. {USIS}
The information explosion : The new electronic media in Japan and Europe. {NASSDOC}
Information for academic library decision making : The case for organisational information management. {JNU}
Information for action : From knowledge to wisdom. {JNU}
Information handling : First principles. {JNU}
Information handling in the National Standard Reference Data System. (NBS, Technical Note 290). [U.S. National Bureau of Standards]. {BIS}
Information in the 1980's : Proceedings : ASLIB seminar for information planners and industry, May 13-14, 1976, Beaconfield. [Association of Special Libraries and Information Bureaux]. {BCL NASSDOC}
Information in 1985 : A forecasting study of information needs and resources. [Organisation for Economic Cooperation and Development]. {BCL BIS CRRI JNU MMTC}
Information in business and administrative systems. {DUL NASSDOC}
Information in the language sciences : Proceedings of the conference held at Airlic House, Warrenton, Virginia, March 4-6, 1966. {NASSDOC}
Information indexing and subject cataloguing : Alphabetical classified, coordinate, mechanical. {DUL IEG IIT}
Information India, 1988 : Global view {IDSA IIPA NIEPA NMML}
Information India, 1990-91 : Global view. {AIU BIS CPR DUL ICA IEG IIT ISI JNU NASSDOC NIEPA NMML ZHL}

Information Industry Market Place : An international directory of information products and services, **1978**; **1982**; **1983**. {USIS}
Information literacy : Revolution in the library. {NASSDOC}
Information maintenance system documentation. {JNU}
Information management. {IIT}
Information management research in Europe : Proceedings of the EURIMS conference, Paris. {JNU}
Information market with special regard to social science information. (FID studies in social science information and documentation). [Hungarian Academy of Science; International Federation for Documentation and Information]. {NASSDOC}
Information needs of the 80's. {JNU}
Information needs of social scientists. [British Library Research and Development Department]. {NASSDOC}
Information networks for on-line bibliography retrieval. [UNESCO]. {BIS}
Information policy for development : National and international responsibilities. [UNESCO]. {NASSDOC}
Information processing. {NASSDOC NIH}
Information processing : Proceedings : International conference on information processing. {JNU}
Information processing : Proceedings : International conference on information processing. {JNU}
Information processing and computer programming : An introduction. {NIH}
Information processing equipment. {JNU}
Information processing laboratory for education and research in library science : Phase-I. {IIT}
Information processing systems. {JNU}
Information processing systems, 2nd edn. {JNU}
Information professional : Survey of an emerging field. {IIT JNU USIS}
Information requirements of mechanical engineers : Report of a recent survey. {DUL}
Information resources : A challenge to American science and industry. {JNU}
Information resources on Nepal {IEG}
Information retrieval. {JNU}
Information retrieval, 2nd edn. {BCL CRRI DUL IEG MMTC NIH}
Information retrieval : British and American. {JNU}
Information retrieval : A critical view. {JNU}
Information retrieval : Computational and theoretical aspects. {BCL CRRI NIH}
Information retrieval : Notes for students. {BCL}
Information retrieval and the computer. {BCL}
Information retrieval and machine translation. {CRRI DUL}
Information retrieval and processing. {BIS CRRI DUL IIMC ISI NASSDOC NIH USIS}
Information retrieval experiment. {BIS IIMC IIT}
Information retrieval management. {JNU}
Information retrieval on-line. {DUL INSA ISI NASSDOC USIS}
Information retrieval research. {IIMC JNU NASSDOC}
Information retrieval systems : Characteristics, testing and evaluation. {TDA}
Information retrieval systems : Characteristics, testing and evaluation, 2nd edn. {CRRI DUL IIT USIS}

Information retrieval systems : Subject authority list, 7th edn. [American Petroleum Institute]. {IIT}

Information retrieval thesaurus of education terms. {AIU}

The information revolution : Annals. [American Academy of Political and Social Science]. {USIS}

Information science : Principles and practice. {NASSDOC}

Information science : Search for identity. {INSA}

Information science : A unified view through a systems approach. [Indian Association of Special Libraries and Information Bureaux]. {DUL MMTC}

Information science and computer basics. {BIS}

Information science and libraries. {CRRI ICHR JNU ZHL}

Information science in action : System design, 2 vols. {DUL}

Information sciences. [United States Air Force Office of Scientific Research]. {JNU}

Information seeking : Assessing and anticipating user needs. {JNU}

Information selection systems retrieving replica copies : A state-of-art report. {JNU}

Information service for the small enterprise : Need, source and organisation. {BIS}

Information service in guidance for career development and planning. {NIPCCD}

Information service in libraries. {CRRI IEG JNU NAI}

Information service in the Parliament of India. {NASSDOC}

Information services : Their organisation and administration. {JNU}

Information services for college librarians. {JNU}

Information services for world trade centres. [World Trade Centre Association]. {TDA}

Information services in India : Papers : IASLIC national seminar, 10th, December 21-24, 1982, Kanpur. [Indian Association of Special Libraries and Information Centres]. {ICA JNU MMTC NASSDOC NIPCCD}

The information society : Issues and answers. [American Library Association]. {JNU}

Information sources : An international selective guide. {DUL ICA IIFT INSA}

Information sources in children's literature : A practical reference guide. {NIPCCD}

Information sources in science and technology : A practical guide to traditional and on-line use. {JNU}

Information storage and retrieval : Theory, system and devices. {CRRI DUL}

Information storage and retrieval : Tools, elements, theories. {DUL ICA IEG MFL NASSDOC USIS}

Information storage and retrieval systems : Origin, development and applications. {NASSDOC}

Information storage and retrieval systems for individual researchers. {ISI MHA USIS}

Information system for modern management. {ICA}

Information systems. {DUL ICA ISI MMTC NASSDOC}

Information systems : Theory and practice. {JNU NIPCCD TDA}

Information systems and networks : Eleventh annual symposium {JNU}

Information systems compatibility. {JNU}

Information systems design for socio-economic development : Retrospect and prospect. [International Federation for Documentation and Information]. {JNU}
Information systems for strategic decisions. {DUL}
Information systems in documentation. {CRRI DUL JNU}
Information systems in UK agriculture. [UK Agriculture Information Review Committee; British Library Research and Development Department]. {BCL}
Information systems, services and centres. {CRRI DUL NASSDOC USIS}
Information technology : Critical choices for library decision makers : Pittsburg conference on electronic information technology and its impact on library and information services, 1981, Pittsburg. {BIS CRRI IIT JNU USIS}
Information technology and its impact on American education. {USIS}
Information technology in local government : A survey of the development of urban and regional information systems in five European countries. [Organisation for Economic Cooperation and Development]. {BCL}
Information technology revolution. {NASSDOC}
Information technology serving society. {USIS}
Information theory and coding. {INSA}
Information trade directory : An international directory of information products and services. {USIS}
Information transfer, 2nd edn. [International Organisation for Standardisation]. {CRRI MMTC}
Information transfer and use in chemistry : Final report of the Chemical Information Review Committee. {BCL}
Information U.S.A. {USIS}
Information work today : Symposium on information work today, September, 1966, Liverpool. {ICA IIMC MHA}
Information work with unpublished reports. {NASSDOC}
The infrastructure of an information society. {JNU}
Insect : Enemies of books. {JNU}
Inside library India : North meets South. {JNU NASSDOC}
Instructional Media Centre : Bold new venture. {USIS}
Instructions concerning erecting of a library. {DUL}
Insurance manual for libraries. [American Library Association]. {BIS}
Integrated online library systems : Principles, planning and implementation. {NASSDOC}
Intellectual foundations of library education. {IIT}
Intellectual skywriting : Literary politics and the New York Review of Books. {USIS}
Intent upon reading : A critical appraisal of modern fiction for children. {DUL}
Interchange of bibliographic information in machine readable form : Papers given at the Western European seminar, May 12-16, 1974, England. [Library Association, London]. {BCL}
Interface : Library automation with special reference to computing activity. {JNU NASSDOC}
Interior designs for libraries. [American Library Association]. {USIS}
Interlibrary communications and information networks. {JNU}
Inter-library cooperation : A sampling of inter-library cooperation programmes. [American Library Association; Committee on Inter Library Co-operation]. {DUL}
Inter-library cooperation in England and Wales. [H.M.S.O., London]. {NASSDOC}

Interlibrary loan involving academic libraries. [American Library Association]. {NASSDOC}

Interlibrary loan procedure manual. [American Library Association]. {DUL NASSDOC USIS}

Inter-Library Resources Centre : Holding of periodicals. {NASSDOC}

Inter-Library Resources Centre : Indian Council of Social Science Research—Jawaharlal Nehru University. [Indian Council of Social Science Research]. {NASSDOC}

Intermediate lexicon for information science : Feasibility study. [Polytechnic of North London]. {BCL JNU}

International academic and specialist publishers directory. {NASSDOC}

International and national library and information services : A review of some recent developments, 2 vols. {IIT NASSDOC NERC}

International aspects of librarianship. {IEG}

International bibliography of directories, 6th edn. {NASSDOC}

International bibliography of non-periodical literature on documentation and information. {JNU}

International books-in-print : English- language titles published outside the United States and the United Kingdom. 2 vols. {NASSDOC}

International circulation of books. [UNESCO]. {NASSDOC}

International computer bibliography, 1968; 1971. {NASSDOC}

International co-operation in orientalist librarianship. {JNU NMML}

International dictionary of acronyms in data processing, library and information systems. {CRRI MFL NASSDOC NMML}

International directory of acronyms in library, information and computer sciences. {NASSDOC USIS}

International directory of dealers of back-sets of periodicals. {NASSDOC}

International directory of libraries and documentation centres in terminology. [Documentation Directorate, Ottawa]. {NASSDOC}

International directory of library, archives and information science associations, 2nd edn. [UNESCO General Information Programme; UNISIST]. {NASSDOC}

International directory of population information, Pt. 2 : Address list. [Carolina Population Center, USA]. {NIH}

International distribution of catalogue cards : Present situation and future prospects 1968; 1969; 1974. [UNESCO]. {CRRI IIMC IIT JNU NERC NIEPA NIPCCD}

International documents for 80's : Their role and use : Proceedings : World symposium on international documentation, 2nd, 1980, Brussels. {JNU NMML}

International guide to library and information science education : A reference source for educational programmes in the information fields world-wide. [International Federation of Library Associations and Institutions]. {NASSDOC}

International guide to library, archival and information science associations. {USIS}

International guide to library, archival and information science associations, 2nd edn. {USIS}

International handbook of contemporary developments in librarianship. {USIS}

International inter-library lending : A review of the literature. [International Federation of Library Associations and Institutions]. {NASSDOC}

International librarianship : Surveys of recent developments in developing countries and in advanced librarianship submitted to the 1971 IFLA press-session seminar for developing countries, August 24—September 1, 1971. [Library Association, London]. {NASSDOC}

International library directory : A world directory of libraries. {ICWA}

International literary market place, 1986-87. {NASSDOC}

International organisation and their activities in the field of scientific and technical information. [UNESCO]. {NASSDOC}

The international provision and supply of publications. [UNESCO]. {NASSDOC}

International scientific organisations : A guide to their library, documentation and information services. [U.S. National Science Foundation, International Science Information Studies]. {DUL}

International seminar on electronic data processing in libraries, Regersburg. {JNU}

International socio-economic information systems : An evaluating directory of DEVSIS-type programs. {NASSDOC}

International standard book numbering system in India. {NASSDOC}

International standard classification of education (ISCED) : Three stage classification system, 2pts. [UNESCO]. {AIU}

International standardisation of library and documentation techniques. [UNESCO]. {ICA}

International standards for computers and information processing. [International Organisation for Standardisation]. {BIS}

International standards for documentation and terminology, 3rd edn. [International Organisation for Standardisation]. {BIS}

International subscription agents : An annotated directory, 2nd edn. [American Library Association]. {DUL}

International system for the transliteration of Arabic characters. (ISO/R 233-1961) (E). [International Organisation for Standardisation]. {NASSDOC}

International system for the transliteration of Greek characters into Latin characters. (ISO/R 843-1968) (E). [International Organisation for Standardisation]. {NASSDOC}

International system for the transliteration of Slavic Cyrillic characters, 2nd edn. (ISO/R 9-1968) (E). [International Organisation for Standardisation]. {NASSDOC}

Interviewing : Strategy, techniques and tactics. {NASSDOC}

Introduction to the Anglo-American cataloguing rules. {MFL NASSDOC ZHL}

Introduction to the Anglo-American cataloguing rules : History and development. [American Library Association]. {USIS}

Introduction to automation for librarians. [American Library Association]. {USIS}

Introduction to bibliography and reference work : A guide to materials and sources. {JNU}

Introduction to bibliography for literary students. {DUL}

Introduction to bookbinding. {CRRI}

Introduction to cataloguing, 2 vols, Vol. 1: Descriptive cataloguing and an overview of catalogues and cataloguing; Vol 2: Entry headings. {IIT JNU NERC NASSDOC NMML ZHL}

Introduction to cataloguing, 2nd edn. {ZHL}

Introduction to cataloguing and classification, 3rd edn. {IIT}

Introduction to cataloguing and classification, 6th edn. {USIS}

Introduction to cataloguing and classification. (Library Science Text Series). {NASSDOC}
Introduction to cataloguing and classification of books. [American Library Association]. {BIS CRRI ICA NAI NMML SPA USIS ZHL}
Introduction to cataloguing and classification of books, 2nd edn. [American Library Association]. {IIFT}
Introduction to cataloguing practice. {ISI JNU NASSDOC NERC NMML}
Introduction to chain indexing. {BCL ICHR IIT JNU NASSDOC}
Introduction to classification and number building in Dewey. {IIFT}
Introduction to Colon Classification. {ICHR IIFT IIT JNU NASSDOC NMML SPA ZHL}
Introduction to computer-based library systems. {JNU NIH}
Introduction to computers and computer programming. {DUL}
Introduction to computers in information science. {JNU}
Introduction to county library practice. {JNU}
Introduction to cybernetics. {NASSDOC}
Introduction to data processing. {JNU}
Introduction to data processing and COBOL. {NASSDOC}
Introduction to the Dewey Decimal Classification {IIFT IIT MFL SPA ZHL}
Introduction to Dewey Decimal Classification for British schools. {DUL}
An introduction to documentation science. {NASSDOC}
Introduction to the eighteenth edition of the Dewey Decimal Classification. {CRRI IIC JNU NIE USIS}
Introduction to historical bibliography, rev edn. {DUL}
An introduction to index language construction : A programmed text. {BCL}
Introduction to indexing and abstracting for technical information systems. {TDA}
Introduction to information science. {DUL NASSDOC}
Introduction to librarianship. {IIT MFL NCAER ZHL}
Introduction to librarianship, 2nd edn. {USIS}
Introduction to library administration. {JNU}
Introduction to library automation. {NASSDOC NMML}
Introduction to library cataloguing, 1958; 1959; 1969. {CRRI IIT NERC NIPCCD NMML}
Introduction to library cataloguing and classification, 4th rev. edn. {DUL}
Introduction to library classification. {NAI}
An introduction to library classification. {CRRI}
Introduction to library classification, 9th edn. {BIS}
Introduction to library research in geography. {DUL}
Introduction to library science. {AIU IIT MFL}
Introduction to library science : Basic elements of library science. {DUL}
Introduction to library services for library media technical assistants. {ICA}
Introduction to minicomputers in federal libraries. [Library of Congress]. {USIS}
Introduction to modern information retrieval. {BIS}
Introduction to operating systems. {NASSDOC}
Introduction to operations research. {NASSDOC}
Introduction to PL-1 programming for library and information science. {BCL IIT JNU}
Introduction to philosophical analysis, rev edn. {NASSDOC}
Introduction to the practice of Dewey Decimal Classification. {NASSDOC}

Introduction to PRECIS for North American usage. {USIS}
Introduction to public librarianship for entrance examination students. {ZHL}
Introduction to public library organisation. {NAI}
An introduction to public library organisation, 2nd edn. {SPA}
Introduction to public library organisation with special reference to India. {NERC}
Introduction to quantitative research methods for librarians, 2nd rev edn. {DUL}
Introduction to reference books, 1948; 1952; 1956. {CRRI JNU SPA}
Introduction to reference work. [American Library Association]. {BIS CRRI DUL ICHR IIFT NMML USIS}
Introduction to reference work, 2 vols, V. 1 : Basic information services; V. 2 : Reference services. {AIU BIS DUL ICHR IIT ISI NASSDOC}
Introduction to reference work, 2nd edn, 2 vols. {CRRI DUL JNU MMTC}
Introduction to reference work, 3rd edn., 2 vols. {CRRI MMTC NIPCCD}
Introduction to reference work, 4th edn., 2 vols. {CRRI IIC USIS}
Introduction to Sears list of subject headings. {IIMC IIT}
Introduction to the study of bibliography, to which is prefixed a memour on the public libraries of America, 2 vols. {DUL}
An introduction to subject indexing. {ICA NIEPA NIH ZHL}
Introduction to subject indexing : A programmed text. 2nd edn. {IIT}
Introduction to subject study. {AIU IIT NASSDOC}
Introduction to technical services for library technicians, 3rd edn. {MHA}
Introduction to technical services for library technicians, 5th edn. {NASSDOC}
Introduction to UDC. {BIS IIT ISI JNU SPA}
Introduction to university library administration, 3rd edn. {DUL IIT NIH ZHL}
Introduction to the University of Chicago library : A brief guide to the location and use of the library's service and resources. {NMML}
Introductory course in informatics/documentations. [UNESCO]. {DUL NASSDOC}
Inventory of bibliographic data bases produced in the UK : Report. [British Library Department of Research and Development]. {JNU}
Investigation concerning the SFS information service and its users. [Finnish Standards Association]. {BIS}
An investigation of man-computer interaction in an online bibliographic information retrieval system. {BCL}
Islam : Outline of a classification scheme. {ZHL}
Islamic libraries. (Mimeo; short bibliography). {NASSDOC}
Islamic sciences : Expansion of Dewey Decimal Classification (16th edn.) for oriental libraries, {ZHL}
Issues in library administration : Papers presented at the U.S.-Japan conference on libraries and information science in higher education, 2nd, 1972. {JNU}
Issues in South East Asian librarianship : A selection of papers and articles. {NASSDOC}
Issues of freedom in American libraries. [American Library Association]. {USIS}
Itself an education. [Library Association, London]. {IIT}
Itself an education : Six lectures on classification, 2nd edn. [Library Association, London]. {NASSDOC NMML}

Jaina grantha bhandars in Rajasthan. {INSA}

Job satisfaction of para-professional librarians : Comparative study of public and technical services departments in selected university libraries. {JNU}
Joint university libraries : Staff handbook. {JNU}
Junior college libraries development needs and prospective. {JNU}
Junior high school library catalog, 2nd edn. {USIS}

Ketab va ketab khana. {JNU}
Key to the computer, 2 vols. V. 1 : Text book; V. 2 : Training manual. {NASSDOC}
Keys to library research on the graduate level : A guide to guides. {JNU}
keywords : A vocabulary of culture and society {NMML}
Khuda Bakhsh Oriental Public Library, Patna. {Khuda Bakhsh Oriental Public Library]. {ZHL}

LIST : Library and information services today : An international registry of research and innovation, vol-4. {USIS}
Land of libraries : Story of a study tour of the USA. [Gurudev Literary Association, Hubli]. {AIU ZHL}
Landscape filling index. [Institute of Landscape Architects]. {SPA}
Languages of indexing and classification : A linguistic study of structures and function. {DUL}
Latin American cooperative acquisitions programme. {IIFT}
Law library administration and reference. {CRRI MMTC}
Layout of periodicals. (ISO/R 8-1954) (E). [International Organisation for Standardisation, Geneva]. {NASSDOC}
Learn to use books and libraries : A programmed text. {JNU}
Learned societies and institutions in India : Activities and publications, including over 4000 research oriented titles. {JNU UGC}
Learning and libraries in ancient India : A study. {JNU}
Learning the library : Concepts and methods for effective bibliographic instruction. {AIU}
Learning, remembering and knowing. {NASSDOC}
Learning to read : Use of orthographic and semantic cues. {NASSDOC}
Lecture notes : NISSAT training course on systems analysis for information sciences, December 12-23, 1978, New Delhi. [Department of Science and Technology, New Delhi]. {BIS}
Lectures on universe of knowledge. {NMML}
Lenin and library cooperation. {NASSDOC*}
Let's read together : Books for family enjoyment, 2nd edn. [American Library Association; Association for Library Service to Children]. {USIS}
Letters to a younger librarian. {DUL NASSDOC}
The librarian and his committee. {CRRI}
Librarian and libraries : In the memory of the Master Moti Lal ji and his Shri Sanmati Pustakalaya. {JNU NASSDOC}
Librarian and library administration. {NAI}
Librarian and the machine : Observations on the applications of machines in administration of college and university libraries. {JNU}
Librarian and reference queries : A systematic approach. {CRRI ISI USIS}
Librarian speaking : Interview with university librarians. {JNU USIS}
Librarians and online services. {BCL IIT}

Librarians' glossary of terms used in librarianship, documentation and the book crafts and reference book, 3rd edn. {CRRI IIT JNU NASSDOC}
Librarians' glossary of terms used in librarianship, documentation and the book crafts and reference book, 4th edn. {ICA IIC MMTC NCDC NCERT NERC NIH NMML ZHL}
Librarians' guide to Broad System of ordering. [British Standards Organisation]. {JNU}
Librarians' guide to Indian periodicals published for free distribution. {NASSDOC}
Librarians' guide to microcomputer technology and applications. {JNU NIEPA USIS}
Librarians' handbook [Library Association London]. 2 vols. {JNU NASSDOC NIPCCD}
A librarian's musing. {JNU}
The Librarians' phone book. {USIS}
Librarians' practical dictionary in twenty- two languages. {JNU}
Librarian's psychological commitments : Human relations in librarianship. {INSA NIPCCD USIS}
Librarianship. {NERC NIPCCD ZHL}
Librarianship. {NIH}
Librarianship : Change or status quo. {CRRI JNU}
Librarianship : Essays on applied bibliography. {CRRI}
Librarianship : Introduction to the profession. {ICA USIS}
Librarianship : Its philosophy and history. {BIS IIT NASSDOC NIH SPA}
Librarianship : Perspectives and prospects. {AIU NIEPA}
Librarianship : A short manual with special reference to developing countries. {IIMC SPA}
Librarianship and bureaucratic organisation : A study in the sociology of library profession in India. {JNU NASSDOC}
Librarianship and documentation : An international perspective. {BIS ICHR ISI NASSDOC NERC}
Librarianship and the Third World : An annotated bibliography of selected literature on developing nations, 1960-1975. {NASSDOC}
Librarianship as a career. {ICA}
Librarianship as a profession (Mimeo short bibliography). {NASSDOC}
Librarianship as a profession : A study of socio-economic background and professional orientation of the libraries in Delhi . Thesis. [Punjab University]. {NASSDOC}
Librarianship as a profession in India. {NASSDOC}
Librarianship in Australia, New Zealand and Oceania. {NASSDOC}
Librarianship in Britain today. [Library Association, London]. {IIT}
Librarianship in developing countries. {NIPCCD}
Librarianship in India and abroad : Retrospect and prospect. {CRRI ICA IIT JNU NASSDOC NCAER NIEPA NIPCCD ZHL}
Libraries and the arts : A symposium of papers and discussions at the seminar held in the College of Librarianship, September 1-6, 1969, Wales. {NASSDOC}
Libraries and automation. {IIT}
Libraries and bibliographic centres in the Soviet Union. {IEG}
Libraries and college climate of learning. {JNU}
Libraries and cultural change, 1970; 1975. {AIU IIT MMTC NASSDOC USIS}

Libraries and data processing : Where do we stand. {JNU}

Libraries and information centres in Britain. [British Council, London]. {NASSDOC*}

Libraries and information centres in the Soviet Union. {NASSDOC*}

Libraries and information science in the electronic age. {NASSDOC}

Libraries and information technology : A national system challenge : A report to the Council of Library Resources. [National Academy of Sciences, Washington]. {USIS}

Libraries and librarians in an age of electronics. {USIS}

Libraries and librarianship in Thailand. {JNU}

Libraries and librarianship of ancient and medieval India. {IIC IIT JNU NAI NERC NMML}

Libraries and library services in the Southeast : A report of the Southeastern states cooperative library survey, 1972-74. {BIS ISI}

Libraries and the life of the mind in America : Addresses delivered at the centennial celebration of the American Library Association, [American Library Association]. {IIT NIPCCD USIS}

Libraries and literature for teenagers. {ICHR}

Libraries and mass education. [Sri Setha Parvathi Bayi Library, Kottayam]. {NASSDOC*}

Libraries and the materials of local history. {CRRI NAI}

Libraries and the organisation of knowledge. {IIT USIS}

Libraries and the public. {NAI}

Libraries and readers in the State of New York. {NASSDOC*}

Libraries and their users : Collected papers in library history. [Library Association, London]. {NIPCCD}

Libraries and their uses. {ICA IIT}

Libraries and universities : Addresses and reports, ed. by E.E. Williams {JNU}

Libraries and work sampling. {BIS}

Libraries architecture and equipment. {IIT ZHL}

Libraries as communication systems. {IIMC USIS}

Libraries as educational tools. [Sri Venkateswara University, Tirupati]. {JNU}

Libraries at large : Tradition, innovation and the national interest : The resource book based on the materials of the National Advisory Commission on Libraries. {JNU USIS}

Libraries, documentation and bibliography in the USSR, 1917-1971 : Survey and critical analysis of Soviet studies. {JNU NASSDOC}

Libraries for all : A world of books and their readers : World congress on libraries for all, 50th, 1977, Brussels. [International Federation of Library Association and Institutions]. {IIT}

Libraries for children. {DUL}

Libraries for the handicapped. {DUL}

Libraries for professional practice. {CRRI IIT}

Libraries for research and industry planning and equipment. {DUL}

Libraries for schools and universities. {CRRI}

Libraries in adult and fundamental education : Report of the Malmo Seminar. [UNESCO]. {IEG NASSDOC ZHL}

Libraries in adult and fundamental education : Report of the Malmo Seminar, (Hindi Translation). [Indian Adult Education Association]. {NIEPA}

Libraries in Britain. {IEG}

Libraries in Britain. {NASSDOC}
Libraries in Delhi : A comprehensive list. {AIU IIT}
Libraries in the East : An international and comparative study. {ICA IIMC JNU NASSDOC NMML}
Libraries in Finland. [Finnish Library Association, Helsinki]. {NASSDOC*}
Libraries in France. {NASSDOC}
Libraries in higher education : The user approach to service. {INSA NIEPA}
Libraries in Hongkong : A directory {ICWA}
Libraries in Hungary. [National Szechenyr Library, Budapest]. {NASSDOC}
Libraries in India. [Ministry of Education, New Delhi]. {BIS NMML}
Libraries in India. [Ministry of Education, New Delhi]. {MHA NASSDOC}
Libraries in the modern world. {AIU IIC SPA}
Libraries in the Netherlands. [Netherlands Librarians Association]. {NASSDOC}
Libraries in Poland. {BIS}
Libraries in the political science : Georg Legh and Guman librarianship, 1933-53, tr. by Marta L. Dosa {JNU}
Libraries in post-industrial society. {IIT}
Libraries in Scandinavia, 2nd edn. {IIT}
Libraries in schools. {JNU}
Libraries in social education : Report of the national seminar on libraries in social education, 2nd, September 26—October 5, 1955. [Indian Adult Education Association]. {NIPCCD}
Libraries in society. {IIT NIEPA}
Libraries in the USSR. {NASSDOC}
Libraries in the USSR. [USSR Embassy in India, New Delhi]. {NASSDOC*}
Libraries in West Malaysia and Singapore : A short history. [University of Malaysia, Kuala Lumpur]. {CRRI NASSDOC}
Libraries of Bengal 1700-1947. {NMML}
Libraries of the future. {JNU NMML SPA USIS}
Libraries of the United Nations : A descriptive guide. [United Nations]. {ICWA IIC IIT JNU NIH}
Libraries, readers and book selection. {USIS}
Libraries serving the CSIR complex. [Indian National Scientific Documentation Centre]. {IIT NASSDOC}
Library : Introduction for library assistants. [Special Library Association, New York]. {IIT}
Library acquisition : A classified bibliographic guide to the literature and reference tools. {JNU}
Library acquisition policies and procedures. {IIT}
Library administration, 2nd edn. {DUL NASSDOC ZHL}
Library administration. {CRRI IIT}
Library administration, 3rd edn. {DUL ICA}
Library administration, 2nd edn. {AIU BIS CRRI DSSW DUL IEG IIC IIT JNU MMTC NAI NASSDOC NIH NMML SPA ZHL}
Library administration : Theory and practice. {DUL ICA NAI NCAER NIH NMML SPA ZHL}
Library administration : Theory and practice, 2nd edn. {DUL JNU NASSDOC NIEPA SPA}
Library administration : Theory and practice, 3rd edn. {CRRI DUL JNU NIH TDA}
Library administration : Theory and practice, 4th edn. {BIS DUL JNU NIEPA ZHL}

Library administration : Theory and practice, 5th edn. {ZHL}
Library administration and management. {JNU NASSDOC}
Library adult education : The biography of an idea. {USIS}
Library and the community. {MFL}
The library and the community, 3rd rev. edn. {USIS}
Library and the community. {ICA}
Library and the community. {JNU NASSDOC NMML}
Library and the community : Units 1-9. [Andhra Pradesh Open University, Hyderabad]. {NASSDOC*}
Library and documentation journals. [International Federation for Documentation and Information]. {NASSDOC}
The library and information manager's guide to online services. {USIS}
Library and information manpower development : Papers and proceedings : Nagpur Seminar. {NASSDOC}
Library and information network in the United Kingdom. [Association of Special Libraries and Information Bureaux]. {CRRI JNU}
Library and information science : Current trends in India. {JNU}
Library and information science and archive administration : A guide to building a basic collection for library schools. {JNU}
Library and information science education in India : Papers and recommendations of an All-India seminar held at the Department of Library Science, University of Delhi, during October-3-8, 1977, {AIU ICA JNU NASSDOC NIEPA}
Library and information science journals in India. (Typed short bibliography). {NASSDOC}
Library and information science literature : SSDC resources. {NASSDOC}
Library and information science manpower development in the Asian Region : Report : Meeting of supervisors of library and documentation schools in the Asian region, Bangalore. {CRRI}
Library and information sciences : An ERIC bibliography [Educational Resources Information Centre]. {NASSDOC}
Library and information service needs of the nation. {JNU}
Library and information services in India : Assessment and effectiveness. [Indian Library Association]. {NASSDOC}
Library and information services in India : The current scenario. {NASSDOC}
Library and information services of management development institutions : A practical guide. {NASSDOC}
Library and information studies in the United Kingdom and Ireland, 1950-1974 : An index to theses. [Association of Special Libraries and Information Bureaux]. {NASSDOC}
Library and library related publications : A directory of publishing opportunities in journals, serials and annuals. {NASSDOC}
Library and society. [Kurukshetra University, Kurukshetra]. {JNU NMML}
Library architecture. [Indian Association of Special Libraries and Information Centres]. {MMTC NIEPA}
Library as a learning service centre. {JNU}
Library assistance to readers. [DUL MHA}
Library assistant's manual. 2nd rev. edn. {IIT}
Library association : Creed of librarian. {IIT}

Library Association. [Committee on Scientific Library Service, Library Association, London]. {IIT}

Library atlas. {JNU}

Library automation : Experience, methodology and technology of the library as an information system. {AIU INSA JNU NASSDOC NIPCCD NMML}

Library automation : Issues and applications. {JNU NASSDOC NMML}

Library automation : A state of art review : Papers : Pre-conference institution on library automation, 1967, San Francisco. [American Library Association]. {USIS}

Library automation-II : The state of art : Papers : Pre-conference institute on library automation, June 22-23, 1973, Las Vegas. [American Library Association, Information Science and Automation Division]. {USIS}

Library automation and information science : A collection of essays. {NASSDOC}

Library automation at the New York Public Library and the Association of New York Libraries for Technical Services. [LARC]. {USIS}

Library automation systems, 2nd edn. {CRRI JNU NIH}

Library binding handbook. [Library Building Institute]. {ISI}

Library binding manual. [American Library Association]. {IIT}

Library book selection. [Indian Library Association]. {BIS DSSW INSA}

Library book selection, 2nd rev edn. {BIS CRRI IIT ISI NMML SPA}

Library book selections. [Sarada Ranganathan Endowment for Library Sciences, Bangalore]. {NASSDOC}

Library building and furniture with special reference to college libraries. {CRRI ICA ICHR INSA MFL NASSDOC NIEPA NIH NIPCCD ZHL}

Library building consultant role and responsibility. {IIT}

Library buildings. {DUL}

Library buildings, 1967-1968. {DUL}

Library buildings : Innovation for changing needs : Proceedings. {AIU}

Library buildings : Planning and design. [ICA IIMC IIT NASSDOC NIEPA NIH NIPCCD ZHL}

Library buildings for the future : Library buildings institute and American libraries trustee association workshop, 1965, Detroit : Proceedings. {DUL}

Library buildings of Britain and Europe. {CRRI IIT NASSDOC}

Library catalogs : Changing damnations. {IIT}

Library catalogue : Fundamentals and procedure. [Madras Library Association]. {BIS}

Library catalogues : Their preservation and maintenance by photographic and automated techniques. {AIU IIT SPA}

Library catalogues of the English renaissance. {DUL}

Library cataloguing and classification. {DUL}

Library cataloguing practice : Solutions to assignments 1-26. [Andhra Pradesh Open University, Hyderabad]. {NASSDOC*}

Library cataloguing practice : Unit 1 : Lessons 1-14. [Andhra Pradesh Open University, Hyderabad]. {NASSDOC}

Library classification. {CRRI IIT NMML}

Library classification : Evolution of a dynamic theory. {AIU BIS IIT ISI JNU MHA NMML}

Library classification : Fundamentals and procedure, with graded examples and exercises. [Madras Library Association]. {BIS}

Library classification : Theory and practice. {IIT}

Library classification for public administration materials. [American Library Association]. {NAI}

Library classification manual. {IIT ZHL}

Library classification practice : Unit 2 : Lessons 1-16. [Andhra Pradesh Open University, Hyderabad]. {NASSDOC*}

Library classification practice : Units 1-13. [Andhra Pradesh Open University, Hyderabad]. {NASSDOC*}

Library classification theory : Units 1-10. [Andhra Pradesh Open University, Hyderabad]. {NASSDOC*}

Library clerical workers and wagers. {BIS}

Library collections : Their origin, selection and development. {DUL}

The library college : Contributions for American higher education at the Jamestown college workshop. {USIS}

Library Computerisation in India : Isaac festschrift. {JNU}

Library co-operation, 1966; 1968; 1977. {AIU ICA IIT NIH}

Library co-operation : Brown university study of university school community library coordination in the State of Rhode Island. {DUL}

Library co-operation in India, 1977; 1978. {NASSDOC}

Library co-operation in the North West : A report. {DUL}

Library development in India. {JNU NMML}

Library development in Pakistan : Resume and recommendation : National seminar, February 7-9, 1974, Lahore. [Society for the Promotion and Improvement of Libraries]. {NASSDOC*}

Library development oriented education. {ICA}

Library development plan : Thirty-year programme for India. [University of Delhi]. {BIS MFL NERC SPA}

Library development plan for Allahabad University. {AIU NASSDOC}

Library disaster preparedness handbook. {JNU}

Library displays : Their purpose, construction and use. {USIS}

Library education : A bibliography. {IIT JNU NASSDOC}

Library education and professional issues : A handbook for library management. {JNU NASSDOC}

Library education and training in developing countries. {ICA NIEPA}

Library education in India, Pakistan and Iran. {NASSDOC*}

Library education programme in developing countries with special reference to Asia : UNESCO pre-IFLA conference seminar on library education programme in developing countries, August 15-18, 1980, Philippines. [Library Association, London]. {IIT NASSDOC}

Library effectiveness : A systems approach. {AIU DUL JNU NASSDOC NMML SPA USIS}

The library environment : Aspects of interior planning : Proceedings : Library equipment institute, 2nd, 1964, St. Louis. {JNU USIS}

Library evaluation. [American Library Association]. {DUL}

Library facility for elementary and secondary schools. {JNU}

Library furniture and equipment. [American Library Association]. {DUL IIT NASSDOC ZHL}

Library furniture and equipment. {IIT NMML ZHL}

Library guidance for teachers. {DUL ZHL}

Library history : An examination guide book, 2nd rev edn. {ICHR IIT}

Library humor : A bibliothecal miscellany to 1970. {NASSDOC}

Library in college instruction. {ZHL}

Library in colleges of commerce and technology. {DUL IIT}

Library in education : With special reference to school libraries. {JNU}

Library in the high school teaching. {JNU}

Library in the information revolution : Proceedings : Congress of South-East Asian librarians, 6th, May 30 - June 3, 1983, Singapore. {JNU}

Library in the primary schools : A report by sub-committee of School Library Association. {JNU}

Library in the school, 4th edn. [American Library Association]. {DUL ZHL}

The library in the university : The University of Tennessee library lectures, 1949-1967. {USIS}

Library, information and archive work. [Ministry of Labour, Great Britain]. {JNU}

Library instruction : A bibliography. {NIPCCD}

Library instruction : Junior and senior high schools. {ZHL}

Library instruction manual, 3rd edn. {ZHL}

Library issues : The sixties. {ICHR USIS}

Library legislation. [Madras Library Association]. {BIS IEG}

Library legislation in India : A historical and comparative study. {BIS ICA IIMC NASSDOC NERC SPA}

Library legislation in India : Problems and prospects. {NASSDOC*}

Library legislation in the Punjab. [Punjab Library Literary Circle]. {IIT}

Library life — American style : A journalist's field report. {USIS}

Library literature : An index to library and information science, 1949-51 to 1982-83. {NASSDOC USIS}

Library literature in Telugu, 1915-1981. {NASSDOC*}

Library local collections. {DUL NAI}

Library management. {JNU}

Library management. {DUL USIS}

Library management, 2nd edn. {BIS DUL USIS}

Library management : Units 1-10. [Andhra Pradesh Open University, Hyderabad]. {NASSDOC*}

Library management and organisation, Vol. I. {DUL ICHR IIFT IIT}

Library management case studies. {JNU}

The library manager's guide to automation, 2nd edn. {NASSDOC USIS}

Library manual. {BIS DSSW ICA IIC IIFT IIMC IIT ISI JNU NCDC NERC NIH ZHL}

Library manual. [Indian Library Association]. {BIS DSSW INSA NERC ZHL}

Library manual, 2nd edn. {BIS CRRI DSSW ICHR IIT INSA MMTC NASSDOC NERC NIPCCD}

Library manual : A study work manual of lessons on the use of books and libraries, 6th edn. {USIS}

Library manual for library authorities, librarians and honorary library workers. {ICA}

Library manual for library authorities, librarians and honorary library workers, 2nd edn. {BIS ISI JNU NIEPA NMML ZHL}

Library materials for elementary science. {DUL}

Library media centre problems : Case studies. {USIS}

Library movement. {AIU}

Library movement in India. {NASSDOC}

Library movement in India. [Delhi Library Association]. {CRRI}

Library movement in India and abroad. {JNU}

Library movement in Kerala : The need for reform and legislation. {NERC}
Library networks, 1978-79. {IIT USIS}

Martin, Susan K., 1980, Library network, 1981-82, 4th edn. {USIS}
Library networks : Promises and performance. {IIT}
The Library of Congress, 2nd edn. {IIC JNU NASSDOC NMML USIS}
The Library of Congress : Its architecture and decoration ed. by Henry Hope Reed. {USIS}
The Library of Congress : A picture story of the world's largest library, rev. edn. {JNU}
The Library of Congress : A portrait of an institution. {USIS}
The Library of Congress in perspective {NASSDOC}
Library of Congress subject headings, 8th edn., 2nd vols. [Library of Congress, Subject Cataloguing Division]. {NASSDOC USIS}
Library of Congress subject headings, 9th edn. [Library of Congress, Subject Cataloguing Division]. {USIS}
Library of Congress subject headings : Principles and application, 2nd edn. (Research studies in library science, No. 19). {NASSDOC}
Library of Congress subject headings : Quarterly cumulative supplement to the 8th edn. [Library of Congress]. {NASSDOC}
Library of Congress subject headings : Quarterly cumulative supplements to the 9th edn., 1979-80. [Library of Congress]. {NASSDOC}
Library of the India Office : A historical sketch. [India Office, London]. {NAI}
Library of Rameses, the Great. {DUL}
Library operations research : Computer programming for circulation. {USIS}
Library organisation. {SPA}
Library organisation. {JNU NASSDOC}
Library organisation. {CRRI ISI MMTC NIEPA}
Library organisation and its development in India, 2nd edn. {NIH}
Library organisation and library administration. {NIEPA NIH}
Library organisation and library administration, 2nd edn. {DUL ICA IIT ISI NIEPA NMML}
Library organisation for higher education : The status and role of university librarian. {AIU JNU NIEPA}
Library personnel administration and supervision, 2nd edn. {DUL}
Library planning : A working memorandum. {DUL}
Library planning and decision-making systems. {DUL NIEPA}
Library practice for colleges of education. {JNU}
Library programme, 1911-61. {ZHL}
Library programmes : How to select, plan and produce them. {USIS}
Library programmes : How to select, plan and produce them, 2nd edn. {USIS}
Library promotion handbook. {IIT USIS}
Library publicity and service. {DUL MHA}
Library resource sharing. {ISI JNU NIH}
Library resources : How to research and write a paper. {IIMC IIT NASSDOC NCAER}
Library resources in Scotland. {JNU}
Library resources of Pakistan. {JNU}

Library resources on East Asia : Reports and working papers for the 10th meeting of the committee on American library resources. [Association for Asian Studies]. {JNU}

Library response to urban change : A study of the Chicago Public Library. [American Library Association]. {USIS}

Library scene in Calcutta : Seminar on the occasion of the 100th meeting of the IASLIC study circle, February 26-27, 1977. [Indian Association of Special Libraries and Information Centres]. {NASSDOC*}

Library science based service. {NERC}

Library science dissertations, 1925-1960 : An annotated bibliography of doctoral studies. {USIS}

Library science in India. [Madras Library Association]. {BIS SPA}

Library science in India today : A symposium. [Bengal Library Association, Calcutta]. {NASSDOC*}

Library science in Indian universities : Report. [University Grants Commission, New Delhi]. {ICA IIC JNU NASSDOC NIEPA}

Library science literature in Andhra Pradesh, 1924-1989. {NASSDOC*}

Library science research, 1974-79. {DUL}

Library science today : Ranganathan festschrift. {BIS CRRI ICHR IIT INSA MFL NIH SPA ZHL}

Library service yearbook and directory. [Punjab Library Association]. {IIT}

Library services : Important documents. {NASSDOC*}

Library services for all. [Mysore Library Association, Bangalore]. {BIS SPA}

Library services for children in New Zealand schools and public libraries : A report. [New Zealand Library Association]. {JNU}

Library services for young people in England and Wales, 1830-1970. {DUL}

Library services in hospitals : A survey of their present provision and possible future development in the Southeast Metropolitan region. {DUL}

Library services in Pakistan : Being the proceedings of the departments of library science. . . . {JNU}

Library services in rural areas. [Library Advisory Council, Wales]. {NIEPA}

Library services in a sparsely populated area. [UNESCO]. {NASSDOC*}

Library services in theory and context. {IIT}

Library service to the disadvantaged. {NIPCCD}

Library service to schools. {JNU}

Library service to schools and children. {JNU NIPCCD}

Library staff. {IIT}

Library staff development and continuing education : Principles and practices. {USIS}

Library statistics : A handbook of concepts, definitions and terminology. [American Library Association, Statistics Coordinating Project]. {USIS}

Library stock and assistance to readers : A textbook. {NAI}

Library supply agencies in Europe. {JNU}

Library surveys. {DUL}

Library surveys : An introduction to their use, planning, procedure and presentation. {CRRI IIT NASSDOC USIS}

Library surveys : An introduction to their use, planning, procedure and presentation, 2nd edn. {JNU NASSDOC}

Library systems analysis guidelines. {DUL ICA IIT JNU NASSDOC NIH NMML USIS}

Library systems and information services. {IIMC NASSDOC}

Library technical service : Operations and management. {JNU}

Library technique. {CRRI DUL}

Library terms. {ISI}

Library tour, 1948 : Europe and America : Impressions and reflections. [Indian Library Association]. {INSA MFL}

Library trustee. {DUL}

Library trustees manual. [Ohio Library Trustees Association]. {JNU}

Library use in further education. {DUL}

Library use of computers : Introduction. [Special Libraries Association, New York]. {IIT USIS}

Library work with children : With special reference to developing countries. {DUL}

Library work with young people : An examination guide book. {DUL}

Library's public : Report of the public library inquiry. [Social Science Research Council]. {IEG}

Life of the book : How the book is written, published, sold and read. {DUL}

Life sciences information network. [National Library of Australia]. {JNU}

Linguistic and information science. {DUL}

List of books for college libraries, 1931-38. [American Library Association]. {ZHL}

List of documents and publications of General Information Programme and UNISIST, 1977-81. [UNESCO]. {JNU}

List of official publications not included in the general catalogue of Government of India publications issued during the period 1-1-1940 to 31-12-1960. {NASSDOC}

List of subject headings, 8 edn., ed by Bertha Margret Frick. {DUL}

List of subject headings for small libraries including practical suggestings for the beginner in subject heading work, 5th edn. {MHA}

List of subject headings for use in dictionary catalogue, 3rd rev. edn. [American Library Association]. {NAI}

List of subject headings in home building and allied fields. [National Housing Centre Library, Washington]. {SPA}

Literature and bibliometrics. {BCL IIT NASSDOC}

Literature of technical services. {DUL}

Literature recommendation : Basic reference list for establishing an industrial library. [U.S. International Cooperation Administration]. {BIS}

Literature search. {UGC}

Literature survey and trends in library cataloguing, 1970-1975. (Mimeo; short bibliography). {NASSDOC}

Lives, works and transformations : A quarter century of book reviews and essays, ed. by Linda Rolens. {USIS}

Living library : Planning public library buildings for cities of 100,000 or less. {CRRI}

Living with books : Art of book selection, 2nd edn. {DUL IIC IIT USIS}

Local history and the library. {IIC NMML SPA}

Local public library administration. [International Managers Association, Illinois]. {SPA USIS}

Local studies librarianship. {NIH}

London education classification. {University of London}. {IIT}

Looking for ideas : A display manual for libraries and bookstores. {USIS}

Looking forward in documentation. [Association of Special Libraries and Information Bureaux]. {BIS}

Louis Round Wilson : Librarian and administrator. {USIS}

The MARC II format : A communications format for bibliographic data, 2 vols. [Library of Congress]. {USIS}

The MARC pilot project : Final report on a project. [US Library of Congress]. {USIS}

MIMC microforms annual, 1977-78. [Microform International Marketing Corporation]. {NASSDOC}

MINIS, MICROS and terminals for libraries and information services. {JNU}

McGraw Hill computer handbook. {RTL}

Machine literature searching. {CRRI}

Macmillan dictionary of information. {NASSDOC}

Macrothesaurus for information processing in the field of economic and social development. {JNU}

Magazine for school libraries, rev edn. {ZHL}

Magazine selection : How to build a community-oriented collection. {USIS}

Maintaining library services : A study in six countries. [Education and Science Department, Great Britain]. {IIMC NIEPA}

Major libraries of the world : A selective guide. {NMML}

Making book work : A course for the school library. {JNU}

Making an Index. {IIT}

The making of books, 5th edn. {INSA}

The making of a code : The issues underlying AACR2 : Papers : International conference on AACR2, March 11-14, 1979, Florida. [American Library Association]. {USIS}

Making of a library : Academic library in transition. {CRRI DUL JNU}

Man-computer problem solving : Experimental evaluation of time-sharing and batch processing. {NASSDOC}

Man-machine communication. {INSA NASSDOC}

Man, machine systems : Information control and decision models of human performance. {JNU}

Man, memory and machines : An introduction to cybernetics. {INSA}

Management dynamics ; The new synthesis. {JNU}

Management for librarians : Based on a course of lectures at the Library Association in 1967. {JNU}

Management for librarians : Fundamentals and issues. {NIEPA USIS}

Management in libraries. {NASSDOC}

Management information and decision support systems in libraries. {JNU NASSDOC}

Management information retrieval : A new indexing language. {BCL NASSDOC}

Management information systems : Selected papers from MIS conferences. {JNU}

The management of archives. {NASSDOC USIS}

The management of the information department. {BCL}

Management of information from archives. {NMML}

Management of information handling systems. {NIEPA}

Management of information resources at the national level. [UNESCO]. {NASSDOC*}

The management of libraries and information centres, 4 vols. {DUL NIPCCD USIS}

Management of library networks : Policy analysis, implementation and control. {IIT}
The management of polytechnic libraries. {NASSDOC}
Management of technical services in libraries. {JNU}
Management of university libraries in India : Principles and practices. {AIU IIT}
Management services : Report on the library system of the Jawaharlal Nehru University. [Institute of Secretariat Training and Management]. {JNU ZHL}
Management techniques for librarians. {AIU IIT JNU NIEPA USIS}
Management techniques for librarians, 2nd edn. {BCL DUL IIT JNU NMML USIS}
Management training for libraries. [Library Association, London]. {NIEPA NIPCCD}
Managing informations systems and technologies : A basic guide for design, selection, evaluation and use. {NASSDOC}
Managing multimedia libraries. {DUL USIS}
Managing the serials explosion : 1982 {JNU NMML}
Managing the special library : Strategies for success within the larger organisation. {NASSDOC}
Manpower in the field of documentation and library services. [UNESCO]. {CRRI ICA}
Manual for college libraries. {UGC}
Manual for cataloguing school libraries. {JNU}
Manual for co-operative libraries and documentation services. {DSSW ICA}
Manual for new members of the staff. [County Library]. {JNU}
Manual for the operation of an information/public relations department in standards organisation. [Industrial Standards Institute]. {BIS}
Manual for the preparation of records in development information systems. [International Development Research Corporation]. {NASSDOC}
Manual for writers of term papers, theses and dissertations. {DUL}
Manual of archival and manuscript processing procedures. {DUL}
Manual of archive administration. {NAI}
Manual of bibliographic control. [UNESCO]. {NASSDOC*}
Manual of book binding. {ZHL}
Manual of book classification and display for public libraries. {BIS MMTC NAI NIH SPA ZHL}
Manual of book selling. {DUL}
Manual of cataloguing and indexing. {NAI}
Manual of cataloguing practice. {IIT JNU NASSDOC NIPCCD NMML ZHL}
Manual of children libraries. {DUL}
Manual of classification. {NMML}
Manual of classification, 3rd edn. {BIS CRRI IIT JNU NAI SPA ZHL}
Manual of classification. 5th edn., ed. by Arthur Maltby {BIS ICA ICHR MMTC NERC NIPCCO NMML ZHL}
Manual of form for theses and term reports, rev edn. {DUL}
Manual of government publications : United States and foreign. {CRRI}
Manual of library classification. {NAI}
Manual of library economy. {JNU}
Manual of library economy, ed. by R.N. Lock. {BIS CRRI DUL MFL MHA NIH SPA}
Manual of library management. [Physical Research Laboratory, Ahmedabad]. {JNU}

Manual of library management. {DUL IIT}
Manual of library organisation. {NAI}
Manual of library routine. {JNU}
A manual of practical book selection for public libraries. {CRRI DUL}
Manual of practical indexing including arrangement of subject catalogues. {NAI}
Manual of procedures for evaluation visits under standards for accredition. {USIS}
Manual of procedures for private law libraries. [American Association of Law Libraries]. {USIS}
Manual of reference work. {DUL SPA}
Manual of style, 11th edn. {INSA}
Manual of style, 12th edn. {INSA}
Manual of technical services processes. {DUL}
Manual of techniques in library organisation. {DUL}
Manual on the use of the Dewey Decimal Classification, 19th edn. {NASSDOC}
Manual on the use of the state publications. [American Library Association]. {CRRI}
Manuals : Stack and reader division reference department. [Library of Congress]. {JNU}
Manuscripts and documents : Their deterioration and restoration. {NASSDOC NMML}
The many faces of information science. {INSA JNU USIS}
Map collection in the United States and Canada : A directory, 2nd edn. [Special Libraries Association, New York]. {USIS}
Map collections in the United States and Canada : A directory, 3rd edn. [Special Libraries Association, New York]. {USIS}
Map librarianship. {NASSDOC NMML}
Map librarianship : An introduction. {USIS}
Marathi granth suchi, 2 vols, Vol. 1 : 1800-1937; Vol. 2 : 1938-1951 {NASSDOC}
March of library science : Kaula festschrift : Papers presented in honour of Prof. P.N. Kaula. {CRRI ICA ICHR IIC IIFT INSA ISI JNU NCAER NIEPA ZHL}
Margin for surprise : About books, children and librarians. {USIS}
Marginal punched cards in college and research libraries. {JNU}
Mariamali Adigal library : 20th Anniversary celebrations souvenir. {NMML}
Marketing of library and information services in India. [Indian Association of Special Libraries and Information Centres]. {NASSDOC}
Marketing the library. {JNU USIS}
Marketing the library service, ed. by A. Wilson. [Library Association, London]. {JNU}
Mass communications : Selected readings for librarians. {NIPCCD}
Mathematical models for library systems analysis. {JNU}
The Maulana Azad Library : A major library of the world, 1977-1988. {DUL JNU UGC ZHL}
Measurement and evaluation : Papers presented at a conference conducted by the University of Illinois, Graduate School of Library Science, September 10-12, 1967. {DUL}
Measurement and evaluation of library services. {IIT USIS}
Measuring the quality of library service. {NIEPA USIS}

Mechanisation information retrieval and processing : Application of punched. {NASSDOC}

Mechanisation of the national library catalogues. [UNESCO]. {NASSDOC}

Mechanised circulation system, Leh University Library. {JNU}

Mechanised in-house information systems. {BCL CRRI NIPCCD}

Mechanised information storage, retrieval and dissemination : Proceedings. {JNU}

Media utilization for the development of women and children. {NIPCCD}

Medical classification, 3rd edn. [Boston Medical Library]. {DUL}

Medical librarianship : Outlines of modern librarianship. {NIH USIS}

Medical librarianship : Principles and practice. {DUL}

Medium term programme, 1981-85. [International Federation of Library Associations and Institutions]. {NASSDOC}

Medium term programme, 1986-91. [International Federation of Library Associations and Institutions, Professional Board]. {NASSDOC}

Melcher on acquisition. [American Library Association]. {AIU NASSDOC}

Melvil Dewey : The man and the classification. {NASSDOC}

Melvil Dewey : The man and the classification. {DUL}

Memoirs. [Madras Library Association]. {NASSDOC}

Men, messages and media : A look at human communication. {NASSDOC}

Men of library science and libraries in India. {SPA USIS}

Mental hospital library. {DUL}

Merging of databases for the production of secondary information publications : Phase-1. {BCL}

Method for writing calendar dates in all-numeric form. (IS : 7900-1976). [Indian Standards Institution]. {NASSDOC}

Methods of analysis and evaluation of information needs : A critical review. {JNU}

Methods of book design : The practices of an industrial craft, 2nd edn. {INSA}

Methods of information handling. {DUL IIMC IIT JNU NASSDOC}

Methods of research : Educational, psychological and sociological. {NASSDOC}

Methods of teaching librarianship. [UNESCO]. {IIMC JNU NASSDOC NIEPA NIPCCD}

Metropolitan libraries : The challenge and the promise. [American Library Association]. {USIS}

Metropolitan public library planning throughout the work. {DUL JNU NASSDOC SPA USIS}

Micro computer in library and information services : An annotated bibliography. {JNU}

Microcomputers : A planning and implementation guide for librarians and information professionals. {JNU}

Microcomputers and libraries : A guide to technology, products and applications. [American Society for Information Science]. {USIS}

Microcopying methods, ed. by Gordon H. Wright. {DUL}

Microfiche reader. {USIS}

Microfilm : The librarians' view, 1976-77. {USIS}

Microfilming of technical drawings and other drawing office equipments : Pt-1 : operation procedures (ISO 3272/I-1983); Pt-II : Quality criteria and control (ISO 3272/II-1978); Pt-III : Unitized 35 mm microfilm carriers (ISO 3272/III-1975). [International Organisation for Standardisation, Geneva]. {NASSDOC}

The microform connection : A basic guide for libraries. {USIS}
Microform librarianship. {NASSDOC}
Microform librarianship, 2nd edn. {IDA ZHL}
Microform retrieval equipment guide. [Bastuibak Archives and Records Service, Washington]. {BIS}
Microform revolution in libraries. {BIS}
Microform, video and electronic media librarianship. {NMML}
Microforms annual, 1982-83 : An international guide to microforms. {NASSDOC}
Microforms annual, 1984-85 : An international guide to microforms. {NASSDOC}
Microforms as an alternative to physical growth in libraries. [University of Poona, Pune]. {NASSDOC*}
Microforms in libraries. [American Library Association]. {NASSDOC}
Microforms in libraries : A reader. {BIS JNU USIS}
Microphotography for libraries. {DUL}
Microphotography in the library. [UNESCO]. {IDA NASSDOC}
Microrecording : Industrial and library applications. {DUL}
Microtext and microreading. [County Technical Library Service, Hertfordshire]. {DUL}
Milestones in cataloguing : Famous cataloguers and their writings, 1835-1969. {USIS}
Miniaturised communications : A review of microforms. [Library Association, London]. {NASSDOC}
Minicomputers and bibliographic information retrieval. [British Library Lending Division]. {BCL}
Minicomputers in libraries, 1979-80; 1981-82 {USIS}
Minimum standards for public library systems, 1966. [Standards committee and subcommittees of the Public Library Association; American Library Association]. {USIS}
Mirror of brass : Compensation and working condition of college and university administrators. {JNU}
Mobile libraries and other public library transport. [Association of Assistant librarians, London]. {BIS}
Modern book production. {DUL}
Modern cataloguing theory and practice. {AIU IIC IIT JNU}
Modern data processing, 2nd edn. {NASSDOC}
Modern design in book binding. {DUL}
Modern documentation and information practices : A basic manual. [International Federation for Documentation and Information]. {BIS DUL ICA NASSDOC NIEPA}
Modern filing methods and equipment. {IIMC}
Modern information systems. {NIH}
Modern libraries for modern colleges. {JNU}
Modern library equipment. {CRRI IIT NIH NMML}
Modern library systems. {NMML}
Modern manuscript library. {NMML}
Modern news library : Documentation of current affairs in newspaper and broadcasting libraries. {IIMC}
Modern outline of library classification, 2nd edn. {BIS CRRI IIT MFL NAI NMML}
Modern programming : PL/I. {DUL}
Modern public libraries : Their planning and design. {CRRI}

Modern public library movement and services in India. {JNU}
Modern researcher, 3rd edn. {NASSDOC}
Modern school library : Its administration as a material centre. {JNU}
Modern techniques of documentation and information work. {NASSDOC}
Modern trends in documentation. {ISI}
Modern trends in librarianship in India. {IIMC IIT NMML}
Modernisation in libraries : Seminar Papers : All India Library Conference, 33rd, December 28-31, 1987, Tiruchirapalli. [Indian Library Association]. {NASSDOC}
Modular planning for college and small university libraries. {DUL}
Monograph on use of library as enrichment to teaching. [State Council for Education Research and Teaching, Hyderabad]. {NASSDOC*}
More case studies in reference work. {DUL IIT}
Moving a library. {USIS}
Moving library materials. {JNU}
Multimedia library : Materials selection and use. {IIFT JNU NIPCCD}
Multimedia library : Materials selection and use, 2nd edn. {NIEPA}
Multitype library cooperation. {NASSDOC USIS}

NASSDOC : How it works. {NASSDOC}
NASSDOC dockets. {NASSDOC}
NASSDOC research information series, 62 vols. {NASSDOC}
NATIS : Design and planning of national information systems. [UNESCO]. {NASSDOC*}
NATIS : National information policy. {NASSDOC*}
NATIS : Preliminary survey of education and training programmes at university level in information and library science. [UNESCO]. {NIEPA}
NCC thesaurus of computing terms, 4th edn, 2 vols, Vol. 1 : Alphabetic; Vol. 2 : Hierarchy listing. {NASSDOC}
NCC thesaurus of computing terms, 7th edn. {NASSDOC}
Names of person : National usages for entry in catalogues. [International Federation of Library Association and Institutions]. {NASSDOC}
National abstracting services : Need, purpose and scope. {JNU}
National agency for International Standard Book Numbering System : A manual. [Raja Rammohun Roy National Educational Resources Centres, New Delhi]. {NASSDOC}
National and international library planning. {DUL}
The National archives : America's Ministry of Documents, 1934-1968. {USIS}
National bibliographical services. {IEG}
National bibliography of Indian literature 1901-1953, 4 vols. [Sahitya Akademi, New Delhi]. {DSSW INSA MFL NASSDOC}
National catalogue of university level books. {DSSW NASSDOC}
National Diet Library : Organisation, functions and activities. [National Diet Library, Japan]. {AIU}
National document handling systems for science and technology. {BIS IIMC NIH USIS}
National Documentation Centre on Mass Communication : Report. [Ministry of Information and Broadcasting, New Delhi]. {IIMC}
National information ; Guide to Indian periodicals, 1953-1956. {DSSW}

National information base for health population and family welfare in India : Manual for preparation of input for computerised bibliographic information base. [National Institute of Health and Family Welfare, New Delhi]. {NIH}

National information literature in SSDC. {NASSDOC*}

National information system : Library and information science manpower development in Asian region : Meeting of supervisors of library and documentation schools in the Asian region, Bangalore. [UNESCO; DRTC]. {JNU}

National Information System for Science and Technology (NISSAT) : Detailed project report, (1985-1990). [Ministry of Science and Technology, New Delhi]. {NASSDOC}

National information system for social sciences. (Typed Short bibliography). {NASSDOC}

National libraries : Their problems and prospects : Symposium on national libraries in Europe, September 8-27, Vienna. [UNESCO]. {AIU BIS CRRI IEG IIMC MFL NASSDOC NIEPA NIPCCD}

National library and information services : Handbook for planners. {CRRI DUL IIT INSA JNU NASSDOC NCAER NIEPA}

National library and information system. {NASSDOC NMML}

National Library Bill, 1972 : Report and evidence : India, Lok Sabha, Joint Committee on the National Library Bill. {AIU NMML}

National library network. {IIT}

National library of India : Critical study. {AIU ICHR IIC IIFT IIMC IIT ISI NERC NIEPA NIH NIPCCD NMML SPA ZHL}

The National Library of India, 1903-1978 : A pictorial history released on the occasion of platinum jubilee of the National Library, Calcutta. [National Library, Calcutta]. {NASSDOC}

National Library of Medicine classification : A scheme for the shelf arrangement of books in the field of medicine and its related sciences, 3rd edn. [U.S. National Library of Medicine]. {USIS}

National library system : A plan for India. {ZHL}

National library week souvenir, 1976. [Kerala Library Association, Trivandrum]. {ICA JNU MMTC}

National policy for university libraries on India : Problems and perspectives. {NASSDOC}

National policy on library and information system : A presentation. [Government of India, Committee on National Policy on Library and Information System]. {NASSDOC*}

National public library system. {NASSDOC}

National seminar on social science documentation in India. {JNU}

National standards for cataloguing and indexing art museum objects and documents. {ZHL}

National transport system for inter-library loan. {JNU}

Nationwide location data base and service. [Library of Congress]. {MMTC}

Need for National Information Policy : Its parameters : Papers : Convention and conference of the society for information science, 4th, December 27-28, 1984, Madras. {NASSDOC*}

Neighbourhood library centres and services. [National Book Trust, New Delhi]. {JNU}

Newbery medal books, with their authors' acceptance : Papers and related material, chiefly from the Horn Book magazine, 1922-55. {USIS}

New definitions of school library service. {JNU}

New dimensions for academic library service. {USIS}

New dimensions in library science. {CRRI DUL ICHR IIT ISI NIEPA}

New directions in staff development moving from ideas to action : The papers : Microworkshop on staff development, June 28, 1970, Detroit. [American Library Association]. {USIS}

New education and school library : Experience of half a century. {DUL ICA JNU NIEPA}

New Education Policy : Libraries and information system : Papers and proceedings. [NCERT; Raja Ram Mohan Roy Library Foundation, Calcutta]. {NMML}

New education policy vis-a-vis library development : Papers presented in the seminar held at New Delhi on February 13, 1986. [Indian Library Association]. {NASSDOC}

New frontiers in library and information science. [Zilla Granthalaya Samsthan, Machilipatnam]. {NASSDOC*}

New India directory of libraries and educational institutions of India, Pakistan, Burma and Ceylon. {AIU IIT}

New introduction to bibliography. {INSA}

New Jersy graduate school of library science, 2 vols. {IIT}

The new librarianship : A challenge for change. {USIS}

New library buildings : Architect-librarian assessment, 1973-74. {DUL}

New library design : Guidelines to planning academic library buildings. {AIU BIS CRRI IIT JNU NIPCCD USIS}

The new library key, 3rd edn. {USIS}

New media and the library in education. {IIT NIH}

New media in public libraries : Survey of current practices. {USIS}

New options for librarians. {NASSDOC*}

New perspectives for reference service in academic libraries. {CRRI IIT NIPCCD}

New school librarian. {JNU}

New trends in international librarianship. {NASSDOC NMML}

New trends in scientific communication. [Indian Association of Special Libraries and Information Centres]. {SPA}

New Zealand national bibliography, 1978. [National Library of New Zealand]. {NASSDOC}

News information : Organisation of press cuttings in the libraries of newspapers and broadcasting services. {IIMC IIT NMML SPA}

Newspaper libraries. (Mimeo short bibliography). {NASSDOC}

Newspaper microfilming : A plea for newsprint documentation. {NASSDOC ZHL}

Non-book material available in Nehru Memorial Museum and Library : A brief survey. {NMML}

Non-book materials : The organisation of integrated collections. [Canadian Library Association]. {NERC USIS}

Non-book materials : The organisation of integrated collections, 2nd edn. [Canadian Library Association]. {NERC USIS}

Non book materials : The organisation of integrated collections, 3rd edn. [Canadian Library Association]. {NASSDOC}

Non-book materials cataloguing rules : Integrated code of practice and draft revision of the Anglo-American Cataloguing Rules. [Library Association Media

Cataloguing Rules Committee; National Council for Educational Technology, London]. {NASSDOC}

Non-book materials in libraries : A practical guide. {ISIR}

Non-print media in academic libraries. [American Library Association]. {USIS}

Notes for serials cataloguing. {NASSDOC*}

Notes on subject bibliography. {DUL IEG MFL}

OCLC : Its governance, function, financing and technology. {JNU}

Of libraries and librarians. [University of Karachi]. {ZHL}

Offset lithography. {DUL}

The old librarians almanac. {NASSDOC*}

On documentation of scientific literature. {JNU}

On-line bibliographic databases : An international directory, 2nd edn. [Association of Special Libraries and Information Bureaux]. {USIS}

On line catalogue. [Library Association, London. {NASSDOC}

The online catalogue : Improving public access to library materials. {USIS}

On-line information retrieval : Concepts, principles and techniques. {JNU}

On-line information retrieval : An introduction and guide to British library's short term experimental information network project, Vol. 1 : Experimental use of non-medical information services; Vol. 2 : Experimental use of medical information services. [British Library]. {BCL}

On-line information retrieval, 1965-76 : A bibliography with a guide to on-line data bases and systems. [Association of Special Libraries and Information Bureaux]. {BCL CRRI NASSDOC}

On-line information retrieval systems : An introductory manual to principles and practices. {BCL CRRI DUL NIH}

The on-line revolution in libraries : Proceedings of the 1977 conference in Pittsburgh. {JNU}

Online search services in the academic library : Planning, management and operation. [American Library Association]. {NASSDOC}

On-line search strategies. {USIS}

Online searching. {IIT}

Online searching : A dictionary and bibliographic guide. {NASSDOC USIS}

Online searching technique and management. [American Library Association]. {USIS}

On machine translation : Selected papers. {USIS}

On research libraries : Statement and recommendations. [American Council of Learned Societies Devoted to Humanistic Studies, Committee on Research Libraries]. {IIT INSA USIS}

On retrieval system theory, 2nd edn. {CRRI DUL IIT}

Operating manual for use in abstracting and coordinate indexing. [Battelle Memorial Institute, Ohio]. {BIS}

Operating systems : A pragmatic approach. {NASSDOC}

Operational research techniques, Vol. 1 : Introduction. {NASSDOC}

Operations research : Implications for libraries. {NASSDOC}

Operations research : An introduction. {NASSDOC}

Operations research : An introduction to modern applications. {NASSDOC}

Operations research : A tool for library management. [American Library Association]. {USIS}

Opinion poll survey among visitors to the New Delhi World Book Fair : A report. [National Book Trust, New Delhi]. {NASSDOC*}

Optical character recognition : Use of OCR techniques in decentralised data collection for bibliographic information systems. [International Development Research Centre, Ottawa]. {NASSDOC}

Optical structures and Universal Classification. {DUL JNU}

Optimum utilisation of knowledge : Making knowledge serve human betterment. {NMML}

Oral communication of technical information. {CRRI}

Oral history collections. {USIS}

Order procedure. {JNU}

Ordering systems for global information networks : Proceedings : International study conference on classification research, 3, January 6-11, 1975, Bombay, [FID/CR; Sarada Ranganathan Endowment for Library Science]. {BIS NASSDOC}

Organisation and administration of college libraries. {DUL ICA}

Organisation and administration of the learning resources centre in the community college. {USIS}

Organisation and retrieval of economic knowledge : Proceedings of the conference held by the International Economic Association. {NASSDOC}

Organisation development for academic libraries. {JNU}

Organisation, functioning and activities of national documentary information systems in the scientific, technical and economic fields. [National Institute for Scientific and Technical Information and Documentation, Romania]. {BIS}

Organisation of data services in India. [Indian Association of Special Libraries and Information Centres]. {NASSDOC}

Organisation of information systems for government and public administration. {BIS JNU}

Organisation of intermediate records storage. [UNESCO]. {NIEPA NMML}

Organisation of knowledge and system of the sciences. {DUL}

Organisation of knowledge in libraries and the subject-approach to books, 2nd edn. {BIS IEG USIS}

Organisation of libraries, 3rd edn. {JNU NIH}

Organisation of the library profession. {CRRI}

Organisation of small libraries : A manual of educational institutions in tropical countries. {JNU NIEPA}

The organisation of the small public library. [UNESCO]. {ICA IEG NASSDOC NERC NIEPA}

Organisation of social science information and documentation : Reports on 11 Asian countries. [UNESCO Regional Adviser for Social Science in Asia and the Pacific, Bangkok]. {NASSDOC}

Organising information : Principle of data base and retrieval. {JNU}

Organising knowledge in libraries : An introduction to classification and cataloguing. {IIC MFL SPA ZHL}

Organising knowledge in libraries : An introduction to information retrieval, 2nd rev edn. {ICA IIFT NASSDOC}

Organising local government documents collection. [American Library Association]. {USIS}

Organising nonprint materials : A guide for librarians. {ICHR IIT JNU NASSDOC ZHL}

Organising resources : Six case studies : Final report of the Schools Council Resources Centre project. {NIPCCD}

Organising village library : A guide book for social education workers and village librarians. [National Council for Educational Research and Training, New Delhi]. {ICA ISI NIPCCD}

Origins of American academic librarianship. {JNU}

Origins of the America's college library, 1838-1900. {JNU}

Our national attic. [U.S. Library of Congress; Smithsonian Institution; National Archives]. {USIS}

Out of the dinosaurs : The evolution of the National Lending Library for Science and Technology. {NASSDOC}

Outline for the courses in problems in cataloguing and classification. {DUL}

Outline for the organisation of hospital libraries. {DUL}

Outline of library classification. {NERC}

PERT and CPM : Principles and applications. {JNU}

PILOT : An on-line library acquisition system. {JNU}

PRECIS : A manual of concept analysis and subject indexing. {CRRI JNU}

PRECIS : A rotated subject index system. [Council of British National Bibliography]. {NASSDOC}

The PRECIS index system : Principles, applications and prospects : Proceedings : International PRECIS workshop, October 15-17, 1976, Maryland. {NASSDOC}

Papers : Advanced working seminar on national information policy and the impact of social and technological change on national information planning, Australia. {CRRI}

Papers : All India library conference, 10th, June 1-4, 1953, Hyderabad. [Indian Library Association]. {NASSDOC}

Papers : All India library conference, 15th, 1963, Mysore. [Indian Library Association]. {NASSDOC}

Papers : All India library conference, 1965, Mysore. [Indian Library Association]. {CRRI}

Papers : All India library conference, 21st, 1975, Bhubaneswar. [Indian Library Association]. {NASSDOC}

Papers : All India library conference, 1980, New Delhi. [Indian Library Association]. {NASSDOC*}

Papers : All India library conference, 1981. [Indian Library Association]. {NMML}

Papers : All India library conference, 1986, [Indian Library Association]. {NMML}

Papers . All India library conference, 32nd, 1987, Anantpur. [Indian Library Association]. {NASSDOC}

Papers : All India public library convention, November, 16-18, 1978, New Delhi. [Delhi Library Association, Delhi]. {MMTC NMML}

Papers : All India seminar on agricultural library and information services, December 29-January 16, 1980. [Andhra Pradesh Agricultural University, Hyderabad; Indian Council of Agricultural Research, New Delhi]. {IIMC}

Papers : All India seminar on libraries and the book trade, February 1982, New Delhi. [Indian Library Association]. {IIMC IIT JNU ZHL}

Papers : All India seminar on library resources in university education and research, 1982, Hyderabad. [Osmania University Library, Hyderabad]. {ZHL}

Papers : All India seminar on national policy for library and information science education, 1983, Nagpur. {NASSDOC}

Papers : Conference on electronic information technology and its impact on library and information service, 4th, 1981, Pittsburg. {IIT}

Papers : Conference on informatics, 1973, Durham. [Association of Special Libraries and Information Bureaux]. {CRRI}

Papers : Conference on informatics, 1974, Oxford. [Association of Special Libraries and Information Bureaux]. {CRRI}

Papers : Conference on informatics, 1975, Cambridge. [Association of Special Libraries and Information Bureaux]. {CRRI}

Papers : Conference on use of computers in libraries and information centres, 1975, London. [Association of Special Libraries and Information Bureaux]. {CRRI}

Papers : DRTC annual seminar on information analysis and consolidation, 1981, Bangalore. [Documentation Research and Training Centre, Bangalore]. {CRRI}

Papers : DRTC refresher seminar, 1983, Bangalore. [Documentation Research and Training Centre, Bangalore]. {JNU}

Papers : DRTC refresher seminar on data accessibility and dissemination, 1980, Bangalore. [Documentation Research and Training Centre, Bangalore]. {CRRI}

Papers : EUSIDIC conference on user education, 1976, Graz. {CRRI}

Papers : European conference on the contribution of users to planning and policy making for information systems and networks, 1978, Germany. {CRRI}

Papers: FID congress on new trends in documentation and information, 1978, Edinburg. {CRRI}

Papers : FID pre-congress seminar on education and training : Theory and provision with a look at new developments and an example of the challenges confronting information workers, 1978, Edinburg. [International Federation for Documentation and Information]. {NASSDOC}

Papers : IASLIC conference, 9th, 1972, Calcutta. [Indian Association of Special Libraries and Information Centre]. {IIT INSA JNU MMTC}

Papers : IASLIC conference, 10th, 1975, Lucknow, Pt. A. : Library documents aspects of utilisation; Pt. B. : Procurement of periodicals : Current problems in India [Indian Association of Special Libraries and Information Centres]. {IIMC}

Papers : IASLIC conference, 14th December 26-29, 1983, New Delhi, I : Information flow in non R and D context; II : Grey literature. [Indian Association of Special Libraries and Information Centres]. {JNU MMTC NASSDOC NCAER NIEPA NIPCCD}

Papers : IASLIC conference on library profession in India : Its status and responsibilities and standardised library practices and job classification, 1969, Bombay. [Indian Association of Special Libraries and Information Centres]. {CRRI}

Papers : IASLIC conference on planning of national information network, 11th, November 2-5, 1977, Dharwar. [Indian Association of Special Libraries and Information Centres]. {CRRI ISI JNU NIEPA NIPCCD}

Papers : IASLIC national seminar, 4th,. 1966, Hyderabad. [Indian Association of Special Libraries and Information Centres]. {NASSDOC}

Papers : IASLIC national seminar, 11th, November 26-29, 1984, Hyderabad, I : Toward a code of professional ethics; II : Document delivery, reproduction, translation. [Indian Association of Special Libraries and Information Centres]. {NASSDOC}

Papers : IASLIC seminar, 6th, November 2-5, 1970, Bangalore. [Indian Association of Special Libraries and Information Centres]. {BIS JNU NMML}

Papers : IASLIC seminar, 7th, December 28-31, 1976, Burdwan. [Indian Association of Special Libraries and Information Centres]. {BIS JNU NASSDOC}

Papers : IASLIC seminar, 9th, October 23-26, 1980, Nagpur, I : Role of information centres in technology transfer; II : Role of State-level and national library association in library development in India. [Indian Association of Special Libraries and Information Centres]. {CRRI INSA JNU NASSDOC}

Papers : IASLIC seminar on information services in India, 1982, Kanpur. [Indian Association of Special Libraries and Information Centres]. {CRRI}

Papers : IASLIC symposium on the development of libraries in India under the Third Five Year Plan with particular reference to special libraries, January 23-25, 1960, Calcutta. [Indian Association of Special Libraries and Information Centres]. {BIS}

Papers : IFLA General Conference, 53rd, August 16-21, 1987, Bringhton. [International Federation of Library Associations and Institutions]. {NASSDOC}

Papers : International library conference on libraries and the challenge of change, April 24-29, 1976, Kingsten. [Jamaica Library Association]. {IIT}

Papers : National conference, 1980, Tirupati. [Indian Association of Academic Librarians]. {ZHL}

Papers : National conference on new horizons for academic libraries, November 8-11, 1978, Boston, {IIT}

Papers : National seminar on assessment of public library development in India, March 3-6, 1986, Madras. [University of Madras, Department of Library Science; University Grants Commission, New Delhi]. {NASSDOC}

Papers : National seminar on library and information manpower development, December 6-9, 1985, Nagpur. [Nagpur University, Department of Library and Information Science; University Grants Commission, New Delhi]. {NASSDOC}

Papers : National seminar on library and information science education in India : New perspective, December 10-12, 1986, Trivandrum. [Kerala State Committee on Science, Technology and Environment]. {NASSDOC}

Papers : Seminar on information for engineering industry, February 10, 1978, New Delhi. [Association of Engineering Industry; Indian National Scientific Documentation Centre, New Delhi]. {BIS}

Papers : Seminar on library and information science education in India, 1977, New Delhi. {JNU}

Papers : Seminar on library buildings in India, February 11-13, 1980, New Delhi. [National Information Systems for Science and Technology, New Delhi]. {BIS CRRI IIT}

Papers : Seminar on library science in Southeast Asia, December 18-20, 1964, Bangkok. [Association of Southeast Asian Institutions of Higher Learning]. {NASSDOC NIEPA}

Papers : Seminar on mechanical engineering information : Provision and use, March 27-29, 1974, Loughborough. {BCL}

Papers : Seminar on reference sources on South Asia, 1979, Jaipur. {JNU}

Papers : Seminar on the rendering of Indic names, 1960-61, Calcutta. [Indian Association of Special Libraries and Information Centres]. {NASSDOC}

Papers : Seminar on the role of the national liberty of India, November 23, 1978, Calcutta. [National Library Employee's Association, Calcutta]. {NASSDOC}

Papers : Seminar on thesaurus in information systems, December 1-5, 1975, Bangalore. [DRTC, Bangalore; Indian National Scientific Documentation Centre, New Delhi]. {BIS CRRI DUL IIMC ZHL}

Papers : Seminar on work flow in libraries, November 21-24, 1966, New Delhi; 3 vols., Vol. 1 : Special libraries; Vol II : University libraries; Vol. III : Government libraries. [Indian National Scientific Documentation Centre, New Delhi]. {NASSDOC NMML SPA}

Papers : Symposium on modern trends in documentation, 1958, California. {CRRI}

Papers : Symposium on new technology in libraries : Prospects and problems for libraries in the Gulf States, 1982, Teheran. [Ministry of Petroleum and Minerals, Teheran]. {CRRI}

Papers : UGC sponsored national seminar on documentation services in university and college libraries, January 12-14, 1986, Jabalpur. {NASSDOC}

Papers : Workshop on computer techniques in information processing. [University of Delhi, Department of Library and Information Science]. {AIU}

Papers : Workshop on norms, guidelines and standards for public libraries. [Zilla Granthalaya Samstha, Eluru]. {NASSDOC*}

Papers and proceedings : IASLIC conference, 8th, December 26-29, 1978, Madras, Pt I : Standardisation of techniques and procedures for information handling; Pt II : Library and information system for rural development. [Indian Association of Special Libraries and Information Centres]. {BIS NIPCCD}

Papers and proceedings : Round table discussion on the concepts of Australian national bibliography, 1983, South Wales. {JNU}

Papers on oriental library collections submitted to a library panel : International congress of orientalists, 27th, August 17, 1967, Ann Arbor, Michigan. {NMML}

Parliaments and information dissemination. {NASSDOC}

Participative management in academic libraries. {DUL NIEPA}

Pathfinder : An operational guide for the school librarian. {JNU}

Pathways for communication : Books and libraries in the information age. {AIU NIEPA}

Patrons are people : How to be a model librarian, 2nd rev edn. [American Library Association]. {DUL USIS}

Patterns in the use of books in large research libraries. {NMML}

Patterns of communication in international meeting : A pilot study of tenth international congress of anthropological and ethnological sciences. {NASSDOC}

People work, communications dynamics for libraries. [American Library Association]. {USIS}

Periodicals administration in libraries : A collection of essays. {IIT NASSDOC NCAER NIPCCD}

Periodicals collection : Its purpose and uses in libraries. {NMML}

Permanence and durability of library catalogue cards. {DUL}

Personal documentation for professionals : Means and methods. {JNU}

Personal filing system for the professional concerned with community planning. {SPA}

Personal issues in reference service. {JNU}

Personnel administration for libraries : A bibliographic essay. [American Library Association]. {BIS DUL}

Personnel administration in libraries. {JNU}

Personnel administration in libraries, 2nd edn. rev. by P.G. Mohrhardt. {JNU NIH USIS}

Personnel administration in public libraries. [American Library Association]. {CRRI}

Personnel development in libraries. [Bureau of Library and Information Science Research, Rutgers University Graduate School of Library Service]. {NIPCCD USIS}

Personnel issues in reference services, {JNU NASSDOC}
Personnel management. {JNU}
Personnel management in libraries. {BIS IIFT IIMC ISI JNU NIEPA ZHL}
Personnel management in libraries. {JNU}
Personnel management in library. {DUL IIT}
Personnel motivation and work efficiency in libraries. {NASSDOC}
Personnel organisation and procedure : A manual suggested for use in public libraries, 2nd edn. [American Library Association]. {DUL USIS}
Perspectives in information science. {JNU}
Perspectives in library and information science : Viswanathan festschrift. 2 vols. {AIU ICHR ISI JNU MMTC NASSDOC NCDC NIEPA NIPCCD SPA ZHL}
Philosophy of classification. {IEG IIT}
Philosophy of librarianship. {CRRI IEG IIT}
Philosophy of library classification. {DUL}
Philosophy of user education. {DUL IIT ISI JNU NASSDOC NIEPA ZHL}
Photo charging : Its operation and installation in British Public Library. {JNU}
Photocopying in libraries : The librarians speak. {IIT}
Photoduplication service. [U.S. Library of Congress]. {DUL}
Photo-offset : Fundamentals. {DUL}
Physical bibliography for librarians, 2nd ed. {AIU ICA INSA}
Physics and astronomy classification scheme. [American Institute of Physics]. {IIT}
Picture file in school, college and public libraries, rev edn. {ZHL}
Pilot project on the mechanisation of documentation services in Asia : Thailand. [UNESCO]. {NASSDOC*}
Pioneer of information science : Selected works. {JNU}
Planning academic and research library buildings. {BIS IIT NASSDOC NIH USIS}
Planning the academic library. {JNU}
Planning the administrative library. {DUL}
Planning agency library manual. [Council of Planning Librarians]. {SPA}
Planning and design of library buildings. {IIT ISI}
Planning and design of library buildings, 2nd edn. {CRRI}
Planning college and university library : A book for campus planners and architects. {USIS}
Planning for innovation through dissemination and utilisation of knowledge. {NASSDOC*}
Planning for a national information and documentation system : Kenya. [UNESCO]. {NASSDOC}
Planning functional college library. {IIT}
Planning in library resource sharing : Proceedings : Seminar on coordination in resource sharing held at Isabella Thouburn College, Lucknow. {NASSDOC}
Planning the library : A guide to those considering problems of library design, book storage and shelving. {DUL}
Planning a library building. {DUL}
Planning library buildings for service : Proceedings : Library building and equipment institute, July 6-8, 1961 : Kent. [American Library Association]. {BIS DUL}

Planning library education programmes : A study of the problems involved in the management and operation of library schools in the developing countries. {MFL NIEPA}

Planning library service. {NASSDOC}

Planning library training programmes. {NIEPA}

Planning library workshops and institutes. [American Library Association]. {USIS}

Planning manual for academic library buildings. {JNU}

Planning national infrastructures for documentation, libraries and archives : Outline of a general policy. {DUL IIMC JNU NASSDOC NIEPA}

Planning national technical information centre for child development in India : A blueprint, Thesis : Associateship in Documentation and Information Science. [Documentation Research and Training Centre]. {NIPCCD}

Planning of great library. {ZHL}

The planning of indexing and abstracting services in the social sciences : Coverage overlap and content. [Bath University Library]. {BCL}

The planning of library and documentation services. [UNESCO]. {AIU ICA NIEPA SPA}

Planning of library and documentation services, 2nd edn. [UNESCO]. {IIMC INSA MFL NASSDOC NCAER NERC NIH NIPCCD NMML TDA}

Planning of national information network : 11th, IASLIC conference at Dharwar, 1977. {JNU}

Planning programming budgeting system : Implications for library management. {JNU}

Planning the public library. [American Society of Planning Officials]. {SPA}

Planning school library development : A report of the school library development project. {DUL NASSDOC}

Planning the university library building : A summary of discussions by librarians, architects and engineers. {NASSDOC ZHL}

Plans for six public library buildings. [American Library Association]. {USIS}

Pointers for public library building planners. {DUL}

Policies of publishers : A handbook for order librarians. {JNU}

Politics, international relations and law : Scope, methodology and classification. {BIS ICHR IEG IIT JNU MFL MHA NASSDOC NMML ZHL}

Position classification and salary administration in libraries. [American Library Association]. {IIT}

Post-war reconstruction of libraries in India. [Punjab Library Association, Lahore]. {ZHL}

Practical administration of public libraries. {IIT NMML USIS}

Practical approach to information and data retrieval. [Boston Industrial Education Institute]. {ISI}

Practical approval plan management. {IIT}

Practical cataloguing. {ICHR IIC IIT ZHL}

Practical cataloguing. [Association of Assistant Librarians, London]. {IIT}

Practical cataloguing. {ZHL}

Practical cataloguing : Classified catalogue. {INSA JNU NCAER}

Practical cataloguing : Classified catalogue, 2nd edn. [ICA ICHR IEC JNU NIPCCD}

Practical cataloguing procedure. {IIT NIPCCD}

Practical classification, V.I : Colon Classification. {NIH NIPCCD ZHL}

Practical current awareness services from libraries. {JNU}
Practical guide to Colon Classification. {AIU IIT JNU NERC NIEPA}
A practical guide to library procedure. {NASSDOC}
Practical guide to library procedure. {CRRI DUL IIT NERC SPA ZHL}
Practical guide to precis writing and indexing. {DUL}
Practical information for seminar members : Working paper : International seminar on the development of public libraries in Asia, October 6-26, 1966, Delhi. [UNESCO]. {NASSDOC}
Practical printing binding. {INSA}
Practical procedure of cataloguing. {ICHR}
Practical procedure of classification. {IIMC}
Practice for alphabetical arrangement. (IS : 382-1952). [Indian Standards Institution]. {NAI NASSDOC}
Practice for layout of library catalogue code. (IS : 1358-1950). [Indian Standards Institution]. {NAI}
Practice for layout of library catalogue code, rev edn., (IS : 1358-1967). [Indian Standards Institution]. {NASSDOC}
Pralekhan {JNU NASSDOC}.
Prediction of the future : The development programme of the University of Delhi. {JNU}
Preface to library science. {BIS}
Preparation and production of technical books. {DUL}
Preparation of manuscripts and correction of proofs. {DUL}
Present state of information retrieval by computer. {JNU}
Presentation of contributions to periodicals. (ISO/R 215-1961) (E). [International Organisation for Standardisation, Geneva]. {NASSDOC}
Presentation of ideas in technical writing. {ICHR IIC NIH}
Presentation of technical information : Based on four public lectures given at University College, London. {DUL}
Preservation challenge : A guide to conserving library materials. {JNU NMML}
Preservation of books in tropical and subtropical countries. {JNU}
Preservation of documents and papers. [Israel Programme for Scientific Transactions, Jerusalem]. {INSA}
Preservation of library materials, archives and documents. {DUL ICHR NASSDOC NERC NIH NIPCCD NMML ZHL}
Preserving manuscripts and other research material in the Braj area of India, (reprinted from the Bulletin of the British Association of Orientalists). [Vrindaban Research Institute]. {NMML}
Press cuttings : Cooperative library guide. {ICA}
Primary school library and its services. [UNESCO]. {DUL IEG NERC NIPCCD}
Primer of book classification, rev. edn. [Association of Assistant Librarians, London]. {INSA ZHL}
Primer of book collecting. {DUL}
Primer of comparative librarianship. {IIT}
A primer on Ranganathan's book number. {NASSDOC*}
Principles and techniques of educational library displays and exhibits. {IIT NMML}
Principles of automated information retrieval. {JNU}
Principles of bibliographical description. {DUL}
Principles of book classification. {DUL}

Principles of cataloguing. {IEG IIT NAI SPA}
Principles of data-base management. {NASSDOC}
Principles of information retrieval. {CRRI DUL ISI MHA USIS}
Principles of library classification with special reference to Colon and Decimal Classification, Pt. 1 : General theory of classification. {CRRI}
Principles of punched card data processing. {JNU}
Print : A manual for librarians and students describing in detail the history, methods and applications of printing and paper making. {DUL}
Printed books : A short introduction to fine typography. {DUL}
Printed reference material. {NASSDOC ZHL}
Printing presses in India : Its beginning and early development. {DUL}
Probabilistic information theory : Discrete and memoryless models. {INSA}
Problems and failures in library automation : Clinic on library applications of data processing, 1978 Illinois, [University Illinois at Urbana-Champaign]. {USIS}
Problems and prospects of fundamental research in multidisciplinary fields : Computer science. [Organisation for Economic Co-operation and Development, Paris; Committee for Science Policy]. {NASSDOC}
Problems and prospects of the research library. {IEG}
Problems in developing academic library collections. {DUL IIT ISI}
Problems in library classification : Dewey 17 and conversion. {ISI}
Problems in library management. {DUL ICA ICHR ISI JNU NIEPA NIH NIPCCD}
Problems in library public relations. {ISI}
Problems in organising library collections. {JNU NERC}
Problems in planning library facilities, Consultants, architects, plans and critiques : Proceedings : Library building institute, July 12-13, 1963, Chicago. [American Library Association]. {BIS DUL NASSDOC*}
Problems in reference service : Case studies in method and policy. {DUL USIS}
Problems of information user needs. [International Federation for Documentation and Information]. {CRRI DUL}
Problems of misplacement, mutilation and theft of books in libraries. {JNU}
Procedural model for the use of bibliographic records in libraries. [Association of Special Libraries and Information Bureaux]. {DUL NASSDOC}
Proceedings : All India library conference, 2nd, 1935, Lucknow. [Indian Library Association]. {NASSDOC}
Proceedings : All India library conference, 5th, April 4-6, 1942, Bombay. [Indian Library Association]. {NASSDOC}
Proceedings : All India library conference, 7th, January 25-28, 1946, Baroda. [Indian Library Association]. {NASSDOC}
Proceedings : All India library conference, 26th, March 6-9, 1980, New Delhi. [Indian Library Association]. {NASSDOC}
Proceedings : All India library conference, 22nd, 1987. [Indian Library Association]. {NASSDOC}
Proceedings : All India library conference, 23rd, 1988. [Indian Library Association]. {NASSDOC}
Proceedings : All Indian library conference, 24, 1989. [Indian Library Association] {NASSDOC}
Proceedings : All India library convention. [Government of India Librarians Association]. {NMML}
Proceedings : Anniversary conference of Library Association, 15th, 1927, Edinburg. [Library Association, London]. {NASSDOC}

Proceedings : Conference on the on-line revolution in libraries, 1978, Pittsburg. {JNU}

Proceedings : Conference on organisation of data services in India and user education and training programmes, 13th, 1981, Waltair. [Indian Association of Special Libraries and Information Centres]. {BIS MMTC NIPCCD}

Proceedings : International and comparative librarianship group conference, June 28-July 1, 1974, {NASSDOC}

Proceedings : International conference of directors of national libraries of Asia and Oceania, 3rd, November 18-23, Colombo. {NASSDOC}

Proceedings : International conference on the application of mini and micro computers in information documentation and libraries, March 13-18, 1983, Tel Aviv. {IIT}

Proceedings : International conference on technical information services for developing countries, March, 1977, Madras. [International Council of Scientific Unions, Committee of Science and Technology in Developing Countries]. {BCL BIS CRRI IIT JNU}

Proceedings : International seminar of conservation of Traditional records, paper and allied materials. [National Archives of India]. {NAT}

Proceedings : International study conference on classification for information retrieval, 1957, {IEC IIT}

Proceedings : International study conference on classification research, 2nd, September 14-18, 1969, Elsinore. {BIS IIT}

Proceedings : International study conference on classification research : Universal classification, 4th, June 28-July 2, 1982, Ausburg. {BIS}

Proceedings : National seminar on strategies for survival by Nigerian academic and research libraries during austere times, November 9-11, 1987, Ibadan. [Nigerian Association of Agricultural Librarians and Documentalists; Nigerian Librarian Association, Academic and Research Libraries Section]. {NASSDOC*}

Proceedings : National symposium on information display, 7th, Technical session. [Society for Information Display]. {JNU}

Proceedings : Regional seminar on measurement and application of micrographics, 3rd, 1987, Pune. {NASSDOC}

Proceedings : Seminar of university librarians in India, 1967, Jaipur. [Rajasthan University]. {DUL IIT}

Proceedings : Seminar on the Anglo-American Cataloguing Rules, 1967. [Library Association, London]. {ZHL}

Proceedings : Seminar on international cooperative information systems, July 9-13, 1979. [International Development Research Centre]. {CRRI USIS}

Proceedings : Seminar on the purpose and function of library in national education, April 7-10, 1961, Nazimabad. [Society for the Promotion and Improvement of Libraries]. {NASSDOC*}

Proceedings and list of government of Indian libraries of Delhi : All India library convention, 3rd, February 10-12, 1982, New Delhi. [Government of India Librarians Association]. {CRRI NASSDOC}

Proceedings and papers : IASLIC seminar on library science in Calcutta, 1977, Calcutta. [Indian Association of Special Libraries and Information Centres]. {JNU}

Proceedings and papers : International conference on delivery mechanisms for engineering and technological information, November 3-5, 1980, Budapest. {BIS}

Proceedings of the General Council : IFLA annual. [International Federation of Library Association and Institutions]. {NASSDOC}

Processing manual : A pictorial work book of catalogue cards, rev. edn. {DUL}

Processing services of the Dallas Public Library : A report on their organisation, operation and administration. {DUL}

The procurement of library furnishings : Specifications BID documents and evaluation : Proceedings : Library equipment institute, 3rd, 1966, New York. [American Library Association]. {USIS}

Procurement of library materials in the federal government : An orientation prepared for Federal Library Committee. {JNU}

Prodh siksha aur pustakalaya. {NIEPA NIPCCD}

Production and distribution of knowledge in the United States. {NASSDOC}

Professional and non-professional duties in libraries, 2nd edn. [Research and Development Committee, Library Association, London]. {IIT ZHL}

Professional associations and development of librarianship : Case studies. [Library Association, London; American Library Association]. {AIU NASSDOC NCAER}

Profession education and training for library and information work : A review. [Library Association, London]. {NASSDOC}

The professional librarian's reader in library automation and technology. {JNU USIS}

A profile of Andhra book readers. {NASSDOC*}

Prognostics : A science in the making surveys and creates the future. {NASSDOC}

Programmed course in cataloguing and classification. {CRRI IIC IIFT IIT INSA NCAER}

Programming and coding digital computers. {NASSDOC}

Programming in COBOL. {NASSDOC}

Progress in educating the library user. {CRRI IIT}

Progress in library science. {CRRI IEG IIFT NIH NMML}

Progress report in chemical literature retrieval. {CRRI}

Prolegomena to library classification. [Madras Library Association]. {CRRI NMML}

Prolegomena to library classification, 2nd edn. [Madras Library Association]. {IEG IIMC ISI MFL NAI}

Prolegomena to library classification, 3rd edn. assisted by M.H. Gopinath, [Madras Library Association]. {AIU ICA IIC INSA JNU NASSDOC NCAER}

Promoting the reading habit. {JNU}

Promotion of reading habits in Pakistan : A study on methods and measures to promote reading habits in Pakistan. [Pakistan National Book Council]. {ZHL}

Proof corrections for printers and authors. (IS : 1250-1958). [Indian Standards Institution]. {NASSDOC}

Proposal for documentation centre at the Central Family Planning Institute, New Delhi : Report. {NASSDOC}

Prospects for library co-operation in New York city : Planning for more effective utilisation of reference and research resources submitted by Nelson Associations Incorporated, New York. {DUL}

Prospects of library services in India : A study. {JNU}

Protecting the library and its resources : A guide to physical protection and insurance : Report on a study conducted by Gage Babcock and Associates, Incorporated. [American Library Association]. {DUL IIT NASSDOC IIT}

Provision and use of library and documentation services : Some contributions. [University of Sheffield Postgraduate School of Librarianship]. {DUL JNU MHA NIH SPA USIS}

Psychology of computer programming. {NASSDOC}

Public knowledge and private ignorance : Towards a library and information policy. {CRRI USIS}

The public librarian as adult learners' advisor : An innovation in human services. {USIS}

Public librarianship : A reader. {USIS}

Public libraries, mimeo short bibliography. {NASSDOC}

Public libraries : Collection of papers on public libraries written at different times. {NASSDOC*}

Public libraries and cultural activities. [Department of Education and Science, Great Britain]. {NIPCCD}

Public libraries and their mission. [UNESCO]. {ICA}

Public libraries and their use. [Department of Education and Science, Great Britain]. {NIPCCD}

Public libraries for Asia : The Delhi seminar. [UNESCO]. {NASSDOC NIEPA ZHL}

Public libraries for every one. {NASSDOC}

Public libraries in Australia : Present conditions and future possibilities. {JNU}

Public libraries in Bihar. [Bihar Library Service Association, Patna].

Public libraries in Denmark, tr. by Megens Hay Larsen from Danish. {NASSDOC}

Public libraries in developing society and planning for national information system : Seminar papers : All India library conference, 28th, October 20-23, 1982, Lucknow. [Indian Library Association]. {ICA NASSDOC NIPCCD ZHL}

Public libraries in India. {JNU}

Pubic libraries in Karnataka : Their scope and development. {AIU}

Public libraries in the urban metropolitan setting. {DUL IIT}

Public libraries system. {NASSDOC*}

Public libraries today. {DUL IIT NASSDOC}

The public library : Circumstances and prospects : Papers presented at the 39th Annual Conference. {IIT USIS}

Public library : Operations and services : A short manual, rev edn. {NASSDOC}

Public library administration. {IIT NIEPA}

Public library administration : An examination guide book. {MFL NERC SPA ZHL}

Public library and the city. {JNU SPA}

Public library and federal policy. {NIPCCD}

Public library as culture and social centres : The origin of the concept. {USIS}

Public library building. {IIT}

Public library buildings : Their financing, design, construction, equipment and operation. {DUL}

The public library comes of age. {CRRI}

Public library development perspectives. [Indian Library Association]. {NASSDOC*}

Public library extension. [UNESCO]. {NASSDOC ZHL}

Public library finance. {CRRI}

Public library finance : A literature review. {JNU}

Public library in American life. {NAI USIS}

The public library in non-traditional education. {NASSDOC USIS}

Public library in perspective : An examination of its origins and modern role. {IIT}

Public library in the United States. {IEG}

Public library in the urban setting : The thirty second conference of the Graduate Library School, July 31-August 2, 1967, 1968. {NMML}

Public library information and referral service. {USIS}

Public library law : An international survey. {ICA NASSDOC NMML}

Public library legislation : A comparative study. [UNESCO]. {JNU NASSDOC NIEPA}

Public library operations and services : A short manual. {CRRI IIT MHA NERC SPA ZHL}

Public library service. [American Library Association]. {USIS}

Public library service : Its post-war reorganisation and development. [Library Association, London]. {NAI}

Public library service : Reorganisation and after. [Department of Education and Science, Great Britain]. {NIPCCD}

Public library services : Bahamas. [UNESCO]. {NASSDOC*}

Public library services for children, [UNESCO]. {IEG JNU NASSDOC NERC NIPCCD}

Public library system : India, Sri Lanka, UK, USA. {BIS IEG IIC JNU NAI NMML ZHL}

Public library system in Andhra Pradesh. [Andhra University]. {NASSDOC}

Public library system in India. {ZHL}

Public library systems in the United States : A survey of multi-jurisdictional systems. [American Library Association]. {USIS}

Public relations for librarians. {ICA MMTC ZHL}

Public relations for public libraries : Creative problem solving. {USIS}

Publications of the United Nations systems. {NASSDOC}

Publicity primer : An ABC of telling all about the public library, 4th edn. {USIS}

Published library catalogues : An introduction to their contents and use. {IIT}

Publishing in the USSR. {DUL}

Punch-card methods in research and documentation with special reference to biology. {CRRI DUL IIMC NASSDOC}

Punched cards : Their application to science and industry. {JNU}

Punjab library primer. [University of Punjab, Lahore]. {ZHL}

Purchase of books by public libraries. [Department of Education and Science, Great Britain]. {NIPCCD}

Purchasing an encyclopaedia : 12 point to consider. [American Library Association]. {USIS}

Pustak chayan evam rachna : Book selection and physical bibliography. {BIS NMML}

Pustak sankhya praveshika : Introduction to book numbers in Hindi. {NASSDOC}

Pustakalaya andolan, Bihar. {NMML}

Pustakalaya aur hum {RTL}

Pustakalaya aur sandarbh seva. {BIS DUL}

Pustakalaya Karyapadhati. {JNU}

Pustakalaya paddhati. {DUL}

Pustakalaya parichay. {BIS}

Pustakalaya parichay, 2nd edn. {BIS NMML}

Pustakalaya-Prakriya, Patna. {NMML}

Pustakalaya prashasan : Sidhant evam vyavahar. {BIS}

Pustakalaya sanghatan evam prashasan. {DUL}

Pustakalaya sangathan evam sanchalan. {DUL IIMC}
Pustakalaya siddhant and vyavahar : College pustakalaya ke sandarbh men. {NMML}
Pustakalaya soochikaran : Ek adhyayan. [Madhya Pradesh Hindhi Granth Academy]. {NMML}
Pustakalaya vargikarna : Siddhant aur prayog. {BIS MFL}
Pustakalaya vargikaran ke mool tatva, 3rd edn. {DUL}
Pustakalaya vigyan ke panch sutra. [Rajasthan Hindi Granth Academy, Jaipur]. {BIS}
Putting knowledge to work : American view of Ranganathan's Five Laws of Library Science. {AIU IIMC JNU NIEPA USIS}

Quality in libraries. [Indian Library Association]. {NASSDOC*}
Quantification : A history of the meaning of measurement in the natural and social sciences. {NASSDOC}
Quantitative measurement and dynamic library service. {BIS IIT}
Quantitative methods for library and information science. {BIS ISI JNU NASSDOC}
Quantitative methods in librarianship : Standards, research and management. {IIT ISI JNU}

Rajasthan ke granthagar. {NASSDOC*}
Rampur Raza Library Bill. [Lok Sabha, New Delhi]. {JNU}
Ranganathan : Method and style : A pastiche of opinions. {JNU}
Ranganathan : A pattern maker : A synthetic study of his contributions. {CRRI ISI JNU NIEPA NIPCCD ZHL}
Ranganathan's philosophy : Assessment, impact and relevance. {JNU NMML}
Rare book collections : Some theoretical and practical suggestions for use by librarians and students. [American Library Association]. {NAI}
Rare book librarianship. {NASSDOC}
Rare book librarianship : A select annotated bibliography. {JNU}
Rare books section in the library. [UNESCO]. {IIMC IIT NASSDOC}
Rashtriya granth-suchi, 1961-63. {NASSDOC}
Reaching readers : The library's responsibility and opportunity : Papers with a summary of discussions and recommendations. Regional conference workshop for librarians, 6th, December 6-13, 1964, Albay. {NASSDOC}
Read faster and understand better, 2 pts. [Central Institute of Indian Languages, Mysore]. {MHA}
Read well and remember. {IIT}
Reader in the academic library. {USIS}
Reader in government documents. {NASSDOC}
Reader in library administration. {DUL USIS}
Reader in library management. {JNU}
Reader in library systems analysis. {USIS}
Reader in research methods for librarianship. {USIS}
Reader instruction in colleges and universities : An introduction handbook. {AIU JNU NIEPA}
Reader instruction methods in academic libraries. {JNU}
Reader's guide to Madras University Library : Platinum jubilee celebration, 1907-1982. [Madras University Library]. {NMML}

Reading habits among college students : The role of library. {NASSDOC}

Reading habits in Pakistan : A report. {ZHL}

Reading in information retrieval. {JNU}

Reading material : Orientation seminar on planning and management for senior administrators of public library services, February 6-10, 1984, New Delhi. {NASSDOC NIEPA}

Reading research and librarianship : A history and analysis. {CRRI IIT JNU}

Reading research in the Centre for Library Science Methodology, 1981-85 and M. [Centre for Library Science and Methodology, Budapest]. {NASSDOC}

Readings in library cataloguing. {NASSDOC NMML SPA ZHL}

Readings in nonbook librarianship. {NMML USIS}

Readings in special librarianship. {USIS}

Recent advances in school librarianship. {NIEPA}

Recommendations for the abbreviation of titles of periodicals (BS. 4148-1967). [British Standards Institution]. {CRRI}

Recommendations for bibliographical catalogue reference. [Indian Standards Institution]. {NAI}

Recommendations for bibliographical references, (IS : 2380-1963). [Indian Standards Institution]. {NASSDOC}

Recommendations for bibliographical references. Essential and supplementary elements, rev. edn., (IS : 2381-1978). [Indian Standards Institution]. {NASSDOC}

Recommendations for the preparation of indexes for books, periodicals and other publications, (BS 3700 : 1964). [British Standards Institution]. {CRRI NASSDOC}

Recommendations for the processing and storage of silver gelatin-type microfilm. (BS : 1153 : 1975). [British Standards Institution]. {CRRI}

Recommendations for the storage of microfilm. (BS : 1153 : 1955). [British Standards Institution]. {CRRI NASSDOC NMML}

Recommendations relating to primary elements in the design of library buildings. [Indian Standards Institution]. {NASSDOC}

Reducing the cost of surveys. {NASSDOC}

Reference : A programmed instruction. [Ohio Library Association]. {USIS}

Reference as the promotion of free enquiry. {JNU}

Reference books for regional reference collection. {NAI}

Reference books in academic libraries : A brief survey. {DUL JNU}

Reference books in the social sciences and humanities. {DUL}

Reference catalogue of Indian books in print, 3 vols. {NASSDOC}

Reference function of the library. {DUL NAL}

Reference guide of India : Who's who incorporating men of library science in India, men of science and technology in India, and men of education in India. {JNU NASSDOC}

Reference librarian in university, municipal and specialised libraries. {BIS CRRI DUL}

Reference library methods. {NAI}

Reference library stack : An informal guide. {CRRI}

Reference library stacks : An enquiry into reference book provision in the rate-supported libraries of England and Wales. {JNU}

Reference manual for machine-readable bibliographic descriptions, 2nd rev edn. [UNESCO]. {NASSDOC}

Reference readiness : A manual for librarians and students. {DUL NASSDOC}

Reference research and the regionalism : Selected papers from 53rd conference of Texas Library Association. {JNU}

Reference resources : A systematic approach. {DUL NASSDOC}

Reference service. {DUL ICA}

Reference service. {JNU NMML}

Reference service, 2nd edn. {BIS CRRI DSSW DUL JNU MHA NASSDOC NIH NMML SPA ZHL}

Reference service : An annotated bibliographic guide supplement, 1976-1982. {JNU}

Reference service and bibliography, Vol. 1, Pts. 1-4. {DSSW DUL}

Reference service and library education : Essays in honour of Neel Chaney. {JNU}

Reference service and sources of information. {NMML}

Reference service in academic libraries in India. {JNU NASSDOC NMML}

Reference service-in-action : Processing and servicing of special material in libraries. [Indian Association of Special Libraries and Information Centres, Calcutta]. {IEG NAI}

Reference services. {DUL USIS}

Reference services and library instruction : A handbook for library management. {NASSDOC}

Reference services and public policy. {NASSDOC}

Reference work. [American Library Association]. {ZHL}

Reference work and its tools. {CRRI ICA NMML SPA}

Reference work and its tools, 2nd edn. {DUL JNU NASSDOC NERC NIEPA NMML}

Reference work and its tools, 3rd ed. {CRRI ICA IIT NIH NIPCCD}

Reference work in the university library. {JNU}

Referral centres and services : A review. [Association of Special Libraries and Information Bureaux]. {CRRI}

Reform and reaction : The big city public library in American life. {USIS}

A register of communications research in Canada, 1974-1975 : Status report. [Canadian Communication Research Information Centre, Ottawa]. {NASSDOC}

Relegation and stock control in libraries. {DUL IIT ZHL}

Reluctant reader. {DUL}

Repair and preservation of records. [National Archives of India]. {NASSDOC}

Repairing of books, 2nd edn. {NAI}

Report : ASLIB meeting on planning and equipment of special libraries, April 6, 1946, London. [Association of Special Libraries and Information Bureaux]. {CRRI}

Report : Advisory committee for libraries. [Ministry of Education, New Delhi]. {NASSDOC}

Report : Asia Pacific information network in social science : Regional advisory group (APINESS/RAG) meeting. [UNESCO Principal Regional Office for Asia and the Pacific, Bangkok]. {NASSDOC}

Report : Asia Pacific POPIN experts working group on population information networking. [U.N. Economic and Social Commission for Asia and the Pacific, Bangkok]. {NASSDOC}

Report : Asian regional seminar on information sources, systems and services in the social sciences, July 11-22, 1983, Philippines [UNESCO Regional Office, Bangkok]. {NASSDOC*}

Report : Australia committee on inquiry on public libraries. {JNU}

Report : Committee appointed by the Government of Andhra Pradesh to review the working of the Andhra Pradesh to review the working of the Andhra Pradesh Public Library Act, 1960, and to suggest amendments to the act. [Government of Andhra Pradesh, Hyderabad]. {NASSDOC*}

Report : Committee appointed for developing the Tagore Memorial Library, Vijayawada. [Zilla Granthalaya Samstha, Machilipatnam]. {NASSDOC*}

Report : Committee on private libraries. [Government of Andhra Pradesh, Hyderabad]. {NASSDOC*}

Report : Committee on the re-organisation of libraries, research centres and museums for the government of Jammu Kashmir. [Punjab Agricultural University, Ludhiana]. {NASSDOC*}

Report : Expert working group on development of population information centres and networks, June 20-23, 1984. [U.N. Economic and Social Commission for Asia and the Pacific]. {NASSDOC}

Report : International conference on cataloguing principles, October 9-14, 1961, Paris. [International Federation of Library Associations and Institutions]. {IIT ISI NIEPA NMML}

Report : National Archives committee on archival legislation. [National Archives of India, New Delhi]. {MFL}

Report : National Library committee to enquire into the strained relations among the members of staff, 1969. [National Library, Calcutta]. {JNU}

Report : National Library reviewing committee, 1968. [National Library, Calcutta]. {JNU}

Report : Orientation course for the libraries of cooperative training colleges and apex level organisations/institutions in India, June 1977, New Delhi. [National Council for Cooperation Training]. {ICA}

Report : Planning conference on information transfer experiments, September 3, 1965, Massachusetts. {USIS}

Report : Regional seminar on curriculum development in information studies, September 17-21, 1985, Bangkok. [UNESCO].

Report : Seminar on documentation and information systems for vocational training, November 5-16, 1985, Pattaya, Thailand. [International Labour Office; Asian and Pacific Skill Development Programme, Islamabad]. {NASSDOC}

Report : Seminar on library education, December 1-4, 1965, Bombay. [Shreemati Nathibai Damodar Thachery Women's University, Bombay]. {AIU NASSDOC}

Report : Seminar on public library system, 1972, Bangalore. {JNU}

Report : Sub-regional workshop for cooperation librarians and documentation officers for S.E. Area, April, 14-29, 1981, Los Banos. [ICA Regional Office and Education Centre for South-East Asia, New Delhi]. {ICA NASSDOC}

Report : University Grants Commission committee on scales of pay and qualification, etc., for library staff in universities and colleges. [University Grants Commission, New Delhi]. {NIEPA}

Report : University Grants Commission library committee. [University Grants Commission, New Delhi]. {SPA}

Report : Western regional conference on library architecture, October 8-10, 1980, Bombay. [Indian Association of Special Libraries and Information Centres]. {JNU NASSDOC}

Report : Working meeting on Asian resources for a population library network, September 13-15, 1973, Bangkok. [UN Economic Commission for Asia and the Far East]. {NIH}

Report : Working group on libraries, 1964, New Delhi. [Planning Commission, New Delhi]. {AIU CRRI JNU MFL MHA NASSDOC NCAER NERC NIEPA NIPCCD NMML}

Report : Workshop on road research and information for South East Asia, 1980, Melbourne. {CRRI}

Report, 1981. [ICA Regional Office and Education Centre for South-East Asia, New Delhi]. {ICA NASSDOC}

Report, 1984-85. [British Library Department of Oriental Manuscripts and Printed Books]. {NMML}

Report of expert consultative services rendered to Cooperative Training Centre in Nepal for organising their library and documentation services. [International Cooperation Alliance Regional Office and Education Centre for South-East Asia, New Delhi]. {ICA}

Report on feasibility of establishing a regional network of social science information and documentation centres in Asia and Pacific. [Institute of Library Science]. {NASSDOC}

Report on feasibility study for a computer based circulation control system. [NASSDOC]. {NASSDOC}

Report on library networks. {DUL}

Report on the library of the Indian Institute of Technology, New Delhi. [Indian Institute of Technology]. {IIT}

Report on the municipal library system. {JNU}

Report on a programme of library education in Israel. (Technical assistance : Special report, No. 1). [UNESCO]. {IEG NASSDOC}

A report on the supply and training of librarians. [Department of Education and Science, Great Britain]. {NIEPA}

Report on a survey made of book charging systems at present in use in England. {JNU}

Report on the testing and analysis of an investigation into the comparative efficiency of indexing systems. {BIS IIT}

Representation and meaning : Experiments with information processing systems. {NASSDOC}

Reproductions reference guide. 2nd edn. {NASSDOC}

Reprographic management handbook. {ISI}

Reprographic services in libraries : Organisation and administration. [American Library Association]. {BIS NMML}

Reprography for librarians. {AIU JNU}

Requiem for the card catalogue : Management issues in automated cataloguing. [Associated College of the Midwest]. {IIT NIPCCD USIS}

Research : An introduction. {NASSDOC}

Research centres directory, 4th edn. {NASSDOC}

Research facilities in Bangalore, Mysore, Ahmedabad. {NMML}

Research facilities in Bombay, Calcutta and Madras. {NIPCCD NMML USIS}

Research facilities in Delhi. {DSSW ICA NIEPA NIPCCD NMML USIS}

Research facilities in Hyderabad. {NIPCCD NMML}

Research facilities in Uttar Pradesh. {NMML}

Research for decision making : Methods for librarians. {DUL}

Research in archives : The use of unpublished primary sources. {NASSDOC USIS ZHL}

Research in library in information science in India : A bibliography of Ph.D, M.Phil. and MLIS dissertation. {NASSDOC NMML}

Research in progress, 4 vols. [Inter University Board of India and Ceylon]. {NASSDOC}

Research information retrieval. {JNU}

Research librarianship : Essays in honour of Robert B. Downs. {JNU NASSDOC USIS}

Research libraries and collections in the United Kingdom : A selective inventory and guide. {DUL ZHL}

Research libraries and technology : A report. [Sloan Foundation]. {USIS}

Research libraries in developing countries. {AIU DUL IEG IIT JNU NASSDOC NIEPA NIPCCD NMML}

Research manual for college studies and papers, rev. edn. {ZHL}

Research methods in information systems : Proceedings of the IFIP WG 8.2 colloquium, manchester Business School, September 1-3, 1984. {NASSDOC}

Research methods in librarianship : Historical and bibliographical methods in library research. {NASSDOC}

Research methods in librarianship : Techniques and interpretation. {ISI}

Research methods in library and information studies. [Library Association, London].{DUL}

Research methods in library science : A bibliographic guide with tropical outlines. {NASSDOC}

Research services directory. {USIS}

Resource sharing in libraries : Why, how when : Next action steps. {IIT INSA NASSDOC}

Resource sharing of libraries in developing countries : Proceedings : IFLA/UNESCO pre-session seminar for librarians from developing countries, August 30-September 3, 1977, [Antwerp University]. {NASSDOC}

Resources of Canadian academic and research libraries. {AIU}

Resources of Canadian university libraries for research in the humanities and social sciences : Report of a survey. [National Conference of Canadian Universities and Colleges, Ottawa]. {DUL NASSDOC}

Responsibilities of libraries and information service. [Organisation for European Economic Co-operation]. {BIS}

Retrieval of information in the humanities and the social sciences. {NIEPA}

Review of national scientific and technical information policy : Germany. [Organisation for Economic Co-operation and Development, Paris]. {CRRI ICA JNU}

Reviews in library book selection. {DUL}

Revolting librarians. {USIS}

Rider's international classification for the arrangement of books on the shelves of the general libraries, Preliminary edn. {DUL}

The right to read and the nation's libraries. [American Association of School Libraries, Children's Services Division; Public Library Association; American Library Association]. {USIS}

Rise and growth of public library movement in India. [Iyyanki Library Awards Committee, Eluru]. {NASSDOC*}

Role of classification in the modern American library : Papers presented at an institute conducted by the University of Illinois Graduate School of Library Science, 1959. {DUL}

Role of libraries in national development. {JNU}

Role of libraries in socio-economic development : Papers : All India library convention, 1st, February 13, 1978, Delhi. [Government of India Librarians Association]. {NASSDOC}

Role of the library in the development of the community : Society for the promotion and improvement of libraries seminar, April 12-18, 1964, Karachi. [Hamdard National Foundation, Karachi]. {NASSDOC}

The role of the library in an electronic society : Proceedings : Library applications of data processing clinic, 1979 Illinois. [University of Illinois at Urbana-Champaign]. {USIS}

Role of the library in national reconstruction : Society for the promotion and improvement of libraries seminar, October 30—November 3, 1967, Rawalpindi. [Hamdard National Foundation, Karachi]. {NASSDOC}

Role of national libraries in developing countries with special reference to Saudi Arabia. {NMML}

Role of school libraries in education. {JNU}

Roles and responsibilities of librarians and library technicians : Report. [Canada Library Association, Ottawa].

Root thesaurus. 2 pts., Pt.-1 : Subject display; Pt.-2 : Alphabetical list. [British Standards Institution]. {NASSDOC}

Rules for the catalog of printed book : Vatican Library. [American Library Association]. {NAI}

Rules for compiling the catalogues of printed books, maps and music in the British Museum. [British Museum, London]. {NAI}

Rules for compiling the catalogues of printed books, maps, etc., in the Imperial Library, Calcutta. [National Library, Calcutta]. {NAI}

Rules for descriptive cataloguing in the Library of Congress. [Library of Congress]. {BIS NAI SPA}

Rules for descriptive cataloguing in the Library of Congress : Supplement 1949-1951. [U.S. Library of Congress]. {ISI}

Rules for descriptive cataloguing in the Library of Congress : Phonorecords. [U.S. Library of Congress]. {IEG 7HL}

Rules for a dictionary catalog. {IIT}

Rules for dictionary catalog, 4th edn. [Library Association, London]. {BIS CRRI JNU MFL NAI NIEPA NMML}

Rules for indexing records. [Imperial Record Department]. {INL}

Rules for making alphabetical indexes. [Indian Standards Institution]. {AIU NASSDOC}

Rules for making alphabetical indexes, rev. edn., (IS : 1275-1976). [Indian Standards Institution]. {NASSDOC}

Rules for press listing. [Imperial Record Department]. {NAI}

Rural library services in India. {NASSDOC*}

The SMART retrieval system : Experiments in automatic document processing. {MHA NASSDOC}

S.R. Ranganathan, 1892-1972 : Papers : Memorial meeting, January 25, 1973. {JNU}

Safeguarding our cultural heritage : A bibliography on the protection of museums, works of art, monuments, archives and libraries in time of war. {JNU}

Sample catalog cards. {IIT}

Sample catalog cards, 2nd edn. [School of Library Science, Columbia University]. {ZHL}

Scheme for classification of information on nutrition coded for machine retrieval. {DUL}

Scheme for the organisation of co-operative libraries. [Plunkett Foundation for Co-operative Studies]. {ICA}

School and children's libraries in Australia. {JNU}

School and college libraries. {JNU}

School librarians' encyclopedic dictionary. {NIEPA}

School libraries : A series of talks delivered. [Ministry of Education, New Delhi]. {NMML}

School libraries : A short manual, {JNU}

School libraries : Theory and practice. {JNU}

School libraries in Puerto Rico : A survey and plan for development. {NASSDOC}

School libraries in West Africa. {JNU NIEPA}

School library. [Department of Education and Science, Great Britain]. {JNU}

School library. {AIU DUL}

The school library : A force for educational excellence. {JNU USIS}

School library : Some practical hints. {ISI MFL}

School library at work : Acquisition, organisation and maintenance of materials in the school library. {JNU}

School library development. [Indian Library Association]. {NASSDOC*}

School library management. {NERC}

School library resource centre. {JNU}

School library service in the United States. {ZHL}

School loan services. {JNU}

School media programmes : Case studies in management, 2nd edn. {NIEPA}

Science and technology policies information exchange systems (SPINES) feasibility study. {JNU}

Science, humanism and libraries. {IIT JNU}

Science information services in India. [Indian National Scientific Documentation Centre, New Delhi]. {NASSDOC*}

Science reference sources, 4th edn. {DUL}

Scientific and technical documentation centres. [UNESCO]. {AIU}

Scientific and technical information : Its impact on the development of science and technology. [UNESCO; UNIDO, Moscow]. {NASSDOC*}

Scientific and technical information in Canada. [Science Council of Canada]. {JNU}

Scientific and technical information resources. {DUL}

Scientific and technical information sources, 1977. {IIT INSA JNU NERC}

Scientific and technical libraries, 2 vols. {JNU}

Scientific and technical libraries : Their organisation and administration. {BIS CRRI IIT INSA}

Scientific and technical libraries : Their organisation and administration, 2nd edn. {BIS ISI INSA JNU}

Scientific and technological information for development. [United Nations Information Systems]. {JNU}

Scientific books, libraries and collectors : A study of bibliography and the book trade in relation to science, 2nd edn. {DUL}

Scientific information. {BCL INSA}

Scientific information and society. {NASSDOC}
Scientific management of library operations. {DUL USIS}
Scientific method : Optimising applied research decision. {NASSDOC}
Scientific periodicals : Their historical development, characteristics and control. {DUL}
Scientific thinking and scientific writing. {DUL}
Scientist approaches to information. [American Library Association]. {BIS}
Scolma directory of libraries and special collections of Africa, 2nd edn. {IIC IIT}
Scope for automatic data processing in the British library, 2 pts. [Department of Education and Science, Great Britain]. {NASSDOC}
Searcher's manual. {IIT USIS}
Secondary school libraries in Uttar Pradesh. [Department of Education, Allahabad University]. {IEG}
Security for computer systems. {NIPCCD}
Selected material in classification : A bibliography. {JNU}
Selecting materials for libraries. {USIS}
Selective Hindi Dewey Decimal Classification and Relative Index tr. by Prabhu Narayan Gour. {DUL}
Selective inventory of social science information and documentation services, 3rd edn. [UNESCO Social and Human Sciences Documentation Centre]. {NASSDOC}
Selective list of activities in the field of information : UNESCO-Intergovernmental conference on scientific and technical information for development, 1979, Paris. {JNU}
Semantics in the organisation of knowledge : A programmed text for students in information retrieval. {NASSDOC}
Seminar and exhibition on information for industry, 1975, Bangalore. {CRRI}
Seminar of college librarians in Rajasthan, Jaipur, 1966. {JNU NMML}
Seminar on library and information services for management. [Liverpool College of Commerce]. {NMML}
A seminar on public library system. [Sarada Ranganathan Endowment for Library Science, Bangalore]. {NASSDOC*}
Serial cataloguing handbook : An illustrative guide to the use of AACR2 and LC rule interpretations. [American Library Association]. {DUL}
Serial publications : Their place and treatment in libraries. {MFL}
Serial publications : Their place and treatment in libraries, 2nd edn. [American Library Association]. {NASSDOC}
Serial publications : Their place and treatment in libraries, 3rd edn. [American Library Association]. {USIS}
Serial publications in the British Parliamentary papers, 1900-1968 : A bibliography. [American Library Association]. {NASSDOC}
Serials automation for acquisition and inventory control. [American Library Association]. {USIS}
Serials librarianship in transition : Issues and development. {NASSDOC}
Serials management and microforms. {IIT}
Serving the older adult : A guide to library programs and information sources. {USIS}
Seven questions about the profession of librarianship : Proceedings of the 26th Annual Conference of the Graduate Library School. {IEG}
Sharing of information : South Asian initiatives. {NASSDOC*}

Shelf access in libraries. [American Library Association]. {DUL NASSDOC}

Shelf work in library. [American Library Association]. {DUL IIT}

Short contents list of periodicals or other documents, (ISO/R 18-1955) (E). [International Organisation for Standardisation, Geneva]. {NASSDOC}

Short list of subject headings. {CRRI}

Shree Iyyanki Venkata Ramanayya commemoration volume : Presented to him on Shashtipurti celebration (60th birthday). {NASSDOC}

Sign systems for libraries : Solving the way finding problems. {BIS IIT USIS}

Simple library cataloguing, 3rd edn. [American Library Association]. {BIS}

Simple library cataloguing, 4th edn. [American Library Association]. {CRRI DSSW MHA SPA ZHL}

Simple library cataloguing, 5th edn. {JNU NASSDOC NMML USIS ZHL}

Simple library cataloguing, 6th rev and rewritten edn., ed. by Arthur Curlly and Jana Varlejs. {MHA NIEPA}

Simplifying work in small public libraries. {Drexel Institute of Technology]. {NASSDOC}

Simulation activities in library, communication and information science, ed. by Patrick R. Penland. {NASSDOC}

Simulation and national development. {NASSDOC}

Simulation modelling : A guide to using SIMSCRIPT. {NASSDOC}

Sizes of correspondence envelopes. (IS : 3338-1965). [Indian Standards Institution]. {NASSDOC}

Skyline of information processing : Proceedings of the 10th anniversary of IFIP, Amsterdom. {JNU}

A small country in the world of standards : ANSINBS symposium on international standards information and ISONET. {BIS}

The small public library building, 2nd edn. [UNESCO]. {CRRI IEG IIMC IIT BIS NASSDOC NERC ZHL}

Small scale bibliographic database. {JNU}

Small technical libraries. [UNESCO]. {DUL ICA NERC NIEPA}

Social bibliography or physical bibliography for libraries. {BIS CRRI DSSW}

Social issues and library problems : Case studies in the social science. {NMML}

Social science information : Problems and prospects. {NASSDOC}

Social science information and documentation : Search and relevance in India. {BIS DUL JNU NASSDOC NIH NIEPA NMML ZHL}

Social science research and libraries : Papers and summary proceedings of the library seminar on research in the social science, January 2-4, 1959. {NMML}

Social science research and library development : Summary proceedings. [Indian Council of World Affairs; Indian School of International Studies]. {NASSDOC*}

The social sciences : Information system. [USSR Academy of Sciences, Moscow]. {NASSDOC*}

The social use of information ownership and access. {BCL NASSDOC USIS}

Sociological foundations of librarianship. {IEG NASSDOC NIEPA NMML ZHL}

Some characteristics of an efficient information retrieval system. {JNU}

Some fundamentals of information retrieval. {BIS CRRI DUL JNU TDA}

Some Oxford libraries. {JNU}

Some practical problems in cataloguing. {DUL}

Some problems in information science. {JNU}

Some statistical indicators of UK abstracting and indexing services. {BCL}

Soochikaran ke siddhant, tr. by Prem Kumar Jayaswal. {BIS DUL NMML}

Sources of information librarianship and information science : A grafton book. {NIH}

South Asian library resources in North America : A survey prepared for the Boston conference, 1974. {NASSDOC}

South Pacific region pilot project on school library development : Training programmes for teachers. {JNU}

Souvenir : AP libraries conference, 1st, 1979, Hyderabad. {NASSDOC*}

Souvenir : AP libraries conference, 2nd, 1980, Narasaropet. {NASSDOC*}

Souvenir : AP libraries conference, 3rd, 1982, Tirupati. {NASSDOC*}

Souvenir : All India library conference, 14th, Indore. [Indian Library Association]. {NASSDOC}

Souvenir : All India library conference, 15th, 1963, Mysore. [Indian Library Association]. {NASSDOC}

Souvenir : All India library conference, 16th, 1966, Chandigarh. [Indian Library Association]. {NASSDOC}

Souvenir : All India library conference, 20th, 1973, Hyderabad. [Indian Library Association]. {NASSDOC}

Souvenir : All India library conference, 21th, 1975, Bhubneswar. [Indian Library Association]. {NASSDOC}

Souvenir : All India library conference, 22nd, 1976, New Delhi. [Indian Library Association]. {NASSDOC}

Souvenir : All India library conference, 24th, 1978, Bangalore. [Department of Public Libraries, Bangalore; Indian Library Association]. {NASSDOC}

Souvenir : All India library conference, 25th, May 14-18, 1979, Trivandrum. [Indian Library Association]. {ICA}

Souvenir : All india library conference, 26th, March 6-9, 1980, New Delhi, [Indian Library Association]. {ICA}

Souvenir : All India library conference, 27th, January 9-12, 1981, Hyderabad. [Academy of Library Science and Documentation, Hyderabad]. {ICA NASSDOC}

Souvenir : All India library conference, 31th, 1985, Baroda. [Indian Library Association]. {NASSDOC}

Souvenir : All India library conference, 32nd, Anantpur. [Indian Library Association]. {NASSDOC}

Souvenir : All India library conference, 33rd, 1987, Tiruchirapalli. [Indian Library Association]. {NASSDOC}

Souvenir : All India library conference, 1988, Calcutta. [Indian Library Association]. {NASSDOC}

Souvenir : All India library conference, 1989, Pune. [Indian Library Association]. {NASSDOC}

Souvenir : Golden jubilee celebration. [Department of Library and Information Science, Andhra University]. {NASSDOC}

Souvenir : IASLIC all India conference, 13th, 1981, Waltaire. [Indian Association of Special Libraries and Information Centres]. {NASSDOC}

Souvenir : IASLIC conference, 7th, December 27-30, 1967, Delhi. [University of Delhi]. {NASSDOC}

Souvenir : IASLIC national seminar, 9th, 1980, Nagpur [IASLIC]. {NASSDOC}

Souvenir : IASLIC national seminar, 11th, 1984, Hydrabad [IASLIC]. {NASSDOC*}

Souvenir : Library education centenary celebration. [Nagpur University]. {NASSDOC*}

Souvenir : Platinum Jubilee. [Central Library, Baroda]. {NASSDOC*}
Souvenir : Shri Sanmati Pustakalaya Trust, Jaipur. {NASSDOC*}
Souvenir : Silver Jubilee. [British Council Library, Madras]. {NASSDOC*}
Souvenir : Silver Jubilee. [City Granthalaya Samstha, Hyderabad]. {NASSDOC*}
Souvenir : Silver Jubilee. [Delhi Public Library, Delhi]. {NASSDOC*}
Souvenir : Silver Jubilee. [State Regional Library, Guntur]. {NASSDOC*}
Soviet libraries and librarianship : Report of the visit of the delegation of U.S. librarians to the Soviet Union, May-June, 1961 under the U.S.-Soviet cultural exchange agreement. [American Library Association]. {NASSDOC NMML}
Special cataloguing with particular reference to music, films, maps, serials and the multi-media computerised catalogue. {CRRI ICHR IIC IIT JNU NASSDOC NMML ZHL}
Special collection in the Library of Congress : A selective guide. [U.S. Library of Congress]. {USIS}
Special librarianship. {JNU}
Special librarianship [Andhra Pradesh Open University, Hyderabad]. {NASSDOC*}
Special libraries. {INSA JNU NERC NMML}
Special libraries : Development of the concept, their organization and their service. JNU}
Special libraries : Guide for management. [Special Libraries Association, New York]. {IIC IIT}
Special libraries : Guide for management, 2nd edn. {MMTC}
Special libraries : How to plan and equip them. [Special Libraries Association, New York]. {BIS NMML}
Special libraries and documentation centres in the Netherlands {IIT JNU NASSDOC SPA}
Special libraries and information bureau : An examination guidebook. {BIS ICA IIC IIFT IIT MFL NMML SPA}
Special libraries and information services in India and in the U.S.A. {IEG IIT NASSDOC}
Special libraries in Canada : A directory. {JNU}
Special libraries of Greater New York, 10th edn. [Special Libraries Association, New York]. {DUL}
Special library and information services in the United Kingdom, 2nd edn. [Library Association, London]. {NIEPA}
Special library methods : An introduction to special librarianship. {IEG NAI}
Special library resources, vol. 4. [Special Libraries Association, New York]. {CRRI}
Special materials in the library. [Library Association, London]. {IIT}
Special problems in classification and cataloguing. {DUL}
Specialised information centres. {BCL CRRI ICA USIS}
Specialised information centres. {JNU}
Specification for the abbreviation of titles of periodicals, 2 pts., Pt. 1 : Principles; Pt. 2 : World abbreviation. [British Standards Institution]. {CRRI NASSDOC}
Specification for alphabetical arrangement and the filing order of numerals and symbols. (BS 1749 : 1969). [British Standards Institution]. {CRRI NASSDOC}
Specification for bibliographic information interchange format for magnet tape. (BS 4748 : 1971). [British Standards Institution]. {CRRI}

Specification for book binding leather. (IS : 2960-1964). [Indian Standards Institution]. {CRRI}

Specification for book numbering. (BS 4762 : 1971). [British Standards Institution]. {NASSDOC}

Specification for data elements for the generation and exchange of serials records. (BS 3532 : 1982). [British Standards Institution]. {CRRI}

Specification for drawing filling equipment, rev. edn. (IS : 2695-1974). [Indian Standards Institution]. {NASSDOC}

Specification for general structure of preliminary pages of a book (tentative). (IS : 790-1956). [Indian Standards Institution]. {NASSDOC}

Specification for librachine (mobile library). (IS : 2661-1964). [Indian Standards Institution]. {NASSDOC}

Specification for library catalogue and abstract card. (IS : 7150-1974) [Indian Standards Institution]. {NASSDOC}

Specification for library furniture and fittings. (IS : 785-1829 (Pt 1) : 1961). 2 pts. Pt. 1 : Timber; Pt. 2 : Steel. [Indian Standards Institution]. {CRRI NASSDOC}

Specification for packages for use of libraries. (IS : 2662-1964). [Indian Standards Institution]. {CRRI}

Specification for page sizes for books. (BS 1413 : 1970). [British Standards Institution]. {NASSDOC}

Specification for the presentation of library directories. (BS 4605 : 1970) [British Standards Institution]. {CRRI NASSDOC}

Specification for the presentation of serial of publications, including periodicals. (BS 2509 : 1970). [British Standards Institution]. {NASSDOC}

Specification for sizes of folders and files. (IS : 5457-1969). [Indian Standards Institution]. {NASSDOC}

Specification for steel filing cabinets for general office purposes, rev. edn. (IS : 3313-1974). [Indian Standards Institution]. {NASSDOC}

Specification for steel shelving cabinets, rev. edn. (IS : 3312-1974). [Indian Standards Institution]. {NASSDOC}

Specification for the title leaves of a book. (BS 4719 : 1971). [British Standards Institution]. {NASSDOC}

Specification for title-page and back of title-page of a book, rev. edn. (IS : 792-1964). [Indian Standards Institution]. {NASSDOC}

Specification for wooden shelving cabinets (adjustable type). (IS : 4116-1967). [Indian Standards Institution]. {NASSDOC}

Stable rules : Science and social transmission. [Organisation for Economic Co-operation and Development, Paris]. {NASSDOC}

Staff communication in libraries. {JNU}

Staff management in library and information work. {IIT NASSDOC NIH}

Staff management in university and college libraries, ed. by G. Chandler. {ISI}

Staff training in libraries : The British experience. {NASSDOC}

Staffing of public libraries : A report. [Department of Education and Science, Great Britain]. {BIS IIT ZHL}

Standard citation forms for published bibliographies and catalog used in rare book cataloguing. [U.S. Library of Congress]. {NASSDOC}

Standard for a book : The Tamils view. {NASSDOC*}

Standard industrial classification manual. {TDA}

Standard international trade classification, 2nd edn. [United Nations Department of Economic and Special Affairs]. {TDA}

Standardization for documentation. {JNU}

Standardisation in computerised information system : Papers for technical session. [Indian Standards Institution]. {JNU}

Standardization in the domain of documentation. [International Organization for Standardization, Hague]. {BIS}

Standardisation in library and information work and services. [Indian Library Association]. {NASSDOC}

Standardisation of library and information services : With special reference to scientific and agricultural libraries. {JNU}

Standards and objectives for school libraries. [Library Association of Australia]. {JNU}

Standards for library functions at the state level, rev edn., [American Association of State Libraries, Standards Revision Committee. {USIS}

Standards for library services : An international survey. [UNESCO]. {BIS IEG JNU NASSDOC NIEPA NMML}

Standards for library services for the blind and visually handicapped. [American Library Association]. {DUL}

Standards for public libraries. (CIFLA publications). {NASSDOC*}

Standards for school library programmes. [American Association of School Librarians]. {JNU}

Standards for teachers college libraries. [New Zealand Library Association]. {JNU}

Standards of bibliographical description. {DUL}

Standards of public library service in England and Wales : Report of the working party appointed by the Minister of Education in March, 1961. {NASSDOC}

State and national planning. {ISI}

State Department of Education responsibilities for school libraries. {JNU}

The State Lenin Library of USSR. {NASSDOC*}

State library policy : Its legislative and environmental contexts. {USIS}

State of the art report on social science documentation in India. {JNU}

State of library resources in Pakistan. {JNU}

State publications and depository libraries : A reference handbook. {USIS}

Statement of principles adopted at the international conference on cataloguing principles, October 1961, Paris. [IFLA Committee on Cataloguing, London]. {NASSDOC}

Statistical design and analysis of experiments. {NASSDOC}

Statistical methods for librarians. {ISI}

Statistical methods for librarians. {ICHR ISI JNU NASSDOC}

Statistical methods for research workers, 14th edn. {NASSDOC}

Statistics and data sources, Pt. 1 : SSDC sources. {NASSDOC}

Statistics of public libraries, 1960-61. {JNU}

Status of American college and university librarian. {JNU}

Status of documentation in India. [Indian National Documentation Centre, New Delhi]. {JNU}

Steady-state, zerogrowth and the academic library : A collection of essays. {DUL NASSDOC NIEPA}

Stock verification in libraries : Problems and solutions. {DUL}

Strategies for change in information programs. {DUL USIS}

Strategies for manipulating Universal Decimal Classification relationships for computer retrieval. {JNU}

Strategies for meeting the information needs of society in the year 2000. {USIS}
Strategies for problem solving : Programmed instruction. {NASSDOC}
String indexing. {JNU NASSDOC}
Structure and governance of library networks : Proceedings of the 1978 conference in Pittsburg. {JNU}
Structure and subject interaction : Toward a sociology of knowledge in the social sciences. {BIS}
Structured information files. {NASSDOC}
Structured programming. {NASSDOC}
Student use of libraries : An inquiry into the needs of students, libraries and the educational process. [American Library Association]. {USIS}
Student's manual of bibliography, 3rd edn. {CRRI}
Studies in coordinate indexing. {JNU}
Studies in library administrative problems : Eight reports from a seminar on library administration. {DUL USIS}
Studies in library management, vol. 2. {DUL ICA NIPCCD}
Studies in library management, vol. 4. {ICA JNU NAL NIEPA NIPCCD}
Studies in library management, vol. 5. {DUL IIT}
Studies in library resources. {JNU}
Studies in micropublishing, 1853-1976. {USIS}
Studies in readership. {IIT}
Study of 1967 annual salaries of members of Special Library Association. [Personnel Committee of Special Libraries Association]. {JNU}
Study of Bengali surnames. [Linguistic Society of India]. {ZHL}
Study of characteristics, costs and magnitude of inter-library loans in academic libraries. [Association of Research Libraries, Washington]. {JNU}
Study of circulation control systems : Public libraries, college and university libraries, special libraries. (Library Technology Project). [American Library Association]. {DUL IIT USIS}
Study of the effect of library use on academic achievement of post-graduate students in the M.S. University of Baroda. {NASSDOC}
Study of factors influencing college students to become librarians. {JNU}
Study of general categories applicable to classification and coding in documentation, rev edn. tr. by Anthony Thompson. [UNESCO]. {BIS DSSW IEG IIT JNU}
A study of indexers reactions to the PRECIS indexing system. [Department of Library and Information Studies, Faculty of Humanities and Social Studies, Liverpool Polytechnic]. {BCL}
Study of information : Inter- disciplinary messages. {JNU}
Study of the information in the Philippine population programs. [Population Center Foundation of the Philippines]. {NIH}
Study of the rules for entry and heading in the Anglo-American Cataloguing Rules, 1967 : British text. [Library Association, London]. {ZHL}
Study of seven academic libraries in Brooklyn and their cooperative potential. {JNU}
Study of subject bibliography with special reference to the social sciences. [School of Library and Information Services, Maryland]. {NASSDOC}

Study on national structures for documentation and library services in countries with different levels of development, with particular reference to the needs of developing countries. [UNESCO]. {ICA}

Study report on the feasibility of an international data bank to the non-aligned countries. [UNESCO]. {NASSDOC}

Study to determine the feasibility of establishing a cooperative technical processing program and direct transmission of interlibrary loans. {DUL}

Studying the community : A basis for planning library adult education services. (Library Community Project). [American Library Association]. {USIS}

Style manual, rev. edn. [Government Printing Office, United States]. {NASSDOC}

Style manual : A guide for the preparation of reports and dissertations. {DUL}

Style manual for authors and printers of Australian Government publications. [Australia Style Manual Committee, 1964]. {DUL}

Style manual for citing microform and non-print media. [American Library Association]. {BIS}

Style manual for writing theses, dissertations and papers in social sciences. {DUL}

Subject access systems : Alternatives in design. {NASSDOC}

Subject analysis : Computer implications of rigorous definition. {BIS JNU}

The subject approach to information, 2nd edn. {IIMC INSA ISIL JNU NASSDOC ZHL}

Subject approach to information, 3rd edn. {JNU NMML}

Subject authorities : A guide to subject cataloguing. {USIS}

Subject bibliography of the social sciences and humanities. {IEG NASSDOC}

Subject catalogue of the library of the Royal Empire Society. {NASSDOC}

Subject catalogues : Headings and structure. [Library Association, London]. {IIT NASSDOC}

Subject cataloguing. : Critique and innovation. {JNU}

Subject classification for the arrangement of libraries and the organisation of information, 3rd edn. {DUL}

Subject classification of law. {DUL}

Subject classifying and indexing of libraries and literature. {IEG IIT MFL}

Subject collections : A guide to special book collections and subject emphasis as reported by university, college, public and special libraries and museums in the United States and Canada, 5th edn. {USIS}

Subject collections in European libraries, 2nd edn. {IIT}

Subject cross reference guide. {JNU}

Subject directory of special libraries and information centres. {IIFT}

Subject guide to books in print, 1970-71; 1974; 1978-79; 1980-81; 1983-84. {NASSDOC}

Subject guide to class 'Ref' : Current reference books. [University of Cambridge Library]. {NASSDOC}

Subject guide to periodical indexes and review indexes. {NIH}

Subject heading for children's materials. [American Library Association]. {ZHL}

Subject headings : The history and theory of the alphabetical subject approach to books. {NAI}

Subject headings : A list with CC and DDC numbers. {NASSDOC}

Subject headings : A practical guide. [Library of Congress]. {CRRI USIS}

Subject headings for financial libraries. [Special Libraries Association, New York]. {ISI}

Subject headings used in the dictionary catalogues, 5th edn. [Library of Congress]. {ZHL}

Subject headings used in the dictionary catalogs of the Library of Congress from 1897 through December 1955, 6th edn. [U.S. Library of Congress]. {BIS IEG USIS}

Subject headings used in the dictionary catalogs of the Library of Congress from 1897 through December 1955 : Supplement to the 6th edn., January 1956-December 1959. [Library of Congress]. {IEG}

Subject headings used in the dictionary catalogs of the Library of Congress, 7th edn. [U.S. Library of Congress. {USIS}

Subject indices list. [Central Reference Library, Calcutta]. {NASSDOC*]

Subject retrieval in the seventies : New directions. {ICHR}

Subject specialisation and cooperative book purchase in the libraries of Great Britain. {DUL}

Substance of library science. {ICHR IIC IIT MFL NIH NERC SPA}

Suchikaran ke siddhant. {DUL}

Suggestions for the organisations of libraries in India. {NASSDOC}

Summary of public library law in England and Wales, Scotland, Northern Ireland and Eira, 2nd edn. [Association of Assistant Librarians, London]. {NASSDOC}

Summoned by books : Essays and speeches, comp. by Marjeanne Jensen Blinn. {USIS}

Supervising library personnel. {DUL}

Supplementary cataloguing rules for the guidance of assistants. [Imperial Record Department]. {NAI}

Supply of foreign books and periodicals to the libraries of the United Kingdom. {DUL}

Surrounded by books : Libraries in primary and middle schools. {JNU NASSDOC}

A survey of the contents of existing national bibliographies. [UNESCO]. {NASSDOC*}

Survey of existing systems and current proposals for the cataloguing and description of non-book materials collected by libraries with preliminary suggestions for their international co-ordination. [UNESCO]. {BIS}

Survey of government documents in Central Secretariat Library 1979-80. (University of Delhi, Department of Library Science, sessional project). {DUL}

Survey of organisations : A machine standardised questionnaire instruments. [Institute of Social Research, Michigan]. {NASSDOC}

Survey of practice training in information science. {JNU}

Survey of public library services in India : Tabulated and analysed : Working group on libraries. [Planning Commission, New Delhi]. {NASSDOC*}

Survey of secondary school libraries in U.P. : Report. [Ministry of Education, New Delhi]. {MHA}

Survey of special libraries serving the Federal Government. [U.S. Department of Health Education and Welfare]. {BIS}

Survey of the University of Delhi library. {AIU DSSW DUL IEG IIC NASSDOC NERC SPA}

Survey of user attitude towards resource and services of three university libraries in Saudi Arabia. {JNU}

Survey research : A decisional approach. {NASSDOC}

Survey research technique. {NASSDOC}

Swedish public libraries in pictures : Country and small town libraries. {IIT}
Syllabus for a documentation course. [International Federation for Documentation and Information]. {BIS}
Syllabus for research methods in librarianship. {DUL}
Symbols and notations for correction of illustration and illustration proofs. (IS : 7140-1971). [Indian Standards Institution]. {NASSDOC}
Synoptic tables concerning the current national bibliographies. {NASSDOC}
Synthesis in D.D.C., 18th edn. [Andhra University, Waltair]. {NASSDOC*}
Syntol, ed. by Susan Artandi, 2 vols. {MFL}
System/360 Assembler language. {NASSDOC}
System analysis. {JNU}
System analysis and design. {JNU}
Systems analysis and design : A Case study approach. {JNU}
System analysis for information retrieval. {BCL}
System analysis for information sciences. [Department of Science and Technology, New Delhi]. {BIS CRRI JNU}
System analysis in libraries. {JNU}
System design and documentation. {JNU}
System development methodology. {DUL}
System of bibliographic classification, 2nd edn. {NAI}
System research : Methodological problems. {JNU}
System scope for library automation and generalised information storage and retrieval at Stanford University. {IIT}
System thinking : Concepts and notions. {JNU}
Systematic analysis of university libraries : Application of cost benefit analysis to the M.I.T. libraries. {AIU DUL IIT JNU NIPCCD SPA}
Systematic bibliography : An introduction. {NASSDOC}
Systematic bibliography : A practical guide to the work of compilation. {ICHR NASSDOC SPA}
Systematic bibliography : A practical guide to the work of compilation, 3rd edn. {NASSDOC}
Systematic bibliography and documentation. {ICA ICHR NASSDOC NIH}
Systematic bibliography in England, 1850-95. {DUL}
Systems analysis. {NASSDOC}
Systems analysis : Definition, process and design. {NASSDOC}
Systems analysis in libraries : A question and answer approach. {BCL DUL}
A systems approach to library program development. {JNU USIS}
Systems bibliography : A thirty years' literature survey. {NASSDOC}
Systems documentation. {JNU}
Systems management. {NASSDOC}
Systems thinking in library and information management. {DUL NIPCCD}

Tabulation of librarianship : Classified tables for the arrangement of all material relating to library economy. {CRRI}
Talks on book collecting. {DUL}
Targets for research in library education. [American Library Association]. {USIS}
Task analysis of library operations. [Association of Special Libraries and Information Bureaux]. {DUL IIT}
Tasks, process and information display design : NATO conference on visual presentation of information, September, 4-8, 1978, Birmingham. {BIS}

Teacher librarian. {JNU}
Teacher librarians handbook. [American Library Association]. {DUL NIEPA ZHL}
Teachers, librarians and children : A study of libraries in education. {IIT}
Teaching and the community college library. {JNU}
Teaching manual for tutor-librarians. {JNU}
Teaching with books : A study of college libraries. [American Library Association]. {ZHL}
Teaching with books : A study of college libraries. {DUL}
Technical and specialised periodicals published in Britain, 1972-73. [Central Office of Information, London]. {NASSDOC}
Technical college libraries : Finchfield. {DUL IIT}
Technical college library : A primer for its development. {AIU DUL IIT}
Technical information sources : A guide to patent specification, standards and technical reports literature. {BIS}
Technical libraries. {IIT}
Technical libraries : Their organisation and management. [Special Libraries Association, New York]. {CRRI ISI}
Technical literature search and the written report. {BCL}
Technical notes : MEDLARS indexing instructions. [National Library of Medicine, Maryland]. {CRRI}
Technical services in libraries : Acquisitions, cataloguing, classification, binding, photographic. {IEG NAI ZHL}
Techniques for document retrieval research : State of art. {JNU}
Technique of union catalogue : A practical guide. [UNESCO]. {IIMC NASSDOC NERC}
Techniques of information retrieval. {AIU BCL IEG IIMC INSA JNU}
Technological change in printing and publishing. {INSA}
Technology in support of library science and information service. [Sarada Ranganathan Endowment for Library Science, Bangalore]. {BIS}
Telecommunications and libraries : A primer for librarians and information managers. {USIS}
Telefascimile in libraries : A report of an experiment in fascimile transmission and an analysis of implication for inter library loan system. {JNU}
Telefascimile services between libraries with the xerox management telescopier. {JNU}
Ten years of United Nations publication, 1945-55 : A complete catalogue. [United Nations]. {DSSW}
Terminology of documentation. [UNESCO]. {JNU NASSDOC NIPCCD ZHL}
Text-book on bibliography. {DUL}
Textbook on mechanised information retrieval. {CRRI}
Theoretical problems of informatics : Forecasting of the development of scientific information activities. [International Federation for Documentation and Information]. {CRRI}
Theoretical problems of information : Criteria of the quality of information systems and processes : Collection of papers. [International Federation for Documentation and Information]. {BIS}
Theoretical problems of information : New trends in information and its terminology. [International Federation for Documentation and Information]. {CRRI}
Theories of bibliographic education : Designs for teachings. {JNU}

Theory and applications of information research : Proceedings : International research forum on information science, 2nd, August 3-6, 1977, Copenhagen. {BCL}

Theory and history of bibliography, tr. by Ralph Robert Shaw. {NASSDOC}

Theory and management of systems. {JNU}

Theory of book selection. {NERC NIPCCD}

Theory of cataloguing, 2nd edn. {ICHR IIT ISIL JNU MMTC NASSDOC NCAER NCDC NERC NIPCCD ZHL}

Theory of cataloguing, 4th edn. {ZHL}

Theory of cataloguing : An examination guide book. {NASSDOC SPA}

Theory of classification. {ICHR IIT MFL NERC ZHL}

Theory of classification. {BIS ICA ISI JNU ZHL}

Theory of classification, 2nd rev. edn. {NASSDOC NMML}

Theory of classification, 3rd edn. {ZHL}

Theory of indexing : Indexing theory as a model for information storage and retrieval. [Computer and Information Science Research Centre, Ohio State University]. {IIT}

Theory of knowledge classification in libraries. {CRRI ICA ICHR IIT JNU NASSDOC NERC SPA ZHL}

Theory of librarianship : Papers in honour of Jesse H. Shera. {NASSDOC*}

Theory of library classification. {DUL}

Theory of subject analysis : A source book. {NASSDOC}

Thesauri and thesauri construction. [Association of Special Libraries and Information Bureaux]. {CRRI NASSDOC}

Thesauri, glossaries, terminologies and dictionaries. {NASSDOC}

Thesauri in retrieval. [Association of Special Libraries and Information Bureaux]. {BCL CRRF DUL IIT NASSDOC}

Thesaurus and faceted classification for engineering and related subjects. {IIT}

Thesaurus construction : A practical manual. {CRRI}

Thesaurus construction and use : A condensed course. [UNESCO]. {NASSDOC}

Thesaurus-making : Grow your own word-stock. {NASSDOC}

Thesaurus of book digests, 1950-1980. {USIS}

Thesaurus of descriptors used for information processing in the ILO library. [ILO]. {NASSDOC}

Thesaurus of ERIC descriptors, with a special chapter on the role and function of thesaurus in education. [U.S. Educational Resources Information Centre]. {USIS}

Thesis and assignment writing. {DUL}

Third European congress on information systems and networks overcoming the language barrier, Luxembourg. {JNU}

Three number author table. {BIS ZHL}

Three thousand books for a public library : Some significant and representative works for basic stock. {NAI}

Title-leaves of a book. (ISO/R 1086-1969) (E). [International Organisation for Standardisation, Geneva]. {NASSDOC*}

Titles in series : A handbook for libraries and students : Supplement to 2nd edn. {NASSDOC}

To know a library : Essays and annual report, 1975-76. {JNU}

Tomorrow's library : Direct access and delivery. {USIS}

Torch-bearer of public library movement : Andhra Pradesh library field workers conference, 1974, Gudiwada. {NASSDOC*}

Toward a better cataloguing code. {IEG}

Toward a federal library and information services network : A proposal. {USIS}

Towards information retrieval. {JNU}

Towards the information society. {DUL}

Towards a national information system : Second annual national colloquium on information retrieval. {IIT}

Toward a national program for library and information services : Goals for action. [U.S. National Commission on Libraries and Information Science]. {USIS}

Toward paperless information system. {BCL DUL IIFT ISI ISIL USIS}

Towards a theory for U.D.C. : Essays aimed at structural understanding and operational improvement. {ICHR NASSDOC}

Training course in documentation techniques in Asia, Tokyo, July 20—August 21, 1970. [Japanese National Commission for UNESCO]. {NASSDOC}

Training for the improvement of library administration. {JNU}

Training in indexing : A course. [Society of Indexers]. {IEG IIFT IIT NASSDOC}

Training manual and work book for use in abstracting and coordinate indexing. [Ohio Battelle Memorial Institute, Ohio]. {BIS}

Transactions : Prague conference on information theory, statistical decision function, random processes, June 3, 1962. {INSA}

Translators and translations : Services and sources. {JNU}

Transliteration of Hebrew (ISO/R 259-1962) (E). [International Organisation for Standardisation, Geneva]. {NASSDOC}

Transnational library relations : The Indo-American experience. {NASSDOC}

Treasures of the Library of Congress. {USIS}

A treatise on book selection. {NERC NIH ZHL}

A treatise on Colon Classification appended with a select bibliography on the scheme. {NASSDOC NMML}

Treatment of special material in libraries. {MFL}

Trends 1985-86 : Report to the Council by the Secretary General. [International Federation of Library Associations and Institutions]. {NASSDOC*}

Trends in information transfer. {ISI NASSDOC}

Trends in special librarianship. {IEG IIT MMTC}

Trends in subject indexing. {NASSDOC NMML}

Trends of information service in India {AIU CRRI ICHR NASSDOC NERC NIH NIPCCD ZHL}

Twenty years of Library Herald : A cumulative index to Vols. 1-20, 1958-59 to 1981. [Delhi Library Association]. {IIT NASSDOC}

UDC, 3rd edn. [British Standards Institution]. {ICCR}

U.D.C. : Theory and practice. {JNU}

UK MARC manual. [Bibliographic Services Division, British Library, London]. {JNU}

UK MARC manual, 2nd edn. [Bibliographic Services Division, British Library, London]. {BIS}

UK MARC project : Proceedings of seminar organised by the cataloguing and indexing group of the Library Association at the University of Southampton, 28-30 March, 1976. {NASSDOC}

U.N. report : Working meeting on Asian resources for a Population Library Information Network, September 13-15, 1973, Bangkok. [U.N. Economic Commission for Asia and the Far East]. {NIH}

UNBIS thesaurus : List of terms used in indexing and cataloguing of documents and other materials relevant to United Nations programmes and activities. [Dag Hammerskjold Library]. {JNU}

UNESCO and library development planning. {DUL}

UNESCO list of documents and publications : 1972/76, 1980-81. [UNESCO]. {NASSDOC}

UNESCO thesaurus, Vol. 1 : Introduction, classified thesaurus permitted index hierarchical display; Vol. 2 : Alphabetical thesaurus. [UNESCO]. {NASSDOC}

UNISIST : A study on the application of scientific and technological information in development. [UNESCO]. {JNU}

UNISIST : Synopsis of the feasibility study on a World Science Information System. [UNESCO; International Council of Scientific Unions]. {BIS DSSW IIMC NASSDOC ZHL}

UNISIST guide for the establishment and evaluation of services for selective dissemination of information. [UNESCO]. {CRRI}

UNISIST guide to standards for information handling. [UNESCO]. {BIS DUL MMTC}

UNISIST guidelines for editors of scientific and technical journals. [UNESCO]. {DUL}

UNISIST guidelines for the establishment and development of monolingual thesauri, 2nd edn. [UNESCO]. {BIS}

UNISIST guidelines for the evaluation of information systems and services. [UNESCO]. {BIS}

UNISIST guidelines for formulating policy on education, training and development of library and information personnel. [UNESCO]. {BIS}

UNISIST guidelines for the organisation of training courses, workshops and seminars in scientific and technical information and documentation. [UNESCO]. {BIS}

UNISIST information policy objectives. [UNESCO]. {JNU}

UNISIST information networks for online bibliographic retrieval. [UNESCO]. {BIS DUL}

UNISIST International Serials Data Systems (ISDS). [UNESCO]. {BIS}

UNISIST international system and networks for technology transfer. [UNESCO]. {BIS}

UNISIST study report on the feasibility of a world science information. [UNESCO]. {BIS DSSW IIMC NASSDOC ZHL}

USA standard : Basic criteria for indexes, rev edn., (USAS Z 39. 4-1968). [American National Standards Institute]. {NASSDOC}

USA standard for compiling book publishing statistics. (USAS Z 39.8-1968). [American National Standards Institute]. {NASSDOC}

USA standard for permanent and durable library catalogue cards. (USAS Z 35.1-1969). [American National Standards Institute]. {NASSDOC}

The undergraduate library. [American Library Association]. {USIS}

Understanding scientific literatures : A bibliometric approach. {INSA}

Union catalogue of Asian publications, 1965-1970. {NASSDOC}

Union catalogue of the books in the libraries of the Botanical Survey of India, 3 vols. [Botanical Survey of India]. {INSA}

Union catalogue of the Central Government of India publications held by libraries in London, Oxford and Cambridge. [Centre of South Asian Studies, University of Cambridge, Mansell]. {NASSDOC}

Union catalogue of the Government of Ceylon publications held by libraries in London, Oxford and Cambridge. [Centre of South Asian Studies, University of Cambridge, Mansell]. {NASSDOC}

Union catalogue of library and information science publications : Delhi libraries. {NASSDOC}

Union catalogue of library science periodical holdings in Delhi University Library system, Jawahar Lal Nehru University Library and National Science Library. [Indian National Scientific Documentation Centre]. {DUL}

Union catalogue of newspapers : Delhi libraries. {NASSDOC}

Union catalogue of social science periodicals/serials, 32 vols. {NASSDOC}

Union catalogues : Their problems and organisation. [UNESCO]. {CRRI}

Union list of current social science periodicals : Delhi libraries. {NASSDOC}

Union list of social science periodicals : Lucknow. {NASSDOC}

Union list of social science periodicals received in Delhi libraries. {NASSDOC}

United Nations document series symbols, 1946-1977 : Cumulative list with index. [United Nations]. {IIFT}

The United Nations family of libraries. {ICA ICHR INSA NASSDOC NMML}

United Nations library : Its origin and development. {JNU NASSDOC USIS}

Universal bibliographic control : A long term policy, a plan for action. {JNU}

Universal Decimal Classification. {ZHL}

Universal Decimal Classification : Its structure, application and tables : Revision procedure. [UNESCO; UNION, Moscow]. {NASSDOC}

The Universal Decimal Classification : Present position and future developments. [UNESCO]. {ICA}

Universal Decimal Classification : Special subject edition for education. {DUL}

Universal Decimal Classification : Special subject edition for metallurgy. {DUL}

Universal Decimal Classification : Structure and methodology. {BIS ICHR IIT JNU ZHL}

Universal Decimal Classification : Ten years supplement to abridged UDC editions, 1958-1968. [UNESCO; FID]. {ICA IIMC IIT NASSDOC}

Universal Decimal Classification : Trilingual abridged edition. {JNU}

Universal reference system, 10 vols. {NMML}

The universe of information. [International Federation of Documentation and Information]. {CRRI}

University and college libraries. [University Grants Commission, New Delhi]. {BIS DUL IEG IIMC IIT JNU NIEPA}

University and college libraries : Containing the report and the proceedings of the Seminar on 'from publisher to reader' held on March 4-7, 1966. [University Grants Commission, New Delhi]. {DUL NASSDOC}

University and research library studies. {AIU DUL IIC IIT ISI JNU SPA}

Univesity librarianship. {JNU}

University libraries and education for librarianship in India. {JNU}

University libraries as information centres : Proceedings of IATUL sixth meeting, 1975. {DCL}

University libraries for developing countries. [UNESCO]. {AIU DUL ICA IIMC IIT JNU NIEPA NMML USIS}

University libraries in Britain : A network. {JNU NIEPA}

University libraries in India : Their organisation and administration. {DUL IIT ISI JNU NERC NIEPA NIPCCD}

University libraries of India : Principles and policy. {AIU DUL IIC JNU NIEPA NMML}

University library : Its management and organisation. {DUL JNU}

University library : Its organisation, administration and functions, 2nd edn. {JNU}

University library administration. {DUL NASSDOC USIS}

University library buildings in India. {AIU BIS DUL IIT JNU MMTC NASSDOC NIEPA}

University library finances in Madhya Pradesh : A comparative study. {NASSDOC}

University library system in India. {JNU NASSDOC NMML}

University science and engineering libraries : Their operations, collections and facilities. {CRRI IIT}

Unreluctant years. [American Library Association]. {ZHL}

Urban information thesaurus : A vocabulary for social documentation. {JNU}

Use of citation data in writing the history of science. {DUL}

Use of computer in libraries : Summary of the proceedings of a seminar held on March 15, 1982, New Delhi. {NASSDOC}

Use of journals in libraries : A cost effectiveness analysis. {JNU}

Use of libraries : A guide to better use of libraries and their resources. {CRRI ICA IIT MMTC NASSDOC NCAER NCDC NIPCCD NMML}

Use of libraries and the literature of human geography. {SPA}

Use of library classification schemes in Indian libraries with special reference to Delhi. {NASSDOC}

Use of library materials : The University of Pittsburgh study. {CRRI USIS}

The use of Library of Congress Classification : Proceedings : Institute of the use of the Library of congress classification, 1966, New York. [American Library Association]. {USIS}

Use of management and business literature. {MMTC}

Use of mechanized methods in documentation work. {JNU}

Use of microprocessors in information analysis and library applications. [Society for Information Science]. {NASSDOC}

Use of microprocessor in information analysis and library applications. {NASSDOC}

Use of reference material. {ZHL}

Use of reports in literature. {INSA JNU}

Use of television by public library. [American Library Association]. {JNU}

User and library information service. [Indian Association of Special Libraries and Information Centres]. {IIFT}

User education : Towards a better use of information resources. {BCL}

User education in libraries. {DUL JNU NASSDOC NIEPA}

User education programmes in Swedish academic libraries : A study of developments in the year 1973-77. {JNU}

User studies : An introduction guide and select bibliography. [Centre for Research of User Studies, University of Sheffield, Sheffield]. {NASSDOC}

User surveys and evaluation of library services [Association of Research Libraries, Washington]. {NASSDOC}

User's manual for the general inquirer. {NASSDOC}

Users of documentation. {JNU}

Uses of libraries. {AIU}
Using books and libraries, 4th edn. {ZHL}
Using books and libraries, 5th edn. {DUL NASSDOC USIS}
Using libraries. {CRRI IIT MFL}
Using libraries : An information guide for students and general users, 3rd edn. {ICA}
Using libraries effectively. {ICA}
Using the library for reference and research. {JNU}
Using your high school library. {JNU}
Using your library. {JNU}

Vargikaran siddhant evam vyavhar. {NASSDOC}
The vertical file and its satelites : A handbook. {DUL USIS}
Video to online : Reference services and the new technology. {JNU}
Vistas in information handling : The augmentation of man's intellect by machine. {MHA}
The vital network : A theory of communication and society. {USIS}
Vocabularium bibliothecari {IEG}
Voluntary education through the public library. [American Library Association]. {NASSDOC*}
Vyavaharik suchikaran vidhi. {NASSDOC}

Weeding library collections, 2nd rev edn. {DUL USIS}
What children read : A survey. [National Book Council of Pakistan, Karachi]. {ZHL}
What computers can do : A guide to the plain man. {DUL}
What else can you do with a library degree. {IIT}
What is the index. {NAI}
What reading does to people. {NAI}
What they say. [Ranganathan Volume Committee, Varanasi]. {NASSDOC*}
Where the time goes. [Association of Special Libraries and Information Bureaux]. {AIU CRRI IIT}
Where to find what : A handbook to reference service. {JNU}
Who's who in librarianship and information science, 2nd edn. {JNU}
Women and librarianship : An investigation into certain problems of library staffing. {DUL}
Women's information network for Asia and Pacific. [United Nations Economic and Social Commission for Asia and Pacific, Bangkok]. {NASSDOC}
Wonderful world of books. {ZHL}
Words that mean business : 3,000 terms for access to business information. {USIS}
Workbook for a successful workshop. [American Library Association]. {USIS}
Working conditions in Canadian public libraries. [Canadian Library Association]. {JNU}
Working document on scientific and technological information in Asia and the Pacific. [UNESCO]. {NASSDOC}
Working documents : Workshop on norms, guidelines and standards for library and information science education. [Nagpur University Department of Library and Information Science, Nagpur]. {NASSDOC}
Working of central museums : Report : Central museums review committee, 1968, New Delhi. {AIU}

Working papers : All India library conference, 25th, May 14-18, 1979, Trivandrum. [Indian Library Association]. {ICA NCDC NMML}

Working papers : Seminar on library buildings in India, February, 1980. [NISSAT].

Working papers : Seminar on use of microforms and space management in libraries. [Sri Venkateshwar University Library, Tirupati].

Working papers and proceedings : DRTC seminar on cataloguing, 1970, Bangalore. [Documentation Research and Training Centre, Bangalore]. {NASSDOC}

Working papers and proceedings : DRTC seminar on reference service. [Documentation Research and Training Centre, Bangalore]. {NASSDOC}

Working papers and proceedings : IASLIC conference, 4th, 1967, Dhanbad. [Indian Association of Special Libraries and Information Centres]. {SPA}

Working papers and proceedings : IASLIC seminar, 2nd, 1965, Chandigarh : Part-I : Users and library information services. [Indian Association of Special Libraries and Information Centres]. {SPA}

Working papers and proceedings of the three symposia, I : General vs special classification schemes; II : Inter library loan and exchange of materials in India; III : Social science documentation in India : IASLIC seminar, 3rd, 1964, Lucknow; [Indian Association of Special Libraries and Information Centres]. {NASSDOC SPA}

Working papers for the symposia : IASLIC conference, 5th, 1963, Pune, Pt. I : Document and data processing in academic research and special libraries in India; Pt. II : Problems and prospects of library associations in India. [Indian Association of Special Libraries and Information Centres]. {NASSDOC}

Working papers for the symposia : IASLIC conference, 6th, 1965, Trivandrum, Pt 1-3 : Colon Classification local documentation lists, library organisation and social science research, 1967; Pt. 4 : Colon Classification, local documentation lists, library organisation and social science research, 1967. [Indian Association of Special Libraries and Information Centres]. {NASSDOC SPA}

Working papers of the two symposia : IASLIC seminar, 4th 1966, Hyderabad, Pt. 1 : Procurement of government publications and technical reports; Pt. 2 : Devaluation : Its impact on the development of libraries in India. [Indian Association of Special Libraries and Information Centres]. {NASSDOC SPA}

Working papers for the symposia : IASLIC seminar, 5th, October 7-9, 1968, Durgapur, Pt. I : Selective dissemination of information for India; Pt. II : Functions and problems of library personnel in special libraries of India. [Indian Association of Special Libraries and Information Centres]. {NASSDOC}

Workshop on computer application to library and information activities. [ILA NISSAT]. {JNU}

World guide to library school and training course in documentation. [UNESCO]. {ICA IIT JNU NASSDOC NERC NIEPA USIS}

World guide to technical information and documentation services. [UNESCO]. {CRRI NMML}

World guide to technical information and documentation services, 2nd edn. [UNESCO]. {JNU NASSDOC}

World guide to terminological activities. {JNU}

World librarianship. {IIT NMML}

A world of information : American society for information science meeting, 35th, October, 23-26, 1972, Washington, D.C. {USIS}

World trends in library education. {AIU IIT NERC NIEPA USIS}

World's great libraries, 1934-1937 2 vols. {NAI}

Writer's reference book : A reference work for authors, freelance journalists and writers for film, radio and television. {DUL}

Writing book reviews. {DUL}

Writing for new readers : A handbook. [Pakistan National Book Council, Karachi]. {ZHL}

Writing, illustrating and editing children's books, rev. edn. {DUL}

Year's work in Indian librarianship, 1987. [Indian Library Association]. {NASSDOC}

You can do it : Manual for librarians. {USIS}

Your future as a librarian. {IIFT}

Your library : Readers guide to Karnatak University Library, Dharwar. {NASSDOC}

Your library : A reference guide. {USIS}

Your library : A reference guide, 2nd edn. {JNU NASSDOC}

Your library : What's in it for you. {CRRI}

Youth library work : Exploratory essays, 2nd edn. {IIT}

4

AUTHOR APPROACH

Abdul Haq, A.M. and Aman, Mohammad M., 1977, **Librarianship and the Third World** : An annotated bibliography of selected literature on developing nations, 1960-1975. {NASSDOC}

Abidi, Syed Ameer Haider, 1967, **Evaluation of selected reference tools published in India**. (University of Delhi, Department of Library Science, Sessional Project). {DUL}

Abkin, Michael H. and Carrol, Tam W., 1976, **Computer library for agricultural systems simulation** : A progress report. {BIS}

Abramson, Norman, 1963, **Information theory and coding**. {INSA}

Abramson, Norman, 1985, **Data communication and information exchange network**. (ASTINFONET). [UNESCO]. {NASSDOC}

Ackoff, Russell L., et al, 1962, **Scientific method** : Optimising applied research decision. {NASSDOC}

Ackoff, Rusell L., et al, 1976, **Designing national scientific and technological communication system**. {USIS}

Ada, Winifred John, 1968, **Special libraries** : Development of the concept, their organization and their service. {JNU}

Adamson, Edith, 1962, **Public library finance** : A literature review. {JNU}

Adamson, Edith, 1963, **Examination of public library finance in Canada in relation to minimum standards of the Canadian Library Association**. {JNU}

Adler, Mortimer J. and Van Doren, Charles, 1972, **How to read a book**, rev. edn. {USIS}

Agarwal, S.N., et al, 1982, **Perspectives in library and information science** : Viswanathan festschrift. 2 vols. {AIU ICHR ISI JNU MMTC NASSDOC NCDC NIEPA NIPCCD SPA ZHL}

Agarwal, Shyam Sunder, 1971, **Pustakalaya soochikaran** : Ek adhyayan. [Madhya Pradesh Hindhi Granth Academy]. {NMML}

Agarwal, Shyam Sunder, 1978, **Granthalaya sangathan**. {BIS}

Aggarwal, D.S., 1985, **Lectures on universe of knowledge**. {NMML}

Aggarwal, J.C. and Agrawal, S.P., 1990, **Documentation encyclopaedia of UNESCO and education**. {NIEPA}

Agrawal, Binod C., 1982, **Patterns of communication in international meeting** : A pilot study of tenth international congress of anthropological and ethnological sciences. {NASSDOC}

Agrawal, O.P., 1977, **Care and preservation of museum objects**. {NASSDOC}

Agrawal, O.P., 1984, **Conservation of manuscripts and painting of South-East Asia**. {NMML}

Note: Based on catalogue entry pattern of libraries surveyed.

Agrawal, S.P., 1987, **Library and information services in India** : The current scenario. {NASSDOC}

Agrawal, S.P., 1987, **Social science information and documentation** : Search and relevance in India. {BIS DUL JNU NASSDOC NIH NIEPA NMML ZHL}

Agrawal, S.P., 1989, **Development of documentation in India** : Social science information. {BIS DSSW DUL ISI JNU NAL NERC NASSDOC NMML SPA ZHC}

Agrawal, S.P., 1989, **Development of library services in India** : Social science information. {BIS DUL ISI JNU NASSDOC NERC NMML ZHL}

Agrawal, S.P. and Aggarwal, J.C., 1989, **Information India, 1988** : Global view {IDSA IIPA NIEPA NMML}

Agrawal, S.P. and Aggarwal, J.C., 1990, **Information India, 1990-91** : Global view. {AIU BIS CPR DUL ICA IEG IIT ISI JNU NASSDOC NIEPA NMML ZHL}

Agrawal, S.P. and Naresh Kanta, 1990, **Child education in India**: Index to scholarly writings in Indian educational journals and newspapers. {NIPCCD}

Agrawal, S.P., ch. ed., 1973-76, **Union catalogue of social science periodicals/serials**, 32 vols. {NASSDOC}

Agrawal, S.P., ch. ed., 1982, **Union list of social science periodicals received in Delhi libraries**. {NASSDOC}

Agrawal, S.P., ch. ed., 1982-88, **NASSDOC research information series**, 62 vols. {NASSDOC}

Agrawal, S.P., ch. ed., 1983, **Union catalogue of newspapers** : Delhi libraries. {NASSDOC}

Agrawal, S.P., ch. ed., 1983, **Union list of current social science periodicals** : Delhi libraries. {NASSDOC}

Agrawal, S.P., ed., 1984, **Inter-Library Resources Centre** : Holding of periodicals. {NASSDOC}

Agrawal, S.P., ch. ed., 1985, **Dr. S.R. Ranganathan** : A bibliography, comp. by O.K. Choudhry. [National Social Science Documentation Centre]. {NASSDOC NMML}

Agrawal, S.P., ch. ed., 1985, **Library and information science literature** : SSDC resources. {NASSDOC}

Agrawal, S.P., ch. ed., 1985, **National information literature in SSDC**. {NASSDOC*}

Agrawal, S.P., ch ed., 1985, **Statistics and data sources**, Pt. 1 : SSDC sources. {NASSDOC}

Agrawal, S.P., ch. ed., 1986, **Union catalogue of library and information science publications** : Delhi libraries. {NASSDOC}

Agrawal, S.P., ch. ed., 1986, **Union list of social science periodicals** : Lucknow. {NASSDOC}

Agrawal, S.P., ch. ed., 1987, **Thesauri, glossaries, terminologies and dictionaries**. {NASSDOC}

Agrawal, S.P., ch. ed., 1987, **NASSDOC** : How it works. {NASSDOC}

Agrawal, S.P., ch. ed., 1987-88, **NASSDOC dockets**. {NASSDOC}

Agrawal, S.P., gen ed., 1989-, **Concepts in communication, informatics and librarianship**. (CICIL series). {JNU NASSDOC}

Agrawal, S.S., 1972, **Catalogue entries and procedure** : A guide to cataloguing work according to ALA and AACR and CCC. {IEG IIT ISI}

Agrawal, Suren, et al, 1972, **Hindi mein bal sahitya** : Children literature in Hindi since independence, Pratham khand 1947-1960. {NASSDOC}

Ahmad, Syed Reyaz, 1979, **Annotated and classified bibliography of project reports submitted to the Department of Library Science, University of Delhi since 1968.** {DUL}

Ahrensfelf, Janet L., et al, 1981, **Special libraries** : Guide for management, 2nd edn. {MMTC}

Aitchison, Jean and Allen, C.G., eds. 1982, **Bibliography of mono and multilingual vocabularies, thesauri, subject headings and classification schemes in the social sciences** : Prepared by the ASLIB Library. [UNESCO]. {NASSDOC}

Aitchison, Jean and Gilchrist, Alan, 1972, **Thesaurus construction** : A practical manual. {CRRI}

Aitchison, Jean, comp., 1977, **UNESCO thesaurus**, Vol. 1 : Introduction, classified thesaurus permitted index hierarchical display; Vol. 2 : Alphabetical thesaurus. [UNESCO]. {NASSDOC}

Aiyepeku, Wilson O., 1983, **International socio-economic information systems** : An evaluating directory of DEVSIS-type programs. {NASSDOC}

Akers, Susan Grey, 1944, **Simple library cataloguing**, 3rd edn. [American Library Association]. {BIS}

Akers, Susan Grey, 1954, **Simple library cataloguing**, 4th edn. [American Library Association]. {CRRI DSSW MHA SPA ZHL}

Akers, Susan Grey, 1969, **Simple library cataloguing**, 5th edn. {JNU NASSDOC NMML USIS ZHL}

Akers, Susan Grey, 1977, **Simple library cataloguing**, 6th rev and rewritten edn., ed. by Arthur Curlly and Jana Varlejs. {MHA NIEPA}

Al-Nahari, Abdulaziz Mohamed, 1984, **Role of national libraries in developing countries with special reference to Saudi Arabia**. {NMML}

Aldrich, Ella V., 1960, **Using books and libraries**, 4th edn. {ZHL}

Aldrich, Ella V., 1967, **Using books and libraries**, 5th edn. {DUL NASSDOC USIS}

Alex, M., 1963, **Making book work** : A course for the school library. {JNU}

Alexander, C. and Burke, A.J., 1958, **How to locate educational information and data,** 4th edn. {NIEPA}

Alexs, Phillip, 1935, **Filing and preserving stock and records,** in libraries and other institutions including museums and art galleries. {JNU}

Allan, Margaret, 1974, **School library resource centre**. {JNU}

Allen, Joan, 1961, **Organisation of small libraries** : A manual of educational institutions in tropical countries. {JNU NIEPA}

Allen, Kenneth W. and Allen, Loren, 1973, **Organisation and administration of the learning resources centre in the community college.** {USIS}

Allison, Anne Manne and Allan, Ann, eds., 1979, **National library network**. {IIT}

Almasy, Elina, et al, 1976, **Comparative survey analysis** : An annotated bibliography, 1967-1978. {NASSDOC}

Aman, Mohammad M., ed., 1980, **Cataloguing and classification of non-Western materials** : Concerns, issues and practices. {IIT}

Amarsinghe, N., ed., 1987, **Proceedings** : International conference of directors of national libraries of Asia and Oceania, 3rd, November 18-23, Colombo. {NASSDOC}

Ambhnwong, Suthilak, 1967, **Libraries and librarianship in Thailand**. {JNU}

Anand Sagar, comp. and ed., 1986, **Directory of publishers and booksellers in India**, based on actual mailing. [Federation of Indian Publishers]. {NASSDOC}

Anderla, Georges, 1986, **Information in 1985** : A forecasting study of information needs and resources. [Organisation for Economic Cooperation and Development]. {BCL BIS CRRI JNU MMTC}

Anders, Mary Edna, 1976, **Libraries and library services in the Southeast** : A report of the Southeastern states cooperative library survey, 1972-74. {BIS ISI}

Andersen, A., et al, 1985, **Libraries and information centres in the Soviet Union**. {NASSDOC*}

Anderson, Beryl L., 1968, **Special libraries in Canada** : A directory. {JNU}

Anderson, Charles B., et al, 1969, **Manual of book selling**. {DUL}

Anderson, Dorothy, 1974, **Universal bibliographic control** : A long term policy, a plan for action. {JNU}

Anderson, Florence, 1963, **Library programme, 1911-61.** {ZHL}

Anderson, Janathan, et al, 1970, **Thesis and assignment writing**. {DUL}

Anderson, M.D., 1971, **Book indexing**. {NASSDOC NIEPA}

Anderson, R.G., 1984, **Concise dictionary of data processing and computer terms,**, 2nd edn. {NCERT}

Anderson, Ursula, 1977, **Management training for libraries**. [Library Association, London]. {NIEPA NIPCCD}

Angelo, Douglas St., et al, 1971, **State library policy** : Its legislative and environmental contexts. {USIS}

Anger, Arthur L., et al, 1972, **Computers science** : The PL/I language. {DUL}

Annette, Mary, 1955, **Manual for cataloguing school libraries**. {JNU}

Anon, n.d., **ABC : Abridged building classification for architects, builders, civil engineers**. [International Council for Building Research Studies and Documentation, Rotterdam]. {BIS}

Anon, n.d., **Abbreviations for titles of periodicals**. [Indian Standards Institution]. {AIU}

Anon, n.d., **Abstracting services in science, technology, medicine agriculture, social science, humanity**. [International Federation for Documentation and Information]. {DEPT JNU}

Anon, n.d., **Agricultural documentation** : Responcibilities of libraries and information services. {IIMC}

Anon, n.d., **Audio-visual materials** : Development of a national cataloguing and information service : Report of joint feasibility study for the British Library and the Council for Educational Technology {IIMC}

Anon, n.d., **Australian government publications, 1974-82**. [National Library of Australia]. {NASSDOC}

Anon, n.d., **Auctralian public affairs information service** : A subject index to current literature, 1977-82. {NASSDOC}

Anon, n.d., **Author catalogue of printed books in European languages**, 8 vols. [National Library, Calcutta]. {NASSDOC}

Anon, n.d., **Automation in union catalogue of periodicals** : India and abroad, typed short bibliography. {NASSDOC}

Anon, n.d., **Bibliography of United Nations thesauri, classification nomenclatures.** [Inter-Organisation Board for Information Systems, Geneva]. {BIS}

Anon, n.d., **Canadian library directory**, 2 vols. [Canada National Library]. {ICWA}

Anon, n.d., **Catalogue of Government of India civil publications** : Subject-wise arranged corrected up to 31st December, 1959 : Supplement for the years 1968-70. [Controller of Publications, Delhi]. {IIFT ISI NASSDOC TDA}

Anon, n.d., **Catalogue of serials** : Indian Institute of Science Library, Bangalore. [INSDOC Union Catalogue Series, 2]. {DUL}

Anon, n.d., **Catalogue of type specimens**. {DUL}

Anon, n.d., **Cataloguing rules of the American Library Association and the Library of Congress, 1949-1958**. [American Library Association; U.S. Library of Congress]. {BIS IEG ZHL}

Anon, n.d., **Classification** : Class A : General works, polygraphy, 3rd edn. [U.S. Library of Congress] {CRRI}.

Anon, n.d., **Classification** : class B, 2nd edn. [U.S. Library of Congress]. {ISI}

Anon, n.d., **Classification** : Class H : Social sciences, 3rd edn. [U.S. Library of Congress]. {CRRI}

Anon, n.d., **Classification** : Class R : Medicine : 3rd edn. [U.S. Library of Congress]. {ISI}

Anon, n.d., **Convention papers** : All India library convention, 5th, May 23-26, 1985, Hardwar. [Government of India Librarians Association]. {NASSDOC}

Anon, n.d., **Cooperative cataloguing manual for the use of contributing libraries.** [U.S. Library of Congress]. {DUL}

Anon, n.d., **Curriculum guide for the school libraries in the elementary school.** [Detroit Public School]. {JNU}

Anon, n.d., **Delhi University Library** : The opening of the new library by S. Radhakrishnan. {JNU}

Anon, n.d., **Dilemma of the urban public library in developing countries.** [International Federation of Library Associations and Institutions; International Council for Adult Education]. {IIMC}

Anon, n.d., **Directory of British publishers**, 1961; 1967. {DUL}

Anon, n.d., **Economic analysis of special libraries with special reference to CSIR libraries**, memeo short bibliography. {NASSDOC}

Anon, n.d., **Editor and publisher international year book** : Encyclopaedia of the newspaper industry. {DUL}

Anon, n.d., **Final report on the ICAR institutions and Agricultural University libraries**. [ICAR]. {IEG}

Anon, n.d., **Final report on mechanised information services in the university library** : Phase-I : Planning. 13 pts. Pt 1 : Mechanised information services in the university library : Introduction and summary; Pt 2 : Summary of symposium on mechanised information services in the university library; Pt 3 : Inventory of available data bases; Pt 4 : Standards for cataloguing of magnetic tape material; Pt 5 : Nature of typical data bases; Pt 6 : Evaluation of generalised file management systems; Pt 7 : Experience with Library of Congress rare tapes; Pt 8 : Experimental on-line mathematics citation data base; Pt 9 : Development programme for a centre for information services; Pt 10 : Preliminary specifications (hardware and software) for a centre for information and documentation services (Interim report); Pt 11 : On the development of social science information; Pt 12 : Joint design and development of library systems; and Pt 13 : Library and human memory. [Institute of Library Research, University of California]. {BIS}

Anon, n.d., **First seminar of university librarians in India, Jaipur.** {NMML}

Anon, n.d., **A guide for authors in the preparation of manuscripts and illustrations**. {IIPA}

Anon, n.d., **A guide to micrographics**. [Bhabha Atomic Research Centre; Micrographic Congress of India]. {NASSDOC*}

Anon, n.d., **IFLA directory** : 1977; 1979; 1982-84; 1984-85; 1986-87; 1988-89. [International Federation of Library Associations and Institutions]. {NASSDOC}

Anon, n.d., **ISBD (B)** : International standard bibliographic description for books. [International Federation of Library Associations and Institutions]. {JNU}

Anon, n.d., **Impact of technology on the library building**. [Educational Facilities Laboratories, New Delhi]. {AIU}

Anon, n.d., **Indian publishers directory**, {NASSDOC}

Anon, n.d., **Industrial technical libraries of paperback books** : Little Libraries. [U.S. State Department]. {BIS}

Anon, n.d., **Information and its dissemination**. [Institute of Petroleum, London]. {BIS}

Anon, n.d., **Information processing** : Proceedings : International conference on information processing. {JNU}

Anon, n.d., **International standards for computers and information processing**. [International Organisation for Standardisation]. {BIS}

Anon, n.d., **International standards for documentation and terminology**, 3rd edn. [International Organisation for Standardisation]. {BIS}

Anon, n.d., **Investigation concerning the SFS information service and its users**. [Finnish Standards Association]. {BIS}

Anon, n.d., **Islamic libraries**, mimeo short bibliography. {NASSDOC}

Anon, n.d., **Librarianship as a profession**, mimeo short bibliography. {NASSDOC}

Anon, n.d., **Library and information science journals in India**, typed short bibliography. {NASSDOC}

Anon, n.d., **Library binding handbook**. [Library Building Institute]. {ISI}

Anon, n.d., **Library in the primary schools** : A report by sub-committee of School Library Association. {JNU}

Anon, n.d., **Literature recommendation** : Basic reference list for establishing an industrial library. [U.S. International Cooperation Administration]. {BIS}

Anon, n.d., **Manual of procedures for evaluation visits under standards for accredition**. {USIS}

Anon, n.d., **Microforms annual, 1982-83** : An international guide to microforms. {NASSDOC}

Anon, n.d., **Microforms annual, 1984-85** : An international guide to microforms. {NASSDOC}

Anon, n.d., **National agency for International Standard Book Numbering System** ; A manual. [Raja Rammohan Roy National Educational Resources Centres, New Delhi]. {NASSDOC}

Anon, n.d., **National Diet Library** : Organisation, functions and activities. [National Diet Library, Japan]. {AIU}

Anon, n.d., **National Documentation Centre on Mass Communication** : Report. [Ministry of Information and Broadcasting, New Delhi]. {IIMC}

Anon, n.d., **National information** : Guide to Indian periodicals, 1953-1956. {DSSW}

Anon, n.d., **National information system for social sciences**, typed short bibliography. {NASSDOC}

Anon, n.d., **New India directory of libraries and educational institutions of India, Pakistan, Burma and Ceylon**. {AIU IIT}

Anon, n.d., **Newspaper libraries**, mimeo short bibliography. {NASSDOC}

Anon, n.d., **Papers** : IASLIC symposium on the development of libraries in India under the Third Five Year Plan with particular reference to special libraries,

January 23-25, 1960, Calcutta. [Indian Association of Special Libraries and Information Centres]. {BIS}

Anon, n.d., **Papers** : Symposium on new technology in libraries : Prospects and problems for libraries in the Gulf States, 1982, Teheran. [Ministry of Petroleum and Minerals, Teheran]. {CRRI}

Anon, n.d., **Practice for layout of library catalogue code**. (IS : 1358-1950). [Indian Standards Institution]. {NAI}

Anon, n.d., **Practice for layout of library catalogue code**, rev edn., (IS : 1358-1967). [Indian Standards Institution]. {NASSDOC}

Anon, n.d., **Proceedings** : All India library convention. [Government of India Librarians Association]. {NMML}

Anon, n.d., **Public libraries**, mimeo short bibliography. {NASSDOC}

Anon, n.d., **Reading research in the Centre for Library Science and Methodology, 1981-85**. [Centre for Library Science and Methodology, Budapest]. {NASSDOC}

Anon, n.d., **Reference catalogue of Indian books in print**, 3 vols. {NASSDOC}

Anon, n.d., **Report, 1984-85**. [British Library Department of Oriental Manuscripts and Printed Books]. {NMML}

Anon, n.d., **Research in progress**, 4 vols. [Inter University Board of India and Ceylon]. {NASSDOC}

Anon, n.d., **Responsibilities of libraries and information service.** [Organisation for European Economic Co-operation]. {BIS}

Anon, n.d., **Rules for descriptive cataloguing in the Library of Congress**. [U.S. Library of Congress]. {BIS NAI SPA}

Anon, n.d., **Rules for descriptive cataloguing in the Library of Congress** : Supplement 1949-1951. [U.S. Library of Congress]. {ISI}

Anon, n.d., **Rules for making alphabetical indexes**. [Indian Standards Institution]. {AIU NASSDOC}

Anon, n.d., **Rules for making alphabetical indexes,** rev. edn., (IS : 1275-1976). [Indian Standards Institution]. {NASSDOC}

Anon, n.d., **Scientific and technical documentation centres**. [UNESCO]. {AIU}

Anon, n.d., **Secondary school libraries in Uttar Pradesh**. [Department of Education, Allahabad University]. {IEG}

Anon, n.d., **Souvenir** : All India library conference, 14th, 1964, Indore. [Indian Library Association]. {NASSDOC}

Anon, n.d., **Souvenir** : All India library conference, 32nd. [Indian Library Association]. {NASSDOC}

Anon, n.d., **Souvenir** : Silver Jubilee. [British Council Library, Madras]. {NASSDOC*}

Anon, n.d., **Specification for the abbreviation of titles of periodicals,** 2 pts., Pt. 1 : Principles; Pt. 2 : World abbreviation. [British Standards Institution]. {CRRI NASSDOC}

Anon, n.d., **Specification for alphabetical arrangement and the filing order of numerals and symbols**. (BS 1749 : 1969). [British Standards Institution]. {CRRI NASSDOC}

Anon, n.d., **Specification for bibliographic information interchange format for magnet tape**. (BS 4748 : 1971). [British Standards Institution]. {CRRI}

Anon, n.d., **Specification for book binding leather**. (IS : 2960-1964). [Indian Standards Institution]. {CRRI}

Anon, n.d., **Specification for book numbering**. (BS 4762 : 1971). [British Standards Institution]. {NASSDOC}

Anon, n.d., **Specification for data elements for the generation and exchange of serials records**. (BS 3532 : 1982). [British Standards Institution]. {CRRI}

Anon, n.d., **Specification for drawing filling equipment,** rev. edn. (IS : 2695-1974). [Indian Standards Institution]. {NASSDOC}

Anon, n.d., **Specification for general structure of preliminary pages of a book (tentative)**. (IS : 790-1956). [Indian Standards Institution]. {NASSDOC}

Anon, n.d., **Specification for librachine (mobile library)**. (IS : 2661-1964). [Indian Standards Institution]. {NASSDOC}

Anon, n.d., **Specification for library catalogue and abstract card**. (IS : 7150-1974) [Indian Standards Institution]. {NASSDOC}

Anon, n.d., **Specification for library furniture and fittings**. (IS : 785-1829 (Pt 1) : 1961). 2 pts. Pt. 1 : Timber; Pt. 2 : Steel. [Indian Standards Institution]. {CRRI NASSDOC}

Anon, n.d., **Specification for packages for use of libraries**. (IS : 2662-1964). [Indian Standards Institution]. {CRRI}

Anon, n.d., **Specification for page sizes for books**. (BS 1413 : 1970). [British Standards Institution]. {NASSDOC}

Anon, n.d., **Specification for the presentation of library directories**. (BS 4605 : 1970) [British Standards Institution]. {CRRI NASSDOC}

Anon, n.d., **Specification for the presentation of serial of publications, including periodicals**. (BS 2509 : 1970). [British Standards Institution]. {NASSDOC}

Anon, n.d., **Specification for sizes of folders and files**. (IS : 5457-1969). [Indian Standards Institution]. {NASSDOC}

Anon, n.d., **Specification for steel filing cabinets for general office purposes,** rev. edn. (IS : 3313-1974). [Indian Standards Institution]. {NASSDOC}

Anon, n.d., **Specification for steel shelving cabinets**, rev. edn. (IS : 3312-1974). [Indian Standards Institution]. {NASSDOC}

Anon, n.d., **Specification for the title leaves of a book**. (BS 4719 : 1971). [British Standards Institution]. {NASSDOC}

Anon, n.d., **Specification for title-page and back of title-page of a book**, rev. edn. (IS : 792-1964). [Indian Standards Institution]. {NASSDOC}

Anon, n.d., **Specification for wooden shelving cabinets (adjustable type)**. (IS : 4116-1967). [Indian Standards Institution]. {NASSDOC}

Anon, n.d., **Standardization in the domain of documentation**. [International Organization for Standardization, Hague]. {BIS}

Anon, n.d., **Study of the Information in the Philippine population programs**. [Population Center Foundation of the Philippines]. {NIH}

Anon, n.d., **Subject guide to books in print,** 1970-71; 1974; 1978-79; 1980-81; 1983-84. {NASSDOC}

Anon, n.d., **Symbols and notations for correction of illustration and illustration proofs**. (IS : 7140-1971). [Indian Standards Institution]. {NASSDOC}

Anon, n.d., **System analysis for information sciences**. [Department of Science and Technology, New Delhi]. {BIS CRRI JNU}

Anon, n.d., **UNESCO list of documents and publications** : 1972/76, 1980-81. [UNESCO]. {NASSDOC}

Anon, n.d., **USA standard** : Basic criteria for indexes, rev edn., (USAS Z 39. 4-1968). [American National Standards Institute]. {NASSDOC}

Anon, n.d., **Use of television by public library**. [American Library Association]. {JNU}

Anon, n.d., **Working papers and proceedings of the three symposia**, I : General vs special classification schemes; II : Inter library loan and exchange of materials in India; III : Social science documentation in India : IASLIC seminar, 3rd, 1964, Lucknow; [Indian Association of Special Libraries and Information Centres]. {NASSDOC SPA}

Anon, 1911, **List of subject headings for use in dictionary catalogue**, 3rd rev. edn. [American Library Association]. {NAI}

Anon, 1913, **Rules for compiling the catalogues of printed books, maps, etc., in the Imperial Library, Calcutta**. [National Library, Calcutta]. {NAI}

Anon, 1914, **Supplementary cataloguing rules for the guidance of assistants**. [Imperial Record Department]. {NAI}

Anon, 1915, **Classification** : Class P : Subclasses PNPR, PS and PZ, Literature, [U.S. Library of Congress]. {DUL}

Anon, 1918, **Rules for press listing**. [Imperial Record Department]. {NAI}

Anon, 1922, **Classification** : Class N : Fine Arts, 3rd edn., [U.S. Libray of Congress]. {ISI}

Anon, 1924, **Classification** : Class J : Political science with supplementary pages, 2nd edn. [U.S. Library of Congress]. {DUL}

Anon, 1927, **Classification** : Class Z : Bibliography and library science, 3rd edn. [U.S. Library of Congress]. {CRRI}

Anon, 1927, **Proceedings** : Anniversary conference of Library Association, 15th, 1927, Edinburg. [Library Association, London]. {NASSDOC}

Anon, 1928, **Cumulative instructions to depository libraries**. {NASSDOC}

Anon, 1928-81, **Cumulated book index** : World list of books in English language, 1928-32 to 1973; 1976 to 1981. {NASSDOC}

Anon, 1930, **Library instruction** : Junior and senior high schools. {ZHL}

Anon, 1931, **Colleges and reference library year book**, No. 3. [American Library Association]. {JNU}

Anon, 1932, **County libraries in Great Britain and Ireland**. [Library Association, London]. {NASSDOC}

Anon, 1933, **Manual of library routine**. {JNU}

Anon, 1935, **Proceedings** : All India library conference, 2nd, 1935, Lucknow. [Indian Library Association]. {NASSDOC}

Anon, 1937, **Classification** : Class P : Subclass PQ : Italian, Spanish and Portuguese literature with supplementary pages, part 2. [U.S. Library of Congress]. {DUL}

Anon, 1941, **Author entry for government publications**. [U.S. Library of Congress]. {NAI}

Anon, 1941, **Memoirs**. [Madras Library Association]. {NASSDOC}

Anon, 1942, **ALA rules for filing catalogue cards**. [American Library Association]. {CRRI IIT}

Anon, 1942, **Proceedings** : All India library conference, 5th, April 4-6, 1942, Bombay. [Indian Library Association]. {NASSDOC}

Anon, 1942, **Rules for indexing records**. [Imperial Record Department]. {NML}

Anon, 1943, **Public library service** : Its post-war reorganisation and development. [Library Association, London]. {NAI}

Anon, 1946, **Manuals** : Stack and reader division reference department. [U.S. Library of Congress]. {JNU}

Anon, 1946, **Proceedings** : All India library conference, 7th, January 25-28, 1946, Baroda. [Indian Library Association]. {NASSDOC}

Anon, 1946-67, **General catalogue of UNESCO publications and UNESCO sponsored publications**. supplements : 1946/59-1964/67. [UNESCO]. {NASSDOC}

Anon, 1947, **ASLIB meeting on planning and equipment of special libraries, April 6, 1946, London**. {CRRI}

Anon, 1947, **Report** : ASLIB meeting on planning and equipment of special libraries, April 6, 1946, London. [Association of Special Libraries and Information Bureaux]. {CRRI}

Anon, 1948, **Classification** : Class P : Subclass PG : Russian literature. [U.S. Library of Congress]. {DUL}

Anon, 1948, **Classification** : Class S : Agriculture, plant and animal industry, fish culture and fisheries, hunting, sports, 3rd edn. [U.S. Library of Congress]. {DUL}

Anon, 1948, **Descriptive list of professional and non-professional duties in libraries** : Primary draft. [American Library Association]. {USIS}

Anon, 1948, **Rules for the catalog of printed book** : Vatican Library. [American Library Association]. {NAI}

Anon, 1948-1981, **Book review digest 1948-73**; **1976-77**; **1979-80**; **1980-81.** {NASSDOC}

Anon, 1949-83, **Library literature** : An index to library and information science, 1949-51 to 1982-83. {NASSDOC USIS}

Anon, 1950, **Bibliographical references.** (BS 1629 : 1950). [British Standards Institution]. {CRRI NASSDOC}

Anon, 1950, **Bibliographical services** : Their present state and possibilities of improvement. [U.S. Library of Congress]. {JNU}

Anon, 1950, **Classification** : Class Q : Science, 5th edn. [U.S. Library of Congress]. {CRRI}

Anon, 1950, **Photoduplication service**. [U.S. Library of Congress]. {DUL}

Anon, 1950, **Planning the library** : A guide to those considering problems of library design, book storage and shelving. {DUL}

Anon, 1950-1974, **Bibliographical services throughout the world,** 1950-54; 1955-59; 1960-64; 1965-69; 1970-74. [UNESCO]. {DSSW DUL IIMC JNU NASSDOC NIEPA ZHL}

Anon, 1950-83, **British national bibliography**, 1950-54 to 1973; 1975 to 83, 2 vols. [British Library Bibliographic Services Division]. {NASSDOC}

Anon, 1951, **Alphabetical arrangement**. (BS 1749 : 1951). [British Standards Institution]. {CRRI}

Anon, 1951, **Army medical library classification** : Medicine. {DUL}

Anon, 1951, **Documentation techniques in the USA**. [Organisation for Economic Co-operation and Development, Paris]. {ISI}

Anon, 1951, **Libraries in India**. [Ministry of Education, New Delhi]. {BIS NMML}

Anon, 1951, **Library binding manual**. [American Library Association]. {IIT}

Anon, 1951, **Position classification and salary administration in libraries**. [American Library Association]. {IIT}

Anon, 1951, **Rules for compiling the catalogues of printed books, maps and music in the British Museum.** [British Museum, London]. {NAI}

Anon, 1951, **Sample catalog cards**, 2nd edn. [School of Library Science, Columbia University]. {ZHL}

Anon, 1951, **Subject headings** : A practical guide. [U.S. Library of Congress]. {CRRI USIS}

Anon, 1952, **Classification** : Class U : Military science, 3rd edn. [U.S. Library of Congress]. {JNU}

Anon, 1952, **Development of public libraries in Latin America** : The Sao Paulo conference. [UNESCO]. {IEG NASSDOC ZHL}

Anon, 1952, **Library trustees manual**. [Ohio Library Trustees Association]. {JNU}

Anon, 1952, **Souvenir** : Silver Jubilee. [State Regional Library, Guntur]. {NASSDOC*}

Anon, 1953, **Cataloguing of musical instruments.** [Government Museum, Madras]. {NAL}

Anon, 1954, **Development of public libraries in Africa** : Ibadan seminar. [UNESCO]. {IEG NASSDOC ZHL}

Anon, 1954, **Layout of periodicals**. (ISO/R 8-1954) (E). [International Organisation for Standardisation, Geneva]. {NASSDOC}

Anon, 1954, **Rules for descriptive cataloguing in the Library of Congress** : Phonorecords. [U.S. Library of Congress]. {IEG ZHL}

Anon, 1954, **Subject headings for financial libraries.** [Special Libraries Association, New York]. {ISI}

Anon, 1955, **Classification schedules for printed, microcopy and phonorecord materials in the Reference Department**, 2nd edn. [New York Public Library]. {DUL}

Anon, 1955, **Descriptive catalogue of documentary films.** [Films Division, Government of India]. {NAL}

Anon, 1955, **Medical classification**, 3rd edn. [Boston Medical Library]. {DUL}

Anon, 1955, **Recommendations for the storage of microfilm**. (BS : 1153 : 1955). [British Standards Institution]. {CRRI NASSDOC NMML}

Anon, 1955, **Short contents list of periodicals or other documents**, (ISO/R 18-1955) (E). [International Organisation for Standardisation, Geneva]. {NASSDOC}

Anon, 1955, **Ten years of United Nations publication, 1945-55** : A complete catalogue. [United Nations]. {DSSW}

Anon, 1955-1983, **Indian books in print** : A bibliography of Indian books in English language, 3 vols, Vol 1 : Author; Vol 2 : Title; Vol 3 : Subject guide. {ICA INSA NASSDOC}

Anon, 1956, **Extensions and corrections to the UDC**. [International Federation for Documentation and Information]. {IIT INSA}

Anon, 1956, **Filing rules for dictionary catalogues of the Library of Congress**. [U.S. Library of Congress]. {IEC NASSDOC}

Anon, 1956, **Handbook on the international exchange of publications**. [UNESCO]. {CRRI IEG}

Anon, 1956, **Public libraries for Asia** : The Delhi seminar. [UNESCO]. {NASSDOC NIEPA ZHL}

Anon, 1956, **Public library service**. [American Library Association]. {USIS}

Anon, 1957, **Design for elementary libraries**. [Department of School, City of South Bend]. {JNU}

Anon, 1957, **Education clearing houses and documentation centres**. [UNESCO]. {JNU}

Anon, 1957, **Exchange of ideas** : East and West meet the challenge : Final report : Seminar on the international exchange of publications in the Indo-Pacific area, 1957, Tokyo. {IEG}

Anon, 1957, **Proceedings** : International study conference on classification for information retrieval, 1957, {IEC IIT}

Anon, 1957, **Survey of secondary school libraries in U.P.** : Report. [Ministry of Education, New Delhi]. {MHA}

Anon, 1958, **Classification of type design**. {DUL}

Anon, 1958, **Microtext and microreading**. [County Technical Library Service, Hertfordshire]. {DUL}

Anon, 1958, **Proof corrections for printers and authors.** (IS : 1250-1958). [Indian Standards Institution]. {NASSDOC}

Anon, 1958, **Report** : University Grants Commission library committee. [University Grants Commission, New Delhi]. {SPA}

Anon, 1958, **Universal Decimal Classification** : Trilingual abridged edition. {JNU}

Anon, 1958-62, **Indian National Bibliography** : Cumulated Index 1958-62. [Central Reference Library, Calcutta]. {NASSDOC}

Anon, 1958-77, **Indian National Bibliography**. [Central Reference Library, Calcutta]. {DSSW INSA NASSDOC}

Anon, 1959, **Catalogue of Government of India civil publications** : Subject-wise arranged corrected up to 31st December, 1959. [Controller of Publications, Delhi]. {NASSDOC NIPCCD}

Anon, 1959, **Plans for six public library buildings**. [American Library Association]. {USIS}

Anon, 1959, **University and college libraries** : Containing the report and the proceedings of the Seminar on 'from publisher to reader' held on March 4-7, 1966. [University Grants Commission, New Delhi]. {DUL NASSDOC}

Anon, 1960, **American libraries** : Report : U.S. field seminar on library reference services for Japanese librarians, June 1960. [International House of Japan]. {DUL NASSDOC}

Anon, 1960, **Basic book collection for elementary grades**. [American Library Association]. {NIEPA USIS}

Anon, 1960, **Cassell's dictionary of publishing in Great Britain, the commonwealth and Ireland**. {ICCR}

Anon, 1960, **Classification of business literature**. [Graduate School of Business Administration Library, Harvard University]. {ISI}

Anon, 1960, **Code of practice relating to primary elements in the design of library buildings**. (IS : 1553-1960). [Indian Standards Institution]. {NASSDOC}

Anon, 1960, **Guidelines for library planners.** [American Library Association]. {IIT}

Anon, 1960, **Indian scientific and technical publications** : Exhibition. (National Library, Calcutta). {DUL}

Anon, 1960, **Information processing** : Proceedings : International conference on information processing. {JNU}

Anon, 1960, **Libraries in India**. [Ministry of Education, New Delhi]. {MHA NASSDOC}

Anon, 1960, **Report** : National Archives committee on archival legislation. [National Archives of India, New Delhi]. {MFL}

Anon, 1960, **Standards for school library programmes**. [American Association of School Librarians]. {JNU}

Anon, 1960, **Studying the community** : A basis for planning library adult education services. (Library Community Project). [American Library Association]. {USIS}

Anon, 1961, **Abstracts and synopses**. [International Organisation for Standardisation, Geneva]. (ISO/R 214-1961) (E). {NASSDOC}

Anon, 1961, **Author table for Indian names**. [National Library, Calcutta]. {NMML}

Anon, 1961, **Cataloguing rules** : Author and title entries. [American Library Association; Library Association, London]. {IIT MFL}

Anon, 1961, **The changing pattern of librarianship**. [Library Association, London]. {ICA}

Anon, 1961, **Documentation, indexing and retrieval of scientific information.** [US Committee on Government Operations]. {JNU}

Anon, 1961, **International system for the transliteration of Arabic characters.** (ISO/R 233-1961) (E). [International Organisation for Standardisation, Geneva]. {NASSDOC}

Anon, 1961, **Library and documentation journals**. [International Federation for Documentation and Information]. {NASSDOC}

Anon, 1961, **Papers** : Seminar on the rendering of Indic names, 1960-61, Calcutta. [Indian Association of Special Libraries and Information Centres]. {NASSDOC}

Anon, 1961, **Presentation of contributions to periodicals**. (ISO/R 215-1961) (E). [International Organisation for Standardisation, Geneva]. {NASSDOC}

Anon, 1961, **Report** : Advisory committee for libraries. [Ministry of Education, New Delhi]. {NASSDOC}

Anon, 1961, **Reproductions reference guide**. 2nd edn. {NASSDOC}

Anon, 1961, **Study of circulation control systems** : Public libraries, college and university libraries, special libraries. (Library Technology Project). [American Library Association]. {DUL IIT USIS}

Anon, 1961, **UDC**, 3rd edn. [British Standards Institution]. {ICCR}

Anon, 1962, **Directory of special and research libraries in India**. [Indian Association of Special Libraries and Information Centres]. {IIT ISI MFL NMML ZHL}

Anon, 1962, **Guide to use of Dewey Decimal Classification**. [Lake Placid Club Education Foundation]. {IIT USIS}

Anon, 1962, **Hospital library in Sweden**, tr. by Frykman. {DUL}

Anon, 1962, **Inter-library cooperation in England and Wales**. [H.M.S.O., London]. {NASSDOC}

Anon, 1962, **International inter-library lending** : A review of the literature. [International Federation of Library Associations and Institutions]. {NASSDOC}

Anon, 1962, **International scientific organisations**, : A guide to their library, documentation and information services. [U.S. National Science Foundation, International Science Information Studies]. {DUL}

Anon, 1962, **Libraries in the Netherlands**. [Netherlands Librarians Association]. {NASSDOC}

Anon, 1962, **Library service yearbook and directory**. [Punjab Library Association]. {IIT}

Anon, 1962, **Practice for alphabetical arrangement**. (IS : 382-1952). [Indian Standards Institution]. {NAI NASSDOC}

Anon, 1962, **Standards of public library service in England and Wales** : Report of the working party appointed by the Minister of Education in March, 1961. {NASSDOC}

Anon, 1962, **Transliteration of Hebrew** (ISO/R 259-1962) (E). [International Organisation for Standardisation, Geneva]. {NASSDOC}

Anon, 1963, **Article and reports reprinted from the Library Association Record for December, 1963.** [Library Association, London]. {NASSDOC}

Anon, 1963, **Automation and the Library of Congress**. [U.S. Library of Congress]. {BIS}

Anon, 1963, **Code of recommended practice for the form and presentation of periodicals of permanent value**. (CP 48 : 1963). [New Zealand Standards Institute, Wellington]. {NASSDOC}

Anon, 1963, **A comprehensive bibliography on operations research, 1957-58**. [Operations Research Society of America]. {INSA}

Anon, 1963, **Delhi Public Library** : Constitution, regulations of Delhi Library Board and rules of the library. [Delhi Library Board]. {NASSDOC}

Anon, 1963, **Does your firm need its own information service** : An enquiry into the economic advantages of an information service in small and medium-sized firms. [Organisation for Economic Cooperation and Development, Paris]. {TDA}

Anon, 1963, **Film cataloguing rules**. [Association of Special Libraries and Information Bureaux]. {SPA}

Anon, 1963, **Glossary of classification terms**. (IS : 2550-1963). [Indian Standards Institutions]. {ISI NASSDOC}

Anon, 1963, **Guide to the Universal Decimal Classification**. (BS 1000 C : 1963). [British Standards Institution]. {AIU IIT JNU NASSDOC}

Anon, 1963, **Indian standard glossary of classification terms**. [Indian Standards Institution]. {NASSDOC}

Anon, 1963, **International library directory** : A world directory of libraries. {ICWA}

Anon, 1963, **Introduction to the University of Chicago library** : A brief guide to the location and use of the library's service and resources. {NMML}

Anon, 1963, **Library furniture and equipment**. [American Library Association]. {DUL IIT NASSDOC ZHL}

Anon, 1963, **Library science in India today** : A symposium. [Bengal Library Association, Calcutta]. {NASSDOC*}

Anon, 1963, **Manual of style**, 11th edn. {INSA}

Anon, 1963, **National libraries** : Their problems and prospects : Symposium on national libraries in Europe, September 8-27, Vienna. [UNESCO]. {AIU BIS CRRI IEG IIMC MFL NASSDOC NIEPA NIPCCD}

Anon, 1963, **Papers** : All India library conference, 15th, 1965, Mysore. [Indian Library Association]. {NASSDOC}

Anon, 1963, **Prospects for library co-operation in New York city** : Planning for more effective utilisation of reference and research resources submitted by Nelson Associations Incorporated, New York. {DUL}

Anon, 1963, **Protecting the library and its resources** : A guide to physical protection and insurance : Report on a study conducted by Gage Babcock and Associates, Incorporated. [American Library Association]. {DUL IIT NASSDOC IIT}

Anon, 1963, **Recommendations for bibliographical references**, (IS : 2380-1963). [Indian Standards Institution]. {NASSDOC}

Anon, 1963, **Report** : International conference on cataloguing principles, October 9-14, 1961, Paris. [International Federation of Library Associations and Institutions]. {IIT ISI NIEPA NMML}

Anon, 1963, **Special libraries of Greater New York**, 10th edn. [Special Libraries Association, New York]. {DUL}

Anon, 1963, **Your library** : Readers guide to Karnatak University Library, Dharwar. {NASSDOC}

Anon, 1963-74, **Annual seminar.** No. 1: 1963; No. 2: 1964; No. 3: 1965; No. 4: 1966; No. 5: 1967; No. 6 : 1968, 2 pts; No. 7: 1969; No. 8: 1970; No. 9: 1971; No. 10: 1972, 2 pts; No. 11: 1974. [Documentation Research and Training Centre, Bangalore]. {IEG IIMC ISI JNU NASSDOC}.

Anon, 1964, **Acquisition, organisation and use of books and related materials.** [Trustees of New South Wales Public Library]. {JNU}

Anon, 1964, **Bibliography of dictionaries and encyclopaedias in Indian languages**. [National Library, Calcutta]. {ZHL}

Anon, 1964, **Code of practice relating to primary elements in the design of buildings for archives**. (IS : 2663-1964). [Indian Standards Institution]. {NASSDOC}

Anon, 1964, **Forecast of the cost of academic library services in Canada, 1965-1975**. [Association of College and University Libraries, Canada]. {JNU}

Anon, 1964, **Glossary of cataloguing terms in Indian regional languages.** [Indian Association of Special Libraries and Information Centres]. {NASSDOC SPA}

Anon, 1964, **Let's read together** : Books for family enjoyment, 2nd edn. [American Library Association; Association for Library Service to Children]. {USIS}

Anon, 1964, **Looking forward in documentation**. [Association of Special Libraries and Information Bureaux]. {BIS}

Anon, 1964, **Planning agency library manual**. [Council of Planning Librarians]. {SPA}

Anon, 1964, **Recommendations for the preparation of indexes for books, periodicals and other publications**, (BS 3700 : 1964). [British Standards Institution]. {CRRI NASSDOC}

Anon, 1964, **Student use of libraries** : An inquiry into the needs of students, libraries and the educational process. [American Library Association]. {USIS}

Anon, 1964, **Transactions** : Prague conference on information theory, statistical decision function, random processes, June 3, 1962. {INSA}

Anon, 1964, **Universal Decimal Classification** : Special subject edition for metallurgy. {DUL}

Anon, 1964, **Working conditions in Canadian public libraries**. [Canadian Library Association]. {JNU}

Anon, 1964, **Working papers** : Seminar on use of microforms and space management in libraries. [Sri Venkateshwar University Library, Tirupati].

Anon, 1964-72, **American library directory, 1964; 1971; 1972.** {IIT INSA JNU}

Anon, 1965, **Catalogue card reproduction.** [American Library Association]. {IIT}

Anon, 1965, **Code of practice for reinforced binding of library books and periodicals**. (IS : 3050-1965). [Indian Standards Institution]. {CRRI NASSDOC}

Anon, 1965, **Code of practice for storage and use of microfilms of permanent value.** (IS : 3130-1965). [Indian Standards Institution]. {NASSDOC}

Anon, 196[illegible], **Education for librarianship in India**. [Indian Association of Special Libraries and Information Centres]. {IIT MFL NASSDOC}

Anon, 1965, **Information sciences**. [U.S. Air Force Office of Scientific Research]. {JNU}

Anon, 1965, **Introduction to cataloguing and classification of books**, 2nd edn. [American Library Association]. {IIFT}

Anon, 1965, **Library science in Indian universities** : Report. [University Grants Commission, New Delhi]. {ICA IIC JNU NASSDOC NIEPA}

Anon, 1965, **Papers** : All India library conference, 15th, 1965, Mysore. [Indian Library Association]. {NASSDOC}

Anon, 1965, **Papers** : Seminar on library science in Southeast Asia, December 18-20, 1964, Bangkok. [Association of Southeast Asian Institutions of Higher Learning]. {NASSDOC NIEPA}

Anon, 1965, **Reaching readers** : The library's responsibility and opportunity : Papers with a summary of discussions and recommendations. Regional conference workshop for librarians, 6th, December 6-13, 1964, Albay. {NASSDOC}

Anon, 1965, **Role of the library in the development of the community** : Society for the promotion and improvement of libraries seminar, April 12-18, 1964, Karachi. [Hamdard National Foundation, Karachi]. {NASSDOC}

Anon, 1965, **Sizes of correspondence envelopes**. (IS : 3338-1965). [Indian Standards Institution]. {NASSDOC}

Anon, 1965, **Souvenir** : All India library conference, 15th, 1965, Mysore. [Indian Library Association]. {NASSDOC}

Anon, 1965, **Universal Decimal Classification** : Special subject edition for education. {DUL}

Anon, 1965, **University and college libraries.** [University Grants Commission, New Delhi]. {BIS DUL IEG IIMC IIT JNU NIEPA}

Anon, 1965, **User and library information service**. [Indian Association of Special Libraries and Information Centres]. {IIFT}

Anon, 1965, **Working papers and proceedings** : IASLIC seminar, 2nd, 1965, Chandigarh : Part-I : Users and library information services. [Indian Association of Special Libraries and Information Centres]. {SPA}

Anon, 1966, **Bibliography on work-flow in libraries**. [Council of Scientific and Industrial Research, New Delhi]. {INSDOC NASSDOC}.

Anon, 1966, **Children's literature** : A guide to reference sources. [U.S. Library of Congress]. {USIS}

Anon, 1966, **Code of practice for library lighting**. (IS : 2672-1966). [Indian Standards Institution]. {NASSDOC}

Anon, 1966, **Code of practice for the processing of microfilms**, Silver halide. (IS : 3083-1966). [Indian Standards Institution]. {NASSDOC}

Anon, 1966, **DDC descriptor frequencies**. [Defence Documentation Centre]. {IIT}

Anon, 1966, **Development of performance standards for library binding**, Phase 1: Report of the survey, April, 1961; Phase 2: Report on a study conducted by library technology project. [American Library Association]. {BIS IIT}

Anon, 1966, **Information handling in the National Standard Reference Data System**. (NBS, Technical Note 290). [U.S. National Bureau of Standards]. {BIS}

Anon, 1966, **INSDOC seminar on work-flow in libraries**, November 21-24, 1966, New Delhi, 3 pts. Pt-1 : Special libraries; Pt-2 : University libraries; Pt-3 : Government libraries. {BIS}

Anon, 1966, **Libraries of the United Nations** : A descriptive guide. [United Nations]. {ICWA IIC IIT JNU NIH}

Anon, 1966, **Library statistics** : A handbook of concepts, definitions and terminology. [American Library Association, Statistics Coordinating Project]. {USIS}

Anon, 1966, **Neighbourhood library centres and services**. [National Book Trust, New Delhi]. {JNU}

Anon, 1966, **Origins of the America's college library, 1838-1900**. {JNU}

Anon, 1966, **Papers** : All India library conference, 1965, Mysore. [Indian Library Association]. {CRRI}

Anon, 1966, **Papers** : IASLIC national seminar, 4th, 1966, Hyderabad. [Indian Association of Special Libraries and Information Centres]. {NASSDOC}

Anon, 1966, **Papers** : Seminar on work flow in libraries, November 21-24, 1966, New Delhi; 3 vols., Vol. 1 : Special libraries; Vol II : University libraries; Vol. III : Government libraries. [Indian National Scientific Documentation Centre, New Delhi]. {NASSDOC NMML SPA}

Anon, 1966, **Personnel organisation and procedure** : A manual suggested for use in public libraries, 2nd edn. [American Library Association]. {DUL USIS}

Anon, 1966, **Practical approach to information and data retrieval**. [Boston Industrial Education Institute]. {ISI}

Anon, 1966, **Practical information for seminar members** : Working paper : International seminar on the development of public libraries in Asia, October 6-26, 1966, Delhi. [UNESCO]. {NASSDOC}

Anon, 1966, **Proceedings** : National symposium on information display, 7th, Technical session. [Society for Information Display]. {JNU}

Anon, 1966, **Reference research and the regionalism** : Selected papers from 53rd conference of Texas Library Association. {JNU}

Anon, 1966, **Report** : Working group on libraries, 1964, New Delhi. [Planning Commission, New Delhi]. {AIU CRRI JNU MFL MHA NASSDOC NCAER NERC NIEPA NIPCCD NMML}

Anon, 1966, **Souvenir** : All India library conference, 16th, 1966, Chandigarh. [Indian Library Association]. {NASSDOC}

Anon, 1966, **Style manual for authors and printers of Australian Government publications**. [Australia Style Manual Committee, 1964]. {DUL}

Anon, 1966, **Working papers for the symposia** : IASLIC conference, 5th, 1963, Pune, Pt. I : Document and data processing in academic research and special libraries in India; Pt. II : Problems and prospects of library associations in India. [Indian Association of Special Libraries and Information Centres]. {NASSDOC}

Anon, 1966, **Working papers of the two symposia** : IASLIC seminar, 4th 1966, Hyderabad, Pt. 1 : Procurement of government publications and technical reports; Pt. 2 : Devaluation : Its impact on the development of libraries in India. [Indian Association of Special Libraries and Information Centres]. {NASSDOC SPA}

Anon, 1966-84, **Annual review of information science and technology**, 19 vols {CRRI NASSDOC USIS}

Anon, 1967, **American national standards for periodicals** : Format and arrangement. (ANSI Z39.5-1967). [American National Standards Institute]. {NASSDOC}

Anon, 1967, **Anglo-American Cataloguing Rules**. [American Library Association]. {NASSDOC}

Anon, 1967, **Application of international classification of diseases and neurology**. [World Health Organisation]. {JNU}

Anon, 1967, **Book development in Asia** : A report on the production and distribution of books. [UNESCO]. {DUL}

Anon, 1967, **Catalogue of publications issued by Government of Uttar Pradesh and obtainable from the book depot, Government Press, Allahabad, for the year ending, 1965-66** : Corrected up to September, 1966. {NASSDOC}

Anon, 1967, **Centres of advanced study in Indian universities**. [University Grants Commission, New Delhi]. {NASSDOC}

Anon, 1967, **Conference on mechanised information storage, retrieval and dissemination**. {NMML}

Anon, 1967, **Developments in classification** : DRTC annual seminar, 2 vols. [Documentation Research And Training Centre]. {NASSDOC}

Anon, 1967, **Fifteen years of activity of the association, 1953-67**. [Delhi Library Association]. {NASSDOC*}

Anon, 1967, **Glossary of cataloguing terms**. (IS : 796-1966). [Indian Standards Institution]. {NAI NASSDOC}

Anon, 1967, **Glossary of terms for wooden furniture.** (IS : 4415-1967). [Indian Standards Institution]. {NASSDOC}

Anon, 1967, **Indian library science abstracts**. [Indian Association of Special Libraries and Information Centres]. {NASSDOC}

Anon, 1967, **Indian standard glossary of cataloguing terms**, rev edn. [Indian Standards Institution]. {ICA IIMC JNU NASSDOC}

Anon, 1967, **Inter-library cooperation** : A sampling of inter-library cooperation programmes. [American Library Association; Committee on Inter Library Co-operation]. {DUL}

Anon, 1967, **The library in the university** : The University of Tennessee library lectures, 1949-1967. {USIS}

Anon, 1967, **Library resources on East Asia** : Reports and working papers for the 10th meeting of the committee on American library resources. [Association for Asian Studies]. {JNU}

Anon, 1967, **List of official publications not included in the general catalogue of Government of India publications issued during the period 1-1-1940 to 31-12-1960**. {NASSDOC}

Anon, 1967, **Minimum standards for public library systems, 1966**. [Standards committee and subcommittees of the Public Library Association; American Library Association]. {USIS}

Anon, 1967, **Proceedings** : Seminar of university librarians in India, 1967, Jaipur. [Rajasthan University]. {DUL IIT}

Anon, 1967, **Recommendations for the abbreviation of titles of periodicals** (BS. 4148-1967). [British Standards Institution]. {CRRI}

Anon, 1967, **School library.** [Department of Education and Science, Great Britain]. {JNU}

Anon, 1967, **Seminar of college librarians in Rajasthan, Jaipur, 1966**. {JNU NMML}

Anon, 1967, **Seminar on library and information services for management**. [Liverpool College of Commerce]. {NMML}

Anon, 1967, **Social science research and library development** : Summary proceedings. [Indian Council of World Affairs; Indian School of International Studies]. {NASSDOC*}

Anon, 1967, **Souvenir** : IASLIC conference, 7th, December 27-30, 1967, Delhi. [University of Delhi]. {NASSDOC}

Anon, 1967, **Standards for library services for the blind and visually handicapped.** [American Library Association]. {DUL}

Anon, 1967, **Standards for teachers college libraries**. [New Zealand Library Association]. {JNU}

Anon, 1967, **Study of 1967 annual salaries of members of Special Library Association**. [Personnel Committee of Special Libraries Association]. {JNU}

Anon, 1967, **Style manual**, rev. edn. [U.S. Government Printing Office]. {NASSDOC}

Anon, 1967, **A survey of the contents of existing national bibliographies**. [UNESCO]. {NASSDOC*}

Anon, 1967, **Working papers and proceedings** : IASLIC conference, 4th, 1967, Dhanbad. [Indian Association of Special Libraries and Information Centres]. {SPA}

Anon, 1967, **Working papers for the symposia** : IASLIC conference, 6th, 1965, Trivandrum, Pt 1-3 : Colon Classification local documentation lists, library organisation and social science research, 1967; Pt. 4 : Colon Classification, local documentation lists, library organisation and social science research, 1967. [Indian Association of Special Libraries and Information Centres]. {NASSDOC SPA}

Anon, 1968, **Library, information and archive work**. [Ministry of Labour, Great Britain]. {JNU}

Anon, 1968, **Abbreviations of generic names in titles of periodicals**. [International Organisation for Standardisation, Geneva]. (ISO/R 833-1968) (E/F). {NASSDOC}

Anon, 1968, **Abbreviations of typical words in bibliographical references**. [International Organisation for Standardisation, Geneva]. (ISO/R 832-1968) (E/F). {NASSDOC}.

Anon, 1968, **American national standards for library statistics**. (ANSI Z39.5-1968). [American National Standards Institute]. {NASSDOC}

Anon, 1968, **Bibliographical references** : Essential elements. (ISO/R 690-1968) (E). [International Organisation for Standardisation, Geneva]. {NASSDOC}

Anon, 1968, **Bibliographies and reference works including abstract journals, library journals, books about books and standard works,** 2 parts, pt 1: A-J. {NASSDOC}

Anon, 1968, **Development of library facilities in universities and colleges**. [University Grants Commission, New Delhi]. {AIU IIT MHA}

Anon, 1968, **Directory of booksellers, publishers, libraries and librarians in India, 1968-69**. {SPA}

Anon, 1968, **Evaluation of the MEDLARE demand research services**. [U.S. National Library of Medicine]. {USIS}

Anon, 1968, **Exhibition of scientific and technical books** : Catalogue. {DUL}

Anon, 1968, **Final report** : UNESCO meeting of experts on the national planning of library services in Asia, December 11-19, 1967, Colombo. {NASSDOC}

Anon, 1968, **Guide for preparation of manuscript of an article in a learned periodical**. (IS : 4731-1968). [Indian Standards Institution]. {NASSDOC}

Anon, 1968, **International system for the transliteration of Greek characters into Latin characters.** (ISO/R 843-1968) (E). [International Organisation for Standardisation, Geneva]. {NASSDOC}

Anon, 1968, **International system for the transliteration of Slavic Cyrillic characters**, 2nd edn. (ISO/R 9-1968) (E). [International Organisation for Standardisation, Geneva]. {NASSDOC}

Anon, 1968, **Libraries in social education** : Report of the national seminar on libraries in social education 6th September 26—October 5, 1955 2nd ed. [Indian Adult Education Association]. {NIPCCD}

Anon, 1968, **Library Association**. [Committee on Scientific Library Service, Library Association, London]. {IIT}

Anon, 1968, **Papers** : FID pre-congress seminar on education and training : Theory and provision with a look at new developments and an example of the challenges confronting information workers, 1978, Edinburg. [International Federation for Documentation and Information]. {NASSDOC}

Anon, 1968, **Planning the public library**. [American Society of Planning Officials]. {SPA}

Anon, 1968, **Report** : National Library reviewing committee, 1968. [National Library, Calcutta]. {JNU}

Anon, 1968, **A report on the supply and training of librarians**. [Department of Education and Science, Great Britain]. {NIEPA}

Anon, 1968, **Standards and objectives for school libraries**. [Library Association of Australia]. {JNU}

Anon, 1968, **Survey of special libraries serving the Federal Government.** [U.S. Department of Health Education and Welfare]. {BIS}

Anon, 1968, **USA standard for compiling book publishing statistics**. (USAS Z 39.8-1968). [American National Standards Institute]. {NASSDOC}

Anon, 1968, **Working of central museums** : Report : Central museums review committee, 1968, New Delhi. {AIU}

Anon, 1968, **Working papers for the symposia** : IASLIC seminar, 5th, October 7-9, 1968, Durgapur, Pt. I : Selective dissemination of information for India; Pt. II : Functions and problems of library personnel in special libraries of India. [Indian Association of Special Libraries and Information Centres]. {NASSDOC}

Anon, 1968-71, **International computer bibliography**, 1968; 1971. {NASSDOC}

Anon, 1969, **Abridged Bliss Classification** : The bibliographic classification of Henry Evelyn Bliss revised for school libraries. [Bliss Classification Working Party]. {DUL}

Anon, 1969, **Aligned list of descriptors** : Alphabetical order. [Organisation for Economic Co-operation and Development, Paris]. {NASSDOC}

Anon, 1969, **American national standards for the abbreviation of titles of periodicals.** (ANSI Z39.5-1969). [American National Standards Institute]. {NASSDOC}

Anon, 1969, **Children's catalogue**, 12th edn. {USIS}

Anon, 1969, **Final report** : Project for evaluating the benefits from university libraries. [University of Durham]. {NIEPA}

Anon, 1969, **Index of a publication**. (ISO/R 999-1969. (E). [International Organisation for Standardisation, Geneva]. {NASSDOC}

Anon, 1969, **International subscription agents** : An annotated directory, 2nd edn. [American Library Association]. {DUL}

Anon, 1969, **Manual for new members of the staff**. [County Library]. {JNU}

Anon, 1969, **Manual of style**, 12th edn. {INSA}

Anon, 1969, **National Library of Medicine classification** : A scheme for the shelf arrangement of books in the field of medicine and its related sciences, 3rd edn. [U.S. National Library of Medicine]. {USIS}

Anon, 1969, **On research libraries** : Statement and recommendations. [American Council of Learned Societies Devoted to Humanistic Studies, Committee on Research Libraries]. {IIT INSA USIS}

Anon, 1969, **Papers** : IASLIC conference on library profession in India : Its status and responsibilities and standardised library practices and job classification, 1969, Bombay. [Indian Association of Special Libraries and Information Centres]. {CRRI}

Anon, 1969, **Physics and astronomy classification scheme**. [American Institute of Physics]. {IIT}

Anon, 1969, **Proceedings of the General Council** : IFLA annual. [International Federation of Library Association and Institutions]. {NASSDOC}

Anon, 1969, **Public library systems in the United States** : A survey of multi-jurisdictional systems. [American Library Association]. {USIS}

Anon, 1969, **Scientific and technical information in Canada**. [Science Council of Canada]. {JNU}

Anon, 1969, **Subject indices list.** [Central Reference Library, Calcutta]. {NASSDOC*]

Anon, 1969, **Thesaurus and faceted classification for engineering and related subjects.** {IIT}

Anon, 1969, **Title-leaves of a book**. (ISO/R 1086-1969) (E). [International Organisation for Standardisation, Geneva]. {NASSDOC*}

Anon, 1969, **USA standard for permanent and durable library catalogue cards.** (USAS Z 35.1-1969). [American National Standards Institute]. {NASSDOC}

Anon, 1969, **Universal Decimal Classification** : Ten years supplement to abridged UDC editions, 1958-1968. [UNESCO; FID]. {ICA IIMC IIT NASSDOC}

Anon, 1969, **Universal reference system**, 10 vols. {NMML}

Anon, 1969, **World guide to technical information and documentation services.** [UNESCO]. {CRRI NMML}

Anon, 1969-1983, **Books in print 1969-71; 1973-74 to 1982-83**. {NASSDOC NIH}

Anon, 1970, **American national standards practice for storage of processed silver-gelatin micro-film**. (ANSI PH5.4-1970). [American National Standards Institute]. {NASSDOC}

Anon, 1970, **Bibliography on documentation**. {JNU}

Anon, 1970, **Biographical directory of librarians in the United States and Canada**, 5th edn. {NASSDOC}

Anon, 1970, **Guide for abbreviations of words in titles of periodicals using Roman alphabet**, rev edn. (IS : 18-1970). [Indian Standards Institution]. {NASSDOC}

Anon, 1970, **Guide to national bibliographical centres.** [UNESCO]. {DUL IIMC NASSDOC USIS}

Anon, 1970, **Information retrieval systems** : Subject authority list, 7th edn. [American Petroleum Institute]. {IIT}

Anon, 1970, **International seminar on electronic data processing in libraries, Regersburg**. {JNU}

Anon, 1970, **Junior high school library catalog**, 2nd edn. {USIS}

Anon, 1970, **Landscape filling index**. [Institute of Landscape Architects]. {SPA}

Anon, 1970, **Library automation at the New York Public Library and the Association of New York Libraries for Technical Services**. [LARC]. {USIS}

Anon, 1970, **Microform retrieval equipment guide**. [Bastuibak Archives and Records Service, Washington]. {BIS}

Anon, 1970, **Papers** : IASLIC seminar, 6th, November 2-5, 1970, Bangalore. [Indian Association of Special Libraries and Information Centres]. {BIS JNU NMML}

Anon, 1970, **Public library services** : Bahamas. [UNESCO]. {NASSDOC*}

Anon, 1970, **Reference service-in-action** : Processing and servicing of special material in libraries. [Indian Association of Special Libraries and Information Centres, Calcutta]. {IEG NAI}

Anon, 1970, **Report** : National Library committee to enquire into the strained relations among the members of staff, 1969. [National Library, Calcutta]. {JNU}

Anon, 1970, **Standards for library functions at the state level**, rev edn., [American Association of State Libraries, Standards Revision Committee. {USIS}

Anon, 1970, **System scope for library automation and generalised information storage and retrieval at Stanford University**. {IIT}

Anon, 1970, **Training course in documentation techniques in Asia, July 20—August 21, 1970, Tokyo**. [Japanese National Commission for UNESCO]. {NASSDOC}

Anon, 1970, **Users of documentation**. {JNU}

Anon, 1970, **Working papers and proceedings** : DRTC seminar on cataloguing, 1970, Bangalore. [Documentation Research and Training Centre, Bangalore]. {NASSDOC}

Anon, 1970-71, **Catalogue of government publications**. [HMSO, Great Britain]. {NASSDOC}

Anon, 1970-1984, **Bowker annual of library and book trade information**. {IIT JNU NASSDOC NCAER NIH USIS}

Anon, 1970-1984, **British books in print** {NASSDOC}

Anon, 1971, **American national standards for directories of libraries and information centres**. (ANSI Z39.5.-1971). [American National Standards Institute]. {NASSDOC}

Anon, 1971, **American national standards for identification number for serial publications**. (ANSI Z39.5-1971). [American National Standards Institute].{NASSDOC}

Anon, 1971, **American national standards for title leaves of a book.** (ANSI Z39.5-1971). [American National Standards Institute]. {NASSDOC}

Anon, 1971, **American national standards for writing abstracts**. (ANSI Z39.5-1971). [American National Standards Institute]. {NASSDOC}

Anon, 1971, **Anglo-American Cataloguing Rules** : North American Text, with supplement of additions and changes. [American Library Association]. {JNU}

Anon, 1971 **Authors and writer's who's who**, 6th. edn. {NMML RTL}

Anon, 1971, **College libraries** : Recommended standards of library provision in colleges of technology and other establishment of further education. [Library Association, London]. {DUL ICA}

Anon, 1971, **Computers and computation**. {NASSDOC}

Anon, 1971, **Directory of college and university libraries in New York State.** [University of the State of New York; State Education Department]. {JNU}

Anon, 1971, **A general description of an approach to computerised bibliographical control.** [International Labour Office, Intergrated Scientific Information System]. {TDA}

Anon, 1971, **Guide for handling, testing and storage of monochrome photographic prints**, (IS : 6299-1971). [Indian Standards Institution]. {NASSDOC}

Anon, 1971, **Libraries as educational tools**. [Sri Venkateswara University, Tirupati]. {JNU}

Anon, 1971, **Libraries in Finland**. [Finnish Library Association, Helsinki]. {NASSDOC*}

Anon, 1971, **National catalogue of university level books**. {DSSW NASSDOC}

Anon, 1971, **Review of national scientific and technical information policy** : Germany. [Organisation for Economic Co-operation and Development, Paris]. {CRRI ICA JNU}

Anon, 1971, **Role of the library in national reconstruction** : Society for the promotion and improvement of libraries seminar, October 30—November 3, 1967, Rawalpindi. [Hamdard National Foundation, Karachi]. {NASSDOC}

Anon, 1971, **Study of characteristics, costs and magnitude of inter-library loans in academic libraries**. [Association of Research Libraries, Washington]. {JNU}

Anon, 1971, **UNISIST** : Synopsis of the feasibility study on a World Science Information System. [UNESCO; International Council of Scientific Unions]. {BIS DSSW IIMC NASSDOC ZHL}

Anon, 1971, **UNISIST study report on the feasibility of a world science information**. [UNESCO]. {BIS DSSW IIMC NASSDOC ZHL}

Anon, 1971, **Working papers and proceedings** : DRTC seminar on reference service. [Documentation Research and Training Centre, Bangalore]. {NASSDOC}

Anon, 1972, **American national standards system for the romanisation of Arabic** 12th rev edn. (ANSI Z39.12-1972). [American National Standards Institute]. {NASSDOC}

Anon, 1972, **American national standards system for the romanisation of Japanese**, rev edn. (ANSI Z39.11-1972). [American National Standards Institute]. {NASSDOC}

Anon, 1972, **Annual report of the Library of Congress, 1972**. [U.S. Library of Congress]. {JNU}

Anon, 1972, **Care of books and documents**. [Library Association, London]. {ZHL}

Anon, 1972, **Code of practice for handling and storage of microtransparencies**, rev. edn., (IS : 3130-1972). [Indian Standards Institution]. {NASSDOC}

Anon, 1972, **Content Analysis** : A technique for systematic inference from communications. {NASSDOC}

Anon, 1972, **A directory of libraries and library training programme in Thailand**. [UNESCO Regional Office for Education in Asia, Bangkok]. {NASSDOC NIEPA}

Anon, 1972, **Education, library science, journalism** : A bibliography of doctoral dissertations, 1857-1970. [Inter-University Board of India and Ceylon, New Delhi]. {JNU NMML}

Anon, 1972, **Examples illustrating Anglo-American Cataloguing Rules** : British text. [Library Association, London]. {ZHL}

Anon, 1972, **Final report** : International congress on the universal availability of publications. [UNESCO]. {NASSDOC}

Anon, 1972, **Guide to selected computer-based information services.** [Association of Special Libraries and Information Bureaux]. {CRRI}

Anon, 1972, **International standard classification of education** (ISCED) : Three stage classification system, 2pts. [UNESCO]. {AIU}

Anon, 1972, **International standardisation of library and documentation techniques**. [UNESCO]. {ICA}

Anon, 1972, **ISBN** : International standard book numbering (incorporating the recommendations for implementing the Standard Book Numbering Scheme). [Standard Book Numbering Agency, London]. {NASSDOC}

Anon, 1972, **Issues in library administration** : Papers presented at the U.S.-Japan conference on libraries and information science in higher education, 2nd, 1972. {JNU}

Anon, 1972, **Libraries and information technology** : A national system challenge : A report to the Council of Library Resources. [National Academy of Sciences, Washington]. {USIS}

Anon, 1972, **Library and information sciences** : An ERIC bibliography [Educational Resources Information Centre]. {NASSDOC}

Anon, 1972, **NCC thesaurus of computing terms**, 4th edn, 2 vols, Vol. 1 : Alphabetic; Vol. 2 : Hierarchy listing. {NASSDOC}

Anon, 1972, **National Library Bill, 1972** : Report and evidence : India, Lok Sabha, Joint Committee on the National Library Bill. {AIU NMML}

Anon, 1972, **Papers** : IASLIC conference, 9th, 1972, Calcutta. [Indian Association of Special Libraries and Information Centre]. {IIT INSA JNU MMTC}

Anon, 1972, **Problems and prospects of fundamental research in multidisciplinary fields** : Computer science. [Organisation for Economic Co-operation and Development, Paris; Committée for Science Policy]. {NASSDOC}

Anon, 1972, **Purchase of books by public libraries**. [Department of Education and Science, Great Britain]. {NIPCCD}

Anon, 1972, **Report** : Seminar on public library system, 1972, Bangalore. {JNU}

Anon, 1972, **Scope for automatic data processing in the British library**, 2 pts. [Department of Education and Science, Great Britain]. {NASSDOC}

Anon, 1972, **Souvenir** : Shri Sanmati Pustakalaya Trust, Jaipur. {NASSDOC*}

Anon, 1972, **Standard industrial classification manual**. {TDA}

Anon, 1972, **World guide to library school and training course in documentation**. [UNESCO]. {ICA IIT JNU NASSDOC NERC NIEPA USIS}

Anon, 1973, **American library directory**: A classified list of libraries in the U.S. and Canada with personnel and statistical data. {ICWA}

Anon, 1973, **Aspects of public library management** : The application of new management processes to the library services. [Library Advisory Council for England]. {NIPCCD ZHL}

Anon, 1973, **Automated information management in public administration** : Present development and impacts. [Organisation of Economic Co-operation and Development, Paris]. {TDA}

Anon, 1973, **Bibliography of publications issued by UNESCO or under its auspices, 1946-1971**. [UNESCO]. {NASSDOC}

Anon, 1973, **Classification research** : India, 1968-1973. [Documentation Research and Training Centre, Bangalore]. {BIS}

Anon, 1973, **A compressed term index language for library and information science.** [Association of Special Libraries and Information Bureaux]. {NASSDOC}

Anon, 1973, **Computer programming problems** : Batch-I. [National Computer Centre, Manchester]. {NASSDOC}

Anon, 1973, **First All India workshop on the methods of teaching and evaluation in library science, May 15-30, 1973, Delhi.** {DUL}

Anon, 1973, **ISIS** : A general description of an approach to computerised bibliographical control. [International Labour Office]. {NASSDOC}

Anon, 1973, **Introduction to indexing and abstracting for technical information systems**. {TDA}

Anon, 1973, **Manpower in the field of documentation and library services.** [UNESCO]. {CRRI ICA}

Anon, 1973, **Non-book materials cataloguing rules** : Integrated code of practice and draft revision of the Anglo-American Cataloguing Rules. [Library Association Media Cataloguing Rules Committee; National Council for Educational Technology, London]. {NASSDOC}

Anon, 1973, **Papers** : Conference on informatics, 1973, Durham. [Association of Special Libraries and Information Bureaux]. {CRRI}

Anon, 1973, **Public libraries and their use.** [Department of Education and Science, Great Britain]. {NIPCCD}

Anon, 1973, **Public library service** : Reorganisation and after. [Department of Education and Science, Great Britain]. {NIPCCD}

Anon, 1973, **Recommendations for bibliographical catalogue reference**. [Indian Standards Institution]. {NAI}

Anon, 1973, **Souvenir** : All India library conference, 20th, 1973, Hyderabad. [Indian Library Association]. {NASSDOC}

Anon, 1973, **Study on national structures for documentation and library services in countries with different levels of development, with particular reference to the needs of developing countries**. [UNESCO]. {ICA}

Anon, 1973, **Subject guide to class 'Ref'** : Current reference books. [University of Cambridge Library]. {NASSDOC}

Anon, 1973, **UNISIST International Serials Data Systems (ISDS).** [UNESCO]. {BIS}

Anon, 1974, **Anglo-American Cataloguing Rules** : British text. [Library Association, London]. {AIU IIT ISI JNU ZHL}

Anon, 1974, **Clinic on library applications of data processing**, 24th, 1974, Illinois. [University of Illinois at Urbana-Champaign]. {USIS}

Anon, 1974, **Design of information in the social sciences** : Size and growth of monograph literature with particular reference to the social sciences. [Bath University Library]. {BCL NASSDOC*}

Anon, 1974, **Directory of co-operative libraries and documentation services.** [ICA, London]. {ICA}

Anon, 1974, **A directory of information resources in the United States Federal Government, with a supplement of government sponsored information analysis centres**. [U.S. Library of Congress, National Referral Centre]. {USIS}

Anon, 1974, **Glossary of terms relating to wooden furniture and fixtures**, rev. edn. (IS : 4415-1974). {NASSDOC}

Anon, 1974, **Granthalaya shastra paribhasha kosh**. {NASSDOC NMML}

Anon, 1974, **Guide to the National Archives of the United States**. [U.S. National Archives and Records Service]. {USIS}

Anon, 1974, **Guidelines for thesaurus structure, construction and use.** [American National Standard Institute]. {CRRI}

Anon, 1974, **ISBD (S)** : International standard bibliographic description for serials. [International Federation o Library Associations and Institutions, Joint Working Group on the International Standard Bibliographic Description for Serials]. {NASSDOC}

Anon, 1974, **Information technology in local government** : A survey of the development of urban and regional information systems in five European countries. [Organisation for Economic Cooperation and Development, Paris]. {BCL}

Anon, 1974, **Libraries in the political science** : Georg Legh and German librarianship, 1933-53, tr. by Marta L. Dosa {JNU}

Anon, 1974, **Library and information service needs of the nation**. {JNU}

Anon, 1974, **NCC thesaurus of computing terms**, 7th edn. {NASSDOC}

Anon, 1974, **Professional and non-professional duties in libraries**, 2nd edn. [Research and Development Committee, Library Association, London]. {IIT ZHL}

Anon, 1974, **Report** : University Grants Commission committee on scales of pay and qualification, etc., for library staff in universities and colleges. [University Grants Commission, New Delhi]. {NIEPA}

Anon, 1974, **Report** : Working meeting on Asian resources for a population library network, September 13-15, 1973, Bangkok. [UN Economic Commission for Asia and the Far East]. {NIH}

Anon, 1974, **Status of documentation in India**. [Indian National Scientific Documentation Centre, New Delhi]. {JNU}

Anon, 1974, **The right to read and the nation's libraries**. [American Association of School Libraries, Children's Services Division; Public Library Association; American Library Association]. {USIS}

Anon, 1974, **U.N. report** : Working meeting on Asian resources for a Population Library Information Network, September 13-15, 1973, Bangkok. [U.N. Economic Commission for Asia and the Far East]. {NIH}

Anon, 1974, **UNISIST information policy objectives.** [UNESCO]. {JNU}

Anon, 1975, **Anglo-American Cataloguing Rules** : Amendment bulletin. [Library Association, London] {ZHL}

Anon, 1975, **Anglo-American Cataloguing Rules** : North American text : Chapter 12 : Audiovisual media and special instructional materials, rev. [American Library Association]. {USIS}

Anon, 1975, **Bangladesh national bibliography**. {NASSDOC}

Anon, 1975, **Conference number and souvenir** : All India library conference, 22nd, January 17-20, 1976, Delhi. [Indian Library Association]. {NASSDOC}

Anon, 1975, **Development of resource sharing networks in the framework of UNISIST World Science Information System**. [National Library of Australia]. {JNU}

Anon, 1975, **Essays and studies in librarianship**. {NASSDOC}

Anon, 1975, **Faculty status for university and college librarian in India** : Basic documents. {JNU NASSDOC ZHL}

Anon, 1975, **The future of cataloguing**. {USIS}

Anon, 1975, **Guidelines for the evaluation of training courses, workshops and seminars in scientific and technical information and documentation.** [UNESCO]. {NASSDOC}

Anon, 1975, **Inter-Library Resources Centre** : Indian Council of Social Science Research—Jawaharlal Nehru University. [Indian Council of Social Science Research]. {NASSDOC}

Anon, 1975, **Library development in Pakistan** : Resume and recommendation : National seminar, February 7-9, 1974, Lahore. [Society for the Promotion and Improvement of Libraries]. {NASSDOC*}

Anon, 1975, **Library of Congress subject headings**, 8th edn., 2nd vols. [U.S. Library of Congress, Subject Cataloguing Division]. {NASSDOC USIS}

Anon, 1975, **Library of Congress subject headings** : Quarterly cumulative supplement to the 8th edn. [U.S. Library of Congress]. {NASSDOC}

Anon, 1975, **Literature survey and trends in library cataloguing, 1970-1975.** (Mimeo; short bibliography). {NASSDOC}

Anon, 1975, **Papers** : All India library conference, 21st, 1975, Bhubaneswar. [Indian Library Association]. {NASSDOC}

Anon, 1975, **Papers** : Conference on informatics, 1975, Cambridge. [Association of Special Libraries and Information Bureaux]. {CRRI}

Anon, 1975, **Papers** : Conference on use of computers in libraries and information centres, 1975, London. [Association of Special Libraries and Information Bureaux]. {CRRI}

Anon, 1975, **Papers** : IASLIC conference, 10th, 1975, Lucknow, Pt. A. : Library documents aspects of utilisation; Pt. B. : Procurement of periodicals : Current problems in India [Indian Association of Special Libraries and Information Centres]. {IIMC}

Anon, 1975, **Papers** : Seminar on thesaurus in information systems, December 1-5, 1975, Bangalore. [DRTC, Bangalore; Indian National Scientific Documentation Centre, New Delhi]. {BIS CRRI DUL IIMC ZHL}

Anon, 1975, **Public libraries and cultural activities.** [Department of Education and Science, Great Britain]. {NIPCCD}

Anon, 1975, **Rampur Raza Library Bill**. [Lok Sabha, New Delhi]. {JNU}

Anon, 1975, **Recommendations for the processing and storage of silver gelatin-type microfilm**. (BS : 1153 : 1975). [British Standards Institution]. {CRRI}

Anon, 1975, **Seminar and exhibition on information for industry, 1975, Bangalore**. {CRRI}

Anon, 1975, **Souvenir** : All India library conference, 21st, 1975, Bhubneswar. [Indian Library Association]. {NASSDOC}

Anon, 1975, **Standard international trade classification**, 2nd edn. [United Nations Department of Economic and Special Affairs]. {TDA}

Anon, 1975, **Standardisation in computerised information system** : Papers for technical session. [Indian Standards Institution]. {JNU}

Anon, 1975, **Toward a national program for library and information services** : Goals for action. [U.S. National Commission on Libraries and Information Science]. {USIS}

Anon, 1975, **UK MARC manual**. {Bibliographic Services Division, British Library, London]. {JNU}

Anon, 1975, **UNISIST guidelines for the organisation of training courses, workshops and seminars in scientific and technical information and documentation.** [UNESCO]. {BIS}

Anon, 1975, **World guide to technical information and documentation services**, 2nd edn. [UNESCO]. {JNU NASSDOC}

Anon, 1975-83, **Microfilming of technical drawings and other drawing office equipments** : Pt-1 : operation procedures (ISO 3272/I-1983); Pt-II : Quality criteria and control (ISO 3272/II-1978); Pt-III : Unitized 35 mm microfilm carriers (ISO 3272/III-1975). [International Organisation for Standardisation, Geneva]. {NASSDOC}

Anon, 1976, **Anglo-American Cataloguing Rules** : North American tech. [Library Association, London]. {NASSDOC NMML USIS}

Anon, 1976, **Anglo-American Cataloguing Rules** : North American text : Chapter 6 : Separately published monographs. [American Library Association]. {JNU}

Anon, 1976, **BIBDATA network** : A draft proposal for an Australian national shared cataloguing system. [National Library of Australia]. {JNU}

Anon, 1976, **Bibliography of selected Indian books, 1970-71**. {NASSDOC}

Anon, 1976, **Canons for making abstracts**. [Indian Standards Institution]. {NASSDOC}

Anon, 1976, **Capital provision for university libraries** : Report of a working party. [University Grants Commission, London]. {IIT JNU NIEPA ZHL}

Anon, 1976, **Collection building in special purpose libraries**. {USIS}

Anon, 1976, **Community college libraries in the United States**. {USIS}

Anon, 1976, **Copyright Act**. {NASSDOC}

Anon, 1976, **A course in administration for managers of information services** : Design, implementation and topical outline. [UNESCO; UNISIST]. {NASSDOC}

Anon, 1976, **Delhi Public Library** : Silver jubilee souvenir, 27th October, 1976. {NASSDOC}

Anon, 1976, **DEVSIS** : The preliminary design of an international information system for the development sciences. [International Development Research Centre, DEVSIS Study Team, Ottawa]. {NASSDOC}

Anon, 1976, **Directory of development documentation and information facilities in Asia and Pacific**. [UN Asian Development Institute, Bangkok]. {IEG IIFT NASSDOC}

Anon, 1976, **Directory of medical libraries in the British Isles**. [Library Association, London, Medical Section]. {NIH}

Anon, 1976, **Directory of suppliers of library requisites**. [IDL Chemicals Limited, Hyderabad]. {NASSDOC*}

Anon, 1976, **Glossary of documentation terms**. (BS : 5408-1976). [British Standards Institution]. {CRRI}

Anon, 1976, **Guide for layout of learned periodicals**, rev edn. (IS : 795-1976). [Indian Standards Institution]. {NASSDOC}

Anon, 1976, **Guide for preparation of abstracts**, rev. edn. (IS : 795-1976). [Indian Standards Institution]. {NASSDOC}

Anon, 1976, **Guidelines for newspaper libraries**. [American Newspaper Publishers Association]. {USIS}

Anon, 1976, **Indexing systems** : IASLIC special course, November 1—December 14, 1976 : Course material. [Indian Association of Special Libraries and Information Centres]. {JNU}

Anon, 1976, **Information policy for development** : National and international responsibilities. [UNESCO]. {NASSDOC}

Anon, 1976, **Information systems design for socio-economic development** : Retrospect and prospect. [International Federation for Documentation and Information]. {JNU}

Anon, 1976, **Inventory of bibliographic data bases produced in the UK** : Report. [British Library, Department of Research and Development]. {JNU}

Anon, 1976, **Library and information science manpower development in the Asian Region** : Report : Meeting of supervisors of library and documentation schools in the Asian region, Bangalore. {CRRI}

Anon, 1976, **Life sciences information network**. [National Library of Australia]. {JNU}

Anon, 1976, **Management services** : Report on the library system of the Jawaharlal Nehru University. [Institute of Secretariat Training and Management, New Delhi]. {JNU ZHL}

Anon, 1976, **Method for writing calendar dates in all-numeric form**. (IS : 7900-1976). [Indian Standards Institution]. {NASSDOC}

Anon, 1976, **Minicomputers and bibliographic information retrieval**. [British Library Lending Division]. {BCL}

Anon, 1976, **NATIS** : Design and planning of national information systems. [UNESCO]. {NASSDOC*}

Anon, 1976, **NATIS** : National information policy. {NASSDOC*}

Anon, 1976, **Papers** : IASLIC seminar, 7th, December 28-31, 1976, Burdwan. [Indian Association of Special Libraries and Information Centres]. {BIS JNU NASSDOC}

Anon, 1976, **The planning of indexing and abstracting services in the social sciences** : Coverage overlap and content. [Bath University Library]. {BCL}

Anon, 1976, **A register of communications research in Canada, 1974-1975** : Status report. [Canadian Communication Research Information Centre, Ottawa]. {NASSDOC}

Anon, 1976, **Report** : Australia committee on inquiry on public libraries. {JNU}

Anon, 1976, **Report** : Committee on the re-organisation of libraries, research centres and museums for the government of Jammu and Kashmir. [Punjab Agricultural University, Ludhiana]. {NASSDOC*}

Anon, 1976, **Souvenir** : All India library conference, 22nd, 1976, New Delhi. [Indian Library Association]. {NASSDOC}

Anon, 1976, **Souvenir** : Silver Jubilee. [Delhi Public Library, Delhi]. {NASSDOC*}

Anon, 1976, **Staffing of public libraries** : A report. [Department of Education and Science, Great Britain]. {BIS IIT ZHL}

Anon, 1976, **Subject cross reference guide.** {JNU}

Anon, 1976, **Thesaurus of descriptors used for information processing in the ILO library**. [ILO]. {NASSDOC}

Anon, 1977, **Bibliography** : Reports from the International Conference on Education, 1975. [UNESCO]. {ICA}

Anon, 1977, **Catalogue of Government of India civil publications** : Subject-wise arranged, corrected up to 31st December, 1977, 8th supplement for the year 1977. {MMTC}

Anon, 1977, **Development index Canada** : Index to 1976 Canadian literature on economic and social development. [International Development Research Centre]. {IIFT}

Anon, 1977, **Guide for the conversion of school libraries into media centres.** [UNESCO]. {DUL ICA JNU NIEPA}

Anon, 1977, **Guide for standard book numbering**. {IS : 8310-1977}. [Indian Standards Institution]. {NAI NASSDOC}

Anon, 1977, **ISBD (CH)** : International standard bibliographic description for cartographic material. [International Federation of Library Association and Institutions]. {NASSDOC}

Anon, 1977, **ISBD (G)** : General international standard bibliographic description : Annotated text. [International Federation of Library Associations and Institution, Working Group on the General International Standard Bibliographic Description]. {NASSDOC}

Anon, 1977, **ISBD (NBM)** : International standard bibliographic description for non-book materials. [International Federation of Library Associations and Institutions, Working Group on the International Standard Bibliographic Description for Non-Book Materials]. {NASSDOC}

Anon, 1977, **Impact of information services on national development.** [COSTED, Bangalore]. {NASSDOC}

Anon, 1977, **Indian trade classification**, 2nd rev edn. [Directorate General of Commercial Intelligence and Statistics, New Delhi]. {TDA}

Anon, 1977, **Information networks for on-line bibliography retrieval.** [UNESCO]. {BIS}

Anon, 1977, **Information services for world trade centres.** [World Trade Centre Association]. {TDA}

Anon, 1977, **Libraries and the life of the mind in America** : Addresses delivered at the centennial celebration of the American Library Association, [American Library Association]. {IIT NIPCCD USIS}

Anon, 1977, **Monograph on use of library as enrichment to teaching**. [State Council for Education Research and Teaching, Hyderabad]. {NASSDOC*}

Anon, 1977, **National information system** : Library and information science manpower development in Asian region : Meeting of supervisors of library and documentation schools in the Asian region, Bangalore. [UNESCO; DRTC]. {JNU}

Anon, 1977, **Papers** : Seminar on library and information science education in India, 1977, New Delhi. {JNU}

Anon, 1977, **Proceedings and papers** : IASLIC seminar on library Scene in Calcutta, 1977, Calcutta. [Indian Association of Special Libraries and Information Centres]. {JNU}

Anon, 1977, **Recommendations relating to primary elements in the design of library buildings**. [Indian Standards Institution]. {NASSDOC}

Anon, 1977, **Report** : Orientation course for the libraries of cooperative training colleges and apex level organisations/institutions in India, June 1977, New Delhi. [National Council for Cooperation Training, New Delhi]. {ICA}

Anon, 1977, **Standards for public libraries**. (CIFLA publications). {NASSDOC*}

Anon, 1977, **Third European congress on information systems and networks overcoming the language barrier, Luxembourg**. {JNU}

Anon, 1977, **UNISIST information networks for online bibliographic retrieval.** [UNESCO]. {BIS DUL}

Anon, 1977-79, **Directory**, 1977; 1979. [International Federation of Library Association and Institutions]. {NASSDOC}

Anon, 1977-81, **List of documents and publications of General Information Programme and UNISIST, 1977-81**. [UNESCO]. {JNU}

Anon, 1977-82, **Canadian Periodical Index**, 1975; 1977 to 1982. (Formerly *Canadian Index to periodicals and documentary films*). [Canadian Library Association]. {NASSDOC}.

Anon, 1977-83, **Communication yearbook**, 1977-78; 1982-83. {RTL}

Anon, 1978, **Anglo-American Cataloguing Rules**, 2nd edn. [American Library Association]. {CRRI IIC ISI JNU MHA NCAER NERC NIH NIPCCD USIS ZHL}

Anon, 1978, **Annotated bibliography of country serials**. [UNCTAD/GATT. International Trade Centre]. {MFL}

Anon, 1978, **Automated centre for scientific and technical information.** [UNESCO]. {ISI}

Anon, 1978, **BEPI** : Bibliography of English publications in India : An integrated author-title-subject index of scholarly and significant publications of the year, 1977-1978. {NASSDOC}

Anon, 1978, **BSO manual** : The development, rationale and use of broad system of ordering. [International Federation for Documentation and Information] {CRRI}

Anon, 1978, **FID congress on new trends in documentation and information, 1978, Edinburg**. [International Federation of Documentation and Information] {CRRI}

Anon, 1978, **Guidelines for curriculum development on information studies**. [UNESCO]. {NASSDOC*}

Anon, 1978, **ISBD (M)** : International standard bibliographic description for monographic publications, rev edn. [International Federation of Library Associations and Institutions]. {NASSDOC}

Anon, 1978, **Information science** : A unified view through a systems approach. [Indian Association of Special Libraries and Information Bureaux]. {DUL MMTC}

Anon, 1978, **International bibliography of directories**, 6th edn. {NASSDOC}

Anon, 1978, **Library services in rural areas.** [Library Advisory Council, Wales]. {NIEPA}

Anon, 1978, **MIMC microforms annual, 1977-78.** [Microform International Marketing Corporation]. {NASSDOC}

Anon, 1978, **Maintaining library services** : A study in six countries. [Education and Science Department, Great Britain]. {IIMC NIEPA}

Anon, 1978, **Management of information resources at the national level.** [UNESCO]. {NASSDOC*}

Anon, 1978, **National library week souvenir, 1976.** [Kerala Library Association, Trivandrum]. {ICA JNU MMTC}

Anon, 1978, **Nationwide location data base and service**. [U.S. Library of Congress]. {MMTC}

Anon, 1978, **New Zealand national bibliography**, 1978. [National Library of New Zealand]. {NASSDOC}

Anon, 1978, **Papers** : All India public library convention, November, 16-18, 1978, New Delhi. [Delhi Library Association]. {MMTC NMML}

Anon, 1978, **Papers**: FID congress on new trends in documentation and information, 1978, Edinburg. {CRRI}

Anon, 1978, **Papers** : Seminar on information for engineering industry, February 10, 1978, New Delhi. [Association of Engineering Industry; Indian National Scientific Documentation Centre, New Delhi]. {BIS}

Anon, 1978, **Recommendations for bibliographical references**. Essential and supplementary elements, rev. edn., (IS : 2381-1978). [Indian Standards Institution]. {NASSDOC}

Anon, 1978, **Report** : Committee appointed by the Government of Andhra Pradesh to review the working of the Andhra Pradesh Public Library Act, 1960, and to suggest amendments to the Act. [Government of Andhra Pradesh, Hyderabad]. {NASSDOC*}

Anon, 1978, **Report** : Committee on private libraries. [Government of Andhra Pradesh, Hyderabad]. {NASSDOC*}

Anon, 1978, **Role of libraries in socio-economic development** : Papers : All India library convention, 1st, February 13, 1978, Delhi. [Government of India Librarians Association]. {NASSDOC}

Anon, 1978, **Souvenir** : All India library conference, 24th, 1978, Bangalore. [Department of Public Libraries, Bangalore; Indian Library Association]. {NASSDOC}

Anon, 1978, **UNISIST** : A study on the application of scientific and technological information in development. [UNESCO]. {JNU}

Anon, 1978, **UNISIST guidelines for the evaluation of information systems and services.** [UNESCO]. {BIS}

Anon, 1978, **UNISIST guidelines for formulating policy on education, training and development of library and information personnel.** [UNESCO]. {BIS}

Anon, 1978, **UNISIST international system and networks for technology transfer.** [UNESCO]. {BIS}

Anon, 1978, **United Nations document series symbols, 1946-1977** : Cumulative list with index. [United Nations]. {IIFT}

Anon, 1978-83, **Information Industry Market Place** : An international directory of information products and services, **1978**; **1982**; **1983**. {USIS}

Anon, 1979, **ALA handbook of organisation, 1979-80.** [American Library Association]. {NASSDOC USIS}

Anon, 1979, **ALA membership directory, 1979-80** [American Library Association]. {NASSDOC USIS}

Anon, 1979, **Computer-based information services in medicines**: A feasibility study : On behalf of the University of Otago medical libraries. [Centerbury Medical Library]. {BCL}

Anon, 1979, **Decision tables in data processing** : A report. [National Computer Centre, Manchester]. {NASSDOC}

Anon, 1979, **Directory of educational documentation and information services**, 3rd edn., [UNESCO]. {NASSDOC NIPCCD}

Anon, 1979, **Directory of information sources in Japan.** {JNU}

Anon, 1979, **Directory of libraries and documentation centres in the United Nations system.** {JNU}

Anon, 1979, **Formation of necessary standards for different types of libraries in India** : Working paper : ILA seminar, 1979, Trivandrum. [Indian Library Association]. {NASSDOC}

Anon, 1979, **Guidelines for the establishment and development of monolingual thesauri.** (BS 5723-1979), [British Standards Institution]. {CRRI}

Anon, 1979, **Guidelines for national bibliographic agency and national bibliography.** [UNESCO]. {NASSDOC}

Anon, 1979, **Implication of modern information technology for national information policy and planning.** [UNESCO]. {NASSDOC}

Anon, 1979, **Information systems in UK agriculture.** [UK Agriculture Information Review Committee; British Library Research and Development Department]. {BCL}

Anon, 1979, **Mariamali Adigal library** : 20th Anniversary celebrations souvenir. {NMML}

Anon, 1979, **Papers** : Seminar on reference sources on South Asia, 1979, Jaipur. {JNU}

Anon, 1979, **Papers** : Seminar on the role of the National Library of India, November 23, 1978, Calcutta. [National Library Employee's Association, Calcutta]. {NASSDOC}

Anon, 1979, **Problems and failures in library automation** : Clinic on library applications of data processing, 1978, Illinois. [University of Illinois at Urbana-Champaign]. {USIS}

Anon, 1979, **Purchasing an encyclopaedia** : 12 point to consider. [American Library Association]. {USIS}

Anon, 1979, **Selective list of activities in the field of information**: UNESCO Intergovernmental conference on scientific and technical information for development, 1979, Paris. {JNU}

Anon, 1979, **Souvenir** : AP libraries conference, 1st, 1979, Hyderabad. {NASSDOC*}

Anon, 1979, **The Library of Congress** : A portrait of an institution. {USIS}

Anon, 1979, **Technical and specialised periodicals published in Britain, 1972-73**. [Central Office of Information, London]. {NASSDOC}

Anon, 1979, **Theoretical problems of informatics** : Forecasting of the development of scientific information activities. [International Federation for Documentation and Information]. {CRRI}

Anon, 1979, **Theoretical problems of information** : New trends in information and its terminology. [International Federation for Documentation and Information]. {CRRI}

Anon, 1979, **UNISIST guidelines for editors of scientific and technical journals.** [UNESCO]. {DUL}

Anon, 1979, **Working papers** : All India library conference, 25th, May 14-18, 1979, Trivandrum. [Indian Library Association]. {ICA NCDC NMML}

Anon, 1980, **AACR2 institute handbook** : The Library of Congress interpretation and application of the Anglo-American Cataloguing Rules, 2nd. edn. [U.S. Library of Congress; American Library Association]. {USIS}

Anon, 1980, **ALA filing rules**. [American Library Association]. {USIS}

Anon, 1980, **ALA year book**: A review of library events, 1979. [American Library Association]. {IIT JNU USIS}

Anon, 1980, **Buildings for small public libraries** : Remodelled and adapted including new designs for branches. [American Library Association]. {DUL}

Anon, 1980, **Catalogue of special collections in National Library, Baghdad**. [National Library, Baghdad]. {NASSDOC}.

Anon, 1980, **Directory of United Nations information systems**, 2 vols. [United Nations Inter-Organisation Board of Information Systems, Geneva]. {MMTC RTL}

Anon, 1980, **Documentation services in departmental libraries** : Papers : All India library convention, 2nd, March 3-6, 1980, New Delhi. [Government of India Librarians Association]. {CRRI NASSDOC NMML}

Anon, 1980, **Essential problems in terminology for informatics and documentation**. [International Federation for Documentation and Information]. {BIS CRRI}

Anon, 1980, **Handbook for information systems and services.** [UNESCO] {IDSA}

Anon, 1980, **Library of Congress subject headings**, 9th edn. [U.S. Library of Congress, Subject Cataloguing Division]. {USIS}

Anon, 1980, **Papers** : All India library conference, 1980, New Delhi. [Indian Library Association]. {NASSDOC*}

Anon, 1980, **Papers** : DRTC refresher seminar on data accessibility and dissemination, 1980, Bangalore. [Documentation Research and Training Centre, Bangalore]. {CRRI}

Anon, 1980, **Papers** : National conference, 1980, Tirupati. [Indian Association of Academic Librarians]. {ZHL}

Anon, 1980, **Papers** : Seminar on library buildings in India, February 11-13, 1980, New Delhi. [National Information System for Science and Technology, New Delhi]. {BIS CRRI IIT}

Anon, 1980, **Papers** : Workshop on computer techniques in information processing. [University of Delhi, Department of Library and Information Science]. {AIU}

Anon, 1980, **Proceedings** : Seminar on international cooperative information systems, July 9-13, 1979. [International Development Research Centre]. {CRRI USIS}

Anon, 1980, **Report** : Workshop on road research and information for South East Asia, 1980, Melbourne. {CRRI}

Anon, 1980, **Science information services in India**. [Indian National Scientific Documentation Centre, New Delhi]. {NASSDOC*}

Anon, 1980, **Souvenir** : All India library conference, 26th, March 6-9, 1980, New Delhi, [Indian Library Association]. {ICA}

Anon, 1980, **Souvenir** : AP libraries conference, 2nd, 1980, Narasaropet. {NASSDOC*}

Anon, 1980, **Souvenir** : IASLIC national seminar, 9th, 1980, Nagpur {NASSDOC}

Anon, 1980, **Technology in support of library science and information service**. [Sarada Ranganathan Endowment for Library Science, Bangalore]. {BIS}

Anon, 1980, **The professional librarian's reader in library automation and technology**. {JNU USIS}

Anon, 1980, **UK MARC manual**, 2nd edn. [Bibliographic Services Division, British Library, London]. {BIS}

Anon, 1980, **UNISIST guide for the establishment and evaluation of services for selective dissemination of information.** [UNESCO]. {CRRI}

Anon, 1980, **UNISIST guide to standards for information handling**. [UNESCO]. {BIS DUL MMTC}

Anon, 1980, **Working papers** : Seminar on library buildings in India, February 11-13, 1980, New Delhi. [NISSA]. {CRRI IIT BISY}

Anon, 1981, **Background papers** : Sub-regional workshop for cooperative librarians and documentation officers for South East Asia, April 14-29, 1981, Los Banos; [ICA Regional Office and Education Centre for South East Asia, New Delhi]. {ICA}

Anon, 1981, **Bombay Booksellers and Publishers Association Members' Directory**. [Bombay Booksellers and Publishers Association] {NASSDOC}

Anon, 1981, **Computer based national information systems** : Technology and public policy issues. [U.S. Office of Technology Assessment]. {USIS}

Anon, 1981, **The concise AACR2** : Being a rewritten and simplified version of Anglo-American Cataloguing Rules, 2nd edn. [American Library Association]. {NASSDOC USIS}

Anon, 1981, **Guidelines on studies of information users**. [UNESCO]. {NASSDOC}

Anon, 1981, **The international provision and supply of publications**. [UNESCO]. {NASSDOC}

Anon, 1981, **Papers** : All India library conference, 27th, 1981, Hyderabad. [Indian Library Association]. {NMML}

Anon, 1981, **Papers** : All India seminar on agricultural library and information services, December 29-January 16, 1980. [Andhra Pradesh Agricultural University, Hyderabad; Indian Council of Agricultural Research, New Delhi]. {IIMC}

Anon, 1981, **Papers** : Conference on electronic information technology and its impact on library and information service, 4th, 1981, Pittsburg. {IIT}

Anon, 1981, **Papers** : DRTC annual seminar on information analysis and consolidation, 1981, Bangalore. [Documentation Research and Training Centre, Bangalore]. {CRRI}

Anon, 1981, **Proceedings and papers** : International conference on delivery mechanisms for engineering and technological information, November 3-5, 1980, Budapest. {BIS}

Anon, 1981, **Promotion of reading habits in Pakistan** : A study on methods and measures to promote reading habits in Pakistan. [Pakistan National Book Council]. {ZHL}

Anon, 1981, **Report** : Sub-regional workshop for cooperative librarians and documentation officers for S.E. Area, April, 14-29, 1981, Los Banos. [ICA Regional Office and Education Centre for South-East Asia, New Delhi]. {ICA NASSDOC}

Anon, 1981, **Report**, 1981. [ICA Regional Office and Education Centre for South-East Asia, New Delhi]. {ICA NASSDOC}

Anon, 1981, **Research services directory**. {USIS}

Anon, 1981, **Root thesaurus**. 2 pts., Pt.-1 : Subject display; Pt.-2 : Alphabetical list. [British Standards Institution]. {NASSDOC}

Anon, 1981, **Souvenir** : All India library conference, 27th, January 9-12, 1981, Hyderabad. [Academy of Library Science and documentation, Hyderabad; Indian Library Association]. {ICA NASSDOC}

Anon, 1981, **Souvenir** : IASLIC all India conference, 13th, 1981, Waltaire. [Indian Association of Special Libraries and Information Centres]. {NASSDOC}

Anon, 1981, **Subject authorities** : A guide to subject cataloguing. {USIS}

Anon, 1981, **Theoretical problems of information** : Criteria of the quality of information systems and processes : Collection of papers. [International Federation for Documentation and Information]. {BIS}

Anon, 1981, **UNBIS thesaurus** : List of terms used in indexing and cataloguing of documents and other materials relevant to United Nations programmes and activities. [Dag Hammerskjold Library]. {JNU}

Anon, 1981, **UNISIST guidelines for the establishment and development of monolingual thesauri**, 2nd edn. [UNESCO]. {BIS}

Anon, 1981, **User surveys and evaluation of library services** [Association of Research Libraries, Washington]. {NASSDOC}

Anon, 1981-83, **Current book review citations**, 1981 to 1983. {USIS}

Anon. 1982, **Changing information** : Concepts and technologies. {JNU USIS}

Anon, 1982, **EUDISED multilingual thesaurus** : Alphabetical list of deseriptors. {NASSDOC}

Anon, 1982, **Final report** : International congress on the universal availability of publications. [UNESCO]. {NASSDOC}

Anon, 1982, **Future development of libraries and information services.** [Department of Education and Science, Great Britain]. {ISI}

Anon, 1982, **Future of libraries** : Panel discussion by librarians, administrators, faculty and students : Papers from the millionth volume celebration. [New York State University]. {NASSDOC}

Anon, 1982, **Granthalaya pragati** : Souvenir : Andhra Pradesh libraries conference, December 10-12, 1982, Tirupati. [Andhra Pradesh Public Library Association]. {NASSDOC*}

Anon, 1982, **Guidelines for curriculum development in records management and administration of modern archives**. [UNESCO]. {NASSDOC}

Anon, 1982, **Guidelines for the preparation of bibliography**. [U.S. National Agricultural Library]. {NASSDOC}

Anon, 1982, **ISO standards handbook, 1982** : Information transfer. [UNESCO]. {NASSDOC}

Anon, 1982, **Information technology and its impact on American education.** {USIS}

Anon, 1982, **Information trade directory** : An international directory of information products and services. {USIS}

Anon, 1982, **Information transfer,** 2nd edn. [International Organisation for Standardisation]. {CRRI MMTC}

Anon, 1982, **Library of Congress subject headings** : Quarterly cumulative supplements to the 9th edn., 1979-80. [U.S. Library of Congress]. {NASSDOC}

Anon, 1982, **Medium term programme, 1981-85**. [International Federation of Library Associations and Institutions]. {NASSDOC}

Anon, 1982, **Papers** : All India seminar on libraries and the book trade, February 1982, New Delhi. [Indian Library Association]. {IIMC IIT JNU ZHL}

Anon, 1982, **Papers** : All India seminar on library resources in university education and research, 1982, Hyderabad. [Osmania University Library, Hyderabad]. {ZHL}

Anon, 1982, **Papers** : IASLIC seminar on information services in India, 1982, Kanpur. [Indian Association of Special Libraries and Information Centres]. {CRRI}

Anon, 1982, **Personnel administration for libraries** : A bibliographic essay. [American Library Association]. {BIS DUL}

Anon, 1982, **Proceedings and list of government of Indian libraries of Delhi** : All India library convention, 3rd, February 10-12, 1982, New Delhi. [Government of India Librarians Association]. {CRRI NASSDOC}

Anon, 1982, **Public libraries in developing society and planning for national information system** : Seminar papers : All India library conference, 28th, October 20-23, 1982, Lucknow. [Indian Library Association]. {ICA NASSDOC NIPCCD ZHL}

Anon, 1982, **Report** : Committee appointed for developing the Tagore Memorial Library, Vijayawada. [Zilla Granthalaya Samstha, Machilipatnam]. {NASSDOC*}

Anon, 1982, **Souvenir** : AP libraries conference, 3rd, 1982, Tirupati. {NASSDOC*}

Anon, 1982, **Study report on the feasibility of an international data bank for the non-aligned countries**. [UNESCO]. {NASSDOC}

Anon, 1982, **Use of computer in libraries** : Summary of the proceedings of a seminar held on March 15, 1982, New Delhi. {NASSDOC}

Anon, 1983 **Directory of World Bank depository libraries**. [International Bank for Reconstruction and Development] {NASSDOC}

Anon, 1983, **Asian regional seminar on information sources, systems and services in the social sciences, July 11-22, 1983, Philippines**. [Unesco Regional Office, Bangkok]. {NASSDOC}

Anon, 1983, **Computerised systems in library and information services.** {NASSDOC}

Anon, 1983, **Educational information** : Problems, issues and strategies for resolving them : Report of a regional workshop. [National Institute for Educational Research]. {NIEPA}

Anon, 1983, **Encyclopaedias and dictionaries of the world**. {NASSDOC}

Anon, 1983, **Fifty years of Government of India Librarians Association.** [Government of India Librarians Association]. {NASSDOC NMML}

Anon, 1983, **Fifty years of Indian Library Association, 1933-83** : Golden jubilee. [Indian Library Association]. {JNU MMTC ZHL}

Anon, 1983, **Guidelines for presentation of abstract sheets in serial publications**. (IS : 10455-1983). [Indian Standards Institution]. {CRRI}

Anon, 1983, **Guidelines for presentation of translations.** (IS : 10454-1983). [Indian Standards Institution]. {NASSDOC}

Anon, 1983, **IENS press handbook**. [Indian and Eastern Newspaper Society, New Delhi]. {JNU}

Anon, 1983, **Library in the information revolution** : Proceedings : Congress of South-East Asian librarians, 6th, May 30 - June 3, 1983, Singapore. {JNU}

Anon, 1983, **Manual of bibliographic control**. [UNESCO]. {NASSDOC*}

Anon, 1983, **Organisation of social science information and documentation** : Reports on 11 Asian countries. [UNESCO Regional Adviser for Social Science in Asia and the Pacific, Bangkok]. {NASSDOC}

Anon, 1983, **Papers** : All India seminar on national policy for library and information science education, 1983, Nagpur. {NASSDOC}

Anon, 1983, **Papers** : DRTC refresher seminar, 1983, Bangalore. [Documentation Research and Training Centre, Bangalore]. {JNU}

Anon, 1983, **Reader's guide to Madras University Library** : Platinum jubilee celebration, 1907-1982. [Madras University Library]. {NMML}

Anon, 1983, **Report** : Asian regional seminar on information sources, systems and services in the social sciences, July 11-22, 1983, Philippines [UNESCO Regional Office, Bangkok]. {NASSDOC*}

Anon, 1983, **The State Lenin Library of USSR**. {NASSDOC*}

Anon, 1983, **Working document on scientific and technological information in Asia and the Pacific**. [UNESCO]. {NASSDOC}

Anon, 1984, **Guide for drafting Indian standards**, 2nd edn. (IS : 12-1984). [Indian Standards Institution]. {NASSDOC}

Anon, 1984, **Need for National Information Policy** : Its parameters : Papers : Convention and conference of the Society for Information Science, 4th, December 27-28, 1984, Madras. {NASSDOC*}

Anon, 1984, **Papers** : IASLIC national seminar, 11th, November 26-29, 1984, Hyderabad, I : Toward a code of professional ethics; II : Document delivery, reproduction, translation. [Indian Association of Special Libraries and Information Centres]. {NASSDOC}

Anon, 1984, **Papers and proceedings** : Round table discussion on the concepts of Australian national bibliography, 1983, South Wales. {JNU}

Anon, 1984, **Reading material** : Orientation seminar on planning and management for senior administrators of public library services, February 6-10, 1984, New Delhi. {NASSDOC NIEPA}

Anon, 1984, **Report** : Expert working group on development of population information centres and networks, June 20-23, 1984. [U.N. Economic and Social Commission for Asia and the Pacific]. {NASSDOC}

Anon, 1984, **Souvenir** : IASLIC national seminar, 11th, 1984, Hydrabad [IASLI]. {NASSDOC*}

Anon, 1985, **Annual report of the Library of Congress for 1985**. [U.S. Library of Congress]. {NASSDOC}

Anon, 1985, **Bachelor degree in library and information science** : A handbook. [Andhra Pradesh Open University, Hyderabad]. {NASSDOC}

Anon, 1985, **Catalogue of back volumes of periodicals in Punjabrao Krishi Vidyapeeth Library, Akola, 1985**. [Punjabrao Krishi Vidyapeeth, Akola]. {NASSDOC}

Anon, 1985, **Conservation in India** : Problems and prospects : Seminar on conservation in India, 1985, Lucknow. {NMML}

Anon, 1985, **Development of research and information system in the Third World** : Report of the proceedings: Research and information system for the non-aligned and other developing countries, 2nd, November 20-22, 1985, New Delhi. [RISNODC]. {NASSDOC}

Anon, 1985, **Directory of institutions and organisations specialising in children's literature**. [International Board on Books for Young People; UNESCO]. {NASSDOC*}

Anon, 1985, **Directory of libraries and information centres in Gujarat**. {Gujarat Granthalaya Seva Sangh, Ahmedabad]. {NASSDOC}

Anon, 1985, **Directory of special and research libraries in India**. 2nd edn. [Indian Association of Special Libraries and Information Centres]. {ICCR ICWA IDSA IIPA NASSDOC NMML UGC}

Anon, 1985, **Directory of United Nations databases and information systems** [United Nations Advisory Committee for Coordination of Information Systems]. {NASSDOC}

Anon, 1985, **Documents on national policy on library and information system**. [Raja Rammohan Roy Library Foundation; Indian Library Association]. {NASSDOC*}

Anon, 1985, **FID directory 1985-86**. [International Federation of Documentation and Information]. {NASSDOC}

Anon, 1985, **ILO thesaurus**. [International Labour Office, Geneva]. {NASSDOC}

Anon, 1985, **Library and the community** : Units 1-9. [Andhra Pradesh Open University, Hyderabad]. {NASSDOC*}

Anon, 1985, **Library cataloguing practice** : Solutions to assignments 1-26. [Andhra Pradesh Open University, Hyderabad]. {NASSDOC*}

Anon, 1985, **Library cataloguing practice** : Unit 1 : Lessons 1-14. [Andhra Pradesh Open University, Hyderabad]. {NASSDOC}

Anon, 1985, **Library classification practice** : Unit 2 : Lessons 1-16. [Andhra Pradesh Open University, Hyderabad]. {NASSDOC*}

Anon, 1985, **Library classification practice** : Units 1-13. [Andhra Pradesh Open University, Hyderabad]. {NASSDOC*}

Anon, 1985, **Library classification theory** . Units 1-10. [Andhra Pradesh Open University, Hyderabad]. {NASSDOC*}

Anon, 1985, **Library management** : Units 1-10. [Andhra Pradesh Open University, Hyderabad]. {NASSDOC*}

Anon, 1985, **Manual of library management**. [Physical Research Laboratory, Ahmedabad]. {JNU}

Anon, 1985, **Medium term programme, 1986-91**. [International Federation of Library Associations and Institutions, Professional Board]. {NASSDOC}

Anon, 1985, **National Information System for Science and Technology (NISSAT)** : Detailed project report, (1985-1990). [Ministry of Science and Technology, New Delhi]. {NASSDOC}

Anon, 1985, **New frontiers in library and information science**. [Zilla Granthalaya Samstha, Machilipatnam]. {NASSDOC*}

Anon, 1985, **Public library development perspectives.** [Indian Library Association]. {NASSDOC*}

Anon, 1985, **Report** : Regional seminar on curriculum development in information studies, September 17-21, 1985, Bangkok. [UNESCO]. {NASSDOC}

Anon, 1985, **Report** : Seminar on documentation and information systems for vocational training, November 5-16, 1985, Pattaya, Thailand. [International Labour Office; Asian and Pacific Skill Development Programme, Islamabad]. {NASSDOC}

Anon, 1985, **Scientific and technological information for development**. [United Nations Information Systems]. {JNU}

Anon, 1985, **Souvenir** : All India library conference, 31st, 1985, Baroda. [Indian Library Association]. {NASSDOC}

Anon, 1985, **Souvenir** : Platinum Jubilee. [Central Library, Baroda]. {NASSDOC*}

Anon, 1985, **Special librarianship**. [Andhra Pradesh Open University, Hyderabad]. {NASSDOC*}

Anon, 1985, **The social sciences** : Information system. [USSR Academy of Sciences, Moscow]. {NASSDOC*}

Anon, 1985, **Use of microprocessors in information analysis and library applications**. [Society for Information Science]. {NASSDOC}

Anon, 1985-1986, **Final report, 1985 and 1986**. [Inter-Governmental Committee for the UNESCO; Inter-Governmental Informatics Programme]. {JNU}

Anon, 1986, **APINESS** : Report : UNESCO/AASSREC regional meeting of experts to develop Asia Pacific Information Network in Social Sciences, May 12-16, 1986, Bangkok. {NASSDOC}

Anon, 1986, **Challenges of new technologies** : All India library convention, 6th, September 1-4, 1986, Shimla, [Government of India Librarian Associations]. {NMML}

Anon, 1986, **Course material** : Workshop on computer application to library and information activities, 2nd, September 8-13, 1986, Ahmedabad. [ILA; Physical Research Laboratory, Ahmedabad]. {NASSDOC}

Anon, 1986, **Directory of social science libraries, information centres and data bases in Sri Lanka**. [Sri Lanka Social Science Documentation Centre]. {NASSDOC}

Anon, 1986, **Glossary of terms used in the Public Libraries Department** : English-Telugu. [Government of Andhra Pradesh, Official Language Commission, Hyderabad]. {NASSDOC*}

Anon, 1986, **IFLA statutes, rules of procedure terms of reference**. [International Fedration of Library Associations and Institutions] {NASSDOC}

Anon, 1986, **Information market with special regard to social science information**. (FID studies in social science information and documentation). [Hungarian Academy of Science; International Federation for Documentation and Information]. {NASSDOC}

Anon, 1986, **International directory of library, archives and information science associations**, 2nd edn. [UNESCO General Information Programme; UNISIST]. {NASSDOC}

Anon, 1986 **International literary market place, 1986-87**. {NASSDOC}

Anon, 1986, **National policy on library and information system** : A presentation. [Government of India, Committee on National Policy on Library and Information System]. {NASSDOC*}

Anon, 1986, **New Education Policy** : Libraries and information system : Papers and proceedings. [NCERT; Raja Rammohan Roy Library Foundation, Calcutta]. {NMML}

Anon, 1986, **Opinion poll survey among visitors to the New Delhi World Book Fair** : A report. [National Book Trust, New Delhi]. {NASSDOC*}

Anon, 1986, **Papers** : All India library conference, 1986. [Indian Library Association]. {NMML}

Anon, 1986, **Papers** : National seminar on library and information science education in India : New perspective, December 10-12, 1986, Trivandrum. [Kerala State Committee on Science, Technology and Environment]. {NASSDOC}

Anon, 1986, **Profession education and training for library and information work** : A review. [Library Association, London]. {NASSDOC}

Anon, 1986, **Report** : Seminar on library education, December 1-4, 1965, Bombay. [Shreemati Nathibai Damodar Thachery Women's University, Bombay]. {AIU NASSDOC}

Anon, 1986, **Souvenir** : Silver Jubilee. [City Granthalaya Samstha, Hyderabad]. {NASSDOC*}

Anon, 1986, **Workshop on computer application to library and information activities.** [ILA NISSAT]. {JNU}

Anon, 1987, **Bangladesh public library directory (1972-1986)**. [Ministry of Education, Cultural Affairs Division, Directorate of Archives and Libraries, Bangladesh National Library, Colombo]. {NASSDOC}

Anon, 1987, **Hundred years of library education.** [Nagpur University, Department of Library and Information Science, Nagpur]. {NASSDOC}

Anon, 1987, **IFLA and the Third World** : The IFLA core on the advancement of librarianship in the Third World. (ALP). {NASSDOC}

Anon, 1987, **IFLA round-table on research on reading, August 13-15, 1987, Manchester** : Preparatory meeting before Brighton Congress. {NASSDOC*}

Anon, 1987, **Papers** : All India library conference, 32nd, 1987, Anantpur. [Indian Library Association]. {NASSDOC}

Anon, 1987, **Papers** : IFLA General Conference, 53rd, August 16-21, 1987, Bringhton. [International Federation of Library Associations and Institutions]. {NASSDOC}

Anon, 1987, **Proceedings** : All India library conference, 32nd, 1987. [Indian Library Association]. {NASSDOC}

Anon, 1987, **Proceedings** : Regional seminar on measurement and application of micrographics, 3rd, 1987, Pune. {NASSDOC}

Anon, 1987, **Report** : Asia Pacific POPIN experts working group on population information networking. [U.N. Economic and Social Commission for Asia and the Pacific, Bangkok]. {NASSDOC}

Anon, 1987, **Souvenir** : All India library conference, 32nd, 1987, Tiruchirapalli. [Indian Library Association]. {NASSDOC}

Anon, 1987, **Souvenir** : Golden jubilee celebration. [Department of Library and Information Science, Andhra University]. {NASSDOC}

Anon, 1987, **Souvenir** : Library education centenary celebration. [Nagpur University]. {NASSDOC*}

Anon, 1987, **Trends 1985-86** : Report to the Council by the Secretary General. [International Federation of Library Associations and Institutions]. {NASSDOC*}

Anon, 1987, **Women's information network for Asia and Pacific**. [United Nations Economic and Social Commission for Asia and Pacific, Bangkok]. {NASSDOC}

Anon, 1988, **Convention and exposition** : Micrographic Congress (India), 2nd, January 20-22, 1988, New Delhi. {NASSDOC}

Anon, 1988, **Directory of members**. [Micrographic Congress of India]. {NASSDOC}

Anon, 1988, **Guidelines for drafting and presentation of India standards**. [Bureau of Indian Standards]. {BIS NASSDOC}

Anon, 1988, **IFLA annual** : Proceedings of the general conferences; Annual reports. [International Federation of Library Associations and Institutions]. {NASSDOC}

Anon, 1988, **Proceedings** : All India library conference, 34th, 1988. [Indian Library Association]. {NASSDOC}

Anon, 1988, **Proceedings** : National seminar on strategies for survival by Nigerian academic and research libraries during austere times, November 9-11, 1987, Ibadan. [Nigerian Association of Agricultural Librarians and Documentalists; Nigerian Librarian Association, Academic and Research Libraries Section]. {NASSDOC*}

Anon, 1988, **Selective inventory of social science information and documentation services**, 3rd edn. [UNESCO Social and Human Sciences Documentation Centre]. {NASSDOC}

Anon, 1988, **Souvenir** : All India library conference, 1988, Calcutta. [Indian Library Association]. {NASSDOC}

Anon, 1989, **Effective methods of promoting reading habits in Asia and the Pacific.** [Asian Cultural Centre for UNESCO, Tokyo]. {NASSDOC*}

Anon, 1989, **Proceedings** : All India library conference, 35th, 1989. [Indian Library Association] {NASSDOC}

Anon, 1989, **Report** : Asia Pacific information network in social science : Regional advisory group (APINESS/RAG) meeting. [UNESCO Principal Regional Office for Asia and the Pacific, Bangkok]. {NASSDOC}

Anon, 1989, **Roles and responsibilities of librarians and library technicians** : Report. [Canada Library Association, Ottawa].

Anon, 1989, **Souvenir** : All India library conference, 1989, Pune. [Indian Library Association]. {NASSDOC}

Anthony, Lawrence James, ed., 1976, **ASLIB seminar for information planners and industry, May 13-14, 1976, Boaconfield**. {BCL NASSDOC}

Anthony, Lawrence James, ed., 1976, **Information in the 1980's** : Proceedings : ASLIB seminar for information planners and industry, May 13-14, 1976, Beaconfield. [Association of Special Libraries and Information Bureaux]. {BCL NASSDOC}

Anwar, H., 1985, **Issues in South East Asian librarianship** : A selection of papers and articles. {NASSDOC}

Arberry, A.J., 1938, **Library of the India Office** : A historical sketch. [India Office, London]. {NAI}

Arberry, A.J., 1967, **India Office Library** : A historical sketch, [Commonwealth Office, London]. {NASSDOC}

Archer, H. Richard, ed., 1965, **Rare book collections** : Some theoretical and practical suggestions for use by librarians and students. [American Library Association]. {NAI}

Arnold, Denis Victor, 1976, **The management of the information department.** {BCL}

Arnold, Robert R., et al, 1972, **Modern data processing,** 2nd edn. {NASSDOC}

Arora, Meena, 1980, **Survey of government documents in Central Secretariat Library 1979-80**. (University of Delhi, Department of Library Science, sessional project). {DUL}

Artandi, Susan B., 1972, **Introduction to computers in information science.** {JNU}

Arvinda Chandra and Saxena, T.P., 1979, **Style manual for writing theses, dissertations and papers in social sciences.** {DUL}

Ash, Lee, comp., 1978, **Subject collections** : A guide to special book collections and subject emphasis as reported by university, college, public and special libraries and museums in the United States and Canada, 5th edn. {USIS}

Asha Rani, 1964, **Exchange of publications and organisation of national exchange centres**. (University of Delhi, Department of Library and Information Science, Sessional Project). {DUL}

Asheim, Lester, 1966, **Librarianship in developing countries**. {NIPCCD}

Ashburner, E.H., **Modern public libraries** : Their planning and design. {CRRI}

Ashby, W. Ross, 1964, **Introduction to cybernetics.** {NASSDOC}

Asheim, Lester, 1957, **The humanities and the library** : Problems in the interpretation, evaluation and use of library materials. [American Library Association]. {AIU USIS}

Ashoor, Mohammed Salem, 1978, **Survey of user attitude towards resource and services of three university libraries in Saudi Arabia**. {JNU}

Ashworth, W., ed., 1955, **Handbook of special librarianship and information work**. [Association of Special Libraries and Information Bureaux]. {BIS IEG}

Ashworth, W., ed., 1962, **Handbook of special librarianship and information work**. 2nd edn. [Association of Special Libraries and Information Bureaux]. {IIT SPA}

Ashworth, W., ed., 1967, **Handbook of special librarianship and information work**, 3rd edn. [Association of Special Libraries and Information Bureaux]. {MHA MMTC NASSDOC NIH}

Asija, S., 1988, **Documentation services in India** : An overview of some selected documentation centres. {NASSDOC}

Askall, Glaister A. 1960, **Glossary of the book** : Terms used in paper making, printing, binding book printing and publishing with notes on illuminated manuscripts bibliographies, private presses and printing societies. {DUL}

Astall, Raland, 1966, **Special libraries and information bureau** : An examination guidebook. {BIS ICA IIC IIFT IIT MFL NMML SPA}

Asundi, A.Y., 1983, **Development of an unified scheme of common subdivisions in general classification systems**. Thesis. [Gulbarga University]. {NASSDOC}

Athar, Shere, 1965, **Khuda Bakhsh Oriental Public Library, Patna**. {Khuda Bakhsh Oriental Public Library]. {ZHL}

Atherten, Pauline, 1977, **Handbook of information systems services**. {JNU}

Atherton, Pauline A., 1973, **Putting knowledge to work** : American view of Ranganathan's Five Laws of Library Science. {AIU IIMC JNU NIEPA USIS}

Atherton, Pauline, 1978, **Handbook for information systems and services.** [UNESCO]. {ICA IIMC NASSDOC NIEPA TDA USIS}

Atherton, Pauline, ed., 1965, **Proceedings** : International study conference on classification research, 2nd, September 14-18, 1969, Elsinore. {BIS IIT}

Atherton, Pauline and Chiristian, Roger W., 1977, **Librarians and online services**. {BCL IIT}

Atkins, Thomas V., ed., 1984, **Cross reference index**, 2nd edn. {USIS}

Atkins, Thomas V., et al, eds., 1974, **Cross reference index** : A subject heading guide. {NASSDOC USIS}

Atkinson, Frank, 1974, **Librarianship** : Introduction to the profession. {ICA USIS}

Atkinson, Jean, 1968, **Handbook for interviewers** : A manual for Government social survey interviewing staff, describing practice and procedures on structured interviewing. {NASSDOC}

Auduson, Herschel V., 1969, **Audio-visual services in the small public library**. {JNU}

Auger, Charles P., ed., 1975, **Use of reports in literature**. {INSA JNU}

Augustine, C.A. and Devarajan, G., 1990, **Public library system in India**. {ZHL}

Augustine, C.A., ed., 1979, **Souvenir** : All India library conference, 25th, May 14-18, 1979, Trivandrum. [Indian Library Association]. {ICA}

Austin, Derek, 1974, **PRECIS** : A manual of concept analysis and subject indexing. {CRRI JNU}

Austin, Derek and Butcher, Peter, 1969, **PRECIS** : A rotated subject index system. [Council of British National Bibliography]. {NASSDOC}

Avebury, Lord, et al, eds., n.d., **Computers and the year 2000**. [National Computer Centre, Manchester]. {NASSDOC}

Avedon, Don M., 1971, **Computer output microfilm,** 2nd edn. [National Microfilm Association]. {USIS}

Avery, Louis and Hulthciss, S.C., 1962, **Advanced data processing in university library.** {JNU}

Avram, Henriette D., et al, 1968, **The MARC II format** : A communications format for bibliographic data, 2 vols. [U.S. Library of Congress]. {USIS}

Avram, Henriette D., et al, 1968, **The MARC pilot project** : Final report on a project. [US Library of Congress]. {USIS}

Awad, Atef Kamel, 1975, **Bibliographical control of patent literature**. (University of Delhi, Department of Library Science, Sessional Project). {DUL}

Awad, Elias M., 1966, **Automatic data processing** : Principle procedures. {JNU}

Azad, Asadollah, 1978, **Job satisfaction of para-professional librarians** : Comparative study of public and technical services departments in selected university libraries. {JNU}

Aziz, Abdul, 1974, **The imperial library of the moghuls**. [Idarah-I Adabiyat-I Delhi]. {INSA NMML}

Baba, Abdul Majid, 1988, **Dewey Decimal Classification, Universal Decimal Classification and Colon Classification** : Development structure, comparison. {NASSDOC}

Baer, Eleanora A., 1971, **Titles in series** : A handbook for libraries and students : Supplement to 2nd edn. {NASSDOC}

Bagari, N.D., 1973, **Pustakalaya paddhati**. {DUL}

Bagg, Thomas C. and Stevens, Mary Elizabeth, 1961, **Information selection systems retrieving replica copies** : A state-of-art report. {JNU}

Bagley, D.E., 1966, **Computer in libraries** : A selected bibliography. {JNU}

Bagley, W.A., n.d. **Facts and how to find them,** 7th edn. {DSSW}

Bagley, W.A., 1948, **Facts and how to find them**. {CRRI MFL}

Bagley, W.A., 1950, **Facts and how to find them**, 4th edn. {BIS DUL}

Bagley, William, 1958, **Facts and how to find them** : A guide to source of information and to the method of systematic research. {JNU}

Bahr, Alic Harrison, n.d., **Book theft and library security systems**. {BIS JNU USIS}

Baker, C.A., 1977, **An investigation of man-computer interaction in an online bibliographic information retrieval system**. {BCL}

Baker, E.A., ed., n.d., **Uses of libraries**. {AIU}

Baker, Robert, K., 1981, **Doing library research** : An introduction for community college students. {USIS}

Bakewell, K.G.B., 1969, **Industrial libraries throughout the world**. {IIFT IIT ISI NASSDOC}

Bakewell, K.G.B., 1972, **Manual of cataloguing practice**. {IIT JNU NASSDOC NIPCCD NMML ZHL}

Bakewell, K.G.B., ed., 1968, **Classification for information retrieval** : Papers presented at an intensive course held in September 1967 at the School of Librarianship. [Liverpool College of Commerce]. {NIH}

Bakewell, K.G.B., n.d., **How to organise information** : A manager's guide to techniques and sources with a check list for secretaries and assistants. {JNU}

Ballou, Hubbard, W., ed., 1968, **Guide to micro reproduction equipment,** 4th edn. [National Microfilm Association]. {NASSDOC}

Balmforth, C.L. and Cox, N.S., eds., 1971, **Interface** : Library automation with special reference to computing activity. {JNU NASSDOC}

Balnaves, John, 1956, **Australian libraries**. {NASSDOC}

Balwinder Kaur, comp., n.d., **Librarians' guide to Indian periodicals published for free distribution**. {NASSDOC}

Bamberger, Richard, 1975, **Promoting the reading habit**. {JNU}

Banerjee, S.B., ed., 1980, **Indian Association of Special Libraries and Information Centres** : Perspective, performance, promise : Silver jubilee commemorative volume. [Indian Association of Special Libraries and Information Centres]. {JNU}

Barden, Bertha R. and Denison, Barbara, n.d., **Guide to the SLA loan collection, classification schemes and subject heading lists**. [Special Libraries Association] {DUL}

Barden, Bertha R., 1937, **Book numbers** : A manual for students with a basic code of rules. {DUL}

Barhydt, Gordon C. and Schmidt, Charles T., n.d., **Information retrieval thesaurus of education terms**. {AIU}

Barker, Ronald and Escarpit, Robert, eds., 1973, **Book hunger**. {DUL}

Barnes, Melvyn, 1978, **Youth library work** : Exploratory essays, 2nd edn. {IIT}

Barnes, R.C.M., 1964, **Present state of information retrieval by computer**. {JNU}

Barquin, Raman C. and Mead, Graham P., n.d., **Towards the information society**. {DUL}

Barr, Keith and Line, Maurice, eds., 1975, **Essays on information and libraries**. {CRRI DUL ICA IIMC INSA JNU NASSDOC NIPCCD ZHL}

Barrett, W.J., 1961, **Glossary of photocopying terms**. {DUL}

Barrocal, Ramon, 1969, **A glossary of technical service terms for library science students**. [School of Library Science, Syracuse University]. {NASSDOC*}.

Barron, D.W., 1971, **Computer operating systems**. {NASSDOC}

Barrow, W.J., 1961, **Permanence and durability of library catalogue cards**. {DUL}

Barrow, W.J., 1972, **Manuscripts and documents** : Their deterioration and restoration. {NASSDOC NMML}

Barton, Mary N. and Watson, Ellen F., 1950, **General reference department staff manual.** [Enoch Pratt Free Library, Baltimore]. {USIS}

Barua, B.P. ed., 1986, **Directory of Indian public libraries** : A selected list of libraries. {NASSDOC}

Barzun, Jacques and Graff, Henry F., 1977, **Modern researcher,** 3rd edn. {NASSDOC}

Batten, W.E., ed., 1975, **Handbook of special librarianship and information work,** 4th edn. [Association of Special Libraries and Information Bureaux]. {CRRI IIT}

Batty, C.D., 1966, **Introduction to Colon Classification**. {ICHR IIFT IIT JNU NASSDOC NMML SPA ZHL}

Batty, C.D., 1966, **Introduction to the Dewey Decimal Classification**. {IIFT IIT MFL SPA ZHL}

Batty, C.D. 1971, **Introduction to the eighteenth edition of the Dewey Decimal Classification.** {CRRI IIC JNU NIE USIS}

Baumel, W.J. and Marcus, M., n.d., **Economics of academic libraries**. [American Council of Education]. {AIU NIEPA USIS}

Bavakutty, M., 1981, **Canons of library classification**. {JNU NIH ZHL}

Bavakutty, M., 1984, **A critical study of the organisation and utilisation of libraries in higher educational institutions in Kerala**. [University of Calicut]. {NASSDOC}

Bavakutty, M., 1986, **College libraries in India** : A case study: Photocopy from :*Library management* 7(1) 1986. {NASSDOC}

Bean, Donald E. and Ellsworth, Ralph E., 1948, **Modular planning for college and small university libraries**. {DUL}

Bean, Jared, 1909, **The old librarians almanac**. {NASSDOC*}

Beard, John Robert, 1967, **Canadian provincial libraries**. {JNU}

Beaubien, Anne K. and George, Mary W., 1982, **Learning the library** : Concepts and methods for effective bibliographic instruction. {AIU}

Becker, Carol A., 1974, **Community information service** : A directory of public library involvement. {JNU}

Becker, Joseph and Hayes, Robert M., 1963, **Information storage and retrieval** : Tools, elements, theories. {DUL ICA IEG MFL NASSDOC USIS}

Becker, Joseph, ed., 1971, **Interlibrary communications and information networks.** {JNU}

Beckett, John A., 1975, **Management dynamics** : The new synthesis. {JNU}

Beeler, M. Fancher, et al, 1974, **Measuring the quality of library service**. {NIEPA USIS}

Beetle, Clara, 1970, **ALA cataloguing rules for author and title entries**. {BIS CRRI DSSW ICA IIFT IIT MFL NIEPA SPA TDA USIS ZHL}

Beetle, Clara, 1970, **Cataloguing rules for author and title entries,** 2nd edn. [American Library Association]. {NAI}

Belongov, G. and Kotov, R., 1971, **Automated information** : Retrieval system. {JNU}

Belson, W.A., 1962, **Studies in readership**. {IIT}

Benewick, Anne J., 1974, **Asian and African collections in British libraries** : Problems and prospects. {DUL NMML}

Benge, Ronald C., 1970-75, **Libraries and cultural change, 1970; 1975**. {AIU IIT MMTC NASSDOC USIS}

Benge, Ronald Charles, 1979, **Culture crisis and libraries in the Third World**. {IIT}

Bennett, Frederick, 1972, **Cataloguing in practice** : Organisation of book acquisition in libraries. {CRRI ICHR NASSDOC NIPCCD}

Benton, Milored, comp., 1973, **Federal library resources** : A user's guide to research collections. {USIS}

Benz, .Magdalena Krommer, 1977, **World guide to terminological activities**. {JNU}

Berelson, Bernard, 1971, **Content analysis in communication research**. {NASSDOC}

Berelson, Bernard, ed., n.d., **Education for librarianship.** {AIU IEG}

Berelson, Bernard and Asheim, Lester, 1949, **Library's public** : Report of the public library inquiry. [Social Science Research Council]. {IEG}

Bergen, Dan and Duryea, E.D., 1964, **Libraries and college climate of learning**. {JNU}

Bergman, Samuel and Bruckner, Steven, 1972, **Introduction to computers and computer programming.** {DUL}

Berman, Sanford, 1984, **Subject cataloguing**. : Critique and innovation. {JNU}

Berriman, S.G., 1969, **Library buildings, 1967-1968**. {DUL}

Berriman, S.G. and Harrison, K.C., 1966, **British public library buildings**. {IIT}

Berry, John N., ed., 1969, **Directory of library consultants**. {USIS}

Berry, Ralph, 1966, **How to write a research paper**. {DUL}

Beswick, Norman, 1975, **Organising resources** : Six case studies : Final report of the Schools Council Resources Centre project. {NIPCCD}

Bhargava, G.D., 1971, **Granthalaya vargikaran**. [Madhya Pradesh Hindi Granth Academi]. {NMML}

Bhargava, G.D.,1977, **Librarianship in India and abroad** : Retrospect and prospect. {CRRI ICA IIT JNU NASSDOC NCAER NIEPA NIPCCD ZHL}

Bhargava, G.D. and Sood, S.P., 1975, **Colon Classification** : Theory and practice. {CRRI ICA ICHR NIPCCD}

Bhargava, G.D. and Tejomurty, A.. eds., 1986, **Dimensions in library and information science**. {JNU}

Bhargava, K.D., 1967, **Repair and preservation of records**. [National Archives of India]. {NASSDOC}

Bhatia, Brajesh, and Goyal, M.M.L., 1971, **Directory of family planning and population libraries in India**. [National Institute of Family Planning]. {NIH}

Bhatia, S.K. and Surender Kumar, comps., 1988, **Directory of libraries in Delhi**. {ICA ICCR IIC IIPA JNU NIEPA NASSDOC}

Bhatia, S.K., ed., 1979, **Libraries in Delhi** : A comprehensive list. {AIU IIT}

Bhatnagar, Manjula, 1977, **Analysis of the current serial publications being subscribed to in the Delhi University Library System (DULS), Jawahar Lal Nehru University Library and Indian Institute of Technology Library**. (University of Delhi, Department of Library Science, Sessional Project, 1977). {DUL}

Bhatt, Narayan Singh, 1986, **Rajasthan ke granthagar**. {NASSDOC*}

Bhattacharya, G., n.d., **A general theory of SIL, POPSI and CLASSAURUS** : Results of current classification research in India. {NASSDOC*}

Bhattacharya, I.S., 1962, **New trends in scientific communication**. [Indian Association of Special Libraries and Information Centres]. {SPA}

Bhattacharya, K.K., 1979, **Modern trends in librarianship in India**. {IIMC IIT NMML}

Bidlack, Russel E., 1955, **City Library of Detroit, 1817-1837**. {JNU}

Biggs, P.T., ed., 1985, **Current research for the information profession, 1985-86**. [Library Association, London]. {NASSDOC}

Bikewell, Kenneth Graham Bartlett, 1978, **A study of indexers reactions to the PRECIS indexing system**. [Department of Library and Information Studies, Faculty of Humanities and Social Studies, Liverpool Polytechnic]. {BCL}

Biligiri, B.S. and Sulochna, C.R., 1973, **Classification for linguistics and languages** : A modified approach based on Decimal Classification. [Central Institute of Indian Languages, Mysore]. {ICHR ZHL}

Binns, Norman, E., 1962, **Introduction to historical bibliography**, rev edn. {DUL}

Binwal, J.C., et al, ed., 1990, **Social science information** : Problems and prospects. {NASSDOC}

Bird, E.A., 1972, **Electronic data processing computers for commercial students.** {NERC}

Bishop, Enid and Waller, Jean M., eds. 1972, **International co-operation in orientalist librarianship**. {JNU NMML}

Black, Donard V., 1983, **Document storage and retrieval techniques appendix** : Indexing techniques, descriptions and background. {JNU}

Black, Dorothy M., 1975, **Guide to lists of Master's theses**. [American Library Association]. {NASSDOC}

Blagden, John, 1980, **Do we really need libraries?** {NIPCCD}

Blagden, John Frederick, 1969, **Management information retrieval** : A new indexing language. {BCL NASSDOC}

Blessum, William T. and Sippl, Charles J., 1972, **Computer glossary for medical and health sciences.** {NASSDOC}

Bliss, H.E., 1936, **System of bibliographic classification**, 2nd edn. {NAI}

Bliss, Henry Evelyn, 1929, **Organisation of knowledge and system of the sciences**. {DUL}

Bliss, Henry Evelyn, 1939, **Organisation of knowledge in libraries and the subject-approach to books,** 2nd edn. {BIS IEG USIS}

Bliss, Henry Evelyn, 1953, **Bibliographic Classification** : Classes L-Z, 3 vols, {CRRI}

Bliss, Henry Evelyn, 1977, **Bibliographic Classification**, 2nd edn., ed. by J. Mills {IIT JNU}

Bloomberg, Marty and Evans, G. Edward, 1976, **Introduction to technical services for library technicians**, 3rd edn. {MHA}

Bloomberg, Marty and Evans, G. Edward, 1985, **Introduction to technical services for library technicians**, 5th edn. {NASSDOC}

Bloomberg, Marty and Weber, Hans, 1976, **Introduction to classification and number building in Dewey**. {IIFT}

Bloomfield, B.C., 1972, **Acquisition and provision of foreign books by national and university libraries in the United Kingdom** : Papers of the Morecamb conference, April 16, 1972. {NMML}

Boaz, Martha, ed., n.d., **Papers** : Symposium on modern trends in documentation, 1958, California. {CRRI}

Boaz, Martha, ed. 1951, **Living library** : Planning public library buildings for cities of 100,000 or less. {CRRI}

Boaz, Martha, ed., 1959, **Modern trends in documentation**. {ISI}

Boaz, Martha, ed., 1979, **Current concepts in library management.** {USIS}

Boaz, Martha, ed., 1981, **Strategies for meeting the information needs of society in the year 2000.** {USIS}

Bobinski, George S., 1969, **Carnegie libraries** : Their history and impact on American public library development. [American Library Association]. {USIS}

Bochm, Eric H., 1967, **CUE system for bibliography and indexing**. {NASSDOC}.

Bohe, Marilyn, 1971, **Flow charting techniques**. {JNU}

Boll, John J., 1970, **Introduction to cataloguing**, 2 vols, Vol. 1: Descriptive cataloguing and an overview of catalogues and cataloguing; Vol 2: Entry headings. {IIT JNU NERC NASSDOC NMML ZHL}

Bolt, A.B. and Wardle, M.E., 1970, **Communicating with a computer**. {NASSDOC}

Bommer, Michael R.W. and Chorba, Ronald W., 1982, **Decision-making for library management**. {JNU NIEPA}

Bonk, Wallace John and Marymagril, Rose, 1979, **Building library collections**, 5th edn. {USIS}

Bonn, G.S., 1966, **Library education and training in developing, countries**. {ICA NIEPA}

Bonn, George S. and Faibisoff, Sulvia, eds., 1978, **Changing times, changing libraries.** {USIS}

Bonny, Harold V., 1939, **A manual of practical book selection for public libraries.** {CRRI DUL}

Boorer, David, 1967, **Mental hospital library**. {DUL}

Booth, Grayce M., 1973, **Functional analysis of information processing** : A structured approach for simplifying systems design. {NASSDOC}

Borcharat, D.H. and Horacek, J.I., 1975, **Librarianship in Australia, New Zealand and Oceania.** {NASSDOC}

Bordin, Ruth B. and Warner, Robert M., 1966, **Modern manuscript library.** {NMML}

Borko, H., 1965, **Conceptual foundations of information systems.** {JNU}

Borko, Harold, 1967, **Automated language processing**. {NASSDOC}

Borko, Harold and Bernier, Charles L., 1975, **Abstracting concepts and methods.** {DEPT JNU}

Borko, Harold and Bernier, Charles L., 1978, **Indexing concepts and methods.** {BCL BIS}

Borko, Harold, ed., 1973, **Targets for research in library education**. [American Library Association]. {USIS}

Bose, H., 1986, **Information science** : Principles and practice. {NASSDOC}

Bose, H., 1987, **U.D.C.** : Theory and practice. {JNU}

Boss, Richard W., 1982, **Automating library acquisitions** : Issues and outlook. {JNU}

Boss, Richard W., 1983, **The library manager's guide to automation**, 2nd edn. {NASSDOC USIS}

Boswell, David, B., 1952, **Text-book on bibliography.** {DUL}

Boulding, Kenneth E. and Senesh, Lawrence, 1983, **Optimum utilisation of knowledge** : Making knowledge serve human betterment. {NMML}

Bourne, Charles P., 1966, **Methods of information handling**. {DUL IIMC IIT JNU NASSDOC}

Bowden, Russel E., ed., 1980, **Library education programme in developing countries with special reference to Asia** : UNESCO pre-IFLA conference seminar on library education programme in developing countries, August 15-18, 1980, Philippines. [Library Association, London]. {IIT NASSDOC}

Bowen, Judith, 1978, **The design and implementation of community information service in the library**. {BCL}

Bowler, Reberta, ed., 1964, **Local public library administration**. [International Managers Association, Illinois]. {SPA USIS}

Bowles, Edmund A., ed., 1967, **Computers in humanistic research**. {NASSDOC}

Boyd, Jessie, et al, 1941, **Books, libraries and you**, {ZHL}

Boyd, Jessie, et al, 1965, **Books, libraries and you** : A handbook on the use of reference books and the reference resources of the library, 3rd edn. {USIS}

Boyle, Deirdre, ed., 1977, **Expanding media**. {IIT}

Bracken, Marlyn C. and Shilling, Charles W., 1967, **Survey of practice training in information science**. {JNU}

Braden, Irene A., 1970, **The undergraduate library**. [American Library Association]. {USIS}

Bradford, S.C., 1953, **Documentation**. {BCL BIS DUL MFL NAI SPA}

Bramley, Gerald, 1975, **World trends in library education**. {AIU IIT NERC NIEPA USIS}

Branscomb, Harvie, 1940, **Teaching with books** : A study of college libraries. [American Library Association]. {ZHL}

Branscomb, Harvie, 1964, **Teaching with books** : A study of college libraries. {DUL}

Brawne, Michael, 1970, **Libraries architecture and equipment**. {IIT ZHL}

Breillat, Pierre, 1965, **Rare books section in the library**. [UNESCO]. {IIMC IIT NASSDOC}

Breivick, Patrica Senn and Gel. E. Gordon, 1989, **Information literacy** : Revolution in the library. {NASSDOC}

Brenni, Vito J., comp. and ed., 1975, **Essays on bibliography.** {NASSDOC}

Breuer, Hans, n.d., **Dictionary for computer languages**. {RTL}

Brimmer, Brenda, et al, 1962, **A guide to the use of United Nations documents, including reference to the specialised agencies and special U.N. bodies.** {MFL USIS}

Brittain, J.M., 1970, **Information and its users** : A review with special reference to the social sciences. {JNU NASSDOC}

Broadbent, K.P., 1980, **Dissemination of scientific information in the People's Republic of China**. [International Development Research Centre, Ottawa]. {NASSDOC}

Broadffield, A., 1946, **Philosophy of classification**. {IEG IIT}

Broadffield, A., 1949, **Philosophy of librarianship**. {CRRI IEG IIT}

Broadus, Robert N., 1973, **Selecting materials for libraries**. {USIS}

Brodman, Estelle, 1968, **Proposal for documentation centre at the Central Family Planning Institute, New Delhi** : Report. {NASSDOC}

Brogan, Gerald E. and Buck, Jeanne T., 1969, **Using libraries effectively**. {ICA}

Brooks, James and Draper, James, 1979, **Interior design for libraries**. [American Library Association]. {USIS}

Brooks, Jean S. and Reich, David L., 1974, **The public library in non-traditional education.** {NASSDOC USIS}

Brooks, Philip C., 1969, **Research in archives** : The use of unpublished primary sources. {NASSDOC USIS ZHL}

Brown, A.G., 1976, **An introduction to subject indexing.** {ICA NIEPA NIH ZHL}

Brown, A.G., 1982, **Introduction to subject indexing** : A programmed text. 2nd edn. {IIT}

Brown, Charles Harvey and Bousfield, H.G., n.d., **Circulation work in college and university libraries**. {JNU}

Brown, Eleanor Frances, 1967, **Bookmobiles and bookmobile service**. {USIS}

Brown, Everett S., 1950, **Manual of government publications** : United States and foreign. {CRRI}

Brown, Harry Faulkner, 1971, **Planning the academic library**. {JNU}

Brown, James Duff, 1939, **Subject classification for the arrangement of libraries and the organisation of information**, 3rd edn. {DUL}

Brown, James W., 1976, **New media in public libraries** : Survey of current practices. {USIS}

Brown, Royston, 1979, **Public library administration.** {IIT NIEPA}

Brownstone, David M. and Franck Irene M., 1982, **The directory of publishing**. {NASSDOC}

Broyard, Anatole, 1974, **Aroused by books.** {USIS}

Brugghen, W. Van Den, 1975, **Syllabus for a documentation course**. [International Federation for Documentation and Information]. {BIS}

Brummel, L., 1956, **Union catalogues** : Their problems and organisation. [UNESCO]. {CRRI}

Bry, Ilse, 1977, **Emerging field of socio-bibliography** : The collected essays of Ilse Bry, comp. and ed. by Lois Afflerback and Marga Franck {BCL IIT}

Bryan, Harrison, 1976, **University libraries in Britain** : A network. {JNU NIEPA}

Bryan, J.F.W., et al, 1956, **Library co-operation in the North West** : A report. {DUL}

Buchanan, Brian W., 1976, **Glossary of indexing terms**. {BCL NASSDOC NERC}

Buchanan, Brian, 1979, **Theory of library classification**. {DUL}

Buck, Paul, 1964, **Libraries and universities** : Addresses and reports, ed. by E.E. Williams {JNU}

Buckland, Michael K., 1963, **Library services in theory and context**. {IIT}

Buckland, Michael K., 1975, **Book availability and the library user**. {JNU NASSDOC USIS}

Buckner, B.C., comp., 1973, **Directory of population libraries and information centres in the United States**. [Carolina Population Centre, University of North Carolina]. {NIH RTL}

Budd, Richard W., et al, 1967, **Content analysis of communication.** {NASSDOC}

Buhler, Curt F., et al, 1949, **Standards of bibliographical description**. {DUL}

Bulick, Stephen, 1982, **Structure and subject interaction** : Toward a sociology of knowledge in the social sciences. {BIS}

Bunch, Allan, 1982, **Community information services** : Their origin, scope and development. {IIT}

Bunch, Allan, 1984, **Basics of information work**. {JNU}

Bundy, Mary Lee and Wasserman, Paul, eds., 1970, **Reader in research methods for librarianship**. {USIS}

Burch, John G., et al, 1979, **Information systems** : Theory and practice. {JNU NIPCCD TDA}

Burchard, John E., et al, eds., 1949, **Planning the university library building** : A summary of discussions by librarians, architects and engineers. {NASSDOC ZHL}

Burke, J.E., 1961, **Planning functional college library**. {IIT}

Burke, Remend A., 1952, **What is the index**. {NAI}

Burkett, J. and Morgan, T.S., 1963, **Special materials in the library**. [Library Association, London]. {IIT}

Burkett, J., ed., 1965, **Special library and information services in the United Kingdom**, 2nd edn. [Library Association, London]. {NIEPA}

Burkett, Jack., 1963, **Special libraries and documentation centres in the Netherlands** {IIT JNU NASSDOC SPA}

Burkett, Jack, 1933, **Library and information network in the United Kingdom**. [Association of Special Libraries and Information Bureaux]. {CRRI JNU}

Burkett, Jack, ed., 1968, **Trends in special librarianship**. {IEG IIT MMTC}

Burkhalter, Barten R., 1968, **Case studies in systems analysis in a university library**. {JNU}

Burlingame, Dwight F., 1978, **College learning resource centre**. {NIEPA}

Burr, Nelson R., 1952, **Safeguarding our cultural heritage** : A bibliography on the protection of museums, works of art, monuments, archives and libraries in time of war. {JNU}

Burrel, T.W., 1969, **Learn to use books and libraries** : A programmed text. {JNU}

Burton, Paul F., 1986, **Micro computer in library and information services** : An annotated bibliography. {JNU}

Busha, Charles H. and Herter, Stephen P., eds., 1980, **Research methods in librarianship** : Techniques and interpretation. {ISI}

Bushnell, George H., 1951, **Reference librarian in university, municipal and specialised libraries**. {BIS CRRI DUL}

Buter, Pierce, 1943, **Reference function of the library**. {DUL NAL}

Butler, Brett and Martin, Susan K. eds., 1975, **Library automation-II** : The state of art : Papers : Pre-conference institute on library automation, June 22-23, 1973, Las Vegas. [American Library Association, Information Science and Automation Division]. {USIS}

Butler, Pierce, 1961, **Introduction to library science**. {AIU IIT MFL}

Byerly, Greg, 1983, **Online searching** : A dictionary and bibliographic guide. {NASSDOC USIS}

Byrne, Brendan, 1985, **Art of systems analysis.** {JNU}

Cabeceiras, James, 1978, **Multimedia library** : Materials selection and use. {IIFT JNU NIPCCD}

Cabeceiras, James, 1982, **Multimedia library** : Materials selection and use, 2nd edn. {NIEPA}

Calder, Rose E., et al, comps., **A guide to library resources in Rangoon**. {IEG}

Calderhead, Particia, ed., 1972, **Libraries for professional practice**. {CRRI IIT}

Caldwell, William, 1956, **Introduction to county library practice**. {JNU}

Caless, T.W., et al, 1970, **Strategies for manipulating Universal Decimal Classification relationships for computer retrieval.** {JNU}

Cameron, William J., 1978, **Bibliographical control of early books**. {JNU}

Camille, Claude and Dehaine, Michel, 1970, **Dictionary of data processing**. {NASSDOC}

Campbell, D.J., 1973, **Small technical libraries**. [UNESCO]. {DUL ICA NERC NIEPA}

Campbell, H.C., 1967, **Metropolitan public library planning throughout the work**. {DUL JNU NASSDOC SPA USIS}

Campbell, H.C., 1973, **Public libraries in the urban metropolitan setting**. {DUL IIT}

Campbell, H.C., 1983, **Developing public library systems and services.** [UNESCO]. {NIEPA}

Campbell, Malcolm James, 1974, **Business information services** : Some aspects of structure organisation and problems. {BCL}

Campey, Lucille H., 1972, **Generating and printing indexes by computer.** [Association of Special Libraries and Information Bureaux]. {CRRI}

Cancaster, F.W., et al, 1980, **Impact of a paperless society on the research library of the future** : A report to the NSF. [Library Research Centre, Illinois]. {ISI}

Cardenas, Alfonso F., et al, eds., 1972, **Computer science**. {NASSDOC}

Carey, G.V., 1951, **Making an Index**. {IIT}

Carey, R.J.P., 1966, **Finding and using technical information.** {MHA}

Cargill, Jennifer S. and Alley, Brian, 1979, **Practical approval plan management.** {IIT}

Carleton, Joecket, 1939, **Current issues in library administration.** {JNU}

Carnell, E.J., 1938, **County libraries** : Retrospect and forecast. {CRRI ZHL}

Carnovsky, Leon, n.d., **Report on a programme of library education in Israel.** (Technical assistance : Special report, No. 1). [UNESCO]. {IEG NASSDOC}

Carnovsky, Leon, 1968, **Public library in the urban setting** : The thirty second conference of the Graduate Library School, July 31-August 2, 1967. {NMML}

Carnovsky, Leon, ed., 1969, **Library networks** : Promises and performance. {IIT}

Carpenter, Michael and Svenonius, E., eds., 1985, **Foundations of cataloguing** : A source book. {NASSDOC}

Carpenter, Ray L. and Vasu, Ellan Storey, 1979, **Statistical methods for librarians**. {ISI}

Carrington, David K. and Stephenson, Richard W., comps., 1978, **Map collections in the United States and Canada** : A directory, 3rd edn. [Special Libraries Association, New York]. {USIS}

Carrington, David K., comp., 1970, **Map collection in the United States and Canada** : A directory, 2nd edn. [Special Libraries Association, New York]. {USIS}

Carroll, Frances Laverne, 1981, **Recent advances in school librarianship.** {NIEPA}

Carter, J., 1961, **ABC for book collectors**. {IIT}

Carter, Launor F., et al, 1967, **National document handling systems for science and technology.** {BIS IIMC NIH USIS}

Carter, Marry Duncan, et al, 1974, **Building library collections,** 4th edn. {USIS}

Carter, Mary Duncan and Bonk, Wallace John, 1969, **Building library collections**, 3rd edn. {USIS}

Casby, Brinkley, comp., n.d., **Directory of library photo duplication services in the United States, Canada and Mexico**. {DUL}

Casey, Robert S., 1958, **Oral communication of technical information**. {CRRI}

Casey, Robert S., 1958, **Punched cards** : Their application to science and industry. {JNU}

Cassata, Mary B. and Totten, Herman L., ed., 1975, **The administrative aspects of education for librarianship** : A symposium. {NIEPA USIS}

Casteleyn, Mary, 1981, **Planning library training programmes**. {NIEPA}

Cave, Roderick, 1976, **Rare book librarianship.** {NASSDOC}

Cecil, Henry L. and Heap, Willard A., 1940, **School library service in the United States.** {ZHL}

Chakmakhchev, A.G., 1970, **International organisation and their activities in the field of scientific and technical information.** [UNESCO]. {NASSDOC}

Chakrabarti, A.K., 1980, **An introduction to documentation science.** {NASSDOC}

Chakrabarti, A.K., 1983, **A treatise on book selection.** {NERC NIH ZHL}

Chakrabarti, Bhubaneswar and Chakraborty, A.R. 1983, **Acronyms, initialisms and abbreviations in library and information science** : An annotated guide. {NASSDOC}

Chakraborti, M.L. 1971, **Bibliography in theory and practice.** {MFL NASSDOC}

Chakraborti, M.L. 1975, **Bibliography in theory and practice,** 2nd rev edn. {ICA ICHR IIMC INSA JNU NIPCCD}

Chakraborty, A.R. and Kapoor, S.K., eds., 1983, **Papers** : IASLIC conference, 14th, December 26-29, 1983, New Delhi, I : Information flow in non R and D context; II : Grey literature. [Indian Association of Special Libraries and Information Centres]. {JNU MMTC NASSDOC NCAER NIEPA NIPCCD}

Chakravarty, N.C., 1962, **Library movement in India.** {NASSDOC}

Chakraverty, N.C., 1966, **Education for librarianship** : A survey. [Indian Association of Special Libraries and Information Centres]. {SPA}

Chambers, A., 1969, **Reluctant reader.** {DUL}

Chambers, Marjori, comp., 1968, **Introduction to Dewey Decimal Classification for British schools.** {DUL}

Chan, Lois M., 1980, **Immroth's guide to the Library of Congress Classification,** 3rd edn. {USIS}

Chan, Lois Mai, 1985, **Cataloguing and classification** : An introduction. {JNU}

Chan, Lois Mai, 1986, **Library of Congress subject headings** : Principles and application, 2nd edn. (Research studies in library science, No. 19). {NASSDOC}

Chan, Lois Mai, et al, eds., 1985, **Theory of subject analysis** : A source book. {NASSDOC}

Chanana, Charanjit, 1973, **Computers in Asia.** {NASSDOC}

Chancellor, John Miller, 1938, **Helping the reader toward self education.** {JNU}

Chandel, A.S., ed., 1987, **Planning in library resource sharing** : Proceedings : Seminar on coordination in resource sharing held at Isabella Thouburn College, Lucknow. {NASSDOC}

Chandler, G., 1967, **How to find out** : A guide to sources of information for all, arranged by the Dewey Decimal Classification, 2nd edn. {MHA}

Chandler, G., 1968, **How to find out about literature.** {DUL}

Chandler, G., 1974, **How to find out** : A guide to sources of information for all, arranged by the Dewey Decimal Classification, 4th rev. edn. {NASSDOC}

Chandler, G., 1982, **How to find out** : Printed and on-line sources, 5th rev edn. {DUL NASSDOC}

Chandler, George, 1966, **Libraries in the modern world.** {AIU IIC SPA}

Chandler, George, 1971, **Libraries in the East** : An international and comparative study. {ICA IIMC JNU NASSDOC NMML}

Chandler, George, 1972, **Libraries, documentation and bibliography in the USSR, 1917-1971** : Survey and critical analysis of Soviet studies. {JNU NASSDOC}

Chandler, George, 1982, **International and national library and information services** : A review of some recent developments. 2 vols. {IIT NASSDOC NERC}

Chandler, George, ed., 1972, **International librarianship** : Surveys of recent developments in developing countries and in advanced librarianship submitted to the 1971 IFLA pre-session seminar for developing countries, August 24—September 1, 1971. [Library Association, London]. {NASSDOC}

Chandrasekharan, K., 1953, **Library science in India**. [Madras Library Association]. {BIS SPA}

Chaplin, A.H., comp., 1967, **Names of person** : National usages for entry in catalogues. [International Federation of Library Association and Institutions]. {NASSDOC}

Chaplin, H., ed., 1976, **Organisation of the library profession**. {CRRI}

Chapman, Edward A., et al, 1970, **Library systems analysis guidelines**. {DUL ICA IIT JNU NASSDOC NIH NMML USIS}

Chapman, R.W., 1950, **Book collecting** : Four broadcast talks. {DUL}

Charen, Thelma, 1975, **Technical notes** : MEDLARS indexing instructions. [National Library of Medicine, Maryland]. {CRRI}

Charles, Compbell, 1963, **Writer's reference book** : A reference work for authors, freelance journalists and writers for film, radio and television. {DUL}

Charles, Rosner, n.d., **Growth of the book-jacket**. {DUL}

Chartrand, Robert Lee and Morentz, James W., eds., 1979, **Information technology serving society.** {USIS}

Chatterjee, Nihar Kanti, 1980, **Directory of research and special libraries in India and Sri Lanka**, 2 vols. {MMTC ZHL}

Chen, Ching-Chih, 1976, **Applications of operations research models to libraries.** {CRRI}

Chen, Ching-Chih, 1976, **Biomedical, scientific and technical book reviewing.** {DUL}

Chen, Ching-Chih, 1987, **Scientific and technical information sources**, 1977. {IIT INSA JNU NERC}

Chen, Ching-Chih, ed., 1978, **Quantitative measurement and dynamic library service.** {BIS IIT}

Chen, Ching-chih and Hernon, Peter, 1982, **Information seeking** : Assessing and anticipating user needs. {JNU}

Chene, Steven Seapho, 1976, **Comparative study of librarian's job satisfaction** : Cataloguer and reference librarians in university libraries. {JNU}

Cheney, Frances Neel and Williams, Wiley J., 1971, **Fundamental reference sources**. [American Library Association]. {DUL INSA JNU MMTC NASSDOC NERC}

Cheney, Frances Neel, 1980, **Fundamental reference sources**. [American Library Association]. {DUL}

Chennaveerian, M.S., et al, eds., 1976, **Compendium of research, 1951-1976**. [Karnatak University]. {NASSDOC}

Chirgwin, F. John and Oldfield, Phyllis, 1983, **Library assistant's manual.** 2nd rev. edn. {IIT}

Chopra, H.R., 1984, **Librarianship as a profession** : A study of socio-economic background and professional orientation of the libraries in Delhi : Thesis. [Punjab University]. {NASSDOC}

Chopra, H.R., 1989, **Librarianship as a profession in India**. {NASSDOC}

Chopra, H.R., Kumar, P.S.G. and Tejomurty, A., 1988, **Directory of library and information science schools in India**. {NASSDOC}

Chopra, R.N., 1979, **Union catalogue of library science periodical holdings in Delhi University Library system, Jawahar Lal Nehru University Library and National Science Library.** [Indian National Scientific Documentation Centre]. {DUL}

Chopra, R.N., 1990, **Dictionary of library scinece**. {JNU}

Choudhary, Anil Roy, 1959, **National standards for cataloguing and indexing art museum objects and documents**. {ZHL}

Christ, Alam G.L., n.d., **MINIS, MICROS and terminals for libraries and information services**. {JNU}

Christien, Roger, 1978, **The electronic library** : Bibliographic data bases, 1978-79, 2nd rev. edn. {USIS}

Chuna, George M. and Chuna, Dorothy G., 1972, **Conservation of library materials** : Manual of bibliography on the care, repair and restoration of library materials, 2 vols. {DUL IIT NMML USIS}

Churchman, C. West, 1971, **Design of inquiry systems** : Basic concepts of systems and organisation. {JNU}

Churchman, C. West, et al, 1969, **Introduction to operations research.** {NASSDOC}

Clack, Doris H., ed., 1975, **Black literature resources** : Analysis and organisation. {IIT ISI}

Clack, Doris Hargrett, 1979, **The making of a code** : The issues underlying AACR2 : Papers : International conference on AACR2, March 11-14, 1979, Florida. [American Library Association]. {USIS}

Clapp, Vener W., 1964, **Future of the research library**. {IEG JNU}

Clark, F.J., 1970, **Information processing**. {NASSDOC NIH}

Clark, Fife, 1970, **Central Office of Information**. {NASSDOC}

Clark, Robert L., ed., 1976, **Archive-library relations.** {ISI}

Clarke, Archibald Leycester, 1933, **Manual of practical indexing including arrangement of subject catalogues**. {NAI}

Clarke, D.A., ed., 1975, **Acquisitions from the Third World.** {DUL NASSDOC}

Clarke, J.D., 1963, **Your future as a librarian**. {IIFT}

Clarke, Marion G.M., 1966, **David Watkinson's library** : Hundred years in Harftord, Connecticat. {DUL}

Clarke, Tom, 1975, **International academic and specialist publishers directory**. {NASSDOC}

Clason, W.E., comp., 1973, **Elsevier's dictionary of library science, information and documentation**. {JNU ZHL}

Clason, W.E., comp., 1976, **Elsevier's dictionary of library science, information and documentation**, 2nd edn. {IIT}

Cleary, Florence D., 1966, **Discovering books and libraries** : A handbook for the upper elementary and junior high school grades. {DUL}

Clements, Jaff, n.d., **Bookbinding**. {ISI}

Cleverdon, Cysil W., 1962, **Report on the testing and analysis of an investigation into the comparative efficiency of indexing systems.** {BIS IIT}

Clifton, H.D., 1971, **Data processing systems design** : Case studies from the application of computers to business. {NASSDOC}

Cloke, J., ed., 1986, **Management for librarians** : Based on a course of lectures at the Library Association in 1967. {JNU}

Clugh, Eric A., 1967, **Bookbinding for librarians**. [Association of Assistant Librarians, London]. {NASSDOC}

Coates, E.J., 1960, **Subject catalogues** : Headings and structure. [Library Association, London]. {IIT NASSDOC}

Coblans, H., et al, 1974, **Science and technology policies information exchange systems (SPINES) feasibility study**. {JNU}

Coblans, Herbert, 1966, **Use of mechanized methods in documentation work.** {JNU}

Coblans, Herbert, 1974, **Librarianship and documentation** : An international perspective. {BIS ICHR ISI NASSDOC NERC}

Coburn, Louis, 1973, **Library media centre problems :** Case studies. {USIS}

Cockerell, Douglas, 1925, **Bookbinding and the care of the books**, 5th edn. {CRRI ZHL}

Cockerell, S.M., 1960, **Repairing of books**, 2nd edn. {NAI}

Codlin, Ellen M., ed., 1982, **ASLIB directory of information sources in the United Kingdom**, vol. 1: Science, Technology & Commerce, 5th edn. {JNU}

Cogoli, John E., 1960, **Photo-offset** : Fundamentals. {DUL}

Cohen, Aaron and Cohen, Elaine, 1979, **Designing and space planning for libraries** : A behavioural guide. {BIS NASSDOC USIS}

Cohen, Aaron and Cohen Elaine, 1982, **Automation, space management and productivity** : A guide for libraries. {IIT USIS}

Cohen, Nathan M., et al, 1963, **Library science dissertations, 1925-1960** : An annotated bibliography of doctoral studies. {USIS}

Colby, Jean Polndexter, 1967, **Writing, illustrating and editing children's books**, rev. edn. {DUL}

Cole, John Y., 1979, **For Congress and the nation** : A chronological history of the Library of Congress. [U.S. Library of Congress]. {USIS}

Cole, John, Y., ed., 1978, **The Library of Congress in perspective** {NASSDOC}

Colin, A.J.T., 1971, **Introduction to operating systems**. {NASSDOC}

Collins, F. Howard, 1956, **Author's and printer's dictionary**. {IIC}

Collins, F. Howard, 1973, **Author's and printer's dictionary**. {DUL}

Collison, R.L., n.d., **Information services** : Their organisation and administration. {JNU}

Collison, R.L., 1951, **Bibliographies** : Subject and national : A guide to their contents, arrangement and use. {MFL}

Collison, R.L., 1957, **Treatment of special material in libraries**. {MFL}

Collison, R.L., 1962, **Bibliographics** : Subject and national : A guide to their contents and use, 2nd ed. {MFL}

Collison, R.L., ed., 1966, **Progress in library science**. {CRRI IEG IIFT NIH NMML}

Collison, Robert, n.d., **Scolma directory of libraries and special collections of Africa**, 2nd edn. {IIC IIT}

Collison, Robert, 1969, **Commercial and industrial records storage**. {NMML}

Collison, Robert, 1971, **Abstract and abstracting services**. {JNU NASSDOC USIS}

Collison, Robert, 1973, **Published library catalogues** : An introduction to their contents and use. {IIT}

Collison, Robert, comp., 1970, **Directory of libraries and special collections on Asia and North Africa**. {NASSDOC NCERT NMML}

Collison, Robert L., 1869, **Library assistance to readers**. [DUL MHA}

Collison, Robert L., 1950, **Cataloguing arrangement and filing of special material in special libraries**. {NAL}

Collison, Robert L., 1959, **Indexes and indexing**. {BIS CRRI IEG IIT MFL MHA SPA}

Collison, Robert L., 1969, **Indexes and indexing** : Guide to the indexing of books and collections of books, periodicals, music recordings, films and other materials, with a reference section and suggestions for further reading, 3rd rev. edn. {USIS}

Collison, Robert L., 1969, **Indexing books** : A manual of basic principles. {IEG IIT INSA NIPCCD}

Collison, Robert L., 1972, **Indexes and indexing** : Guide to the indexing of books and collections of books, periodicals, music recordings, films and other materials, with a reference section and suggestions for further reading, 4th edn. {JNU NASSDOC NIPCCD NMML}

Collison, Robert Lewis, 1957, **Book collection** : An introduction to modern methods of literary and bibliographical detection. {DUL}

Colvin, Laura C., 1973, **Cataloguing sampler** : Comparative and interpretive guide. {IIT}

Comarona, John P. and Warren, Margaret J., 1982, **Manual on the use of the Dewey Decimal Classification**, 19th edn. {NASSDOC}

Comb, Lewis C. Brans, n.d., **Case for faculty status for academic librarians.** {JNU}

Comey, A.C. and McNamara, Katherine, 1937, **State and national planning.** {ISI}

Conant, Ralph W., ed., 1965, **Public library and the city.** {JNU SPA}

Conlon, Eileen, 1964, **Books lead the way** : Library and reading skill-text. {JNU}

Conning, Arthur M., 1983, **Guide to the computerisation of population documentation storage and retrieval systems**. [United Nations]. {NASSDOC}

Conroy, Barbara, 1978, **Library staff development and continuing education** : Principles and practices. {USIS}

Continolo, G., n.d., **Modern filing methods and equipment.** {IIMC}

Converse, Jean M. and Schuman, Howard, 1974, **Conversations at random** : Survey research as interviewers see it. {NASSDOC}

Cook, C. Donald, comp., 1982, **AACR2 decisions and rule interpretations :** A consolidation of the decision and rule interpretations for the Anglo-American Cataloguing Rules, 2nd. edn. assisted by Glenna E. Stevens. [Canadian Library Association]. {USIS}

Cook, Margaret G., 1975, **The new library key,** 3rd edn. {USIS}

Cook, Michael, 1986, **Management of information from archives**. {NMML}

Cooke, A.S., ed., 1931, **County libraries manual**. [Library Association, London]. {NASSDOC}

Cooper, M.J., 1969, **What computers can do** : A guide to the plain man. {DUL}

Coplan, Kate, 1974, **Effective library exhibits** : How to prepare and promote good displays, 2nd edn. {CRRI USIS}

Corbett, Edmund V., 1950, **Introduction to public librarianship for entrance examination students.** {ZHL}

Corbett, Edmund V., 1957, **Photo charging** : Its operation and installation in British Public Library. {JNU}

Corbett, Edmund V., 1978, **Fundamentals of library organisation and administration** : A practical guide. {NCDC NERC NIEPA ZHL}

Corbin, John, 1981, **Developing computer based library systems.** {JNU}

Corrigan, Dorothy D., 1967, **Workbook for a successful workshop**. [American Library Association]. {USIS}

Corrigan, Phillip, 1967, **Introduction to Sears list of subject headings**. {IIMC IIT}

Cortz, Edwin M. and Kazlaushas, Edwin John, 1986, **Managing informations systems and technologies** : A basic guide for design, selection, evaluation and use. {NASSDOC}

Costello, John C., n.d., **Training manual and work book for use in abstracting and coordinate indexing**. [Ohio Battelle Memorial Institute, Ohio]. {BIS}

Costello, John C., et al, n.d., **Operating manual for use in abstracting and coordinate indexing**. [Battelle Memorial Institute, Ohio]. {BIS}

Cousineau, Marie Josee, comp., 1986, **International directory of libraries and documentation centres in terminology**. [Documentation Directorate, Ottawa]. {NASSDOC}

Coward, R.E. and Yelland, H., eds., 1975, **Interchange of bibliographic information in machine readable form** : Papers given at the Western European seminar, May 12-16, 1974, England. [Library Association, London]. {BCL}

Cowles, Betty M. and Orr, Robert W., 1952, **Library instruction manual**, 3rd edn. {ZHL}

Cowley, J., ed., 1985, **The management of polytechnic libraries.** {NASSDOC}

Cowley, J.D., 1939, **Bibliographic description and cataloguing**. {DUL}

Cowley, J.D., 1947, **Use of reference material**. {ZHL}

Cowley, J.D., 1970, **Bibliographical description and cataloguing**. {NASSDOC}.

Cowley, John, 1982, **Personnel management in library**. {DUL IIT}

Cowley, John, ed., 1975, **Libraries in higher education** : The user approach to service. {INSA NIEPA}

Cox, N.S.M., 1966, **Computer and the library**. {IIT}

Craster, H.H.E., 1941, **Bedlican library extension scheme**. {NAL}

Cravan, Timothy, 1986, **String indexing**. {JNU NASSDOC}

Crix, F.C., 1975, **Reprographic management handbook**. {ISI}

Croghan, Antony, 1968, **Faceted classification for an essay on the literature of the performing arts.** {DUL}

Cronin, Richard, 1981, **Congressional research service**. {USIS}

Crookall, R.E., 1961, **School libraries in West Africa**. {JNU NIEPA}

Cross, Otti, n.d., **Library terms**. {ISI}

Crutchky, Brooke, 1967, **Preparation of manuscripts and correction of proofs**. {DUL}

Cundiff, Ruby Ethel, 1954, **Manual of techniques in library organisation**. {DUL}

Cunninghan, Eileen R., 1967, **Classification for medical literature**. 5th edn. {DUL}

Curran, Ann T. and Auram, Henriette D., n.d., **Identification of data elements in bibliographic records**. {BIS}

Currie, Dorothy H., 1965, **How to organise a children's library**. {DUL}

Curwin, Henry, 1968, **History of booksellers** : The old and new. {DUL}

Cutter, C.A., nd. **Cutter's three figure author table**. {IIT ISI}

Cutter, C.A., 1891, **Rules for a dictionary catalog**. {IIT}

Cutter, C.A., 1953, **Rules for dictionary catalog**, 4th edn. [Library Association, London]. {BIS CRRI JNU MFL NAI NIEPA NMML}

D'Olier, J.H. and Delmas, B., 1975, **Planning national infrastructures for documentation, libraries and archives** : Outline of a general policy. {DUL IIMC JNU NASSDOC NIEPA}

Dadzie, E.W. and Strickland, J.T., n.d., **Directory of archives, libraries and schools of librarianship in Africa**. {IIMC}

Daedalus, 1976, **In praise of books**. [Academy of Arts and Sciences, Cambridge]. {USIS}

Dahl, O.J., et al, 1972, **Structured programming**. {NASSDOC}

Daily, Jay E., 1972, **Organising nonprint materials** : A guide for librarians. {ICHR IIT JNU NASSDOC ZHL}

Daily, Jay, E., 1975, **Cataloguing phonorecordings** : Problems and possibilities. {BIS}

Daiute, Robert J. and Gorman, Kenneth A., 1974, **Library operations research** : Computer programming for circulation. {USIS}

Dale, Doris Cruger, 1970, **United Nations library** : Its origin and development. {JNU NASSDOC USIS}

Daniel, Gore, 1978, **To know a library** : Essays and annual report, 1975-76. {JNU}

Daniel, Hawthorne, 1961, **Public libraries for every one**. {NASSDOC}

Daniel, Ruth and Mills, J., 1975, **Classification of library and information science**. {DUL}

Danton, J. Periam, 1949, **Education for librarianship.** [UNESCO]. {IEG NASSDOC}

Danton, J. Periam, 1959, **Climate of book selection** : Social influences on school and public libraries. {DUL}

Danton, J. Periam, 1963, **Book selection and collections** : A comparison of German and American university libraries. {JNU}

Danton, J. Periam, 1970, **Between MLS and PHD** : A study of sixth year specialist programmes in accredited library schools. {DUL}

Danton, J. Periam, 1973, **Dimensions of comparative librarianship.** [American Library Association]. {NASSDOC}

Darley, Lionel S., 1965, **Introduction to bookbinding**. {CRRI}

Das, A.R., n.d., **Union catalogue of the books in the libraries of the Botanical Survey of India**, 3 vols. [Botanical Survey of India]. {INSA}

Dasgupta, A.K., 1967, **Essays in personnel bibliography** : A bibliography of the writings on and by S.R. Ranganathan. {DUL NASSDOC NMML}

Date, Shankar Ganesh, ed., 1943, **Marathi granth suchi**, 2 vols, Vol. 1 : 1800-1937; Vol. 2 : 1938-1951 {NASSDOC}

Datta, Bimal Kumar, 1956, **A practical guide to library procedure**. {NASSDOC}

Datta, Bimal Kumar, 1962, **Practical guide to library procedure**. {CRRI DUL IIT NERC SPA ZHL}

Datta, Bimal Kumar, 1970, **Libraries and librarianship of ancient and medieval India**. {IIC IIT JNU NAI NERC NMML}

Datta, N., 1985, **Academic status for university and college librarians in India**. {JNU}

David, Kaser, ed., 1966, **Books in America's past** : Essays honouring Rudolph H. Gjelsness. {DUL}

Davies, D.W., 1974, **Public library as culture and social centres** : The origin of the concept. {USIS}

Davies, Ruth Ann, 1969, **The school library** : A force for educational excellence. {JNU USIS}

Davinson, D.E., 1969, **Periodicals collection** : Its purpose and uses in libraries. {NMML}

Davinson, Donald, 1965, **Academic and legal deposit libraries**, 2nd. edn. {DEPT DUL ICHR MFL ZHL}

Davinson, Donald 1980, **Reference service**. {DUL ICA}

Davinson, Donald Edward, 1975, **Bibliographic control**. {AIU DUL NASSDOC}

Davis, Charles H. and Lundeen, Gerald W., 1974, **Illustrative computer programming for libraries**. {JNU}

Davis, Charles H. and Lundeen, Gerald W., 1981, **Illustrative computer programming for libraries** : Selected examples for information specialists, 2nd edn. {NASSDOC USIS}

Davis, Charles H. and Ruse, James E., 1979, **Guide to information science**. {BCL JNU}

Davis, Harold S., ed., 1971, **Instructional Media Centre** : Bold new venture. {USIS}

Davis, Richard A. and Bailey, Catherine A., 1964, **Bibliography of use studies**. {JNU}

Davis, William S., 1981, **Information processing systems**, 2nd edn. {JNU}

Davison, Fla Keith, 1966, **Theory of classification**. {ICHR IIT MFL NERC ZHL}

Davison, Keith, 1966, **Classification practice in Britain** : Report on a survey of classification opinion, etc. {DUL}

De Grolier, E., 1962, **Study of general categories applicable to classification and coding in documentation**, rev edn. tr. by Anthony Thompson. [UNESCO]. {BIS DSSW IEG IIT JNU}

De Grolier, Eric, 1979, **Organisation of information systems for government and public administration**. {BIS JNU}

De Hart, Florence E, 1979, **Librarian's psychological commitments** : Human relations in librarianship. {INSA NIPCCD USIS}

De Rossi, Claude J., 1975, **Exploring the world of data processing.** {NASSDOC}

De Reuck, Anthony and Knight, Julie, eds., 1967, **Communication in science** : Documentation and automation. [CIBA Foundation]. {MHA}

Dean, John, 1972, **Planning library education programmes :** A study of the problems involved in the management and operation of library schools in the developing countries. {MFL NIEPA}

Dearden, James, 1969, **Books are for people** : Librarian's life educational explorers. {IIT}

Debons, Anthony, 1981, **Information professional** : Survey of an emerging field. {IIT JNU USIS}

Debons, Anthony, ed., 1974, **Information science** : Search for identity. {INSA}

Debons, Anthony and Cameron, William J., 1975, **Perspectives in information science**. {JNU}

Debons, Anthony and Larson, Arvid G., eds., n.d., **Information science in action** : System design, 2 vols. {DUL}

Delaney, Jalk J., 1968, **New school librarian**. {JNU}

Delavenay, Emile, 1974, **For books**. [UNESCO]. {ICA}

Delbigio, G. and Ruckenbaver, E. Inis, 1978, **Descriptive cataloguing rules**. [International Atomic Energy Agency, Vienna]. {BIS}

Denison, Barbara, comp. 1968, **Selected material in classification** : A bibliography. {JNU}

Dennis, Donald D., 1965, **Simplifying work in small public libraries**. {Drexel Institute of Technology]. {NASSDOC}

Dent, Flu W., 1966, **Practical cataloguing**. {ICHR IIC IIT ZHL}

Deprospo, Ernest R., 1969, **Library building consultant role and responsibility**. {IIT}

Desai, Z.A., 1978, **Centres of Islamic learning in India**. [Ministry of Information and Broadcasting, New Delhi]. {NASSDOC}

Deshmukh, P.P., 1990, **Standardisation of library and information services** : With special reference to scientific and agricultural libraries. {JNU}

Deshpande, K.S., 1958, **Land of libraries** : Story of a study tour of the USA. [Gurudev Literary Association, Hubli]. {AIU ZHL}

Deshpande, K.S., 1985, **University library system in India**. {JNU NASSDOC NMML}

Devarajan, G. and Rahelamma, A.V., 1990, **Library computerisation in India** : Isaac festschrift. {JNU}

Devsare, H.K., n.d., **Indexing of children's magazines in Hindi with particular reference to its impact on society and social sciences**. (typed copy). {NASSDOC}

Dewe, A. and Deunelle, J., n.d., **Papers** : European conference on the contribution of users to planning and policy making for information systems and networks, 1978, Germany. {CRRI}

Dewe, Michael, 1968, **Library supply agencies in Europe**. {JNU}

Dewey, Harry, 1957, **Introduction to library cataloguing and classification**, 4th rev. edn. {DUL}

Dewey, Melvil, 1935, **Dewey Decimal Classification and Relative Index,** 6th edn. {NAI}

Dewey, Melvil, 1936, **Abridged Decimal Classification and Relative Index**, 5th. edn. {DEPT ZHL}

Dewey, Melvil, 1942, **Dewey Decimal Classification and Relative Index.** 14th edn., 2 vols. {USIS ZHL}

Dewey, Melvil, 1951, **Dewey Decimal Classification and Relative Index**. 15th edn. {IEG IIT NAI USIS}

Dewey, Melvil, 1959, **Abridged Dewey Decimal Classification and Relative Index**, 8th. edn. {USIS}

Dewey, Melvil, 1964, **Dewey Decimal Classification and Relative Index**. 16th edn. 2 vols. {CRRI NASSDOC NMML SPA USIS}

Dewey, Melvil, 1965, **Abridged Dewey Decimal Classification and Relative Index**, rev. edn. {USIS}

Dewey, Melvil, 1967, **Dewey Decimal Classification and Relative Index**, 17th edn., 2 vols. {CRRI NASSDOC NMML SPA USIS}

Dewey, Melvil, 1971, **Abridged Dewey Decimal Classification and Relative Index**, rev. edn. {USIS}

Dewey, Melvil, 1971, **Dewey Decimal Classification and Relative Index,** 18th edn., 3 vols. {JNU IIMC ISI NASSDOC NIEPA USIS}

Dewey, Melvil, 1976, **Selective Hindi Dewey Decimal Classification and Relative Index** tr. by Prabhu Narayan Gour. {DUL}

Dewey, Melvil, 1979, **Dewey Decimal Classification and Relative Index,** 19th edn., 3 vols. {CRRI ICHR ISI JNU MHA NAI NMML NASSDOC USIS ZHL}

Dewey, Melvil, 1982, **Dewey decimal Classification** : 301-307, sociology : Expanded version based on edition 19. {NASSDOC}

Dewey, Melvil, 1989, **Dewey Decimal Classification**, 20th edn. 4 vols, V. 1. : Introduction tables; V. 2. : Schedules 000-599; V. 3. : Schedules 600-990; V. 4. : Index manual, 20th edn. {NASSDOC}

Dhir, S.C. and Anand, S.K., 1979, **Directory of health science libraries in South-Asia**. {NIH}

Dhyani, Pushpa, n.d., **Guide to Dewey Decimal Classification**. {DUL}

Dhyani, Pushpa, 1979, **Use of library classification schemes in Indian libraries with special reference to Delhi**. {NASSDOC}

Dhyani, Pushpa, 1983, **Classification schemes and Indian libraries**. {DUL IIFT IIT ISI NERC NMML}.

Dhyani, Pushpa, 1990, **Information science and libraries.** {CRRI ICHR JNU ZHL}

Dial, O. Eugene, 1968, **Computer programming and statistics for basic research**. {NASSDOC}

Diaz, Albert J., ed., 1975, **Microforms in libraries** : A reader. {BIS JNU USIS}

Dickinson, Ass Don, 1916, **Punjab library primer**. [University of Punjab, Lahore]. {ZHL}

Diehl, Edith, 1965, **Bookbinding** : Its background and technique, 2 vols. {DUL}

Dierickx, Harold and Hopkinson, Alan, eds., 1981, **Reference manual for machine-readable bibliographic descriptions**, 2nd rev edn. [UNESCO]. {NASSDOC}

Dikshit, S.R. and Dikshit, S.D., comps., 1970-72, **All India booksellers and publishers directory, 1970, 1971, 1972.** {ICCR JNU NASSDOC}

Dimitrov, Th. and Maruli, L., 1982, **International documents for 80's** : Their role and use : Proceedings : World symposium on international documentation, 2nd, 1980, Brussels. {JNU NMML}

Diringer, David, 1967, **Illuminated book** : Its history and production. 2nd edn. {DUL}

Dixit, R.S., 1990, **Geography of marketing and commercial activities in India** : Documentation on research information. {IIT}

Dodd, K.N., 1969, **Computer programming and languages**. {DUL}

Doednikoff, Basic, 1973, **Information retrieval.** {JNU}

Dohlbery, Ingetraut, 1978, **Optical structures and Universal Classification**. {DUL JNU}

Dolby, J.L., et al, 1969, **Computerised library catalogues** : Their growth, costs and utility. {IIT JNU NMML USIS}

Domanovszky, A., 1975, **Functions and objects of author and title cataloguing** : A contribution to cataloguing theory. {NMML}

Donohue, Joseph C., 1973, **Understanding scientific literatures** : A bibliometric approach. {INSA}

Dority, G. Kim, 1984, **Guide to reference books for small and medium sized libraries, 1970-82**. {NASSDOC}

Dorothy, Harrop, n.d., **Modern book production**. {DUL}

Doss, Milburn Price, 1955, **Information processing equipment**. {JNU}

Doubleday, W.E., 1933, **Manual of library classification**. {NAI}

Dougherty, Richard M. and Heinritz, Fred J., 1966, **Scientific management of library operations**. {DUL USIS}

Douglas, M.P., 1949, **Teacher librarians handbook**. [American Library Association]. {DUL NIEPA ZHL}

Douglas, Mary Peacock, 1974, **Primary school library and its services**. [UNESCO]. {DUL IEG NERC NIPCCD}

Downg, J.C. and Sharp, N.F., 1969, **Proceedings** : Seminar on the Anglo-American Cataloguing Rules, 1967. [Library Association, London]. {ZHL}

Downs, Robert B., n.d., **American library resources** : A bibliographical guide: Supplement: 1961-1970. {NASSDOC}

Downs, Robert B., n.d., **Resources of Canadian academic and research libraries**. {AIU}

Downs, Robert B., 1956, **Books that changed the world**. [American Library Association]. {USIS}

Downs, Robert B., 1958, **Status of American college and university librarian**. {JNU}

Downs, Robert B., 1966, **How to do library research**. {ICA IIT JNU NIH USIS}

Downs, Robert B., 1977, **Books that changed America**. {USIS}

Downs, Robert B., 1978, **Books that changed the world**, 2nd edn., [American Library Association]. {USIS}

Doyle, James M. and Grimes, George H., 1976, **Reference resources** : A systematic approach. {DUL NASSDOC}

Doyle, Lauren B., 1975, **Information retrieval and processing.** {BIS CRRI DUL IIMC ISI NASSDOC NIH USIS}

Dranov, Paula, 1976, **Microfilm** : The librarians' view, 1976-77. {USIS}

Dranov, Paula, 1977, **Automated library circulation systems.** {IIT}

Dresser, Maxwell, 1957, **Using the library for reference and research.** {JNU}

Drewry, John E., n.d., **Book reviewing.** {DUL}

Drewry, John Eldridge, 1966, **Writing book reviews**. {DUL}

Drury, Francis K.W., 1930, **Book selection**. [American Library Association]. {ZHL}

Duchein, Michel, 1977, **Archive buildings and equipment**. {DUL}

Duckworth, Walter E., 1962, **Guide to operational research**. {NASSDOC}

Dudley, Edward, ed., 1974, **S.R. Ranganathan, 1892-1972** : Papers : Memorial meeting, January 25, 1973. {JNU}

Dudley, Edward, ed., 1983, **Development of national library and information service.** [Library Association, London]. {NIEPA}

Duff, Brown James, 1949, **Manual of library economy**. {JNU}

Duff, Brown James, 1977, **Manual of library economy**, ed. by R.N. Lock. {BIS CRRI DUL MFL MHA NIH SPA}

Dugdale, Kathleen, 1962, **Manual of form for theses and term reports**, rev edn. {DUL}

Duggal, K.S., 1982, **Indian broadcast media yearbook**. {NASSDOC}

Duke, Richard D., 1961, **Personal filing system for the professional concerned with community planning**. {SPA}

DuMont, Rosemary Ruhig, 1977, **Reform and reaction** : The big city public library in American life. {USIS}

Dunkin, Paul S., 1969, **Cataloguing**. [American Library Association]. {USIS}

Dunkin, Paul Shaner, 1973, **How to catalogue a rare book**, 2nd edn. {JNU}

Dupuy, Trevor N., 1968 **Modern libraries for modern colleges**. {JNU}

Dupuy, Trevor N., 1968, **Ferment in college libraries** : The impact of information technology. {JNU}

Durey, Peter Spayers, 1965, **Moving library materials.** {JNU}

Durey, Peter, 1976, **Staff management in university and college libraries**, ed. by G. Chandler. {ISI}

Durr, W.T. and Rosenberg, Paul, comp., 1977, **Urban information thesaurus** : A vocabulary for social documentation. {JNU}

Dutt, Newton Mohun, 1928, **Baroda and its libraries**. [Central Library, Baroda]. {NAI NASSDOC}

Dutta, D., 1958-1969, **Introduction to library cataloguing**, 1958; 1959; 1969. {CRRI IIT NERC NIPCCD NMML}

Dutta, D.N., 1962, **Library classification** : Theory and practice. {IIT}

Dutta, D.N. 1975, **Libraries and their uses.** {ICA IIT}

Dutta, D.N., 1978, **Library classification manual**. {IIT ZHL}

Dutta, D.N., 1978, **Manual of library management.** {DUL IIT}

Dutta, Rajeshwari, 1970, **Union catalogue of the Central Government of India publications held by libraries in London, Oxford and Cambridge**. [Centre of South Asian Studies, University of Cambridge, Mansell]. {NASSDOC}

Duyvis, F. Donker and Schippers, M.E., n.d. **Document reproduction services** : Their efficient organisation and management. [UNESCO]. {IIMC NASSDOC}

Dyer, C., 1970, **Role of school libraries in education**. {JNU}

Dyer, C., 1970, **School libraries** : Theory and practice. {JNU}

Earuqui, Jalees A., ed., 1974, **Reading habits in Pakistan** : A report. {ZHL}

East, H., 1979, **Some statistical indicators of UK abstracting and indexing services**. {BCL}

Easterby, Ronald, ed., 1978, **Tasks, process and information display design** : NATO conference on visual presentation of information, September 4-8, 1978, Birmingham. {BIS}

Eastlick, John T., ed., 1958, **Encyclopaedia of librarianship**. {SPA ZHL}

Eastlick, John T., ed., 1971, **The changing environment of libraries** : Papers delivered at the 1970-71 colloquim series. [American Library Association]. {USIS}

Eastwood, C.R., 1967, **Mobile libraries and other public library transport**. [Association of Assistant librarians, London]. {BIS}

Eaton, F. Thelma and Strout, Donald Everett, eds., 1959, **Role of classification in the modern American library** : Papers presented at an institute conducted by the University of Illinois, Graduate School of Library Science, 1959. {DUL}

Eaton. Thelma, 1963, **Cataloguing and classification** : An introductory manual, 3rd edn. {DUL}

Ebeling, Elinor H., comp., 1966, **Manual of technical services processes**. {DUL}

Eckard, Helen Mary, n.d., **Statistics of public libraries**, 1960-61. {JNU}

Eddison, Elizabeth B. and Lyman, Lois B., eds. and comps., 1981, **Words that mean business** : 3,000 terms for access to business information. {USIS}

Edelman, H., ed., 1986, **Libraries and information science in the electronic age**. {NASSDOC}

Edgar, Mansfield, 1966, **Modern design in book binding.** {DUL}

Edsall, Marian S., 1980, **Library promotion handbook.** {IIT USIS}

Edwards, Margaret A., 1974, **The fair garden and the swarm of beasts** : The library and the young adult. {USIS}

Edwards, Tom, ed., 1978, **A comparative analysis of the major abstracting and indexing services for library and information science**. [UNESCO]. {NASSDOC}

Edwards, Tom, ed., 1982, **A comparative analysis of the major abstracting and indexing services for library and information science** : With notes on their coverage of archive material. [UNESCO]. {NASSDOC}

Egan, Margret Elizabeth, 1954, **Communication of specialised information**. {JNU}

Ekbole, Gopal Rao, 1987, **Public libraries system**. {NASSDOC*}

El-Benhawy, Mohamad Amil, 1970, **Dictionary of library terms** : English-Arabic. {JNU}

El-Hadidy, Barbara and Horne, Estic E., 1984, **The infrastructure of an information society**. {JNU}

Eliott, Charles A., 1951, **Library publicity and service**. {DUL MHA}

Elisworth, Ralph E., 1969, **Economics of book storage in college and university libraries**. {NASSDOC}

Elithorn, Alick and Jones, David, eds., 1973, **Artificial and human thinking**. {NASSDOC}

Ellinger, Werner B., n.d., **Subject classification of law**. {DUL}

Elliott, Charles A., 1954, **Library technique**. {CRRI DUL}

Elliott, C.K., 1971, **Guide to the documentation of psychology**. {NIH}

Ellis, Alec, 1971, **Library services for young people in England and Wales, 1830-1970**. {DUL}

Ellis, Lee Robert, 1966, **Continuing education for adults through the American Public Library, 1833-1964**. [American Library Association]. {USIS}

Ellsworth, Ralph E., 1973, **Planning manual for academic library buildings**. {JNU}

Ellsworth, Ralph E. and Wagener, Hobart E., n.d., **School library**. {AIU DUL}

Ellsworth, Ralph Eugene, 1960, **Planning college and university library** : A book for campus planners and architects. {USIS}

Emerick, Paul L. and Wilkinson, Joseph W., 1970, **Computer programming for business and social science**. {NASSDOC}

Ennis, Philip H. and Winger, Howard W., eds., 1962, **Seven questions about the profession of librarianship** : Proceedings of the 26th Annual Conference of the Graduate Library School. {IEG}

Enright, B.J., 1972, **New media and the library in education**. {IIT NIH}

Enser, A.G.S., 1950, **Branch library practice**. {CRRI}

Eric, Bailey, 1965, **Economics of book selling**. {DUL}

Erickson, E. Walfred, 1961, **College and university library surveys**, 1938-52. {JNU}

Ernest, Roe, 1966, **Teachers, librarians and children** : A study of libraries in education. {IIT}

Escarpit, Robert, 1966, **Book revolution**. {DUL}

Escreet, P.K., 1971, **Introduction to the Anglo-American cataloguing rules**. {MFL NASSDOC ZHL}

Esdaile, A., 1967, **Esdaile's manual of bibliography**, rev edn., by Roy Stockes. {MFL}

Esdaile, Arundell, 1946, **British Museum Library**. {NAL NMML}

Esdaile, Arundell, 1964, **Student's manual of bibliography,** 3rd edn. {CRRI}

Esdaile, Arundell, n.d., **World's great libraries,** 1934-1937 2 vols. {NAI}

Estabrook, Leigh, ed., 1977, **Libraries in post-industrial society.** {IIT}

Estes, Rice, 1953, **Study of seven academic libraries in Brooklyn and their cooperative potential**. {JNU}

Evans, A.J., et al, 1977, **Education and training of users of scientific and technical information** : UNISIST guide for teachers. [UNESCO]. {BCL ISI NASSDOC}

Evans, Frank B., comp., 1979, **The history of archives administration** : A select bibliography. [UNESCO] {NASSDOC}

Evans, G. Edward, 1976, **Management techniques for librarians**. {AIU IIT JNU NIEPA USIS}

Evans, G. Edward, 1979, **Developing library collections**. {USIS}

Evans, G. Edward, 1983, **Management techniques for librarians**, 2nd edn. {BCL DUL IIT JNU NMML USIS}

Evans, Lynn, 1976, **Automatic aids to profile construction** : Expansion of search terms by thesaurus. [Institute of Electrical Engineers]. {BCL}

Evans, Lynn, 1976, **Merging of databases for the production of secondary information publications** : Phase-1. {BCL}

Eyre, John and Tonks, Peter, 1971, **Computers and systems** : Introduction for librarians. {IIT NASSDOC}

Fairthorne, Robert Arthur, 1961, **Towards information retrieval.** {JNU}

Falk, Leslie K., n.d., **Procurement of library materials in the federal government** : An orientation prepared for Federal Library Committee. {JNU}

Fang, Josephine Riss and Songe, Alice H., 1973, **Handbook of national and international library associations**. [American Library Association]. {NASSDOC USIS}

Fang, Josephine Riss and Nauta, Paul, eds., 1985, **International guide to library and information science education** : A reference source for educational programmes in the information fields world-wide. [International Federation of Library Associations and Institutions]. {NASSDOC}

Fang, Josephine Riss and Songe, Alice H., 1976, **International guide to library, archival and information science associations**. {USIS}

Fang, Josephine Riss and Songe, Alice H., 1980, **International guide to library, archival and information science associations**, 2nd edn. {USIS}

Farber, Evan Ira and Walling, Ruth, 1974, **Academic library** : Essays in honour of Guy R. Lyle. {JNU}.

Fargo, Lucile F., 1945, **Activity book number two** : Library projects for children and young people. [American Library Association]. {NIEPA}

Fargo, Lucile F., 1947, **Library in the school**, 4th edn. [American Library Association]. {DUL ZHL}

Fargo, Lucile F., 1964, **Activity book for school libraries.** {JNU}

Farr, M.A.L., et al, 1973, **Security for computer systems**. {NIPCCD}

Fasana, Paul J. and Veaner, Allen, 1971, **Collaborative library systems development**. {JNU}

Fay, Adra M., 1950, **Supervising library personnel**. {DUL}

Fayen, Emily Gallup, 1973, **The online catalogue** : Improving public access to library materials. {USIS}

Fegan, E.S. and Cant M., 1958, **Chetenham classification**. {JNU}

Fellows, Doracas, 1926, **Cataloguing rules with explanations and illustrations**, 2nd edn. {NAI}

Fenton, F.H., 1960, **Reference library stacks** : An enquiry into reference book provision in the rate-supported libraries of England and Wales. {JNU}

Fenwick, Sara Innis, 1960, **New definitions of school library service**. {JNU}

Fenwick, Sara Innis, 1966, **School and children's libraries in Australia**. {JNU}

Fenwick, Sara Innis, 1975, **Library services for children in New Zealand schools and public libraries** : A report. [New Zealand Library Association]. {JNU}

Ferguson, John, 1971, **Libraries in France**. {NASSDOC}

Fhessle, Barbara Ruth, 1965, **Focus on information and communication.** {JNU}

Finer, Ruth, 1979, **Referral centres and services** : A review. [Association of Special Libraries and Information Bureaux]. {CRRI}

Finn, David, et al, 1978, **Teaching manual for tutor-librarians**. {JNU}

Fisher, Margery, 1962, **Intent upon reading** : A critical appraisal of modern fiction for children. {DUL}

Fisher, Ronald A., 1970, **Statistical methods for research workers**, 14th edn. {NASSDOC}

Fitzgerald, John M. and Fitzgerald, Andra F., 1973, **Fundamentals of systems analysis**. {JNU}

Fjallbrant, Nancy and Malley, Ian, 1984, **User education in libraries**. {DUL JNU NASSDOC NIEPA}

Fjallbrant, Nancy, 1977, **User education programmes in Swedish academic libraries** : A study of developments in the year 1973-77. {JNU}

Flannery, Anne and Mack, James D., 1966, **Mechanised circulation system, Leigh University Library**. {JNU}

Fleet, Anne, 1973, **Children's libraries**. {DUL}

Fleischer, Eugene and Goodman, Helen, 1980, **Cataloguing audio-visual materials** : A manual based on the Anglo-American Cataloguing Rules-2. {IIT}

Fleischer, Eugene B., 1978, **Style manual for citing microform and non-print media.** [American Library Association]. {BIS}

Flyate, D.M., ed., 1968, **Preservation of documents and papers**. [Israel Programme for Scientific Transactions, Jerusalem]. {INSA}

Folcarelli, Ralph F., et al, 1982, **The microform connection** : A basic guide for libraries. {USIS}

Ford, Geoffrey, 1979, **User studies** : An introduction guide and select bibliography. [Centre for Research of User Studies, University of Sheffield, Sheffield]. {NASSDOC}

Ford, Stephen, 1973, **The acquisition of library materials**. [American Library Association]. {DUL ICA USIS}

Forsyth, Alexandra I., et al, 1970, **Computer science** : Fortran language programming. {DUL}

Fosdick, Howard, 1981, **Computer basics for librarians and information scientists**. {USIS}

Foskett, A.C., 1970, **Guide to personal indexes** : Using edgenotched and peek-a-boo cards, 2nd edn. {BIS IEG IIT JNU NASSDOC}

Foskett, A.C., 1971, **The subject approach to information**, 2nd edn. {IIMC INSA ISIL JNU NASSDOC ZHL}

Foskett, A.C., 1973, **Universal Decimal Classification.** {ZHL}

Foskett, A.C., 1977, **Subject approach to information**, 3rd edn. {JNU NMML}

Foskett, D.J., 1962, **Library association** : Creed of librarian. {IIT}

Foskett, D.J., 1963, **Classification and indexing in the social sciences**. {DSSW IEG IIMC IIT NAI NASSDOC NIEPA SPA USIS}

Foskett, D.J., 1963, **London education classification.** {University of London]. {IIT}

Foskett, D.J., 1964, **Science, humanism and libraries**. {IIT JNU}

Foskett, D.J., 1967, **Information service in libraries**. {CRRI IEG JNU NAI}

Foskett, D.J., 1970, **Library systems and information services**. {IIMC NASSDOC}

Foskett, D.J., 1971, **Classification and indexing in the social sciences**, 2nd edn. {BIS ICA JNU NASSDOC}

Foskett, D.J., 1976, **NATIS** : Preliminary survey of education and training programmes at university level in information and library science. [UNESCO]. {NIEPA}

Foskett, D.J., 1984, **Pathways for communication** : Books and libraries in the information age. {AIU NIEPA}

Foskett, D.J. and Palmer, B.I., 1961, **Essays in librarianship** : In memory of William Charles Berwick Sayers. {MFL}

Fothergill, Richard and Butchart, I., 1972, **Non-book materials in libraries** : A practical guide. {ISIR}

Foubert, Charles Henri, 1982, **The IDOC documentation handbook**. [IDOC]. {NASSDOC}

Foulkes, John, ed., 1986, **Down loading bibliographic records.** {NASSDOC*}

Fowles, Jib, ed., 1978, **Handbook of futures research.** {NASSDOC}

Fox, Gertrude, 1964, **List of subject headings in home building and allied fields.** [National Housing Centre Library, Washington]. {SPA}

Fox, Peter, 1974, **Reader instruction methods in academic libraries**. {JNU}

Francis, Simon, ed., 1971, **Libraries in the USSR**. {NASSDOC}

Frank, O., ed., 1961, **Modern documentation and information practices** : A basic manual. [International Federation for Documentation and Information]. {BIS DUL ICA NASSDOC NIEPA}

Frarey, Carlyle J., 1959, **Processing services of the Dallas Public Library** : A report on their organisation, operation and administration. {DUL}

Fredson, Bowers, 1949, **Principles of bibliographical description**. {DUL}

Freeman, Patricia, 1975, **Pathfinder** : An operational guide for the school librarian. {JNU}

Freeman, Robert R., et al, eds., 1968, **Information in the language sciences** : Proceedings of the conference held at Airlic House, Warrenton, Virginia, March 4-6, 1966. {NASSDOC}

French, Ruth, ed., n.d., **Toward a better cataloguing code**. {IEG}

Frick, B.M., 1959, **Outline for the courses in problems in cataloguing and classification**. {DUL}

Friedman, Joan and Jeffreys, Alan, 1967, **Cataloguing and classification in British university libraries** : A survey of practices and procedures. [Sheffield University Post Graduate School of Librarianship]. {DUL IIT}

Fry, Bernard, 1979, **Government publications** : Their role in the national programme for library and information services. [U.S. National Commission on Libraries and Information Science]. {USIS}

Fry, George, et al, 1961, **Circulation systems selection manual for college and university libraries.** {JNU}

Fullard, Harold and Darby, H.C., eds., 1973, **Library atlas**. {JNU}

Furlong, Norman, 1966, **Library practice for colleges of education**. {JNU}

Fussler, Herman H., 1974, **Research libraries and technology** : A report. [Sloan Foundation]. {USIS}

Fussler, Herman H. and Simon, Julian L., 1969, **Patterns in the use of books in large research libraries**. {NMML}

Fussler, Herman, ed., 1954, **Functions of the library in the modern college** : Conference of the Graduate Library School, 19th, 1954, Chicago. {IIT SPA}

Futas, Elizabeth, 1977, **Library acquisition policies and procedures**. {IIT}

Gakhar, Attam Prakash, 1982, **Librarians' guide to Broad System of ordering**. [British Standards Institution]. {JNU}

Galvin, Hoyt R. and Devereaux, Kathryn A., eds., 1955, **Planning a library building**. {DUL}

Galvin, Hoyt R. and Van Buren, Martin, 1959, **The small public library building**, 2nd edn. [UNESCO]. {CRRI IEG IIMC IIT BIS NASSDOC NERC ZHL}

Galvin, Thomas J., 1965, **Problems in reference service** : Case studies in method and policy. {DUL USIS}

Galvin, Thomas J., 1971, **Current problems in reference service**. {DUL JNU NERC USIS}

Gangadhara Rao, P., 1983, **Synthesis in D.D.C., 18th edn.** [Andhra University, Waltair]. {NASSDOC*}

Gangadhara Rao, P. and Raghavan, Q.S., eds., 1986, **Papers** : National seminar on assessment of public library development in India, March 3-6, 1986, Madras. [University of Madras, Department of Library Science; University Grants Commission, New Delhi]. {NASSDOC}

Ganguly, N., 1933, **Librarian and library administration**. {NAI}

Garde, P.K., 1970, **The United Nations family of libraries**. {ICA ICHR INSA NASSDOC NMML}

Gardin, J.C., 1965, **SYNTOL**, ed. by Susan Artandi, 2 vols. [New Jerrsy Graduate School of Library Science]. {IIT MFL}

Gardiner, Jewel, 1954, **Administering library service in the elementary school**, 2nd edn. [American Library Association]. {DUL NIEPA ZHL}

Gardner, Frank M., 1951, **Letters to a younger librarian**. {DUL NASSDOC}

Gardner, Frank M., 1957, **Delhi Public Library** : An evaluation report. {DSSW DUL}

Gardner, Richard K., 1981, **Library collections** : Their origin, selection and development. {DUL}

Garfield, E., 1979, **Citation indexing** : Its theory and application in science, technology and humanities. {NASSDOC NIH}

Garfield, Eugene, 1964, **Use of citation data in writing the history of science**. {DUL}

Garfield, Eugene, 1981, **Essays of an information scientist.** {CRRI JNU}

Garnoosky, Leon, ed., n.d., **International aspects of librarianship**. {IEG}

Garvey, Mona, 1969, **Library displays** : Their purpose, construction and use. {USIS}

Garvin, Paul L., 1972, **On machine translation** : Selected papers. {USIS}

Gaskell, Philip, 1972, **New introduction to bibliography**. {INSA}

Gates, Arthur I., 1947, **Improvement of reading**. 3rd edn. {ZHL}

Gates, Hilary and Brookes, Alison, comp.s, 1986, **A directory of library and information retrieval software for micro-computers**, 2nd edn. {NASSDOC}

Gates, J.K., 1962, **Guide to the use of books and libraries**. {DUL IIT MFL}

Gates, J.K., 1968, **Introduction to librarianship.** {IIT MFL NCAER ZHL}

Gates, J.K., 1969, **Guide to the use of books and libraries**, 2nd edn. {NIH USIS}

Gates, J.K., 1976, **Introduction to librarianship,** 2nd edn. {USIS}

Gates, J.K., 1979, **Guide to the use of books and libraries**, 4th edn. {USIS}

Gaur, Ganesh, comp., 1975, **Catalogue of Punjabi printed books added to the India Office Library, 1902-1964**. [India Office Library, London]. {NASSDOC}

Gautreaux, Agnes A. and Lally, Mary, comps., 1949, **Aviation subject headings** : A concise list for civil aviation libraries or collections. {DUL}

Gaver, Mary Virginia, 1962, **Every child needs a school library**. {JNU}

Gaver, Mary Virginia, 1963, **Effectiveness of centralized library services in elementary schools**. {JNU}

Gaver, Mary Virginia and Velazquer, Gonzal, 1963, **School libraries in Puerto Rico** : A survey and plan for development. {NASSDOC}

Gawrecki, Drahoslav, 1968, **Compact library shelving**. [American Library Association]. {DUL NASSDOC USIS}

Geer, H.T., 1955, **Charging system**. [American Library Association]. {DUL IIFT IIT ZHL}

Geerge, Mackaness, 1956, **Art of the book collecting in Australia** {JNU}

Gehrke, U., 1975, **Planning for a national information and documentation system** : Kenya. [UNESCO]. {NASSDOC}

Gelfand, M.A., 1971, **University libraries for developing countries**. [UNESCO]. {AIU DUL ICA IIMC IIT JNU NIEPA NMML USIS}

Gellatly, P., ed., 1980, **Serials librarianship in transition** : Issues and development. {NASSDOC}

Genaway, David, C., 1984, **Integrated online library systems** : Principles, planning and implementation. {NASSDOC}

George, K.M., 1985, **Indian libraries** : Trends and prospectives. {JNU NMML}

George, Mann, 1951, **Print** : A manual for librarians and students describing in detail the history, methods and applications of printing and paper making. {DUL}

Georgi, C. and Bellanti, Robert, eds., 1985, **Excellence in library management**. {NASSDOC*}

Gerard, David, 1978, **Libraries in society**. {IIT NIEPA}

Gerard, David E., ed., 1970, **Libraries and the arts** : A symposium of papers and discussions at the seminar held in the College of Librarianship, September 1-6, 1969, Wales. {NASSDOC}

Gerould, James Thayer, n.d., **College library building** : Its planning and equipment. {DUL}

Gessford, J.E., 1980, **Modern information systems**. {NIH}

Getz, Malcolm, 1979, **An economic view of public libraries** [U.S. National Bureau of Economic Research]. {USIS}

Ghazi, Muhammad Ismail, 1963, **A librarian's musing**. {JNU}

Ghosh, G.B. and Banerjee, B.N., 1974, **Trends of information service in India**. {AIU CRRI ICHR NASSDOC NERC NIH NIPCCD ZHL}

Gibson, Strickland, 1914, **Some Oxford libraries**. {JNU}

Gidwani, N.N. and Navalani, K., 1974, **A guide to reference materials on India**, 2 vols. {INSA NAI NASSDOC NCAER NERC ZHL}

Gidwani, N.N., ed., 1973, **Comparative librarianship** : Essays in honour of Prof. D.N. Marshall. {ICHR IIC JNU NASSDOC NIPCCD NMML ZHL}

Gilchrist, Alan, 1971, **Thesauri in retrieval**. [Association of Special Libraries and Information Bureaux]. {BCL CRRF DUL IIT NASSDOC}

Giljarevskij, R.S., 1968-74 **International distribution of catalogue cards** : Present situation and future prospects 1968; 1969; 1974. [UNESCO]. {CRRI IIMC IIT JNU NERC NIEPA NIPCCD}

Gillespie, John T. and Spirt, Diana L., 1983, **Administering the school library media centre.** {JNU}

Girja Kumar, 1965, **Politics, international relations and law** : Scope, methodology and classification. {BIS ICHR IEG IIT JNU MFL MHA NASSDOC NMML ZHL}

Girja Kumar, 1986, **Library development in India**. {JNU NMML}

Girja Kumar, 1990, **Crisis management of libraries in India**. {NASSDOC}

Girja Kumar, and Krishan Kumar, 1976, **Bibliography**. {CRRI ICA ISI JNU NASSDOC NIPCCD NMML}

Girja Kumar and Krishan Kumar, 1976, **Soochikaran ke siddhant**, tr. by Prem Kumar Jayaswal. {BIS DUL NMML}

Girja Kumar and Krishan Kumar, 1976, **Suchikaran ke siddhant**. {DUL}

Girja Kumar and Krishan Kumar, 1977, **Theory of cataloguing**, 2nd edn. {ICHR IIT ISIL JNU MMTC NASSDOC NCAER NCDC NERC NIPCCD ZHL}

Girja Kumar and Krishan Kumar, 1978, **Granthvigyan**. {CRRI NMML}

Girja Kumar and Krishan Kumar, 1982, **Theory of cataloguing**, 4th edn. {ZHL}

Girja Kumar and Krishan Kumar, 1983, **Philosophy of user education**. {DUL IIT ISI JNU NASSDOC NIEPA ZHL}

Girja Kumar, et al, 1978, **Role of libraries in national development**. {JNU}

Gleaves, Edwin S. and Tucker, John Mark, 1983, **Reference service and library education** : Essays in honour of Neel Chaney. {JNU}

Gleiter, Karin, ed., 1975, **International directory of population information**, Pt. 2 : Address list. [Carolina Population Center, USA]. {NIH}

Gliden, Sophia Hall, 1942, **Library classification for public administration materials.** [American Library Association]. {NAI}

Godden, Irene P., 1984, **Library technical service** : Operations and management. {JNU}

Goel, N.K., et al, 1964, **Directory of libraries and who's who in library profession in Delhi**. [Delhi Library Association]. {BIS CRRI DSSW ICCR ICWA IEG IIC NMML ZHL}

Goil, N.K., ed., 1973, **Dictionary of pseudonyms in Indian literature**. [Delhi Library Association]. {NASSDOC}

Goil, N.K., n.d., **College libraries in India** : Needed a policy for development. {AIU IEG}

Going, Mona E., comp. and ed., 1963, **Hospital libraries and work with the disabled in the community**. {DUL}

Goldberg, Robert L., 1976, **A systems approach to library program development.** {JNU USIS}

Goldberg, Walter, n.d., **Management information systems** : Selected papers from MIS conferences. {JNU}

Goldhor, Herbert, ed., n.d., **Measurement and evaluation** : Papers presented at a conference conducted by the University of Illinois, Graduate School of Library Science, September 10-12, 1967. {DUL}

Good, Carter V. and Scates, Dughlas E., 1954, **Methods of research** : Educational, psychological and sociological. {NASSDOC}

Goodell, John S. and Kemper, Robert E., eds., 1975, **Libraries and work sampling**. {BIS}

Goodman, Frederick, 1970, **Thesaurus of ERIC descriptors, with a special chapter on the role and function of thesaurus in education.** [U.S. Educational Resources Information Centre]. {USIS}

Goodrum, Charles A., 1980, **Treasures of the Library of Congress.** {USIS}

Goodrum, Charles A. and Dalrymple, Helen W., 1982, **The Library of Congress**, 2nd edn. {IIC JNU NASSDOC NMML USIS}

Gopalakrishnan, P. and Narayanan, K.S., 1975, **Computers in India**. {NASSDOC}

Gopinath, M.A., **Colon Classification for macro documents in history**. {DUL}

Gorden, Raymond L., 1969, **Interviewing** : Strategy, techniques and tactics. {NASSDOC}

Gordon, M., et al, 1984, **Dictionary of new information technology acronyms**. {JNU}

Gore, Daniel, 1973, **Bibliography for beginners**, 2nd edn. {NASSDOC}.

Gore, Daniel, et al, eds., 1979, **Requiem for the card catalogue** : Management issues in automated cataloguing. [Associated College of the Midwest]. {IIT NIPCCD USIS}

Gorkhoff, Boris I., n.d., **Publishing in the USSR**. {DUL}

Gorman, Michael, 1968, **Study of the rules for entry and heading in the Anglo-American Cataloguing Rules, 1967** : British text. [Library Association, London]. {ZHL}

Gorman, Michael, and Linford, John E., 1971, **Description of the BNB/MARC record** : A manual of practice. {JNU}

Gorst, S.M., 1953, **Scheme for the organisation of co-operative libraries.** [Plunkett Foundation for Co-operative Studies]. {ICA}

Goschen, Viscount, n.d., **Library movement**. {AIU}

Goswami, Badri Prasad, n.d., **Problems of misplacement, mutilation and theft of books in libraries**. {JNU}

Goswami, Badri Prasad, 1972, **Personnel motivation and work efficiency in libraries**. {NASSDOC}

Gough, Chet and Taverekere, Srikantaiad, 1978, **Systems analysis in libraries** : A question and answer approach. {BCL DUL}

Gour, P.N., 1980, **Glossary of library science technical terms**. {JNU NASSDOC RTL}

Gournay, Bernard, 1963, **French bibliographical digest** : Public administration. {MFL}

Gover, Harvey R., 1981, **Keys to library research on the graduate level** : A guide to guides. {JNU}

Govrilova, S.A., 1979, **Universal Decimal Classification** : Its structure, application and tables : Revision procedure. [UNESCO; UNION, Moscow]. {NASSDOC}

Goyal, S.P., 1973, **International directory of dealers of back-sets of periodicals.** {NASSDOC}

Goyal, Satpaul, ed, n.d., **Indian librarianship**. {JNU}

Grabbe, Eugene M., et al, eds., 1961, **Handbook of automation, and computation and control**. {IDSA}

Gradiner, Frank M., 1971, **Public library legislation** : A comparative study. [UNESCO]. {JNU NASSDOC NIEPA}

Gray, John and Perry, Brian, 1975, **Scientific information**. {BCL INSA}

Gray, Max, 1969, **Documentation standards**. {BIS DUL NIEPA}

Greenberg, Alan M., 1981, **Author index to Library of Congress classification** : Class P, Subclass PN, PR, PS, PZ. {BIS}

Grieder, T.E.D., 1978, **Acquisition** : Where, what and how. {CRRI DUL NIEPA}

Grimshaw, Ernest, 1960, **Teacher librarian**. {JNU}

Gringhuis, Drik, n.d., **Here comes the book mobile.** {JNU}

Grishiani, J.M., et al, 1984, **System research** : Methodological problems. {JNU}

Grisnshaw, E., 1963, **Using your library**. {JNU}

Groenewegena, H.W. and Marshall, J., 1976, **Optical character recognition** : Use of OCR techniques in decentralised data collection for bibliographic information systems. [International Development Research Centre, Ottawa]. {NASSDOC}

Grogan, Denis, 1967, **Case studies in reference work**. {DUL IIT NIH}

Grogan, Denis, 1972, **More case studies in reference work**. {DUL IIT}

Grosch, Audrey N., 1979-82, **Minicomputers in libraries**, 1979-80; 1981-82 {USIS}

Gross, Elizabeth Henry, 1983, **Children's service in public libraries** : Organisation and administration, with collaboration of Gene Inyart Namovicz. {NASSDOC}

Grounds, Roger, 1971, **Agriculture** : Library of knowledge. {ICA}

Grove, Pearce S. and Clement, Evelyn G., eds., 1972, **Bibliographic control of nonprint media.** [American Library Association]. {NASSDOC}

Grove, Pearce S., ed., 1975, **Non-print media in academic libraries**. [American Library Association]. {USIS}

Grundt, Leonard, 1968, **Efficient patterns for adequate library service in a large city** : A survey of Boston. {JNU}

Guha, B., ed., 1986, **In the library and information science horizon** : A collection of essays in honour of Dr. V.A. Kamath, presented by the Bombay Science Librarians Association (BOSLA). {JNU NASSDOC}

Guha, Bimalendu, 1978, **Documentation and information** : Services, techniques and systems. {AIU BCL BIS IIMC ISI JNU MFL NASSDOC NCDC NERC NIEPA NIH NMML}

Guha, Bimalendu, 1988, **Documentation and information** : Services, techniques and systems, 2nd edn. {DUL ICA IIT JNU MHA NIH NIPCCD ZHL}

Guinchat, Claire and Menou, Michel, 1983, **General introduction to the techniques of information and documentation work.** [UNESCO]. {JNU NMML}

Gujarati, B.S., 1963, **Library organisation**. {SPA}

Gujarati, B.S., 1964, **Librarianship.** {NERC NIPCCD ZHL}

Gujarati, B.S., 1966, **Library administration**, 2nd edn. {DUL NASSDOC ZHL}

Gujarati, B.S., 1970, **Library organisation and its development in India**, 2nd edn. {NIH}

Gujarati, Balwant Singh, 1961, **Library in education** : With special reference to school libraries. {JNU}

Gunjal, S.R. and Sangam, S.L., 1986, **Dictionary of library and information science** : English-Kannada. [University of Gulbarga, Gulbarga]. {NASSDOC}

Gunjal, S.R. and Sangam, S.L., 1987, **College library** : Problems and prospects. [Gulbarga University, Gulbarga]. {NASSDOC}

Gunther, A., 1962, **Microphotography in the library**. [UNESCO]. {IDA NASSDOC}

Gupta, B.L., comp., 1989, **Library services** : Important documents. {NASSDOC*}

Gupta, B.M., et al, eds., 1984-89, **Handbook of libraries, archives and information centres in India**, 8 vols. : Vol. 1 : Libraries and archives; Vol. 2 : Libraries and archives; Vol. 3 : Information policy system and network; Vol. 4 : Asia-Pacific co-operative information systems and networks and programmes; Vol. 5 : Information technology industry and networks; Vol. 6 : International co-operative information systems, network and programmes; Vol. 7 : Science and technology information systems and centres; Vol. 8 : Social sciences information systems and centres. {DSIW IDSA JNU NASSDOC NCAER NMML}

Gupta, Chandra Prakash, n.d., **Pustakalaya prashasan** : Sidhant evam vyavahar. {BIS}

Gupta, K.R., 1980-82, **All India directory of book trade**, vol. 1: Libraries; vol. 2; Booksellers and publishers {NASSDOC NCAER NCERT}

Gupta, Pawan K. and Usha Pawan, 1986, **Library and information science** : Current trends in India. {JNU}

Gupta, R.C., 1975, **Indian Press Index** : Procedure manual. (University of Delhi, Department of Library Science, Sessional project, 1975). {DUL}

Gupta, R.D., 1970, **Preserving manuscripts and other research material in the Braj area of India**, (reprinted from the Bulletin of the British Association of Orientalists). [Vrindaban Research Institute]. {NMML}

Gupta, S.R., 1978, **Evaluation of collection of Jawahar Lal Nehru University Library from the point of view of Indian reference sources**. (University of Delhi, Department of Library and Information Science Sessional Project). {DUL}

Gupta, S.R., 1990, **Stock verification in libraries** : Problems and solutions. {DUL}

Gupta, Shamsher, 1973, **Evaluation of Indian reference sources published during last ten years available in Delhi University Library**. (University of Delhi, Department of Library and Information Science, Sessional Project). {DUL}

Gurney, Gene and Apple, Nick, 1981, **The Library of Congress** : A picture story of the world's largest library, rev. edn. {JNU}

Guruswamy Naidu, N., 1990, **Public library finance**. {CRRI}

Guthman, Judith, ed., 1969, **Metropolitan libraries** : The challenge and the promise. [American Library Association]. {USIS}

Gyawali, Bharat M. and Standrodd, Garland L., n.d., **Information resources on Nepal**. {IEG}

Hagler, Ronald and Simmons, Peter, 1982, **Bibliographic record and information technology**. {DUL JNU}

Haines, Helen E., 1965, **Living with books** : Art of book selection, 2nd edn. {DUL IIC IIT USIS}

Hakam Singh, 1962, **Library legislation in the Punjab**. [Punjab Library Literary Circle]. {IIT}

Hakam Singh and Narang, S.P., 1973, **Current trends in library organisation**. {JNU}

Hale, Barbara M., 1970, **Subject bibliography of the social sciences and humanities**. {IEG NASSDOC}

Haleda, Prithvi, ed., 1983, **Computer directory of India, 1983.** {NASSDOC}

Haleda, Prithvi, ed., 1984, **Computer directory of India, 1984.** {NCERT}

Hall, Anna Gertrude, n.d., **Library trustee**. {DUL}

Hall, David E., 1971, **Union catalogue of Asian publications, 1965-1970**. {NASSDOC}

Hall, J.L., comp., 1977, **On-line information retrieval, 1965-76** : A bibliography with a guide to on-line data bases and systems. [Association of Special Libraries and Information Bureaux]. {BCL CRRI NASSDOC}

Hall, James L. and Brown, Marjorie J., 1981, **On-line bibliographic databases** : An international directory, 2nd edn. [Association of Special Libraries and Information Bureaux]. {USIS}

Haltery, Loweld H. and McCormik, Edmaral M., 1962, **Information retrieval management**. {JNU}

Haman, Albert C. and Bakin, Marg K., comps., 1964, **Library materials for elementary science**. {DUL}

Hamburg, Morris, et al, 1974, **Library planning and decision-making systems**. {DUL NIEPA}

Hamer, Philip M., ed., 1961, **A guide to archives and manuscripts in the United States**. [U.S. National Historical Publications Commission]. {USIS}

Hamilton, Beth A. and Ernst, William B. Jr., eds., 1977, **Multitype library cooperation**. {NASSDOC USIS}

Hammer, Donald P., ed., 1976, **The information age, its development, its impact**. {DUL USIS}

Hammond, George P., 1972, **Guide to the manuscript collections of the Bancroft Library**, 2 Vols. {JNU}

Hanley, E.R., 1939, **College and university library building**. [American Library Association]. {IIT}

Hanson, J.C.M., 1939, **A Comparative study of cataloguing rules** : Based on Anglo-American code of 1908. {NASSDOC*}

Hants, Roy Stokes, 1982, **The function of bibliography**. {AIU NASSDOC}

Harbo, Ols, ed., 1980, **Theory and applications of information research** : Proceedings : International research forum on information science, 2nd, August 3-6, 1977, Copenhagen. {BCL}

Harleston, Robekah M. and Stoffle, Carla J., 1974, **Administration of government documents collections.** {USIS}

Harlow, Jacquis, 1963, **Research information retrieval.** {JNU}

Harmon, Robert B., 1976, **Developing the library collection in political science.** {JNU}

Haroon, Mohammed, 1984, **Cataloguing of Indian Muslim names.** {NASSDOC NMML}

Harper, William L., 1973, **Data processing documentation** : Standards, procedures and applications. {USIS}

Harris, Jessica Lee, 1970, **Subject analysis** : Computer implications of rigorous definition. {BIS JNU}

Harrison, Colin and Oates, Rosemary, 1981, **The basics of librarianship**. {ISIL}

Harrison, Helen P., 1973, **Film library techniques** : Principles of administration. {NMML USIS}

Harrison, K.C., n.d., **Libraries in Britain**. {IEG}

Harrison, K.C., 1963, **Library and the community**. {MFL}

Harrison, K.C., 1963, **Public libraries today**. {DUL IIT NASSDOC}

Harrison, K.C., 1964, **Facts at your fingertips** : Everyman's guide to reference books. {MFL}

Harrison, K.C., 1964, **First steps in librarianship.** {CRRI ICHR IIT MFL SPA}

Harrison, K.C., 1966, **Library and the community**. {ICA}

Harrison, K.C., 1969, **Libraries in Scandinavia**, 2nd edn. {IIT}

Harrison, K.C., 1973, **Public relations for librarians**. {ICA MMTC ZHL}

Harrison, K.C., 1977, **The library and the community**, 3rd rev. edn. {USIS}

Harrod, L.M., 1971, **Librarians' glossary of terms used in librarianship and the book crafts and reference book**, 3rd edn. {CRRI IIT JNU NASSDOC}

Harrod, L.M., 1977, **Librarians' glossary of terms used in librarianship, documentation and the book crafts and reference book**, 4th edn. {ICA IIC MMTC NCDC NCERT NERC NIH NMML ZHL}

Harrod, Leonard Montague, 1969, **Library work with children** : With special reference to developing countries. {DUL}

Harrod, Leonard Mortague and Prytherch, R.J., ed., 1984, **Harrod's librarians' glossary and reference book**. {NCERT}

Harrod, Leonard Montague, ed., 1978, **Indexers on indexing** : Selection of articles published in the Indexer. {BIS}

Harter, Stephen P., 1986, **On-line information retrieval** : Concepts, principles and techniques. {JNU}

Harvey, John M., 1976, **Specialised information centres.** {BCL CRRI ICA USIS}

Harvey, John, M., 1966, **Data processing in public and university libraries**. {DUL IIT}

Hastings, N.A. and Mello, J.M., 1978, **Decision networks**. {JNU}

Hattery, Lowell H. and Bush, George P., 1973, **Technological change in printing and publishing**. {INSA}

Hattery, Lowell H. and Bush, George P. eds., n.d., **Automation and electronics in publishing**. {DUL}

Haughney, John D., 1968, **Effective catalogues**. {NIPCCD}

Havelock, Ronald G., 1968, **Bibliography on knowledge utilisation and dissemination**. [University of Michigan]. {NASSDOC}

Havelock, Ronald G., et al, 1971, **Planning for innovation through dissemination and utilisation of knowledge**. {NASSDOC*}

Hawkes, Nigel, 1971, **Computer revolution**. {NASSDOC}

Haworth, Carol S., 1964, **Documentation of semi-automatic bibliographic information retrieval**. {JNU}

Hayes, R.M. and Shoffner, R.M., 1964, **Economics of book catalogue production**. {DUL}

Hayes, Robert M. and Becker, Joseph, 1970, **Handbook of data processing for libraries** : A comprehensive guide to the use of modern data processing equipment in libraries. {CRRI IIT INSA NASSDOC NCAER NIH NMML USIS}

Hayes, Robert M. and Becker, Joseph, 1971, **Glossary from handbook of data processing for libraries**. {USIS}

Hayes, Robert M. and Becker, Joseph, 1974, **Handbook of data processing for libraries**, 2nd edn. {BIS CRRI DUL ISI JNU USIS}

Headicar, B.M., 1935, **Manual of library organisation**. {NAI}

Heaps, H.S., 1978, **Information retrieval** : Computational and theoretical aspects. {BCL CRRI NIH}

Heiliger, Edward M. and Henderson, Paul B., 1971, **Library automation** : Experience, methodology and technology of the library as an information system. {AIU INSA JNU NASSDOC NIPCCD NMML}

Heintze, Ingeborg, 1963, **The organisation of the small public library**. [UNESCO]. {ICA IEG NASSDOC NERC NIEPA}

Helms, Harry, ed., 1983, **McGraw Hill computer handbook**. {RTL}

Henderson, James W. and Rosenthal, Joseph A., eds., 1968, **Library catalogues** : Their preservation and maintenance by photographic and automated techniques. {AIU IIT SPA}

Henderson, M.M., et al, **Cooperation, convertibility and compatibility among information systems** : A literature review. {BIS}

Hendricks, Donald D., 1966, **Comparative costs of book processing in a processing centre and in five individual libraries**. {DUL}

Hendricks, Donald D., 1973, **Report on library networks**. {DUL}

Henley, J.P., 1970, **Computer based library and information systems**. {BIS IIT JNU NASSDOC NIH}

Henley, J.P., 1972, **Computer based library and information systems**, 2nd edn. {DUL NIH}

Henry, W.M., 1980, **Online searching**. {IIT}

Herald, Alther Canley, 1963, **Processing manual** : A pictorial work book of catalogue cards, rev. edn. {DUL}

Herbert, Clara W., 1939, **Personnel administration in public libraries**. [American Library Association]. {CRRI}

Herbert, Ward, ed., 1976, **New library buildings** : Architect-librarian assessment, 1973-74. {DUL}

Herdman, Margaret M., 1947, **Classification** : An introductory manual, 2nd edn. {DUL NASSDOC}

Hernon, Peter, et al, 1973, **Library and library related publications** : A directory of publishing opportunities in journals, serials and annuals. {NASSDOC}

Hewitt, A.R., 1947, **Summary of public library law in England and Wales, Scotland, Northern Ireland and Eira**, 2nd edn. [Association of Assistant Librarians, London]. {NASSDOC}

Hewitt, A.R., 1957, **Guide to resources for Commonwealth studies in London, Oxford and Cambridge with bibliographical and other information.** {IEG JNU NIEPA}

Hewitt, Roy, 1969, **Library management case studies.** {JNU}

Hewitt-Bates, F. S.A.M., 1954, **Bookbinding.** {NASSDOC}

Heys, H., 1965, **Preparation and production of technical books.** {DUL}

Hice, G.F., 1974, **System development methodology.** {DUL}

Hickec, Doralyn J., 1972, **Problems in organising library collections.** {JNU NERC}

Hickiny, Norman, 1985, **Book worms** : The insect pests of books. {JNU}

Hicks, Warren B. and Tillin, Alma, 1970, **Developing multi-media libraries.** {JNU}

Hicks, Warren B. and Tillin, Alma M., 1977, **Managing multimedia libraries.** {DUL USIS}

Higgins, Gavin, ed., 1980, **Printed reference material.** {NASSDOC ZHL}

Hildesheimer, Francoise, 1983, **Guidelines for the preparation of general guides to national archives.** [UNESCO]. {NASSDOC}

Hill, H.C., 1973, **Information processing and computer programming** : An introduction. {NIH}

Hill, Henry H., et al, eds., 1956, **Books and publishing**, vol. 3. {DUL}

Hillard, James M., 1975, **Where to find what** : A handbook to reference service. {JNU}

Hillian, Margret P., 1955, **Libraries for research and industry planning and equipment.** {DUL}

Hills, Philip J., ed., 1982, **Trends in information transfer.** {ISI NASSDOC}

Hingwe, K.S., 1967, **Reference books in academic libraries** : A brief survey. {DUL JNU}

Hingwe, K.S., 1982, **Management of university libraries in India** : Principles and practices. {AIU IIT}

Hjelmquist, Bengt, comp., n.d., **Swedish public libraries in pictures** : Country and small town libraries. {IIT}

Hoadley, Irene Braden and Clark, Alice S., eds., 1974, **Quantitative methods in librarianship** : Standards, research and management. {IIT ISI JNU}

Hobbs, John L., 1962, **Local history and the library.** {IIC NMML SPA}

Hobbs, John L., 1984, **Libraries and the materials of local history.** {CRRI NAI}

Hobson, Anthony, 1970, **Great libraries.** {NMML USIS}

Hodson, J.H., 1972, **Administration of archives.** {JNU ZHL}

Hoffmann, Christa F., 1980, **Getting ready for AACR2** : The cataloguer's guide. {JNU USIS}

Holloway, A.M., et al, 1976, **Information work with unpublished reports.** {NASSDOC}

Holmes, P.L., 1978, **On-line information retrieval** : An introduction and guide to British library's short term experimental information network project, Vol. 1 : Experimental use of non-medical information services; Vol. 2 : Experimental use of medical information services. [British Library]. {BCL}

Holmes, W. Robert and Raj Gopal, S., 1967, **Research facilities in Delhi.** {DSSW ICA NIEPA NIPCCD NMML USIS}

Holmes, W. Robert and Raj Gopal, S., 1967, **Research facilities in Hyderabad.** {NIPCCD NMML}

Holmes, W. Robert and Raj Gopal, S., 1968, **Research facilities in Bangalore, Mysore, Ahmedabad.** {NMML}

Holmes, W. Robert and Raj Gopal, S., 1968, **Research facilities in Bombay, Calcutta and Madras.** {NIPCCD NMML USIS}

Holroyd, Gileon, ed., 1974, **Studies in library management**, vol. 2. {DUL ICA NIPCCD}

Homanyunfarokh, Ruknuddin, n.d., **Ketab va ketab khana.** {JNU}

Hoover, Ryan E., ed., 1980, **The library and information manager's guide to online services.** {USIS}

Hoover, Ryan, E., ed., 1982, **On-line search strategies**. {USIS}

Hopper, Rohn, 1974, **Manual for the operation of an information/public relations department in standards organisation**. [Industrial Standards Institute]. {BIS}

Horecky, Paul L., **Libraries and bibliographic centres in the Soviet Union**. {IEG}

Horn, Jack, n.d., **Computer and data processing** : Dictionary and guide. {RTL}

Horne, Thomas Hartwell, 1981, **Introduction to the study of bibliography, to which is prefixed a memour on the public libraries of America**, 2 vols. {DUL}

Horner, John, 1973, **Special cataloguing with particular reference to music, films, maps, serials and the multi-media computerised catalogue**. {CRRI ICHR IIC IIT JNU NASSDOC NMML ZHL}

Horowitiz, Blanche, 1975, **A family planning library manual**. [Planned Parenthood Federation of America]. {NIH}

Horsnell, Verina, 1974, **Intermediate lexicon for information science** : Feasibility study. [Polytechnic of North London]. {BCL JNU}

Horsnell, Verina, ed., 1974, **Papers** : Conference on informatics, 1974, Oxford. [Association of Special Libraries and Information Bureaux]. {CRRI}

Horton, Carolyn, 1967, **Cleaning and preserving bindings and related materials**. [American Library Association]. {DUL IIT}

Horton, Carolyn, 1969, **Cleaning and preserving bindings and related materials,** 2nd edn. [American Library Association]. {USIS}

Hospers, John, ed., 1971, **Introduction to philosophical analysis**, rev edn. {NASSDOC}

Hostrop, Richard W., 1968, **Teaching and the community college library**. {JNU}

Hott, Richard W., 1971, **Basic system analysis**. {JNU}

Houghton, A.G. and Nixon, M., 1976, **National transport system for inter-library loan**. {JNU}

Houghton, Bernard, 1967, **Information work today** : Symposium on information work today, September, 1966, Liverpool. {ICA IIMC MHA}

Houghton, Bernard, 1969, **Standardization for documentation**. {JNU}

Houghton, Bernard, 1972, **Out of the dinosaurs** : The evolution of the National Lending Library for Science and Technology. {NASSDOC}

Houghton, Bernard, 1972, **Technical information sources** : A guide to patent specification, standards and technical reports literature. {BIS}

Houghton, Bernard, 1975, **Scientific periodicals** : Their historical development, characteristics and control. {DUL}

Houghton, Bernard, 1977, **The evaluation of a programme designed for teaching on-line information retrieval techniques** : Final report for the period

June-September 1976. [Liverpool Polytechnic, Department of Library and Information Studies]. {BCL}

Houghton, Bernard and Convey, John, 1977, **On-line information retrieval systems** : An introductory manual to principles and practices. {BCL CRRI DUL NIH}

Houghton, Bernard, ed., 1968, **Computer based information retrieval systems**. {DUL INSA NASSDOC}

Houle, Cyril O., ed., 1951, **Libraries in adult and fundamental education** : Report of the Malmo Seminar. [UNESCO]. {IEG NASSDOC ZHL}

Houle, Cyril O., ed., 1957, **Libraries in adult and fundamental education** : Report of the Malmo Seminar, (Hindi Translation). [Indian Adult Education Association]. {NIEPA}

House, William C., 1972, **Operations research** : An introduction to modern applications. {NASSDOC}

Howcraft, B. and Wagner, I., 1980, **Press cuttings** : Cooperative library guide. {ICA}

Howerton, P.W., 1963, **Vistas in information handling** : The augmentation of man's intellect by machine. {MHA}

Howerton, Paul W., 1963, **Information handling** : First principles. {JNU}

Howerton, Paul W., ed., 1974, **Management of information handling systems.** {NIEPA}

Hrgg, H.N., 1961, **Report on a survey made of book charging systems at present in use in England.** {JNU}

Huck-Tee, Edward Lim, 1970, **Libraries in West Malaysia and Singapore** : A short history. [University of Malaysia, Kuala Lumpur]. {CRRI NASSDOC}

Hudson, Kenneth and Micholls, Ann, 1975, **Directory of museum**. {ICCR}

Huen, P. Lim Pui, comp., 1973, **Directory of microfilm facilities in Southeast Asia**, 2nd edn. {JNU}

Hug, William E., ed., 1974, **Strategies for change in information programs**. {DUL USIS}

Hulme, E. Wyndham, 1950, **Principles of book classification**. {DUL}

Humphrey, K.W., 1966, **Report on the library of the Indian Institute of Technology, New Delhi**. [Indian Institute of Technology]. {IIT}

Humphry, John A., 1963, **Library co-operation** : Brown university study of university school community library coordination in the State of Rhode Island. {DUL}

Hunnisett, R.F., 1972, **Indexing for editors.** { NASSDOC NMML}

Hunt, K.G., 1955, **Subject specialisation and cooperative book purchase in the libraries of Great Britain**. {DUL}

Hunt, K.G., 1967, **Association of metropolitan chief librarians.** {JNU}

Hunter, Eric J., 1972, **Anglo-American Cataloguing Rules, 1967** : An introduction. {JNU NERC}

Hunter, Eric J., 1974, **Cataloguing**. {NASSDOC}

Hunter, Eric J., 1979, **Cataloguing**, 2nd rev. edn. {IIT}

Hunter, Eric J. and Fox, Nicholas J., 1980, **Examples illustrating AACR2** : Anglo-American Cataloguing Rules, 2nd ed. [Library Association, London]. {NASSDOC}

Hurt, Peyton, 1968, **Bibliography and footnotes** : A style manual for students and writers. 3rd edn. [University of California]. {NASSDOC}

Hussain, Khateeb M., 1973, **Development of information systems for education.** {AIU INSA}

Hussain, Mahmud, 1974, **Of libraries and librarians**. [University of Karachi]. {ZHL}

Hutchings, F.G.B., 1969, **Librarianship** : A short manual with special reference to developing countries. {IIMC SPA}

Hutchins, Margaret, 1944, **Introduction to reference work**. [American Library Association]. {BIS CRRI DUL ICHR IIFT NMML USIS}

Hutchins, Robert M., 1954, **Great books** : The foundation of liberal education. {USIS}

Hutchins, W.J., 1971, **Generation of syntactic structures from a semantic base.** {JNU}

Hutchins, W.J., 1975, **Languages of indexing and classification** : A linguistic study of structures and function. {DUL}

Hyman, Richard Joseph, 1982, **Shelf access in libraries**. [American Library Association]. {DUL NASSDOC}

Ian, Lovecy, 1984, **Automating library procedures** : A survivor's handbook. {NMML}

Ijari, S.R., 1983, **A development plan for public library system in the Karnataka State**. Thesis. (Karnataka University). {NASSDOC}

Immroth, John Philip, 1968, **Guide to Library of Congress classification**. {USIS}

Immroth, John Philip, 1971, **A guide to Library of Congress classification**, 2nd edn. {USIS}

Immroth, John Philip, 1980, **Guide to Library of Congress classification**, 3rd edn., by Lois Mai Chan. {USIS}

Inamdar, N.B. and Ramaiah, L.S., eds., 1990, **National policy for university libraries on India** : Problems and perspectives. {NASSDOC}

Ingraham, Mark H., 1968, **Mirror of brass** : Compensation and working condition of college and university administrators. {JNU}

Ingram, K.E. and Jefferson, Albert A., 1976, **Papers** : International library conference on libraries and the challenge of change, April 24-29, 1976, Kingsten. [Jamaica Library Association]. {III}

Insha, Ibne, 1967, **Developing reading habits in Asian conditions.** {ZHL}

Ireland, Norma Olin, 1952, **Picture file in school, college and public libraries**, rev edn. {ZHL}

Irving, Richard D. and Katz, Bill, 1988, **Reference services and public policy**. {NASSDOC}

Irwin, Raymond, 1949, **Librarianship** : Essays on applied bibliography. {CRRI}

Irwin, Raymond, 1966, **English library** : Sources and history. {JNU}

Isaac, K.A., 1990, **Literature search**. {UGC}

Isaac, Stephen and Michael, William B, 1972, **Handbook in research and evaluation** : A collection of principles, methods and strategies useful in the planning, design and evaluation of studies in education and the behavioural sciences. {NASSDOC}

Isenberg, Arthur, 1968, **A profile of Andhra book readers**. {NASSDOC*}

Iyengar, T.K.S., 1977, **New dimensions in library science**. {CRRI DUL ICHR IIT ISI NIEPA}

Jacker, Corinne, 1964, **Man, memory and machines** : An introduction to cybernetics. {INSA}

Jackson, Eugene B. and Jackson, Ruth L., 1978, **Industrial information systems** : A manual for higher management and their information officer, librarian/associates. {USIS}

Jackson, Lucille, ed., 1951, **Technical libraries** : Their organisation and management. [Special Libraries Association, New York]. {CRRI ISI}

Jackson, Miles M., ed., 1970, **Comparative and international librarianship** : Essays on themes and problems. {AIU IIT}

Jackson, Miles M., ed., 1981, **Contemporary developments in librarianship** : An international handbook. [Library Association, London]. {IIT NASSDOC}

Jackson, Miles M., ed., 1981, **International handbook of contemporary developments in librarianship.** {USIS}

Jackson, Sidney L,. et al, eds., 1976, **A century of service** : Librarianship in United States and Canada. [American Library Association]. {USIS}

Jackson, Wills, 1953, **Communication theory**. {JNU}

Jafar, S.M., 1971, **Research facilities in Uttar Pradesh**. {NMML}

Jagjit Singh, 1967, **Great ideas in information theory, language and cybernetics**. {INSA}

Jahoda, Gerald, 1970, **Information storage and retrieval systems for individual researchers.** {ISI MHA USIS}

Jahoda, Gerald and Braunagel, J.S., 1980, **Librarian and reference queries** : A systematic approach. {CRRI ISI USIS}

Jain, H.C., 1972, **Law library administration and reference**. {CRRI MMTC}

Jain, M.K., 1989, **Indiana** : A bibliography of bibliographical sources. {NASSDOC}

Jain, M.K., 1990, **Handbook of government libraries**. {CRRI}

Jain, Nem Chand, 1975, **National abstracting services** : Need, purpose and scope. {JNU}

Jain, T.C., 1971, **Professional associations and development of librarianship** : Case studies. [Library Association, London; American Library Association]. {AIU NASSDOC NCAER}

Janker, Frederic, 1964, **Indexing theory, indexing methods and search devices**. {IIT JNU USIS}

Jast, L. Stanley, 1928, **Planning of great library**. {ZHL}

Jayaswal, P.K., 1990, **Librarianship and bureaucratic organisation** : A study in the sociology of library profession in India. {JNU NASSDOC}

Jayne, Sears, et al, 1956, **Library catalogues of the English renaissance**. {DUL}

Jefferson, G., 1966-1977, **Library co-operation, 1966; 1968; 1977.** {AIU ICA IIT NIH}

Jefferson, George, 1965, **Public library administration** : An examination guide book. {MFL NERC SPA ZHL}

Jefferson, George and Burnett, C.C.K. Smith, 1978, **College library** : A collection of essays. {DUL NIEPA}

Jeffreys, A.E., 1974, **Mechanisation of the national library catalogues**. [UNESCO]. {NASSDOC}

Jeffreys, A.E. and Wison, T.D., 1970, **UK MARC project** : Proceedings of seminar organised by the cataloguing and indexing group of the Library Association at the University of Southampton, March 28-30, 1976. {NASSDOC}

Jelinek, Frederick, 1968, **Probabilistic information theory** : Discrete and memoryless models. {INSA}

Jell, Hans and Machesney, Robert, 1965, **International bibliography of non-periodical literature on documentation and information**. {JNU}

Jenkins, Frances Briggs, 1965, **Science reference sources**, 4th edn. {DUL}

Jenkinson, Hilary, 1973, **Manual of archive administration**. {NAI}

Jennett, Sean, 1973, **The making of books**, 5th edn. {INSA}

Jennings, Jerdson T., 1930, **Voluntary education through the public library.** [American Library Association]. {NASSDOC*}

Jenssen, Gudbrand, n.d., **A small country in the world of standards** : ANSINBS symposium on international standards information and ISONET. {BIS}

Jesse, W.H., 1952, **Shelf work in library**. [American Library Association]. {DUL IIT}

Jessup, Libby, F., et al, 1962, **Manual of procedures for private law libraries.** [American Association of Law Libraries]. {USIS}

Job, M.M., 1978, **Theory of book selection**. {NERC NIPCCD}

Joginder Singh and Sethi, A.R., eds., 1987, **Indian library directory**; 4th edn. [Indian Library Association]. {JNU NMML}

John, Peter W., 1971, **Statistical design and analysis of experiments**. {NASSDOC}

Johnson, A.F., 1962, **Practical cataloguing**. [Association of Assistant Librarians, London]. {IIT}

Johnson, A.F., 1968, **Programmed course in cataloguing and classification**. {CRRI IIC IIFT IIT INSA NCAER}

Johnson, Arthur W., 1978, **Manual of book binding**. {ZHL}

Johnson, E.D., 1966, **Communication** : An introduction to the history of writing, printing, books and libraries, 3rd edn. {IIC MHA}

Johnson, E.D., 1973, **Communication** : An introduction to the history of writing, printing, books and libraries, 4th edn. {USIS}

Johnson, Edward R. and Mann, Stuart H., **Organisation development for academic libraries**. {JNU}

Johnson, Edwin G. and Corliss, William R., 1971, **Human factors applications in tele-operator design and operation**. {INSA}

Johnson, Elmer D., 1965, **History of libraries in the Western world.** {NASSDOC}

Johnson, Herbert Weber, et al, 1972, **How to use the business library** : With sources of business information, 4th edn. {USIS}

Johnson, R.S., 1971, **Foreign theses in British libraries**. [University of Birmingham]. {NASSDOC}

Johnson, Richard A., et al, 1973, **Theory and management of systems**. {JNU}

Jolley, J.L., 1968, **Data university**. {JNU}

Jolley, L., 1961, **Principles of cataloguing**. {IEG IIT NAI SPA}

Joncich, M.I. and Lancaster, F.W., 1977, **Measurement and evaluation of library services**. {IIT USIS}

Jones, Clara Station, ed., 1978, **Public library information and referral service**. {USIS}

Jones, Frances M., 1983, **Defusing censorship** : The librarian's guide to handling censorship conflicts. {JNU}

Jones, Karen Spark, 1971, **Automatic keyword classification for information retrieval**. {BCL BIS NASSDOC}

Jones, Karen Spack, ed., 1981, **Information retrieval experiment.** {BIS IIMC IIT}

Jones, Karen Spack and Kay, Martin, 1973, **Linguistic and information science**. {DUL}

Jones, Ken, 1984, **Conflict and change in library organisation** : People, power and service. {DUL JNU}

Jones, Mander, 1962, **Books and related materials**. {JNU}

Jones, Noragh and Jordon, Peter, 1982, **Staff management in library and information work**. {IIT NASSDOC NIH}

Jordain, Philip B., 1969, **Condensed computer encyclopedia**. {IDSA}

Jordan, Robert Thayer, 1970, **Tomorrow's library** : Direct access and delivery. {USIS}

Josey, E.J., ed., 1975, **New dimensions for academic library service**. {USIS}

Josey, E.J., ed., 1979, **The information society** : Issues and answers. [American Library Association]. {JNU}

Joshi, M., 1985, **Microforms as an alternative to physical growth in libraries.** [University of Poona, Pune]. {NASSDOC*}

Judge, Peter and Gerrie, Brenda, 1987, **Small scale bibliographic database.** {JNU}

Juggal Kishore, 1981, **Personnel management in libraries**. {JNU}

Kabir, Abulfazal M. Fazle, 1987, **Libraries of Bengal 1700-1947**. {NMML}

Kaimann, Richard A., 1973, **Structured information files**. {NASSDOC}

Kaiser, Frances E., 1959, **Translators and translations** : Services and sources. {JNU}

Kalia, D.R., n.d., **American libraries** : Lessons for developing countries. (Mimeographed). {NASSDOC*}

Kalia, D.R., n.d., **Public libraries** : Collection of papers on public libraries written at different times. {NASSDOC*}

Kalia, D.R., 1955, **National public library system**. {NASSDOC}

Kalia, D.R., 1965, **Survey of public library services in India** : Tabulated and analysed : Working group on libraries. [Planning Commission, New Delhi]. {NASSDOC*}

Kalia, D.R., 1988, **Classification schedule for area studies**. {NASSDOC*}

Kalia, D.R. and Jain, M.K., 1975, **A bibliography of bibliographies on India**. {ICA}

Kalia, D.R. and Surender Kumar, 1988, **Directory of scientific and technical libraries in India.** {DUL}

Kan, Lai-Bing, comp., 1963, **Libraries in Hongkong** : A directory {ICWA}

Kane, Lucile M., 1966, **Guide to the care and administration of manuscripts**, 2nd edn. [American Association for State and Local History]. {NMML}

Kapoor, Pran, comp. and ed., 1979, **Directory of business Information research centres in India.** [National Industrial Documentation and Manpower Centre, New Delhi]. {NASSDOC}

Kapoor, S.K. and Chatterjee Amitabha, eds., 1988, **Marketing of library and information services in India**. [Indian Association of Special Libraries and Information Centres]. {NASSDOC}

Kapoor, S.K. and Ghosh, S.B., eds., 1977, **Papers** : IASLIC conference on planning of national information network, 11th, November 2-5, 1977, Dharwar. [Indian Association of Special Libraries and Information Centres]. {CRRI ISI JNU NIEPA NIPCCD}

Kapoor, S.K. and Ghosh, S.B., eds., 1977, **Planning of national information network** : 11th, IASLIC conference at Dharwar, 1977. {JNU}

Kapoor, S.K., ed., 1977, **Library scene in Calcutta** : Seminar on the occasion of the 100th meeting of the IASLIC study circle, February 26-27, 1977. [Indian Association of Special Libraries and Information Centres]. {NASSDOC*}

Kapoor, S.K., ed., 1979, **Applications of management techniques to library and information system**. {JNU NIPCCD}

Kapoor, S.K., ed., 1979, **Papers and proceedings** : IASLIC conference, 8th, December 26-29, 1978, Madras, Pt I : Standardisation of techniques and procedures for information handling; Pt II : Library and information system for rural development. [Indian Association of Special Libraries and Information Centres]. {BIS NIPCCD}

Kapoor, S.K., et al, eds., n.d., **Proceedings** : Conference on organisation of data services in India and user education and training programmes, 13th, 1981, Waltair. [Indian Association of Special Libraries and Information Centres]. {BIS MMTC NIPCCD}

Kapoor, S.K., et al, eds., 1980, **Papers** : IASLIC seminar, 9th, October 23-26, 1980, Nagpur, I : Role of information centres in technology transfer; II : Role of State-level and national library association in library development in India. [Indian Association of Special Libraries and Information Centres]. {CRRI INSA JNU NASSDOC}

Kapoor, S.K., et al, eds., 1981, **Organisation of data services in India**. [Indian Association of Special Libraries and Information Centres]. {NASSDOC}

Kapp, Reginold O., 1961, **Presentation of technical information** : Based on four public lectures given at University College, London. {DUL}

Kapur, Gopal K., 1970, **IBM 360 assembler language programming**. {NASSDOC}

Keren, Carl and Perlmutter, Linda, n.d., **Proceedings** : International conference on the application of mini and micro computers in information, documentation and libraries, March 13-18, 1983, Tel Aviv. {IIT}

Karetzkey, Stephen, 1982, **Reading research and librarianship** : A history and analysis. {CRRI IIT JNU}

Kartashou, N.S., ed., 1983, **Lenin and library cooperation**. {NASSDOC*}

Karunakaran Nayar, 1947, **Libraries and mass education**. [Sri Setha Parvathi Bayi Library, Kottayam]. {NASSDOC*}

Kashyap, S.C., 1986, **Parliaments and information dissemination**. {NASSDOC}

Kashyap, Subhash C., 1988, **Information service in the Parliament of India**. {NASSDOC}

Kasliwal, Kastoor Chand, comp., 1967, **Jaina grantha bhandars in Rajasthan**. {INSA}

Kathpalia, Yash Pal, 1973, **Conservation and restoration of archive materials**. {NASSDOC}

Katz, Bill and Fraley, Ruth A., 1983, **Video to online** : Reference services and the new technology. {JNU}

Katz, Bill and Fraley, Ruth A., eds., 1986, **Personnel issues in reference services**, {JNU NASSDOC}

Katz, William A., 1969, **Introduction to reference work**, 2 vols, V. 1 : Basic information services; V. 2 : Reference services. {AIU BIS DUL ICHR IIT ISI NASSDOC}

Katz, William A., 1974, **Introduction to reference work**, 2nd edn, 2 vols. {CRRI DUL JNU MMTC}

Katz, William A., 1978, **Introduction to reference work**, 3rd edn., 2 vols. {CRRI MMTC NIPCCD}

Katz, William A., 1979, **Your library** : A reference guide. {USIS}

Katz, William A., 1982, **Introduction to reference work**, 4th edn., 2 vols. {CRRI IIC USIS}

Katz, William A., 1984, **Your library** : A reference guide, 2nd edn. {JNU NASSDOC}

Katz, William A. and Swarf, Roderick G., eds., 1964, **Problems in planning library facilities**, Consultants, architects, plans and critiques : Proceedings : Library building institute, July 12-13, 1963, Chicago. [American Library Association]. {BIS DUL NASSDOC*}

Katz, William Armstrong, 1971, **Magazine selection** : How to build a community-oriented collection. {USIS}

Katzan, Harry, 1971, **Computer organisation and the system/370**. {NASSDOC}

Katzan, Harry, 1973, **Operating systems** : A pragmatic approach. {NASSDOC}

Katzan, Harry, 1976, **System design and documentation**. {JNU}

Katzer, Zeffery, et al, 1978, **Evaluating information** : A guide for users of social science research. {NCAER}

Kaufman, Paul, 1969, **Libraries and their users** : Collected papers in library history. [Library Association, London]. {NIPCCD}

Kaul, B.K., 1962, **Examination of current practices in Delhi college libraries and suggestion for improvement.** {JNU}

Kaul, H.K., ed., 1975, **Handbook of Indian writers**. {ICCR MMTC NASSDOC UGC}

Kaul, Neelima, comp., 1980, **Handbook of information scientists and librarians in India**. {BIS CRRI IIPA IIT ISI MMTC NASSDOC NCAER NIEPA NMML RTL}

Kaul, R.K., 1980, **Indic names** : Documentation list. {BIS NASSDOC ZHL}

Kaula, P.N., 1970, **National library of India** : Critical study. {AIU ICHR IIC IIFT IIMC IIT ISI NERC NIEPA NIH NIPCCD NMML SPA ZHL}

Kaula, P.N., 1985, **A treatise on Colon Classification appended with a select bibliography on the scheme**. {NASSDOC NMML}

Kaula, P.N., ed., 1965, **Library science today** : Ranganathan festschrift {BIS CRRI ICHR IIT INSA MFL NIH SPA ZHL}

Kaula, P.N., ed., 1965, **What they say**. [Ranganathan Volume Committee, Varanasi]. {NASSDOC*}

Kaula, P.N., ed., 1968, **Library movement in India**. [Delhi Library Association]. {CRRI}

Kaula, Prithvi N., 1971, **Library buildings** : Planning and design. {ICA IIMC IIT NASSDOC NIEPA NIH NIPCCD ZHL}

Kawatra, P.S., 1984, **Fundamentals of documentation** : With special reference to India. {DSSW DUL ICA ISI NCDC NMML}

Kee, S. Janice and Smith, Dorothy K., eds., 1955, **Book selection** : Proceedings of a work conference. {DUL}

Keen, Peter F. and Scott-Morten, Michael S., 1978, **Decision support systems** : An organisational perspective. {JNU}

Keeth, Kent H., comp., 1965, **A directory of libraries in Malaysia.** [University of Malaya Library, Kaula Lumpur]. {NASSDOC}

Kelierhals, W. and Kamp, C., 1964, **Manual for co-operative libraries and documentation services**. {DSSW ICA}

Kelley, Grace O., 1938, **Classification of books** : An inquiry into its usefulness to the reader. {DUL}

Kemp, Alasdair, 1979, **Current awareness service**. {JNU}

Kempe, Mary E., 1977, **Documentation training needs in Eastern Africa**. {ICA}

Kennedy, James R., ed., 1972, **Guide to reference sources on Africa, Asia, Latin America and the Caribbean, Middle East and North Africa and Russia and East Europe** : Selected and annotated. {NASSDOC}

Kenneth, Day, ed., 1966, **Book typography, 1815-1965, in Europe and the United States of America**. {DUL}

Kenney, Brigitte L., 1959, **Cooperative centralised processing** : A report of the establishment and first year of operation of the South West Mission Library Service. {DUL}

Kennlison, W.C. and Spilman, A.J.B., 1963, **Dictionary of printing paper making and book binding**. {DUL}

Kennon, Mary Frances and Doyle, Leila Ann, 1962, **Planning school library development** : A report of the school library development project. {DUL NASSDOC}

Kent, A. and Galvin, T.J., 1977, **Library resource sharing.** {ISI JNU NIH}

Kent, Allen, 1962, **Textbook on mechanised information retrieval**. {CRRI}

Kent, Allen, 1965, **Specialised information centres.** {JNU}

Kent, Allen, 1971, **Information analysis and retrieval**. {CRRI JNU MHA NASSDOC NIPCCD}

Kent, Allen, ed., 1960, **Information retrieval and machine translation**. {CRRI DUL}

Kent, Allen, ed., 1974, **Resource sharing in libraries** : Why, how when : Next action steps. {IIT INSA NASSDOC}

Kent, Allen, et al, 1979, **Use of library materials** : The University of Pittsburg study. {CRRI USIS}

Kent, Allen, et al, eds., 1967, **Electronic handling of information** : Testing and evaluation. {DUL INSA}

Kent, Allen and Galvin, Thomas J., eds., 1978, **The on-line revolution in libraries** : Proceedings of the 1977 conference in Pittsburgh. {JNU}

Kent, Allen and Galvin, Thomas J., eds., 1979, **Structure and governance of library networks** : Proceedings of the 1978 conference in Pittsburg. {JNU}

Kent, Allen and Galvin, Thomas J., eds., 1982, **Information technology** : Critical choices for library decision makers : Pittsburg conference on electronic information technology and its impact on library and information services 4th, 1981, Pittsburg. {BIS CRRI IIT JNU USIS}

Kent, Allen and Lancom, Harold, eds., n.d., **Encyclopaedia of library and information science**, 41 vols. {ACA IOSA IEG IIT INSA JNU NASSDOC NCERT NIH ZHL}

Kenyon, Frederic G., 1951, **Books and readers in ancient Greece and Rome**, 2nd edn. {DUL}

Keren, Carl and Perlmutter, Linda, 1985, **Applications of mini and micro computers in information, documentation and libraries**. {JNU NASSDOC}

Kerlsztury D., n.d., **Famous Hungarian libraries**. [National Szecheni Library]. {NASSDOC}

Kesarwani, S.K. and Bhat, S.G. eds., n.d., **Abstracting, indexing and current awareness services in environmental science**. {INSA}

Kesavan, B.S., 1961, **India's national library**. [National Library, Calcutta]. {IIT JNU MFL ZHL}

Kesavan, B.S., 1967, **University libraries and education for librarianship in India**. {JNU}

Kesavan, B.S., 1968, **Documentation in India**. {JNU}

Kesavan, B.S., ed., 1978, **National bibliography of Indian literature 1901-1953,** 4 vols. [Sahitya Akademi, New Delhi]. {DSSW INSA MFL NASSDOC}

Kesavan, B.S, et al, eds., n.d., **Rashtriya granth-suchi**, 1961-63. {NASSDOC}

Kessler, Margaret and Hall-Quest, Alfred L., 1941, **Library guidance for teachers.** {DUL ZHL}

Khan, H.A. and Ijari, S.R., 1990, **Current problems and trends in library and information services** : Professor K.S. Deshpande felicitation volume. {DUL}

Khan, Mohammad A.S., comp., 1983, **Directory of Islamic libraries and librarians**. [Islamic Library Association, California]. {ZHL}

Khan, Noorul Hassan, Kamleshwar Nath and Sardana, J.L., 1984, **Cataloguing practice** : Classified catalogue code and Anglo- American cataloguing rules. {IIMC JNU NASSDOC NIH}

Khan, Sadiq Ali, 1982, **Library services in Pakistan** : Being the proceedings of the departments of library science. . . . {JNU}

Khandwala, Vidyut K. and Naidu, M.K.R., eds., 1965, **Directory of libraries, publishers, booksellers in the city of Bombay**. [SNDT Women University Library]. {NASSDOC}

Khandwala, Vidyut K. and Sales-Pontes, A. Hilda, 1982, **Report** : Western regional conference on library architecture, October 8-10, 1980, Bombay. [Indian Association of Special Libraries and Information Centres]. {JNU NASSDOC}

Khandwala, Vidyut K., ed., 1982, **Library architecture**. [Indian Association of Special Libraries and Information Centres]. {MMTC NIEPA}

Khanna, J.K., 1981, **Personnel management in libraries**. {BIS IIFT IIMC ISI JNU NIEPA ZHL}

Khanna, J.K., 1984, **Fundamentals of library organisation**. {DSSW IIMC}

Khanna, J.K., 1987, **Library and society**. [Kurukshetra University, Kurukshetra]. {JNU NMML}

Khanna, J.K. and Bhagal, S.R., 1986, **Colon Classification** : Enumerated and expanded schedules alongwith theoretical formulations. {NASSDOC}

Khanna, J.K. and Kapil, D.D., 1982, **Colon Classification**. {CRRI ICHR IIFT IIT}

Khawar, Rafiq, comp., 1963, **Writing for new readers** : A handbook. [Pakistan National Book Council, Karachi]. {ZHL}

Khosla, Raj K., 1973, **Reference guide of India** : Who's who incorporating men of library science in India, men of science and technology in India, and men of education in India. {JNU NASSDOC}

Khosla, Raj K., ed., 1973, **Directory of booksellers, publishers, libraries and librarians in India**, including who's who, 2nd edn, {ICA IDSA JNU NASSDOC NMML}

Khosla, Raj K. and Gaur, M.K., eds., 1967, **Men of library science and libraries in India**. {SPA USIS}

Khurshid, A., 1987, **Library education in India, Pakistan and Iran.** {NASSDOC*}

Khurshid, Anis, 1976, **What children read** : A survey. [National Book Council of Pakistan, Karachi]. {ZHL}

Khurshid, Anis, 1982, **State of library resources in Pakistan**. {JNU}

Kibirige, Harry M., 1983, **Information dilemma**. {NIEPA}

Kies, Cosette, 1974, **Problems in library public relations.** {ISI}

Kim, Ung C., 1976, **Policies of publishers** : A handbook for order librarians. {JNU}

Kimber, Richard T., 1968, **Automation in libraries**. {AIU BIS IIT ISI JNU NASSDOC NCAER NIH SPA}

Kimber, Richard T., 1974, **Automation in libraries**, 2nd edn. {USIS}

Kimey, 1967, **Abbreviated citation**. {DEPT}

King, Donald W., 1981, **Telecommunications and libraries** : A primer for librarians and information managers. {USIS}

King, Marion, 1954, **Books and people** : Five decades of New York's oldest library. {NAI}

Kingery, Robert E. and Tauber, Maurice F., eds., 1963, **Book catalogs.** {USIS}

Kipp, Laurence, 1961, **Indian libraries and India Wheat Loan Education Exchange Programme** : A report. {JNU}

Kipp, Laurence and Kipp, Re Cedlia, 1968, **Prediction of the future** : The development programme of the University of Delhi. {JNU}

Kirby, John, 1985, **Creating the library identity** : A manual of design. {NASSDOC}

Kirkendall, Carolyn A., ed., 1981, **Directions for the decade** : Library instruction in the 1980's : Conference on library orientation for academic libraries, 10th, May 8-9. 1980. [Eastern Michigan University]. {USIS}

Kirkwood, Letla H., 1961, **Charging systems**. {USIS}

Kirsch, Robert, 1978, **Lives, works and transformations** : A quarter century of book reviews and essays, ed. by Linda Rolens. {USIS}

Kiss, Jeno, 1972, **Libraries in Hungary**. [National Szechenyi Library, Budapest]. {NASSDOC}

Kister, Kenneth F., 1968, **Social issues and library problems** : Case studies in the social science. {NMML}

Knapp, Particia B., n.d., **College teaching and the college library**. {AIU JNU}

Knight, Douglas M. and Nourse, E. Shapley, eds., 1969, **Libraries at large** : Tradition, innovation and the national interest : The resource book based on the materials of the National Advisory Commission on Libraries. {JNU USIS}

Knight, G. Norman, 1979, **Indexing, the art of** : A guide to the indexing of books and periodicals. {BCL NASSDOC}

Knight, G. Norman, ed., 1970, **Training in indexing** : A course. [Society of Indexers]. {IEG IIFT IIT NASSDOC}

Kochen, Manfred, 1963, **Techniques for document retrieval research** : State of art. {JNU}

Kochen, Manfred, 1965, **Some problems in information science**. {JNU}

Kochen, Manfred, 1974, **Principles of information retrieval.** {CRRI DUL ISI MHA USIS}

Kochen, Manfred, ed., 1967, **The growth of knowledge** : Readings on organisation and retrieval of knowledge. {NIEPA USIS}

Kochenburger, Ralph J. and Turcio, Corolyn J., 1974, **Computers in modern society**. {NASSDOC}

Kodiyan, Cicily, 1987, **Libraries in the USSR**. [USSR Embassy in India, New Delhi]. {NASSDOC*}

Kohen, Manfred, ed., 1975, **Information for action** : From knowledge to wisdom. {JNU}

Kohl, D.F., 1985, **Administration, personnel, buildings and equipment** : A handbook for library management. {NASSDOC}

Kohl, D.F., 1986, **Cataloguing and catalogue** : A handbook for library management. {NASSDOC}

Kohl, D.F., 1986, **Circulation, interlibrary loan, patron use and collection maintenance** : A handbook for library management. {NASSDOC}

Kohl, David F., 1985, **Acquisition, collection development and collection use**. {JNU}

Kohl, David F., 1985, **Reference services and library instruction** : A handbook for library management. {NASSDOC}

Kohl, David F., 1986, **Library education and professional issues** : A handbook for library management. {JNU NASSDOC}

Kohn, Rita T. and Tepper, Krysta, 1981, **You can do it** : Manual for librarians. {USIS}

Kolatkar, Ram S., 1970, **Finding the facts** : Newspaper information retrieval system. {IIMC JNU NIPCCD}

Konkar, S., 1985, **Dissemination services provided by special libraries in Pune.** [University of Poona, Pune]. {NASSDOC*}

Konnur, M.B., 1990, **Transnational library relations** : The Indo-American experience. {NASSDOC}

Koops, William R.H. and Stellingwerff, Johannes, eds., 1977, **Developments in collection building in university libraries in Western Europe**: Symposium on . . ., March 31-April 2, 1976, Amsterdam. {IIT}

Kramer, N. and De Smit, Jacob, 1977, **System thinking** : Concepts and notions. {JNU}

Krishan Kumar, 1973, **Research libraries in developing countries**. {AIU DUL IEG IIT JNU NASSDOC NIEPA NIPCCD NMML}

Krishan Kumar, 1979, **Theory of classification**. {BIS ICA ISI JNU ZHL}

Krishan Kumar, 1981, **Introduction to cataloguing practice**. {ISI JNU NASSDOC NERC NMML}

Krishan Kumar, 1981, **Theory of classification**, 2nd rev. edn. {NASSDOC NMML}

Krishan Kumar, 1982, **Library manual**. {BIS DSSW ICA IIC IIFT IIMC IIT ISI JNU NCDC NERC NIH ZHL}

Krishan Kumar, 1983, **Introduction to cataloguing,** 2nd edn. {ZHL}

Krishan Kumar, 1983, **Theory of classification**, 3rd edn. {ZHL}

Krishan Kumar, 1984, **Reference service**. {JNU NMML}

Krishan Kumar, 1987, **Library administration and management**. {JNU NASSDOC}

Krishan Kumar, 1987, **Library organisation**. {JNU NASSDOC}

Krishan Kumar and Vashishth, C.P., eds., 1980, **Proceedings** : All India library conference, 26th, March 6-9, 1980, New Delhi. [Indian Library Association]. {NASSDOC}

Krishnamurty, P.G., 1979, **National information base for health population and family welfare in India** : Manual for preparation of input for computerised bibliographic information base. [National Institute of Health and Family Welfare, New Delhi]. {NIH}

Krishnamurty, P.G., 1980, **Directory of health science libraries and documentation centres in India**. [National Institute of Health and Family Welfare, New Delhi]. {NIH}

Kroll, Morton, 1960, **Elementary and secondary school libraries of the Pacific North West**. {JNU}

Kroll, Morton, 1961, **College, university and special libraries of the Pacific North West**. {JNU}

Kronick, David A., 1962, **History of scientific and technical periodicals** : The origins and development of the scientific and technical press. {DUL}

Kruzas, Authony T., ed., 1963, **Directory of special libraries and information centres**. {ICCR ICWA IIPA}

Kruzas, Anthony Thomas, ed., 1974, **Encyclopaedia of information systems and services**. {MHA}

Kruzas, Anthony Thomas, ed., 1978, **Encyclopaedia of information system and services** : A guide to information storage and retrieval services, data base produces and publishers, online vendors, 3rd edn. {USIS}

Kruzas, Anthony Thomas, ed., 1981, **Encyclopaedia of information system and services** : An international guide to computer readable data bases, data base producers and publishers, online vendors and time sharing companies, 4th edn. {USIS}

Krzys, Richard, 1983, **World librarianship.** {IIT NMML}

Kubat, Libor and Zeman, Jiri, eds., 1975, **Entropy and information in science and philosophy.** {INSA}

Kudelkar, Janardan S., n.d., **The Baroda library movement** : A short account of the origin and growth of the Central Library Department of the Baroda State. [Central Library, Baroda]. {NASSDOC}

Kuhn, Hermann, 1986, **Conservation and restoration of works of art and antiquities,** tr. by Alexandra Trone. {NMML}

Kujoth, J.S., 1969, **Subject guide to periodical indexes and review indexes**. {NIH}

Kujoth, Jean S., 1968, **Readings in nonbook librarianship**. {NMML USIS}

Kujoth, Jean Spealman, 1969, **Libraries, readers and book selection**. {USIS}

Kumar, P.S.G., n.d., **Practical classification**, V.I : Colon Classification. {NIH NIPCCD ZHL}

Kumar, P.S.G., 1977, **Indian library chronology**. {BIS JNU NERC NIPCCD}

Kumar, P.S.G., 1987, **Computerisation in Indian libraries.** {NASSDOC}

Kumar, P.S.G., comp., 1987, **Research in library in information science in India** : A bibliography of Ph.D, M.Phil. and MLIS dissertation. {NASSDOC NMML}

Kumar, P.S.G., ed., 1985, **Papers** : National seminar on library and information manpower development, December 6-9, 1985, Nagpur. [Nagpur University, Department of Library and Information Science; University Grants Commission, New Delhi]. {NASSDOC}

Kumar, P.S.G., ed., 1987, **Hundred years of library education and its future** : Pre-seminar volume : ILA-IASLIC-GILA-IATLIS library education centenary seminar, October 10-12, 1987, Nagpur. [Nagpur University, Department of Library and Information Science, Nagpur]. {NASSDOC}

Kumar, P.S.G., ed., 1988, **Library and information manpower development** : Papers and proceedings : Nagpur Seminar. {NASSDOC}

Kumar, P.S.G., ed., 1989, **Working documents** : Workshop on norms, guidelines and standards for library and information science education. [Nagpur University Department of Library and Information Science, Nagpur]. {NASSDOC}

Kunz, Werener, 1977, **Methods of analysis and evaluation of information needs** : A critical review. {JNU}

Kurth, William H. and Grim, Ray W., 1966, **Moving a library**. {USIS}

Kutuzona, N.P., et al, 1979, **Mechanisation information retrieval and processing** : Application of punched. {NASSDOC}

Kyle, Barbara and Vickery, B.C., 1961, **The Universal Decimal Classification** : Present position and future developments. [UNESCO]. {ICA}

La Montagstne, Leo E., 1961, **American library classification with special reference to the Library of Congress**. {DUL}

Ladd, Dorothy P. and Gabriel, Michael R., 1980, **Microform revolution in libraries**. {BIS}

Lahood, Charles G. and Sullivan, Robert C., 1975, **Reprographic services in libraries** : Organisation and administration. [American Library Association]. {BIS NMML}

Lal, S.S., comp., 1985, **Herald of Library Science** : Trend report, citation and index, 1962-83. {NASSDOC}

Lamberton, D.M., ed., 1971, **Economics of information and knowledge** : Selected readings. {NASSDOC}

Lamberton, Donald M., ed., 1974, **The information revolution : Annals.** [American Academy of Political and Social Science]. {USIS}

Lamp, J.P., 1955, **Commercial and technical libraries.** {BIS}

Lancaster, F.W., 1968, **Information retrieval systems** : Characteristics, testing and evaluation. {TDA}

Lancaster, F.W., 1978, **Guidelines for the evaluation of information systems and services.** [UNESCO]. {JNU}

Lancaster, F.W., 1978, **Toward paperless information system.** {BCL DUL IIFT ISI ISIL USIS}

Lancaster, F.W., 1979, **Information retrieval systems** : Characteristics, testing and evaluation, 2nd edn. {CRRI DUL IIT USIS}

Lancaster, F.W., 1980, **The role of the library in an electronic society** : Proceedings : Library applications of data processing clinic, 1979, Illinois. [University of Illinois at Urbana-Champaign]. {USIS}

Lancaster, F.W., 1982, **Libraries and librarians in an age of electronics.** {USIS}

Lancaster, F.W., 1985, **Thesaurus construction and use** : A condensed course. [UNESCO]. {NASSDOC}

Lancaster, F.W., 1988, **If you want to evaluate your library.** [Library Association, London]. {NASSDOC}

Lancaster, F.W. and Cleverdon, C.W., eds., 1977, **Evaluation and scientific management of libraries and information centres.** {NIEPA}

Lancaster, F.W. and Fayen, E.G., 1973, **Information retrieval on-line.** {DUL INSA ISI NASSDOC USIS}

Lancaster, F.W. and Smith, L.C., n.d., **Compatibility issues affecting information systems and services.** {JNU}

Lancaster, G.T., n.d., **Programming in COBOL.** {NASSDOC}

Landau, T., 1963, **Library furniture and equipment.** {IIT NMML ZHL}

Landau, T., 1972, **Who's who in librarianship and information science,** 2nd edn. {JNU}

Landau, T., ed., 1958, **Encyclopaedia of librarianship**, 3rd edn. {SPA ZHL}

Landau, T., ed., 1967, **Encyclopaedia of librarianship**, rev. edn. {BIS CRRI DSSW IAMR IDSA IEG IIT MFL NASSDOC NCERT NIEPA}

Landry, Bertrand Clovis, 1971, **Theory of indexing** : Indexing theory as a model for information storage and retrieval. [Computer and Information Science Research Centre, Ohio State University]. {IIT}

Lane, Margaret T., 1981, **State publications and depository libraries** : A reference handbook. {USIS}

Langmead, Staphen and Beckman, Margaret, 1970, **New library design** : Guidelines to planning academic library buildings. {AIU BIS CRRI IIT JNU NIPCCD USIS}

Langridge, D.W., 1976, **Classification and indexing in the humanities.** {DUL JNU NASSDOC ZHL}

Langridge, Derek, 1973, **Approach to classification for students of librarianship.** {IIC JNU NASSDOC}

Langwell, W.H., 1974, **Conservation of books and documents.** {NERC}

Larsen, Knud, n.d., **National bibliographical services**. {IEG}

Larsgaard, Mary, 1978, **Map librarianship** : An introduction. {USIS}

Lawrie, Jean Elizabeth, 1970, **Elementary school libraries.** {JNU}

Leduss, S.T.G.S.V. and Stokolova, N.A., 1974, **About a method of constructing information languages having grammar.** {DEPT JNU}

Lee, C.P., 1971, **Library resources** : How to research and write a paper. {IIMC IIT NASSDOC NCAER}

Lee, Charles, 1958, **The hidden public** : The story of the book-of-the- Month Club. {USIS}

Lee, John A.N., 1967, **Anatomy of a compiler**. {NASSDOC}

Lee, Sul H., 1973, **Planning programming budgeting system** : Implications for library management. {JNU}

Lee, Sul H., ed., 1988, **Acquisitions budgets and material costs** : Issues and approaches. {NASSDOC}

Leeds, Herbert D. and Winberg, Gerald M., 1966, **Computer programming fundamentals,** 2nd edn. {NASSDOC}

Leerburger, Benedict A., 1982, **Marketing the library**. {JNU USIS}

Lehmann-Haupt, Hellmut, et al, 1967, **Bookbinding in America** : Three essays. {DUL}

Lehmann-Haupt, Hellmut, 1957, **Life of the book** : How the book is written, published, sold and read. {DUL}

Lehnus, Donal J., 1971, **How to determine author and title entries according to AACR** : An interpretive guide with card examples. {AIU USIS}

Lehnus, Donald J., 1974, **Milestones in cataloguing** : Famous cataloguers and their writings, 1835-1969. {USIS}

Leigh, Robert D., n.d., **Public library in the United States**. {IEG}

Leimkuhler, F.F., 1967, **Mathematical models for library systems analysis**. {JNU}

Leimkuhler, F.F. and Cooper, M.D., n.d., **Analytical planning for university libraries**. [University of California]. {IIT}

Leitch, L. and Billewicz, W.Z., 1963, **Scheme for classification of information on nutrition coded for machine retrieval**. {DUL}

Leonard, Lawrence E., et al, 1969, **Centralised book processing** : A feasibility study based on Colorado academic libraries. {USIS}

Leong, C.L.H., 1989, **Serial cataloguing handbook** : An illustrative guide to the use of AACR2 and LC rule interpretations. [American Library Association]. {DUL}

Lesko, Matthew, 1983, **Information U.S.A.** {USIS}

Lewanski, Richard C., ed. and comp., 1978, **Subject collections in European libraries**, 2nd edn. {IIT}

Lewin, Evan, 1967, **Subject catalogue of the library of the Royal Empire Society**. {NASSDOC}

Lewis, Chester M., n.d., **Special libraries** : How to plan and equip them. [Special Libraries Association, New York]. {BIS NMML}

Lewis, Chester M. and Affen, Hauser William H., 1956, **Microrecording** : Industrial and library applications. {DUL}

Lewis, M. Joy, 1969, **Libraries for the handicapped**. {DUL}

Lewis, P.R., 1982, **The fall and rise of national bibliography**. [Sarada Ranganathan Endowment for Library Science, Bangalore]. {NASSDOC*}

Leyland, Eric, 1961, **Libraries in schools**. {JNU}

Libetz, Ben Anni, 1964, **Citations for physics literature** : Experimental issue : Citations of Journal of Applied Physics : The physical review. {DUL}

Licklider, J.C., 1965, **Libraries of the future**. {JNU NMML SPA USIS}

Liebaers, Herman, 1975, **Book promotion through libraries**. {DUL}

Lincoln, Alan Jary, 1984, **Crime in the library** : A study of patterns, impact and security. {JNU}

Lincoln, Cynthia Mary, ed., 1976, **University libraries as information centres** : Proceedings of IATUL sixth meeting, 1975. {DCL}

Linderman, Wilfred B., 1967, **Conference on the present status and future prospects of reference information work**. {JNU}

Line, Maurice, B., 1969, **Library surveys** : An introduction to their use, planning, procedure and presentation. {CRRI IIT NASSDOC USIS}

Line, Maurice B., 1982, **Library surveys** : An introduction to their use, planning, procedure and presentation, 2nd edn. {JNU NASSDOC}

Line, Maurice, B., 1986, **College students and the library** : Report of a survey in May 1964 of the use of libraries and books, by students in five teacher training colleges. {JNU}

Line, Maurice B., et al, 1971, **Experimental information service in the social sciences** : Report on work carried out in 1970, [University Library, Bath University of Technology]. {NASSDOC}

Lipsman, Claire K., 1972, **The disadvantaged and library effectiveness**. [American Library Association]. {USIS}

Llewellyn, Raney M., ed., 1936, **Microphotography for libraries**. {DUL}

Lock, Reginald Northwood, 1961, **Library administration**. {CRRI IIT}

Lock, Reginald Northwood, 1973, **Library administration**, 3rd edn. {DUL ICA}

Lockwood, Deborah, L., comp., 1979, **Library instruction** : A bibliography. {NIPCCD}

Lodewycks, K.A., 1961, **Essentials of library planning**. {DUL}

Loizeaux, Marie Duvernoy, 1959, **Publicity primer** : An ABC of telling all about the public library, 4th edn. {USIS}

Lolley, John L., 1974, **Your library** : What's in it for you. {CRRI}

Long, Harriet Catherine, 1925, **County library service**. {JNU}

Long, Nicholas, 1975, **Information and referral services** : Research findings. [U.S. Department of Health, Education and Welfare]. {NASSDOC}

Longley, Dennis and Shain, Michael, 1985, **Macmillan dictionary of information**. {NASSDOC}

Loosjes, T.P., 1973, **On documentation of scientific literature**. {JNU}

Lowell, Milred Hawksworth, n.d., **The management of libraries and information centres**, 4 vols. {DUL NIPCCD USIS}

Lowy, George, 1965, **Searcher's manual**. {IIT USIS}

Lubrans, John, ed., 1974, **Educating the library user**. {USIS}

Lubrans, John, ed., 1977, **Reader in library systems analysis**. {USIS}

Lubrans, John, ed., 1978, **Progress in educating the library user**. {CRRI IIT}

Lucas, Henry C., 1976, **The analysis, design and implementation of information systems**. {TDA}

Lucy, Te-Chu Lee, 1985, **Library automation and information science** : A collection of essays. {NASSDOC}

Luczynska, Alfreda and Krystyna, Remerowa, comps., n.d., **Libraries in Poland**. {BIS}

Luhn, H.P., 1963, **Automation and scientific communication** : Short papers contributed to the theme sessions of the 26th annual meeting of the American Documentation Institute at Chicago. {JNU}

Luhn, Hans Peter, 1968, **Pioneer of information science** : Selected works. {JNU}

Lunati, Rinaldo, 1975, **Book selection** : Principles and procedures. {DUL}

Lunin, Lois F., et al, 1981, **Information Community** : An alliance for progress : Proceedings : ASIS annual meeting, 44th, 1981. {NASSDOC}

Luquire, W., 1986, **Coordinating cooperative collection development** : A national prospective. {JNU NASSDOC}

Luquire, W., ed., 1984, **Experiences of library network administrators** : Papers based on the symposium 'From our past : Towards 2000'. {NASSDOC}

Lydall, G.O.E., 1955, **Practical guide to precis writing and indexing**. {DUL}

Lydenberg, H.M., 1932, **History of the New York Public Library.** {NAI}

Lydenberg, Harry Miller and Archer, John, 1980, **Care and repair of books**, 4th rev edn. {DUL ISI}

Lyle, Guy R., 1935, **College library publicity**. {USIS}

Lyle, Guy R., 1961, **Administration of the college library**. {DUL NERC}

Lyle, Guy R., 1970, **Librarian speaking** : Interview with university librarians. {JNU USIS}

Lyle, Guy R., 1974, **The administration of the college library**, 4th edn. {DUL NIEPA USIS}

Lyle, Guy R., 1986, **College library publicity**. {DUL}

Lynch, Michael Felix, 1974, **Computer-based information services in science and technology** : Principles and techniques. {BCL}

Lynes, Alice, 1974, **How to organise a local collection.** {NASSDOC}

Lynn, Jeannete Murphy, 1965, **Alternative classification for catholic books**. {DUL}

Mabbs, A.W., 1974, **Organisation of intermediate records storage**. [UNESCO]. {NIEPA NMML}

Mac Cafferty, Maxine, n.d., **Papers** : USIDIC conference on user education, 1976, Graz. {CRRI}

Mac Cafferty, Maxine, 1977, **Thesauri and thesauri construction**. [Association of Special Libraries and Information Bureaux]. {CRRI NASSDOC}

Mac Cafferty, Maxine, 1977, **User education** : Towards a better use of information resources. {BCL}

Mac Closkey, Monro, 1968, **Our national attic**. [U.S. Library of Congress; Smithsonian Institution; [U.S. National Archives]. {USIS}

Mac Donald, Teresa, 1970, **Union catalogue of the Government of Ceylon publications held by libraries in London, Oxford and Cambridge**. [Centre of South Asian Studies, University of Cambridge, Mansell]. {NASSDOC}

Machlup, Fritz and Mansfield, Una, n.d., **Study of information** : Inter- disciplinary messages. {JNU}

Mackee, Monique, 1983, **Handbook of comparative librarianship**, 3rd edn. {NASSDOC}

Macledo, Robert D., n.d., **County rural libraries** : Their policy and organisation. {JNU}

Macleish, Archibald, 1971, **Champion of a cause** : Essays and addresses on librarianship. [American Library Association]. {USIS}

Mac Pherson, H.D., 1936, **Some practical problems in cataloguing**. {DUL}

Mac Robert, T.M., 1957, **Printed books** : A short introduction to fine typography. {DUL}

Madan, Som Nath, 1987, **Computer and library services**. {NASSDOC*}

Madhu Bala, 1973, **Analysis of Indian library conferences and seminars since 1947.** {JNU}

Madison, Charles A., 1966, **Book publishing in America**. {DUL}

Magnanand and Vaish, J.D., n.d., **Higher secondary school libraries**. {DUL IEG}

Magnoti, Shirley, 1982, **Library science research, 1974-79**. {DUL}

Mahajan, S.G., 1979, **History of the public library movement in western Maharashtra, 1805-1921** : Thesis. (Poona University). {NASSDOC}

Mahajan, S.G., 1984, **History of public library movement in Maharashtra**. {JNU NASSDOC*}

Mahajan, S.G. and Riswadker, M.R., 1984, **National seminar on social science documentation in India**. {JNU}

Mahapatra, Piyushkanti, 1985, **Computer in library services**. {JNU NASSDOC NMML}

Mahapatra, Piyushkanti, 1966, **Folklore library**. {IIMC NASSDOC NMML}

Maheu, Mary Helen, 1958, **Certification of school librarians** : A compilation of State requirements, 1958. {NASSDOC}

Maheu, Mary Helen, 1960, **State Department of Education responsibilities for school libraries**. {JNU}

Maizell, Robert E., et al, 1971, **Abstracting scientific and technical literature**. {BIS CRRI IIMC ISI JNU USIS}

Majeed Khan, M.A., 1982, **Handbook of library science education in India**. [Andhra Pradesh Library Association, Hyderabad]. {NASSDOC}

Majumdar, 1987, **India's national library** : Systematisation. [National Library, Calcutta]. {NASSDOC}

Majumdar, Gopal Kumar, 1974, **Newspaper microfilming** : A plea for newsprint documentation. {NASSDOC ZHL}

Majumdar, S., 1980, **Evaluation of reference service in JNU library**. {JNU}

Makkar, G.C., 1974, **Three number author table**. {BIS ZHL}

Malhan, Inder Vir and Kapoor, Shabad, 1982, **Library education** : A bibliography. {IIT JNU NASSDOC}

Malinconico, Michael and Fasana, Paul J., 1979, **The future of the catalog** : The library's choices. {USIS}

Maloney, James J., ed., 1983, **Online searching technique and management**. [American Library Association]. {USIS}

Maloney, R. Kay, ed., 1977, **Personnel development in libraries**. [Bureau of Library and Information Science Research, Rutgers University Graduate School of Library Science]. {NIPCCD USIS}

Maltby, Arthur, ed., 1968, **Economics and commerce** : The sources of information and their organisation. {NASSDOC}

Maltby, Arthur, ed., 1972, **Classification in the 1970's** : A discussion of the development and prospects for the major schemes. {AIU IIC JNU NASSDOC NIPCCD ZHL}.

Maltha, D.J., 1976, **Technical literature search and the written report**. {BCL}

Mangla, P.B., ed., 1981, **Library and information science education in India** : Papers and recommendations of an All-India seminar held at the Department of Library Science, University of Delhi, during October 3-8, 1977, {AIU ICA JNU NASSDOC NIEPA}

Mangla, P.B., ed., 1985, **Building library collections and national policy for library** : Seminar papers : All India library conference, 30th, January 28-31, 1985, Jaipur. [Indian Library Association]. {NASSDOC}

Mangla, P.B., et al, eds., 1983, **Fifty years of librarianship in India** : Past, present and future : Papers : All India library conference, 29th, December 5-9, 1983. [Indian Library Association]. {MMTC NASSDOC ZHL}

Manhieimer, Martha L., 1973, **Style manual** : A guide for the preparation of reports and dissertations. {DUL}

Manhieimer, Martha L., 1980, **Cataloguing and classification** : A workshop, 2nd edn. {NASSDOC NIPCCD}

Mann, Margaret, 1943, **Introduction to cataloguing and classification of books**. [American Library Association]. {BIS CRRI ICA NAI NMML SPA USIS ZHL}

Mann, Peter, 1982, **From author to reader** : A social study of books. {AIU}

Mann, Thomas, 1987, **Guide to library research methods**. {JNU}

Manzoor, Suhail, 1982, **Systems bibliography** : A thirty years' literature survey. {NASSDOC}

Marchant, Maurice P., 1976, **Participative management in academic libraries**. {DUL NIEPA}

Margen, A. Marry, ed., 1973, **British government publications** : An index to chairmen and authors, 1941-1960. [Library Association, London]. {NASSDOC}

Marjarum, E. Warne, 1947, **How to use a book.** {JNU}

Marjorie, Fiske, 1959, **Book selection and censorship** : A study of school and public libraries in California. {JNU}

Markley, Arme Ethelyn, and Fruge, Grete W., 1963, **Special problems in classification and cataloguing.** {DUL}

Markuson, B.E., 1964, **Libraries and automation**. {IIT}

Marshall, D.N., 1983, **History of libraries** : Ancient and mediaeval. {JNU}

Marshall, Faya Dix, 1979, **School librarians' encyclopedic dictionary**. {NIEPA}

Marshall, Lee, ed., 1951, **Books are for our time.** {DUL}

Marshall, Margaret R., n.d., **Libraries and literature for teenagers**. {ICHR}

Martell, Charles R., 1983, **Client-centred academic library** : An organisational model. {JNU}

Martin, James, 1982, **Principles of data-base management.** {NASSDOC}

Martin, Laura Katherine, 1950, **Magazine for school libraries**, rev edn. {ZHL}

Martin, Lowell, 1946, **Personnel administration in libraries**. {JNU}

Martin, Lowell A., 1967, **Baltimore reaches out** : Library service to the disadvantaged. {JNU}

Martin, Lowell A., et al, 1969, **Library response to urban change** : A study of the Chicago Public Library. [American Library Association]. {USIS}

Martin, Murray, S., 1978, **Budgetary control in academic libraries**. {AIU DUL}

Martin, Nella Jane, 1948, **Subject headings used in the dictionary catalogues**, 5th edn. [U.S. Library of Congress]. {ZHL}

Martin, Susan K., 1978, **Library networks, 1978-79**. {IIT USIS}

Martin, Susan K., 1980, Library network, 1981-82, 4th edn. {USIS}

Martin, William, ed., 1975, **Library service to the disadvantaged.** {NIPCCD}

Martinson, T.m L., 1972, **Introduction to library research in geography**. {DUL}

Martyn, John, 1987, **Libraries and information centres in Britain**. [British Council, London]. {NASSDOC*}

Maruskin, Albert F., 1980, **OCLC : Its governance, function, financing and technology**. {JNU}

Mary, R. Kenney, 1967, **Abbreviated citation** : A bibliographical problem. {DUL}

Mason, Donald, 1968, **Document reproduction in libraries**. {DUL}

Mason, Donald, 1978, **Information management**. {IIT}

Mason, Merilyn Gell, 1983, **The federal role in library and information services**. {USIS}

Mathews, Anne J., 1983, **Communicate** : A librarian's guide to interpersonal relations. [American Library Association]. {USIS}

Mathur, Lalit Mohan, 1970, **Principles and techniques of educational library displays and exhibits**. {IIT NMML}

Matthews, Joseph, R., 1980, **Choosing an automated library system** : A planning guide. [American Library Association]. {USIS}

Matthis, Raimund E. and Taylor, Desmond, 1971, **Adopting the Library of Congress classification system** : A manual of methods and techniques for application or conversion. {DUL}

Maureen, J., 1966, **Guide to scientific periodicals** : Annotated bibliography. {DUL}

Maurois, Andre, 1961, **Public libraries and their mission**. [UNESCO]. {ICA}

Maxwell, Margaret F., 1980, **Handbook for AACR2** : Explaining and illustrating Anglo-American Cataloguing Rules, 2nd ed. [American Library Association]. {USIS}

Mayes, Paul, ed., 1978, **Periodicals administration in libraries** : A collection of essays. {IIT NASSDOC NCAER NIPCCD}

Mc Cabe, Gerard B. and Kreissman, Bernard, eds., 1983, **Advances in library administration and organisation**. {IIT}

Mc Canse, Ralph Alan, 1963, **Art of the book review** : A comprehensive working outline. {DUL}

Mc Clure, Charles R., 1980, **Information for academic library decision making** : The case for organisational information management. {JNU}

Mc Collough, Ethel Farguhar and Van Buren, Maud, 1931, **Essentials in library education**. [American Library Association]. {NASSDOC*}

Mc Colvin, L.R., 1909, **Library staff**. {IIT}

Mc Colvin, L.R., 1937, **Libraries and the public**. {NAI}

Mc Colvin, L.R., et al, 1939, **Library stock and assistance to readers** : A textbook. {NAI}

Mc Colvin, Lionel R., 1947, **Public libraries in Australia** : Present conditions and future possibilities. {JNU}

Mc Colvin, Lionel R., 1950, **Public library extension**. [UNESCO]. {NASSDOC ZHL}

Mc Colvin, Lionel R., 1952, **Reference library stack** : An informal guide. {CRRI}

Mc Colvin, Lionel R., 1957, **Public library services for children,** [UNESCO]. {IEG JNU NASSDOC NERC NIPCCD}

Mc Colvin, Lionel R., 1961, **Libraries for children**. {DUL}

Mc Colvin, Lianol R., 1961, **Libraries in Britain**. {NASSDOC}

Mc Colvin, Lionel R. and Revie, James, 1949, **British libraries**. {MHA}

Mc Comb, Dana Quick, n.d., **Public library buildings** : Their financing, design, construction, equipment and operation. {DUL}

Mc Coy, Donald R., comp., 1978, **The National Archives** : America's Ministry of Documents, 1934-1968. {USIS}

Mc Cullough, Kathleen, et al, 1977, **Approval plans and academic libraries** : An interpretive survey. {IIT}

Mc Daniel, Herman, ed., 1970, **Applications of decision tables** : A reader. {NASSDOC}

Mc Diarmid, W.W., et al, 1942, **Administration of the American public library.** [American Library Association]. {NAI}

Mc Garry, K.J., 1972, **Mass communications** : Selected readings for librarians. {NIPCCD}

Mc Garry, K.J., 1975, **Communication knowledge and the librarian**. {CRRI DUL NASSDOC}

Mc Garry, K.J., 1981, **Changing context of information** : An introductory analysis. {NIEPA}

Mc Garry, K.J. and Burrel, T.W., 1972, **Semantics in the organisation of knowledge** : A programmed text for students in information retrieval. {NASSDOC}

Mc Garry, K.J., and Burrel, T.W., 1973, **Communication studies**. {CRRI}

Mc Gaw, Howard F., 1952, **Marginal punched cards in college and research libraries**. {JNU}

Mc Innis, Raymond G., 1978, **New perspectives for reference service in academic libraries**. {CRRI IIT NIPCCD}

Mc Kee, B., 1989, **Planning library service.** {NASSDOC}

Mc Kerrow, Ronald B., 1965, **Introduction to bibliography for literary students.** {DUL}

Mc Lean, M., ed., 1985, **The information explosion** : The new electronic media in Japan and Europe. {NASSDOC}

Mc Livaine, Betsy, 1983, **A consumers', researchers' and students' guide to government publications**. {USIS}

Mc Maron, et al, 1969, **Information processing laboratory for education and research in library science** : Phase-I. {IIT}

Mc Mustrie, Douglas C., 1943, **Book** : The story of printing and bookmaking, 3rd rev ed. {DUL}

Meachan, Mary, 1978, **Information sources in children's literature** : A practical reference guide. {NIPCCD}

Meadow, Charles T., 1970, **Man-machine communication**. {INSA NASSDOC}

Meadow, Charles T., 1973, **Analysis of information systems.** {BIS CRRI DUL NIH NIPCCD USIS}

Meadows, A.J., 1982, **Dictionary of new information technology**. {IIPA}

Mechanic, Sylvia, 1971, **Annotated list of selected United States government publications available to depository libraries.** {NASSDOC}

Mechluip, Fritz, 1972, **Production and distribution of knowledge in the United States.** {NASSDOC}

Meckler, Alan M. and Mc Mullin, Ruth, 1975, **Oral history collections**. {USIS}

Meetham, A.R., ed., 1968, **Encyclopaedia of linguistics, information and control**. {NASSDOC NCERT}

Mehta, S.P., 1975, **Art and science of book preservation.** {BIS IIT MFL ZHL}

Melin, Johns, **Libraries and data processing** : Where do we stand. {JNU}

Melton, Jessica S., 1963, **Automatic processing of metallurgical abstracts for purpose of information retrieval.** {JNU}

Meltzer, Morton F., 1967, **The information center** : Management's hidden asset. [American Management Association]. {USIS}

Melville, Annette, comp., 1980, **Special collection in the Library of Congress** : A selective guide. [U.S. Library of Congress]. {USIS}

Meredith, Patrick, 1961, **Learning, remembering and knowing**. {NASSDOC}

Merril, W.S., 1939, **Code for classifiers**. 2nd edn. [American Library Association]. {BIS CRRI IIT NAI USIS ZHL}

Merritt, Le Roy C., 1958, **Reviews in library book selection**. {DUL}

Merritt, Le Roy Charles, 1970, **Book selection and intellectual freedom**. {USIS}

Mery, Richard E., 1975, **Staff communication in libraries**. {JNU}

Metcalf, Keyes D., 1964, **Co-operation among Maine libraries** : A report prepared for the larger libraries of Maine. {DUL}

Metcalf, Keyes D., 1965, **Planning academic and research library buildings**. {BIS IIT NASSDOC NIH USIS}

Metcalf, Keyes D., ed., 1960, **Studies in library administrative problems** : Eight reports from a seminar on library administration. {DUL USIS}

Metcalfe, J., 1957, **Information indexing and subject cataloguing** : Alphabetical classified, coordinate, mechanical. {DUL IEG IIT}

Metcalfe, J., 1959, **Subject classifying and indexing of libraries and literature.** {IEG IIT MFL}

Metcalfe, John, 1976, **Information retrieval** : British and American. {JNU}

Metcalfe, John, ed., 1965, **Alphabetical subject indication of information**. {IIT USIS}

Methics, Lorraine M. and Watson, Peter G., 1976, **Computer based reference service**. {JNU}

Mevissen, W., 1958, **Public library building**. {IIT}

Mews, Hazel, 1942, **Reader instruction in colleges and universities** : An introduction handbook. {AIU JNU NIEPA}

Mews, Hazel, 1951, **Books are tools** : The organisation of small technical libraries for South African industry. {JNU}

Meyriat, Jean and Beauchet, Micheline, 1968, **Guide for the establishment of national social science documentation centres in developing countries.** [UNESCO] {IEG JNU NMML}

Mikhailov, A.I., n.d., **Problems of information user needs**. [International Federation for Documentation and Information]. {CRRI DUL}

Mikhailov, A.I., 1982, **Scientific and technical information** : Its impact on the development of science and technology. [UNESCO; UNIDO, Moscow]. {NASSDOC*}

Mikhailov, A.I. and Giljarevaskij, R.S., n.d., **Introductory course in informatics/documentations**. [UNESCO]. {DUL NASSDOC}

Mildreth, C.R., ed., 1989, **On line catalogue**. [Library Association, London. {NASSDOC}

Millard, Patrica, ed., 1968, **Modern library equipment**. {CRRI IIT NIH NMML}

Miller, Bertha M. and Field, Elinor W., eds., 1955, **Newbery medal books, with their authors' acceptance** : Papers and related material, chiefly from the Horn Book magazine, 1922-55. {USIS}

Miller, Bertha Mahony and Field, Elinor Whitney, eds., 1957, **Caldecott medal books,** with the artists' acceptance: papers and related material chiefly from the Horn Book Magazine, 1938-1957. {USIS}

Miller, Shirley, 1971, **The vertical file and its satelites** : A handbook. {DUL USIS}

Miller, William, 1950, **The book industry** : A report of the public library enquiry. {CRRI}

Mills, J., 1960, **Modern outline of library classification,** 2nd edn. {BIS CRRI IIT MFL NAI NMML}

Milstead, Jessica L., 1984, **Subject access systems** : Alternatives in design. {NASSDOC}

Minaikit, Nonglak, 1968, **Annotated bibliography on librarianship in Thailand.** {JNU}

Misra, Jogesh, 1965, **Censorship** : A literature survey. (University of Delhi, Department of Library Science. Sessional Project). {DUL}

Misra, Jogesh, 1979, **History of libraries and librarianship in modern India since 1850**. {JNU NERC NMML}

Mitchell, Ruth K., 1971, **Information science and computer basics**. {BIS}

Mittal, R.L., 1964, **Library administration** : Theory and practice. {DUL ICA NAI NCAER NIH NMML SPA ZHL}

Mittal, R.L., 1969, **Library administration** : Theory and practice, 2nd edn. {DUL JNU NASSDOC NIEPA SPA}

Mittal, R.L., 1970, **Advances in library and information science**. {CRRI ICA NCAER NCDC}

Mittal, R.L., 1971, **Public library law** : An international survey. {ICA NASSDOC NMML}

Mittal, R.L., 1973, **Library administration** : Theory and practice, 3rd edn. {CRRI DUL JNU NIH TDA}

Mittal, R.L., 1978, **Library administration** : Theory and practice, 4th edn. {BIS DUL JNU NIEPA ZHL}

Mittal, R.L., **Library administration** : Theory and practice, 5th edn. {ZHL}

Mittal, R.L. and Gupta, Shamsher, 1966, **Dictionary catalogue** : A practical manual. {ICHR IIT IIMC NERC NIPCCD}

Mittal, S.R., 1964, **Organising village library** : A guide book for social education workers and village librarians. [National Council for Educational Research and Training, New Delhi]. {ICA ISI NIPCCD}

Mohanrajan, P.A., 1983, **Ascent of a university library**. {NMML}

Mohanrajan, P.A., ed., 1984, **New trends in international librarianship**. {NASSDOC NMML}

Mohinder Pratap Chand, 1978, **Colon Classification** : Its structure and working. {ISI NERC NMML}

Mohinder Singh, 1967, **Government publications of India** : A survey of their nature, bibliographical control and distribution systems. {MFL NASSDOC NIPCCD}

Mohinder Singh, 1969, **Outline of library classification**. {NERC}

Mohinder Singh, 1982, **Government of India publications**. {MHA}

Mohinder Singh, comp., 1975, **Learned societies and institutions in India** : Activities and publications, including over 4000 research oriented titles. {JNU UGC}

Moir, P.H., ed., 1952, **Talks on book collecting**. {DUL}

Momoh, O.A., 1975, **Catalogue of new accessions in the headquarter's library, National Archives of India, April 1966 to March 1974**. {NAI}

Monroe, Margaret Ellen, 1963, **Library adult education** : The biography of an idea. {USIS}

Montgomery, A.C., 1986, **Acronyms and abbreviations in library and information work**, 3rd edn. [Library Association, London]. {NASSDOC}

Montgomery, A.C., ed. 1982, **Acronyms and abbreviations in library and information work** : A reference handbook of British usage, 2nd. edn. {JNU}

Montgomery, Edward B., ed., 1968, **Foundations of access to knowledge** : A symposium. {NASSDOC}

Montgomery, K. Leon, 1975, **Document retrieval systems** : Factors effecting search time. {DUL IIT NASSDOC USIS}

Moodey, Edgar C., 1977, **Fraser-Hickson library** : An informal history. {IIT}

Mookerjee, S.K., 1969, **Development of libraries and library science in India.** {ICA IIC IIT NASSDOC NERC NIH NIPCCD NMML}

Mookerjee, S.K. and Sengupta, B., 1972, **Library organisation and library administration**. {NIEPA NIH}

Mookerjee, S.K. and Sengupta, B., 1977, **Library organisation and library administration**, 2nd edn. {DUL ICA IIT ISI NIEPA NMML}

Moon, Eric and Nyren, Karl, eds., 1970, **Library issues** : The sixties. {ICHR USIS}

Moon, Eric, ed., 1969, **Book selection and censorship in the sixties**. {DUL IIT USIS}.

Moore, Everett L., 1964, **Issues of freedom in American libraries**. [American Library Association]. {USIS}

Moore, Everett Leroy, 1968, **Junior college libraries development needs and prospective.** {JNU}

Moranjian, Lorig and Boss, Richard W., 1980, **Fee based information services** : A study of a growing industry. {IIT USIS}

Morehouse, H.G., 1966, **Telefascimile services between libraries with the xerox management telescopier**. {JNU}

Morehouse, Ward, ed., 1965, **Foreign area studies and the college library** : Bibliographies, reference service, acquisitions programmes and other activities and services for undergraduate librarians in African, Asian, Latin American and Russian studies. [Foreign Area Materials Center, University of the State of New York]. {NASSDOC}

Moreland, Carroll C. and Usmani, M. Adil, eds., n.d., **Proceedings** : Seminar on the purpose and function of library in national education, April 7-10, 1961, Nazimabad. [Society for the Promotion and Improvement of Libraries]. {NASSDOC*}

Morpurgo, J.E., 1969, **Book and journal services for doctors and nurses** : An interim report on a National Book League investigation. {DUL}

Morris, John, 1986, **Library disaster preparedness handbook**. {JNU}

Morrison, Perry, D., 1969, **Career of the academic librarian** : A study of the social origins. {JNU}

Morrow, Carolyn Clark and Dual, Carole, 1986, **Conservation treatment procedure** : A manual of step by step procedures for the maintenance and repair of library materials. {NASSDOC}

Morrow, Carolyn Clark and Walker, Gay, 1983, **Preservation challenge** : A guide to conserving library materials. {JNU NMML}

Morse, Grant W., 1966, **Concise guide to library research**. {JNU}

Morse, Philip M., 1968, **Library effectiveness** : A systems approach. {AIU DUL JNU NASSDOC NMML SPA USIS}

Mortensen, C. David and Sereno, Kenneth K., 1973, **Advances in communication research**. {NASSDOC}

Mortimore, Arthur D., 1966, **Branch libraries**. {ICA}

Mortin-Labatut, Girele and Sly, Mureen, 1982, **Manual for the preparation of records in development information systems**. [International Development Research Centre]. {NASSDOC}

Morton, E.H., 1974, **Development of library services** : Trinidad and Tobago. [UNESCO]. {ISI}

Morton, Leslie T., 1979, **How to use a medical library**. {NIH}

Mosher, Frederic J., ed., 1954, **Freedom of book selection** : Proceedings : Conference on intellectual freedom, 2nd, June 20-21, 1953. [American Library Association]. {AIU USIS}

Mossberg, Thomas, et al, 1976, **ADDLIB** : A packaged computer programme for processing, etc. {JNU NIH}

Motiwale, Sushila A. and Jagtar Singh, eds., 1986, **Papers** : UGC sponsored national seminar on documentation services in university and college libraries, January 12-14, 1986, Jabalpur. {NASSDOC}

Mott, Thomas H. Jr., et al, 1972, **Introduction to PL-1 programming for library and information science.** {BCL IIT JNU}

Mount, Ellis, 1975, **University science and engineering libraries** : Their operations, collections and facilities. {CRRI IIT}

Muhammad, Riaz, 1989, **Advanced indexing and abstracting practices**. {NASSDOC}

Muhammad, Riaz, 1989, **Modern techniques of documentation and information work**. {NASSDOC}

Mukherjee, A.K., 1960, **Book selection and systematic bibliography** {IIT MFL NMML SPA}

Mukherjee, A.K., 1964, **Reference work and its tools**. {CRRI ICA NMML SPA}

Mukherjee, A.K., 1965, **School library** : Some practical hints. {ISI MFL}

Mukherjee, A.K., 1966, **Librarianship** : Its philosophy and history. {BIS IIT NASSDOC NIH SPA}

Mukherjee, A.K., 1969, **Fundamentals of special librarianship and documentation**. [Indian Association of Special Libraries and Information Centres]. {AIU DUL IIT}

Mukherjee, A.K., 1971, **Reference work and its tools**, 2nd edn. {DUL JNU NASSDOC NERC NIEPA NMML}

Mukherjee, A.K., 1974, **Book selection** : Principles, practices and tools. {ICHR IEG}

Mukherjee, A.K., 1975, **Reference work and its tools**, 3rd ed. {CRRI ICA IIT NIH NIPCCD}

Mukherjee, A.K., 1979, **Guide to selected reference tools and Indological source materials** : Classified and annotated. {DUL NASSDOC}

Mukherjee, Ajit Kumar, 1957, **Manual of reference work**. {DUL SPA}

Mukherjee, B.B., 1973, **Preservation of library materials, archives and documents**. {DUL ICHR NASSDOC NERC NIH NIPCCD NMML ZHL}

Mukherji, Sudhir Kumar, 1939, **Study of Bengali surnames**. [Linguistic Society of India]. {ZHL}

Mukhopadhyay, Ajoy, 1976, **Guide to Colon Classification practical.** {CRRI ICHR}

Mullis, A.A., ed., 1983, **ISDS manual**. (International Serial Data System). {NASSDOC}

Mullish, Henry, 1971, **Modern programming** : PL/I. {DUL}

Mumford, W.A. comp., 1939, **Three thousand books for a public library** : Some significant and representative works for basic stock. {NAI}

Mumfort, Erid, et al, eds., 1985, **Research methods in information systems** : Proceedings of the IFIP WG 8.2 colloquium, Manchester Business School, September 1-3, 1984. {NASSDOC}

Munby, A., 1960, **Cambridge college libraries** : Aid for research studies. {JNU}

Murdick, Robert G. and Ross, Jod E., 1977, **Information system for modern management.** {ICA}

Murfin, Marjorie E. and Wynar, Lubomyr R., 1984, **Reference service** : An annotated bibliographic guide supplement, 1976-1982. {JNU}

Murphey, R.W., 1958, **How and where to look it up**. {IIT}

Murphy, Marcy and Johns, Claude J., 1977, **Handbook of library regulations**. {INSA JNU USIS}

Murty, A.T., 1979, **Document bibliography**. {NIPCCD NASSDOC}

Muscutt, H.C., 1963, **Display techniques**. {DUL}

Mushtaq Ahmed, 1958, **Evaluation of reading materials for neo-literates and a study of their reading needs and interests**. {NMML}

Muthuswamy, A.T., 1969, **ABC of library science**. {NASSDOC}

Mwinyimvua, E.A., comp. and ed., 1984, **Directory of libraries in Tanzania**. [National Central Library, Tanzania]. {NASSDOC}

Myers, Gerald E., 1977, **Insurance manual for libraries**. [American Library Association]. {BIS}

Myller, Rolf, 1966, **The design of the small public library**. {USIS}

Myrick, William J., 1975, **Coordination** : Concept or reality. {DUL}

Myson, William, 1963, **Librarianship as a career**. {ICA}

Nadvi, Salman Shamsi, 1973, **Hindustan ke mashraqi kutubkhane**. {NMML}

Nagaraj, M.N. and Ghosh, A.K.. eds., 1978, **The National Library of India, 1903-1978** : A pictorial history released on the occasion of platinum jubilee of the National Library, Calcutta. [National Library, Calcutta]. {NASSDOC}

Nagarajan, S., ed., 1988, **Use of microprocessor in information analysis and library applications**. {NASSDOC}

Nagarajan, S., et al, eds., 1989, **Distributed data bases** : Plan for interaction and online search. {NASSDOC*}

Narang, Rita, 1974, **Chain procedure** : An annotated bibliography. {JNU}

Narasimhan, P.V.A. and Majeed Khan, M.A., 1980, **Andhra Pradesh Public Libraries Act, 1960 with latest amendments and commentaries.** [Andhra Pradesh Public Library Association]. {NASSDOC*}

Narasimharao, K.V.V.L., 1988, **Handbook of AP Government Oriental Manuscripts Library and Research Institute**. [Andhra Pradesh Government Oriental Manuscripts Library and Institute, Hyderabad], {NASSDOC*}

Narasimharao, K.V.V.L. and Oommen, Chinna, 1972, **Read faster and understand better,** 2 pts. [Central Institute of Indian Languages, Mysore]. {MHA}

Narayana Rao, B., 1982, **Academic libraries in India** : An enquiry into their organisation and professional aspect. {JNU}

Narayana Rao, Kodati and Ramachandra Rao, T., 1981, **Rise and growth of public library movement in India**. [Iyyanki Library Awards Committee, Eluru]. {NASSDOC*}

Narula, Manju, 1973, **State of the art report on social science documentation in India**. {JNU}

Nasatir, David, 1973, **Data archives for the social sciences** : Purposes, operations and problems. {ZHL}

Nasso, Christine, ed., 1976, **Contemporary authors** : A bibliographical guide to current authors and their work, 2 vols. {RTL}

Nathan, Henry, 1973, **Stable rules** : Science and social transmission. [Organisation for Economic Co-operation and Development, Paris]. {NASSDOC}

Naude, Gabriel, 1961, **Instructions concerning erecting of a library**. {DUL}

Naude, Gabriel, 1976, **Advice on establishing a library**. {DUL NIPCCD}

Naur, Peter, 1974, **Concise survey of computer methods**. {NASSDOC}

Navalani, K. and Gidwani, N.N., 1981, **Practical guide to Colon Classification**. {AIU IIT JNU NERC NIEPA}

Naylor, Thomas H., et al, 1968, **Computer simulation techniques**. {NASSDOC}

Neal, Harcon, et al, 1969, **Administration and change** : Continuing education in library administration. {JNU}

Neal, K.W., 1965, **Technical college libraries** : Finchfield. {DUL IIT}

Neal, K.W., 1973, **British academic libraries.** {JNU}

Neal, K.W., 1975, **Introduction to library administration.** {JNU}

Needham, C.D., 1966, **Organising knowledge in libraries** : An introduction to classification and cataloguing. {IIC MFL SPA ZHL}

Needham, C.D., 1971, **Organising knowledge in libraries** : An introduction to information retrieval, 2nd rev edn. {ICA IIFT NASSDOC}

Needham, Christopher D. and Herman, Esther, eds., 1970, **Study of subject bibliography with special reference to the social sciences**. [School of Library and Information Services, Maryland]. {NASSDOC}

Neelameghan, A., 1975, **Presentation of ideas in technical writing**. {ICHR IIC NIH}

Neelameghan, A., et al, n.d., **Colon Classification** : Schedule of basic subjects, 7th edn. {DUL}'

Neelameghan, A., and Seetharam, S., n.d., **Colon Classification for macro documents in mathematics.** {DUL}

Neelameghan, A., ed., 1977, **Guidelines for formulation of a policy on education, training and development of library and information personnel** : All India seminar on library and information science education, October 3-8, 1977, Delhi. [Indian Standards Institution]. {NASSDOC}.

Neelameghan, A., ed., 1979, **Ordering systems for global information networks** : Proceedings : International study conference on classification research, 3rd, January 6-11, 1975, Bombay, [FID/CR; Sarada Ranganathan Endowment for Library Science]. {BIS NASSDOC}

Neeland, Frances, 1967, **Bibliography on information science and technology for 1966**. {JNU}

Negus, Ron, 1972, **Guide to Computer Bureau Services**. {NASSDOC}

Nelson, Edward C., 1967, **Reference books for regional reference collection**. {NAI}

New, Peter C., 1975, **Reprography for librarians**. {AIU JNU}

New, Peter G., 1978, **Education for librarianship** : Decisions in organising a system of professional education. {NIEPA}

Newbury, K.M., ed., n.d., **Design in the library**. [Library Association London]. {ISI}

Newhouse, Joseph P. and Alexender, Arthur J., 1972, **Economic analysis of public library services**. {ISI}

Newman, Simon M., 1965, **Information systems compatibility**. {JNU}

Nicholas, Charles L., 1964, **Library of Rameses, the Great**. {DUL}

Nicholas, David, 1975, **Characteristics of social science serials** : The construction and analysis of a file : Social science serial titles. [Bath University]. {BCL}

Nicholas, David and Ritchies, Maureen, 1978, **Literature and bibliometrics**. {BCL IIT NASSDOC}

Nichols, H., 1979, **Local studies librarianship**. {NIH}

Nichols, Harold, 1976, **Map librarianship**. {NASSDOC NMML}

Nicolaus, John J., 1964, **Automated approach to technical information retrieval** : Library application. {JNU}

Nobile, Philip, 1974, **Intellectual skywriting** : Literary politics and the New York Review of Books. {USIS}

Norris, Dorothy May, 1939, **History of cataloguing and cataloguing methods, 1100-1880, with an introductory survey of ancient times**. {CRRI}

Norris, Willa, et al, 1972, **Information service in guidance for career development and planning**. {NIPCCD}

O'Connor, V.C. Scott, 1920, **Eastern library**. {ZHL}

O'Connor, V.C. Scott, 1950, **Ek mashriqui kutubkhana** : Kutub- khana Khuda Bakhsh, tr. by Mubarizuddin Rifat. {NMML}

O'Connor, V.C. Scott, 1977, **Eastern library** : An introduction to the Khuda Bakhsh Oriental Public Library, 2nd edn. {JNU NMML}

O'Connor, V.C. Scott, 1985, **An eastern library** : An introduction to the Khuda Bakhsh Oriental Public Library, 3rd edn. {NASSDOC*}

O'Hara, Frederick J., ed., 1973, **Reader in government documents**. {NASSDOC}

Oberman, Cerise and Strauch, Katina, eds., 1982, **Theories of bibliographic education** : Designs for teachings. {JNU}

Oboler, Eli M., 1977, **Ideas and the university library** : Essays of an unorthodox academic librarian. {DUL}

Oddy, R.N., et al, eds., 1981, **Information retrieval research**. {IIMC JNU NASSDOC}

Oehlerts, Donald E., 1962, **Study to determine the feasibility of establishing a cooperative technical processing program and direct transmission of interlibrary loans**. {DUL}

Ohdedar, A.K., 1966, **Growth of the library in modern India, 1498-1836**. {ICHR IIT NMML ZHL}

Ohdedar, A.K., 1975, **Systematic bibliography and documentation**. {ICA ICHR NASSDOC NIH}

Olding, R.K., ed., 1967, **Readings in library cataloguing**. {NASSDOC NMML SPA ZHL}

Olle, James G., 1967, **Library history** : An examination guide book, 2nd rev edn. {ICHR IIT}

Olle, James G., 1984, **A guide to sources of information in libraries**. {NASSDOC}

Olligg, P.J., 1966, **Theory of cataloguing** : An examination guide book. {NASSDOC SPA}

Olney, John C., 1963, **Library cataloguing and classification**. {DUL}

Optner, Stanford L., ed., 1973, **Systems analysis**. {NASSDOC}

Orne, Jerrold, ed., 1971, **Research librarianship** : Essays in honour of Robert B. Downs. {JNU NASSDOC USIS}

Orr, James Mconnell, 1977, **Libraries as communication systems**. {IIMC USIS}

Orr, N.M., 1972, **Designing library buildings for activity**. {CRRI ICA ICHR ISI MMTC NASSDOC}

Osborn, Andrew D., 1955, **Serial publications** : Their place and treatment in libraries. {MFL}

Osborn, Andrew D., 1973, **Serial publications** : Their place and treatment in libraries, 2nd edn. [American Library Association]. {NASSDOC}

Osborn, Andrew D., 1980, **Serial publications** : Their place and treatment in libraries, 3rd edn. [American Library Association]. {USIS}

Osborn, Egar and Sharr, F.A., 1950, **County library practice**. [Library Association, London]. {CRRI ZHL}

Osborn, Jeanne, 1982, **Dewey Decimal Classification** : A study manual. {USIS}

Osburn, Charles B., ed., 1979, **Academic research and library resources :** Changing patterns in America. {DEPT IIT JNU NIPCCD}

Overhagem, Carl F.J. and Herman, R. Joyce, eds., 1965 **Report** : Planning conference on information transfer experiments, September 3, 1965, Massachusetts. {USIS}

Overton, C. David, 1951, **Gramophone recording library**. {CRRI}

Overton, David, 1983, **Planning the administrative library**. {DUL}

Pacay, Philip, 1977, **ED art library manual** : A guide to resources and practice. {IIT}

Packer, Katherine H. and Phillips, Delores, eds., 1969, **Code and the cataloguer** : Proceedings of the colloquium on the Anglo-American Cataloguing Rules held at the School of Library Science, University of Toronto on March 31 and April 1, 1967. {NASSDOC}

Paice, D.B., 1977, **Information retrieval and the computer**. {BCL}

Palmer, Archie M., 1972, **Research centres directory**, 4th edn. {NASSDOC}

Palmer, B.I., 1951, **Fundamentals of library classification**. {BIS CRRI NAI SPA}

Palmer, B.I., 1962, **Itself an education**. [Library Association, London]. {IIT}

Palmer, B.I., 1966, **From little acorns** : The library profession in Britain. {IEG NERC}

Palmer, B.I., 1971, **Itself an education** : Six lectures on classification, 2nd edn. [Library Association, London]. {NASSDOC NMML}

Palmer, Richard Phillips, 1973, **Case studies in library computer systems**. {ISI USIS}

Palouec, Lora and Goodman, Elezabeth B., 1969, **Elementary school library in action**. {JNU}

Panchanathan, A., 1984, **Guide to Saraswati Mahal**. [Saraswati Mahal Library, Tanjore]. {NASSDOC*}

Pandey, B.D., 1979, **Report of expert consultative services rendered to Cooperative Training Centre in Nepal for organising their library and documentation services**. [International Cooperation Alliance Regional Office and Education Centre for South-East Asia, New Delhi]. {ICA}

Pandey, S.K., 1986, **Cataloguing theory**. {JNU}

Pandey, S.K., 1986, **Depth schedules for Indian philosophy and religions for DDC**. {JNU}

Panwar, B.S. and Vyas, S.D., 1986, **Library management**. {JNU}

Panwar, Bhanwar Singh and Vyas, Shree Dhar, 1970, **Directory of libraries, publishers and booksellers of Udaipur city and who's who.** {NMML RTL}

Pao, M.L., 1989, **Concepts of information retrieval.** {NASSDOC}

Parish, Charles, 1966, **History of the Birmingham Library.** {JNU}

Parker, J. Stephen, 1985, **UNESCO and library development planning.** {DUL}

Parkhi, R.S., 1945, **The Decimal and Colon Classifications** : A summary and a comparison. {NASSDOC}

Parkhi, R.S., 1950, **Principles of library classification with special reference to Colon and Decimal Classification**, Pt. 1 : General theory of classification. {CRRI}

Parkhi, R.S., 1964, **Decimal Classification and Colon Classification in perspective.** {CRRI IEG IIT ISI NAL NERC NMML}

Parkhi, R.S., 1965, **Dvibindu vargikaran paddhatiche yatharth darshan** {NMML}

Parkhi, R.S., 1972, **Library classification** : Evolution of a dynamic theory. {AIU BIS IIT ISI JNU MHA NMML}

Parkin, Andrew, 1980, **System analysis.** {JNU}

Parkin, Anorew, 1980, **Systems management.** {NASSDOC}

Parper, C.C. and Turley, R.V., 1986, **Information sources in science and technology** : A practical guide to traditional and on-line use. {JNU}

Parsons, C.J., 1973, **Library use in further education.** {DUL}

Parsons, S.A.J., 1972, **How to find out about engineering.** {CRRI}

Pask, Gordon, 1975, **Cybernetics of human learning and performance** : A guide to theory and research. {NASSDOC}

Pasty, Cullen and Kirby, John, 1986, **Design and production of media presentation for libraries.** {JNU}

Pathak, Vijay, and Ramaiah, L.S. 1986, **Bibliography of research in library and information in India.** {NMML}

Patil, G.M., 1967, **Bibliography technical** : An illuminating exposition. {NASSDOC}

Patil, P.K., n.d., **Pubic libraries in Karnataka** : Their scope and development. {AIU}

Patil, P.K., 1972, **Bibliographical services for Indian studies** : A guide to printed sources of information. [Mysore Institute of Development Studies]. {NASSDOC}

Patterson, Maureen L.P., ed., 1975, **South Asian library resources in North America** : A survey prepared for the Boston conference, 1974. {NASSDOC}

Peaks, Gilbert L., et al, 1957, **Progress report in chemical literature retrieval.** {CRRI}

Pearson, J.D., ed., 1971, **Papers on oriental library collections submitted to a library panel** : International congress of orientalists, 27th, August 17, 1967, Ann Arbor, Michigan. {NMML}

Peereault, Jean M., 1978, **Idea of order in bibliography.** {JNU}

Pemberton, John E., 1971, **British official publications.** {NASSDOC}

Pemberton, John E., 1982, **Bibliographic control of official publications.** {IIT}

Penland, Patrick R., 1972, **Communication manual for libraries.** {JNU}

Penland, Patrick R., 1974, **Communication in science and technology.** {INSA}

Penland, Partick R. and Mathai, Aleyamma, 1978, **Library as a learning service centre.** {JNU}

Penna, C.V., 1970, **Planning of library and documentation services**, 2nd edn. [UNESCO]. {IIMC INSA MFL NASSDOC NCAER NERC NIH NIPCCD NMML TDA}

Penna, C.V. and Sewell, P.H., 1967, **The planning of library and documentation services.** [UNESCO]. {AIU ICA NIEPA SPA}

Penna, C.V., et al, eds., 1977, **National library and information services** : Handbook for planners. {CRRI DUL IIT INSA JNU NASSDOC NCAER NIEPA}

Perkins, David, ed., 1979, **Guidelines for collection development.** [American Library Association]. {USIS}

Perlman, M., ed., 1977, **Organisation and retrieval of economic knowledge** : Proceedings of the conference held by the International Economic Association. {NASSDOC}

Perreault, Jean M., 1969, **Introduction to UDC**. {BIS IIT ISI JNU SPA}

Perreault, Jean M., 1969, **Towards a theory for U.D.C.** : Essays aimed at structural understanding and operational improvement. {ICHR NASSDOC}

Perreault, Jean M. and Dohlberg, Ingetraut, eds., 1983, **Proceedings** : International study conference on classification research : Universal classification, 4th, June 28-July 2, 1982, Ausburg. {BIS}

Perry, J.W. and Kent, Allen, n.d., **Documentation and information retrieval** : An information to basic principle and cost analysis. {JNU}

Perry, James W., et al, 1956, **Machine literature searching**. {CRRI}

Perti, R.K., ed., 1987, **Proceedings** : International seminar on conservation of traditional records, paper and allied materials. [National Archives of India]. {NAT}

Peter, Braphy, 1986, **Management information and decision support systems in libraries**. {JNU NASSDOC}

Peters, Jean, ed., 1961, **The bookmen's glossary**. 5th edn. {NCERT}

Peters, Jean, ed., 1983, **The bookmen's glossary**. 61th edn. {NASSDOC}

Petrova, L.G., et al, eds., 1965, **Collection of materials on the preservation of library resources**. {INSA NASSDOC}

Petru, William C., ed., 1967, **Library** : Introduction for library assistants. [Special Library Association, New York]. {IIT}

Pettee, Julla, 1947, **Subject headings** : The history and theory of the alphabetical subject approach to books. {NAI}

Phebe, Snow, 1960, **How a book is made**. {DUL}

Philips, G.M. and Taylor, P.J., 1969, **Computers**. {DUL}

Phillips, David, 1972, **Book display.** {USIS}

Phillips, W. Howard, 1951, **Primer of book classification,** rev. edn. [Association of Assistant Librarians, London]. {INSA ZHL}

Picache, U.G., 1986, **Report on feasibility of establishing a regional network of social science information and documentation centres in Asia and Pacific.** [Institute of Library Science]. {NASSDOC}

Picken, F.M. and Mathews, D.A., 1979, **Medical librarianship** : Outlines of modern librarianship. {NIH USIS}

Pierce, William S., 1980, **Furnishing the library interior**. {BIS USIS}

Piercy, Esther J., 1974, **Commonsense cataloguing** : A manual for the organization of books and other materials in school and small public libraries, 2nd rev ed., by Marian Sannar. {USIS}

Pinehes, Stella, 1966, **Library work with young people** : An examination guide book. {DUL}

Pipics, Zoltan, ed., 1969, **Librarians' practical dictionary in twenty- two languages**. {JNU}

Plaister, Jean M., 1982, **Computing in LASER regional library cooperation** : London and South Eastern library region. [Library Association, London]. {DUL}

Plant, Marjorie, n.d., **Supply of foreign books and periodicals to the libraries of the United Kingdom**. {DUL}

Plaster, C.D., 1939, **Floor and floor coverings**. [American Library Association]. {NAI}

Plotnik, Arthur, 1975, **Library life — American style** : A journalist's field report. {USIS}

Plumbe, Wilfred J., 1964, **Preservation of books in tropical and subtropical countries**. {JNU}

Plump, Philip W., 1965, **Central library storage of books** : An essay awarded the Sevensma prize, 1962. {IIT}

Pocock, Guy, 1942, **Brush up your reading**. {ZHL}

Polak, Fred L., 1971, **Prognostics** : A science in the making surveys and creates the future. {NASSDOC}

Politt, A.S., 1989, **Information storage and retrieval systems** : Origin, development and applications. {NASSDOC}

Pollack, Bary W., 1972, **Compilers techniques**. {NASSDOC}

Pollard, A.F.C., 1926, **Decimal Bibliographical Classification of the Institut International de Bibliographies**. {BIS}

Pollett, Dorothy and Haskell, Peter C., eds., 1979, **Sign systems for libraries** : Solving the way finding problems. {BIS IIT USIS}

Pomassel, Gerhand, 1975, **Synoptic tables concerning the current national bibliographies**. {NASSDOC}

Ponder, John, 1971, **Management in libraries.** {NASSDOC}

Pool, Ithiel de Sola, et al, eds., 1973, **Handbook of communication**. {NASSDOC}

Poole, Frazer G. and Trezza, Alphonse F., eds., 1969, **The procurement of library furnishings** : Specifications BID documents and evaluation : Proceedings : Library equipment institute, 3rd, 1966, New York. [American Library Association]. {USIS}

Poole, Frazer G., ed., 1965, **The library environment** : Aspects of interior planning : Proceedings : Library equipment institute, 2nd, 1964, St. Louis. {JNU USIS}

Poole, Herbert, ed., 1977, **Academic libraries by the year 2000**. {DEPT DUL ISI JNU USIS}

Porat, Marc Uri, 1977, **The information economy** : Definition and measurement. {USIS}

Potter, William Gray and Sirkin, Arlne Farber, eds., 1981, **Serials automation for acquisition and inventory control.** [American Library Association]. {USIS}

Powell, Judith W. and Lelieuvre, Robert B., 1979, **People work, communications dynamics for libraries**. [American Library Association]. {USIS}

Powell, Lawrence Clark, 1960, **Books in my baggage** : Adventures in reading and collecting. {JNU}

Powell, Ronald R., 1985, **Basic research methods for librarians**. {JNU}

Prasad, K.N., 1983, **Development of terminology in the field of library classification with special reference to Indian school of thought**: A case study in terminology development : Thesis. (Karnatak University). {NASSDOC}

Prasher, R.G., 1971, **Indian library literature** : An annotated bibliography. {ICHR NASSDOC NIPCCD NMML}

Prasher, R.G., 1990, **Index and indexing systems**. {JNU}

Prasher, Ram Gopal, et al, 1971-72, **Indian books** : An annual bibliography. {NASSDOC}

Pratt, Gordon, 1976, **Information economics** : Costs and prices of machine-readable information in Europe. [Association of Special Libraries and Information Bureaux]. {BCL}

Press, Jaques Cattel, ed., 1979, **The Librarians' phone book**. {USIS}

Price, Wilson T., 1972, **Introduction to data processing**. {JNU}

Priolker, Anant Kakba, 1958, **Printing presses in India** : Its beginning and early development. {DUL}

Pritchard, Alan, 1969, **Guide to computer literature** : An introductory survey of the sources of information. {NASSDOC}

Prostano, Emanuel T., 1974, **School media programmes** : Case studies in management, 2nd edn. {NIEPA}

Pruett, Nancy Jones, 1986, **Scientific and technical libraries**, 2 vols. {JNU}

Pry, Barnard M. and Mohrarot, Foster E., 1963, **Guide to information sources in space science and technology**. {DUL}

Prytherch, R., ed., 1986, **Staff training in libraries** : The British experience. {NASSDOC}

Prytherch, Ray, 1986, **Handbook of library training practice**. {NASSDOC}

Prytherch, Ray, comp., 1983, **Sources of information librarianship and information science** : A grafton book. {NIH}

Punnoose, Kunnuparampil P., 1977, **Book dealers in India, Pakistan, Sri Lanka** : A directory of dealers in second hand and antiquarian books in the sub-continent of South Western Asia. {NMML}

Purton, Rowland W., 1962, **Surrounded by books** : Libraries in primary and middle schools. {JNU NASSDOC}

Pushp Lata, 1979, **Planning national technical information centre for child development in India** : A blueprint, Thesis : Associateship in Documentation and Information Science. [Documentation Research and Training Centre]. {NIPCCD}

Qaisar, Mahmood Hasan, 1965, **Islamic sciences** : Expansion of Dewey Decimal Classification (16th edn.) for oriental libraries, {ZHL}

Quattlebaum, Marguerite V., ed., n.d., **Subject headings used in the dictionary catalogs of the Library of Congress from 1897 through December 1955**, 6th edn. [U.S. Library of Congress]. {BIS IEG USIS}

Quattlebaum, Marguerite V., ed., n.d., **Subject headings used in the dictionary catalogs of the Library of Congress from 1897 through December 1955** : Supplement to the 6th edn., January 1956-December 1959. [U.S. Library of Congress]. {IEG}

Quattlebaum, Marguerite V., ed., 1966, **Subject headings used in the dictionary catalogs of the Library of Congress**, 7th edn. [U.S. Library of Congress]. {USIS}

Quinn, J.H. and Aconib, H.M., 1937, **Manual of cataloguing and indexing**. {NAI}

Qureshi, Ishrat Ali, 1990, **The Maulana Azad Library** : A major library of the world, 1977-1988. {DUL JNU UGC ZHL}

Rader, Hannelore B., 1976, **Faculty involvement in library instruction**. {JNU}

Radford, K.J., 1978, **Information systems for strategic decisions.** {DUL}

Radhakrishnan, S. and Iyengar, T.K.S., eds., 1977, **Proceedings** : International conference on technical information services for developing countries, March, 1977, Madras. [International Council of Scientific Unions, Committee of Science and Technology in Developing Countries]. {BCL BIS CRRI IIT JNU}

Raffel, J.A. and Shiskho, Robert, 1969, **Systematic analysis of university libraries** : Application of cost benefit analysis to the M.I.T. libraries. {AIU DUL IIT JNU NIPCCD SPA}

Rajagopalan, T.S. and Ramaswami, K., n.d., **Libraries serving the CSIR complex**. [Indian National Scientific Documentation Centre]. {IIT NASSDOC}

Rajagopalan, T.S., comp., 1973, **Essays in library science**, 3rd edn. {JNU}

Rajagopalan, T.S., ed., 1968, **Ranganathan's philosophy** : Assessment, impact and relevance. {JNU NMML}

Rajagopalan, T.S., ed., 1988, **Year's work in Indian librarianship, 1987**. [Indian Library Association]. {NASSDOC}

Rajan, T.N., 1981, **Indexing systems** : Concepts, models and techniques. [Indian Association of Special Libraries and Information Centres]. {BIS CRRI JNU MFL MMTC NASSDOC}

Rajaraman, V., 1971, **Computer programming in Fortran IV**. {NASSDOC}

Rajjan Lal, 1980, **Practical cataloguing procedure**. {IIT NIPCCD}

Rajjan Lal and Kidwai, Nasira, 1980, **Vyavaharik suchikaran vidhi**. {NASSDOC}

Raju, A.A.N., 1974, **Handbook of pseudonymous authors in Telugu**. {NASSDOC*}

Raju, A.A.N., 1984, **Decimal, Universal Decimal and Colon Classification** : A study in comparison. {ICA NASSDOC NERC NIEPA SPA}

Raju, A.A.N., 1988, **History of library movement in Andhra Pradesh, 1900-1956**. {NASSDOC*}

Rajwant Singh, 1984, **University library buildings in India**. {AIU BIS DUL IIT JNU MMTC NASSDOC NIEPA}

Ram Shobhit Prasad Singh, 1990, **Fundamentals of library administration and management**. {NMML}

Ramachandra Rao, T., 1974, **Torch-bearer of public library movement** : Andhra Pradesh library field workers conference, 1974, Gudiwada. {NASSDOC*}

Ramakrishnan, M.N., 1986, **Indexing systems and techniques**. {NASSDOC}

Ramanujam Nair, P., 1974, **Library movement in Kerala** : The need for reform and legislation. {NERC}

Ramsden, Michael John, 1974, **An introduction to index language construction** : A programmed text. {BCL}

Randall, William, ed., 1944, **Acquisition and cataloguing of books** : Papers presented before the library institute at the University of Chicago, July 29 to August 9, 1940. {JNU NAI ZHL}

Ranganathan, S.R., n.d., **Indian library manifesto**. {IDSA}

Ranganathan, S.R., n.d., **Library catalogue** : Fundamentals and procedure. [Madras Library Association]. {BIS}

Ranganathan, S.R., 1937, **Prolegomena to library classification**. [Madras Library Association]. {CRRI NMML}

Ranganathan, S.R., 1939, **Colon Classification**, 2nd edn. {DSSW}

Ranganathan, S.R., 1940, **Reference service and bibliography**, Vol. 1, Pts. 1-4. {DSSW DUL}

Ranganathan, S.R., 1942, **School and college libraries**. {JNU}

Ranganathan, S.R., 1944, **Post-war reconstruction of libraries in India**. [Punjab Library Association, Lahore]. {ZHL}

Ranganathan, S.R., 1945, **Classified catalogue code**, 2nd edn. [Madras Library Association]. {CRRI DSSW NAI}

Ranganathan, S.R., 1945, **Elements of library classification**. {ZHL}

Ranganathan, S.R., 1946, **National library system** : A plan for India. {ZHL}

Ranganathan, S.R., 1947, **Library development plan for Allahabad University**. {AIU NASSDOC}

Ranganathan, S.R., 1948, **Preface to library science.** {BIS}
Ranganathan, S.R., 1950, **Classification, coding and machinery for search.** {DUL}
Ranganathan, S.R., 1950, **Colon Classification**. 3rd edn. [Madras Library Association]. {CRRI}
Ranganathan, S.R., 1950, **Library development plan** : Thirty-year programme for India. [University of Delhi]. {BIS MFL NERC SPA}
Ranganathan, S.R., 1950, **Library tour, 1948** : Europe and America : Impressions and reflections. [Indian Library Association]. {INSA MFL}
Ranganathan, S.R., 1951, **Classification and communication**. {ISI NERC}
Ranganathan, S.R., 1951, **Classified catalogue code**, 3rd edn. {DSSW}
Ranganathan, S.R., 1951, **Philosophy of library classification**. {DUL}
Ranganathan, S.R., 1952, **Colon Classification**. 4th edn. [Madras Library Association]. {ISI}
Ranganathan, S.R., 1952, **Dictionary Catalogue Code**, 2nd edn. [Madras Library Association]. {CRRI}
Ranganathan, S.R., 1952, **Library book selection**. [Indian Library Association]. {BIS DSSW INSA}
Ranganathan, S.R., 1952, **Social bibliography or physical bibliography for libraries**. {BIS CRRI DSSW}
Ranganathan, S.R., 1953, **Depth classification and reference service and reference material**. [Indian Library Association]. {INSA ISI}
Ranganathan, S.R., 1953, **Library legislation**. [Madras Library Association]. {BIS IEG}
Ranganathan, S.R., 1955, **Heading and canons.** {BIS IEG ISI}
Ranganathan, S.R., 1957, **Colon Classification**, 5th edn. (DSSW IEG NCAER}
Ranganathan, S.R., 1957, **Prolegomena to library classification**, 2nd edn. [Madras Library Association]. {IEG IIMC ISI MFL NAI}
Ranganathan, S.R., 1958, **Classified catalogue code**, with additional rules for dictionary catalogue code, 4th edn. [Madras Library Association]. {DSSW IEG NERC}
Ranganathan, S.R., 1959, **Library administration**, 2nd edn. {AIU BIS CRRI DSSW DUL IEG IIC IIT JNU MMTC NAI NASSDOC NIH NMML SPA ZHL}
Ranganathan, S.R., 1960, **Elements of library classification**, 2nd edn. {INSA NERC SPA}
Ranganathan, S.R., 1960, **Library manual for library authorities, librarians and honorary library workers**. {ICA}
Ranganathan, S.R., 1961, **Reference service**, 2nd edn. {BIS CRRI DSSW DUL JNU MHA NASSDOC NIH NMML SPA ZHL}
Ranganathan, S.R., 1962, **Elements of library classification**, 3rd edn. {BIS CRRI IIT ISI NASSDOC}
Ranganathan, S.R., 1963, **Documentation and its facets** : Being a symposium of seventy papers by thirty-two authors. {BIS DUL DSSW IIFT JNU NMML SPA}
Ranganathan, S.R., 1963, **Five laws of library science**. {BIS CRRI IIT MHA NAI NCAER NMML SPA ZHL}
Ranganathan, S.R., 1963, **Organisation of libraries**, 3rd edn. {JNU NIH}
Ranganathan, S.R., 1964, **Library classification** : Fundamentals and procedure, with graded examples and exercises. [Madras Library Association]. {BIS}
Ranganathan, S.R., 1964, **Suggestions for the organisations of libraries in India**. {NASSDOC}

Ranganathan, S.R., 1965, **Classified catalogue code**, with additional rules for dictionary catalogue code, 5th edn. {AIU BIS CRRI DSSW ICHR IIT ISI MHA NAI NASSDOC NMML SPA ZHL}

Ranganathan, S.R., 1966, **Library book selection**, 2nd rev edn. {BIS CRRI IIT ISI NMML SPA}

Ranganathan, S.R., 1966, **Library manual**, 2nd edn. {BIS CRRI DSSW ICHR IIT INSA MMTC NASSDOC NERC NIPCCD}

Ranganathan, S.R., 1966, **Library manual for library authorities, librarians and honorary library workers**, 2nd edn. {BIS ISI JNU NIEPA NMML ZHL}

Ranganathan, S.R., 1967, **A descriptive account of Colon Classification.** {BIS DSSW DUL ISI JNU NAL NASSDOC NERC NMML SPA ZHL}

Ranganathan, S.R., 1967, **Prolegomena to library classification**, 3rd edn. assisted by M.H. Gopinath, [Madras Library Association]. {AIU ICA IIC INSA JNU NASSDOC NCAER}

Ranganathan, S.R., 1968, **Pustakalaya vargikaran ke mool tatva**, 3rd edn. {DUL}

Ranganathan, S.R., 1969, **Colon Classification**, 6th edn., reprinted 1960; 1963; 1964; 1969. {AIU BIS CRRI DSSW GPF ICHR IDSA IIFT IIMC IIT INSA ISI JNU MHA NAL NASSDOC NERC NIPCCD NMML SPA UGC ZHL}

Ranganathan, S.R., 1969, **Colon Classification** : A perview, 7th edn. {JNU}

Ranganathan, S.R., 1969, **Library science based service.** {NERC}

Ranganathan, S.R., 1970, **Colon Classification for library science.** {DUL}

Ranganathan, S.R., 1973, **New education and school library** : Experience of half a century. {DUL ICA JNU NIEPA}

Ranganathan, S.R., 1974, **Cataloguing practice**, 2nd edn. {ICA ICHR IEG JNU NERC NMML ZHL}

Ranganathan, S.R., 1980, **Pustakalaya vigyan ke panch sutra**. [Rajasthan Hindi Granth Academy, Jaipur]. {BIS}

Ranganathan, S.R., 1987, **Colon Classification**, 7th edn. {JNU}

Ranganathan, S.R., 1989, **Library book selections**. [Sarada Ranganathan Endowment for Library Sciences, Bangalore]. {NASSDOC}

Ranganathan, S.R. and Bhattacharya, G., 1970, **Conflict of authorship.** [Sarada Ranganathan Endowment for Library Science]. {ZHL}

Ranganathan, S.R. and Das Gupta, S., 1951, **Indian library directory**, 3rd edn. [Indian Library Association]. {BIS INSA NASSDOC}

Ranganathan, S.R. and Girja Kumar, 1960, **Social science research and libraries** : Papers and summary proceedings of the library seminar on research in the social science, January 2-4, 1959. {NMML}

Ranganathan, S.R. and Nagar, M.L., 1951, **Granthalaya pratikriya**. {JNU}

Ranganathan, S.R. and Neelameghan, A., n.d., **Book science** : Depth classification. {DUL}

Ranganathan, S.R. and Neelameghan, A., 1966, **Library services for all**. [Mysore Library Association, Bangalore]. {BIS SPA}

Ranganathan, S.R. and Neelameghan, A., 1974, **Physical bibliography for librarians**, 2nd ed. {AIU ICA INSA}

Ranganathan, S.R. and Neelameghan, A., eds., 1972, **Public library system** : India, Sri Lanka, UK, USA. {BIS IEG IIC JNU NAI NMML ZHL}

Ranganathan, S.R. and Neelameghan, A., eds., 1972, **A seminar on public library system**. [Sarada Ranganathan Endowment for Library Science, Bangalore]. {NASSDOC*}

Ranganathan, S.R. and Sivaraman, K.M., 1951, **Library manual**. [Indian Library Association]. {BIS DSSW INSA NERC ZHL}

Ranganathan, S.R., ed., 1953, **Papers** : All India library conference, 10th, June 1-4, 1953, Hyderabad. [Indian Library Association]. {NASSDOC}

Ranganathan, S.R., ed., 1973, **Documentation** : Genesis and development. {AIU CRRI DUL ICA ICHR IIMC ISI JNU MFL MHA MMTC NASSDOC NIEPA NIPCCD NMML}

Ranganathan, S.R., et al, 1968, **Free book service for all** : An international survey. {ICA ISI JNU MFL NMML SPA}

Rangra, V.K., 1982, **International dictionary of acronyms in data processing, library and information systems**. {CRRI MFL NASSDOC NMML}

Rathbone, Robert R., 1972, **Communicating technical information.** {CRRI}

Ravichandrarao, I.K., 1983, **Quantitative methods for library and information science.** {ISI BIS JNU NASSDOC}

Ravilious, C.P., 1975, **Survey of existing systems and current proposals for the cataloguing and description of non-book materials collected by libraries with preliminary suggestions for their international co-ordination**. [UNESCO]. {BIS}

Rawski, Conrad H. and Towaid, A., eds., 1973, **Theory of librarianship** : Papers in honour of Jesse H. Shera. {NASSDOC*}

Ray, Colin, 1979, **Library service to schools and children.** {JNU NIPCCD}

Ray, Sheila G., 1982, **Library service to schools**. {JNU}

Rayward, W. Boyd, 1967, **Systematic bibliography in England, 1850-95**. {DUL}

Rayward, W. Boyd, 1975, **The universe of information**. [International Federation of Documentation and Information]. {CRRI}

Rayward, W. Boyd, ed., 1978, **The public library** : Circumstances and prospects : Papers presented at the 39th Annual Conference. {IIT USIS}

Razvi, M.H., 1973, **Aligarh Muslim University library** : An approach paper on Fifth Five Year Plan including statistical analysis. {JNU}

Reagon, Agnes Lytton, 1959, **Study of factors influencing college students to become librarians**. {JNU}

Redfern, Brian, ed., 1977, **Studies in library management**, vol. 4. {ICA JNU NAL NIEPA NIPCCD}

Rees, Alan M., et al, n.d., **Feasibility study for continuing education of medical librarians** : Interim report. {DUL}

Rees, Alan, ed., 1974, **Contemporary problems in technical library and information centre management** : A state-of-the-art. [American Society for Information Science]. {USIS}

Rehrauer, George, 1975, **The film user's handbook** : A basic manual for managing library film services. {USIS}

Reichmann, Felix and Tharpe, Josephine M., 1972, **Bibliographic control of microforms**. {ISI JNU}

Reilly, Jane A., 1981, **The public librarian as adult learners' advisor** : An innovation in human services. {USIS}

Renford, Beverly and Hendrickson, Linnea, 1980, **Bibliographic instruction** : A handbook. {IIT}

Rescoe, A., 1962, **Cataloguing made easy**. {DUL}

Reynolds, Dennis, 1985, **Library automation** : Issues and applications. {JNU NASSDOC NMML}

Reynolds, J.D., ed., 1967, **Library buildings.** {DUL}

Reynolds, Michael M., ed., 1970, **Reader in the academic library**. {USIS}

Rhodes, Dennis E., 1969, **History of printing in the India, Pakistan, Ceylon, Burma and Thailand.** {DUL}

Rice, Betty, 1972, **Public relations for public libraries** : Creative problem solving. {USIS}

Rice, James, 1984, **Introduction to library automation.** {NASSDOC NMML}

Rice, Margaretta G., 1966, **Audio-visual aids for teaching the use of school library**. {JNU}

Richardson, Ernest Cushing, 1964, **Classification** : Theoretical and practical, 3rd edn. {DUL}

Richmond, Phyllis A., 1965, **Aspects of recent research in the art and science of classification**. {DUL}

Richmond, Phyllis A., 1981, **Introduction to PRECIS for North American usage.** {USIS}

Riddle, Jean, et al, 1970, **Non-book materials** : The organisation of integrated collections. [Canadian Library Association]. {NERC USIS}

Riddle, Jean, et al., 1979, **Non-book materials** : The organisation of integrated collections, 2nd edn. [Canadian Library Association]. {NERC USIS}

Rider, Fremond, n.d., **Rider's international classification for the arrangement of books on the shelves of the general libraries**, Preliminary edn. {DUL}

Rigby, M., 1974, **Computers and the UDC** : A decade of progress, 1963-1973. [International Federation for Documentation and Information]. {NIH}

Rigby, Malcolm, 1981, **Automation and the UDC**, 1948-1980, 2nd edn. [International Federation for Documentation and Information]. {CRRI}

Riggs, Fred W., 1986, **Help for social scientists** : A new kind of information process. {NASSDOC}

Rizzo, John R., 1980, **Management for librarians** : Fundamentals and issues. {NIEPA USIS}

Robbins-Carter, Jane, ed., 1982, **Public librarianship** : A reader. {USIS}

Roberts A.D., 1948-1956, **Introduction to reference books, 1948**; **1952**; **1956**. {CRRI JNU SPA}

Roberts, Stephen, et al, eds., 1978, **Research libraries and collections in the United Kingdom** : A selective inventory and guide. {DUL ZHL}

Robinow, Beatrix H., 1967, **Outline for the organisation of hospital libraries.** {DUL}

Robinson, A.M. Lewin, 1966, **Systematic bibliography** : A practical guide to the work of compilation. {ICHR NASSDOC SPA}

Robinson, A.M. Lewin, 1971, **Systematic bibliography** : A practical guide to the work of compilation, 3rd edn. {NASSDOC}

Robinson, F., 1969, **System analysis in libraries**. {JNU}

Robotham, John S. and Lafleur, Lydia, 1976, **Library programmes** : How to select, plan and produce them. {USIS}

Robotham, John S. and Lafleur, Lydia, 1981, **Library programmes** : How to select, plan and produce them, 2nd edn. {USIS}

Rodgers, Frank, comp., 1971, **Serial publications in the British Parliamentary papers, 1900-1968** : A bibliography. [American Library Association]. {NASSDOC}

Rogers, Harold A., 1970, **Dictionary of data processing terms** : {UGC}

Rogers, Rutherford D. and Weber, David C., 1971, **University library administration**. {DUL NASSDOC USIS}

Rokhan, Stein, n.d., **Data archives for the social science**. {DSSW}

Rolland, E. Stevens, ed., n.d., **Historical and bibliographical methods in library research**. {ICHR}

Rorvig, Mark E., 1981, **Microcomputers and libraries** : A guide to technology, products and applications. [American Society for Information Science]. {USIS}

Rose, Ernstine, 1954, **Public library in American life.** {NAI USIS}

Rose, J., 1974, **The cybernetic revolution.** {INSA NASSDOC}

Rosenberg, Kenyon C. and Feinstein, Paul T., 1983, **Dictionary of library and educational technology,** 2nd rev edn. {NASSDOC}

Rosove, Perry E., 1967, **Developing computer based information systems.** {JNU}

Ross, Robert, 1974, **Research** : An introduction. {NASSDOC}

Rossoff, Martin, 1964, **Using your high school library**. {JNU}

Rossoft, Martin, 1955, **Library in the high school teaching**. {JNU}

Roth, Harold, L., ed., 1964, **Planning library buildings for service** : Proceedings : Library building and equipment institute, July 6-8, 1961, Kent. [American Library Association]. {BIS DUL}

Rouse, William B., 1980, **Management of library networks** : Policy analysis, implementation and control. {IIT}

Rout, R.K., 1986, **Library legislation in India** : Problems and prospects. {NASSDOC*}

Rowland, Arthur Ray, 1964, **Reference services.** {DUL USIS}

Rowland, Arthur Ray, 1969, **Catalogue and cataloguing.** {IIFT IIT NMML SPA}

Rowland, J.F.B., 1978, **Information transfer and use in chemistry** : Final report of the Chemical Information Review Committee. {BCL}

Rowley, J.E. and Rowley, Petter J., 1981, **Operations research** : A tool for library management. [American Library Association]. {USIS}

Rowley, J.E., 1979, **Mechanised in-house information systems**. {BCL CRRI NIPCCD}

Rowley, J.E. and Turner, C.M.D., 1978, **The dissemination of information**. {BCL DUL ISI NASSDOC ZHL}

Rowley, Jennifer E., 1982, **Abstracting and indexing**. {ISI JNU}

Rowley, Jennifer E., 1988, **Abstracting and indexing,** 2nd edn. {NASSDOC}

Roy, A.K. and Kapoor, S.K., eds., 1982, **Information services in India** : Papers : IASLIC national seminar, 10th, December 21-24, 1982, Kanpur. [Indian Association of Special Libraries and Information Centres]. {ICA JNU MMTC NASSDOC NIPCCD}

Roy, R. Paul Mohan, 1984, **Systematic bibliography** : An introduction. {NASSDOC}

Rozsa, Gyorgy, 1973, **Scientific information and society**. {NASSDOC}

Rubin, Martin L., 1970-71, **Handbook of data management**, 6 vols, vol 1 : Introduction to the system life cycle; vol 2 : system life cycle standards; vol. 3 : system life cycle standards forms methods, by Peter Zuckerman; vol 4. Advanced technology input and output; vol. 5 : Advanced technology systems concepts; vol. 6 : Data processing administration. {NASSDOC}

Rubin, Martin L., 1970-71, **Handbook of data processing management,** 6 vols. {NASSDOC}

Rubin, Martin L., ed., 1979, **Documentation standards and procedures for on-line systems**. {CRRI}

Rubinoff, Morris, ed., 1965, **Towards a national information system** : Second annual national colloquium on information retrieval. {IIT}

Rue, Eloise and Laplanie, Effie, 1952, **Subject heading for children's materials.** [American Library Association]. {ZHL}

Rufsvold, Margaret I., 1949, **Audio-visual school library service** : A handbook for librarians. [American Library Association]. {ZHL}

Ruggles, Melville J. and Swank, Paynard C., 1962, **Soviet libraries and librarianship** : Report of the visit of the delegation of U.S. librarians to the Soviet Union, May-June, 1961 under the U.S.- Soviet cultural exchange agreement. [American Library Association]. {NASSDOC NMML}

Rugh, Archie, ed., 1983, **International books-in-print** : English- language titles published outside the United States and the United Kingdom. 2 vols. {NASSDOC}

Ruok, Alice, 1959, **Easy ways to displays** : A library publicity handbook. {JNU}

Sabine, Gordon and Sabine, Patricia, 1983, **Books that made the difference** : What people told us. {USIS}

Sabor, Josefa E., 1969, **Methods of teaching librarianship**. [UNESCO]. {IIMC JNU NASSDOC NIEPA NIPCCD}

Sachdev, Surinder Mohan, 1976, **Evaluation of the reference sources in the field of Hindi language and literature serving the needs of post-graduates and faculty of Delhi University campus college libraries**. (University of Delhi, Department of Library and Information Science, Sessional Project). {DUL}

Sachdeva, Mohinder Singh, 1975, **Colon Classification** : Theory and practice. {ICA MHA MMTC NIPCCD}

Sackman, Harold, 1970, **Man-computer problem solving** : Experimental evaluation of time-sharing and batch processing. {NASSDOC}

Sadhu, S.H. and Saraf, B.N., 1967, **Library legislation in India** : A historical and comparative study. {BIS ICA IIMC NASSDOC NERC SPA}

Saffady, William, 1979, **Computer output microfilm** : Its library applications. {JNU}

Saffady, William,1983, **Introduction to automation for librarians.** [American Library Association]. {USIS}

Sager, Donald J., 1968, **Reference** : A programmed instruction. [Ohio Library Association]. {USIS}

Saha, J., 1969, **Special libraries and information services in India and in the U.S.A.** {IEG IIT NASSDOC}

Sahai, S.N. 1976, **Bibliographic methods and reading behaviour**. {ICHR NASSDOC NERC NIPCCD}

Sahai, Shrinath, 1973, **Library and the community**. {JNU NASSDOC NMML}

Saifuddin, comp., 1962, **Subject headings** : A list with CC and DDC numbers. {NASSDOC}

Saini, B.S., 1976, **Library organisation for higher education** : The status and role of university librarian. {AIU JNU NIEPA}

Saith, S.S., 1968, **East African School of Librarianship.** [UNESCO]. {NASSDOC*}

Salmon, Stephen R., 1975, **Library automation systems**, 2nd edn. {CRRI JNU NIH}

Salmon, Stephen R., ed., 1969, **Library automation** : A state of art review : Papers : Pre-conference institute on library automation, 1967, San Francisco. [American Library Association]. {USIS}

Salton, Gerard, 1975, **Dynamic information and library processing.** {CRRI DUL ICHR INSA ISI NASSDOC USIS}

Salton, Gerard and Mc Gill, Michael J., 1983, **Introduction to modern information retrieval.** {BIS}

Salton, Gerald, ed., 1971, **The SMART retrieval system** : Experiments in automatic document processing. {MHA NASSDOC}

Samhel, Rothstein, 1955, **Development of reference services through academic traditions, public library practices and special librarianship**. {JNU}

Samore, Theodore, ed., 1968, **Problems in library classification** : Dewey 17 and conversion. {ISI}

Samuelson, Kjell, 1968, **Mechanised information storage, retrieval and dissemination** : Proceedings. {JNU}

Sanders, Brenda M., n.d., **Library services in hospitals** : A survey of their present provision and possible future development in the Southeast Metropolitan region. {DUL}

Sandhu, S.N., 1969, **Critical evaluation of the bibliographical sources for manuscript in modern Indian languages**. (University of Delhi, Department of Library Science. Sessional Project). {DUL}

Sandre, Mildred W., 1942, **County library primer**. {JNU}

Sankaranarayanan, N., 1964, **Book distribution and promotion problems in South Asia**. {DUL}

Santa, Beauel M. and Hardy, Lois Lynn, 1955, **How to use the library**. {JNU}

Saracevic, Tefko, and Wood, Judith B, 1981, **Consolidation of information** : A handbook on evaluation, restructuring and repackaging of scientific and technical information. [UNESCO]. {CRRI}

Saracevic, Tefko, ed., 1970, **Introduction to information science**. {DUL NASSDOC}

Sarada, K., 1986, **Rural library services in India**. {NASSDOC*}

Sardana, J.L., 1983, **Universal Decimal Classification** : Structure and methodology. {BIS ICHR IIT JNU ZHL}

Sardana, J.L. and Sehgal, R.L., 1982, **Statistical methods for librarians**. {ICHR ISI JNU NASSDOC}

Sardana, J.L., ed., 1984, **Continuing education for librarians** : Paper : All India seminar for librarians, February 13, 1984, New Delhi. [Indian Library Association]. {NASSDOC}

Sardar, Z., 1988, **Building information systems in the Islamic world**. {NASSDOC}

Sardar, Ziauddin, 1979, **Islam** : Outline of a classification scheme. {ZHL}

Sarin, Ashok Kumar, 1987, **Use of journals in libraries** : A cost effectiveness analysis. {JNU}

Sarkar, P.K., 1977, **Administration of technical libraries**. {BIS CRRI ICHR NCAER ZHL}

Satija, M.P., 1979, **An epostle to dean Shera on the gravity of notation in colon classification**. {NASSDOC}

Satija, M.P., 1987, **A primer on Ranganathan's book number**. {NASSDOC*}

Satija, M.P. and Agrawal, S.P., 1990, **Book numbers** : Some Indian methods. {NASSDOC}

Satija, M.P. and Comarona, John P., 1987, **Introduction to the practice of Dewey Decimal Classification**. {NASSDOC}

Satija, Mohinder Partap, 1978, **Ranganathan** : Method and style : A pastiche of opinions. {JNU}

Saual, Margaret and Melcher, Daniel, 1971, **Melcher on acquisition.** [American Library Association]. {AIU NASSDOC}

Saunders, Helen E., 1968, **Modern school library** : Its administration as a material centre. {JNU}

Saunders, W.L., ed., 1966, **Provision and use of library and documentation services** : Some contributions. [University of Sheffield Postgraduate School of Librarianship]. {DUL JNU MHA NIH SPA USIS}

Saunders, W.L., ed., 1967, **Librarianship in Britain today**. [Library Association, London]. {IIT}

Saunders, W.L., ed., 1968, **University and research library studies**. {AIU DUL IIC IIT ISI JNU SPA}

Savage, A.W., 1977, **Personnel management.** {JNU}

Savage, E.A., 1949, **Manual of book classification and display for public libraries**. {BIS MMTC NAI NIH SPA ZHL}

Savage, Ernest A., 1942, **The librarian and his committee.** {CRRI}

Savary, M.J., 1968, **Latin American cooperative acquisitions programme**. {IIFT}

Saxon, James A. and Stayer, Wesley W., 1967, **Basic principles of data processing**. {JNU}

Sayers, Frances Clarke, 1965, **Summoned by books** : Essays and speeches, comp. by Marjeanne Jensen Blinn. {USIS}

Sayers, W.C. Berwick, 1938, **Introduction to library classification**. {NAI}

Sayers, W.C. Berwick, 1939, **Library local collections**. {DUL NAI}

Sayers, W.C. Berwick, 1950, **An introduction to library classification**. {CRRI}

Sayers, W.C., Berwick, 1955, **First steps in annotation in catalogues,** 2nd rev ed. {DUL}

Sayers, W.C. Berwick, 1955, **Manual of classification**. {NMML}

Sayers, W.C. Berwick, 1958, **Introduction to library classification**, 9th edn. {BIS}

Sayers, W.C. Berwick, 1962, **Manual of classification**, 3rd edn. {BIS CRRI IIT JNU NAI SPA ZHL}

Sayers, W.C. Berwick, 1967, **Manual of children libraries**. {DUL}

Sayers, W.C. Berwick, 1975, **Mannual of Classification**. 5th edn., ed. by Arthur Maltby {BIS ICA ICHR MMTC NERC NIPCCO NMML ZHL}

Schad, J.G. and Tanis, N.E., 1974, **Problems in developing academic library collections**. {DUL IIT ISI}

Schaetz, Chaire K., n.d., **Some characteristics of an efficient information retrieval system**. {JNU}

Schatz, Birdie B., 1968, **Joint university libraries** : Staff handbook. {JNU}

Scheele, Martin, 1961, **Punch-card methods in research and documentation with special reference to biology.** {CRRI DUL IIMC NASSDOC}

Scheeter, George, 1967, **Information retrieval** : A critical view. {JNU}

Schellenberg, T.R., 1965, **The management of archives**. {NASSDOC USIS}

Scheuk, Gretchen Knief, 1954, **County and regional library development**. {NASSDOC}

Schieber, William D. and Schofler, Ralph M., 1968, **Telefascimile in libraries** : A report of an experiment in fascimile transmission and an analysis of implication for inter library·loan system. {JNU}

Schimmelpfeng, Richard H. and Cook, C. Donald, 1968, **The use of Library of Congress Classification** : Proceedings : Institute on the use of the Library of Congress classification, 1966, New York. [American Library Association]. {USIS}

Schlessinger, Bernard S., ed., 1983, **The basic business library** : Core resources. {USIS}

Schmalz, Larry C. and Sippl, Charles J., 1972, **Computer glossary for students and teachers.** {NASSDOC}

Schmeckebier, K.F. and Eastin, R.B., 1961, **Government publications and their use**, rev edn. {MFL}

Schmittroth, John, ed., 1982, **Encyclopaedia of information systems and services**, 5th edn. {USIS}

Schnake, M.A., 1973, **Data-processing concepts**. {NASSDOC}

Schneider, George, 1961, **Theory and history of bibliography**, tr. by Ralph Robert Shaw. {NASSDOC}

Schramm, Wilbur, 1973, **Men, messages and media** : A look at human communication. {NASSDOC}

Schuchmann, M., 1958, **Bibliography of standards on documentation**. {BIS ISI}

Schumacher, August, 1973, **Development plans and planning** : Bibliographic and computer aids to research. {JNU}

Schunk, Russell J., 1945, **Pointers for public library building planners.** {DUL}

Schur, H., 1973, **Education and training of information specialists.** {BCL CRRI ICA}

Schutz, H., 1975, **Function and organisation of a national documentation centre in developing country**. [FID/DC Working Group]. {ICA JNU NASSDOC}

Schur, H. and Saunders, W.L., 1968, **Education and training for scientific and technological library and information work.** {IIT SPA}

Schutze, Gertrude, 1965, **Documentation source book**. {BIS DUL MHA NASSDOC NIH}

Schutze, Gertrude, 1972, **Information and library science source book** : Supplement to documentation source book. {NERC}

Schwerin, Kurt, n.d., **Classification for international law and relations,** 2nd edn. {IEG}

Scott, Andrew M., et al, 1966, **Simulation and national development**. {NASSDOC}

Seal, Alan and Bryant, Philip, 1982, **Full and short entry catalogues** : Library needs and uses. [Centre for Catalogue Research]. {NASSDOC}

Sears, Donald A., (1984), **Harbrace guide to the library and the research paper**, 4th ed. {IIMC}

Sears, Minnie Earl, 1944, **List of subject headings for small libraries including practical suggestings for the beginner in subject heading work**, 5th edn. {MHA}

Sears, Minnie Earl, 1959, **List of subject headings**, 8th edn., ed by Bertha Margret Frick. {DUL}

Seely, Pauline A., ed., 1968, **ALA rules for filing catalogue cards**, 2nd. edn. [American Library Association]. {BIS IIT JNU NIEPA NMML USIS}

Sehgal, R.L., 1985, **Vargikaran siddhant evam vyavhar**. {NASSDOC}

Sellen, B.C., ed., 1984, **New options for librarians**. {NASSDOC*}

Sellen, Betty Carol, ed., 1980, **What else can you do with a library degree**. {IIT}

Semprevivo, Philip C., 1976, **Systems analysis** : Definition, process and design. {NASSDOC}

Sen, N.B., ed., 1965, **Development of libraries in new India**. {ICA IIC IIT NASSDOC SPA}

Sengupta, B., 1964, **Cataloguing** : Its theory and practice. {CRRI ICHR MHA NMML SPA ZHL}

Sengupta, B., 1970, **Cataloguing** : Its theory and practice, 2nd edn. {JNU NERC}

Sengupta, B., 1974, **Cataloguing** : Its theory and practice, 3rd rev. edn. {IIT ISIL}

Sengupta, B., 1981, **Indian reference and information services**. {ICA NIH}

Sengupta, B. and Ohdedar, A.K., 1977, **Library classification**. {CRRI IIT NMML}

Sengupta, Benoyendra, 1974, **Book selection.** {ICA IIT ISIL JNU NERC ZHL}

Sengupta, Benoyendra and Chatterjee, Mridula, 1977, **Documentation and information retrieval**. {DUL MHA ZHL}

Sethi, A.R., and Moodgal, H.M.K., 1978, **Indian book review index,** 1975-76. {JNU NASSDOC}

Sewa Singh, 1986, **Reference service in academic libraries in India**. {JNU NASSDOC NMML}

Sewell, P.H., ed., 1963, **Five year work in librarianship.** [Library Association, London]. {IIT}

Sewell, P.H., et al, 1977, **Establishing a legislative framework for the implementation of NATIS**. [UNESCO]. {NASSDOC}

Seymour, Whitney North and Layne, Elizabeth N., 1979, **For the people** : Fightings for public libraries. {USIS}

Sfrigai, Frances and Jacor, Marry, 1968, **PILOT** : An on-line library acquisition system. {JNU}

Shaffer, Kenneth R., 1961, **Book collection** : Policy case studies in public and academic libraries. {DUL}

Shaffer, Kenneth Raymond, 1963, **Library personnel administration and supervision**, 2nd edn. {DUL}

Shaffer, Kenneth, R., 1971, **Decision making** : A seminar in public library management. {USIS}

Shah, Ambalal P., ed., n.d. **Catalogue of Sanskrit and Prakrit manuscripts**, 4 parts. [Lalbhai Dalpatbhai Institute of Indology]. {INSA}

Shankman, Florence V. and Kranyik, Robert, 1964, **How to teach reference and research skills.** {JNU}

Shantilata, 1985, **Learning to read** : Use of orthographic and semantic cues. {NASSDOC}

Sharify, Nasser, 1959, **Cataloguing of Persian works including rules for transliteration, entry and description**. [American Library Association]. {JNU NASSDOC}

Sharma, B.N., 1977, **Dvibindu vargikaran ka sankshipt parichay**. {NMML}

Sharma, B.N., 1977, **Pustakalaya siddhant and vyavahar** : College pustakalaya ke sandarbh men. {NMML}

Sharma, C.D., 1972, **Practical cataloguing** : Classified catalogue. {INSA JNU NCAER}

Sharma, C.D., 1972, **Practical cataloguing** : Classified catalogue, 2nd edn. [ICA ICHR IEC JNU NIPCCD}

Sharma, C.D., 1973, **Classified catalogue code in theory and practice.** {CRRI}

Sharma, C.D., 1976, **Book selection and physical bibliography.** {CRRI}

Sharma, C.D., 1978, **Use of libraries** : A guide to better use of libraries and their resources. {CRRI ICA IIT MMTC NASSDOC NCAER NCDC NIPCCD NMML}

Sharma, C.D. and Boonlia, Naresh, n.d., **Information services for college librarians.** {JNU}

Sharma, C.D. and Dave, Meenakshi, 1990, **Classified catalogue code in theory and practice** {DUL}

Sharma, C.D. and Vyas, Kailash, 1983, **Developing horizons in library and information science**, 2 vols. {AIU IIT ISI JNU NASSDOC NMML SPA}

Sharma, C.K., n.d., **Book selection and bibliography**. {ICHR}

Sharma, C.K., 1983, **Library management and organisation**, Vol. I. {DUL ICHR IIFT IIT}

Sharma, C.K., 1984, **Cataloguing**. {NASSDOC}

Sharma, C.K., 1990, **Modern library systems**. {NMML}

Sharma, Chandra Kant, 1978, **Granthalaya mein sandhrab seva**. {JNU NMML}

Sharma, Chandra Kant, 1975, **Pustak chayan evam rachna** : Book selection and physical bibliography. {BIS NMML}

Sharma, Chandra Kant, 1977, **University library** : Its management and organisation. {DUL JNU}

Sharma, H.D., 1972, **Library building and furniture with special reference to college libraries**. {CRRI ICA ICHR INSA MFL NASSDOC NIEPA NIH NIPCCD ZHL}

Sharma, H.D. and Singh, B.N., 1990, **Manual for college libraries**. {UGC}

Sharma, H.D., ed., 1984, **Indian books** : A bibliography of Indian books published or reprinted in 1983 in the English language, comp. by Ram Lal. [Indian Bibliographic Centre, Varanasi]. {NASSDOC}

Sharma, H.D., et al, n.d., **Indian reference sources** : An annotated guide to Indian reference books. {ICHR IIC NASSDOC ZHL}

Sharma, Hari Krishan, 1977, **Organisation and administration of college libraries.** {DUL ICA}

Sharma, J.K., 1973, **Directory of library schools and lecturers in librarianship in Australia**. {NASSDOC*}

Sharma, J.S., 1965, **Substance of library science**. {ICHR IIC IIT MFL NIH NERC SPA}

Sharma, J.S., 1977, **Fundamentals of library science** : A modern approach. {ICA ISI JNU ZHL}

Sharma, J.S., 1981, **Library organisation**. {CRRI ISI MMTC NIEPA}

Sharma, Jagdish Saran, 1977, **Fundamentals of bibliography with special reference to India**. {JNU NASSDOC}

Sharma, Jagdish Saran, 1986, **Library movement in India and abroad**. {JNU}

Sharma, Jagdish Saran and Grover, D.R., 1987, **Reference service and sources of information**. {NMML}

Sharma, Jai Kishore, 1973, **Directory of book trade in India**. JNU RTL}

Sharma, M.S., 1987, **International standard book numbering system in India**. {NASSDOC}

Sharma, Madhusudan, 1990, **Fundamentals of library and information science**. {NMML}

Sharma, Pandey S.K., **Pustakalaya aur hum** {RTL}

Sharma, Pandey S.K., 1979, **Dewey Decimal Classification for Indology** : Expansion and modification of Dewey Decimal Classification (18) for classifying Indological books with special reference to Indian philosophy and Indian religions. {DSSW ICHR IIC IIT INSA JNU MHA NIPCCD ZHL}

Sharma, Pandey S.K., 1985, **Public libraries in India**. {JNU}

Sharma, Pandey S.K. and Gupta, O.P., 1986, **Dictionary of library and information science** : English-Hindi; Hindi-English. {NASSDOC}

Sharma, Pandey Suraj Kant, 1976, **Expansion and modification of Dewey Decimal Classification (18) for classifying Indological books with special reference to Indian philosophy and Indian religions.** {NASSDOC}

Sharma, Ram Saroop, ed., 1974, **Bibliography and documentation**. {ICHR IIT JNU NIPCCD}

Sharma, Ravindra N., ed., 1981, **Indian librarianship** : Perspectives and prospects. {IEG NASSDOC}

Sharma, Ravindra N., ed., 1981, **Librarianship** : Perspectives and prospects. {AIU NIEPA}

Sharma, Ravindra Nath, 1986, **Indian academic libraries and Dr. S.R. Ranganathan** : A critical study. {JNU NMML}

Sharma, Satinder, 1982, **Contemporary approach to school library**. {DUL NASSDOC}

Sharp, H.A., 1950, **Cataloguing** : A textbook for the use in libraries, 4th edn. {IIT ZHL}

Sharp, H.A., 1964, **Cataloguing** : A textbook for use in libraries. {ICA MFL NAI NIPCCD ZHL}

Sharp, Harold S., 1963, **Readings in special librarianship**. {USIS}

Sharp, Harold S., 1964, **Reading in information retrieval**. {JNU}

Sharp, Henry A., 1938, **Branch libraries** : Modern problems and administration. {JNU}

Sharp, John R., 1965, **Some fundamentals of information retrieval**. {BIS CRRI DUL JNU TDA}

Sharp, John Raymond, 1970, **Information retrieval** : Notes for students. {BCL}

Sharr, F.A., 1962, **Library services in a sparsely populated area.** [UNESCO]. {NASSDOC*}

Shashi Bala, 1982, **Non-book material available in Nehru Memorial Museum and Library** : A brief survey. {NMML}

Shastri, A., 1967, **Pustakalaya andolan, Bihar**. {NMML}

Shastri, A., 1967, **Pustakalaya-Prakriya, Patna**. {NMML}

Shastri, Dwarka Prasad, 1958, **Pustakalaya aur sandarbh seva**. {BIS DUL}

Shastri, Dwarka Prasad, 1959, **Pustakalaya parichay**. {BIS}

Shastri, Dwarka Prasad, 1974, **Pustakalaya parichay**, 2nd edn. {BIS NMML}

Shastri, Dwarka Prasad, 1974, **Pustakalaya vargikarna** : Siddhant aur prayog. {BIS MFL}

Shaw, Charles B., comp., 1940, **List of books for college libraries, 1931-38.** [American Library Association]. {ZHL}

Shaw, Robert J., ed. 1967, **Libraries buildings for the future Proceedings** : Library buildings institute and American libraries trustee association workshop, 1965, Detroit. {DUL}

Shearer, Benjamin F. and Shearer, Barbara Smith, comps., 1981, **Finding the source** : A thesaurus index to the reference collection. {NASSDOC USIS}

Shera, J.H., 1970, **Sociological foundations of librarianship**. {IEG NASSDOC NIEPA NMML ZHL}

Shera, J.H., et al, 1975, **Information systems in documentation.** {CRRI DUL JNU}

Shera, Jesse H., 1949, **Foundations of the public library** : The origins of the public library movement in New England, 1629-1855. {USIS}

Shera, Jesse H., 1958, **Information resources** : A challenge to American science and industry. {JNU}

Shera, Jesse H., 1965, **Libraries and the organisation of knowledge**. {IIT USIS}

Shera, Jesse H., 1966, **Documentation and the organisation of knowledge**, ed. by D.J. Foskett. {DUL NASSDOC NMML USIS}

Shera, Jesse H., 1972, **Foundations of education for librarianship.** {AIU IIFT ISI NIPCCD USIS ZHL}

Shera, Jesse H., 1976, **Introduction to library science** : Basic elements of library science. {DUL}

Shera, Jesse H., ed., n.d., **Advances in documentation and library science**. 3 vols. {BIS}

Shera, Jesse, H., et al, 1956, **Documentation in action**. {BIS DUL NASSDOC}

Shera, Jesse H. and Egan, M.E., 1956, **Classified catalogue** : Basic principles and practices. [American Library Association]. {CRRI NASSDOC}

Shericlam, Thomas B. and Farrell, William R., 1974, **Man, machine systems** : Information control and decision models of human performance. {JNU}

Sherman, Philip M., 1970, **Programming and coding digital computers**. {NASSDOC}

Sherman, Steve, 1971, **ABC's of library promotion.** {DEPT JNU}

Sherrie, Heather and Jones, Phyllis Mander, comps., 1950, **Short list of subject headings**. {CRRI}

Sherrod, John, 1975, **Information systems and networks** : Eleventh annual symposium {JNU}

Shiart-Shibbs, B., 1985, **Changing technology and education for librarianship and information science**. {NASSDOC}

Shiflett, Orvin Lee, 1981, **Origins of American academic librarianship**. {JNU}

Shores, Hous, 1976, **Reference as the promotion of free enquiry**. {JNU}

Shores, Louis, 1939, **Basic reference books** : An introduction to the evaluation study and use of reference materials with special emphasis on some 300 titles. {JNU}

Shores, Louis, 1954, **Basic reference sources**. [American Library Association]. {CRRI NAI USIS}

Shores, Louis, 1972, **Basic reference sources** : An introduction to materials and methods. {DUL USIS}

Shores, Louis, et al, ed., 1966, **The library college** : Contributions for American higher education at the Jamestown college workshop. {USIS}

Shukla, Lalita S., 1974, **Basic foundations of library science**. {CRRI JNU ZHL}

Shypla, Bana Bihari, 1984, **Fundamental theories in abstracting and fundamental laws in library science**. {JNU}

Siddiqui, Akhtar H., n.d., **Library resources of Pakistan**. {JNU}

Sieburth, J.F., 1988, **Online search services in the academic library** : Planning, management and operation. [American Library Association]. {NASSDOC}

Sigel, Efrem, et al, 1982, **Books, libraries and electronics** : Essays on the future of written communication. {USIS}

Sigmund, Frauendorter Wein, 1960, **Classification scheme of agricultural science**, 3rd rev edn. {DUL}

Silva, M., ed., 1985, **Sharing of information** : South Asian initiatives. {NASSDOC*}

Silva, Mail, 1970, **Special libraries**. {INSA JNU NERC NMML}

Simmon, Ross, 1976, **Reader in library management**. {JNU}

Simon, Herbert A. and Siklossy, Leurent, 1972, **Representation and meaning** : Experiments with information processing systems. {NASSDOC}

Simpson, I.S., 1975, **Basic statistics for librarians**. {ISI JNU}

Simpson, I.S., 1983, **Basic statistics for librarians**, 2nd edn. {IIT}

Simpson, Murray, C.T., 1976, **Rare book librarianship** : A select annotated bibliography. {JNU}

Simsova, S. and Mackee, Monique, 1970, **Handbook of comparative librarianship**. {NASSDOC}

Simsova, S. and Mackee, Monique, 1975, **Handbook of comparative librarianship,** 2nd edn. {BIS IICL ISI NIPCCD}

Simsova, Sylva, 1982, **Primer of comparative librarianship**. {IIT}

Sinclair, Dorothy, 1965, **Administration of the small public library**. [American Library Association]. {NASSDOC}

Singer, Howard W. and Smith, Richard Daniel, eds., 1970, **Deterioration and preservation of library materials** : Conference of the Graduate Library School, 34th, August 4-6, 1969, Chicago. {AIU CRRI IIT INSA JNU NASSDOC NMML}

Singer, T.E.R., ed., n.d., **Information and communication practice in industry**. {IEG}

Singh A.P., 1987, **Conservation and museum techniques.** {NMML}

Singh, R.S.P., 1973, **Pustakalaya sanghatan evam prashasan**. {DUL}

Singh, R.S.P., 1981, **Glimpses of librarianship**. {JNU}

Singh, R.S.P., 1988, **Public libraries in Bihar**. [Bihar Library Service Association, Patna].

Singh, S.N. and Prasad, H.N., 1985, **Cataloguing manual** : AACR-2, {JNU}

Singh, S.P., 1975, **Automation in iibraries.** {ICHR NASSDOC NIPCCD SPA}

Singla, M.L., 1988, **Report on feasibility study for a computer based circulation control system**. [NASSDOC]. {NASSDOC}

Sippl, Charles J., 1966, **Computer dictionary and handbook.** {NASSDOC}

Sippl, Charles J. and Sippl, Roger J., 1983, **Computer dictionary and handbook**, 3rd edn. {NASSDOC RTL}

Sircar, Pankti, 1970, **Evaluation of the acquisition policy and procedure of periodicals in the Indian Institute of Foreign Trade Library and Rattan Tata Library**. {DUL}

Sivaramamurti, C., 1959, **Directory of museums in India**. [Ministry of Scientific Research and Cultural Affairs, New Delhi]. {ICCR NASSDOC}

Sivaswami Iyyar, P.S., 1931, **The five laws of library science**. [Madras Library Association, Madras]. {NASSDOC*}

Slamecka, Vladimir, 1965, **Coming age of information technology** : Studies in coordinate indexing. {DUL}

Slater, M., 1964, **Technical libraries.** {IIT}

Slater, M., ed., 1990, **Research methods in library and information studies**. [Library Association, London].{DUL}

Slavens, Thomas P., ed., 1981, **Retrieval of information in the humanities and the social sciences**. {NIEPA}

Slocum, R.B., 1962, **Sample catalog cards**. {IIT}

Slote, Stanley J., 1982, **Weeding library collections**, 2nd rev edn. {DUL USIS}

Small, Herbert, 1982, **The Library of Congress** : Its architecture and decoration ed. by Henry Hope Reed. {USIS}

Smeaton, J., 1959, **School libraries** : A series of talks delivered. [Ministry of Education, New Delhi]. {NMML}

Smith, C. and Walker, R., n.d., **Library resources in Scotland**. {JNU}

Smith, D.L., 1967, **How to find out in architecture and building**. {SPA}

Smith, D.L. and Baxter, E.G., 1965, **College library administration**. {DUL IIT SPA}

Smith, Datus C., 1966, **Guide to book publishing**. {DUL}

Smith, Datus C., 1977, **Economics of book publishing in developing countries.** {DUL}

Smith, David, 1980, **Systems thinking in library and information management.** {DUL NIPCCD}

Smith, G.L. and Meyer, R.S., eds., 1969, **Library use of computers** : Introduction. [Special Libraries Association, New York]. {IIT USIS}

Smith, J.C. and Hisson, N.J., 1965, **Information maintenance system documentation.** {JNU}

Smith, Jessie Carney, 1977, **Black academic libraries and research collections** : An historical survey. {DUL IIT NIPCCD}

Smith, Josephine Metcalfe, 1968, **A chronology of librarianship**. {USIS}

Smith, Lillian H., n.d., **Unreluctant years**. [American Library Association]. {ZHL}

Smith, Paul, 1980, **Use of libraries and the literature of human geography**. {SPA}

Smith, Robert Irvine and Combell, Bob, 1981, **Information technology revolution.** {NASSDOC}

Smith, Roger H., 1963, **The American reading public** : What it reads, why it reads. {USIS}

Soergel, Dagobert, 1974, **Indexing languages and thesauri** : Construction and maintenance. {CRRI IIT NASSDOC}

Soergel, Dagobert, 1985, **Organising information** : Principle of data base and retrieval. {JNU}

Sogani, Kamal Chand and Vijay Narain, eds., 1973, **Librarian and libraries** : In the memory of the Master Moti Lal ji and his Shri Sanmati Pustakalaya. {JNU NASSDOC}

Sood, P.K., 1988, **Reading habits among college students** : The role of library. {NASSDOC}

Sood, S.P. and Jotwani, D., 1981, **Pralekhan** {JNU NASSDOC}.

Soule, Charles C., n.d., **How to plan a library building for library work.** {IEG}

Spencer, Donlad D., ed., 1968, **Computer programmer's dictionary handbook**. {RTL}

Spencer, J., 1976, **Business information in London** : A study of the demand and supply of business information in 13 London business libraries. [Association of Special Libraries and Information Bureaux]. {NASSDOC}

Speterson, Martin, 1966, **Scientific thinking and scientific writing**. {DUL}

Spiker, Sina K., n.d., **Indexing your book** : A practical guide for authors. {DUL}

Spiller, David, 1971, **Book selection** : An introduction to principles and practice, 2nd ed. {BIS}

Spiller, David, 1986, **Book selection** : An introduction to principles and practice. {NASSDOC}

Spivack, Jane, F., 1982, **Careers in information.** {USIS}

Spreitzer, Francis, ed., 1985, **Microforms in libraries**. [American Library Association]. {NASSDOC}

Sprowls, R. Clay, 1968, **Computers** : A programming problem approach, rev. edn. {DUL}

Srinath, Laxmipuram Srinivasascher, 1975, **PERT and CPM** : Principles and applications. {JNU}

Srivastava, A.P., 1969, **Education for library science and documentation** : Iran. [UNESCO]. {NASSDOC*}

Srivastava, A.P., 1973, **Theory of knowledge classification in libraries**. {CRRI ICA ICHR IIT JNU NASSDOC NERC SPA ZHL}

Srivastava, A.P., 1977, **Ranganathan** : A pattern maker : A synthetic study of his contributions. {CRRI ISI JNU NIEPA NIPCCD ZHL}

Srivastava, S.S., 1971, **Survey research technique**. {NASSDOC}

Srivastava, Shyam Nath, 1980, **University libraries in India** : Their organisation and administration. {DUL IIT ISI JNU NERC NIEPA NIPCCD}

Srivastava, Shyam Nath and Verma, Subhash Chandra, n.d., **Pustakalaya sangathan evam sanchalan.** {DUL IIMC}

Stabley, Don H., 1967, **System/360 Assembler language.** {NASSDOC}

Stagle, James R., 1971, **Artificial intelligence** : The heuristic programming approach. {NASSDOC}

Stamper, Ronald, 1973, **Information in business and administrative systems**. {DUL NASSDOC}

Stater, Margaret, 1989, **Information needs of social scientists**. [British Library Research and Development Department]. {NASSDOC}

Staveley, Ronald, 1962, **Notes on subject bibliography**. {DUL IEG MFL}

Staveley, Ronald, ed., n.d., **Guide to unpublished research materials**. {IEG}

Stavley, Ronald, et al, 1967, **Introduction to subject study**. {AIU IIT NASSDOC}

Stebbins, K.B., 1966, **Personnel administration in libraries**, 2nd edn. rev. by P.G. Mohrhardt. {JNU NIH USIS}

Steele, Colin, 1976, **Major libraries of the world** : A selective guide. {NMML}

Steele, Colin, ed., 1978, **Steady-state, zerogrowth and the academic library** : A collection of essays. {DUL NASSDOC NIEPA}

Stefferud, Alfred, ed., 1972, **Wonderful world of books**. {ZHL}

Stene, Elizabeth, 1967, **Training for the improvement of library administration**. {JNU}

Stenstrom, Ralph H., 1970, **Cooperation between types of libraries, 1940-1968** : An annotated bibliography. [American Library Association]. {NASSDOC}

Stephen, Parker J., 1984, **Library and information science and archive administration** : A guide to building a basic collection for library schools. {JNU}

Sterling, T.D. and Rollack, S.V., 1970, **Computing and computer science** : A first course with PL/I. {DUL}

Steurat, Robert D., 1982 : **Information needs of the 80's**. {JNU}

Steven, Mary Elizabeth, 1965, **Automatic indexing** : A state of the art report. [U.S. National Bureau of Standards]. {USIS}

Stevens, N.D., ed., 1971, **Library humor** : A bibliothecal miscellany to 1970. {NASSDOC}

Stevens, Norman D., n.d., **Comparative study of three systems of information retrieval**. [Graduate School of Library Science, New Brunswick]. {BIS MHA}

Stevens, Rolland E., 1966, **Reference books in the social sciences and humanities.** {DUL}

Stevens, Rolland E. and Smith, Linda C., 1986, **Reference work in the university library**. {JNU}

Stevens, Rolland E., ed., 1971, **Research methods in librarianship** : Historical and bibliographical methods in library research. {NASSDOC}

Stevenson, Gordon and Kramer-Greene, Judith, eds., n.d., **Melvil Dewey** : The man and the classification. {DUL}

Stevenson, Gordon and Kramer-Greene, Judith, eds., 1983, **Melvil Dewey** : The man and the classification. {NASSDOC}

Stewart, James D., n.d., **Report on the municipal library system**. {JNU}

Stewart, James D., 1947, **Tabulation of librarianship** : Classified tables for the arrangement of all material relating to library economy. {CRRI}

Stibic, V., 1983, **Personal documentation for professionals** : Means and methods. {JNU}

Stirling, John K., 1987, **Univesity librarianship.** {JNU}

Stockham, K.A., n.d., **The government and control of libraries**, 2nd edn. {DUL ICHR}

Stoff, C.A., 1955, **School libraries** : A short manual, {JNU}

Stokes, Adrian V., 1982, **Concise encyclopaedia of information technology**. {CRRI JNU NASSDOC RTC}

Stockes, Roy, 1965, **Bibliographical control and service**. {DUL IIT MFL NASSDOC}

Stone, Elizabeth W., 1969, **Factors related to the professional development of librarians**. {USIS}

Stone, Elizabeth W., 1974, **Continuing library education as viewed in relation to other continuing professional movements**. [American Society for Information Science]. {NIEPA}

Stone, Elizabeth W., ed., 1971, **New directions in staff development moving from ideas to action** : The papers : Microworkshop on staff development, June 28, 1970, Detroit. [American Library Association]. {USIS}

Stone, Elizabeth W., et al, 1974, **Continuing library and information science education** : Final report to the National Commission on Libraries and Information Science (with bibliography). {USIS}

Stone, Phillip J., 1968, **User's manual for the general inquirer**. {NASSDOC}

Stone, Phillip, J., et al, 1966, **General inquirer** : A computer approach to content analysis. {NASSDOC}

Stone, Sue, ed., 1980, **Humanities information research** : Proceedings of a seminar. {JNU}

Strable, Edward G., ed., 1966, **Special libraries** : Guide for management. [Special Libraries Association, New York]. {IIC IIT}

Strassberg, Richard, 1974, **Manual of archival and manuscript processing procedures**. {DUL}

Strauss, Lucille J., et al, 1964, **Scientific and technical libraries** : Their organisation and administration. {BIS CRRI IIT INSA}

Strauss, Lucille J., et al., 1972, **Scientific and technical libraries** : Their organisation and administration, 2nd edn. {BIS ISI INSA JNU}

Strauss, William, et al, 1968, **Guide to laws and regulation on federal libraries** : A compilation and analysis. {USIS}

Strout, Ruth French, ed., 1964, **Library catalogs** : Changing damnations. {IIT}

Struening, Elmer L. and Guttentag, Marcia, eds., 1975, **Handbook of evaluation research**, 2 vols. {NASSDOC}

Stueart, Robert D., 1972, **Area specialist bibliographer** : An inquiry into his role. {NASSDOC}

Stueart, Robert D. and Eastlick, John Taylor, 1977, **Library management**. {DUL USIS}

Stueart, Robert D. and Eastlick, John Taylor, 1981, **Library management**, 2nd edn. {BIS DUL USIS}

Stueart, Robert D. and Johnson, Richard D., 1979, **Papers** : National conference on new horizons for academic libraries, November 8-11, 1978, Boston, {IIT}

Subbaiah, R., 1988, **Agricultural librarianship in India.** {NASSDOC}

Subramanyan, Krishna, 1981, **Scientific and technical information resources.** {DUL}

Sudame, G.R., 1972, **Study of the effect of library use on academic achievement of post-graduate students in the M.S. University of Baroda.** {NASSDOC}

Sudman, Seymour, 1967, **Reducing the cost of surveys.** {NASSDOC}

Surinder Kumari, 1975-76, **Indian Standards Institution and its role in the development of library and documentation standards.** (University of Delhi, Department of Library and Information Science, Sessional project 1975-76). {BIS}

Suseela Kumar, 1974, **Changing concepts of reference service.** {AIU DUL ICHR IIT MHA NERC NIPCCD NMML}

Sutherland, John W., 1973, **General systems philosophy for the social and behavioural sciences,** ed. by Erwinlaszlo. {NASSDOC}

Sutton, S.C., 1967, **Guide to the India Office Library** : With a note on the India Office Records. [India Office Library]. {NMML}

Sutton, S.C., 1968, **Guide to the India Office Library** : With a note on the India Office Records, 2nd edn. [India Office Library]. {IEG IIT JNU MFL NASSDOC NMML RTL}

Swanson, Don R. and Bookstein, Abraham, eds., 1972, **Operations research** : Implications for libraries. {NASSDOC}

Swanson, Don R., ed., 1965, **Intellectual foundations of library education.** {IIT}

Swaran Kumar, 1963, **East and West.** : Delhi Public Library, India, as seen against the background of the Rochester Public Library. {NASSDOC*}

Swartzburg, Susan Garretson, ed., 1983, **Conservation in the library** : A handbook of use and care of traditional and non-traditional materials. {JNU NMML}

Swihart, Stanley J. and Heeley, Beryl F., 1973, **Computer systems in the library** : A handbook for managers and designers. {CRRI NASSDOC NIPCCD}

Swisher, Robert and Mc Clure, Charles R., 1984, **Research for decision making** : Methods for librarians. {DUL}

Syenawine, Wayne, n.d., **Library evaluation.** [American Library Association]. {DUL}

Sykes, Paul, 1979, **Public library in perspective** : An examination of its origins and modern role. {IIT}

Szweda, Ralph A., 1981, **Information processing systems.** {JNU}

Taha, Handy A., 1971, **Operations research** : An introduction. {NASSDOC}

Tait, James A., 1969, **Authors' and titles** : An analytical study of the author concept in codes of cataloguing rules in the English language from that of the British Museum. {NMML}

Tait, James A. and Anderson, F. Douglas, 1968, **Descriptive cataloguing** : A students introduction to the Anglo-American Cataloguing Rules, 1967. {NASSDOC}

Tait, James A. and Anderson, F. Douglas, 1971. **Descriptive cataloguing** : A students introduction to the Anglo-American Cataloguing Rules, 1967, 2nd edn. {IIC IIT}

Taneja, Ram D., n.d., **Information service for the small enterprise** : Need, source and organisation. {BIS}

Tapingkae, A., 1974, **Directory of selected scholars and researchers in Southeast Asia**. [Regional Institute of Higher Education and Development, Singapore]. {NASSDOC}

Taraboi, Vasile, 1973, **Organisation, functioning and activities of national documentary information systems in the scientific, technical and economic fields.** [National Institute for Scientific and Technical Information and Documentation, Romania]. {BIS}

Tast, Margret, 1984, **South Pacific region pilot project on school library development** : Training programmes for teachers. {JNU}

Taube, Mortimer, n.d., **Studies in coordinate indexing**. {JNU}

Taube, Mortimer, 1961, **Computers and common sense** : The myth of thinking machines. {JNU}

Taube, Mortimer and Wooster, Harold, eds., 1958, **Information storage and retrieval** : Theory, system and devices. {CRRI DUL}

Tauber, Maurice F. and Orne, Jerrold, eds., 1976, **Education and libraries** : Selected papers. {AIU USIS}

Tauber, Maurice F., et al, 1953, **Technical services in libraries** : Acquisitions, cataloguing, classification, binding, photographic. {IEG NAI ZHL}

Tauber, Maurice F. and Feinberg, Hilda, 1971, **Book catalogs**. {NASSDOC}

Tauber, Maurice Falcolm, 1967, **Louis Round Wilson** : Librarian and administrator. {USIS}

Tauber, Maurice Falcolm and Irlene, R. Stephens, eds., 1967, **Library surveys**. {DUL}

Taverekere, Srikantaid and Hoffman, Herbert H., 1978, **Introduction to quantitative research methods for librarians**, 2nd rev edn. {DUL}

Taylor, David C., 1982, **Managing the serials explosion** : 1982 {JNU NMML}

Taylor, Hugh, 1980, **Arrangement and description of archival materials**. {IIT}

Taylor, James C. and Bowers, David G., 1967, **Survey of organisations : A machine standardised questionnaire instruments.** [Institute of Social Research, Michigan]. {NASSDOC}

Taylor, James L., 1966, **Library facility for elementary and secondary schools**. {JNU}

Taylor, L.J., ed., 1976, **Librarians' handbook** [Library Association London]. 2 vols. {JNU NASSDOC NIPCCD}

Taylor, Margaret S., 1948, **Fundamentals of practical cataloguing**. {BIS CRRI ICA IIFT MHA NAI NASSDOC ZHL}

Taylor, Margaret T., 1973, **Basic reference sources** : A self study manual. {DUL USIS}

Taylor, Margaret T. and Powell, Ronald R., 1981, **Basic reference sources** : A self study manual, 2nd edn. {USIS}

Taylor, P.J., 1978, **British library research and development reports** : Information guides. {JNU}

Taylor, Peter J. and Crown, Blaise, 1983, **Information management research in Europe** : Proceedings of the EURIMS conference, Paris. {JNU}

Taylor, Peter J., ed., 1976, **Library and information studies in the United Kingdom and Ireland, 1950-1974** : An index to theses. [Association of Special Libraries and Information Bureaux]. {NASSDOC}

Taylor, Robert S., 1972, **Making of a library** : Academic library in transition. {CRRI DUL JNU}

Tayyab, R. and Chanadana, K., comps., 1985, **A dictionary of acronyms and abbreviations in library and information science**, 2nd edn. [Canadian Library Association, Ottawa]. {NASSDOC}

Teague, S.J., 1977, **Microform librarianship**. {NASSDOC}

Teague, S.J., 1979, **Microform librarianship**, 2nd edn. {IDA ZHL}

Teague, S. John, 1985, **Microform, video and electronic media librarianship**. {NMML}

Tedd, L.A., 1977, **Introduction to computer-based library systems**. {JNU NIH}

Tedd, L.A., 1979, **Case studies in computer based bibliographic information services**. {BCL}

Teh-Wci, Hu, et al, 1975, **Benefit-cost analysis of alternative library delivery systems**. {JNU}

Tejomurty, A., 1981, **University library finances in Madhya Pradesh** : A comparative study. {NASSDOC}

Thakur, B.S. and Agrawal, Binod C., 1990, **Media utilization for the development of women and children**. {NIPCCD}

Thayer, Lee, ed. and comp., 1967, **Communication theory and research** : Proceedings of the first international symposium. {NASSDOC}

Thempson, Anthony, comp., n.d., **Vocabularium bibliothecari** {IEG}

Thiagrajan, R., 1978, **Lecture notes** : NISSAT training course on systems analysis for information sciences, December 12-23, 1978, New Delhi. [Department of Science and Technology, New Delhi]. {BIS}

Thieravht, Robert J. and Reynolds, George W., 1966, **Systems analysis and design** : A Case study approach. {JNU}

Thillainayagam, V., 1968, **Standard for a book** : The Tamils view. {NASSDOC*}

Thomas, Alan G., 1975, **Great books and book collectors**. {NASSDOC*}

Thomas, Carl, et al, 1950, **Adult education activities for public libraries**. [UNESCO]. {IEG ZUL}

Thomas, Diana M., 1981, **Effective reference librarian**. {IIT ISI NASSDOC}

Thomas, Joy, 1952, **Book selling**. {DUL}

Thomas, Nancy G. and O'Neil, Rosanna, comp., 1986, **Notes for serials cataloguing**. {NASSDOC*}

Thomas, P.A., 1970, **Procedural model for the use of bibliographic records in libraries**. [Association of Special Libraries and Information Bureaux]. {DUL NASSDOC}

Thomas, P.A., 1971, **Task analysis of library operations**. [Association of Special Libraries and Information Bureaux]. {DUL IIT}

Thomas, P.A., 1973, **Bibliographic information in library systems**. [Association of Special Libraries and Information Bureaux]. {CRRI JNU}.

Thomas, P.A. and Ward, V.A., 1973, **Where the time goes**. [Association of Special Libraries and Information Bureaux]. {AIU CRRI IIT}

Thomas, P.A. and Ward, V.A., 1974, **Analysis of managerial activities in libraries**. [Association of Special Libraries and Information Bureaux]. {DUL IIT}

Thompson, Anthony, 1963, **Library buildings of Britain and Europe**. {CRRI IIT NASSDOC}

Thompson, Anthony H., 1983, **Guide to production and use of audio-visual aids in library and information science teaching.** [UNESCO]. {NASSDOC*}

Thompson, Elizabeth H., 1943, **ALA glossary of library terms**. [American Library Association]. {BIS CRRI ZHL}

Thompson, Elizabeth, H. 1971, **ALA glossary of library terms with a selection of terms in related fields**. [American Library Association]. {IIT NASSDOC}

Thompson, G.A., 1969, **Technical college library** : A primer for its development. {AIU DUL IIT}

Thompson, Godfrey, 1973, **Planning and design of library buildings**. {IIT ISI}

Thompson, Godfrey, 1977, **Planning and design of library buildings**, 2nd edn. {CRRI}

Thompson, James, 1968, **History of the principles of librarianship.** {IIT}

Thompson, James, 1980, **Introduction to university library administration**, 3rd edn. {DUL IIT NIH ZHL}

Thompson, James, 1982, **End of libraries**. {IIT}

Thomson, Sarah Katharin, 1970, **Interlibrary loan involving academic libraries**. [American Library Association]. {NASSDOC}

Thomson, Sarah Katharin, 1979, **Interlibrary loan procedure manual**. [American Library Association]. {DUL NASSDOC USIS}

Thornley, Arthur, 1968, **Going into print** : Notes for the guidance of authors in preparing copy for the printer, correcting proofs, etc. {DUL}

Thornton, J.L., 1930, **Cataloguing in special libraries** : A survey of methods. {CRRI MFL NAL}

Thornton, J.L., 1940, **Special library methods** : An introduction to special librarianship. {IEG NAI}

Thornton, J.L., 1941, **Chronology of librarianship**. {CRRI}

Thornton, J.L., 1963, **Medical librarianship** : Principles and practice. {DUL}

Thornton, John L. and Tully, R.I.J., 1962, **Scientific books, libraries and collectors** : A study of bibliography and the book trade in relation to science, 2nd edn. {DUL}

Thorsen, Leif, 1972, **Public libraries in Denmark**, tr. by Megens Hay Larsen from Danish. {NASSDOC}

Tiihonen, Pertti, n.d., **Influence of television on the use of libraries**. {IIMC}

Tirkha, R.N. and Arneja, M.S., 1983, **Library development oriented education**. {ICA}

Titchler, Therea, 1926, **Cataloguing for small libraries**, 3rd edn. {ZHL}

Tiwari, Bhaskar Nath, n.d., **Adult education and libraries**. {AIU}

Tiwari, Bhaskar Nath, n.d., **Prodh siksha aur pustakalaya**. {NIEPA NIPCCD}

Tolly, Roy D., 1979, **Information choice and policies** : Proceedings : American society for information science annual meeting, 42nd, October 14-18, 1979, Minneapoles. {USIS}

Tomlinson, N., 1963, **Librarianship.** {NIH}

Tory, Bruce E., 1957, **Offset lithography**. {DUL}

Toser, Marie A., 1964, **Library manual** : A study work manual of lessons on the use of books and libraries, 6th edn. {USIS}

Tou, Julius T., 1969, ed., **Advances in information systems science**, 9 vols. {CRRI MHA DUL NASSDOC USIS}

Tou, Julius T. and Wilcox, Richard H., eds., n.d., **Computer and information science** : Collected papers on learning, adaptation and control in information systems. {DUL}

Tower, Isable L., comp., 1947, **Special library resources**, vol. 4. [Special Libraries Association, New York]. {CRRI}

Town, Laurence, 1973, **Bookbinding by hand for students and craftsmen**, 2nd edn. {BIS}

Townley, Helen M., 1978, **System analysis for information retrieval.** {BCL}

Townley, Helen M. and Goe, Ralph C., 1980, **Thesaurus-making** : Grow your own word-stock. {NASSDOC}

Trehan, G.L., 1965, **Administration and organisation of school libraries.** {NASSDOC}

Trehan, G.L., 1969, **Administration and organisation of college libraries in India.** {AIU DUL JNU SPA ZHL}

Trehan, G.L., 1975, **Learning and libraries in ancient India** : A study. {JNU}

Trehan, G.L., 1981, **Inside library India** : North meets South. {JNU NASSDOC}

Trehan, G.L., 1982, **Modern public library movement and services in India.** {JNU}

Trehan, G.L., 1985, **College library management** : Academic library system, services and use. {JNU}

Trehan, G.L. and Malhan, I.V., 1980, **School library management.** {NERC}

Trehan, G.L., et al, 1982, **Prospects of library services in India** : A study. {JNU}

Trezza, Alphonse F., 1982, **Toward a federal library and information services network** : A proposal. {USIS}

Trezza, Alphonse F., ed., 1967, **Library buildings** : Innovation for changing needs : Proceedings. {AIU}

Trinkner, Charles L., 1962, **Better libraries make better schools.** {JNU}

Tripathi, S.M., 1969, **Modern cataloguing theory and practice.** {AIU IIC IIT JNU}

Tripathi, S.M., 1976, **Adhunik granthalaya vargikaran** : Sidhantik vivechan. (Modern library classification : Theoretical analysis). {BIS}

Tripathi, S.M., 1983, **Adhunik granthalaya** : Vyavastha avam sanchalan ke mooltatva. {NASSDOC}

Trivedi, Dinkar, ed., 1973, **Directory of Indian publishers.** [Federation of Publishers and Booksellers Association in India]. {IIPA NASSDOC RTL UGC}.

Trollhani, Lilian and Wittmann, Alfred, 1964, **Dictionary of information processing**, including fields of application. {RTL}

Tull, Donald S. and Albaum, Gerald S., 1973, **Survey research** : A decisional approach. {NASSDOC}

Turabian, Kate L., 1966, **Manual for writers of term papers, theses and dissertations.** {DUL}

Turner, Mary C., 1961, **Bookman's glossary**, 4th edn. {DUL}

Turock, Betty J., 1982, **Serving the older adult** : A guide to library programs and information sources. {USIS}

Umapathy Setty, K. 1977, **Librarianship** : Change or status quo. {CRRI JNU}

Umapathy, K.S., 1978, **Information sources** : An international selective guide. {DUL ICA IIFT INSA}

Umapathy, K.S., 1984, **Problems in library management.** {DUL ICA ICHR ISI JNU NIEPA NIH NIPCCD}

Uppal, O.P., n.d., **Practical procedure of cataloguing.** {ICHR}

Uppal, O.P., n.d., **Practical procedure of classification.** {IIMC}

Uppal, O.P., 1987, **AACR2** : Practice and theory. {JNU NASSDOC}

Urquhart, J.A., 1976, **Relegation and stock control in libraries.** {DUL IIT ZHL}

Usmani, M. Adil, 1978, **Bibliographical services throughout Pakistan.** {ZHL}

Vaillancourt, Pauline M., 1980, **International directory of acronyms in library, information and computer sciences.** {NASSDOC USIS}

Vajpayee, Hanuman Prasad, 1958, **Pustakalaya Karyapadhati**. {JNU}

Vakata, Yuri, et al, 1979, **Organising local government documents collection**. [American Library Association]. {USIS}

Valls, J., 1974, **Pilot project on the mechanisation of documentation services in Asia** : Thailand. [UNESCO]. {NASSDOC*}

Van Gigch, John P., 1978, **Applied general systems theory**. {JNU}

Van Orden, Phyllis and Phillips, Edith B., eds., 1979, **Background readings in building library collections**, 2nd edn. {USIS}

Van Rijsbergen, C.J., 1979, **Information retrieval,** 2nd edn. {BCL CRRI DUL IEG MMTC NIH}

Van Winger, Peter and Davis, Stephen Paul, 1982, **Standard citation forms for published bibliographies and catalog used in rare book cataloguing**. [U.S. Library of Congress]. {NASSDOC}

Vanghan, John, ed., 1973, **Papers** : Advanced working seminar on national information policy and the impact of social and technological change on national information planning, Australia. {CRRI}

Vanners, Robert G., 1965, **Principles of punched card data processing.** {JNU}

Vanwijngaerden, Frans, ed., 1978, **Handbook on the international exchange of publications,** 4th edn, [UNESCO]. {JNU NASSDOC USIS}

Varma, A.K., 1984, **Trends in subject indexing.** {NASSDOC NMML}

Varma, A.K., 1986, **AACR2** : Entries and procedure. {NASSDOC}

Vasarhelyi, Paul, n.d., **DARE Equal : UNESCO computerised data retrieval system for documentation in the social and human sciences**. {NASSDOC}

Vashishth, C.P., 1967, **Documents of the UN and the specialised agencies** : A study of problems regarding their acquisition and organisation with special reference to India. (University of Delhi Department of Library and Information Science sessional project). {DUL}

Vashishth, C.P., ed., 1983, **Twenty years of Library Herald** : A cumulative index to Vols. 1-20, 1958-59 to 1981. [Delhi Library Association]. {IIT NASSDOC}

Vashishth, C.P., ed., 1986, **New education policy vis-a-vis library development** : Papers presented in the seminar held at New Delhi on February 13, 1986. [Indian Library Association]. {NASSDOC}

Vashishth, C.P., ed., 1986, **Quality in libraries**. [Indian Library Association]. {NASSDOC*}

Vashishth, C.P., ed., 1986, **School library development**. [Indian Library Association]. {NASSDOC*}

Vashishth, C.P., ed., 1987, **ILA members directory**. [Indian Library Association]. {NASSDOC}

Vashishth, C.P., ed., 1987, **Modernisation in libraries** : Seminar Papers : All India Library Conference, 33rd, December 28-31, 1987, Tiruchirapalli. [Indian Library Association]. {NASSDOC}

Vashishth, C.P., ed., 1989, **Library and information services in India** : Assessment and effectiveness. [Indian Library Association]. {NASSDOC}

Vashishth, C.P., ed., 1989, **Standardisation in library and information work and services**. [Indian Library Association]. {NASSDOC}

Vaswani, H.P., comp., 1964, **Books of India, 1963** : A reference catalogue of Indian book published in English in 1963. {NASSDOC}

Vaughan, Anthony, ed., 1979, **Studies in library management**, vol. 5. {DUL IIT}

Veaner, Allen B., 1970, **Evaluation of micropublications** : A handbook for librarians. [American Library Association]. {NASSDOC}

Veaner, Allen B., ed., 1977, **Studies in micropublishing**, 1853-1976. {USIS}

Venderborght, G., 1979, **Guidelines for preparation of texts of dissertations for their presentation and publication**. {DUL}

Venkatappaiah, V., 1982, **Public library system in Andhra Pradesh**. [Andhra University]. {NASSDOC}

Venkatappaiah, V., 1986, **Glossary of library and information science** : English-Telugu and Telugu-English. [Zilla Granthalaya Samstha, Machilipatnam]. {NASSDOC*}

Venkatappaiah, V. and Vashishth, C.P., 1990, **Indian library legislation**, 2 vols., Vol. 1 : Union Library Bills and Acts; Vol. 2 : State Library Bills and Acts. {NASSDOC}

Venkatappaiah, V., comp., n.d., **Library science literature in Andhra Pradesh, 1924-1989**. {NASSDOC*}

Venkatappaiah, V., ed., 1979, **March of library science** : Kaula festschrift : Papers presented in honour of Prof. P.N. Kaula. {CRRI ICA ICHR IIC IIFT INSA ISI JNU NCAER NIEPA ZHL}

Venkatappaiah, V., ed., 1989, **Papers** : Workshop on norms, guidelines and standards for public libraries. [Zilla Granthalaya Samstha, Eluru]. {NASSDOC*}

Venkatappaiah, V., et al, eds., 1990, **Dimensions of library and information science** : Kaula festschrift. {NASSDOC}

Venkatarangayya, M., ed., 1942, **Shree Iyyanki Venkata Ramanayya commemoration volume** : Presented to him on Shashtipurti celebration (60th birthday). {NASSDOC}

Varma, A.K., 1988, **Classified Catalogue Code** : Entries and procedure. {JNU}

Verma, Subash Chandra, 1977-78, **Library co-operation in India, 1977; 1978**. {NASSDOC}

Verma, Subash Chandra, 1985, **National library and information system**. {NASSDOC NMML}

Vernon, D.C., 1975, **Use of management and business literature**. {MMTC}

Vernon, Jackson William, 1988, **Studies in library resources.** {JNU}

Vernon, Ken, 1986, **Library and information services of management development institutions** : A practical guide. {NASSDOC}

Verona, Eva, 1971, **Statement of principles adopted at the international conference on cataloguing principles,** October 1961, Paris. [IFLA Committee on Cataloguing, London]. {NASSDOC}

Verona, Eva, 1975, **Corporate headings** : Their use in library catalogues and national bibliographies : A comparative and critical study. [International Federation of Library Associations and Institutions]. {JNU NASSDOC ZHL}

Verry, H.R., 1967, **Microcopying methods**, ed. by Gordon H. Wright. {DUL}

Vervliet, H.D.L., 1979, **Resource sharing of libraries in developing countries** : Proceedings : IFLA/UNESCO pre-session seminar for librarians from developing countries, August 30-September 3, 1977, [Antwerp University]. {NASSDOC}

Vett, Fritz, 1975, **The community college library**. {DUL USIS}.

Vickery, B.C., 1959, **Classification and indexing in science**. {CRRI DUL IIT NAI}

Vickery, B.C., 1960, **Faceted classification**. [Association of Special Libraries and Information Bureaux]. {CRRI}

Vickery, B.C., 1965, **On retrieval system theory**, 2nd edn. {CRRI DUL IIT}

Vickery, B.C., 1970, **Techniques of information retrieval**. {AIU BCL IEG IIMC INSA JNU}

Vickery, B.C., 1973, **Information systems**. {DUL ICA ISI MMTC NASSDOC}

Viet, Jean, 1973, **EUDISED multilingual thesaurus for information processing in the field of education**. {NASSDOC}

Viet, Jean, 1978, **Macrothesaurus for information processing in the field of economic and social development**. {JNU}

Viguers, Ruth Hill, 1964, **Margin for surprise** : About books, children and librarians. {USIS}

Vijaya Kumar, P., 1981, **Library literature in Telugu, 1915-1981**. {NASSDOC*}

Vishva Bandhu, n.d., **Catalogue of Vishvesharananda Vedic Research Institute manuscript collection**, 2 vols. {INSA}

Vishwanathan, C.G., 1955, **Introduction to public library organisation.** {NAI}

Vishwanathan, C.G., 1957, **High school library** : Organisation and administration. {DUL NERC}

Vishwanathan, C.G., 1959, **Cataloguing** : Theory and practice, 2nd edn. {CRRI NAI}

Vishwanathan, C.G., 1961, **An introduction to public library organisation,** 2nd edn. {SPA}

Viswanathan, C.G., 1961, **Public library operations and services** : A short manual. {CRRI IIT MHA NERC SPA ZHL}

Vishwanathan, C.G., 1965, **Cataloguing** : Theory and practice, 3rd edn. {ISI MMTC NASSDOC SPA ZHL}

Vishwanathan, C.G., 1970. **Cataloguing** : Theory and practice, 4th edn. {AIU ICA IIFT ISI MMTC NASSDOC NERC NIEPA SPA ZHL}

Viswanathan, C.G., 1972, **University libraries of India** : Principles and policy. {AIU DUL IIC JNU NIEPA NMML}

Vishwanathan, C.G., 1976, **Elements of information science.** {DUL NAI NIEPA}

Vishwanathan, C.G., 1978, **Introduction to public library organisation with special reference to India**. {NERC}

Vishwanathan, C.G., 1983, **Cataloguing** : Theory and practice, 5th edn. {ICHR IEG IIT MHA MMTC NCAER NCDC ZHL}

Viswandhan, C.G., 1985, **Public library** : Operations and services : A short manual, rev edn. {NASSDOC}

Viswanathan, C.G., 1988, **A book on books.** {NASSDOC}

Voegelin, C.F. and Voegelin, F.M., 1977, **Classification and index of the world's languages**. {JNU}

Voight, Melvin J. and Harris, Michael J., 1970-86, **Advances in librarianship**, 14 vols. {IEG NASSDOC NCAER NIH NMML USIS}

Voigt, Molvin J., n.d., **Scientist approaches to information**. [American Library Association]. {BIS}

Von, Bertalanffy, Ludwig, 1968, **General system theory** : Foundations, development, applications. {NASSDOC*}

Von Busse, Gisela, ed., 1964, **Handbook on the international exchange of publications**, 3rd edn. [UNESCO]. {NASSDOC NMML}

Vosper, Robert and Koops, Willram R.H., 1977, **Libraries for all** : A world of books and their readers : World congress on libraries for all, 50th, 1977, Brussels. [International Federation of Library Association and Institutions]. {IIT}

Vosper, Robert and Newskirk, Leone I., 1976, **National and international library planning**. {DUL}

Vyas, S.D., 1990, **Management of technical services in libraries**. {JNU}

Wainwright, Jane, 1975, **Computer provision in British libraries**. {JNU}

Waldo, Willis H., 1965, **Better report writing,** 2nd rev edn. {DUL}

Walford, A.J., ed., n.d., **Guide to reference material,** 3 vols. [Library Association, London]. {INSA NASSDOC NIPCCD ZHL}

Walker, Elinor, comp., 1969, **Book bait** : Detailed notes on adult books popular with young people. 2nd edn. [American Library Association]. {USIS}

Wall, Rayond Alwyn, ed., 1974, **Papers** : Seminar on mechanical engineering information : Provision and use, March 27-29, 1974, Loughborough. {BCL}

Wallace, Sarah Leslie, 1956, **Patrons are people** : How to be a model librarian, 2nd rev edn. [American Library Association]. {DUL USIS}

Wallace, Sarah Leslie, ed., 1962, **Friends of the library** : Organisation and activities. [American Library Association]. {NASSDOC USIS}

Wallick, Clair H., 1970, **Looking for ideas** : A display manual for libraries and bookstores. {USIS}

Walls, Chamberlin Mary, 1959, **Guide to art reference books**. {DUL}

Walsh, Patricia M., 1979, **Serials management and microforms.** {IIT}

Walton, Robert A., 1983, **Microcomputers** : A planning and implementation guide for librarians and information professionals. {JNU}

Waples, Douglas and Carnovsky, Leon, 1939, **Libraries and readers in the State of New York**. {NASSDOC*}

Waples, Douglas, et al, 1940, **What reading does to people**. {NAI}

Ward, Eads Martha and Marquardt, Dorothy A., 1964, **Authors of books for young people**. {DUL}

Ward, Patricia Layzell, 1966, **Women and librarianship** : An investigation into certain problems of library staffing. {DUL}

Wardle, D.B., 1971, **Document repair**. [Society of Archivists]. {NMML}

Warncke, Ruth, 1976, **Planning library workshops and institutes.** [American Library Association]. {USIS}

Warner, J., 1928, **Reference library methods**. {NAI}

Wasserman, Paul, 1965, **Librarian and the machine** : Observations on the applications of machines in administration of college and university libraries. {JNU}

Wasserman, Paul, 1972, **The new librarianship** : A challenge for change. {USIS}

Wasserman, Paul and Bundy, Mary Lee, eds., 1970, **Reader in library administration**. {DUL USIS}

Wasserman, Paul, ed., 1972, **Frontiers in librarianship** : Proceedings of Change Institute, 1969. [Change Institute, University of Maryland]. {JNU NIPCCD}

Wasserman, Paul, et al, eds, 1974, **LIST** : Library and information services today : An international registry of research and innovation, vol-4. {USIS}

Watson, James and Hill, Anne, 1986, **Dictionary of communication and media studies**. {JNU NASSDOC}

Weber, David C., 1976, **Century of cooperative programme among academic libraries**. {BIS}

Webster, O., 1965, **Read well and remember**. {IIT}

Wedgeworth, R., et al., eds., 1980, **ALA world encyclopaedia of library and information services**. [American Library Association]. {IIT NASSDOC NCERT NERC USIS}

Wegman, Edward, 1982, **International circulation of books**. [UNESCO]. {NASSDOC}

Weihs, Jean, 1989, **Non book materials** : The organisation of integrated collections, 3rd edn. [Canadian Library Association]. {NASSDOC}

Weinberg, Gerald M., 1971, **Psychology of computer programming.** {NASSDOC}

Weiner, Margery, 1974, **Answering any questions** : How to set up an information office. {BCL DUL}

Weisman, Herman M., 1972, **Information systems, services and centres**. {CRRI DUL NASSDOC USIS}

Weiss, Edward C., ed., 1977, **The many faces of information science**. {INSA JNU USIS}

Weiss, Harry B. and Carruthers, Ralph H., 1945, **Insect** : Enemies of books. {JNU}

Weiss, Irving and Weiss, Anne De Lavergne, eds., and comps., 1981, **Thesaurus of book digests, 1950-1980.** {USIS}

Welch, Helen, M., 1963, **Literature of technical services**. {DUL}

Wellard, J.H., 1937, **Book selection** : Its principles and practice. {NAI}

Wellard, James Howard, 1940, **The public library comes of age.** {CRRI}

Wellisch, H.H., ed., 1977, **The PRECIS index system** : Principles, applications and prospects : Proceedings : International PRECIS workshop, October 15-17, 1976, Maryland. {NASSDOC}

Wellisch, Hans and Wilson, Thomas D., n.d., **Subject retrieval in the seventies** : New directions. {ICHR}

Wellisch, J.B., et al, 1974, **Public library and federal policy**. {NIPCCD}

Wendel, Thomas M. and Williams, William H., 1969, **Introduction to data processing and COBOL**. {NASSDOC}

Werner, Mevissen, 1958, **Buchereibau** : Public library building. {DUL}

Wersig, Gernot and Neveling, Ulrich, comps., 1976, **Terminology of documentation**. [UNESCO]. {JNU NASSDOC NIPCCD ZHL}

Wessel, Andrew E., 1975, **Computer-aided information retrieval**. {BIS CRRI NIH USIS}

Wessel, Andrew E., 1976, **The social use of information ownership and access.** {BCL NASSDOC USIS}

Wessel, Andrew E., 1979, **Implementation of complex information system.** {CRRI IIT USIS}

West, Celeste and Katz, Elizabeth, eds., 1972, **Revolting librarians**. {USIS}

West, Roland, 1965, **Individualised reading instructions** : Its implication for teacher and librarian. {JNU}

Westin, Alen F. and Baker, Michal A., 1972, **Databanks in a free society** : Computers, record keeping and privacy : Report. [National Academy of Sciences, Washington]. {USIS}

Westlake, Duncan R., 1987, **GEAC** : A guide for librarians and system managers. {NASSDOC}

Whatley, Allen, ed., 1974, **Proceedings** : International and comparative librarianship group conference, June 28-July 1, 1974, {NASSDOC}

Whatley, H.A., ed., 1972, **British librarianship and information science**, 1966-70. {JNU NMML}

Whatmore, Geoffrey, 1964, **News information** : Organisation of press cuttings in the libraries of newspapers and broadcasting services. {IIMC IIT NMML SPA}

Whatmore, Geoffrey, n.d., **Modern news library** : Documentation of current affairs in newspaper and broadcasting libraries. {IIMC}

Wheeler, Helen R., 1968, **Basic book collection for the community college library.** {JNU}

Wheeler, Helen Rippier, 1965, **The community college library** : A plan for action. {DUL USIS}

Wheeler, Joseph L. and Githens, Alfred Morton, 1941, **The American public library building** : Its planning and design with special reference to its administration and service. [American Library Association]. {USIS}

Wheeler, Joseph L. and Goldhor, Herbert, 1962, **Practical administration of public libraries.** {IIT NMML USIS}

Whetton, Harry, ed., 1963, **Practical printing binding.** {INSA}

Whitchall, Tom, 1986, **Practical current awareness services from libraries.** {JNU}

White, Carl M., 1965, **Survey of the University of Delhi library**. {AIU DSSW DUL IEG IIC NASSDOC NERC SPA}

White, Carl M., ed., 1964, **Bases of modern librarianship** : A study of library theory and practice in Britain, Canada, Denmark, the Federal Republic of Germany and the United States. {IIT JNU NIPCCD NMML SPA}

White, Douglas, et al, 1969, **Operational research techniques,** Vol. 1 : Introduction. {NASSDOC}

White, Herbert S., 1984, **Managing the special library** : Strategies for success within the larger organisation. {NASSDOC}

Whitehouse, Franck, 1971, **Documentation** : How to organise and control information processes in business and industry. {JNU}

Whitehouse, Frank, 1978, **Systems documentation**. {JNU}

Whitestone, Patricia, 1977, **Photocopying in libraries** : The librarians speak. {IIT}

Whittaker, Kenneth, 1965, **Using libraries.** {CRRI IIT MFL}

Whittaker, Kenneth, 1972, **Using libraries** : An information guide for students and general users, 3rd edn. {ICA}

Wiio, Osmo, 1984, **Information and communication system** : Introduction to the concepts of information, communication and research. {JNU}.

Wijasuriya, D.E.K. and Huck-Tee, Lim, 1975, **Barefoot librarian** : Library development in Southeast Asia with special reference to Malaysia. {NIEPA}

Wilcox, Jerome K., ed., 1940, **Manual on the use of the state publications**. [American Library Association]. {CRRI}

Wild, Friedemann, 1972, **Libraries for schools and universities**. {CRRI}

Wildman, Panline G., 1980, **Order procedure**. {JNU}

Willemin, Silvere, 1966, **Technique of union catalogue** : A practical guide. [UNESCO]. {IIMC NASSDOC NERC}

Williams, Bernard J.S., 1970, **Miniaturised communications** : A review of microforms. [Library Association, London]. {NASSDOC}

Williams, Cecil B. and Stevenson, Allan H., 1951, **Research manual for college studies and papers**, rev. edn. {ZHL}

Williams, Edwin E., 1962, **Resources of Canadian university libraries for research in the humanities and social sciences** : Report of a survey. [National Conference of Canadian Universities and Colleges, Ottawa]. {DUL NASSDOC}

Williams, Edwin E., ed., n.d., **Problems and prospects of the research library**. {IEG}

Williams, Edwin Everitt, 1953. **Farminton plan handbook**. [Association of Research Libraries]. {USIS}

Williams, James G. and Pope, Elspeth, 1976, **Simulation activities in library, communication and information science**, ed. by Patrick R. Penland. {NASSDOC}

Williams, James G., et al, eds., 1972, **Classified Library of Congress subject headings**, 2 vols., V. 1: Classified list; V. 2: Alphabetical list. {IIT JNU NASSDOC NIH}

Williams, James G., et al, eds., 1982, **Classified Library of Congress subject headings**, 2nd edn., Part A : Classified list; Part B : Alphabetical list. {IIT JNU NASSDOC}

Williams, Martha E., et al, comps. and eds., 1982, **Computer readable data bases** : A directory and data sourcebook. 2 vols. [American Society for Information Science]. {USIS}

Williams, Patrick and Pearce, Joan T., 1978, **The vital network** : A theory of communication and society. {USIS}

Williams, Raymond, 1976, **keywords** : A vocabulary of culture and society {NMML}

Williams, William F., 1966, **Principles of automated information retrieval**. {JNU}

Williamson, Hugh, 1966, **Methods of book design** : The practices of an industrial craft, 2nd edn. {INSA}

Wilson, Brian J., ed., 1968-70, **ASLIB directory** : Information sources in medicine, the social sciences and the humanities. 2 vols. {IIT NASSDOC}

Wilson, John H., ed., 1973, **A world of information** : American society for information science meeting, 35th, October 23-26, 1972, Washington, D.C. {USIS}

Wilson, Louis Round, 1944, **Library planning** : A working memorandum. {DUL}

Wilson, Louis Round, et al, 1951, **Library in college instruction**. {ZHL}

Wilson, Louis Round and Tauber, Maurice F., 1945, **University library** : Its organisation, administration and functions, 2nd edn. {JNU}

Wilson, Patrick, 1977, **Public knowledge and private ignorance** : Towards a library and information policy. {CRRI USIS}

Wilson, Pauline, 1977, **Community elite and the public library** : The use of information in leadership. {IIT NIPCCD}

Wilson, T.D., 1971, **Introduction to chain indexing**. {BCL ICHR IIT JNU NASSDOC}

Wilson, Vivian, 1970, **Strategies for problem solving** : Programmed instruction. {NASSDOC}

Wilson, T.D. and Stephenson, J., 1969, **Dissemination of information** : An examination guidebook. {BIS DUL MFL NIPCCD}

Winchell, C.M., 1967, **Guide to reference books**, 8th edn, [American Library Association]. {JNU NASSDOC}

Winkler, Paul Walter, 1980, **Introduction to the Anglo-American cataloguing rules** : History and development. [American Library Association]. {USIS}

Winser, Marian Marley, 1959, **Handbook for library trustees**. {DUL}

Winstanley, Baroda, 1959, **School loan services.** {JNU}

Winterich, John Tracy and Randall, David A., 1966, **Primer of book collecting**. {DUL}

Winton, Harry N.M., comp. and ed., 1972, **Publications of the United Nations systems**. {NASSDOC}

Wisdom, Aline C., 1974, **Introduction to library services for library media technical assistants**. {ICA}

Withers, E.N., 1976, **Standards for library services** : An international survey. [UNESCO]. {BIS IEG JNU NASSDOC NIEPA NMML}

Withington, Frederic G., 1978, **Environment for systems programmes.** {JNU}

Wittmann, Alfred, and Klos, Joel, 1977, **Dictionary of data processing**, 3rd. rev edn. {NASSDOC}

Wofford, Azile, 1959, **School library at work** : Acquisition, organisation and maintenance of materials in the school library. {JNU}

Wofford, Azile, 1967, **Book selection for school libraries** {JNU}

Wolman, Perctz, 1975, **Guidelines on the conduct of a national inventory of current research and development projects**. {DUL}

Wolman, Yecheskel, 1983, **Chemical information** : A practical guide to utilisation. {CRRI}

Wolters, Marthin F., ed., 1972, **Key to the computer**, 2 vols. V. 1 : Text book; V. 2 : Training manual. {NASSDOC}

Wood, D.N. and Hamilton, D.R.L., 1967, **Information requirements of mechanical engineers** : Report of a recent survey. {DUL}

Woods, Lawrence A. and Pope, Nolan F., 1983, **Librarians' guide to microcomputer technology and applications.** {JNU NIEPA USIS}

Woodworth, David, comp., 1971, **Directory of publishers of British journals**. {NASSDOC}

Woodworth, David, ed., 1973, **Guide to current British journals**, Vol. 1, 2nd edn. [Library Association, London]. {NASSDOC}

Woodworth, David P., ed., 1982, **Current British journals, 1982.** [British Library Lending Division]. {NASSDOC}

Woolf, Harry, ed., 1961, **Quantification** : A history of the meaning of measurement in the natural and social sciences. {NASSDOC}

Worth, Wilfred Ash, 1979, **Special librarianship**. {JNU}

Woy, James, ed., 1980, **Encyclopaedia of business information sources**. {USIS}

Wright, Alice E., 1973, **Library clerical workers and wagers**. {BIS}

Wright, Gordon H., ed., 1966, **Library in colleges of commerce and technology.** {DUL IIT}

Wulfekoelter, G., ed., 1961, **Acquisition work** : Process involved in building library collections. {DUL IEG SPA}

Wyer, James I., 1930, **Reference work**. [American Library Association]. {ZHL}

Wyman, Forest Paul, 1970, **Simulation modelling** : A guide to using SIMSCRIPT. {NASSDOC}

Wynar, Bodhan, 1962, **Syllabus for research methods in librarianship**. {DUL}

Wynar, Bohdan, S., 1967, **Introduction to bibliography and reference work** : A guide to materials and sources. {JNU}

Wynar, Bohdan, S. 1967, **Introduction to cataloguing and classification**, 3rd edn. {IIT}

Wynar, Bohdan S., 1968, **Library acquisition** : A classified bibliographic guide to the literature and reference tools. {JNU}

Wynar, Bohdan S., 1974, **Research methods in library science** : A bibliographic guide with tropical outlines. {NASSDOC}

Wynar, Bohdan S., 1976, **Best reference books**. {JNU}

Wynar, Bohdan S., et al, eds., 1971, **American reference books annual.** {NASSDOC}

Wynar, Bohdan S., et al, eds., 1980, **Introduction to cataloguing and classification**, 6th edn. {USIS}

Wynar, Bohdan S., et al, eds., 1985, **Introduction to cataloguing and classification**. (Library Science Text Series). {NASSDOC}

Yadubaities, E.A., ed., 1981, **English-Russian glossary of computer systems and networks terminology**. {NASSDOC}

Yefimova, A.N., et al, eds., 1974, **Books in the service of society** : Collection of articles of Soviet authors. [Ministry of Culture of the USSR, Main Library Inspectorate]. {NASSDOC}

Yehawine, Wayne S., ed., 1958, **Contemporary library design.** {DUL}

Yong, Heartsill, et al, eds., 1983, **The ALA glossary of library and information science.** [American Library Association]. {USIS}

Yorke, D.A., 1977, **Marketing the library service,** ed. by A. Wilson. [Library Association, London]. {JNU}

Young, M.L., et al, eds., 1975, **Subject directory of special libraries and information centres.** {IIFT}

Young, M.L. and Young, H.C., eds., 1974-79, **Directory of special libraries and information centres 1974; 1979.** {IIFT}

Young, M.L. and Young, H.C., eds., 1981-83, **Directory of special libraries and information centres 1981 to 1983.** {USIS}

Young, Micki Jo, et al, 1978, **Introduction to minicomputers in federal libraries.** [U.S. Library of Congress]. {USIS}

Youssef, Leon A., 1975, **System analysis and design.** {JNU}

Yrumpeter, Marg C. and Rounds, Richards, 1985, **Basic budgeting practices for librarians.** {JNU}

Zell, Hans M., 1975, **African books in print** : An Index by author, title and subject, Pt. 1: English language and African language. {NASSDOC}

Zemanck, H., 1972, **Skyline of information processing** : Proceedings of the 10th anniversary of IFIP, Amsterdom. {JNU}

Zemsky, Robert, 1979, **Microfiche reader.** {USIS}

Zidoemba, Dominique, 1977, **Directory of documentation, libraries and archives services in Africa**, 2nd edn. [UNESCO]. {JNU NASSDOC}

Zimmerman, Irena, 1971, **Current national bibliographies of Latin America** : A state-of-the-art study. [Centre for Latin America, University of Florida]. {NASSDOC}

Ziskind, Sylvia, 1977, **Reference readiness** : A manual for librarians and students. {DUL NASSDOC}

Zubair, Mohamad, 1951, **Practical cataloguing.** {ZHL}

Zubair, Mohamad and Agrawal, S.P., 1954, **Pustak sankhya praveshika** : Introduction to book numbers in Hindi. {NASSDOC}

Zwirn, Jerrold, 1983, **Congressional publications** : A research guide to legislation, budgets and treaties. {USIS}

5

ADDED ENTRIES TO AUTHOR APPROACH*

5.1 PERSONAL AUTHOR

Abdul Aziz
See Aziz, Abdul

Aconib, H.M., *jt author*
See Quinn, J.H. and Aconib, H.M.

Affen, Hauser William H., *jt author*
See Lewis, Chester M. and Affen, Hauser William H.

Afflerback, Lois, *compiler and editor*
See Bry, Ilse, 1977

Aggarwal, J.C., *jt author*
See Agrawal, S.P. and Aggarwal, J.C.

Agrawal, Binod C., *jt author*
See Thakur, B.S. and Agrawal, Binod C.

Agrawal, S.P.
See also Agrawal, Suren

Agrawal, S.P., *jt author*
See Aggarwal, J.C., and Agrawal, S.P.; Satija, M.P. and Agrawal, S.P.; Zubair, Mohamad and Agrawal, S.P.

Agrawal, Suren
See also Agrawal, S.P.

Ahmed, Mushtaq
See Mushtaq Ahmed

Albaum, Gerald S., *jt author*
See Tull, Donald S. and Albaum, Gerald S.

Alexander, Arthur J., *jt author*
See Newhouse, Joseph P. and Alexander, Arthur J.

Allan, Ann, *jt editor*
See Allison, Anne Manne

Allen, C.G., *jt editor*
See Aitchison, Jean and Allen, C.G.

Allen, Loran, *jt author*
See Allen, Kenneth W. and Allen, Loren

Alley, Brian, *jt author*
See Cargill, Jennifer S. and Alley, Brian

Aman, Mohammed M., *jt author*
See Abdul Haq, A.M. and Aman, Mohammed, M.

Amil El-Benhawy Mohamad
See El-Benhawy, Mohamad Amil

Anand, S.K., *jt author*
See Dhir, S.C. and Anand, S.K.

Anderson, F. Douglas, *jt author*
See Tait, James A. and Anderson, F. Douglas

Apple, Nick, *jt author*
See Gurney, Gene and Apple, Nick

Archer, John, *jt author*
See Lydenberg, Harry Miller and Archer, John

Arneja, M.S., *jt author*
See Tirkha, R.N. and Arneja, M.S.

Artandi, Susan, *editor*
See Gardin, J.C.

Asheim, Lester, *jt author*
See Berelson, Bernard and Asheim, Lester

---

* Note: *See* and *See also* refer to entries in main Author Approach.
See under and *See also under* refer to entries in the Section.
Based on catalogue entry pattern of libraries surveyed.

Richard H., eds.
Wilkinson, Joseph W., *jt author*
See Emerick, Paul L., and Wilkinson, Joseph W.
Williams, E.E., *editor*
See Buck, Paul, 1967
Williams, Wiley J., *jt author*
See Cheney, Frances Neel and Williams, Wiley J.
Williams, William H., *jt author*
See Wendel, Thomas M. and Williams, William H.
Wilson, A., *editor*
See Yorke, D.A., 1977
Wilson, Louis Round
See Tauber, Mauris Falcolm
Wilson, Thomas D., *jt author*
See Wellisch, Hans and Wilson, Thomas D.
Winberg, Gerald M., *jt author*
See Leeds, Herbert D. and Winberg, Gerald M.
Winger, Howard W., *jt author*
See Ennis, Philip H. and Winger Howard W.
Winger, Peter Van
See Van Winger, Peter
Wison, T.D., *jt author*
See Jeffreys, A.E. and Wison, T.D.
Wittmann, Alfred, *jt author*
See Trollhani, Lilian and Wittmann, Alfred
Wood, Judith B., *jt author*
See Saracevic, Tefka and Wood, Judith B.
Wooster, Harold, *jt editor*
See Taube, Mortimer and Wooster, Harold, eds.
Wynar, Lubomyr R., *jt author*
See Murfin, Marjorie E. and Wynar, Lubomyr R.

Yelland H., *jt editor*
See Coward, R.E. and Yelland, H., eds.
Young, H.C., *jt editor*
See Young, M.L. and Young, H.C., eds.

Zeman, Jiri, *jt editor*
See Kubat, Libor and Zeman, Jiri, eds.

5.2 CORPORATE AUTHOR

5.2.1 Institutions

A A L
= Association of Assistant Librarians
A A L L
= American Association of Law Libraries
A A S
= Association of Asian Studies
A A S S R E C
= Association of Asian Social Science Research Councils
A C E
= American Council of Education
A C L S
= American Council of Learned Societies
A C U L
= Association of College and University Libraries
A D I
= American Documention Institute
A G L I S
= Association of Government Librarians and Information Scientists (formerly GILA)
A I P
= American Institute of Physics
A I U
= Association of Indian Universities
A L A
= American Library Association
A L P
See Anon, 1987
A L S D
= Academy of Library Science and Documentation Hyderabad

A L T A
= American Libraries Trustee Association
A M A
= American Management Association
A M U
= Aligarh Muslim University (Aligarh University)
A N P A
= American Newspaper Publishers' Association
A N S I
= American National Standards Institute
A N S I N B S
= American National Standards Institute National Bureau of Standards
A P
= Andhra Pradesh (India)
A P A U
= Andhra Pradesh Agricultural University
A P I
= American Petroleum Institute
A P I N E S S
= Asia Pacific Information Network in Social Sciences
A P L A
= Andhra Pradesh Library Association
A P O U
= Andhra Pradesh Open Unversity
A P P L A
= Andhra Pradesh Public Library Association
A S I S
= American Society of Information Science
A S L I B
= Association of Special Libraries and Information Bureaux
A S P O
= American Society of Planning Officials
Academy of Art and Sciences, Cambridge
See Daedalus, 1976
Academy of Library Science and Documentation, Hyderabad
See Anon, 1981
Air Force Office of Scientific Research (U.S)
See Anon, 1965
Aligarh University Library
See Razvi, M.H. 1973
Allahabad University, Department of Education
See Anon, n.d.
American Academy of Political and Social Sciences
See Lamberton, Donald M., ed., 1974
American Association for State and Local History
See Kane, Lucile, M., 1966
American Association of Law Libraries
See Jessup, Libby,F., et al, 1962
American Association of School Libraries
See Anon, 1960
American Association of School Libraries, Children's Services Division,
See Anon, 1974
American Association of State Libraries, Standards Revision Committee
See Anon, 1970
American Council of Education
See Baumel, W.J. and Marcus, M., n.d.
American Council of Learned Societies Devoted to Humanistic Studies, Committee on Research Libraries
See Anon, 1969
American Institute of Physics
See Anon, 1969
American Library Association
See Akers, Susan Grey, 1944; Anon, n.d., Anon, 1911; Anon, 1931; Anon, 1942; Anon, 1948; Anon, 1951; Anon, 1956; Anon, 1959; Anon, 1960; Anon, 1961; Anon, 1963; Anon, 1964; Anon, 1964-72; Anon, 1965; Anon, 1966; Anon, 1967; Anon, 1969; Anon, 1974; Anon, 1975; Anon, 1976; Anon, 1977; Anon, 1978; Anon, 1979; Anon, 1980; Anon, 1981; Anon, 1982; Archer, H. Richard, ed., 1965; Asheim, Lester, 1957; Beetle, Clara, 1970; Black, Dorathy M.,

1975; Bobinski, George S., 1969; Borko, Harold, ed., 1973; Braden, Irene A., 1970; Branscomb, Harvie, 1940; Brooks, James and Draper, James, 1979; Cheney Frances Neel, 1980; Cheney, Frances Neel and Williams, Wiley J., 1971; Clack, Doris Hargrett, 1979; Corrigan, Dorothy D., 1967; Danton J. Periam, 1973; Downs, Robert B., 1956; Downs Robert B., 1978; Drury, Francis K.W., 1930; Eastlick, John T., ed., 1971; Ellis, Lee Robert, 1966; Fang, Josephine Rise and Songe, Alice H., 1973; Fargo, Lucile F., 1945; Fargo, Lucile F., 1947; Fleischer, Eugene B., 1978; Ford, Stephen, 1973; Gardiner, Jewel, 1954; Gawrwcki, Drahoslav, 1968; Geer, H.T., 1955; Gliden, Sophia Hall, 1942; Grove, Pearce S. and Clement, Evelyn G., eds., 1972; Grove, Pearce S., eds., 1975; Guthman, Judith, ed., 1969; Hanley, E.R., 1939; Herbert, Clara W., 1939; Horton, Carolyn, 1967; Horton, Carolyn, 1969; Hutchins, Margaret, 1944; Hyman, Richanrd Joseph, 1982; Jackson, Sidney L., et al, eds., 1976; Jain, T.C, 1971; Jennings, Jerdson, T., 1930; Jesse, W.H., 1952; Josey, E.J., ed., 1979; Katz, William, A. and Swarf, Roderick D., eds., 1964; Lahood, Charles G. and Sullivan, Robert C., 1975; Leong C.L.H., 1989; Lipsman, Claire K., 1972; Macleish, Archibald 1971; Maloney, James J., 1983; Mann, Margaret, 1943; Martin, Lowell A., et al, 1969; Mathews, Anne J. 1983; Matthews Joseph, R., 1980; Maxwell, Margaret F., 1980; Mc Collough, Ethel Farguhar and Van Buren, Maud, 1931; Mc Diarmid, W.W., et al., 1942; Merril, W.S., 1939; Moore, Everett L., 1964; Mosher, Frederic J., 1954; Myers, Gerald E., 1977; Osborn, Andrew D., 1973; Osborn, Andrew D., 1980; Perkins, David, ed., 1979; Plaster, C.D., 1939; Pöole, Frazer, G. and Trezza, Alponse, F., eds., 1969; Potter, William Gray and Sirkin, Arlne Farber, eds., 1981; Powell, Judith W. and Lelieuvre, Robert B., 1979; Rodgers, Frank, comp., 1971; Roth, Harold, L., ed., 1964; Rowley, J.E. and Rowley, Petter J., 1981; Rue, Eloise and Laplanie Effie, 1952; Rufsvold, Margaret I., 1949; Ruggles, Miville J. and Swank, Paynard C., 1962; Saffady, William, 1983; Salmon, Stephen R., ed., 1962; Saual, Margaret, and Melcher, Daniel, 1971; Schimmelpfeng, Richard H. and Cook, C. Donald, 1968; Seely, Pauline A., ed., 1968; Sharify, Nasser, 1959; Shaw, Charles B., comp., 1940; Shera, Jesse H. and Egan, M.E, 1956; Shores, Louis, 1954; Sieburth, J.F. 1988; Sinclair, Dorothy, 1965; Smith, Lillian H., n. d.; Spreitzer, Francis, ed., 1985; Stenstrom, Ralph H., 1970; Stone, Elizabeth W., ed., 1971; Syenawine, Wayne, n.d.; Thompson, Elizabeth H., 1943; Thomposn, Elizabeth, H., 1971; Thomson, Sarah Katharin, 1970; Thomson, Sarah Katharin, 1979; Vakata, Yuri, et al, 1979; Veaner, Allen B., 1970; Voigt, Melvin J., n.d.; Waker, Elinor, comp, 1969; Wallace, Sarah Leslie, 1956; Wallace, Sarah Leslie, ed., 1962; Warncke, Ruth, 1976; Wedgeworth, R., et al, eds., 1980; Wheeler, Joseph L. and Githens, Alfred Morton 1941; Wilcox, Jerome K., ed., 1940; Winchell, C.H., 1967; Winkler, Paul Walter, 1980; Wyer, James I., 1930; Yong, Heartsill, et al, eds., 1983

American Library Association, Committee on Inter Library Co-operation

See Anon, 1967

Finish Standards Association
See Anon, n.d.
Foreign Area Meterials Centre, University of the State of New York
See Morehouse, Ward, ed., 1965
Foreign Trade Library
See Sircar, Pankit, 1970

GATT
= General Agreement on Tariffs and Trade
GATT
See Anon, 1978
GILA
Government of India Libraries Association *(now changed to* AGLIS = Association of Governemnt Librarians And Information Scientists)
Gage Balecocl and Associates, Incorporated
See Anon, 1963
Government Museum, Madras
See Anon, 1953
Government of India Librarians Association
See under Association of Government Librarians and Information Scientists
Graduate School of Business Administration Library, Harvard University
See Anon, 1960
Graduate School of Library Science, New Brunswick
See Stevens, Norman D., n.d.,
Graduate Schoole of Library Science, New Jersey
See Gordin, J.C., 1965
Great Britain
See under United Kingdon
Gujarat Granthalaya Seva Sangh, Ahmedabad
See Anon, 1985
Gulbarga University, Gulbarga
See Asundi, A.Y., 1983; Gunjal, S.R. and Sangam, S.L., 1986; Gunjal, S.R. and Sangam, S.L., 1987
Gurudev Liberary Association, Hubli
See Deshpande, K.S., 1958

HMSO
= Her/His Majesty Stationary Office
HMSO, London
See Anon, 1962; Anon, 1970-71
Hamdard National Foundation, Karachi
See Anon, 1965; Anon, 1971
Harvard University, Graduate School of Business Administration Library
See Anon, 1960
Herald of Library Science (Periodical)
See Lal, S.S., comp., 1985
Horn Book Magazine (Periodical)
See Miller, Bertha M. and Field, Elinor W., eds., 1955; Miller, Bertha Mahony and Field, Elinor Whitney, eds., 1957
Hungarian Academy of Science
See Anon, 1986

IASLIC
= Indian Association of Special Libraries and Information Centres
IATLIS
= Indian Association of Teachers of Library and Information Science
ICA
= International Cooperative Alliance
ICAR
= Indian Council of Agricultural Research
IDOC
= *See* Forubert, Charles Henri, 1982
IDL Chemicals Limited, Hyderabad
See Anon, 1976
IEA
= International Economic Association
IENS
= Indian and Eastern Newspaper Society
IFIP
= International Federation of Information Processing
IFLA
= Inertnational Federation of Library Associations And Institutions
ILA
= Indian Library Association
INSDOC
= Indian National Scientific Doumentation Centre

University of Tennessee Library
See Anon, 1967
Uttar Pradesh Government Press
See Anon, 1967

Vishvesharananda Vedic Research Institute, Hoshiarpur
See Vishva Bandhu, n.d.
Vrindaban Research Institute
See Gupta, R.D., 1970

World Bank
See Anon, 1983

World Health Organisation
See Anon, 1967
World Trade Centre Association
See Anon, 1977

Zilla Granthalaya Samstha, Eluru
See Venkatappaiah, V., 1989
Zilla Granthalaya Samatha, Machilipatnam
See Anon, 1982; Anon, 1985; Venkatappaiah, V., 1986

5.2.2 Meetings

AAS
= Association of Asian Studies
AASSREC
Assiociation of Asian Social Science Research Councils
AASSREC Regional Meeting of Experts (jointly with UNESCO) to develop Asia Pacific Information Network in Social Sciences, May 12-16, 1986, Bangkok
See Anon, 1986
ADI
= American Documentation Institute
ALA
= American Library Association
ALA Conference on Intellectual Freedom, 2nd, June 20-21, 1953
See Mosher, Frederic J., ed., 1954
ALTA
= American Libraries Trustee Association
ANSINBS Symposium on International Stardard and ISONET,
See Jenssen, Gudbrand, n.d.
A.P.
= Andhra Pradesh (India)
APINESS
= Asia Pacific Information Network in Social Sciences
ASIS
= American Society of Information Science
ASLIB
= Association of Special Libraries and Information Bureaux
ASLIB Conference on Informatics
1973, Durham
See Anon, 1973,
1974, Oxford
See Horsnell, Verina, ed., 1974
1975, Cambridge
See Anon, 1975
ASLIB Meeting on Planning and Equipment of Special Libraries, April 6, 1946, London
See Anon, 1947
ASLIB Seminer for Information Planners and Industry, May 13-14, 1976, Boaconfield
See Anthony, Lawrence James, ed., 1976
Advanced Working Seminar on National Information Policy and the Impact of Social and Technological Change on National Information Planning, Australia
See Vanghan, John, ed., 1973
All India Conference of Indian Association of Special Libraries and Information Centres, 13th, 1981, Waltaire
See Anon, 1981; Kapoor, S.K., et al, eds., n.d.
See also under IASLIB Conference
All India Library Conference
2nd, 1935, Lucknow
See Anon, 1935
5th, April 4-6, 1942, Bombay

1979, Illinois
See Anon, 1979; Lancaster, F.W., 1980

Library Association (London). Auniversary Conference, 15th, 1927, Edinburg
See Anon, 1927

Library Building and Equipment Institute, July 6-8, Kent
See Roth, Harold, L. ed., 1964

Library Building Institute,
See Anon, n.d.

Library Building Institute, July 12-13, 1963, Chicago
See Katz, William A. and Swarf, Roderick., ed., 1964

Library Building Institute and American Libraries Trustee Association Workshop, 1965, Detroit
See Shaw, Charles B. comp., 1940

Library Education Centenary Seminar jointly organised by ILA-AISLIC-GILA-IATLIS, October 10-12, 1987, Nagpur
See Kumar, P.S.G., ed., 1987

Library Equipment Institute, 2nd, 1967, St. Louis
See Poole, Frazer, G., ed., 1965

Library Institute, July 29, August 9, 1940, Chicago,
See Randall, William, ed., 1949

Library Seminar on Research in the Social Sciences, January 2-4, 1959,
See Ranganathan, S.R. and Girja Kumar, 1960

Malmo Seminar on Libraries in Adult and Fundamental Education,
See Houghton, Cyril O., ed., 1957

Meeting of American Society of Information Science,
35, October 23-26, 1972, Washington, D.C.
See Wilson, John H., ed., 1973
42nd, October 14-18, 1979, Minneapoles
See Tolly, Roy D., 1979
44th, 1981
See Lunin, Lois F., et al, 1981

Meeting of Committee on American Library Resources, Association of Asian Studies, 10th,
See Anon, 1967

Meeting of Experts on the National Planning of Library Services in Asia, December 11-19, 1967, Colombo
See Anon, 1968

Meeting of IATUL, 6th, 1975
See Lincoln, Cynthia Mary, ed., 1976

Meeting of Supervisors of Library and Documentation Schools in the Asian Region, Banagalore
See Anon, 1976

Meeting on Planning and Equipment of Special Libraries,
April 6, 1949, London
See Anon, 1947

Micrographic Congress(India), 2nd, January 20-22, 1988 New Delhi
See Anon, 1988

Microworkshop on Staff Development, June 28, 1970, Detroit
See Stone, Elizabeth W., ed., 1971

Morecamb Conference, April 16, 1972
See Bloomfield, B.C., 1972

NATO
= North Atlantic Treaty Organization

NATO Conference on Visual Presentation of Information,
September 4-8, 1978, Birmingham
See Easterby, Ronald, ed., 1978

NISSAT
= National Information System in Science and Technology

NISSAT Trainning Course on Systems Analysis for Information Sciences, December 12-23, 1978, New Delhi
See Thiagrajan, R., n.d.

Nagpur Seminar
See Kumar, P.S.G, ed., 1985; Kumar, P.S.G., ed., 1987; Kumar, P.S.G., ed., 1988

National Colloquium on Information Retrieval, 2nd,
See Rubinoff, Morris, ed., 1965

National Conference of Canadian Universities and Colleges, Ottawa

6

LIBRARY INDEX

{AIU}
Association of Indian Universities
[Formerly Inter-University Board of India and Ceylon]
AIU House, 16, Kotla Road
New Delhi-110002

{BCL}
British Council Library
British High Commission
AIFACS Building, Rafi Marg
New Delhi-110001

{BIS}
Bureau of Indian Standards
[Formerly Indian Standards Institution]
9 Bahadur Shah Zafar Marg
New Delhi-110002

{CPR}
Centre for Policy Research
Dharma Marg, Chanakayapuri
New Delhi-110021

{CRRI}
Central Road Research Institute
Delhi-Mathura Road
New Delhi-110020

{DEPT}
Department of Library and Information Science
University of Delhi
Delhi-110007

{DSSW}
Delhi School of Social Work
University of Delhi
3, University Road
Delhi-110007

{DUL}
Delhi University Library System
Central Library
University of Delhi
Delhi-110007

{GPF}
Gandhi Peace Foundation
221/223 Deendayal Upadhyaya Marg
New Delhi-110002

{ICA}
International Cooperative Alliance
Regional Office and Education Centre for South East Asia,
Post Box No. 7011
New Delhi-110065

{IAMR}
Institute of Applied Manpower Research
Indraprastha Estate
New Delhi-110002

{ICCR}
Indian Council for Cultural Relations
Azad Bhavan
Indraprastha Estate
New Delhi-110002

{ICHR}
Indian Council of Historical Research
35, Ferozeshah Road
New Delhi-110001

{ICWA}
Indian Council of World Affairs
Sapru House
Barakhamba Road
New Delhi-110001

{IDSA}
Institute of Defence Studies and Analysis
Sapru House
Barakhamba Road
New Delhi-110001

{IEG}
Institute of Economic Growth
University Enclave
Delhi-110007

{IIC}
India International Centre
40, Max Mueller Marg
New Delhi-110003

{IIFT}
Indian Institute of Foreign Trade
B-21, Institutional Area, South of IIT
New Delhi-110016

{IIMC}
Indian Institute of Mass Communication
Sector XIII, Institutional Area
Shaheed Jit Singh Marg
New Delhi-110067

{IIPA}
Indian Institute of Public Administration
Indraprastha Estate
New Delhi-110002

{IIT}
Indian Institute of Technology
Central Library
Hauz Khas
New Delhi-110016

{ILI}
Indian Law Institute
Bhagwan Das Road
New Delhi-110001

{INSA}
Indian National Science Academy
Bahadur Shah Zafar Marg
New Delhi-110002

{ISI}
Indian Statistical Institute
Delhi Centre
7 S.J.S. Sansanwal Marg
New Delhi-110016

{JNU}
Jawaharlal Nehru University
New Mehrauli Road
New Delhi-110067

{MFL}
Ministry of Finance Library
North Block
New Delhi-110001

{MHA}
Ministry of Home Affairs Library
North Block
New Delhi-110001

{MMTC}
Minerals and Metals Trading Corporation of India
Express Building, Post Box 7051
Bahadur Shah Zafar Marg
New Delhi-110002

{NAI}
National Archives of India
Janpath
New Delhi-110001

{NASSDOC} {NASSDOC}*
National Social Science Documentation Centre
ICSSR, 35 Ferozeshah Road
New Delhi-110001

* Indicates D.R. Kalia collection and S.P. Agrawal collection donated to the library. These collections were not fully processed by the time this survey was conducted.

{NCAER}
National Council of Applied Economic Research
Parisila Bhawan
Indraprastha Estate
New Delhi-110002

{NCDC}
National Cooperative Development Corporation
4, Siri Institutional Area
New Delhi-110016

{NCERT}
National Council of Educational Research and Training
NIE Campus
Sri Aurobindo Marg
New Delhi-110016

{NERC}
Raja Rammohan Roy National Educational Resources Centre
1-W-3 Curzon Road Barracks
Kasturba Gandhi Marg
New Delhi-110001

{NIEPA}
National Institute of Educational Planning and Administration
17-B, Aurobindo Marg
New Delhi-110016

{NIH}
National Institute of Health and Family Welfare
National Documentation Centre
New Mehrauli Road
New Delhi-110067

{NIPCCD}
National Institute of Public Cooperation and Child Development
5, Siri Institutional Area
New Delhi-110016

{NMML}
Nehru Memorial Museum and Library
Teen Murti House
New Delhi-110011

{RTL}
Rattan Tata Library
Delhi School of Economics
Univeristy of Delhi
Delhi-110007

{SPA}
School of Planning and Architecture
4, Block B,
Indraprastha Estate
New Delhi-110002

{TDA}
Trade Development Authority
16, Sansad Marg
Bank of Baroda Bldg.
P.O. Box 767
New Delhi-110001

{UGC}
University Grants Commission
Bahadur Shah Zafar Marg
New Delhi-110002

{USIS}
United States Information Service
American Centre Library
24, Kasturba Gandhi Marg
New Delhi-110001

{ZHL}
Dr. Zakir Husain Library
Jamia Millia Islamia,
Jamia Nagar
New Delhi-110025

CICIL LIST

CONCEPTS IN COMMUNICATION, INFORMATICS & LIBRARIANSHIP (CICIL)

General Editor: S.P. AGRAWAL

CICIL-1 Development of Library Services in India: Social Science Information
S.P. Agrawal Rs. 150

CICIL-2 Development of Documentation in India: Social Science Information
S.P. Agrawal Rs. 250

CICIL-3 UNESCO and Social Sciences: Retrospect and Prospect
S.P. Agrawal and **J.C. Aggarwal** Rs. 250

CICIL-4 INDIANA : A Bibliography of Bibliographical Sources
M.K. Jain Rs. 200

CICIL-5 Dimensions of Library and Information Science: Kaula Festschrift
V. Venkatappaiah (Eds.) Rs. 600

CICIL-6 Book Numbers: Some Indian Methods
M.P. Satija and **S.P. Agrawal** Rs. 100

CICIL-7 National Policy for University Libraries in India: Problems and Perspectives
N.B. Inamdar and **L.S. Ramaiah** (Ed.) Rs. 250

CICIL-8 Media Utilisation for the Development of Women and Children
B.S. Thakur and **Binod C. Agrawal** Rs. 150

CICIL-9 Terrorism: An Annotated Bibliography
Susheela Bhan (Ed.) Rs. 275

CICIL-10 Transnational Library Relations: The Indo-American Experience
M.B. Konnur Rs. 175

CICIL-11 Geography of Marketing and Commercial Activities in India (Documentation on Research Information)
R.S. Dixit Rs. 130

CICIL-12 Information India 1988: Global View
S.P. Agrawal and **J.C. Aggarwal** Rs. 200

CICIL-13 Women's Education in India: Historical Review, Present Status and Perspective Plan
S.P. Agrawal and **J.C. Aggarwal** Rs. 360

CICIL-14 Cultural Communication in India: Role and Impact of Phonograms
J.M. Ojha (in press)

CICIL-15 Second Historical Survey of Educational Development in India: Select Documents 1985-1989
S.P. Agrawal and **J.C. Aggarwal** Rs. 490

CICIL-16 Documentation Encyclopaedia of UNESCO and Education
J.C. Aggarwal and **S.P. Agrawal** Rs. 800 (set of 2 parts)

CICIL-17 Attitude Towards Information: A Study of Post-Graduate Teachers and Researchers in Social Sciences
N.G. Satish (in press)

CICIL-18 Librarianship and Bureaucratic Organisation: A Study in the Sociology of Library Profession in India
P.K. Jayaswal Rs. 175

CICIL-19 Literature Search
K.A. Isaac Rs. 150

CICIL-20 Child Education in India: Index to Scholarly Writings in Indian Educational Journals and Newspapers since independence
S.P. Agrawal and **Naresh Kanta** Rs. 100

CICIL-21 Lok Sabha and Vidhan Sabha Elections in India 1989 & 1990: Process and Results with Comparative Study of Manifestos
S.P. Agrawal and **J.C. Aggarwal** Rs. 250

CICIL-22 Islamic Studies in India: A Survey of Human, Institutional and Documentary Sources
Mohamed Taher Rs. 180

CICIL-23 Panchayati Raj: An Annotated Bibliography
N.B. Inamdar, N.G. Satish and **Anil Takalkar** 290

CICIL-24 Information India 1989-90: Global View
S.P. Agrawal and **J.C. Aggarwal** Rs. 500

CICIL-25 First Handbook of Psychological and Social Instruments
Udai Pareek and **T. Venkateswara Rao** (in press)

CICIL-26 Educational and Social Uplift of Backward Classes: At What Cost and How? Mandal Commission and After
S.P. Agrawal and **J.C. Aggarwal** Rs. 275

CICIL-27 Mass Media and New Horizons: Impact of TV & Video an Urban Milieu **H.R. Trivedi** Rs. 180

CICIL-28 Indian Writings on Education : An Indicator to Indian Educational Journals Grouped by Subject Deseriptors 1979 to 1986 (in two parts) **S.P. Agarwal** Rs. 900 (per set)

CICIL-29 Nation in Crisis
S.P. Agrawal and **J.C. Aggarwal** Rs. 200

CICIL-30 Information India 1990-91: Global View
S.P. Agrawal and **J.C. Aggarwal** Rs. 500

CICIL-31 Development of University Libraries in India After Independence
O.P. Gupta Rs. 270

CICIL-32 Handbook on Child : With Historical Background
Pramila Pandit Barooah Rs. 320

CICIL-33 Weaker Section in Indian Society : Undiscovered Past, Uncertain Present and Unpredictable Future Index to Writings in Indian Scholarly Journals and 10 National Newspapers Classified under 1500 Descriptors 1886 1990
S.P. Agrawal and **Rajeev Kumar Sharma** Rs. 600

CICIL-34 Communication Informatics and Librarianship in India : An Introductory Guide to Publications Based on a Survey of Libraries in Capital of City India
S.P. Agrawal and **Pushpa Rani Sharma** Rs. 720